The Trans Canada Trail

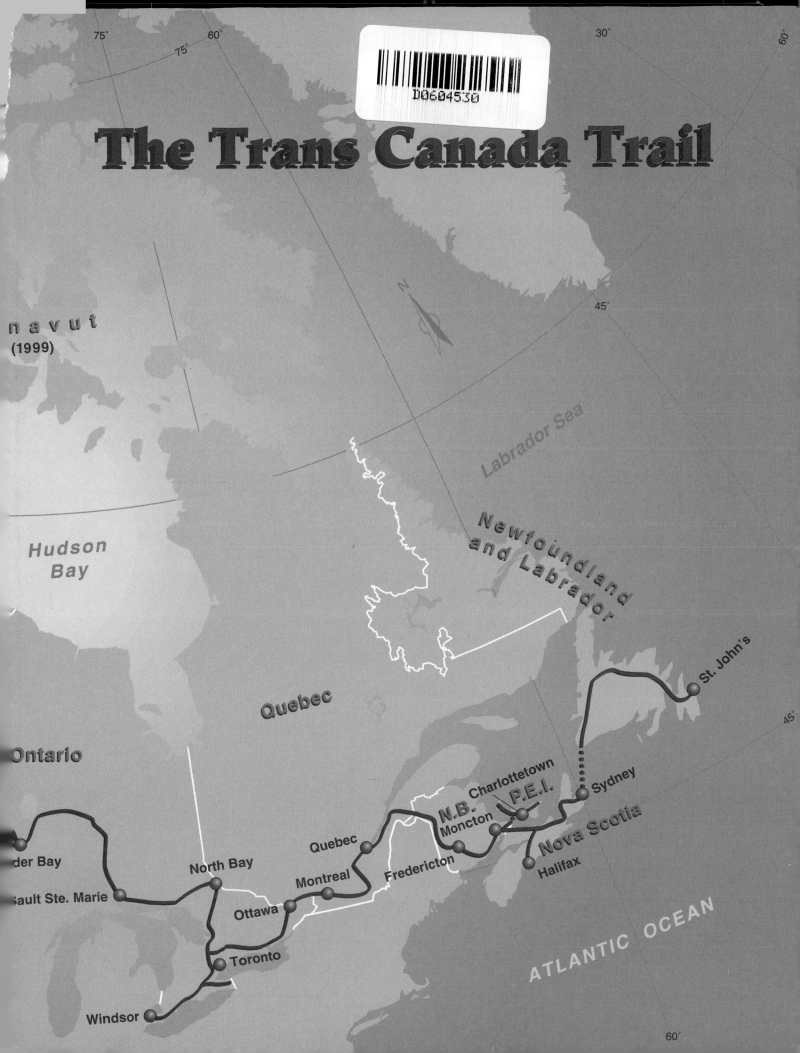

OUR
ENVIRONMENT

OUR ENVIRONMENT

A Canadian Perspective

Dianne Draper

The University of Calgary

ITP Nelson

ITP an International Thomson Publishing company

Toronto • Albany • Bonn • Boston • Cincinnati • Detroit • London • Madrid • Melbourne
Mexico City • New York • Pacific Grove • Paris • San Francisco • Singapore • Tokyo • Washington

I(T)P® **International Thomson Publishing**
The ITP logo is a trademark under licence
www.thomson.com

Published in 1998 by
ITP Nelson
A division of Thomson Canada Limited
1120 Birchmount Road
Scarborough, Ontario M1K 5G4
www/nelson.com/nelson.html

Cover photo: Douglas Provincial Park, Saskatchewan, by Darwin Wiggett/First Light
Endpapers map: Deborah Crowle

Canadian Cataloguing in Publication Data

Draper, Dianne Louise, 1949–
    Our environment : a Canadian perspective

Includes bibliographical references and index.
ISBN 0-17-605552-5

1. Canada – Environmental conditions. 2. Environmental policy – Canada.
I. Title.

GE160.C3D73 1998   363.7'00971   C97-932152-2

Team Leader and Publisher   Michael Young
Executive Editor   Charlotte Forbes
Senior Production Editor   Bob Kohlmeier
Project Editor   Evan Turner
Production Coordinator   Brad Horning
Cover art, cover design, interior design Liz Harasymczuk
Art Direction   Suzanne Peden
Composition Analyst   Janet Zanette
Input Operator   June Reynolds

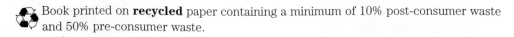 Book printed on **recycled** paper containing a minimum of 10% post-consumer waste and 50% pre-consumer waste.

2 3 4 (WCB) 01 00 99 98

Brief Contents

PART 1
OUR ENVIRONMENT

**Chapter 1   Our Environment: Problems
and Challenges**   2

The Changing Global Environment   3
Linkages: People as Part of Ecosystems   7
Major Causes of Environmental Problems   7
Sustainability Challenges   13

**Chapter 2   Environmental Studies:
Science, Worldviews, and Ethics**   25

Science and the Environment   26
Worldviews and Values   35
Environmental Values and Ethics   44

**PART 2   THE ECOSPHERE
WE LIVE IN**

**Chapter 3   Earth's Life-Support
Systems**   50

Matter and Energy: Basic Building Blocks of
    Nature   51
Earth's Life Support Systems   54

Roles of Species in Ecosystems   65
Energy Flow in Ecosystems   69
Matter Cycling in Ecosystems   71
Terrestrial and Aquatic Ecosystems   76
Responses to Environmental Stress   81
Human Impacts on Ecosystems   84
Working with Nature   85

**Chapter 4   Human Population Issues
and the Environment**   88

Basic Population Concepts   89
Human Population Growth   91
Projecting Future Population Growth   95
Demographic Transition   97
Facing the Problems of World Population
    Growth   108
Population and Environmental Sustainability   111

**PART 3
RESOURCES FOR CANADA'S
FUTURE**

Chapter 5   Our Changing Atmosphere   116
Human Activities and Impacts on the
    Atmosphere   121
Responses to Atmospheric Changes   143
Future Challenges   149

**Chapter 6   Agroecosystems and Land
Resources**   154

Canada's Agricultural Land Base   156
Human Activities and Impacts on Agricultural
    Lands   159
Responses to Environmental Impacts and
    Change   168
Future Challenges   180

Chapter 7   Fresh Water   **184**

Water Supply and Distribution   186
Water Uses and Pressures on Water Quality   188
Human Activities and Impacts on Fresh Water
    Environments   194
Responses to Environmental Impacts and
    Change   208
Future Challenges   218

Chapter 8   Oceans and Fisheries   **222**

Canada's Marine Environments   225
Human Activities and Impacts on Marine
    Environments   236
Responses to Environmental Impacts and
    Change   260
Future Challenges   267

Chapter 9   Forests   **272**

The Earth's Forests   277
The Ecological Importance of Old-Growth
    Forests   289
Human Activities and Impacts on Forest
    Environments   292
Responses to Environmental Impacts and
    Change   307
Future Challenges   316

Chapter 10   Mining   **324**

Human Activities and Impacts on Natural
    Environments   326
Responses to Environmental Impacts and
    Change   342
Future Challenges   346

Chapter 11   Energy   **352**

Human Activities and Impacts on Natural
    Environments   354
Responses to Environmental Impacts and
    Change   371
Energy Futures   379

**Chapter 12   Wild Species and Natural
Spaces**   **383**

Human Activities and Impacts on Canadian
    Species and Natural Environments   389
Responses to Environmental Impacts and
    Change   402
Future Challenges   415

PART 4
GETTING TO TOMORROW

**Chapter 13   Lifestyle Choices and
Sustainable Communities**   **420**

Urban Environmental Conditions and Trends   421
Toward Sustainable Communities   439
Progress toward Urban Sustainability?   445

**Chapter 14   Meeting Environmental
Challenges**   **449**

Progress in Safeguarding Canada's
    Environment   451
Regulatory Efforts to Safeguard Our
    Environment   455
ENGO Actions to Safeguard Our Environment   460
Challenges for the Future   463
The Importance of Individuals   470

Contents

Brief Contents   v
List of Figures   xvii
Preface   xxi
Acknowledgments   xxiv

PART 1
OUR ENVIRONMENT

Chapter 1   Our Environment: Problems and Challenges   2

Chapter Objectives   3
Introduction   3
The Changing Global Environment   3
Linkages: People as Part of Ecosystems   7
Major Causes of Environmental Problems   7
  Human Population Growth   10
  Abuse of Resources and Natural Systems   11
  Pollution   12
  Related Themes   13
Sustainability Challenges   13
  Guiding Principles of Sustainability   15
    Ecological Sustainability   16
      Ecological Footprints   17
      An Ecosystem Approach   18
      Carrying Capacity   20
    Social Sustainability   21
    Economic Sustainability   21
    The Precautionary Principle   22
    Environmental Stewardship   22
    Monitoring for Sustainability   22
    Toward Sustainability   23
Chapter Questions   23
References   24

Chapter 2   Environmental Studies: Science, Worldviews, and Ethics   25

Chapter Objectives   26
Introduction   26
Science and the Environment   26
  Science: What Is It?   27
    Assumptions in Science   28
    Thinking Scientifically   28
    Scientific Measurement   28
  The Methods of Science   29
  Misunderstandings about Science   31
    Use of Language   31
    Value-Free Science   31
    The Scientific Method   32
    Complexity, Values, and Worldviews   33
  Science and Environmental Decision Making   34
Worldviews and Values   35
  Expansionist and Ecological Worldviews   35
    The Expansionist Worldview   35
    The Ecological Worldview   36
    Conservation in the Early Twentieth Century   36
  Environmentalism   39
    Deep Ecology, Green Alternatives, and Sustainable Development   41
    Toward the Future   43
Environmental Values and Ethics   44
  Environmental Values   44
  Environmental Ethics   45
Chapter Questions   47
References   47
Additional Information Sources   48

PART 2
THE ECOSPHERE WE LIVE IN

Chapter 3   Earth's Life-Support Systems   50

Chapter Objectives	51
Introduction	51
Matter and Energy: Basic Building Blocks of Nature	51
Matter	51
Matter Quality	53
Energy	53
Energy Quality	53
Physical and Chemical Changes in Matter	54
The Law of Conservation of Matter	54
First and Second Laws of Energy	54
Earth's Life-Support Systems	54
Earth's Major Components	54
Connections on Earth	56
Ecology	57
Biodiversity	60
Types of Organisms	60
Components and Structure of Ecosystems	61
Tolerance Ranges of Species	64
Limiting Factors in Ecosystems	65
Roles of Species in Ecosystems	65
Types of Species in Ecosystems	65
Ecological Niche	66
Interactions between Species	66
Energy Flow in Ecosystems	69
Food Chains and Food Webs	69
Productivity of Producers	70
Matter Cycling in Ecosystems	71
Nutrient Cycles	71
Carbon Cycle	71
Nitrogen Cycle	71
Phosphorus Cycle	73
Hydrologic Cycle	74
Rock Cycle	75
Terrestrial and Aquatic Ecosystems	76
The Geography of Life	76
Life on Land: Major Terrestrial Biomes	76
Life on Earth: Major Aquatic Biomes	77
Oceans	77
Freshwater Ecosystems	79
Freshwater Rivers and Streams	80
Inland Wetlands	80
Responses to Environmental Stress	81
The Constancy of Change	81
Changes in Population Size	81
Biological Evolution, Adaptation, and Natural Selection	83
Speciation and Extinction	83
Ecological Succession	84
Human Impacts on Ecosystems	84
Working with Nature	85
Chapter Questions	86
References	86
Additional Information Sources	87

Chapter 4:   Human Population Issues and the Environment   88

Chapter Objectives	89
Introduction	89
Basic Population Concepts	89
Population and Technology	89
Human Demography	91
The Human Population Growth	91
Population Dynamics	93
Exponential Growth	94
Projecting Future Population Growth	95
Doubling Time	95
The Logistic Growth Curve	97
The Demographic Transition	97
The Four-Stage Model	97
Diseases and Death in Industrial Society	99
Zero Population Growth	99
Carrying Capacity	100
Limiting Factors	100
Age Structure	100

The Dependency Ratio 105
Fertility Rates and Lag-Time Effects 105
Future Population Trends 106
Cultural Factors 107
Life Expectancy 108
Facing the Problems of World Population
Growth 108
Increasing the Marriage Age 108
Birth Control in Developing Nations 109
National Birth Rate Reduction Programs 110
Migration 111
Population and Environmental Sustainability 111
Chapter Questions 112
References 112
Additional Information Sources 113

PART 3
RESOURCES FOR CANADA'S FUTURE

Chapter 5   Our Changing Atmosphere   116

Chapter Objectives 117
Introduction 117
Human Activities and Impacts on the
Atmosphere 121
Stratospheric Ozone Depletion 121
The Ozone Layer 121
Depletion of the Ozone Layer 121
Ozone-Depleting Substances 122
Volcanoes and Ozone Depletion 123
Antarctic Ozone Depletion 124
Tropical and Mid-Latitude Ozone
Depletion 124

Ozone Depletion Impacts on the
Atmosphere 124
Ultraviolet Radiation and Its Impacts 125
Climate Change 126
Greenhouse Gases and Climate 126
Human Activities and the Greenhouse
Effect 127
Carbon Dioxide 127
Methane 127
Nitrous Oxide 128
Chlorofluorocarbons 128
Predicting Climate Change 128
Impacts of an Enhanced
Greenhouse Effect 130
Indicators and Effects of Climate
Change 130
Some Other Influences on Climate 134
El Niño and the Southern
Oscillation (ENSO) 134
The Greenhouse Effect in the Future 135
Other Atmospheric Changes 137
Acidic Deposition 137
What Is Acid Rain? 137
Sources of Acidic Pollutants 138
Effects of Acidic Deposition 138
Signs of Progress 140
Airborne Contaminants 142
Responses to Atmospheric Changes 143
International Actions 143
Protecting the Ozone Layer 143
Controlling Greenhouse Gas Emissions 143
Canadian Law, Policy, and Practice 145
Canadian Partnerships and Local Actions 148
Future Challenges 149
Chapter Questions 151
References 151
Additional Information Sources 153

**Chapter 6   Agroecosystems and Land
Resources   154**

Chapter Objectives 155
Introduction 155
Canada's Agricultural Land Base 156
Socioeconomic Changes in Canadian
Agriculture 157
Jurisdiction and Tenure 159

Human Activities and Impacts on Agricultural
   Lands   159
    Soil Quality   161
       Soil Organic Matter Levels   161
       Wind, Water, and Tillage Erosion   161
       Soil Structure   162
       Soil Salinization   163
       Chemical Contamination   163
    Water Quality   163
    Agriculture and Biodiversity   164
    Greenhouse Gases   166
    Energy Use   168
Responses to Environmental Impacts and
   Change   168
    International Initiatives   169
       Desertification   169
    Canadian Efforts to Achieve Sustainable
       Agriculture   172
       An Illustration: Sustainable
          Agriculture in Manitoba   172
    Nontraditional Agricultural Activities   176
       Organic Farming   176
       Game Farming and Ranching   176
       Agricultural Biotechnology   177
    Partnerships   178
Future Challenges   180
Chapter Questions   182
References   182
Additional Information Sources   183

CHAPTER 7   Fresh Water   **184**

Chapter Objectives   185
Introduction   185

Water Supply and Distribution   186
    Earth's Freshwater Resources   186
    Canada's Freshwater Resources   186
Water Uses and Pressures on Water Quality   188
    Water Uses   188
    Pressures on Water Quality   190
    The Importance of Water   192
       Water as a Common Link   192
       Water as a Source of Conflict   192
       Water as a Hazard   193
Human Activities and Impacts on Freshwater
   Environments   194
    Domestic and Urban Uses and Impacts   194
       Safe Drinking Water and Sanitation
          Facilities   194
       Demand for Water   196
       The Great Lakes and St. Lawrence
          River Basin: A Case Study   197
    Agricultural Uses and Impacts   200
    Industrial Uses and Impacts   202
       Groundwater Contamination   202
       Impacts on Beluga Whales   204
       Acidic Deposition   204
    Hydroelectric Generation and Impacts   204
    Recreational Uses and Impacts   207
Responses to Environmental Impacts and
   Change   208
    International Initiatives   208
       Agenda 21   208
       The Ramsar Convention   208
       Agreements between Canada and the
          United States   209
          The Great Lakes Water Quality
            Agreements   209
          Remedial Action Plans   210
    Canadian Law, Policy, and Practice   210
       Water Legislation and Policy
          Responses   210
          Inquiry on Federal Water Policy   211
          Shared Jurisdiction   211
       Financial Constraints   212
       Research and Application   212
       Ecological Monitoring and
          Assessment Network   212
       Environmental and Water Quality
          Guidelines   212
       Great Lakes Cleanup Fund and Great
          Lakes 2000   213

Northern River Basins Study   213
Canadian Partnerships and Local Action   214
    Flood Damage Reduction Program   214
    Watershed Planning   214
    Fraser River Action Plan   215
    North American Waterfowl
        Management Plan   216
    Making a Difference Locally   216
Future Challenges   218
Chapter Questions   219
References   219
Additional Information Sources   221

CHAPTER 8   Oceans and Fisheries   222

Chapter Objectives   223
Introduction   223
    The *Irving Whale* Recovery Project   223
Canada's Marine Environments   225
    Canada's Arctic Ocean Environment   225
        Biophysical Characteristics   225
        Threats to Ecosystem Integrity   227
            Hydroelectric Development   227
            Long-Range Transport of
                Pollutants   227
            Climate Change   229
            Overhunting   229
            Nonrenewable Resource
                Extraction   229
    Canada's Pacific Ocean Environment   229
        Biophysical Characteristics   229
        Threats to Ecosystem Integrity   230
            Global Change   230

        Marine Pollution   230
    Canada's Atlantic Ocean Environment   230
        Biophysical Characteristics   230
        Threats to Ecosystem Integrity   232
            Lack of Knowledge   232
            Anthropogenic Impacts and
                Marine Pollution   232
            Commercial Fishing   232
            Sea-Level Rise   232
    Summary of Concerns Facing Canada's
        Ocean Regions   233
Human Activities and Impacts on Marine
    Environments   236
    Fisheries   236
        The 1995 Canada–Spain Turbot
            Dispute   236
        The Northern Cod Moratorium   238
        Pacific Herring and Salmon Stocks 242
            Pacific Herring   243
            Coastal Salmon   245
    Pollution   247
        Industrial and Chemical Effluents 247
        Municipal Sewage   254
    Marine Shipping, Ocean Dumping, and
        Plastics   255
        Marine Shipping   255
        Ocean Dumping   255
        Plastics   255
    Coastal Development   256
        Urban Runoff   256
        Physical Alterations   258
    Offshore Hydrocarbon Development   259
    Atmospheric Change   260
Responses to Environmental Impacts and
    Change   260
    International Initiatives   261
        United Nations Convention on the
            Law of the Sea   261
        Agenda 21   262
    Canadian Law, Policy, and Practice   262
        Revised Oceans and Fisheries
            Legislation   262
        Coastal Zone Management Efforts   264
    Canadian Partnerships and Local Actions 265
Future Challenges   267
Chapter Questions   268
References   268
Additional Information Sources   271

Chapter 9   Forests   **272**

Chapter Objectives   273
Introduction   273
   Focal Point: Clayoquot Sound   275
The Earth's Forests   277
   Global Distribution, Products, and
     Demand   277
   Forests in Canada   278
     Harvesting Systems   282
      Tree Plantations   284
     The Timber Bias   284
     The Falldown Effect   287
The Ecological Importance of Old-Growth
   Forests   289
   The Life Cycle in the Old-Growth Forest 289
     Standing Live Trees, Snags, and Fallen
      Trees   289
   Carbon Storage   290
   Keys to Diversity   290
     Biological Diversity   291
   The Need for Protection   291
Human Activities and Impacts on Forest
   Environments   292
   A Brief Historical Overview of the Forest
     Industry   293
     First Nations and European Settlers 293
     Timber Exports and Government
      Ownership   293
     Changing Market Demands, Changing
      Industry   293
     The Shifting Frontier and
      Conservation Concerns   294
     Licensing and Increasing
      Concentration of Forest Holdings 294
     Growth in Pulp and Paper   295
     Sustained Yield Focus   295
     Continuing Concentration of Control
      over Harvesting Rights   295
   Timber Production Activities and Impacts 295
     Habitat, Wildlife, and Life-Support
      Impacts   296
     Degradation and Deforestation of
      Tropical Forests   300
   Pollution   303
   Sociocultural Dimensions   304
   Tourism and Recreation   304
   Other Human Impacts   306

Responses to Environmental Impacts and
   Change   307
   International Initiatives   307
     UNCED Forest Principles   307
     Agenda 21   308
     UNCED Conventions and Other
      Responses   308
   Canadian Policy, Practice, and
     Partnerships   309
     Canada's National Forest Strategy 309
     Canada's Model Forest Program 313
     Criteria and Indicators of Sustainable
      Forest Management   313
     Local Partnerships and Responses 315
      Wildlife and Forestry Activity 315
      An Ecoadventure in Clayoquot
       Sound   316
Future Challenges   316
Chapter Questions   320
References   321
Additional Information Sources   323

Chapter 10   Mining   **324**

Chapter Objectives   325
Introduction   325
   Mining in Canada   326
Human Activities and Impacts on Natural
   Environments   326
   Historical Overview   326

Value and Distribution of Mineral
    Resources in Canada 328
      Canada's First Diamond Mine 329
  Environmental Impacts of Mining 332
    Mineral Exploration 333
    Mine Development and Mineral
      Extraction 336
    Processing of Minerals 338
    Mine Closure and Reclamation 339
Responses to Environmental Impacts and
  Change 342
    Market Forces 342
    Partnerships for Environmental
      Sustainability 344
Future Challenges 346
    Stewardship 346
    Protection and Monitoring 347
    Knowledge Building 349
Chapter Questions 350
References 350
Additional Information Sources 351

Chapter 11   Energy 352

Chapter Objectives 353
Introduction 353
  A Future without Fossil Fuels? 353
Human Activities and Impacts on Natural
  Environments 354
    Energy Supply and Demand in Canada 354
    How Do We Use Energy? 355
      Net Useful Energy 355
    Energy Resources 356
      Fossil Fuels 358
        Oil 358
        Heavy Oil 358
        Coal 361
        Natural Gas 362
        The 1970s Energy Crisis 364
      Biomass 364
      Hydroelectricity 365
      Nuclear 367
Responses to Environmental Impacts and
  Change 371
    Emerging Energy Resources 371
      Solar and Wind Energy 371
      Hydrogen 371

    Barriers to the Adoption of Alternative
      Technologies 373
    Improving Energy Efficiency 374
      Transportation Efficiency 374
      Industrial Efficiency 376
      Home Efficiency 376
    Organized Initiatives 378
Energy Futures 379
Chapter Questions 380
References 380
Additional Information Sources 382

**Chapter 12   Wild Species and Natural
Spaces** 383

Chapter Objectives 384
Introduction 384
  The Importance of Biodiversity 388
Human Activities and Impacts on Canadian
  Species and Natural Environments 389
    Human Activity and Biodiversity 389
    Habitat Alteration Due to Physical
      Changes 389
      Forestry, Agriculture, and Other
        Human Activities 389
      Fragmentation 390

Chemical Changes   390
Climate Change   390
Habitat Alteration Due to Competition
    from Non-Native Biota   393
Habitat Alteration Due to Harvesting   393
Habitat Alteration Due to Toxic
    Contaminants   393
Habitat Alteration Due to Cumulative
    Agents of Change   393
Species at Risk   394
Spaces at Risk   397
Responses to Environmental Impacts and
    Change   402
    International Calls to Action   402
        International Treaties   402
        In Situ Conservation   404
            Protected Areas   404
            Restoration and Rehabilitation   408
        Ex Situ Conservation   409
            Plants   409
            Animals   410
        Sustainable Use of Biological
            Resources   410
        Improving Understanding of
            Biodiversity   411
    Canadian Law, Policy, and Practice   411
        Protecting Canadian Species   412
        Protecting Canadian Spaces   412
    Partnerships for the Future   413
Future Challenges   415
Chapter Questions   416
References   417
Additional Information Sources   418

PART 4
GETTING TO TOMORROW

**Chapter 13   Lifestyle Choices and
Sustainable Communities   420**

Chapter Objectives   421
Introduction   421
Urban Environmental Conditions and Trends   421
    Atmosphere and Climate   422
        Microclimate   422
        Air Quality   423
    Noise   424
    Water   425
        Cities and the Hydrologic Cycle   425
        Water Supply and Water Quality   425
        Water Use and Wastewater Treatment   426
        Water and Recreation   428
    Energy   429
        Sustainable Housing   429
        Depending Less on Our Cars   430
    Materials Use   432
        Solid Waste   432
        Land Contamination   434
    Urbanization of Land   435
        Green Space in the City   435
        Loss of Agricultural Land   437
Toward Sustainable Communities   439
    Cities and Sustainability   439
    Making Canadian Cities More Sustainable   439
        Urban Form   440
        Conservation   441
            Water Conservation   441
            Energy Conservation   441
            Conservation of Materials   441
            Conservation of Ecosystems and
                Natural Features   442
        Reduction of Environmental Impacts   442
            Air Quality   442
            Water Quality   444
            Waste Management and
                Cleaning Up   444
        Transportation   444
        Planning   445
Progress toward Urban Sustainability?   445
Chapter Questions   446
References   447
Additional Information Sources   448

Chapter 14   Meeting Environmental Challenges   **449**

Chapter Objectives   450
Introduction   450
Progress in Safeguarding Canada's
    Environment   451
    Air Quality Issues   451
    Water Quality Issues   451
    Biological Diversity   452
    Climate Change   452
    Sector Industries   453
        Agriculture   453
        Forests   453
        Minerals and Metals   454
        Energy   454
        Fisheries   454
Regulatory Efforts to Safeguard Our
    Environment   455
    Atlantic Canada   455
    Central Canada   455

Western Canada and the North   457
ENGO Actions to Safeguard Our Environment   460
Challenges for the Future   463
    Resources Management   463
    Conservation   464
    Waste Reduction   465
    Urban Centres and Transportation
        Systems   465
    Pollution Control   466
    Cleanup of Past Environmental Problems 467
    Changes in Decision-Making Processes   467
The Importance of Individuals   470
Chapter Questions   473
References   473
Additional Information Sources   474

Glossary   475
Copyright Acknowledgments   485
Photo Credits   487
Index   489

List of Figures

Figure 1–1   A week on Earth   5

Figure 1–2   Human–environment connections   10

Figure 1–3   Growth in total world population since 1750 and projected from the late 1990s to 2100   10

Figure 1–4   Conflicting trends: growing ecological footprints and shrinking Earthshares   20

Figure 2–1   The scientific method   32

Figure 2–2   Key early figures in 20th-century conservation   38

Figure 2–3   Worldviews in the political sphere of the 1990s   44

Figure 3–1   Atomic structure   52

Figure 3–2   The general structure of the Earth   55

Figure 3–3   Schematic diagram of energy balance on the Earth   57

Figure 3–4   Levels of biological organization   58

Figure 3–5   Map of world biomes   59

Figure 3–6   Ecozones of Canada   60

Figure 3–7   The five-kingdom system of classification   62

Figure 3–8   Classification of organisms and trophic levels in ecosystems   63

Figure 3–9   Energy flows and matter recycling connect energy, chemicals, and organisms in an ecosystem   64

Figure 3–10   Pacific Ocean sea otters: a keystone role   66

Figure 3–11   Resource partitioning and niches among *Dendroica* species (wood warblers)   69

Figure 3–12   A simplified Great Lakes food web   70

Figure 3–13   A simplified diagram of the carbon cycle   73

Figure 3–14   A simplified diagram of the nitrogen cycle   73

Figure 3–15   A simplified diagram of the phosphorus cycle in terrestrial and aquatic environments   74

Figure 3–16   A simplified diagram of the hydrologic cycle   75

Figure 3–17   Generalized effects of altitude and latitude on climate and biomes   77

Figure 3–18   Zonation in the marine environment   78

Figure 3–19   Basic life zones in eutrophic and oligotrophic lakes   79

Figure 3–20   "S" and "J" curves of population growth   81

Figure 3–21   Selected population change dynamics   82

Figure 4–1   World population growth, 1750–2100   93

Figure 4–2   Doubling times and population growth rates   95

Figure 4–3   Logistic growth curve   97

Figure 4–4   Demographic transition   98

Figure 4–5   Generalized age structure diagrams for expanding, stable, and declining populations   104

Figure 4–6   Age structure diagrams for less developed and highly developed countries   104

Figure 4–7   World decline in total fertility rate, 1950–2020   108

Figure 5–1   Distribution of ozone in the atmosphere   121

Figure 5–2   How ozone-depleting substances destroy stratospheric ozone   123

Figure 5–3   Total ozone trend, 30°–65°N   125

Figure 5–4   Atmospheric concentration of carbon dioxide since 1959, and gross world product since 1960   127

Figure 5–5   A simplified general circulation model for Canada: Temperature projections for winter and summer seasons (doubled carbon dioxide concentrations)   129

Figure 5–6   Effects of climate change   133

Figure 5–7   Spatial and seasonal distribution of precipitation anomalies associated with the El Niño–Southern Oscillation   135

Figure 5–8   The pH scale   137

Figure 5–9   Potential of soils and bedrock to reduce acidity of atmospheric deposition in Canada   140

Figure 6–1   Agricultural areas within Canada   156

Figure 6–2   Change in number and size of farms in Canada, 1901–1991   158

Figure 6–3   The use of farmland in Canada, 1971–1991   158

Figure 6–4   Risk of wind and water erosion in Canada   162

Figure 6–5   Distribution of wetlands in Canada   166

Figure 6–6   World drylands and desertification   172

Figure 7–1   Drainage regions of Canada   187

Figure 7–2   Water withdrawal in Canada, 1972–1991   189

Figure 7–3   Daily municipal water use in Canada, by sector, for selected years 1983–1991   196

Figure 7–4   Use of water in Canadian homes   196

Figure 7–5   Residential water use per person by region, 1991   197

Figure 7–6   Schematic example of flood risk areas   214

Figure 8–1   *Irving Whale* Recovery Project: schematic map of barge route to Halifax   223

Figure 8–2   Canada's marine environment   226

Figure 8–3   Biomagnification of PCBs in the Arctic   228

Figure 8–4a   World's most-fished species   234

Figure 8–4b   National percentage of total world fish catch   234

Figure 8–4c   World total fish production in marine waters, 1950–1993   234

Figure 8–5   Common threats to Canada's marine environment sustainability   235

Figure 8–6   Evidence of overfishing of NAFO-managed groundfish stocks by European Union vessels   237

Figure 8–7   Newfoundland cod harvests showing the 1968 "killer spike" and impact on inshore fishers' catches   240

Figure 8–8   Variations in sea surface temperature off the west coast of Vancouver Island, 1951–1993   244

Figure 8–9   Spawning biomass, commercial catch, and economic value of Pacific herring, 1951–1993   244

Figure 8–10   Montreal-area factories involved in the St. Lawrence River cleanup plans   252

Figure 8–11   Urban runoff in the Fraser River basin   257

Figure 8–12   FAO fishing area boundaries   261

Figure 8–13   FREMP sampling sites in the Lower Fraser River basin   265

Figure 9–1	Clayoquot Sound area: location and selected statistics, 1995	275
Figure 9–2	Principal forest zones of the world	278
Figure 9–3	Forest regions of Canada	279
Figure 9–4	Ownership of timber-productive forest lands in Canada	281
Figure 9–5	Major systems of tree harvesting	282
Figure 9–6	Timber volume production	285
Figure 9–7	The falldown effect	287
Figure 9–8	Evolution of wood products development	288
Figure 9–9	Annual area and volume of timber harvest in Canada	296
Figure 10–1	Principal mining regions of Canada	330
Figure 10–2	Great Slave Lake area and location of proposed BHP diamond mine	331
Figure 10–3	Conceptual land use conflicts and constraints for mining	333
Figure 10–4	The mining process and the environment	335
Figure 10–5	Cross-section of a mine shaft	338
Figure 10–6	Decline in sulphur dioxide emissions per kilotonne of metal production at selected smelters in Eastern Canada since 1980	340
Figure 11–1	Energy consumption: global and Canadian	355
Figure 11–2	Changes in types of energy consumed in Canada, 1958–1992	356
Figure 11–3	Canada's important oil-producing basins	359
Figure 11–4	World distribution of coal	362
Figure 11–5	Natural gas pipelines in Canada	363
Figure 11–6	Major hydroelectric dams in Canada	366
Figure 11–7a	Canadian nuclear plant locations around the world	370
Figure 11–7b	CANDU reactors in Canada	370
Figure 12–1	Risk to biodiversity for Canada	387
Figure 12–2	Degree to which human has changed Canada's ecosystems	391
Figure 12–3	Canada's national park system	406
Figure 12–4	Proportion of federal, provincial, and other protected areas in Canada	407
Figure 12–5	Distribution of internationally designated protected areas within Canada	409
Figure 13–1	Per capita urban solid waste production, energy use, water use, and gross domestic product in Canada, 1991	422
Figure 13–2	Ground-level ozone in selected Canadian cities, 1985–1994	424
Figure 13–3a	Municipal population served by type of sewage treatment in Canada	428
Figure 13–3b	Total population served by a sewage system in Canada	428
Figure 13–4	Toronto Healthy House	431
Figure 13–5	Materials in the solid waste stream, 1992	434
Figure 14–1	Growth in establishment of protected areas in Canada	453
Figure 14–2	Greenhouse gas emissions 1980–1995: comparison to stabilization target	453
Figure 14–3	Wanted: three planet Earths	463
Figure 14–4	Toward environmental sustainability	470

PREFACE

Throughout the more than two decades that I have been teaching courses in environmental science and resources management within the Canadian university system, there has been a conspicuous absence of a Canadian perspective in introductory textbooks. For the most part, texts have been American in orientation, with maps that showed nothing above the 49th parallel and with only occasional reference to Canadian environmental issues. The opportunity to write this book provided an occasion to begin to redress what I perceived as a significant information gap in Canadian environmental education at the university and college level.

Though environmental education is a lifelong process, and though no one textbook or course can cover in depth every element relevant to the understanding of environmental issues, this book is intended as a learning tool so that students, today and tomorrow, may be better informed and better able to make scientifically grounded and socially balanced decisions on environmental issues. Canadian students generally care a great deal about the world they live in, and many want to be challenged to think critically about, and to act responsibly with respect to, the environment. It is my hope that this book helps make environmental science meaningful and relevant to Canadian (and other) students so that they may meet the challenge of sustaining a healthy and productive Earth environment.

OBJECTIVES

The purpose of *Our Environment: A Canadian Perspective* is to provide a contemporary introduction to scientific concepts that are important to the study and the understanding of the ecological functioning of our global environment and to present current information about the diverse environmental issues and problems encountered in Canada. If our efforts to resolve environmental issues are to succeed, we need to think critically and in an integrated fashion about them and about the associated relationships between people and Earth's ecosystems. Thus, information presented here integrates both physical and human dimensions and reflects a broad interdisciplinary approach to the study of global and local environments.

Canadians' experiences with environmental issues vary from east to west and north to south. This book is intended to help students understand the evolution of environmental concern in Canada as well as the variability of environmental problems in different resource sectors and regions of the nation. In addition, the range of examples selected from across the country and internationally is intended to help students appreciate the diversity of opinions about, and approaches that have been taken to resolve, specific environmental concerns in Canada and beyond.

While it is true that Canadians have achieved some notable successes in certain environmental matters, it is also true that we cannot become complacent about what remains to be done. In this regard, a number of key themes thread through the text, including the importance of observation and critical reflection on environmental matters, the place of stewardship and cooperative problem solving in environmental action, and a focus on sustainability and the future.

ORGANIZATION

The book contains fourteen chapters. These are grouped into four parts. In Part 1, students are introduced to the broad field of environmental science through discussion of our changing global environment and the major causes of environmental problems. The role of science in understanding our environment and in moving toward a sustainable future is considered, as are the roles of worldviews, environmental values, and ethics.

In Part 2, the focus is on fundamental features and interconnections of the ecosphere, as well as on human population issues and the impact that human numbers have on the environment, both nationally and internationally.

Part 3 focuses on Canada's natural resource base. Chapters on the atmosphere, agroecosystems and land resources, fresh water, oceans and fisheries, forests, mining, energy, and wild species and natural spaces each deal with human activities and impacts on these resource sectors and environments. Each chapter also identifies a range of Canadian responses to the challenges encountered through resource development and use of environments. These responses identify international and national actions, and discuss the activities, partnerships, and local actions of individuals, environmental nongovernmental organizations, industry, and government.

Part 4 considers issues associated with the impacts of our lifestyle choices and some of the ways in which we can move toward sustainable environments in the future.

FEATURES

Our Environment contains several special features to help students in their environmental education. Each chapter begins with a list of *Chapter Objectives* so that students are aware of the concepts they will come to understand as they read and study the chapter. *Key terms* appear in bold throughout the text; definitions for these terms are found in the text and/or the *Glossary*. *Case studies* within each chapter not only provide real illustrations of environmental problems but also demonstrate how people have applied the principles and concepts discussed in the text to the resolution of environmental issues at several geographic scales. These cases should help students understand the economic, social, political, and environmental interconnections in environmental science.

Enviro-Focus boxes identify a range of personal interest/impact issues ranging from the increase in skin cancer cases in Canada and the revival of agricultural hemp for use in clothing, to the competition between wild species and humans for habitat in Banff National Park. *Future Challenges* sections, in the resource sector chapters, are intended to stimulate our thinking about local environmental problems to the future of the world we live in and share with others.

Each chapter ends with a list of *Chapter Questions*. Some questions review material presented in the chapter; others engage students in the development of their observational and critical thinking skills. A list of *References* containing research sources and additional readings appears at the end of each chapter also. Included in these lists are *Internet links* and *Web sources* that encourage students to explore topics in more depth.

INSTRUCTOR'S RESOURCES TO FACILITATE TEACHING AND LEARNING

A rich variety of instructional resources supplement the book, giving instructors the tools to create a dynamic, exciting, and effective course.

Instructor's Manual   The Instructor's Manual consists of two parts. Part 1 includes a section on using the text's support package and integrating items such as the video and Web site into the classroom. The bulk of Part 1 provides teaching suggestions, chapter lecture outlines, and activities and exercises for students on a chapter-by-chapter basis. Part 2 is a hard copy of the test bank.

Computerized Test Bank   Multiple-choice, true/false, short-answer, and fill-in-the-blanks questions are included for every chapter. Instructors can customize their own tests using the test generator.

CTV Video   The CTV video accompanying the text provides short (3–5-minute) clips from a variety of CTV programs that relate to the subject matter of the chapters. The video clips are a great way of introducing topics to students and generating discussion.

CD-ROM   The art program for *Our Environment* has been placed on a CD in separate chapter files, allowing instructors to use the art as visual aids in teaching the course.

Web Site A robust Web site—environment.nelson.com—accompanies *Our Environment.* Instructors and students alike will find this site useful in researching and learning about the world's environment. Pages on the Web site will include "Environmental Science on the Web"; "Education and Careers in Environmental Science"; "Interactive Chapter Quizzes" (with which students can check their understanding of the material covered in the course); "Enviro-Updates" (which cover issues concerning the environment in the news); "Search Engines," for researching environmental information; and "Chapter Links" to environmental organizations and community resources.

HELPING TO BUILD THE TRANS CANADA TRAIL

The 15 000-kilometre Trans Canada Trail represents a grand vision of Canadians' love of their land. Many Canadians are cooperating to finance and build, metre by metre, the world's longest shared-use recreational trail. The dedication and effort that this visionary project embodies as it winds its way through every province and territory is an important touchstone in environmental terms, too. With the purchase of this book, you the reader support the Trans Canada Trail initiative and contribute to a sustainable, apolitical, pan-Canadian effort that strives not only to protect and preserve our environment but to educate Canadians about their environment as they come close to nature on the trail. The combination of education and vision-based action to effect change is a powerful force. It is my hope that this book may contribute to the sustaining of the Earth, our home.

ACKNOWLEDGMENTS

This author and book have benefited greatly from the assistance of many people. I would like to extend special thanks to my highly capable research assistant, Colin Crance, for the knowledge, skill, and dedication he brought to this project. It was a privilege to work with him. Sincere thanks also are extended to Donna McGrath for her timely research efforts.

I am deeply indebted to the talented members of the production team at ITP Nelson. Their vital contributions ensured that this book is as good as it can be. I would like to express my sincere gratitude to Charlotte Forbes, Brad Horning, Bob Kohlmeier, Mike Thompson, Evan Turner, and Michael Young. Their belief in this book was of great importance to me and I am very grateful for their support, advice, and professional assistance. Others at ITP Nelson helped in other ways, and I'd like to thank them, too: Vicki Gould, Sue Peden, Dolores Pritchard, June Reynolds, Tim Sellers, and Janet Zanette.

I would like to thank the reviewers who made important suggestions for improvement. Although remaining deficiencies are mine, my thanks are extended to Jeffrey Atkinson, Brock University; Suzanne Greaves, University of Western Ontario; David Hackett, Nipissing University; Owen Hertzman, Dalhousie University; Brenda Koenig, Trent University; Tom Meredith, McGill University; Chris Olsen, Lakeland College; and Michael Tripp, University of Victoria.

During the 1994 fall term I was fortunate to be granted a Killam Resident Fellowship, which enabled me to devote additional time to the writing of this book. I would like to extend my appreciation to all those associated with the granting and administration of this fellowship, as well as to Karyn Butler, Wayne Davies, Walter Jamieson, and Bruce Mitchell for their support. At the University of Calgary, Steven Randall (Dean, Faculty of Social Sciences) and his staff, and Steven Franklin (Head), Elaine Heinz, Debbie Little, Susan Moisik, and Robin Poitras (of the Department of Geography) provided various kinds of support. Thank-you for your help.

Several individuals provided specific information and made other contributions that enabled me to enrich this text. Their important role is acknowledged gratefully in the alphabetical listing that follows: Nigel Bankes, Jim Bauer, Leslie Beckmann, Marilyn Blache, Anne Breau, Dagmar Budikova, Alice Chambers, Louise and Horace Draper, Jenny Feick, Mary Granskou, Tony Hamilton, Dawn Mitchell, Stan Orchard, Ann Scarfe, John Thomson, and Pat Wells. I would like to extend my thanks also to each of the government officials and nongovernmental environmental organization representatives who responded to my questions and provided information about the environmental activities in which they were engaged.

DIANNE DRAPER

Our Environment

"... although it is only a little planet it is hugely beautiful and surely the finest place in the world to be."

Lawrence Collins (in Brower, 1975, p. 127)

CHAPTER 1

Our Environment: Problems and Challenges

Chapter Contents

CHAPTER OBJECTIVES 3
INTRODUCTION 3
THE CHANGING GLOBAL
  ENVIRONMENT 3
LINKAGES: PEOPLE AS PART OF
  ECOSYSTEMS 7
MAJOR CAUSES OF ENVIRONMENTAL
  PROBLEMS 7
  Human Population Growth 10
  Abuse of Resources and Natural
    Systems 11
  Pollution 12
  Related Themes 13
SUSTAINABILITY CHALLENGES 13
  Guiding Principles of Sustainability 15
    Ecological Sustainability 16
      Ecological Footprints 17
      An Ecosystem Approach 18
      Carrying Capacity 20
    Social Sustainability 21
    Economic Sustainability 21
    The Precautionary Principle 22
    Environmental Stewardship 22
  Monitoring for Sustainability 22
  Toward Sustainability 23
Chapter Questions 23
References 24

Chapter Objectives

After studying this chapter you should be able to

- identify a range of local, regional, and international environmental issues of relevance to Canada
- appreciate the ways humans are linked with Earth's ecosystems
- describe the root causes of environmental problems
- discuss the concepts of sustainable development and sustainability
- identify and summarize the guiding principles of sustainability

INTRODUCTION

From the feel of earth under our feet, to the light of sun and sky in our eyes; from the flaming colours that greet us in autumn woods, to the shimmering oceans, lakes, and streams that flow around us—Canadians know they inhabit some special places on a beautiful planet. The problem is that many of our activities in this country and on this planet are rapidly altering its beauty and its ecological functioning. Exponential growth in population and resource use has caused forests, wetlands, and grasslands to disappear, topsoil to be blown or washed away, oceans and water bodies to be poisoned, and wildlife species to be driven to extinction. The good news is that we are learning to think and act differently to sustain, rather than degrade, our planet.

This book is about environmental problems and challenges that face us as Canadian and global citizens, and about efforts that individuals, groups, industries, and government agencies are making to solve existing problems and to improve the ways we interact with our planet and its ecosystems. Although many problems are significant ones, and some people feel powerless to change them, it is important to remember that individual and combined actions do make a difference. Each one of us can improve our ecological knowledge and understanding of how the world works so that our individual decisions and actions in the future will be less harmful to the environment. Industries and governments, too, can be challenged to develop new approaches to conserving the planet's basic life-support systems and to ensure the long-term sustainability of species and resources.

In addition to providing an overview of the nature of environmental problems facing people in Canada and elsewhere (Figure 1–1), in this chapter we introduce some of the linkages humans have with Earth's interconnected ecosystems and identify some of the root causes of environmental problems. We also consider concepts associated with the term sustainability and some of the principles that help us work toward it.

THE CHANGING GLOBAL ENVIRONMENT

Television and video programs probably have brought each of us face to face with the tragic images of environmental refugees fleeing famine, disease, and death as ecological deterioration overtakes their homelands. Through news photography we have seen large numbers of wildlife killed due to poaching, pesticide poisoning, or

Four dimensions of our environment: landforms, wildlife, atmosphere, and water bodies.

other environmental changes. Whether these images are of the encroaching Sahel desert in Africa, burning tropical rain forests in Central and South America, thousands of dead ducks on a lake in Manitoba, scrap tires burning in Ontario, or Newfoundland fishers without cod to catch, they carry the same message—in a very short time, humans have greatly accelerated environmental change.

While it is true that the Earth's history reveals periods of major environmental changes (such as when glaciation transformed landscapes, and catastrophic volcanic eruptions and floods destroyed species and ecosystems), these events generally occurred over long time frames and provided for relative stability in ecological processes. In contrast, human activities have increased the pace of environmental change and have had dramatic impacts on the quality and productivity of the planet's **ecosystems.** Canadians are becoming increasingly aware of how human demands for resources have resulted in such events as the collapse of the Atlantic cod fishery as well as the reduction of old-growth temperate rain forests, prairie grasslands, and Ontario's Carolinian forests to small fragments of their former expanses.

Similarly, as people have pursued their economic development goals, environmental quality concerns have increased. For instance, acidic atmospheric pollutants

from Canadian and American industrial sources have destroyed fish in many lakes in eastern Canada; Arctic country foods (local meat and fish) have been contaminated by polychlorinated biphenyls (PCBs); and Labrador has been the recipient of long-range transport of radioactive particles from Chernobyl. Polluted soils and water, Arctic haze, large die-offs of neotropical migrant birds, and increased levels of greenhouse gases such as carbon dioxide in the atmosphere, have resulted from discharges of industrial and community wastes as well as from agricultural, forestry, and mining practices.

Such results of our activities have alerted people to the fact that we are not separate from our **environment** but are an integral part of Earth's interconnected ecosystems. Perhaps we can understand the profound impacts that population growth and economic development have on the global ecosystem (the **ecosphere**) when we realize that "the world's population has multiplied almost fivefold since the early 1900s [and that during that same time period] the world's economy has grown by 20 times, the consumption of fossil fuels by 30 times, and industrial production by 50 times" (Government of Canada, 1996a).

Ecosystems have finite productive capacities and assimilative abilities, and they are affected by human activities. As human populations grow, for example, they

PART 1:
OUR ENVIRONMENT

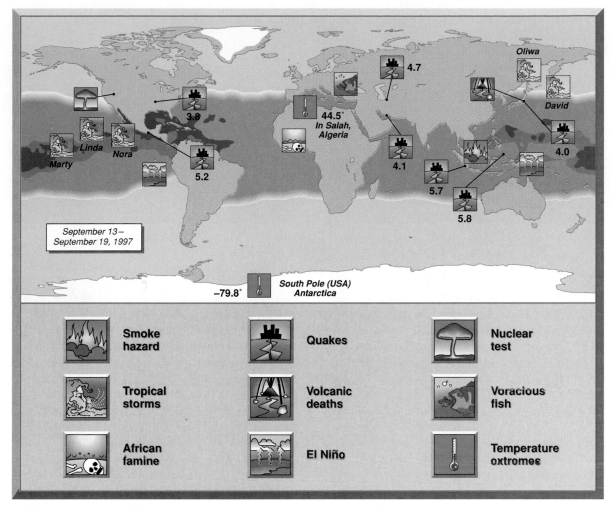

Smoke hazard: Illegal blazes set by farming operations to clear tropical rain forests produced smoke so thick that they caused an unprecedented health hazard across parts of Sumatra and Borneo. The Malaysian government considered plans to evacuate the entire population of Kuala Lumpur.

Tropical storms: The 160-km/h winds of super-typhoon Oliwa caused mudslides that left at least six people dead or missing. Typhoon David, tropical storm Marty, and hurricane Nora caused no damage, while hurricane Linda (the most powerful storm in the history of the eastern Pacific) caused only minor coastal flooding in western Mexico.

African famine: The Niger government announced that 71 000 villagers were threatened by drought-induced famine in the southern region of Oualan.

Quakes: Iran, 4.1 (11:09 p.m., Sept. 14), 250 km southeast of Shiraz, and 4.7 (4:45 p.m., Sept. 16), near Gorgan and Bander-Gaz; Indonesia, 5.7 (1:27 p.m., Sept. 15), centered beneath the Indian Ocean, 145 km southeast of Manna; Niijima Island, Japan, 4.0 (2:33 p.m., Sept. 16), following a tremor of 3.4 a minute earlier; Southern Mexico, 5.2 (10:38 a.m., Sept. 15), centered just offshore beneath the Pacific Ocean; Arkansas, 3.8 (11:31 a.m., Sept. 15), centered on the New Madrid Fault in the northeastern section of the state.

Volcanic deaths: Four members of a climbing expedition were killed by poisonous gas seeping from Japan's Mount Adatara, east of Tokyo, after ignoring warnings issued by vulcanologists.

El Niño: Waters affected by the El Niño ocean warming now encompass an area one and half times the size of the continental USA.

Nuclear test: Despite criticisms from activists and some members of Congress, the U.S. Department of Energy proceeded with an underground nuclear explosion at its Nevada test site.

Voracious fish: the appearance of the alien rotan fish in Western Ukraine has had a devastating impact on native marine life. A single individual requires as much as 30 kg of other fish (including its own species) to gain 1 kg of weight. The resilience of the rotan, which requires 20 times less oxygen than other species, is best illustrated by its ability to revive a day after being left in open air. In one such instance, the first individual to rebound in a group ate up the others, according to Itar-Tass news agency.

Temperature extremes: Hot spot for the week was the Algerian city of In Salah at 44.5°C (112°F); the coldest was at the U.S. Amundsen–Scott research station in Antarctica at −79.8°C (−112°F).

Figure 1–1

A week on Earth

SOURCE: Adapted from *Earthweek: A diary of the planet* (1997, September 19). http://www.slip.net/~earthenv/history/

The productive capabilities of different environments are affected by natural limitations (deserts) and human activities (deforestation).

increase demands on energy supplies for industrial development, transportation, and housing. If we are to succeed in maintaining the productivity and quality of our environment, it is important to acknowledge our relationship with Earth's ecosystems and to act in ways that will not put intolerable pressure on natural resources and life support systems of the ecosphere. Impacts of human activities often transcend political boundaries and can lead to serious social, economic, and environmental problems. This is why Vancouverites should care about what happens in the Arctic, why New Brunswickers should be concerned about pollution in Eastern Europe, and why Inuit

The Swainson's hawk, like many species, is at risk from a range of threats, including pesticide poisoning.

in the Northwest Territories should be concerned about the Brazilian rain forest.

Many people in the Western world are concerned about current impacts of their own activities on the environment, as well as about how future environmental changes might affect their health and socioeconomic well-being. Among the questions that concern Canadians are whether their well water might be contaminated with pesticides; if enough trees are being replanted to replace all those that have been cut; whether sufficient high-quality habitat is being protected for wildlife; to what degree air and water pollution from other countries is affecting Canada's resources; whether exotic species introduced accidentally (or deliberately) can be controlled; and how social, economic, and environmental aspects can be balanced in areas where such activities as mining, fishing, agriculture, and forestry are conducted.

Many Canadians are concerned about environmental problems that occur beyond our borders, too. Among these concerns are effects of nuclear disasters such as Chernobyl; impacts of acid precipitation on forests in Germany and lakes in Sweden and Norway; drought and starvation in African nations; destruction of the world's tropical forests and the associated loss of thousands of unique plant and animal species; impacts of oil tanker spills on sea life; and the ozone hole, greenhouse gases, and global climate change in general.

The 1993 World Scientists' Warning to Humanity identified critical stresses facing the Earth's environment and noted what we must do to avoid irretrievably mutilating our home on this planet (Enviro-Focus 1). This warning was part of a long-term campaign by the Union of Concerned Scientists to increase awareness of the threat that global environmental degradation poses to humanity's life-support systems. By 1993, more than 1670 scientists from 71 countries, including 104 Nobel laureates, had signed the warning. Among Canadian scientists who signed the warning were Paul-Yves Denis, Gerhard

One example of the impact that human activity can have on wildlife.

Herzberg, Digby McLaren, Brenda Milner, Lawrence Mysak, John Polyani, and Betty Roots. In addition to these scientists, many people are aware that achieving the future we desire for human society and the plant and animal kingdom means we must improve how we cooperatively plan and manage environmental resources.

LINKAGES: PEOPLE AS PART OF ECOSYSTEMS

Although our intellectual characteristics separate us from other species, humans play essentially the same role as any other species within ecosystems. That is, humans rely—as do other species— on clean air, water, soil, and a continuing supply of plant and animal products, some of which they consume and convert to meet their own physiological needs. The wastes humans discharge become part of the Earth's cycles of decay and renewal (see Chapter 3).

Humans, however, are unlike other species in that we have the ability to cause drastic changes in the ecosystems on which we depend. Our technologies enable us to extract and use resources and ecosystem products faster than the **biosphere** can renew them. This causes a decline in the natural productivity of ecosystems that may be permanent and irreversible. If this happens, we are said to be living off the capital of our environment rather than the interest. This is a significant reason for learning to sustain environmental resources so that they will be available in the future.

Unlike other species, humans have been successful in minimizing or overcoming factors such as extreme climates, other predators, and diseases that formerly limited

our numbers. These successes have contributed to an expanding world population that continues to put increasing pressure on Earth's natural resources, life support, and socioeconomic systems. It is important to recognize that humans are an integral part of Earth's ecosystems and are subject to the same constraints as other living creatures. The way we lead our lives has a significant impact on the environment we share with them.

Our interdependence is confirmed also: consider how quickly our lives would end without the plants and animals that produce products on which we rely every day— the oxygen we breathe, food we eat, timber for the houses we live in, our cotton and linen clothing, the fibres in the pages of this book, our shoe leather, and the wool of our sweaters and socks, to name a few (Figure 1–2). In the past, people used the environment's resources to provide food, clothing, and shelter, and other commodities that benefited the human race. Often, we measured our progress by our success in exploiting these resources— fish, animals, land, water, and trees—but without realizing that all of these things were interconnected. The use of one environmental resource always affects the status of another resource or ecosystem, either immediately or in the longer term.

With growing understanding of how the Earth works as a system, people began to realize how much a part of the ecosystem they were and began to appreciate the importance of caring for the entirety of their ecosystem, their Earth home. People also began to realize how much knowledge would be needed to understand the effects of our ongoing activities so that we could determine which ones were sustainable, that is, which activities would help maintain environmental resources so they continued to provide benefits for people and other living things.

Today we have accepted the environment as one of our major social and political issues and, with the help of technology, are trying to find solutions to the problems our activities have created. Part of the task of determining appropriate solutions is to understand the major causes of environmental problems we face.

MAJOR CAUSES OF ENVIRONMENTAL PROBLEMS

There is general agreement among environmental scientists that the complex and interrelated root causes of environmental problems include human population growth, abuse of resources and natural systems, and pollution. Each of these major causes and several related themes are discussed in the following sections.

World Scientists' Warning to Humanity

Introduction Human beings and the natural world are on a collision course. Human activities inflict harsh and often irreversible damage on the environment and on critical resources. If not checked, many of our current practices put at serious risk the future that we wish for human society and the plant and animal kingdoms, and may so alter the living world that it will be unable to sustain life in the manner that we know. Fundamental changes are urgent if we are to avoid the collision our present course will bring about.

The Environment The environment is suffering critical stress:

The Atmosphere. Stratospheric ozone depletion threatens us with enhanced ultraviolet radiation at the earth's surface, which can be damaging or lethal to many life forms. Air pollution near ground level, and acid precipitation, are already causing widespread injury to humans, forests, and crops.

Water Resources. Heedless exploitation of depletable ground water supplies endangers food production and other essential human systems. Heavy demands on the world's surface waters have resulted in serious shortages in some 80 countries, containing 40 percent of the world's population. Pollution of rivers, lakes, and ground water further limits the supply.

Oceans. Destructive pressure on the oceans is severe, particularly in the coastal regions which produce most of the world's food fish. The total marine catch is now at or above the estimated maximum sustainable yield. Some fisheries have already shown signs of collapse. Rivers carrying heavy burdens of eroded soil into the seas also carry industrial, municipal, agricultural, and livestock waste—some of it toxic.

Soil. Loss of soil productivity, which is causing extensive land abandonment, is a widespread by-product of current practices in agriculture and animal husbandry. Since 1945, 11 percent of the earth's vegetated surface has been degraded—an area larger than India and China combined—and per capita food production in many parts of the world is decreasing.

Forests. Tropical rain forests, as well as tropical and temperate dry forests, are being destroyed rapidly. At present rates, some critical forest types will be gone in a few years, and most of the tropical rain forest will be gone before the end of the next century. With them will go large numbers of plant and animal species.

Living Species. The irreversible loss of species, which by 2100 may reach one-third of all species now living, is especially serious. We are losing the potential they hold for providing medicinal and other benefits, and the contribution that genetic diversity of life forms gives to the robustness of the world's biological systems and to the astonishing beauty of the earth itself.

Much of this damage is irreversible on a scale of centuries, or permanent. Other processes appear to pose additional threats. Increasing levels of gases in the atmosphere from human activities, including carbon dioxide released from fossil fuel burning and from deforestation, may alter climate on a global scale. Predictions of global warming are still uncertain—with projected effects ranging from tolerable to very severe—but the potential risks are very great.

Our massive tampering with the world's interdependent web of life—coupled with the environmental damage inflicted by deforestation, species loss, and climate change—could trigger widespread adverse effects, including unpredictable collapses of critical biological systems whose interactions and dynamics we only imperfectly understand.

Uncertainty over the extent of these effects cannot excuse complacency or delay in facing the threats.

Population The earth is finite. Its ability to absorb wastes and destructive effluent is finite. Its ability to provide food and energy is finite. Its ability to provide for growing numbers of people is finite. And we are fast approaching many of the earth's limits. Current economic practices which damage the environment, in both developed and underdeveloped nations, cannot be continued without the risk that vital global systems will be damaged beyond repair.

Pressures resulting from unrestrained population growth put demands on the natural world that can overwhelm any efforts to achieve a sustainable future. If we are to halt the destruction of our environment, we must accept limits to that growth. A World Bank estimate indicates that world population will not stabilize at less than 12.4 billion, while the United Nations concludes that the eventual total could reach 14 billion, a near tripling of today's 5.4 billion. But, even at this moment, one person in five lives in absolute poverty without enough to eat, and one in ten suffers serious malnutrition.

No more than one or a few decades remain before the chance to avert the threats we now confront will be lost and the prospects for humanity immeasurably diminished.

Warning We the undersigned, senior members of the world's scientific community, hereby warn all humanity of what lies ahead. A great change in our stewardship of the earth and the life on it is required, if vast human misery is to be avoided and our global home on this planet is not to be irretrievably mutilated.

What We Must Do Five inextricably linked areas must be addressed simultaneously:

1. **We must bring environmentally damaging activities under control to restore and protect the integrity of the earth's systems we depend on.** We must, for example, move away from fossil fuels to more benign, inexhaustible energy sources to cut greenhouse gas emissions and the pollution of our air and water. Priority must be given to the development of energy sources matched to Third World needs—small-scale and relatively easy to implement.

   We must halt deforestation, injury to and loss of agricultural land, and the loss of terrestrial and marine plant and animal species.

2. **We must manage resources crucial to human welfare more effectively.** We must give high priority to efficient use of energy, water, and other materials, including expansion of conservation and recycling.

3. **We must stabilize population. This will be possible only if all nations recognize that it requires improved social and economic conditions, and the adoption of effective, voluntary family planning.**

4. **We must reduce and eventually eliminate poverty.**

5. **We must ensure sexual equality, and guarantee women control over their own reproductive decisions.**

The developed nations are the largest polluters in the world today. They must greatly reduce their overconsumption, if we are to reduce pressures on resources and the global environment. The developed nations have the obligation to provide aid and support to developing nations, because only the developed nations have the financial resources and the technical skills for these tasks.

Acting on this recognition is not altruism, but enlightened self-interest: whether industrialized or not, we all have but one lifeboat. No nation can escape from injury when global biological systems are damaged. No nation can escape from conflicts over increasingly scarce resources. In addition, environmental and economic instabilities will cause mass migrations with incalculable consequences for developed and underdeveloped nations alike.

Developing nations must realize that environmental damage is one of the gravest threats they face, and that attempts to blunt it will be overwhelmed if their populations go unchecked. The greatest peril is to become trapped in spirals of environmental decline, poverty, and unrest, leading to social, economic, and environmental collapse.

Success in this global endeavor will require a great reduction in violence and war. Resources now devoted to the preparation and conduct of war—amounting to over $1 trillion annually—will be badly needed in the new tasks and should be diverted to the new challenges.

A new ethic is required—a new attitude towards discharging our responsibility for caring for ourselves and for the earth. We must recognize the earth's limited capacity to provide for us. We must recognize its fragility. We must no longer allow it to be ravaged. This ethic must motivate a great movement, convincing reluctant leaders and reluctant governments and reluctant peoples themselves to effect the needed changes.

The scientists issuing this warning hope that our message will reach and affect people everywhere. We need the help of many.

We require the help of the world community of scientists—natural, social, economic, political;

We require the help of the world's business and industrial leaders;

We require the help of the world's religious leaders; and

We require the help of the world's peoples.

We call on all to join us in this task.

SOURCE: The Union of Concerned Scientists. (1993). *World scientists' warning to humanity.* Cambridge, MA: Union of Concerned Scientists. Reprinted with permission.

Figure 1–2
Human–environment connections: an anthropocentric view of planet Earth's provision for human life and activities

HUMAN POPULATION GROWTH

The population bomb, or exponential doubling of the Earth's human population, is the fundamental issue of the environment—environmental damage occurs simply because of the very large number of people now on Earth. For most of the world's history, human numbers have been low: within the past 150 years, however, a dramatic increase in population has occurred (Figure 1–3). It was not until 1800 that the human population reached its first billion and it took another 130 years to double to 2 billion. Between 1930 and 1975, in only 45 years, the population doubled again to 4 billion. Sometime between July 1986 and July 1987, the 5 billionth person was added to Earth's population and, by 2030, 10 billion people could inhabit the planet.

In the financial world, exponential rates of increase are considered to be a good thing. For example, if you were promised compensation for a 30-day job, starting at one cent for the first day and doubling each succeeding day, on the final day you would be paid over $5 million! As far as population is concerned, however, exponential rates of increase intensify the competition between people as they try to gain their share of the Earth's water, land, food, and other resources. United Nations statistics indicate that four-fifths of the more than five billion people now

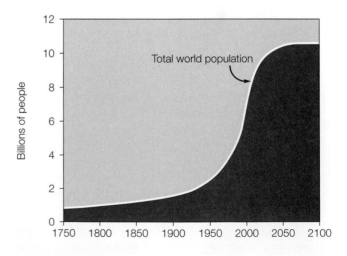

Figure 1–3
Growth in total world population since 1750 and projected from the late 1990s to 2100

Developing countries such as Bangladesh struggle with the problems associated with overcrowding.

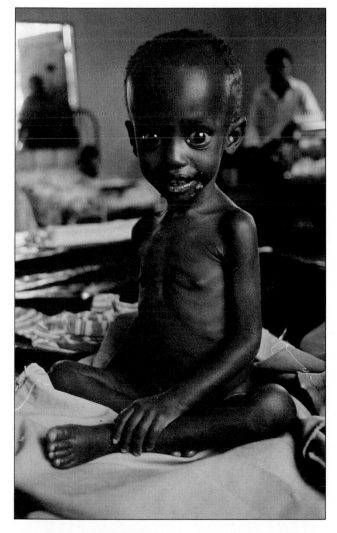

Children are among the hardest-hit victims of food and other resource shortages.

living on Earth do not have adequate food, housing, and safe drinking water. Each day, almost 110 000 people die from starvation or related illnesses. While most of the severe stress occurs in developing countries, even in industrialized nations such as Canada there are people who do not have enough food to eat and who cannot afford a warm, dry place in which to live.

When human populations exceed their environmental resources, particularly the capacity of land to produce food resources, malnutrition and starvation result. Following the Sahel drought (1973–74) in Africa, for example, about 500 000 people died of starvation and several million more were affected permanently by malnutrition. In parts of Africa in the 1980s, human population growth created such demand for food from agricultural lands that their future productivity was threatened.

This situation illustrates a classic conflict in values: which is more important, the survival of people alive today, or the conservation of the environment on which future food production and human life depend? Part of the answer requires technical and scientific knowledge to determine whether agricultural production can continue to increase without destruction of the land on which it is based. Such knowledge provides an important basis for a decision that depends on our values. Ultimately, however, unless we can limit the total number of people on Earth to a number the environment can sustain, we cannot expect to solve other environmental problems. Given that the issue of the rapidly increasing human population underlies almost all environmental problems, we revisit population topics in more detail in Chapter 4.

ABUSE OF RESOURCES AND NATURAL SYSTEMS

People have defined *resources* as anything useful that serves our needs and is available at a price we are willing to pay. **Renewable resources** (such as forests, solar energy, and lobsters) are replaced by environmental processes in a time frame that is meaningful to humans. Provided they are not used more quickly than they are restored, these resources will continue to supply human needs into the future. **Nonrenewable resources** are finite in supply or are replaced so slowly (in human terms) by the environment that, practically speaking, their supply is finite. As nonrenewable resources such as coal, oil, and other fossil fuels are used, their supply is depleted.

Frequently, people have used living environmental resources such as trees, fish, and wildlife, faster than they were replenished by natural processes. We have extracted nonliving resources such as oil, minerals, and groundwater without thinking about their limits or the need for recycling. Technology has allowed us to extract and use resources so efficiently that we have been able to satisfy our wants in addition to our needs. Not surprisingly, the combination of resource demands and vast human numbers has resulted in people exerting an environmental impact greater than any other species. This is particularly true of about 20 percent of the world's population that lives in developed nations (Western Europe, the former U.S.S.R., the United States, Australia, Japan, and Canada) and uses nearly 80 percent of the world's resources each year. In the next two to three decades, as developing nations strive to attain standards of living closer to those of developed nations, it is anticipated that resource use and associated impacts will rise sharply.

POLLUTION

Media coverage of dramatic events such as the 1984 release of methyl isocyanate from Union Carbide's pesticide production facility in Bhopal, India, the 1986 Chernobyl nuclear plant disaster in the Soviet Union, the 1989 *Exxon Valdez* oil spill in Prince William Sound in Alaska, and the 1991 oil slick in the Persian Gulf has promoted international awareness of pollution problems.

Far more insidious, however, are the less dramatic but long-term releases of toxic chemicals, sewage, carcinogens, hormone residues, pesticides, nuclear contaminants, and other harmful substances into our atmosphere, rivers, oceans, and soils. These sorts of industrial and municipal pollution problems have resulted in dead fish on stream banks, vanishing species, recreational beach closures, restrictions on shellfish consumption, dying lakes and forests, birth defects, and other debilitating or fatal conditions such as organ and nerve damage, and lung and bone marrow cancers.

Pollutants, substances that affect adversely the physical, chemical, or biological quality of the Earth's environment or that accumulate in the cells or tissues of living organisms in amounts that threaten the health or survival of these organisms, may originate from natural or human (cultural) sources. Volcanoes, fires ignited by lightning, decomposition of swamp materials, and other natural processes contribute to pollution of Earth's air, water, and soil. But, when human populations grew, technological capabilities advanced, and our consumption of resources and consumer goods increased, large numbers and volumes of cultural pollutants were released into the environment. Increasingly it has become more difficult for the environment to absorb and process these substances.

Many pollution problems are global in scope: increases in greenhouse gases, a decline in stratospheric ozone, and acidification of soils, forests, and lakes are among the most prominent of current global pollution issues. International cooperative action, including overcoming political inertia and socioeconomic barriers that hamper progress, is required to solve these global pollution problems. Other pollution issues occur at regional scales (such as industrial pollution in Eastern Europe) and local scales (such as air pollution in Mexico City) and also require cooperative efforts to resolve.

Historically, humans have discharged their wastes without due regard for the long-term and cumulative impacts on the environment. Our challenge for the future is to change our attitudes and work toward sustainability as a primary goal.

RELATED THEMES

In identifying major causes of environmental problems, we must not forget that life on planet Earth involves complex interrelationships between living things—the land, ocean waters and fresh waters, and the atmosphere. The effects of human activity on Earth are now so extensive that global (not just local) environmental change is under way, and no one is entirely sure how these interrelationships will evolve. We know that the actions of many people at different locations have contributed to changes in concentrations of stratospheric ozone and greenhouse gases; we do not know exactly how these global changes will alter the Earth's climate. What is certain, however, is that because human actions are changing the environment at the global level, we need to ensure that our ways of thinking about and understanding the Earth and its systems have a global perspective.

We need to remember, too, that most people in the developed world, including most Canadians, live in urban areas, in cities and towns that continue to expand over the land, spreading over farmland and natural areas, altering drainage patterns, endangering wildlife, and so on. Urban areas have not been studied intensely from an environmental quality perspective, but they do experience air pollution, waste-disposal problems, social unrest, and other environmental stresses. Increasingly, the livability and quality of the urban world and the balance we strike between economic development and urbanization will be an important focus in sustainable future environments.

To solve contemporary environmental problems, and to move toward future sustainable environments, we need more than facts and scientific understanding regarding a particular issue. While knowledge is an integral part of environmental decision making, so too are our value systems and ethical concerns about social justice and moral commitments to other living things and to future genera-

Even in Canada, where population pressures are less intense, urban growth and development continue to encroach on limited agricultural land and natural habitats.

tions. Sustainability is a function of how many people depend on an environment and of our values (what kind of life or standard of living do we want for ourselves and our descendants? what kind of environment do we want for them? for people in developing nations?). If we know what our values are and which potential solutions are socially just, we should be able to apply our scientific knowledge and determine an acceptable, sustainable solution for each specific problem.

SUSTAINABILITY CHALLENGES

Sustainability is a major theme and challenge related directly to the future of our lives and that of this planet. As a concept, **sustainability** refers to the ability of an ecosystem to maintain ecological processes and functions, **biodiversity,** and productivity over time (Kaufmann et al., 1994). In practice, the meaning of *sustainability* has varied, but there is agreement that people must learn how to sustain environmental resources so that they continue to provide benefits to us, other living things, and the larger environment of which we are a part.

If Canadians as well as people in other countries are to enjoy an acceptable quality of life in the future, the message of sustainability must be carried out through our actions. Considerable importance is attached to sustainability because it offers an approach to "looking at decisions in a holistic way where there is parallel care and respect for people and for the enveloping ecosystem of which everyone is a part" (Hodge, Holtz, Smith & Hawke Baxter, 1995).

The idea of **sustainable development** was brought into the public domain with the 1980 publication of the *World Conservation Strategy* (International Union for the Conservation of Nature and Natural Resources [IUCN], United Nations Environment Programme [UNEP] & World Wildlife Fund [WWF], 1980). The *World Conservation Strategy* (WCS) aimed to achieve sustainable development through the conservation of living resources. Living resource conservation had three main objectives: (a) maintaining essential ecological processes and life support systems, (b) preserving genetic diversity, and (c) ensuring the sustainable utilization of species and ecosystems.

The WCS promoted integration of conservation and development to ensure that "modifications to the planet do indeed secure the survival and wellbeing of all people" and "to meet the needs of today without foreclosing the achievement of tomorrow's [needs]" (IUCN et al., 1980, p. 1). To be sustainable, the WCS declared, development must be sensitive to short- and long-term alternatives; take social, economic, and ecological factors into account; and include living and nonliving resources.

The 1992 Earth Summit illustrates that despite the appearance of cooperation among international leaders, political inertia often can be overcome only by the actions of individuals and nongovernmental organizations.

Publication of *Our Common Future* (World Commission on Environment and Development, 1987), also known as the Bruntland Report, propelled the concept of sustainable development into widespread usage and prominence as a global objective. Generally, the underlying message of most definitions of this concept entails the need for people to live equitably within the means of the ecosphere (Wackernagel & Rees, 1996). Unfortunately, in popular usage *sustainable development* became somewhat of an oxymoron and sometimes was misused or misunderstood because the two words contained in the term meant different things to different people. Some people tuned in to the *sustainable* part of the term and understood that sustainable development called for ecological and social transformation to a world of environmental stability and social justice. Other people identified more with the *development* part of the term and interpreted it to mean more sensitive growth, or a reformed version of the status quo.

The trouble with the popularity of the term *sustainable development* is that it fails to distinguish clearly between true development and mere growth (cited in Wackernagel & Rees, 1996). *Growth* generally means increasing in size, while *development* means improving or getting better. If we apply this understanding, we then have the sense that sustainable development is progressive social betterment without growing beyond ecological carrying capacity. To put it slightly differently, sustainable development leads to improvement in the quality of life while living within the carrying capacity of supporting ecosystems (World Conservation Union (IUCN) et al., 1991). Still, the term is problematic because, for example, people in wealthy societies such as ours may have to consume less while the poor consume more. Not everyone accepts the implications of such a concept.

To reduce the misunderstanding associated with sustainable *development*, the term *sustainability* often is used. Sustainability echoes the need to balance environmental and developmental concerns, to take an ecological approach to decisions, and to stay within carrying capacity. As the concept is applied, and people work toward a sustainable future, one important mechanism to help achieve their goals is increased cooperation and collaborative effort among individuals, organizations, and nations.

A good example of cooperative global action toward sustainability was the development and subsequent adoption at the 1992 Rio de Janeiro Earth Summit of treaties dealing with climate change and biological diversity, and of *Agenda 21* and the Earth Charter. National representatives attending the Earth Summit (officially, the second United Nations Conference on Environment and Development [UNCED]) discussed and debated a number of international environmental problems including deterioration of the Earth's atmosphere and oceans from pollution, forest destruction, and loss of biodiversity.

Negotiations on these topics, treaties, and agreements began years before the Earth Summit was held. *Agenda 21*, for example, is a complex document outlining actions and programs to support sustainable development for the 21st century. Although developed nations did not commit nearly enough financial assistance to help developing countries industrialize without harming the environment, *Agenda 21* itself was developed through the collective action and shared responsibility of both developed and developing nations. For a brief overview of *Agenda 21*, see the summary description in Box 1–1.

Attended by more than 100 heads of state (including Canada's prime minister), the Earth Summit was the largest international gathering ever to concentrate on serious environmental issues. Because the Earth Summit and the Global Forum (a parallel citizens' conference held in conjunction with the United Nations meeting) received so much international attention, they not only increased worldwide awareness of global issues, but also became the

PART 1:
OUR ENVIRONMENT

most visible expression of international awareness of sustainability ever seen. Progress (or lack of it) in achieving the objectives established at the 1992 Earth Summit was considered at the Earth Summit + 5 sessions held in New York in June 1997 (see also Box 5–4).

Canada has been involved in international efforts to define and refine the concept of sustainability and in domestic efforts to promote the concept. Table 1–1 identifies some the of major milestones in international growth of the sustainability concept as well as selected Canadian efforts to support sustainability.

GUIDING PRINCIPLES OF SUSTAINABILITY

If we intend to attain sustainability in Canada, it is vital that we view development as progressive improvement in human and environmental affairs, and that we identify how to achieve this improvement. As Table 1–2 indicates,

if development is viewed in this way, activities that increase the capacity of the environment to meet human needs and protect and maintain life-support systems should result in healthy people and environments. These and other desired benefits, however, must be maintained indefinitely to be considered sustainable.

Since sustainability deals with a future condition (and we know how difficult it is to predict the future accurately), it is uncertain whether we can achieve sustainability. We can, however, improve the likelihood of reaching sustainability by simultaneously rejecting development activities and processes that are unsustainable and taking actions that experience has shown are sustainable. Efforts to achieve sustainability will entail a complex mixture of activities, of which some incorporate social, economic, and environmental objectives, others involve exploitation of Earth's material resources, and still others depend on intellectual resources to help people reach their full potential and enjoy a reasonable standard of living (Government of Canada, 1996).

BOX 1-1
AGENDA 21: A BRIEF OVERVIEW

Agenda 21 is a plan of action for the world's governments and citizens. It sets forth strategies and measures aimed at halting and reversing the effects of environmental degradation and promoting environmentally sound and sustainable development throughout the world. The Agenda contains some 40 chapters and totals more than 800 pages. In the words of UNCED's Secretary General, Maurice Strong: "It is the product of intensive negotiations among Governments on the basis of proposals prepared by the UNCED Secretariat, drawing on extensive inputs from relevant United Nations agencies and organizations, expert consultations, intergovernmental and non-governmental organizations, regional conferences and national reports, and the direction provided through four sessions of the Preparatory Committee of the Conference." It is "based on the premise that sustainable development is not just an option but an imperative, in both environmental and economic terms and that while the transition towards sustainable development will be difficult, it is entirely feasible."

UNCED has grouped Agenda 21's priority actions under seven social themes, designed to promote a prospering, just, habitable, fertile, shared and clean world, managed through wide and responsible public participation. These themes are entitled:

1. The Prospering World (revitalizing growth with sustainability)
2. The Just World (sustainable living)
3. The Habitable World (human settlements)
4. The Fertile Word (global and regional resources)
5. The Shared World (global and regional resources)
6. The Clean World (managing chemicals and waste)
7. The People's World (people participation and responsibility)

For an overview of Agenda 21 and summaries of these themes, the reader is referred to UNCED's publication, *The Global Partnership for Environment and Development: A Guide to Agenda 21*. IRDC has also published *IDRC, An Agenda 21 Organization: A Backgrounder on Current Activities*, in which it states that although the Centre has been active in many of Agenda 21's key areas, it will not try to cover all of them.

"As an Agenda 21 organization", it says, "IDRC's comparative advantage is in capacity-building (one of the highest priorities of Agenda 21): (helping) developing countries and local communities to put in place the knowledge, the people, the organization and linking it all together to enhance their decisions and policies."

NOTE: *Agenda 21* is available on the World Wide Web. One site to check is the United Nations Division for Sustainable Development, where clicking on the hyperlink (underlined text line) of the United Nations Conference on Environment and Development will lead you to the Gopher menu that provides connections to *Agenda 21* (A-21) documentation in English, French, and Spanish. The Uniform Resource Locator (URL) address is: http://www.un.org/dpcsd/dsd/

SOURCE: International Development Research Centre. (1993). *Agenda 21: Green paths to the future.* Ottawa: International Development Research Centre. Reprinted with permission.

TABLE 1-1

MAJOR MILESTONES: SUSTAINABLE DEVELOPMENT AND SUSTAINABILITY

Year(s)	Document or Process	Agency
1980	***World Conservation Strategy*** • The concept of sustainable development was first introduced.	International Union for the Conservation of Nature and Natural Resources, United Nations Environment Programme, and World Wildlife Fund
1987	***Our Common Future*** (the Bruntland Report) • Sustainable development gained international prominence as a global objective. • In 1985, the Bruntland Commission had held hearings in most regions of Canada; input from citizens and officials helped shape the report.	World Commission on Environment and Development
1989	Preparatory discussions began for the United Nations Conference on Environment and Development (UNCED).	United Nations
1989, 1990	***Round tables on the environment and the economy*** • National, provincial, and territorial round tables were established in response to the Bruntland Report. • Round tables provided a forum for discussion of cross-sectoral issues.	National, provincial, and territorial governments in Canada
1991	***Caring for the Earth*** • A more broadly based version of the WCS was developed. • In 1986, Canada had supported the IUCN Conference on Conservation and Development that reviewed and evaluated the WCS and led to publication of *Caring for the Earth*.	International Union for the Conservation of Nature and Natural Resources
1992	***Earth Summit*** (UNCED) held in Rio de Janeiro, Brazil • Treaties and agreements signed included these: *Climate Change:* to curb CO_2 emissions and reduce greenhouse effect, for which no timetable was set; *Biological Diversity:* to decrease the rate of extinction of world's endangered species; *Agenda 21:* a complex action plan for sustainable development in the 21st century; and *Earth Charter* (the Rio Declaration): a statement of philosophy about environment and development.	United Nations
1995	***Earth Charter*** • A new, more progressive, and inspiring Earth Charter was adopted to celebrate the United Nations' 50th anniversary.	United Nations

SOURCE: Adapted from Government of Canada. (1996a). *The state of Canada's environment—1996.* Ottawa: Supply and Services Canada.

One of the major premises or principles of sustainable actions, found in the initial WCS and reiterated through *Our Common Future* and *Agenda 21* of the Earth Summit, involves ethical issues such as equity and respect for the rights and welfare of other people (Box 1–2). Other major principles are those of ecological sustainability, social sustainability, and economic sustainability, as well as the precautionary principle. These principles are discussed below.

Ecological Sustainability

Ecosystems are the source of all life's vital requirements—water to drink, air to breathe, sun for warmth, soils for plant growth—and are the structures within which these life-supporting processes occur (see Chapter 3). If an ecosystem is damaged (for instance, if soils cannot regenerate, or if carbon, oxygen, and other elements cannot circulate) its ability to sustain the life of people, plants, and

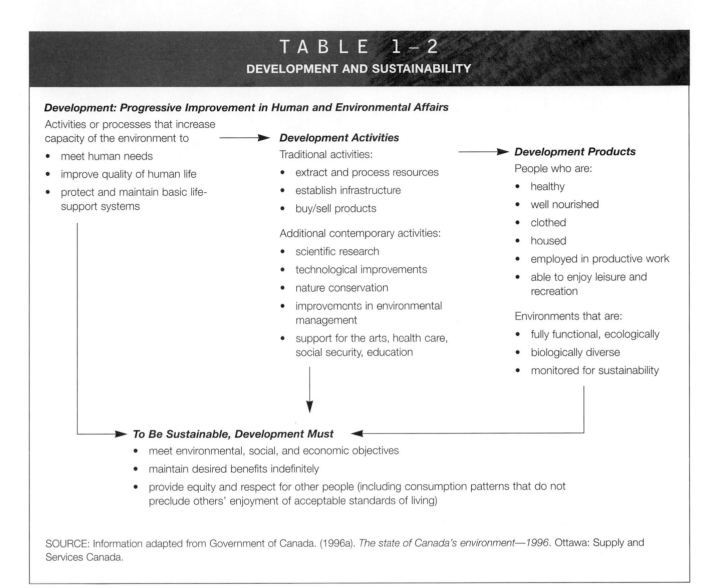

TABLE 1-2
DEVELOPMENT AND SUSTAINABILITY

Development: Progressive Improvement in Human and Environmental Affairs

Activities or processes that increase capacity of the environment to

- meet human needs
- improve quality of human life
- protect and maintain basic life-support systems

Development Activities

Traditional activities:

- extract and process resources
- establish infrastructure
- buy/sell products

Additional contemporary activities:

- scientific research
- technological improvements
- nature conservation
- improvements in environmental management
- support for the arts, health care, social security, education

Development Products

People who are:

- healthy
- well nourished
- clothed
- housed
- employed in productive work
- able to enjoy leisure and recreation

Environments that are:

- fully functional, ecologically
- biologically diverse
- monitored for sustainability

To Be Sustainable, Development Must

- meet environmental, social, and economic objectives
- maintain desired benefits indefinitely
- provide equity and respect for other people (including consumption patterns that do not preclude others' enjoyment of acceptable standards of living)

SOURCE: Information adapted from Government of Canada. (1996a). *The state of Canada's environment—1996*. Ottawa: Supply and Services Canada.

animals may be reduced or destroyed. Since people are dependent on Earth's ecosystems, we need to learn how ecosystems support us and how environmental change affects ecosystems. Furthermore, because "the human economy is a fully dependent sub-system of the ecosphere" (Wackernagel & Rees, 1996, p. 4), it is vital that we understand the significance of incorporating ecological sustainability in our efforts to develop in a sustainable manner.

Ecological Footprints A dramatic metaphor for humanity's continuing dependence on nature and the Earth's capacity to support a humane existence for all in the future, an **ecological footprint** describes the link between people's lifestyles and ecosystems. Ecological footprints allow people to visualize the impacts of their consumption patterns and activities on ecosystems.

The ecological footprint for a particular human population or economy is an estimate of the total area of land and water (ecosystems) needed to produce all the resources consumed and to assimilate all the wastes discharged by that population or economy—a measure of the requirements to support a particular lifestyle indefinitely. Calculating an ecological footprint is complex, given that world trade in foodstuffs, forest resources, and minerals, as well as the products manufactured from those raw materials, facilitates international interaction between people and ecosystems. In Box 1–3, the ecological footprint concept is described briefly and the footprint of the Lower Fraser Valley in British Columbia is noted.

The concept of ecological footprints is important in guiding our efforts to achieve sustainability because it helps people understand that their individual actions can and do affect the global environment. While it is true that small communities in the developing world may have smaller ecological footprints (because they rely less on trade and technology) and may live at a level close to the carrying capacity of their local environmental resources,

The environment is something in which all people share a common interest and by which all may be affected. Not surprisingly, ethical questions are at the heart of many environmental issues.

Ethics refers to the principles that define a person's duty to other persons and, indeed, to other living things with which we share this planet. Such principles are based on respect for the rights and welfare of other people, including those whom we may never meet and those who are as yet unborn. It is in accordance with ethics that people decide if an action is right or wrong.

Socioeconomic development that affects the environment and sometimes entire ecosystems therefore also has ethical dimensions. Decisions about development are usually based on estimates of the present and future costs and benefits to society. Such assessments take into account the likely environmental, economic, and social effects. To assess options, every effort is made to define effects in measurable terms and to identify who may gain and who may lose. Such a process is an indispensable means of assembling relevant information and can provide an invaluable basis for identifying the ethical dimensions involved.

However, many ethical issues cannot be quantified. It is difficult to fit ethical factors into the conventional framework of environmental decision-making in the same way as more tangible factors such as economic and biophysical data. What is necessary, then, is for people to consider the broad implications of any development: whether, on balance, a proposal or project is right or wrong in respect of its present and future impacts on other people, on other species, and on ecosystems. Access to full and accurate information about the development and about experiences with similar activities will guide people in deciding about the options that are available. Views on ethics are an essential supplement to the hard, measurable data in the decision-making process.

SOURCE: Government of Canada. (1996a). *The state of Canada's environment—1996.* Ottawa.

The ecological footprint for residents of the Lower Fraser Valley is estimated at 19 times the land area they occupy.

chlorofluorocarbons (CFCs), destruction of stratospheric ozone, and global climate change are among the results. Whether it is disposal of community waste or discharge of industrial pollutants, experience has shown us that environmental carelessness at any one location may have impacts that extend over considerable distances and time periods. Realizing our individual actions contribute to these environmental problems is an important step to understanding that all humans are connected to the one Earth that supports us. In that one Earth we share a common natural heritage and have a responsibility to care for that heritage. The ecological footprint approach helps us see the ecological reality of our actions and challenges and directs us toward more sustainable lifestyles.

An Ecosystem Approach If we think of ecological footprint analysis as a practical tool to help us assess the sustainability of our current activities, then we can conceive of an ecosystem approach as a guide to help us apply our

Urban infrastructure such as transportation systems contribute to a city's ecological footprint.

the same cannot be said of small communities in the industrialized world. Even in the Canadian North, for instance, where just a few decades ago people in small communities lived in harmony with their local environment and extracted quality **country food,** they now purchase imported foodstuffs and goods from southern Canada (in part because of concern about bioaccumulation of toxins in some fish and animal species eaten—see Chapter 3).

In urban centres, people's everyday activities and actions contribute to disruptions in ecological processes. Our individual actions and those activities associated with our local and regional industrial processes have affected the global environment—emissions of carbon dioxide and

BOX 1-3
THE ECOLOGICAL FOOTPRINT CONCEPT

Probably most of us have looked at our footprints in the sand on a beach, in the dirt of a field, or in new-fallen snow, but how many of us have considered looking at the footprints our communities leave on their surroundings? That's one of the ideas William Rees and Mathis Wackernagel have been exploring since 1990 through the Task Force on Planning Healthy and Sustainable Communities at the University of British Columbia.

As most Canadians live in cities and towns, we tend to forget that human life is very tightly entwined with nature. Urban living tends to break our connections with the ecosystems that provide us with a host of basic materials we need for life, from the air we breathe to the wood we use to build houses and make paper products. Ecosystems also absorb our wastes, protect us from ultraviolet radiation, and provide a wide range of other functions.

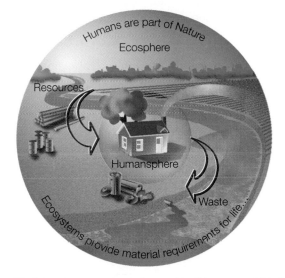

City living, however, tends to provide little sense of this intimacy with the Earth. We probably buy most of our foods—imported from all over the world—from grocery stores, and flush our wastes down the toilet or place them in garbage cans for collection by sanitation engineers. Ironically, we might even be able to shop at a wilderness store in the mall!

In considering a city's impact or footprint on the environment, it's important to include our basic reliance on ecosystems as well as the more obvious buildings, roads, industrial parks, and housing areas that are spread over the landscape. Ecological footprints measure the load that any given community or population imposes on the ecosystems that support it. Footprints are expressed in terms of the land area necessary to sustain current levels of resource consumption and waste discharge by that population. According to Wackernagel and Rees (1996, p. 9), "ecological footprint analysis is an accounting tool that enables us to estimate the resource consumption and waste assimilation requirements of a defined human population or economy in terms of a corresponding productive land area."

Much of the work involved in determining the footprint is aimed at estimating carrying capacity—for example, how much land would it take to produce all the goods and services that are used by people living in a city. It's impossible to take every factor into account, and the calculations are complex, but a rough idea of a city's—or your individual—ecological footprint can be revealing.

Wackernagel and Rees estimated the ecological footprint for residents of British Columbia's densely populated Lower Fraser Valley (Vancouver to Hope) and determined that this region depends on a land area 19 times larger than that contained within its boundaries to satisfy current consumption levels of food, forest products, energy, and carbon dioxide assimilation. By their calculations, each individual Canadian requires 4.27 hectares of land to support her or his current lifestyle. The footprint for an average American was estimated at 5.1 hectares.

"If everyone lived like today's North Americans, it would take at least two additional planet Earths to produce the resources, absorb the wastes, and otherwise maintain life-support. Unfortunately, good planets are hard to find ..." (Wackernagel and Rees, 1996, p. 15).

SOURCES: Government of Canada. (1996a). *The state of Canada's environment—1996.* Ottawa: Supply and Services Canada.

Government of Canada. (1996b). 1996 Report of Canada to the United Nations Commission on Sustainable Development. http://www.ec.gc.ca/agenda21/96/part1.html

Wackernagel, M., & Rees, W. (1996). *Our ecological footprint: Reducing human impact on the earth.* Gabriola Island, BC: New Society

understanding of ecological constraints to make more effective decisions about achieving sustainability. An ecosystem approach requires a fundamental shift in thinking; it reflects a whole Earth ethic in which our decisions and actions recognize the dependencies that exist within and among ecosystems and consider all the connections between biological and physical components of the Ecosphere. This, too, is a practical element in working toward a sustainable future. For example, we cannot improve the management of east coast fish stocks unless we understand both the aquatic environment of which the fish are a part and the human activities that affect that environment.

To achieve our desired sustainable future, our thinking about people as part of ecosystems needs to change. We need to promote a holistic approach to human interactions with ecosystems and the environment, and to be guided by an ecosystem approach that respects ecosystems, organisms, and people. If we adopt an ecosystem approach (see Chapter 12) and adhere to ethical principles (see Chapter 2), we should see new attitudes and practices combining to safeguard the future of the Earth.

Carrying Capacity In simplistic terms, **carrying capacity** is the number of organisms that an area can support indefinitely. An expanded definition, which reflects the importance of all ecosystem components and ecological processes, indicates that carrying capacity is the capability of an ecosystem to support healthy organisms while maintaining its productivity, adaptability, and capability for renewal (IUCN et al., 1991).

The concept of carrying capacity is sometimes used to suggest how many people can be supported by the environment over time, or to define what levels of human impact might be sustainable. However, the carrying capacity idea was developed by population biologists in their study of nonhuman populations, so the concept applies to human populations only by analogy. As a result, and because there is no universally agreed-on equation to calculate the carrying capacity for human populations, we do not know the human carrying capacity of the Earth at this time. Carrying capacity calculations increase in complexity when wealthier countries import locally scarce resources (such as water, fertilizers, and fossil fuels) to supplement their natural carrying capacity. The carrying capacity of ecosystems in poorer nations is defined by their natural limitations.

Despite these difficulties, the carrying capacity concept is useful in debating whether ecosystems define natural limits to growth and whether humans already have exceeded the Earth's carrying capacity. Some people, Wackernagel and Rees (1996) among them, believe that growth in population and in per capita consumption are shrinking the Earth's carrying capacity. Their ecological

footprint analysis has shown two conflicting trends, one where the available ecologically productive land (and water) has decreased from over 5 hectares at the beginning of this century to less than 1.5 hectares per person in 1994, and the other where the ecological footprints of North Americans have kept growing, to over 4 hectares per person (Figure 1–4). This suggests that growth in both population and consumption (particularly in high-income countries) needs to be controlled if sustainability objectives such as greater equity among the world's people and other species are to be achieved.

In contrast to this viewpoint, many other people believe that technology and resource substitution provide endless possibilities for providing the raw materials on which economic activity is based, for continued growth, and for environmental cleanup (Government of Canada, 1996). This perspective equates sustainable development with expansion and rapid economic growth in all nations on the assumption that economic growth and diversification will assist developing countries to mitigate the resulting environmental stresses.

Regardless of which perspective people support, there can be little debate about the impacts of human, resource-related, economic development activity—widespread environmental degradation, serious depletion of some resources and resource stocks, and loss of many species. Many of these environmental changes are permanent and irreversible, and, since the economy is dependent on the ecosphere (the bottom line of the economy, so to speak), it follows that we may have overshot local and global carrying capacity and that current economic growth patterns may not be sustainable. If we believe that social and economic benefits attained through economic

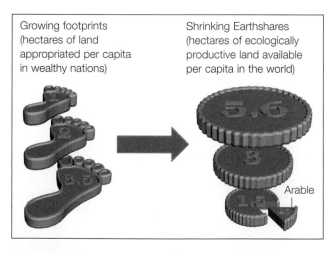

Growing footprints (hectares of land appropriated per capita in wealthy nations)

Shrinking Earthshares (hectares of ecologically productive land available per capita in the world)

Arable

Figure 1–4

Conflicting trends: growing ecological footprints and shrinking Earthshares

SOURCE: Adapted from Wackernagel, M., & Rees, W. (1996). *Our ecological footprint: Reducing human impact on the earth*. Gabriola Island, BC: New Society Publishers, p. 14. Reproduced by permission.

growth (such as increased average life spans, reduced physical work effort, and the multitude of consumer products available) are outweighed by the environmental costs and the danger of living at the ecological edge, then we must conclude that humans are living unsustainably, especially those in material-rich western societies.

As we have seen in analyzing ecological footprints and estimating carrying capacity, however, it is difficult to measure all the dimensions of humanity's load on the Earth, and there is no easy way to determine where the balance between environmental costs and benefits lies. However, ecological sustainability is a fundamental principle in the drive to contribute to improved decisions that will enable the world to move toward sustainable futures. Social sustainability, the subject of the next section, also is essential in planning for sustainability.

Social Sustainability

Social constraints on development are just as difficult to measure as ecological limits, and just as important. Reflecting the values attached to human health and well-being, social constraints (or social norms) are based on the traditions, religion(s), and customs of people and their communities. Sometimes these powerful social values are written in law, and sometimes they are intangible (for example, what is considered right or wrong in a community, or what are the important beliefs about the environment and life in general). Other noneconomically motivated social norms are more concrete, such as class systems, language, and educational systems.

Like many other nations, Canada is undergoing rapid social and economic changes. Today's pervasive pressures for change, as well as the multicultural nature of Canada's varied communities, have compounded the difficulties in defining, measuring, and evaluating the changes occurring in social norms and in the limits they entail regarding development. Development activities may be considered socially sustainable if they conform with a community's social norms or do not stretch them beyond the community's tolerance for change. Conversely, socially unsustainable development may be indicated when antisocial behaviour occurs, such as property damage, violence, and other community disruptions (Government of Canada, 1996).

While most norms will change over time, some social norms are extremely persistent; no matter what development activity is proposed, people will oppose or resist it. Even though they are not measured easily (if at all), these are the norms or constraints that must be respected in assessing whether social sustainability will be achieved. For instance, in communities where traditional ways of life are dependent on the natural resource base (minerals, fish, land, and forests), people often are extremely resistant to change. Their strong social norms insist, for example, that the values they place on fish and fishing for a livelihood must be respected, even though outsiders (often developers) do not appreciate these same values. Unless and until these values are addressed in development decision making, people in such communities will continue to resist change.

The strength of social norms and their potential to place constraints on development activity means that they must be taken into account in planning for sustainability. The people in affected communities must be part of the process of defining social limits to development and to sustainability. As many of the examples discussed in later chapters demonstrate, the importance of cooperation and collaboration with groups or communities concerned cannot be underestimated if we are to move toward a sustainable future.

Economic Sustainability

Even though it is at least as difficult to predict and is affected by as many variables, economic sustainability is more easily measured than social or ecological sustainability. This is because economic sustainability requires that economic benefits (defined usually in monetary terms) exceed or at least balance costs.

Economic sustainability reflects the interplay of supply and demand factors. In general, supply side factors include the availability, cost, and transport of raw materials, as well as the energy, labour, and machinery costs relating to their extraction or processing. "As it is ecological factors that ultimately limit sustainability, economic development must use resources in ways that do not permanently damage the environment and must not impair the capacity of renewable resources to continually replenish their stocks" (Government of Canada, 1996). In relation to the supply side, this statement suggests that economic sustainability will be attained only if we use nonrenewable resources sparingly, if we reduce the content of nonrenewable resources in the goods produced, and if we reduce the energy consumed in their production.

On the demand side, sustainability is threatened because of the increasing rate of human consumption of resources. Nowadays, whether prices are high, reflecting the heightened value of a scarce resource, or low because of efficient harvesting technology, stocks continue to be overharvested. That is, if prices stay high, harvesters may maintain pressure on the resource in order to generate maximum profit, and if prices are low while demand is high, overharvesting may reduce stocks to below-recovery levels. Neither high nor low market prices for resources are particularly good indicators of sustainability (Government of Canada, 1996).

Balancing costs and benefits to achieve sustainability is a complex task. In the pollution control field, for example, regulations may require a plant owner to install costly new equipment or to adjust production procedures to meet new emissions standards. Balancing costs and benefits is difficult when, as is frequently the case,

Intense competition for shrinking resources, such as Pacific salmon, often results in overharvesting.

unexpected cost savings derive from installation of such new equipment or procedures.

Economic, ecological, and social sustainability are equally important principles. Economic sustainability, however, may receive disproportionate emphasis (in the media, at least) because it is the basis of "salaries, wages, pensions, and returns on investment—indeed, all systems for the distribution of income within a society" (Government of Canada, 1996a. In light of this statement, we may say that development activity is unsustainable unless it supports socially acceptable income levels. Similarly, development that emphasizes jobs and income to the exclusion of ecological benefits is not sustainable either.

The Precautionary Principle

We know that Canada and many other nations lack adequate data and records regarding trends and other environmental changes that concern us. Environmental information collected in the past is not always relevant today because it was not directed toward the problems and issues that concern us now, nor was it collected with sustainability objectives in mind. Appreciating that lack of data is currently (and, for some time into the future, likely to continue to be) a serious hindrance to environmental protection and achievement of sustainability, countries attending the 1992 Earth Summit, including Canada, adopted the precautionary principle.

The precautionary principle provides instruction that when there are threats of serious or irreversible damage, the "lack of full scientific certainty shall not be used as a reason for postponing cost-effective measures to prevent environmental deterioration" (Government of Canada, 1996a). This principle means that, as long as the weight of evidence suggests action is appropriate, a country should take such action to protect its environment. For instance, if action were not being taken already in regard to the controversial issue of global climate change, the precautionary principle would provide impetus for such action to commence even though disagreement existed about the specific details regarding climate change.

Environmental Stewardship

Environmental stewardship is reflected in Canada's many local groups that have rolled up their sleeves and provided hands-on conservation, rehabilitation, and other care for threatened and special places in their communities. As well, these groups have pressured decision makers to act in environmentally responsible ways (Lerner, 1994). Through active participation in caring for and maintaining the well-being of a place, many people have learned that they are part of nature. They have learned also how vital it is to maintain ecosystems not only for the benefits they bring to people and other organisms, but also for the sake of ecosystems themselves.

Stewardship is an important principle in achieving sustainability. The perception that governments and corporations in Canada have not been able to protect the environment effectively has persisted over the past decade or so. That perception, as well as fears that damage to the environment and human health could be irreversible, has prompted individuals and groups of people to demand comprehensive, proactive planning for environmental quality and sustainability in their region and the country (Lerner, 1994).

Stewardship permits people to take leadership roles and act responsibly on the sense of urgency that often accompanies a threat to a locally valued place or environment. Local people who feel a sense of stewardship or responsibility may be found cleaning up their natural areas, challenging polluters to do things differently, and forcing action and accountability from their governments. Stewardship also promotes working in partnership with other individuals and environmental nongovernmental groups, as well as with government or private sector programs. Stewardship helps everyone understand the importance of accountability in regard to ecosystem sustainability. In short, stewardship is "active earthkeeping" (Lerner, 1993) that helps promote and attain the public good.

MONITORING FOR SUSTAINABILITY

As the preceding brief descriptions of ecological, social, and economic sustainability principles have noted, there is a great deal of uncertainty associated with attaining sustainable futures. However, every action we take to move toward sustainability can teach us about what works and what doesn't work. If we consistently record, monitor, evaluate, and report on these efforts, we may learn how to improve our progress. Using an ecosystem approach to monitor development activities and the policies that guided them and assessing the long-term and cumulative impacts of development activity will contribute to improved decision making about similar factors in the future. Monitoring and related actions also will provide the background for comparison of environmental, social, and economic parameters of change.

PART 1:
OUR ENVIRONMENT

Toronto residents demonstrate stewardship in a local effort to clean up the Don River.

TOWARD SUSTAINABILITY

Attaining sustainability and sustainable futures for Canadians is an important national goal that requires political will as well as individual and corporate action. New ways of thinking—about the ecosphere and about our local environment, about ecosystems and the interactions and interdependencies that characterize them, and about how sustainability can be achieved now and for the future—are bringing about new attitudes as well as new means of achieving desired, sustainable futures. These new attitudes and means involve deliberate collaborative and cooperative stewardship efforts and, as we will see throughout the chapters regarding Canada's resources, have been delivering some exciting results.

> The notion of sustainable development as an achievable goal provides the only possible basis for a viable future for Canadians. More profits, jobs, and goods will be to no avail if they are gained at the cost of a compromised life support system. Sustainability is a concept whose time has come. We must seize the challenge. The ideal may always elude us, but, as long as we continue to search, consult, and face up to hard choices, we will leave behind a better world for our children and our grandchildren. (Government of Canada, 1996)

Another important outcome of monitoring efforts could be the establishment of a set of comprehensive questions about the expected environmental, social, and economic impacts of proposed developments. If all decision makers routinely would apply such a tool, sustainability would be enhanced and our thinking and planning for the future could be done on a more rational basis. Monitoring could also provide a link to global understanding and cooperation to move toward sustainability.

Chapter Questions

1. Briefly compare and contrast the concepts of sustainable development and sustainability.

2. From the environmental issues or problems cited in the chapter, list at least three that affect Canada at each of the local, regional, and international levels. Compile two or three additional examples of different scales of environmental problems (from your hometown, your campus, or from a local or national newspaper).

3. Which one of the environmental problems on your list do you think is most serious? Discuss the reasons why you identified this as the most serious problem. What is the root cause of this problem?

4. Discuss the guiding principles of sustainability, commenting specifically on how each principle contributes in the effort to move toward sustainability.

Brower, D. (Ed.). (1975). *Only a little planet.* New York: Friends of the Earth/Ballantine Books.

Earthweek. (1997, September 19). http://www.earthweek.com

Government of Canada. (1996a). *The state of Canada's environment—1996.* Ottawa: Supply and Services Canada.

Government of Canada. (1996b). 1996 report of Canada to the United Nations Commission on Sustainable Development. http://www.ec.gc.ca/agenda21/96/part1.html

Hodge, T.S., Holtz, S., Smith, C., & Hawke Baxter, K. (1995). *Pathways to sustainability: Assessing our progress.* Ottawa: National Round Table on Environment and the Economy.

International Development Research Centre. (1993). *Agenda 21: Green paths to the future.* Ottawa: International Development Research Centre.

International Union for the Conservation of Nature and Natural Resources (IUCN), United Nations Environment Programme (UNEP) & World Wildlife Fund (WWF). (1980). *World Conservation Strategy: Living resource conservation for sustainable development.* Gland, Switzerland: International Union for the Conservation of Nature and Natural Resources.

Kaufmann, M.R., Graham, R.T., Boyce, Jr., D.A., Moir, W.H., Perry, L., Reynolds, R.T., Bassett, R.L., Mehlhop, P., Edminster, C.B., Block, W.M., & Corn, P.S. (1994). *An ecological basis for ecosystem management.* Fort Collins, CO: U.S. Department of Agriculture Forest Service, Rocky Mountain Forest and Range Experiment Station and Southwestern Region. USDA Forest Service General Technical Report RM-246.

Lerner, S. (Ed.). (1993). *Environmental stewardship: Studies in active earthkeeping.* Waterloo, ON: University of Waterloo Department of Geography Publication Series No. 39.

Lerner, S. (1994). Local stewardship: Training ground for an environmental vanguard. *Alternatives,* 20(2), pp. 14–19.

United Nations. Division for Sustainable Development. (1996). http://www.un.org./dpcsd/dsd

Union of Concerned Scientists. (1993). *World scientists' warning to humanity.* Cambridge, MA: Union of Concerned Scientists.

Wackernagel, M., & Rees, W. (1996). *Our ecological footprint: Reducing human impact on the earth.* Gabriola Island, BC: New Society Publishers.

World Commission on Environment and Development. (1987). *Our common future.* Oxford: Oxford University Press.

World Conservation Union (IUCN), United Nations Environment Programme (UNEP) & World Wildlife Fund (WWF). (1991). *Caring for the earth: A strategy for sustainable living.* Gland, Switzerland: International Union for the Conservation of Nature and Natural Resources.

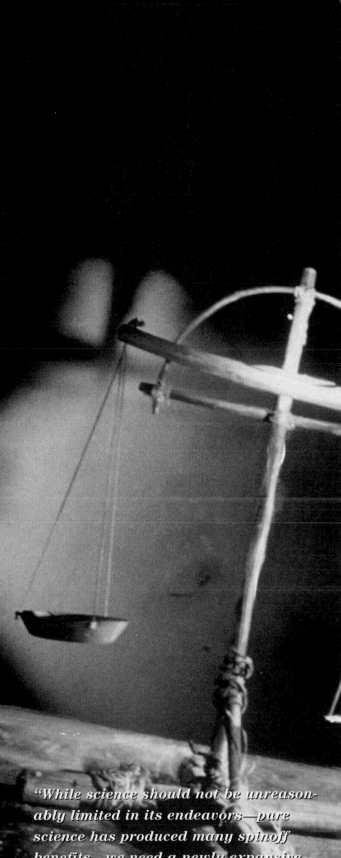

"While science should not be unreasonably limited in its endeavors—pure science has produced many spinoff benefits—we need a newly expansive framework within which science can pursue its new mission, to safeguard the planet; and society within it ..."

Norman Myers (1990, p. 174)

CHAPTER 2

Environmental Studies: Science, Worldviews, and Ethics

Chapter Contents

CHAPTER OBJECTIVES   26
INTRODUCTION   26
SCIENCE AND THE ENVIRONMENT   26
  Science: What Is It?   27
    Assumptions in Science   28
    Thinking Scientifically   28
    Scientific Measurement   28
  The Methods of Science   29
  Misunderstandings about Science   31
    Use of Language   31
    Value-Free Science   31
    The Scientific Method   32
    Complexity, Values, and
      Worldviews   33
  Science and Environmental
    Decision Making   34
WORLDVIEWS AND VALUES   35
  Expansionist and Ecological
    Worldviews   35
    The Expansionist Worldview   35
    The Ecological Worldview   36
    Conservation in the Early 20th
      Century   36
  Environmentalism   39
    Deep Ecology, Green Alternatives, and
      Sustainable Development   41
    Toward the Future   43
ENVIRONMENTAL VALUES AND ETHICS   44
  Environmental Values   44
  Environmental Ethics   45
Chapter Questions   47
References   47
Additional Information Sources   48

Chapter Objectives

After studying this chapter you should be able to

- appreciate why a scientific understanding of our environment is important in making decisions about sustainability

- outline the basic methods of science

- identify the different values and worldviews present in environmental controversies

- discuss the key historical approaches to conservation as well as current approaches to environmentalism

- understand the practical and moral reasons for valuing environments

- describe the concerns associated with environmental ethics

Introduction

In Chapter 1 we noted some fundamental features of life near the end of the 20th century: how people have changed and are changing the global environment; how ecosystems increasingly are under threat from human population growth and resource consumption, pollution, and other environmental abuses; how uncertainty surrounding global changes accentuates the importance of the concept and principles of sustainability as a counterbalance to these changes; and how both knowledge and values are vital in solving contemporary environmental problems.

In this chapter, the historical and current roles and influences of science, worldviews, and ethics in environmental studies are discussed. The significance of interdisciplinary science in generating new environmental knowledge and understanding is stressed, as is the importance of human attitudes, values, and beliefs in addressing root causes of environmental problems. Attention is given, also, to the growth in support for environmental action, particularly the environmental revolution.

Science and the Environment

Early inhabitants of Canada often depended on their knowledge of the environment for their survival; careful observations of wildlife habits and migration routes, weather patterns, and other natural events were crucial to those inhabitants' continued well-being. To some extent this reliance on environmental knowledge continues among professions dependent on the natural environment (such as fishing, hunting, and trapping), but for most Canadians the environment is merely what we encounter in everyday life. Especially for those Canadians living in urban environments, whose lives do not appear to depend directly on the environment, the environment is probably not something we think about scientifically each day.

However remote it might seem to urban Canadians, the environment continues to play a vital role in our everyday lives. However unaccustomed we might be to thinking scientifically about the environment, it is something that each of us can do, to our own benefit and that of our sustainable future. Why should we want to think scientifically about the environment?

There are several reasons why science, as a process of refining our understanding of how the natural world works, is important. The systematic observation and analysis underlying science has provided us with a great

Prior to European settlement, Indigenous peoples depended directly on the land for life's necessities.

deal of understanding about ecosystems and their functioning. This is the kind of knowledge that can be applied to prevent negative effects or better manage human impacts on the environment. With improved knowledge and understanding, we can learn how to avoid inappropriate choices and identify courses of action that will be positive and sustainable in the long term.

Environmental decision making reflects the interactions of society, politics, culture, economics, and values, as well as scientific information. To understand why thinking critically (scientifically) about the environment is important to making decisions about environmental sustainability, the next sections discuss what science is (and isn't), the importance scientists place on measurement, the methods of science, and the role of science in decision making. Since science alone is not sufficient to resolve environmental problems, social science aspects of environmental management are considered later in the chapter. Different worldviews (ways of perceiving reality) are identified, as well as the role of the 1960s environmental revolution in stimulating a reassessment of human relationships with the natural world.

SCIENCE: WHAT IS IT?

Science is a process used to investigate the world that surrounds us, a systematic attempt to understand the universe. In repeatedly asking questions about how the natural environment works, conducting orderly observations (including experiments), and analyzing their findings, scientists are attempting to reduce the complexity of our world to general principles that provide new insights or can be used to solve problems. Thinking about environmental issues involves thinking scientifically.

Science provides one way of looking at the world, a perspective that complements the way we think in everyday life. (Science is not the only way of viewing the world, however. Religious, moral, aesthetic, cultural, and personal values, for example, provide different and valuable ways of perceiving and making sense of the world around us.) In general, scientists focus on rigorous observation, experimentation, and logic in developing an integrated and objective understanding of our world. However, science is not value free: that is, scientists have their own values, interests, and cultural backgrounds that may influence their interpretation of data. This means that we need to be able to evaluate the statements they (and others) make about the environment: Are these statements based on observations and data? An objective interpretation of data? An expert opinion? Or are they subjective opinion? In order to determine an answer for ourselves, we need to understand more about what science is and is not.

Modern science does not deal with metaphysical questions (what is the purpose of life?) or with questions that involve morals or values (what is beauty?), but rather with things that are observable and testable. In terms of the natural world, scientists must be able to make observations from which they develop a **hypothesis** (explanation) that can be accepted until it is disproved. Such hypotheses are based on certain assumptions that scientists make about the world.

Scientific views, such as Darwin's theory of evolution, can conflict with or complement generally accepted social beliefs.

Assumptions in Science

Scientists make five basic assumptions about the natural world they study: (1) people can understand the patterns of events in the natural world through careful observation and analysis; (2) the same rules or patterns of behaviour that describe events in the natural world apply throughout the universe; (3) science is based on inductive reasoning that begins with specific observations of, and extends to generalizations about, the natural world; (4) these generalizations can be subjected to tests that try to disprove them—if no such test can be devised, then a generalization still cannot be treated as a scientific statement (because it is true only until new, contrary evidence is found); and (5) existing scientific theories can be disproven by new evidence, but science can never provide absolute proof of the truth of its theories (Botkin & Keller, 1995).

Thinking Scientifically

Scientists make use of two kinds of reasoning, inductive and deductive. When scientists draw conclusions about their observations of the natural world by means of logical reasoning, they are engaging in **deductive reasoning** (thinking). In this process, a specific conclusion flows logically from the definitions and assumptions (the premises) set initially by the scientists. If a conclusion follows logically from the premises, it is said to be proved. Deductive proof does not require that the premises be true, only that the reasoning is logical. This means that logically valid but untrue statements can result from false premises, as the following example illustrates:

Humans are the only tool-using organisms.

The Egyptian vulture uses tools.

Therefore, the Egyptian vulture is a human being.

The final statement must be true if the two preceding statements are true, but we know that this conclusion is ridiculous and untrue. If the second statement is true (and it is: some African populations of Egyptian vultures break ostrich eggs by dropping rocks on them), then the first statement cannot be true and the conclusion must be false. Because the rules of deductive logic deal only with the process of moving from premises to conclusions, in this example the conclusion that the Egyptian vulture is human follows logically from the series of statements (but it is still nonsensical).

This problem of false conclusions is why science requires not only logical reasoning but also correct premises. If these three statements were expressed conditionally, they would be scientifically correct:

If humans are the only tool-using organisms,

and the Egyptian vulture uses tools,

then the Egyptian vulture is a human being.

When a scientist (or anyone else) draws a general conclusion based on a limited set of observations, that person is engaging in **inductive reasoning.** Let's say, for example, that we are observing fruits with particular characteristics such as tomatoes, and we observe that such fruits are always red. We may make the inductive statement (generalization) that "all tomatoes are red." This really means that all the tomatoes we have ever seen are red. Since it is highly unlikely we will observe all the world's tomatoes, we don't know if the next observation we make may turn up a fruit that is like a tomato in all respects except that it is yellow. In inductive reasoning, then, people (scientists included) can only state what is usually true—that there is a very high degree of probability that all swans are white—but we cannot say so with absolute certainty. Inductive reasoning produces new knowledge, but is error prone.

Probability is one way scientists express how certain (or uncertain) they are about the quality of their observations and how confident they are of their predictions. If they are highly confident in their conclusions, scientists may state the degree of certainty as "there is a 99.9-percent probability that ..." This is about as close as scientists can get to stating proof of their theories—but it is still not proof.

Proving something using inductive reasoning is different from demonstrating proof using deductive reasoning, and science needs both types to help analyze whether the conclusions reached are valid. Both ways of thinking are complementary and important in improving understanding of our environment.

Scientific Measurement

Perhaps more than anyone else, scientists appreciate that every measurement they make is an approximation. Depending on the instruments used and the people who use the instruments, all measurements contain some limitations. These limitations or uncertainties can be reduced, but they can never be eliminated completely.

To make their measurements meaningful, particularly to decision makers, scientists provide an estimate of the uncertainty associated with their measurements. Consider the case of a wildlife biologist who is asked to determine the impact on a caribou herd if the flow rate of a river they cross during their migration were to double due to a proposed hydroelectric development. If the wildlife biologist calculates that doubling the flow in the river will reduce the caribou population by 100 animals, decision makers still do not have enough information to determine if construction of the hydro plant should proceed. In addition to information about the average population size of the particular herd affected (what proportion of the herd does 100 animals represent?), decision makers need to know the uncertainty associated with the loss of 100 animals. If the uncertainty were 1 percent, their decision might be different than if it were 10 percent.

The drowning of 9600 caribou in northern Quebec in October 1984 is thought to have resulted from increased flow in the Caniapiscau River, due in part to the operation of dam systems.

In addition to uncertainty, scientists may encounter systematic and random measurement errors during their research. Random errors occur by chance, but if a scientist's instrument had been calibrated incorrectly and consistently provided inaccurate readings, a systematic error would result. Obviously it is important to avoid such errors and to make and report measurements as accurately and precisely as possible.

If a scientist's measurement is accurate, it will correspond to the value that scientists already have accepted for that feature; if that scientist's measurement is precise, the feature will have been measured with a high degree of exactness. Note that it is possible to make very precise measurements that are not accurate. For instance, the accepted value for the boiling point of water at sea level is 100.000°C (or 212.000°F); if you measure the boiling point of water as 99.885°C, your measurement is as precise as the accepted one (because both are recorded to the nearest .001°), but your measurement is still (slightly) inaccurate. It is important, too, not to mislead others by reporting measurements with more precision than is warranted.

Careful choice of research and statistical procedures, adoption of standard measurement procedures, and improvements in instrumentation will all help to reduce measurement errors and uncertainties. Given that errors

will continue to occur in research, however, it is important to be informed about and understand the nature of measurement uncertainties so that we may read reports of scientific research critically and evaluate their validity.

The increased use of aerial photography and satellite remote sensing during the past 20 years has contributed greatly to our ability to map, inventory, and monitor the environment (thus reducing error and uncertainty). Similarly, the data storage, display, and analysis capabilities of Geographic Information Systems (GISs) have been vital in enabling researchers to contribute to environmental management decisions. As satellite transmitters became small enough to slip over the shoulders of peregrine falcons, researchers were able to track some of these birds as they migrate more than 14 000 kilometres from their breeding grounds in Alaska and northern Canada to their wintering grounds in Central and South America. The data gathered using this technology not only fill large gaps in knowledge based on previous leg-banding programs, but also enable production of flight path maps to determine whether peregrines are travelling to areas where potentially dangerous pesticides are used. In turn, this information has helped in decision making about removing the bird from the endangered species list (Yoon, 1996).

THE METHODS OF SCIENCE

As noted above, **observations**—made through any of our five senses or instruments that extend those senses—are the fundamental basis of science. When scientists check for accuracy in science, they compare their observations with those made by many other scientists, and when all (or almost all) of them agree that an observation is correct, they call it a **fact.**

Observations and facts provide a basis for **inferences**—conclusions derived either by logical reasoning from premises and/or evidence, or by insight or analogy based on evidence. Before inferences are accepted as facts, they must be tested (accepting untested inferences is sloppy thinking). When scientists test an inference, they convert it into a hypothesis, a statement that they can try to disprove. By attempting systematically to demonstrate that certain statements are *not* valid, that is, are not consistent with what has been learned from observation, scientists learn which general principles governing the operation of the natural world are true. Invalid statements are rejected, while statements that have not been proven to be invalid are retained until such time as they are found to be incorrect.

Hypotheses are stated typically in the form of "If ... then" statements—for example, "*If* I apply more fertilizer, *then* my pumpkin plants will produce larger pumpkins." This statement relates two conditions, namely the amount of fertilizer applied and the size of pumpkins produced.

Because each of these conditions can vary, they are called *variables*. The size of pumpkins is called the **dependent variable** because it is assumed to depend on the amount of fertilizer applied, which is the **independent variable.** The independent variable sometimes is called a **manipulated variable** (because scientists deliberately change it) and, because it responds to changes in the manipulated variable, the dependent variable is called a **responding variable.**

Many variables may exist in growing pumpkin plants. Some can be assumed to be irrelevant, such as the position of the planet Mars, while others such as length of the growing season, average temperatures during the growing period, and daylight hours are potentially relevant. To test the stated hypothesis (above), a scientist would want to run a **controlled experiment.** A controlled experiment is designed to test the effects of independent variables on a dependent variable by changing only one independent variable at a time. For each variable tested, there are two setups, an experiment and a control, that are identical except for the independent variable being tested. If there are differences in the outcome between the experiment and the control (relating to the dependent variable) then these differences are attributed to the effects of the independent variable tested. It can be a challenge to properly design control tests and to isolate a single variable from all other variables.

It is also important to ensure that variables are defined in ways that their exact meaning can be understood by all scientists. The vagueness of the variable "size of pumpkins," for example, might cause one scientist to interpret it as weight, another as diameter. Both independent and dependent variables must be defined operationally prior to carrying out an experiment. **Operational definitions** tell scientists what to look for or what to do in order to carry out the measurement, construction, or manipulation of variables. That way, scientists know how to duplicate an experiment and how to check on the results reported: for example, they would know whether "size of pumpkins" was to be measured in kilograms or in centimetres.

Keeping accurate records of independent and dependent variables during experiments is an important element in science. These values, or data, are referred to as either **quantitative data** (numerical) or **qualitative data** (non-numerical). In the pumpkin example, above, qualitative data would record the size of pumpkins as small, medium, or large, while quantitative data would record each pumpkin's weight in grams or diameter in centimetres. There is a long-standing bias in science toward quantitative data, but many fields with relevance to environmental issues collect data in qualitative forms (for instance, sociology, psychology, animal behaviour, human geography, and environmental policy).

Scientific research continues to contribute to the growing body of knowledge pertaining to the natural envi-

Data collected is an integral part of the scientific method. Here a researcher tests for dissolved oxygen.

ronment. As knowledge accumulates in both quantitative and qualitative dimensions, scientists develop explanations or models that illustrate how the natural environment works. Different types of models exist, from actual working models, to mental, computer, mathematical, and laboratory models. All models may be revised or replaced as knowledge increases and currently accepted hypotheses are modified in light of new understanding. Models that offer broadly conceived, logically coherent, and very well supported concepts are labelled **theories.** Einstein's theory of relativity and Newton's theory of gravity are examples of strongly supported theories that are unlikely to be rejected in the future. However, science does not guarantee that future evidence will not cause even these theories to be revised.

It is worth noting that while theories usually grow out of research, theories also may guide research. In fact, scientists make their observations in the context of existing theories. On occasion, scientific revolutions occur when a growing discrepancy between observations and accepted theories forces replacement of old theories by new or revised ones.

MISUNDERSTANDINGS ABOUT SCIENCE

Use of Language

As we have seen, researchers use a variety of scientific methods, as well as their imagination and insight, to increase knowledge and understanding about the natural world. We also appreciate that while scientists may disprove things, they cannot establish absolute truth or proof. So, when you encounter statements that something has been "proven scientifically," it is important to recognize this inaccurate use of scientific language. The claim being made implies falsely that science yields absolute proof or certainty. This situation may occur when people do not understand the nature and limitations of science, or when language is misused deliberately.

Also, be alert to use of the term *theory*. In everyday language, people use the term to indicate a guess or a lack of knowledge ("it's *just* a theory") and do not accord theory the prestige it is given in science. Development of a *theory* is among the greatest achievements in science. It is only after considerable debate, speculation, and sometimes controversy that scientists develop theories based on their consensus about explanations of phenomena.

The significance of scientific consensus often is undervalued by the public and the media as well; this consensus gives even more credence to the message of the World Scientists' Warning to Humanity (Chapter 1).

Value-Free Science

Earlier in this chapter it was noted that science is not value free, that scientists are influenced by their social environment. This does not mean that objectivity is not a goal of scientists, but it means we need to recognize that scientists have biases that must be identified explicitly. Perhaps we need to estimate the effects of these biases, too. Controversial issues, from endangered species preservation to genetic engineering (Enviro-Focus 2) and vehicle emission standards, give rise to conflicts among science, scientists, technology, and society. While it is appropriate for different scientists and other individuals to express their values, science does not permit sloppy or fuzzy thinking. It is necessary to think critically and logically about science and social issues, for without such thinking it is more likely that pseudoscientific (false) ideas of the Earth and how it works will be believed. Pseudoscience constitutes a very weak basis for making vitally important environmental decisions with long-term, serious consequences.

ENVIRO-FOCUS 2

More Engineering for Bananas

Biotechnologists at the Boyce Thompson Institute for Plant Research in New York have genetically engineered bananas to act as a source of cheap, readily available vaccines for immunizing developing nation children against life-threatening diseases.

According to a *New Scientist* report, researchers initially used genetically engineered potatoes to produce hepatitis B antigens that successfully established an immune response in laboratory rats and mice. Engineered potatoes also produced antigens for the Norwalk virus and *Escherichia coli*, a cause of diarrhea in developing countries. However, potatoes were not considered a viable food choice because they are not eaten raw and cooking them would destroy the vaccine.

The researchers decided to use bananas, which are grown extensively in developing countries. Banana purée vaccine would cost a few cents a dose. Standard vaccines cost $100 to $200 per dose.

Institute president Charles Arntzen says enough genetically engineered bananas could be grown on a ten-hectare plantation to provide sufficient vaccine for all Mexican children under five years old.

Researchers are presently waiting for approval from the U.S. Food and Drug Administration and the Mexican government.

Arntzen hopes that in addition to hepatitis B and *Escherichia coli*, the institute will be able to create banana vaccines to protect children from measles, yellow fever, diphtheria and polio.

SOURCE: Odhiambo, D. (1997). More engineering for bananas. *Alternatives,* 23(2), p. 3. Reprinted by permission.

"Dolly," the result of genetic engineering, is evidence of science pushing the frontiers of knowledge.

Given that science is an open process of continual investigation and advancing knowledge, sometimes it is difficult to determine which scientific ideas will become accepted and which will not. Evidence for ideas and models at the frontiers of science is more ambiguous than for those ideas accepted by the scientific community, but some of these frontier-type ideas will be picked up before they have been verified fully (or discarded). In particular, media reports on scientific issues frequently deal with new discoveries, frontier science, and science beyond the fringe. As potential consumers of such information, we need to be able to analyze both media and scientific reports and decide if they are based on objective interpretation of observations and data or on subjective opinion (Box 2–1). While expert opinion is valuable, accepting a statement as fact simply because it was made by a scientist is contrary to the nature of science (particularly if that person has not studied the topic as a scientist).

The Scientific Method

Usually students are informed that the series of steps scientists take to carry out their research is called the **scientific method**, and that it consists of steps similar to those in Figure 2–1. However, it is important to realize that not all research fits into such a neatly defined, step-

Figure 2–1
The Scientific Method

a. Common Steps in the Scientific Method

1. Observe and develop a question about your observations.
2. Develop a hypothesis—a tentative answer to the question.
3. Design a controlled experiment or model defining independent and dependent variables to test your hypothesis.
4. Collect data and record it in an organized manner (such as a table or graph).
5. Interpret the data.
6. Draw a conclusion from the data.
7. Compare your conclusion with your hypothesis to determine whether your results support or disprove your hypothesis.
8. If you accept your hypothesis, conduct further tests to support it.
9. If you reject your hypothesis, make additional observations and construct a new hypothesis.

b. Feedback Processes in Scientific Investigation

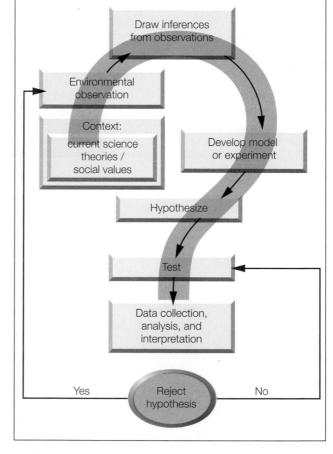

by-step process. While discovering general principles about how the world works is quite often a result of inductive reasoning, accidental discoveries (serendipity), creativity, and flashes of insight also play roles in advancing knowledge and understanding.

PART 1:
OUR ENVIRONMENT

BOX 2-1

THINKING CRITICALLY

With all the competing views and claims about environmental issues, how can we know what to believe? How can we determine what evidence or interpretation is valid and what we should do about an issue? Critical thinking skills help us avoid jumping to conclusions by developing a rational basis for systematically recognizing and evaluating the messages that are conveyed. Critical thinking skills include the ability to recognize assumptions, hidden ideas, and meanings, to separate facts and values, and to assess the reasons and conclusions presented in arguments. These are useful tools in our everyday lives, not just in terms of the environment.

Each one of us has used critical thinking skills at some point—a common experience is questioning the information conveyed on television ads. What does a particular beverage company mean when it labels its product as "good tasting"? According to whose taste buds? What does the product's "new and improved taste" mean—more salt and sugar? In addition to your "well-being," what motivations are behind the ads? If you've ever asked questions like these, you've used critical thinking skills!

Critical thinking involves questioning and synthesizing what has been learned; it is a deliberate effort to think and plan how to think about or analyze a problem rationally. To do this well, we need to be willing to question authority (because even experts are wrong sometimes); to be open-minded and flexible enough to consider different points of view and explanations; to seek full information about an issue; to focus on the main point(s); to be sensitive to the knowledge, feelings, and positions of people involved in discussion of an issue; and to take a stand on an issue when the evidence warrants it, remembering that we, too, could be wrong and have to rethink our assessment later.

There are a number of steps we need to practise, and many questions to ask ourselves while discussion is ongoing, if our critical thinking is to be effective:

1. Examine the claims made: On what premise or basis are they made? Is there evidence to support the claims? What conclusions are drawn from the evidence? Are the conclusions true?

2. Identify and clarify use of language: Are the terms used clear and unequivocal or do they have more than one meaning? Is everyone using the same meaning? Are there any ambiguities in the language used? Could those ambiguities be deliberate? Are all the claims true simultaneously?

3. Separate facts and values or opinions: If the claims that are made can be tested, then they are factual statements and should be verifiable by evidence. If claims are made about the worth or lack of worth of something, they are value statements or opinions and may not be able to be verified objectively.

4. Identify the assumptions and determine potential reasons for the assumptions, evidence, or conclusions people present: Does anyone have a personal agenda or "an axe to grind" on a particular issue? Are there gender, racial, economic, or other issues clouding the discussion?

5. Establish the reliability or credibility of an information source: What special knowledge or information do the experts bring? What makes the experts qualified in this specific issue? How can the accuracy, truth, or plausibility of the information they offer be determined? Is information being withheld?

6. Recognize the basic beliefs, attitudes, and values that each person, group, or agency holds: In what ways do these beliefs and values influence the way these people view themselves and the world around them? Are any of these beliefs and values contradictory?

If we can examine, using the preceding questions, the logic of the arguments people offer about an environmental issue we should be able to determine what to believe even when facts seem confused and experts disagree. This is not to say that critical thinking is easy, but the skills come with practice and we will improve with time. Look for opportunities to think for yourself and use those critical thinking skills.

SOURCE: Adapted from unpublished work by Karen J. Warren, Philosophy Department, MacAlester College, St. Paul, MN. Used by permission.

The myth of a single scientific method dies hard, even though the disciplines of science undertake research differently. For instance, chemists or physicists use a different research logic to guide their research than biologists or geographers use to guide their research. Even within single disciplines, evolutionists conduct their research differently than ecologists, and hydrologists work differently than geomorphologists. In reality, there are many methods of science rather than one scientific method.

Complexity, Values, and Worldviews

In science, the more complex a system or problem being studied, the less certain are the hypotheses, models, and theories used to explain it. When we combine this fact with the knowledge that most environmental problems involve such complex mixtures of data (or lack of data), hypotheses, and theories in the physical and social sciences, we realize that we really don't have sufficient information to understand them well or fully. It is in this context that advocates of any particular action (or inaction) regarding an environmental issue or problem can use incomplete information to support their beliefs, claiming scientific support for their perspective. Alternatively, an insistence that we fully understand a problem before taking action may lead to "paralysis by analysis." If we think this way, the inherent limitations of science and the complexities of environmental problems force us into an unresolvable situation.

Since environmental problems are not about to go away, there comes a point when people have to evaluate available information and make a political or economic decision about what to do (or not do). Often, these decisions are based on intuition, or gut feelings, or values, or common sense (claimed by all sides, of course!). This explains why we find different values and worldviews at the heart of most environmental controversies—people with different worldviews and values can take the same information, examine it in a logically consistent fashion, and come to completely different conclusions. (Worldviews, values, and ethics are examined later in this chapter.)

SCIENCE AND ENVIRONMENTAL DECISION MAKING

Just as we can identify a series of steps in the scientific method, the process of making decisions about the environment may be portrayed as a series of steps (Table 2–1). While this procedure can help guide rational decision making, it is rather simplistic. In real-world environmental issues, for example, it is often the case that scientific data are incomplete and sometimes their interpretation is controversial. Consequences of particular courses of action are very difficult to anticipate, and unin-

Environmental decision making should incorporate all possible worldviews and values. Matthew Coon-Come spoke for the Cree during the James Bay hydroelectric development hearings.

tended consequences are even more difficult to envision. Different groups have conflicting interests, and often the issues of concern are emotionally charged—the best course of action or solution frequently seems to depend on a personal point of view or the economic bottom line. In short, while there are no easy answers to making appropriate environmental decisions, it is essential that we develop sound, critically evaluated approaches to environmental decisions that include sustainability principles.

Science and environmental science have key roles in positively promoting societal awareness and understanding of the importance of making environmentally sound decisions. For instance, scientific research has identified a range of health effects of human exposure to toxic substances. Governments have used this data to make difficult decisions about regulating human exposure to hazardous substances. This is a good example of how addressing environmental issues from both scientific and societal perspectives can be powerful means for mutual gain. In addition, some Canadian scientific research, including the Ballard hydrogen fuel cell technology (see Chapter 11), is of global significance. International attention generated about the fuel cell has heightened people's understanding that social goals (such as reduced atmospheric pollution) can be achieved through science and public action to embrace appropriate new technology.

In Canada, governments play decisive roles in science through involvement in international research agreements, and through domestic support of various research agencies, research councils, Crown agencies, and private-sector interests. In 1997, for instance, Ballard Power Systems Ltd. signed an $8-million agreement with the federal government to develop the hydrogen fuel cell–powered engine for use in cars. Even though downsizing has

TABLE 2–1
A SIMPLIFIED DECISION-MAKING PROCESS

Steps in Environmental Decision Making

1. State the issue as clearly and concisely as possible.
2. Research the issue, gathering the pertinent scientific data and information.
3. Identify all possible courses of action.
4. Predict the outcome of each course of action with reference to the positive and negative consequences of each.
5. Predict the probability of occurrence of each course of action.
6. Evaluate the alternatives and choose the most sustainable one.

reduced monetary support for environmental research, government agendas still drive many research programs. Since most environmental policy decisions are made through the political process, decisions generally are made by political leaders and citizens, and only rarely by the scientists who possess some of the best understanding of environmental problems. This gap emphasizes the need for environmental and scientific education of all those in government and business, particularly policy makers, as well as all citizens.

WORLDVIEWS AND VALUES

Worldviews are "sets of commonly shared values, ideas, and images concerning the nature of reality and the role of humanity within it" (Taylor, 1992, pp. 31–32). Each society's worldview is reflected in and transmitted through its culture. Beliefs, ideas, values, and assumptions about knowledge that each culture transmits help to shape attitudes toward nature and human–environment relationships. These attitudes, in turn, lead to lifestyles and behaviours that may or may not be compatible with natural systems and that may or may not cause environmental problems.

Groups of many political persuasions and as diverse as ecofeminists, deep ecologists, and advocates of maximum resource development have adopted the term *sustainable development* as a guiding force in their activities. However, each of these groups operates with a different, sometimes conflicting, worldview. Different worldviews lead to different interpretations of sustainability and, in turn, to different decisions about use of the environment to achieve various goals. The two major competing worldviews that characterize Western society— expansionist and ecological—are described briefly below.

EXPANSIONIST AND ECOLOGICAL WORLDVIEWS

Two approaches to conservation in the early part of the 20th century have evolved into two major competing worldviews that exist today. The first of these, the expansionist or Western worldview, is based on the values of the 18th-century Enlightenment tradition. The newer and still evolving ecological worldview is based on values of the Counter-Enlightenment and Romantic traditions. A little of the historical nature of both worldviews follows in order that we may understand their contemporary forms and their links to sustainability.

The Expansionist Worldview

The Enlightenment was a period of profound economic, political, and social changes in society. Capitalism, an economic system based on accumulation of (personal) wealth, gained wide acceptance. Democracy, established through political revolutions in North America and France, asserted the rights of individuals to determine their own destinies through law making, owning property, and developing the resources on private property.

The shift to an industrial society in Europe, and the Industrial Revolution (beginning in England at the end of the 18th century), brought urbanization, accelerated use of resources, and pollution. As workers clustered in industrial areas and separated physically from direct, daily contact with the land, knowledge of nature and the sense of the earth was no longer transmitted to succeeding generations. Their quality of life declined in urban areas as coal-burning industries polluted the air, as sewage and other wastes were poured into rivers and streams, and as contagious diseases spread quickly in the crowded, poor conditions.

Many Europeans who migrated to North America during this era took their expansionist worldview with them. The roots of this worldview emphasized the following: faith in science and technology to control nature for human ends; belief in the inherent rights of individuals; accumulation of wealth so that material wants could be satisfied and progress occur; and exploitation of nature and resources to achieve these ends. Arriving in a new land that seemed to have unlimited natural resources, and having the technological means to make maximum use of this resource base, these settlers aggressively exploited their surroundings. Rolling along with their frontier mentality, European settlers spread across the continent, trying to tame the wilderness. Many of the Native North Americans whose land was taken over and whose cultures were fragmented or destroyed as settlement spread had lived lifestyles based on a very different worldview, on a deep respect for the land and its animals.

Crowded and unsanitary urban conditions in 19th-century Europe were a direct result of the Industrial Revolution.

Early European immigrants to North America extensively exploited surrounding natural resources.

The Ecological Worldview

People who espouse the contemporary ecological worldview have built their opposition to the fundamental assumptions of the expansionist worldview on historical and philosophical traditions from both Western and non-Western sources. To varying degrees, people have accepted concepts from India and China that stressed the unity of human life with nature; beliefs from Aboriginal people about the importance of kinship and relatedness of all life forms; and ideas from the early animistic and mystic traditions of Celtic, Nordic, and Germanic societies (Taylor, 1992).

As well, the Counter-Enlightenment and Romantic thought of the late 18th and early 19th centuries influenced the ecological worldview. In particular, the ecological viewpoint protested the Enlightenment assumption that the universe was a great machine that rationalized and mechanized humans and nature and separated them from their intrinsic spiritual value. According to the expansionist worldview at that time, quantities (measurability) mattered, not qualities. Values, emotions, instincts, and all nonmeasurable aspects of the environment were of secondary importance compared to science and reason. Body and mind, and spirit and nature, were separate entities. Against this thinking, Romanticism (part of the Counter-Enlightenment position) emphasized the importance of emotional, instinctual, and irrational dimensions. Romantics reacted against society's trend toward things urban and technological and instead celebrated the world of nature and all that was not artificial. They tried to unify those elements expansionists had separated—to unite body and mind, and the supernatural and natural (Taylor, 1992).

During this same Counter-Enlightenment period, the roles of human emotions, independence, and freedom of expression were elevated, sometimes above the claims of reason and science. Poets such as William Wordsworth extolled the values of beauty and tranquillity in nature and denounced artificial and urban realms. Other writers of the 1800s, such as Thoreau and Emerson, promoted individuals' rights to access universal truths through personal communion with nature and criticized the existing political structures for standing in the way of these truths. In about 1864, George Perkins Marsh also warned of the destructive effects of the dominant cultural beliefs and practices on the environment.

Conservation in the Early 20th Century

The conservation movement was a reaction to "the excesses and wastefulness of an expanding industrial society," but, by the early 20th century, conservationists were viewing the problems from two competing worldviews (Taylor, 1992). "Wise management" conservationists such as Clifford Sifton in Canada (Box 2–2) and Gifford Pinchot in the United States were allied with the expansionist worldview and pitted against the "righteous management" conservationists such as American John Muir and, later, Aldo Leopold and Rachel Carson (Figure 2–2). Both Leopold and Carson spoke of human responsibility for the Earth, echoing the older Christian concept of **stewardship.** Some of the key perspectives of each approach to conservation are presented in Table 2–2. (For a definitive history of the conservation movement, see the book by Hays listed in the References section of this chapter.)

In addition to the features noted in Table 2–2, members of the wise management school of preservation made it known that they were not preservationists but promoted sustainable exploitation, where forests, soils, water, and wildlife would be harvested as if they were renewable crops. In contrast, righteous management conservationists rejected the expansionist emphasis on viewing the world principally in economic and utilitarian terms. Preservationists believed that, in nature, humans could realize their inner spiritual, aesthetic, and moral sensibilities. Believing that physical nature, particularly wilderness, was a benchmark against which to judge the state of human society, the preservationists suggested that large areas of the natural world should be preserved and protected against human interference (Taylor, 1992).

During the period 1900 to 1960, the values of the Enlightenment tradition remained dominant in conservation theory in both Canada and the United States. Nature was seen as a storehouse of resources used to satisfy the continually increasing material needs of an ever growing human population. The expansionist worldview equated material growth with development, which, in turn, was seen as a prerequisite for human happiness and prosperity. Proponents of the expansionist worldview continue to believe that scientific and technological advances will ensure increased global standards of living, employ

Clifford Victor Sifton was born in 1861 on a farm about two kilometres east of the tiny village of Arva, just north of London, Ontario. Although little is known of his early childhood, he had an outstanding record at school. Working intensely to overcome partial deafness, Clifford won the gold medal when he graduated from Victoria College in Cobourg, Ontario, in 1880.

Ambitious and well educated, Sifton articled with a Winnipeg law firm and was called to the Manitoba bar in 1882. His legal practice in Brandon soon flourished, and he became the city solicitor. Like his father before him, Clifford Sifton entered politics, running as a Liberal candidate in the North Brandon riding. Successful in his bid for the seat, Sifton entered the Manitoba legislature in 1888, rising to become attorney general in the government of Thomas Greenway in 1891.

In 1890 the Manitoba government decided to implement a system of nondenominational "national schools." Sifton gained national prominence as he defended the province's position of phasing out the French language and Roman Catholic schools in Manitoba. In January 1896, Sifton masterminded Greenway's victory in the provincial election, and in June 1896, the Liberals under Wilfrid Laurier won the federal election. It was Sifton who negotiated a settlement of the school issue with Greenway and Laurier in November 1896. Immediately following that settlement, Laurier appointed Clifford Sifton minister of the interior and superintendent general of Indian affairs in the federal Cabinet.

As minister of the interior, Sifton earned his place in Canadian history for his aggressive promotion of immigration to settle the west. But he also was one of the few public officials who knew about the conservation movement in other countries and realized Canada should do something—even though its resources seemed inexhaustible, they were not unlimited. Almost as soon as he became minister of the interior, Sifton placed forests under federal control, and in 1902 created a separate forestry branch of the Department of the Interior. Sifton also had organized the Canadian Forestry Association in 1900 and toured the country promoting forest conservation and starting local branches of the organization. The movement reached its climax when Prime Minister Laurier presided over the first Canadian Forestry Convention in 1906.

By this time, conservation had gained national importance in Canada, as it had in the United States. Sifton was one of Canada's delegates to Theodore Roosevelt's North American Conference on Conservation of Natural Resources held in Washington, D.C., in February 1909. In May 1909, the Canadian government established a Commission of Conservation and appointed Sifton as chairman. Comprising federal and provincial government representatives, business leaders, and scientists, the commission had no formal power. As its chair, Sifton felt the commission should first organize in-depth studies in all resource fields to see what needed to be done and then try to influence public opinion so that people would demand government action on conservation. The commission set up a wide range of studies on topics including fisheries, forestry, lands, minerals, game and fur-bearing animals, water and water power, and public health.

In Sifton's day, conservation focused more on efficient management and the best way to exploit resources, rather than on preservation. The forest industry, for example, was governed by only a few, poorly enforced government regulations. Timber companies, determined to make maximum profit as quickly as possible, resisted any regulations that might limit their financial return. Accused of mining rather than cultivating and harvesting the forests, the timber companies' logging practices resulted in large areas of dry slash that frequently caught fire. One estimate indicated that 20 times as much timber was destroyed by fire as was harvested (Hall, 1976).

The Commission of Conservation was determined to demonstrate that in the long term, Canada would benefit from sensible conservation regulations. Sifton believed that forests should be preserved not just for the sake of their beauty but also because, in practical business terms, conservation techniques made economic sense. Although Sifton believed strongly in government regulation and in state ownership of resources, he maintained that resources should be developed privately. A successful businessman himself, Sifton argued that private enterprise operated in its own self-interest and that government control was needed to protect the public interest.

Sifton campaigned strongly against free trade and the practice of selling Canada's resources to the United States. In 1910, on behalf of the commission, Sifton persuaded the Canadian government to veto an American plan to construct a hydroelectric dam on the St. Lawrence River at the Long Sault Rapids above Cornwall. Sifton was convinced the project would lock Canada into permanently supplying power for American industries. Following a similar dispute over another power project, Sifton resigned from the commission in 1918. Without his leadership, the commission carried little influence and was abolished by the government in May 1921.

Sifton's public contributions to Canadian life were recognized by King George V, who knighted him on January 1, 1915. Following the First World War, Sifton was no longer in government, but he remained interested in Canadian transportation problems. His political influence was still evident, as he served from 1924 to 1928 on the Canadian National Advisory Committee on the development of the St. Lawrence Seaway for shipping and hydroelectric purposes. Once again the nationalistic Sifton argued that the international section of the river should not be developed for hydropower until Canadian demand was sufficient to warrant development.

In the 1920s, Sifton continued to build his business interests and to groom his five sons to take over his financial empire, which included the *Manitoba Free Press*. Sir Clifford Sifton died in a New York hospital from the effects of abdominal cancer, on April 17, 1929. Two days later, the father of conservation in Canada was buried in Toronto's Mount Pleasant Cemetery.

SOURCES: Hall, D.J. (1976). *Clifford Sifton*. Don Mills, ON: Fitzhenry & Whiteside.

Hall, D.J. (1988). Sir Clifford Sifton. *Canadian Encyclopedia*, 2nd ed., pp. 1999–2000.

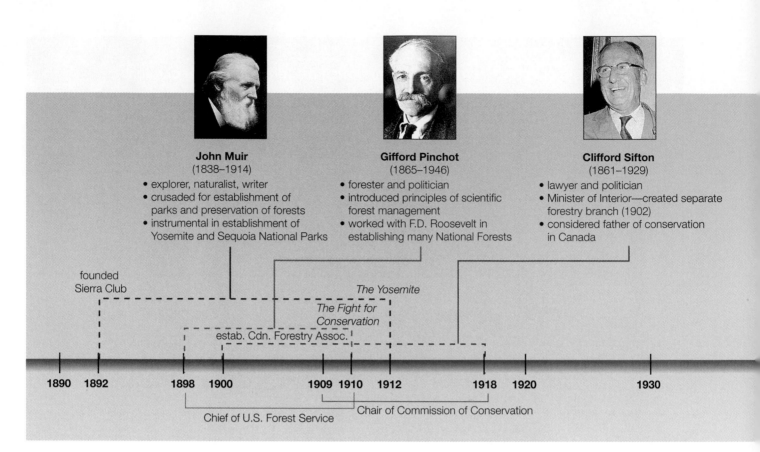

John Muir
(1838–1914)
- explorer, naturalist, writer
- crusaded for establishment of parks and preservation of forests
- instrumental in establishment of Yosemite and Sequoia National Parks

Gifford Pinchot
(1865–1946)
- forester and politician
- introduced principles of scientific forest management
- worked with F.D. Roosevelt in establishing many National Forests

Clifford Sifton
(1861–1929)
- lawyer and politician
- Minister of Interior—created separate forestry branch (1902)
- considered father of conservation in Canada

founded
Sierra Club

The Yosemite

The Fight for Conservation

estab. Cdn. Forestry Assoc.

1890 1892   1898 1900   1909 1910 1912   1918 1920   1930

Chief of U.S. Forest Service

Chair of Commission of Conservation

Figure 2–2
Key early figures in 20th-century conservation

TABLE 2–2
A COMPARISON OF EARLY-TWENTIETH-CENTURY APPROACHES TO CONSERVATION

Expansionist Worldview	Ecological Worldview
"Wise management" is based on the values of the Enlightenment tradition: • Nature is a resource to be used, not preserved. • Conservation must work together with the dominant values of the surrounding society, not against them. • The primary value of natural areas lies in their value to modern society. • Conservation should work against the wastefulness and environmentally disruptive excesses of a developing society. • Conservation is equated with sustainable exploitation.	"Preservation" or "righteous management" is based on the values of the Counter-Enlightenment tradition: • The universe is nondualistic, a totality with all of its parts interrelated and interlocked. • The biotic community and its processes must be protected. • Nature is intrinsically valuable—animals, trees, rock, etc., have value in themselves. • Human activities must work within the limitations of the planet's ecosystems. • Preservation works against the dominant societal values. • Nature provides a forum to judge the state of human society.

SOURCE: Adapted from Taylor, D.M. (1992). Disagreeing on the basics: Environmental debates reflect competing world views. *Alternatives*, 18(3), p. 29. Reprinted by permission.

PART 1:
OUR ENVIRONMENT

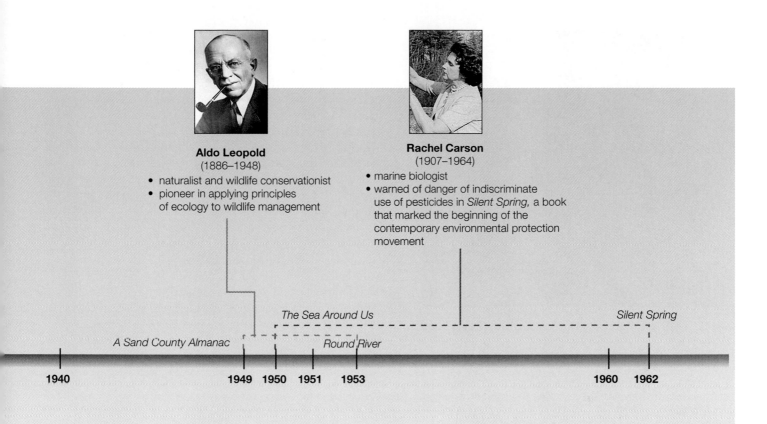

Aldo Leopold
(1886–1948)
- naturalist and wildlife conservationist
- pioneer in applying principles of ecology to wildlife management

Rachel Carson
(1907–1964)
- marine biologist
- warned of danger of indiscriminate use of pesticides in *Silent Spring*, a book that marked the beginning of the contemporary environmental protection movement

The Sea Around Us

A Sand County Almanac

Round River

Silent Spring

1940   1949 1950 1951 1953   1960 1962

renewable and other environmentally friendly sources of energy, increase food production, solve the problems created by previous technologies, create substitutes for depleted resources, and replace damaged environments (Taylor, 1992). Although the expansionist worldview originated with capitalism, today both capitalist and socialist countries apply the basic tenets of the expansionist position.

ENVIRONMENTALISM

In the 1960s and 1970s, a reassertion of Counter-Enlightenment and Romantic values occurred within the conservation movement. In fact, during this time of environmental revolution, both Canadian and American governments began to recognize the value of qualitative and ecocentric approaches to conservation. The late 1960s and early 1970s were years of idealism and optimism—environmental awareness (including interest in worldviews held by other cultures) was growing among all segments of the population, major issues such as pollution and nuclear power were receiving media attention (Table 2–3), and various pieces of legislation respecting environmental protection were promulgated. The first Earth Day and environmental teach-in, bringing together scientists, environmentalists, politicians, students, government offi-

cials, and citizen groups, was held in the United States on April 20, 1970. In 1971 the Canadian government established the Department of the Environment. Since then, Environment Week in Canada has been an important way to promote environmental awareness and the benefits of environmental protection among Canadians (Box 2–3).

It appears, however, that long-lasting change in understanding nature and the place of humans in the environment had not occurred during the first wave of environmentalism (1968–76), for, when political winds shifted and inflation and an economic downturn began to drive the monetary costs of a clean environment upward, many people (especially in the economically disadvantaged regions of the country) began to argue for their jobs and employment rather than environmental controls (Paehlke, 1992).

By the 1980s, the idealism of the 1960s and 1970s had given way to an emphasis on individual well-being, especially economic well-being. In both Canada and the United States, ecocentric values in conservation were increasingly difficult to maintain as the idea of limits to growth was rejected, ecocentric values were pitted against development values, and economic goals took precedence in environmental and resource management decisions (Taylor, 1992). For example, in 1987, when *Our Common Future* (the Bruntland Report) was published and nations were challenged to develop sustainable development strategies,

April 22, 1970: New Yorkers celebrate the first Earth Day with the closure of Fifth Avenue to vehicular traffic.

the Canadian government replied "within the framework of the Expansionist" worldview (Taylor, 1992, p. 28). Neoconservative or expansionist values were dominant once again, although poll after poll showed North Americans wanted to continue efforts to ensure a clean, safe environment for their children and themselves (see, for example, Dunlap, 1987).

This latent interest in environmental matters and concern for the state of (Canada's) environment generated a second wave of environmentalism from 1985 onward. Not only were Counter-Enlightenment and Romantic values back again, but this time deep ecology and sustainable development entered the debate (Paehlke, 1992; Taylor, 1992). As illustrated in Table 2–3, issues of concern in the second wave of environmentalism often were global in perspective (particularly global warming and ozone depletion), and frequently dealt with nature, wilderness, and biodiversity. Earth Day 1990, the 20th anniversary of the first Earth Day, was celebrated worldwide as a global expression of support for

TABLE 2-3

ENVIRONMENTAL ISSUES AND CHARACTERISTICS OF THE FIRST AND SECOND WAVES OF ENVIRONMENTALISM

Environmental Issues	Characteristics and Emphases
First Wave (1968–76) • pollution • energy crisis • offshore oil drilling, tanker spills • nuclear power • population • resource depletion, especially of oil • urban neighbourhood preservation	**First Wave (1968–76)** • tendency for individuals and groups to alienate themselves, to detach from social, political, and economic order • antitechnological character • tendency to millennialism (escapism) • regulatory, "end-of-pipe" solutions favoured by decision makers (standards for emissions) • building awareness of problems
Second Wave (1985 onward) • global warming • ozone depletion • new wilderness and habitat concerns: old growth forests, tropical rainforests, animal rights • waste reduction, recycling • hazardous wastes, carcinogens, pollution • resource depletion, especially of forests, fisheries, and bio-diversity • oil tanker spills • urban planning, automobiles, land use • indoor air quality	**Second Wave (1985 onward)** • re-emergence of preservationist issues • globalized concerns • acceptability of some environmental ideas within economic and political elites • professional character of major environmental organizations • split between those inclined to compromise and those opposed • multiple tools approach

SOURCE: Adapted from Paehlke, R. (1992). Eco-history: Two waves in the evolution of environmentalism. *Alternatives*, 19(1), p. 22.

PART 1:
OUR ENVIRONMENT

environmental action. Continuing interest in global water issues is evidenced in the recent establishment of World Water Day and the World Water Council (Box 2–4).

Deep Ecology, Green Alternatives, and Sustainable Development

Neither deep ecology nor sustainable development were articulated widely prior to the second wave of environmentalism. Among the assertions that deep ecology makes are that humans are only one species among many, and that nature and nonhuman species are as valuable in their own right as are humans (Devall & Sessions, 1985). These assertions are labelled, respectively, the principle of self-realization (an awareness of one's ultimate inseparability and wholeness with the nonhuman world) and the principle of biocentric equality (all organisms and entities in the ecosphere have intrinsic worth and are part of the interrelated web of life). In the deep ecologist's view, at least implicitly, these principles mean that sometimes wild nature must be chosen over human habitat and human well-being. In contrast, sustainable development gives priority to global *human* needs (Paehlke, 1992).

Throughout North America and Europe, other green alternatives have developed, including social ecology and ecofeminism, that criticize the epistemological and normative assumptions underlying modern society. Like deep ecology, ecofeminism is based on the biocentric equality principle but also tries to address the "hierarchical and dominance relationships that it sees as endemic to patriarchy" (Taylor, 1992, p. 30). Ecofeminism argues that the ongoing domination of nature and the ongoing domination of women are systemically related (Salleh, 1984; Hessing, 1993). Similarly, social ecologists argue that all forms of human domination are related directly to the issues of ecology. That is, social ecology indicates that as long as various modes of hierarchy and domination occur in human society, then the domination of nature will continue and lead the planet to ecological extinction (see, for example, Bookchin, 1980).

Ecological worldview adherents have found also that the study of general systems theory has been useful in that its view of the universe as a systemic hierarchy, or as organized complexity, pictures a "myriad of wholes within wholes, all of them interconnected and interacting"

On March 22, 1996, while over 500 children and adults were celebrating World Water Day activities at the Canadian Museum of Nature in Ottawa, the interim board of governors of the World Water Council was meeting for the first time in Marseilles, France, to approve the resolution to create the World Water Council. A nonprofit, nongovernmental, nonpolitical, and nonsectarian forum, the World Water Council's mission is to:

[p]romote awareness about critical water issues at all levels including the highest decision-making level and the general public, and to facilitate the efficient conservation, protection, development, planning, management and use of water in all its dimensions on a sustainable basis for the benefit of all life on this earth. (Shady, 1996a, 10)

The World Water Council was formed because of the serious challenges facing the world's fresh water resources including growing water scarcity; deteriorating water quality; increasing difficulty in accessing clean, reliable sources of water for drinking and food production in many parts of the world; and the lack of an integrated global institutional framework to deal efficiently and effectively with common world water problems (Shady, 1996a).

As established in 1992 by the United Nations General Assembly, World Water Day also provides an opportunity to raise awareness of global water challenges. In terms of water shortages, for instance, the rapid growth in world population has caused increasing demands for fresh water. Globally, 1700 m³ per capita per year of renewable fresh water is considered adequate to meet the needs of the population and its environment. A water shortage occurs when the availability of water drops below 1700 m³ per capita per year and, when water supplies fall below 1000 m³ per capita per year, people face a water *scarcity* condition. In 1950, only 12 countries totalling less than 20 million inhabitants faced water shortages of one form or another; by 1990, 26 countries with a total of 300 million inhabitants faced water shortages. Forecasts indicate that 30 years from now, one-third of the world's population will suffer from chronic water shortages (Dowdeswell, 1996), and by 2050, up to 65 countries with about 7 billion inhabitants will face water shortages. That means about 65 percent of the world's projected population, mostly in developing nations, will not have sufficient water to meet their needs (Shady, 1996b).

Globally, water quality deterioration has increased as industrialization, urbanization, and intensification of agriculture have resulted in large volumes of waste production and a concomitant rise in water pollution. Both the decline in water quality (exacerbated by lack of treatment facilities and safe wastewater disposal facilities), and the resultant reduction in availability of water suitable for human consumption and for sustaining the biodiversity of ecosystems, are major environmental problems. Most rivers, lakes, and, to some extent, groundwater, are considered contaminated with one or more chemical, biological, or physical contaminants beyond levels safe for use by humans, animals, and other biota (Shady, 1996b). This situation is critical, given that about 80 percent of all diseases and more than one-third of all deaths in developing countries are caused by contaminated water (Dowdeswell, 1996).

During the UN Decade for Water Supply and Sanitation in the 1980s, availability of water and sanitation improved considerably, but in 1995, about 1.3 billion people still lacked an adequate supply of clean water (Government of Canada, 1996). Many cities in the rapidly growing coastal regions and megacities of the developing world are unable to provide safe, clean water and adequate sanitation facilities. Poor and disadvantaged groups of people, women and children particularly, are most affected by lack of access to and inability to pay for clean water. Unequal accessibility is evident also in cases where feudal landowners and influential farmers gain more rights and access to irrigation water than landowners of smaller farms and tenant farmers. Such inequities, combined with finite fresh water resources and increasing demand, generate concern that major clashes over dwindling supplies of water may trigger future conflicts within and between nations (Dowdeswell, 1996; Shady, 1996b).

Currently, a wide range of national institutions, municipal and regional governments, nongovernment organizations (NGOs), and private sector and international organizations are active in global water issues. On the one hand, this broad participation is appropriate, as managing fresh water resources involves a complex set of scientific, technological, economic, social, and political factors that extend across regional, national, and international borders. On the other hand, and in spite of many United Nations organizations involved in water issues,[1] no single institution exists with an overall mandate to integrate all relevant dimensions of global water issues. The World Water Council hopes to acquire this role. In the meantime, as exemplified in the Ottawa celebrations for World Water Day, many organizations, companies, and governments are likely to continue to promote awareness of the importance of water through festivals and other water-based activities and celebrations at the local level.

---

[1] Among the United Nations organizations involved in water issues are Food and Agriculture Organization (FAO), United Nations Development Programme (UNDP), United Nations Children's Fund (UNICEF), World Health Organization (WHO), World Meteorological Organization (WMO), United Nations Environment Programme (UNEP), and United Nations Educational, Scientific and Cultural Organisation (UNESCO).

SOURCES: Dowdeswell, E. (1996, March 22). Message from Ms. Elizabeth Dowdeswell, UNEP executive director, for World Water Day, 22 March 1996. gopher://gopher.undp.org.70/00/ungophers/unep/news_releases/1996/nr_96_12.

Government of Canada. (1996). *The state of Canada's environment—1996.* Ottawa: Supply and Services Canada.

Shady, A. (1996a). The World Water Council is now official. *Water News*, 15(2), p. 10.

Shady, A. (1996b). World Water Day—March 22: A day to raise awareness of global water challenges. *Water News*, 15(1), pp. 1, 9.

The long-standing protest at Greenham Common, in England, against U.S. nuclear missile storage may be seen as an early expression of ecofeminism.

Increasing awareness and changing attitudes result in a broader acceptance of environmental initiatives, such as the Blue Box recycling campaign.

(Taylor, 1992, p. 31; see also Prigogine & Stengers, 1984). This perspective has appeared in James Lovelock's Gaia hypothesis, which explains the Earth and its living organisms in terms of a single, indivisible, self-regulating process (Lovelock, 1988). Lovelock's theory provided impetus to the concern that human expansionist activities at local levels were threatening Gaia's health and all the life contained on the planet.

Toward the Future

The second wave of environmentalism brought a remarkable change to recent political reality. Even in a more complicated political climate, and in light of the highly complex body of thought that comprises environmentalism, environmental ideas now are widely held or asserted within the North American and international political elites. Compare the 1970s, when volunteer-staffed recycling depots were barely tolerated by municipal governments, with today's blue box, composting, and other recycling programs that generate economic returns for municipalities. Contrast the attitude of business persons in the 1970s toward environmentalism—it had nothing to do with business life other than to create annoying regulations—to that of today,

when being perceived as an environmentally concerned company is important to the corporate image and perhaps to business success (Paehlke, 1992). Unfortunately, in some instances these changes reveal that the concept of sustainable development has been "co-opted by individuals and institutions to perpetuate many of the worst aspects of the expansionist model under the masquerade of something new" (Taylor, 1992, p. 32). However, sustainable development does carry the hope that society will be able to transform its political, economic, and social institutions in keeping with what is socially and environmentally sustainable.

The expression of worldviews in the political sphere of the 1990s may be illustrated as in Figure 2–3. The horizontal axis shows that political opinions held by environmentalists or nonenvironmentalists can be either left or right. The vertical axis places ecological (sustainability) and expansionist (economic) worldviews at opposite ends, with sustainable development somewhere in the middle. There is tension between these ecological–sustainable development–expansionist values and ways of looking at the world; the challenge for the future is to identify and reach win–win conditions that will allow simultaneous improvement in equity, economy, and ecology.

Sustainable development seems to provide an opportunity for a "trialogue" between enthusiasts of economic growth, environmentalists, and advocates of greater equity among peoples and within nations. However, the real challenge lies in integrating new ideas for ecological protection and sustainability with a workable set of transformations of society and economy (Paehlke, 1992). For many people, current environmental problems reflect a cultural or worldview crisis, a concern for current national and international policies and values as they affect the long-term viability of social and natural systems. Thus, understanding the struggle between the entrenched expansionist worldview and the emerging ecological

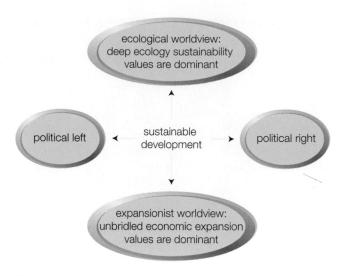

Figure 2–3
Worldviews in the political sphere of the 1990s

SOURCE: After Paehlke, R. (1992). Eco-history: Two waves in the evolution of environmentalism. *Alternatives,* 19(1), p. 22.

worldview is important in helping us move toward both environmental and societal sustainability in the future.

Making decisions about the environment and planning effectively to meet the needs of the future require us to place a value on aspects of the environment. In turn, placing a value on aspects of the environment requires the following: knowledge and understanding of the science involved; knowledge of how the uses and aesthetics of the environment are judged; and our moral commitments to other living things and future generations. As we attempt to deal with the exploding human population, the needs of an urban world, sustaining resources for future generations, and preserving our environment on a global level, we need to know how we are changing the environment, how we can rectify the problems we have caused, and what factors are most important to us. To these ends, the following section provides a brief discussion of environmental values and environmental ethics.

ENVIRONMENTAL VALUES AND ETHICS

ENVIRONMENTAL VALUES

Placing a value on some aspect of our environment— healthy fish populations in Canada's rivers and oceans, or clean air in industrialized regions of the country, or scenic

beauty, or the existence of natural landscapes—may be based on utilitarian, ecological, aesthetic, or moral categories of justification. The utilitarian and ecological categories deal with practical reasons such as economic benefit or our own survival. A **utilitarian justification** for the conservation of nature is that the environment, an ecosystem, a habitat, or a species provides individuals with direct economic benefits or is directly necessary to their survival. Fishers, for example, derive their livelihood from the oceans and need a supply of fish so that they may continue to earn their living.

An **ecological justification** for conserving nature is based on the knowledge that a species, an ecological community, an ecosystem, or the Earth's biosphere provides specific functions necessary to the persistence of our life, or of benefit to life. The ability of trees in forests to remove carbon dioxide produced through burning fossil fuels is a public benefit and an important element in the argument to maintain large areas of forest. Enlightened self-interest also would suggest that dealing with the problems of polluted air in parts of Eastern Europe (caused by burning lignite and poor quality coal) would be beneficial ecologically. Similarly, even if individuals did not benefit immediately, there is value in action designed

Family fishing endeavours in Canada's coastal communities depend on a continuing supply of marine resources.

PART 1:
OUR ENVIRONMENT

to counter the production of greenhouse gases that may lead to climate change that affects the entire Earth.

Aesthetic arguments for the conservation and protection of nature are made on the basis that nature is beautiful and that beauty is of profound importance and value to people. In an effort to add beauty to their surroundings, many people spend hours gardening, and city workers plant trees, shrubs, and flowers in parks and on boulevards. On a larger scale, many people find the Canadian wilderness beautiful and would rather live in a world with wilderness than without it. Psychological, medical, and social benefits accrue from aesthetic values of the environment. For example, research has shown that patients recover more quickly if their hospital room has a view of trees and natural landscapes (Krakauer, 1990). The value of natural sounds and areas as restorative environments (Hartig, Mang & Evans, 1990), and the value of wilderness as sacred space (Graber, 1976) are examples of the importance of the aesthetic values of the environment.

A **moral justification** for conserving nature is that aspects or elements of the environment have a right to exist, independent of human desires, and that it is our moral obligation to allow them to continue or to help them persist. An example of moral justification is the assertion that the Fraser River in British Columbia and the Red Deer River in Alberta (examples of the few remaining "wild" rivers in populated areas of Canada) have rights to exist. Similar moral arguments have been extended to many nonhuman organisms such as trees and wildlife. The 1982 United Nations General Assembly World Charter for Nature states that species have a right to exist.

A new discipline, **environmental ethics,** analyzes these issues and the concerns about our moral obligations to future generations with respect to the environment. Environmental ethics is introduced briefly in the following section.

ENVIRONMENTAL ETHICS

During the 1970s, philosophers began to develop environmental ethics, a field in which the value of the physical and biological environment was studied. This new field is not like traditional ethical studies (which dealt with relationships between people), but it is a large and complex academic subject; only a few aspects are considered here.

As was noted above, there are both practical and moral reasons for placing values on our environments, but the need for new environmental ethics has arisen because of the diverse changes our human activities and technological society are bringing to the world. For instance, humans are having new effects on nature, are developing new knowledge of the environment, and are creating an expanded set of moral concerns. Environmental ethics indicates that an examination of the utilitarian, ecological, aesthetic, and moral consequences of these technological actions is necessary.

With regard to our new knowledge of nature, science has been able to show us how we have changed and are changing our surroundings in ways that were not understood previously. Scientists have demonstrated that burning fossil fuels and large-scale clearing of forests have changed the amount of carbon dioxide in the atmosphere, which may change the global climate. This global perspective is an impetus to examine new moral issues. Also, the extension of moral and legal rights to animals, trees, and objects such as rocks is seen as a natural expansion of civilization to begin incorporating the environment in ethics.

Concern with environmental ethics involves discussion of the rights of animals and plants, of nonliving things, and of large systems that are important to our life support. One important statement of ethics that influences our ethical thinking is Aldo Leopold's land ethic. In *A Sand County Almanac*, Leopold (1949) affirmed that *all* resources (plants, animals, and earth materials) have a right to exist, to continue to exist, and to continue to exist in a natural state in at least some locations. This land ethic indicates that humans are no longer conquerors of the land but are citizens and protectors of the environment. As citizens and protectors, humans should show love and reverence in their relationships with the land; land is not merely an economic commodity to be used up and discarded. Leopold's land ethic assumes that we are responsible ethically to other individuals and society, as well as to the larger environment of which we are a part (including plants, animals, soils, the atmosphere, and water). Note that such responsibility places some limits on the freedom of actions of individuals and societies in their struggle for existence.

Leopold's land ethic suggests each of us is a steward of our environment; our role as stewards includes the moral responsibility to sustain nature for ourselves and for future generations. Certain implications result; for example, although the land ethic assigns rights to animals to survive as a species, it does not necessarily assign those same rights of survival to an individual member of a species (a deer or chicken, for example). This means we must distinguish between an ideal and a realistic land ethic. Another implication is that, because wilderness has intrinsic value, as morally responsible stewards we must maintain it for itself and because our own survival depends on it. Whether or not we agree with the land ethic, we need to consider if ethical values should be extended to nonhuman biological communities. Our position will be determined depending on our values and our understanding of natural systems and other environmental factors.

Given that human effects on today's environment carry consequences for the future, any discussion of environmental ethics also involves the rights of future generations and what we owe them. This issue has become increasingly important because the impacts of technology have the potential to affect the environment for hundreds to thousands of years. Radioactive wastes from nuclear plants, long-term climate changes resulting from land use changes and technology, extinctions of large numbers of species as a result of human activities including destruction of forests, and the direct effects of human population increases are among the issues of particular concern for the future. Depending on what we know about these issues, we will make value judgments about them, about the rights of future citizens, and about the idea of stewardship of the earth—our decisions will reflect these influences. If we think it is important to consider the future as well as stewardship in our decision making, then we are more likely to consider ourselves as merely the latest in a long line of humans who are the stewards or shepherds of the Earth.

In response to the potentially major changes that these issues imply, some people have reacted by hiding their heads in the sand, seeking a simpler life, and rejecting all science, technology, and progress. A better, longer-term, response that might produce solutions would be to use science and technology to the best of our abilities, keeping in mind our environmental ethics. Ernest Partridge (1981), a philosopher concerned with environmental ethics, has commented that scientific knowledge and discipline need to be augmented by critical moral sense and passionate moral purpose if we are to save the future.

Ultimately, there are many ways each individual can become involved in acting on personal environmental ethics. Environmentalism encompasses a wide range of conservative to radical approaches to making a difference in the world around us. In a simple way, every one of us

The use of living animals in scientific experimentation generates controversy. Is their use justifiable?

can address environmental issues personally by adjusting our lifestyles and attitudes toward consumerism. However, by using the best available scientific instruments and methods, and being sensitive to ethical implications of our actions, we can best understand, conserve, and contribute to appropriate management of our environment and its resources.

Chapter Questions

1. What is the scientific method? Why is it appropriate to think of it as a general guide to scientific thinking?

2. Scientific knowledge may be acquired through inductive and deductive reasoning; identify the ways in which these processes are similar and different.

3. Discuss the value of critical thinking in the environmental science field.

4. Select a current environmental controversy and identify (list) the social, economic, aesthetic, and ethical issues involved in it.

5. Concerning the environment: (a) What are the most important environmental benefits and harmful conditions passed on to you by each of your parents' and your grandparents' generations? (b) What obligations, if any, do you have to future generations? (c) For how many generations do your responsibilities extend?

6. Find an article from a local or national newspaper about a controversial topic and make a list of any ambiguous or loaded words used in the article (words that convey an emotional reaction or value judgment). In your opinion, is the article an objective one? Why or why not?

references

Botkin, D.B., & Keller, E.A. (1995). *Environmental science: Earth as a living planet.* New York: John Wiley & Sons.

Devall, B., & Sessions, G. (1985). *Deep ecology: Living as if nature mattered.* Salt Lake City, UT: Peregrine Books.

Dowdeswell, E. (1996, March 22). Message from Ms. Elizabeth Dowdeswell, UNEP executive director, for World Water Day, 22 March 1996. gopher://gopher.undp.org.70/00/ungo.hers/unep/news_releases/1996/nr_96_12.

Environment Canada. (1996). About Environment Week. http://www.ec.gc.ca/env1996/en

Environment Canada. (1997a). No fees … no fines! http://www.ec.gc.ca/special/emissions_e.htm

Environment Canada. (1997b). *Environment Canada to sponsor Emissions Inspection Clinics for the 12th year.* http://www.ec.gc.ca/press/emissions_n_e.htm

Government of Canada. (1996). *The state of Canada's environment—1996.* Ottawa: Supply and Services Canada.

Graber, L.H. (1976). *Wilderness as sacred space.* Washington, DC: Association of American Geographers.

Hall, D.J. (1976). *Clifford Sifton.* Don Mills, ON: Fitzhenry & Whiteside.

Hall, D.J. (1988). Sir Clifford Sifton. *Canadian Encyclopedia,* 2nd ed., pp. 1999–2000.

Hartig, T., Mang, M., & Evans, G.W. (1990). Perspectives on wilderness: Testing the theory of restorative environments. In A.T. Easley, J.F. Passineau & B.L. Driver (Compilers). *The use of wilderness for personal growth, therapy and education,* pp. 86–95. Fort Collins, CO: U.S. Department of Agriculture, Rocky Mountain Forest and Range Experiment Station, General Technical Report RM-193.

Hessing, M. (1993). Women and sustainability: Ecofeminist perspectives. *Alternatives,* 19(4), pp. 14–21.

Krakauer, J. (1990). Trees aren't mere niceties—they're necessities. *Smithsonian,* 21, pp. 160–71.

Leopold, A. (1949). *A Sand County almanac.* New York: Oxford University Press.

Lovelock, J. (1988). *The ages of Gaia: A biography of our living Earth.* New York: W.W. Norton and Company.

Myers, N. (1990). *The Gaia atlas of future worlds: Challenge and opportunity in an age of change.* New York: Doubleday.

Odhiambo, D. (1997). More engineering for bananas. *Alternatives,* 23(2), p. 3.

Paehlke, R. (1992). Eco-history: Two waves in the evolution of environmentalism. *Alternatives,* 19(1), pp. 18–23.

Partridge, E. (1981). *Responsibilities to future generations: Environmental ethics.* Buffalo, NY: Prometheus Books.

Salleh, A.K. (1984). Deeper than deep ecology: The eco-feminist connection. *Environmental Ethics,* 6(4), pp. 65–77.

Shady, A. (1996a). The World Water Council is now official. *Water News,* 15(2), p. 10.

Shady, A. (1996b). World Water Day—March 22: A day to raise awareness of global water challenges. *Water News,* 15(1), pp. 1, 9.

Taylor, D.M. (1992). Disagreeing on the basics: Environmental debates reflect competing world views. *Alternatives*, 18(3), pp. 26–33.

Warren, K.J., cited in Cunningham, W.P., & Saigo, B.W. (1995). *Environmental science: A global concern.* Dubuque, IA: Wm. C. Brown Publishers.

Yoon, C.K. (1996, August 28). Peregrine migration secrets unfold. *The Globe and Mail*, p. A6.

additional information sources

Bookchin, M. (1980). *Toward an ecological society.* Montreal: Black Rose Books.

Dunlap, R.E. (1987, July/August). Public opinion on the environment in the Reagan era. *Environment,* 29, pp. 7–11, 32–37.

Environment Canada. (1996). Action 21.
http://www.cciw.ca/action21/

Hays, S. (1959). *Conservation and the gospel of efficiency.* Cambridge, MA: Harvard University Press.

Prigogine, I., & Stengers, I. (1984). *Order out of chaos: Man's new dialogue with nature.* Toronto: Bantam Books.

The Ecosphere We Live In

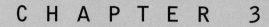

C H A P T E R   3

Earth's Life-Support Systems

Chapter Contents

CHAPTER OBJECTIVES   51
INTRODUCTION   51
MATTER AND ENERGY: BASIC BUILDING
  BLOCKS OF NATURE   51
    Matter   51
        Matter Quality   53
    Energy   53
        Energy Quality   53
    Physical and Chemical Changes in
        Matter   54
        The Law of Conservation of
            Matter   54
        First and Second Laws of Energy   54
EARTH'S LIFE-SUPPORT SYSTEMS   54
    Earth's Major Components   54
        Connections on Earth   56
    Ecology   57
    Biodiversity   60
    Types of Organisms   60
    Components and Structure of
        Ecosystems   61
        Tolerance Ranges of Species   64
        Limiting Factors in Ecosystems   65
ROLES OF SPECIES IN ECOSYSTEMS   65
    Types of Species in Ecosystems   65
        Ecological Niche   66
        Interactions between Species   66
ENERGY FLOW IN ECOSYSTEMS   69
    Food Chains and Food Webs   69
    Productivity of Producers   70
MATTER CYCLING IN ECOSYSTEMS   71
    Nutrient Cycles   71
        Carbon Cycle   71
        Nitrogen Cycle   71
        Phosphorus Cycle   73
        Hydrologic Cycle   74
        Rock Cycle   75
TERRESTRIAL AND AQUATIC
  ECOSYSTEMS   76

"All life exists in a thin layer wrapped around the globe, caught between the molten heat of the earth's interior and the cold immensities of space. The biosphere, the only part of the entire universe known to support life ... proportionately is no thicker than the shine on a billiard ball."

Lean and Hinrichsen (1992, p. 11)

The Geography of Life   76
Life on Land: Major Terrestrial Biomes   76
Life on Earth: Major Aquatic Biomes   77
   Oceans   77
   Freshwater Ecosystems   79
   Freshwater Rivers and Streams   80
   Inland Wetlands   80
RESPONSES TO ENVIRONMENTAL
   STRESS   81
   The Constancy of Change   81
      Changes in Population Size   81
      Biological Evolution, Adaptation, and
         Natural Selection   83
      Speciation and Extinction   83
      Ecological Succession   84
HUMAN IMPACTS ON ECOSYSTEMS   84
WORKING WITH NATURE   85
Chapter Questions   86
References   86
Additional Information Sources   87

Chapter Objectives

After studying this chapter you should be able to

- identify and describe the Earth's major components

- outline the components and structure of ecosystems

- discuss ecosystem functions and their interconnections

- explain how ecosystem population dynamics work

- identify the major forces of change and adaptation affecting the Earth

- identify the key features of living systems that help humans learn to live sustainably

INTRODUCTION

The environmental problems and challenges we face have no easy answers or simple solutions. However, improving our understanding of how the world we live in works, and applying that knowledge, may help us make decisions that are directed toward sustainable environments and futures. With that broad goal in mind, this chapter focuses on some fundamental features and vital interconnections of Earth's life-support systems.

MATTER AND ENERGY: BASIC BUILDING BLOCKS OF NATURE

MATTER

Matter is the material of which things are made, the stuff of life. Everything on Earth is composed of matter—everything that is solid, liquid, or gaseous, including our bodies, the air we breathe, oceans or lakes we fish or swim in, animals we see grazing, vegetables grown in our gardens or farmers' fields, and minerals extracted from the Earth. Matter is anything that has mass and takes up space. Essentially, the Earth is a closed system for matter. With the possible exception of meteors and meteorites that enter the Earth's atmosphere and add matter to the biosphere, most of the matter that will be incorporated into objects in future generations already is present and has been present since the planet came into being.

Scientists note that Earth's matter is found in three chemical forms: **elements** (the simplest building blocks of matter that make up all materials), **compounds** (two or more different elements held together in fixed proportions by the attraction in the chemical bonds between their constituent atoms), and **mixtures** (combinations of elements, compounds, or both). All matter is built from the 109 known chemical elements (92 naturally occurring and 17 synthetic); each element has its own unique atomic structure.

Scientists also tell us that all elements (and all matter) are composed of three types of building blocks: atoms, ions, and molecules. **Atoms** are the smallest particles that exhibit the unique characteristics of that particular element. In turn, atoms consist of subatomic, electrically charged particles known as **ions.** These ions are of three types: **protons** (which are positively charged), **neutrons** (uncharged or electrically neutral), and **electrons** (negatively charged) (Figure 3–1a). A set number of protons and neutrons, which have approximately the same mass, cluster in the centre of the atom and comprise its nucleus. Electrons, which have little mass in comparison to protons and neutrons, continually and rapidly orbit the nucleus; they are held in orbit by attraction to the positive charge of the nucleus.

An atom of any given element, say hydrogen, is distinguished from that of other elements such as carbon or oxygen by the number of protons in that atom's nucleus (called its **atomic number**). Hydrogen, which is the simplest element, has only 1 proton in its nucleus and has an atomic number of 1. Carbon, in contrast, has six protons and an atomic number of 6. An even larger atom, uranium, has 92 protons and an atomic number of 92.

Scientists describe the mass of an atom in terms of its mass number, which is the number of neutrons plus the number of protons in its nucleus. All atoms of a particular element have the same number of electrons and protons but they may have different numbers of neutrons, which change the mass or weight of the atom (Figure 3–1b). These different forms of the same atom are called isotopes of that element, and they may exhibit different characteristics (such as radioactivity in the case of the isotopes of hydrogen and uranium).

Molecules are formed when two or more atoms of the same or different elements combine. In nature, some elements are found as molecules, including oxygen (O_2), nitrogen (N_2), and hydrogen (H_2). Molecules composed of two or more different elements are known as compounds. In chemical notations such as that above, O alone would represent one atom of oxygen; 2 O would represent two atoms of oxygen that have joined to form a molecule of oxygen. When we see the chemical formula H_2O, we know that this compound, water, is formed of two hydrogen

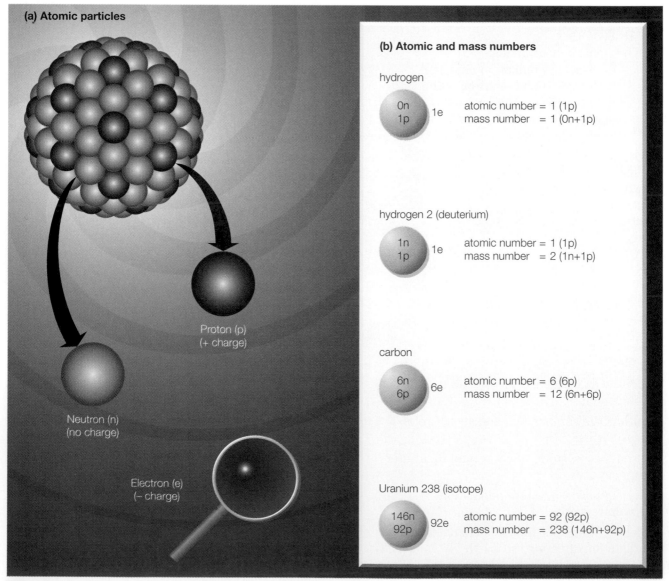

Figure 3–1
Atomic structure

PART 2:
THE ECOSPHERE WE LIVE IN

atoms and one oxygen atom. Similarly, glucose sugar, $C_6H_{12}O_6$, is a compound formed of six carbon atoms, 12 hydrogen atoms, and six oxygen atoms. Other examples include ammonia (NH_3), carbon monoxide (CO), carbon dioxide (CO_2), methane (CH_4), nitrogen (N_2), nitrous oxide (N_2O), nitric oxide (NO), nitrogen dioxide (NO_2), nitric acid (HNO_3), ozone (O_3), sulphur dioxide (SO_2), and sulphuric acid (H_2SO_4).

Matter Quality

Based on its availability and concentration, matter may be of high or low quality. **High-quality matter** (such as coal and salt deposits) usually is found near the Earth's surface in an organized or concentrated form, so that its potential for use as a resource is great. **Low-quality matter** usually has little potential for use as a resource because it is dispersed or diluted (in the oceans or atmosphere), and hard to reach (deep underground). An aluminum can is a more concentrated, higher quality form of aluminum than the aluminum ore from which it was derived. That's why it's less costly in terms of energy, water, and money to recycle an aluminum can than to produce a new one from aluminum ore.

ENERGY

Energy, the ability or capacity to do work, is what enables us to move matter (such as our arms or legs or a basketball) from one place to another or to change matter from one form to another (such as to boil liquid water to produce steam, or to cook food on a barbecue using natural gas). Energy comes in many forms including light, heat, electricity, chemical energy in coal and sugar, moving water and air masses, and nuclear energy from isotopic nuclei. Energy

is used for many purposes such as to build shelters and warm or cool them, to process and transport food, and to keep our body's cells active and functioning properly.

Two types of energy exist: kinetic and potential. Matter has **kinetic energy** because of its motion and mass. Wind (a moving air mass), for example, has kinetic energy as do flowing streams, moving cars, heat, and electricity. Forms of electromagnetic radiation such as visible light, microwaves, ultraviolet radiation, and cosmic rays also are types of kinetic energy. **Potential energy,** stored and potentially available for use, includes the chemical energy stored in gasoline molecules and food molecules, as well as water stored behind a dam. Burning gasoline in our car engines changes the chemical bonds of its molecules into heat, light, and mechanical or kinetic energy that moves the cars.

Energy Quality

Energy quality is a measure of its ability to perform useful work. **High-quality energy** sources include electricity, nuclear fission (uranium), concentrated sunlight, high-velocity wind, natural gas, gasoline, coal, and food. These energy sources are concentrated and have great ability to perform useful tasks such as in industrial processes and to run electrical devices such as lights and motors. In contrast, **low-quality energy** is dispersed and has little ability to do useful work. Even though it contains more stored heat than all Saudi Arabia's high-quality oil deposits, the Atlantic Ocean's energy is too widely dispersed to accomplish tasks such as moving vehicles or heating things to high temperatures (Miller, 1994). Since we do not need to use high-quality energy sources for all our tasks, we can avoid unnecessary energy waste (and save money) by matching the quality of energy used to the specific task performed.

Harnessing energy resources involves making informed choices among competing alternatives.

PHYSICAL AND CHEMICAL CHANGES IN MATTER

When we melt snow to boil water for a cup of tea or hot chocolate during a winter camping trip, we have not altered the chemical composition of the H_2O molecules but we have changed water from a solid to a liquid state. This **physical change** has caused the water molecules to organize themselves differently in space. In lighting our camp stoves and burning their fuel, however, we initiated a **chemical change** or reaction between the carbon contained in the fuel and oxygen from the atmosphere. This chemical reaction produced carbon dioxide gas and energy ($C + O_2$ yields CO_2 + energy). In addition to showing that camp stove fuel is a high-quality, useful energy resource, this example demonstrates how burning carbon-containing compounds such as wood, coal, or natural gas adds carbon dioxide, a greenhouse gas, to the atmosphere.

The Law of Conservation of Matter

Under ordinary circumstances, matter is neither created nor destroyed, but it is recycled repeatedly. Matter is transformed and combined in different ways, but it doesn't disappear—everything goes somewhere. That's why it's inaccurate to talk about consuming or using up resources, because we're using, discarding, reusing, or recycling the same atoms. We can physically rearrange the atoms into different spatial patterns or chemically combine them into different combinations, but we're not creating or destroying them. This is the **law of conservation of matter,** and, in affluent societies such as Canada's, it means that every disposable consumer good thrown away remains with us in one form or another. This is why we hear about the need to emphasize waste reduction and pollution prevention.

First and Second Laws of Energy

The **first law of thermodynamics** (or the **first law of energy**) states that during a physical or chemical change energy is neither created nor destroyed. However, it may be changed in form and it may be moved from place to place. When one form of energy is converted to another form in any physical or chemical change, energy input always equals energy output—we can't get something for nothing in terms of energy quantity.

The **second law of thermodynamics** (or the **second law of energy**) indicates that with each change in form, some energy is degraded to a less useful form and given off to the surroundings, usually as low-quality heat. That is, in the process of doing work, high-quality energy is converted to more dispersed and lower quality energy. If we used all of our camp stove fuel in making our cup of tea or hot chocolate, we would have lost energy quality (the amount of useful energy available for the future).

An incandescent light bulb provides another example that illustrates how we lose energy quality. When electrical energy flows through the filament wires, it changes into about 5 percent useful light and 95 percent low-quality heat. This heat enters the environment and is dispersed by the random motion of air molecules (thus the suggestion that light bulbs really should be called heat bulbs). With each transfer of energy in these processes, heat is given off to the immediate surroundings and dissipates to the external environment and, eventually, through Earth's atmosphere to space. Effectively, the second law of energy means that we can never recycle or reuse high-quality energy to perform useful work.

EARTH'S LIFE-SUPPORT SYSTEMS

EARTH'S MAJOR COMPONENTS

The Earth's environment consists of four interconnected environmental spheres or layers. Surrounding the inner (solid) and outer (molten) cores and the mantle of the Earth are the **lithosphere, hydrosphere, atmosphere,** and **biosphere** or **ecosphere** (Figure 3–2).

Although knowledge of the interior of the Earth is incomplete and imperfect, the **lithosphere** generally is said to consist of the upper zone of the Earth's mantle (to a depth of about 40 to 50 kilometres beneath the crust) as well as the inorganic mixture of rocks and mineral matter contained in the Earth's crust.

On the crust of the Earth lies the **hydrosphere,** the Earth's supply of moisture in all its forms—liquid (both fresh and saltwater), frozen, and gaseous. The hydrosphere includes the surface waters in oceans, lakes, rivers, and swamps; underground water wherever it is located; frozen water in the form of ice, snow, and high cloud crystals; water vapour in the atmosphere; and the moisture that is stored temporarily in the tissues and organs of all living organisms. The hydrosphere impinges on and overlaps significantly with the other spheres.

The **atmosphere** completely surrounds the solid and liquid Earth. Relative to Earth's radius, the atmosphere is a very thin layer of gases consisting mostly of nitrogen (78 percent) and oxygen (21 percent) plus small quantities of water vapour and argon, and minute amounts of other gases such as carbon dioxide and ozone (Table 3–1).

Due to the forces of gravity and compressibility of gases, the two lowest layers of the atmosphere (troposphere and stratosphere) together make up about 99 percent of its mass. The **troposphere** (containing about 80 percent of the atmospheric mass) is the lowest layer of the atmosphere and the zone in which most weather events

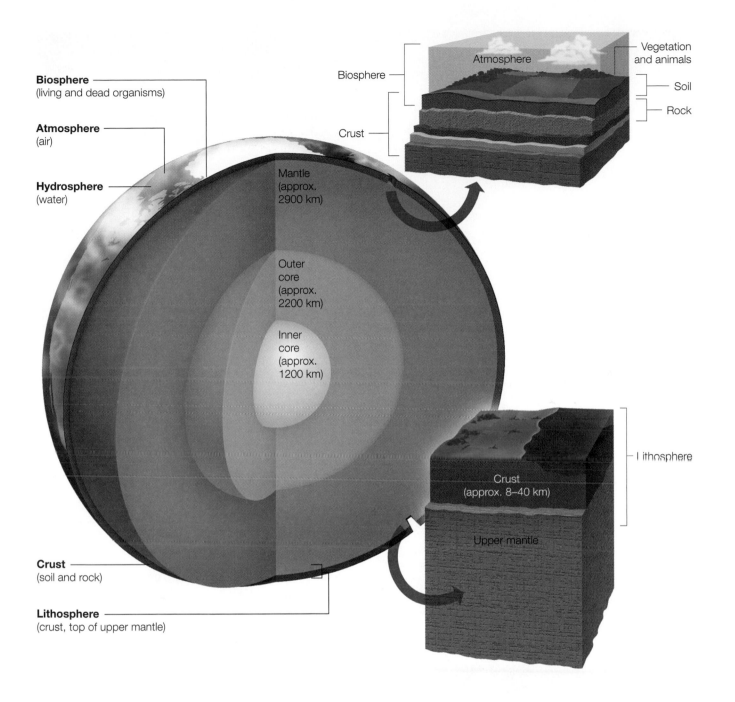

Biosphere
(living and dead organisms)

Atmosphere
(air)

Hydrosphere
(water)

Mantle
(approx.
2900 km)

Outer
core
(approx.
2200 km)

Inner
core
(approx.
1200 km)

Crust
(soil and rock)

Lithosphere
(crust, top of upper mantle)

Biosphere

Atmosphere

Vegetation
and animals

Soil

Rock

Crust

Lithosphere

Crust
(approx. 8–40 km)

Upper mantle

Figure 3–2
The general structure of the Earth

occur. Its height above sea level varies from an average of about 6 kilometers at the poles to about 18 kilometers over the equator, and it also varies seasonally, being higher in summer than in winter. The next layer, the **stratosphere,** contains about 19 percent of the atmospheric mass and extends to about 50 kilometers above the Earth's surface.

The stratosphere and troposphere have very similar compositions except that in the stratosphere the volume of water vapour is about one thousand times lower, and ozone is nearly one thousand times higher than in the troposphere. It is this ozone that protects life on Earth's surface by absorbing most incoming solar ultraviolet radiation. If the **ozone layer** were a band of pure gas surrounding the globe at sea-level pressure and temperature, it would be no more than three millimetres thick, or about the thickness of three Canadian dimes (Government of Canada, 1991).

The ecosphere consists of the incredibly diverse plant and animal organisms that inhabit the Earth and

TABLE 3-1
PRINCIPAL GASES OF EARTH'S ATMOSPHERE

Component	Symbol or Formula	Percent of Volume of Dry Air	Concentration (in parts per million of air)
Uniform Gases			
nitrogen	N_2	78.08	
oxygen	O_2	20.94	
argon	A	0.934	
neon	Ne	0.00182	18.2
helium	He	0.00052	5.2
methane	CH_4	0.00015	1.5
krypton	Kr	0.00011	1.1
hydrogen	H_2	0.00005	0.5
Important Variable Gases			
water vapour	H_2O	0–4	
carbon dioxide	CO_2	0.03	353
carbon monoxide	CO		< 100
ozone	O_3		< 2
sulphur dioxide	SO_2		< 1
nitrogen dioxide	NO_2		<0.2

SOURCES: Cunningham, W.P., & Saigo, B.W. (1995). *Environmental science: A global concern* (3rd ed.). Dubuque, IA: Wm. C. Brown Publishers, p. 353; McKnight, T. (1990). *Physical geography: A landscape appreciation* (3rd ed.). Englewood Cliffs, NJ: Prentice Hall, p. 53.

their interactions with each other and with the atmosphere, hydrosphere, and lithosphere. While most living things inhabit the interface between atmosphere and lithosphere (a zone about 5 kilometres thick) some live largely or entirely within the hydrosphere or atmosphere

Because they occupy aquatic *and* terrestrial habitats, amphibians are sensitive indicators of environmental health.

and many others move freely from one sphere to another. The ecosphere extends vertically about 32 kilometres from the ocean floors to above the tops of the highest mountains. Yet, if the Earth were an apple, the web of life within which we live would be no thicker than the apple's skin (Miller, 1994). The field of ecology tries to determine how this thin skin of air, water, soil, and organisms works.

Connections on Earth

Life on Earth is dependent on three pervasive and interconnected factors: energy flow, matter cycling, and gravity. In particular, it is the one-way flow of high-quality energy from the sun through the materials and living things of the ecosphere, and then into the environment as low-quality energy (and eventually back out into space) that is the ultimate source of energy in most ecosystems. In addition, living organisms require the cycling of critical elements such as carbon, phosphorus, nitrogen, water, and oxygen through the ecosphere. Gravity is important in that it keeps the planet's atmospheric gases from escaping into space and it draws chemicals downward in the matter cycles.

Although energy reaches the Earth continuously as sunlight, less than 0.023 percent of the total energy reaching the atmosphere each day is actually captured by living things through photosynthesis (Kaufman & Franz, 1993). The remainder of the energy is reflected by cloud cover and does not reach the surface, or is radiated by the Earth's surface back into space as heat (Figure 3–3). The Earth is an open system for energy, continuously receiving and using energy from the sun and radiating waste heat into space.

ECOLOGY

Basic ecological knowledge is an important foundation of environmental awareness and also is a basis for using and managing Earth's resources in an environmentally sound and sustainable manner. Part of such ecological knowledge is knowing how the biosphere works, and how natural systems function and respond to change.

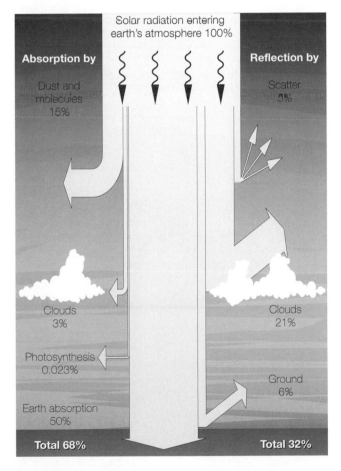

Figure 3–3

Schematic diagram of energy balance on the Earth

SOURCE: Adapted from Fellman, J., Getis, A., & Getis, J. (1995). *Human geography: Landscapes of human activities.* Dubuque, IA: Wm. C. Brown Publishers, p. 454.

Ecology, from the Greek words *oikos* (house, or place to live) and *logos* (study of), is defined as the study of the interactions of living organisms with one another and with their nonliving environment of matter and energy. As part of determining how Earth's living systems maintain the integrity of the ecosphere, ecologists may study individual species, as well as the structure and function of natural systems at the population, community, and ecosystem levels. Other scientists and social scientists such as geologists, earth scientists, and geographers focus on understanding the patterns and distributions of living and nonliving elements of the environment and on the interrelationships of people, other organisms, and their environments.

One of the characteristics of life on Earth is its high degree of organization (Figure 3–4). Starting at the simplest level, atoms are organized into molecules, which in turn are organized into cells. In multicelled organisms, cells are organized into tissues, tissues into organs (such as the brain or liver), organs into organ or body systems (such as the nervous system or digestive system), and organ systems into individual multicellular **organisms** (such as bears, whales, humans, orchids, and cacti).

An individual organism is a single member of a **species,** defined as a group of organisms that resemble one another in appearance, behaviour, chemical makeup and processes, genetic structure, and that produce fertile offspring under natural conditions. While estimates as to how many species there are on Earth vary between 5 and 100 million (mostly insects, microscopic organisms, and small sea creatures), most of the world's species remain unknown. Only about 1.4 million species have been discovered and described (Huyghe, 1993), and for the great majority of these species little is known about their roles and interactions.

Canola in a prairie field, brook trout in a particular stream, or people in Canada—a group of individuals of the same species living and interacting in the same geographic area at the same time—is called a **population.** Although all members of the same population share common structural, functional, and behavioural traits, individuals in a population vary slightly in their genetic makeup and thus exhibit slightly different behaviours and appearances. This is known as **genetic diversity.** The place where the organism or population lives—whether oceans, forests, streams, or soils—is its **habitat.** Populations of different species interact, making up a biological **community,** such as an alpine meadow community or a prairie community.

A community and its members interact with each other and with their nonliving environment of matter and energy, making up an **ecosystem.** Wetlands, estuaries, and the Great Lakes are examples of aquatic (water) ecosystems, while grasslands, high mountain deserts, and Carolinian forests are examples of terrestrial (land)

Figure 3–4
Levels of biological organization

These zebras are visually similar, but each individual is genetically different.

A prairie grassland in the Milk River area of Alberta.

ecosystems. A broad, regional type of ecosystem characterized by distinctive climate and soil conditions and a distinctive kind of biological community adapted to those conditions is referred to as a **biome.** The geography of the biosphere, that is, of global terrestrial ecosystems or world biomes, is illustrated in Figure 3–5. In Canada, 15 terrestrial and five marine biomes, also called ecozones, have been identified (Figure 3–6). Finally, the highest

level of organization is the biosphere or ecosphere, which consists of all communities of living things on Earth, of all Earth's ecosystems together.

Generally the biosphere is not studied as a single large system; instead, the smaller but still globally interrelated ecological systems frequently are the focus of investigation. Ecosystems vary in size and location, but all

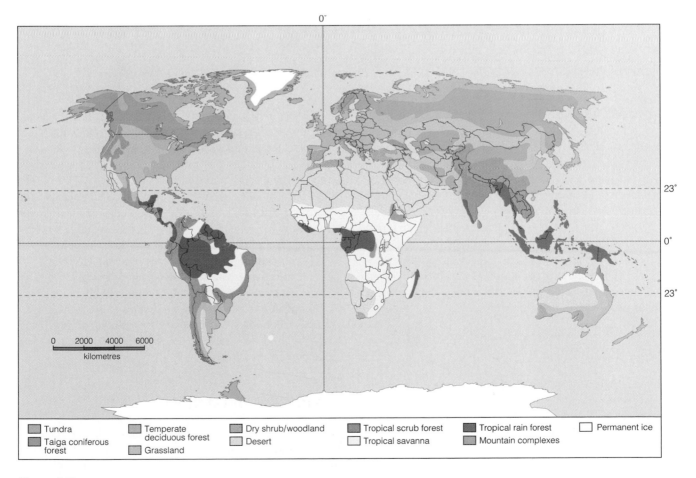

| Tundra | Temperate deciduous forest | Dry shrub/woodland | Tropical scrub forest | Tropical rain forest | Permanent ice |
| Taiga coniferous forest | Grassland | Desert | Tropical savanna | Mountain complexes | |

Figure 3–5
Map of world biomes

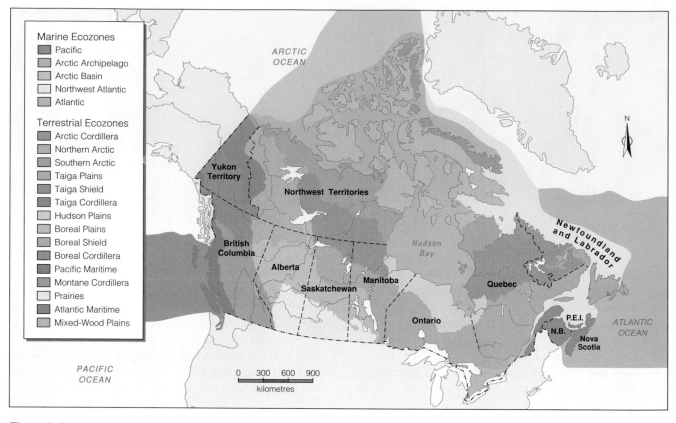

Figure 3–6
Ecozones of Canada

Marine Ecozones
- Pacific
- Arctic Archipelago
- Arctic Basin
- Northwest Atlantic
- Atlantic

Terrestrial Ecozones
- Arctic Cordillera
- Northern Arctic
- Southern Arctic
- Taiga Plains
- Taiga Shield
- Taiga Cordillera
- Hudson Plains
- Boreal Plains
- Boreal Shield
- Boreal Cordillera
- Pacific Maritime
- Montane Cordillera
- Prairies
- Atlantic Maritime
- Mixed-Wood Plains

SOURCE: Government of Canada. (1996). *The state of Canada's environment—1996.* Ottawa: Supply and Service Canada. Figure II.2.

are dynamic entities, always changing as a result of changes in their external environments. These changes may be natural, as in grassland fires or changes in precipitation levels in a forest, or they may be human induced, such as in spraying a field or forest with an insecticide. Unless the change is one that exceeds the threshold limits of the individual ecosystem or the biosphere, ecosystems usually can compensate for the stresses of external changes without incurring permanent change. The buildup of greenhouse gases, stratospheric ozone depletion, and the rapid loss of biological diversity, however, are examples of potentially disastrous and permanent changes to the ecosphere.

BIODIVERSITY

Biological diversity or biodiversity, nature's insurance against ecological disasters, includes genetic diversity, species diversity, and ecological diversity. Genetic diversity, as noted above, is the variation in genetic makeup among individuals within a single species. **Species diversity** refers to the number of different species and the relative abundance of each in different habitats on Earth. **Ecological diversity** is the variety of biological commu-

nities—forests, deserts, grasslands, streams, lakes, oceans—that interact with one another and with their physical and chemical (nonliving) environments.

This abundant variety of genes, species, and ecosystems provides humans with food, energy, fibres, raw materials, medical products, and industrial chemicals, and also generates billions of dollars annually for the global economy. We depend totally on this largely unknown biocapital for life forms and ecosystems, as well as for recycling, purification, and natural pest-control services.

Human cultural diversity sometimes is included as part of Earth's biodiversity. In the same manner as genetic material contained within other living species provides for future adaptability, so might the variety of human cultures represent our adaptability and survival options in the face of changing conditions.

TYPES OF ORGANISMS

For hundreds of years, biologists regarded living things as falling into two broad categories—plants and animals. When microscopes revealed that at the cellular level many organisms did not fit well into either category, a five-kingdom classification system was devised. This system,

PART 2:
THE ECOSPHERE WE LIVE IN

Diversity within genus and species is illustrated in these photos. All four bears belong to the genus *Ursus:* (clockwise from top right) black bear *(Ursus americanus),* polar bear *(Ursus maritimus),* grizzly bear *(Ursus arctos horribilis),* and Kodiac brown bear *(Ursus arctos middendorffi).* The two latter are subspecies of the brown bear, whose coastal and island populations (the Kodiak browns) are genetically distinct from the interior and arctic populations (the grizzlies).

while not perfect, consists of Prokaryotae, Protista, Fungi, Plantae, and Animalia. Bacteria are neither plants nor animals; they are **prokaryotic,** meaning they lack a nuclear envelope and other internal cell membranes. They have their own kingdom, Prokaryotae (Figure 3–7). The four remaining kingdoms are composed of organisms with a **eukaryotic** cell structure. Eukaryotic cells have a high degree of internal organization: a nucleus (genetic material surrounded by a membrane) and several other internal parts enclosed by membranes.

Most of the major groups (phyla) of eukaryotic organisms are single-celled or relatively simple multicellular organisms. They are classified as members of the kingdom Protista and include algae, protozoa, slime moulds, and water moulds. In addition to the Protista, three specialized groups of multicellular organisms form the Fungi, Plantae, and Animalia kingdoms.

These organisms differ from each other in several ways, including their nutrition. Members of the Fungi kingdom (such as mushrooms and yeasts) secrete digestive enzymes into their food and then absorb the predi-

gested nutrients, while members of the Plantae kingdom (such as ferns, conifers, and flowering plants) use radiant energy to manufacture food molecules by photosynthesis. Members of the Animalia kingdom ingest their food and digest it inside their bodies. Most members of the Animalia kingdom are **invertebrates** (they have no backbone, such as jellyfish, worms, insects, and spiders). Animals with backbones, the **vertebrates,** include fish (shark, tuna), amphibians (frogs, salamanders), reptiles (turtles, alligators), birds (eagles, robins, puffins, and ducks), and mammals (elephants, whales, bats, warthogs, and humans).

COMPONENTS AND STRUCTURE OF ECOSYSTEMS

The ecosphere and its ecosystems can be divided into two parts: the living or **biotic** components such as plants and animals, and the nonliving or **abiotic** components such as water, air, solar energy, and nutrients necessary to support life. Living organisms in ecosystems usually

Kingdom

| Prokaryotae | Protista | Animalia | Plantae | Fungi |

(1.3 →)　　　　(1.1 →)　　　　(.7 →)　　　　(.4 →)　　　　(.4 →)

Time (billions of years from present)

Figure 3–7
The five-kingdom system of classification. The prokaryotes were the first organisms to appear; the fungi were the most recent.

are classified as either producers, consumers, or decomposers depending on their nutritional needs and feeding type (Figure 3–8).

Given that sunlight is the source of energy that powers almost all life processes on Earth, **producers** or **autotrophs** (self-feeders) are the self-nourishing organisms that perform photosynthesis. Although hundreds of chemical changes take place sequentially during photosynthesis, in most temperate-zone plants, photosynthesis can be summarized in the following way: $6H_2O + 6CO_2$ + solar energy yields $C_6H_{12}O_6$ (sugar) + $6O_2$. Using solar energy, autotrophs convert relatively simple inorganic substances such as water, carbon dioxide, and nutrients into complex chemicals such as carbohydrates (sugars and starches), lipids (oils, waxes), and proteins. By incorporating the chemicals they produce into their own bodies, producers become potential food resources for other organisms. On land, green plants are the most significant producers; in aquatic ecosystems, algae and certain types of bacteria are important producers. A special group of bacteria **(chemototrophs)** convert the energy found in inorganic chemical compounds in aquatic and other environments into energy without sunlight. In the pitch-black thermal vent areas of deep oceanic trenches, for instance, nonphotosynthetic bacteria use the heat energy (generated by decay of radioactive elements deep in the Earth's core) from the vents to convert dissolved hydrogen sulphide (H_2S) and carbon dioxide (CO_2) into more complex nutrient molecules. Through **chemosynthesis,** these bacteria produce food energy for their nutritional needs and for other consumers in this special ecosystem.

All other organisms in ecosystems are **consumers** or **heterotrophs** (other-feeders) eating the cells, tissues, or waste products of other organisms. Heterotrophic organisms obtain the food energy and bodybuilding materials they need either directly or indirectly from autotrophs and thus indirectly from the sun. Unable to manufacture their own food, heterotrophs live at the expense of other plants and animals. They are categorized broadly as macroconsumers or microconsumers.

Macroconsumers, who feed by ingesting or engulfing particles, parts, or entire bodies of other organisms (living or dead), include herbivores, carnivores,

PART 2:
THE ECOSPHERE WE LIVE IN

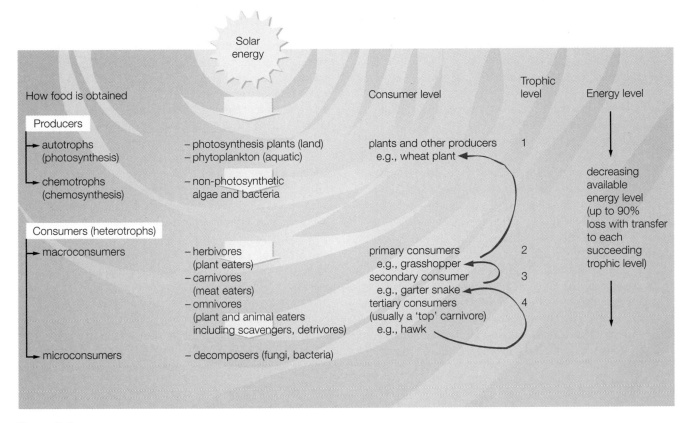

How food is obtained		Consumer level	Trophic level	Energy level
Producers				
→ autotrophs (photosynthesis)	– photosynthesis plants (land) – phytoplankton (aquatic)	plants and other producers e.g., wheat plant	1	
→ chemotrophs (chemosynthesis)	– non-photosynthetic algae and bacteria			decreasing available energy level (up to 90% loss with transfer to each succeeding trophic level)
Consumers (heterotrophs)				
→ macroconsumers	– herbivores (plant eaters)	primary consumers e.g., grasshopper	2	
	– carnivores (meat eaters)	secondary consumer e.g., garter snake	3	
	– omnivores (plant and animal eaters including scavengers, detrivores)	tertiary consumers (usually a 'top' carnivore) e.g., hawk	4	
→ microconsumers	– decomposers (fungi, bacteria)			

Solar energy

Figure 3–8

Classification of organisms and trophic levels in ecosystems

omnivores, scavengers, and detrivores. **Herbivores (plant-eaters)** or **primary consumers,** such as deer, eat green plants directly. **Carnivores** (meat-eaters) or **secondary consumers,** such as bobcats and certain snakes, feed indirectly on plants by eating herbivores. Most carnivores are animals, but the Venus flytrap is an example of a plant that traps and consumes insects. Consumers that eat both plants and animals, including black bears, pigs, and humans, are **omnivores. Tertiary** consumers are carnivores such as hawks that eat secondary (other carnivorous) consumers.

Many heterotrophs consume dead organic material. Those that consume the entire dead organism, such as vultures and hyenas, are known as **scavengers.** Consumers that ingest fragments of dead or decaying tissues or organic wastes are called **detritivores** or **detritus feeders.** Examples are earthworms, shrimp, dung beetles, and maggots. **Microconsumers** or **decomposer** organisms such as fungi and bacteria live on or within their food source, completing the final breakdown and recycling of the complex molecules in detritus into simpler compounds (which we call rot or decay). Decomposers play the major role in returning nutrients to the physical environment, providing an important source of food for worms and insects in the soil and water.

Awareness of the crucial importance of decomposers to the continuation of life in ecosystems has developed relatively recently. As understanding of their performance and function has improved, so has appreciation of the vital link that decomposers play in the cycle that returns chemical nutrients to the physical environment in a form that

Decomposers, including these fungi, are an important mechanism in the process of returning nutrients to ecosystems.

can be used by producers. Given that organisms constantly remove necessary chemicals from the environment, it is not difficult to imagine how quickly nutrients in the soil would be depleted if decomposers did not recycle nutrients continually after the death of producers and consumers. How quickly the Earth would be covered in plant litter, dead animal bodies, animal wastes, and garbage if decomposers did not act on them.

Both producers and consumers use chemical energy stored in glucose and other nutrients to drive their life processes. This energy is released by **aerobic respiration,** which uses oxygen to convert nutrients such as glucose back into carbon dioxide and water. A complex process, the net chemical change for aerobic respiration (glucose + O_2 yields CO_2 + H_2O + energy) is the opposite of that for photosynthesis.

Any individual organism depends on the flow of matter and energy through its body, while the community of organisms in an ecosystem survives by a combination of matter recycling and one-way energy flow. Energy, chemicals, and organisms are the main structural components of an ecosystem and are linked by energy flow and matter recycling (Figure 3–9).

Tolerance Ranges of Species

Every population in an ecosystem exhibits a range of tolerance to variations in its physical and chemical environment. While a speckled trout population may do best at water temperatures between 14°C and 19°C, for example, a few individual trout can survive temperatures as high as 24°C or 25°C for short periods of time because of small differences in their genetic makeup, health, and age (Kaufman and Franz, 1993). Beyond the range of tolerance, however, no trout will survive. The **law of tolerance** notes that the presence, number, and distribution of a species in an ecosystem are determined by whether the levels of one or more physical or chemical factors fall within the range tolerated by the species.

Some organisms have wide ranges of tolerance to some factors and narrow ranges of tolerance to other factors. Generally, the least tolerance is exhibited during the juvenile or reproductive stages of an organism's life cycle. Highly tolerant species can live in a range of habitats with different conditions, and other species can adjust their tolerance to physical factors such as temperature, if change is gradual. This adjustment to slowly changing

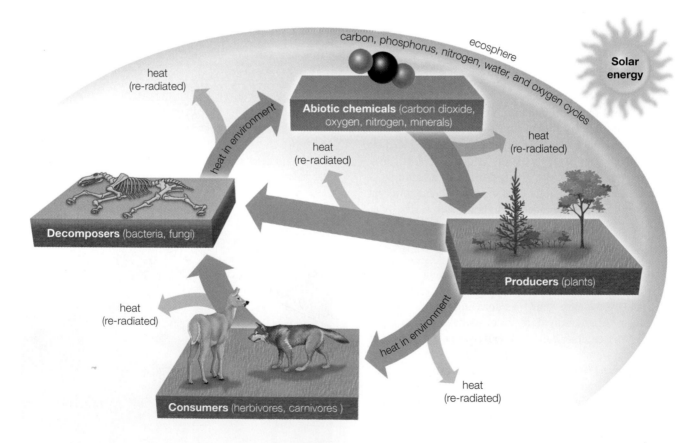

Figure 3–9

Energy flows and matter recycling connect energy, chemicals, and organisms in an ecosystem

PART 2:
THE ECOSPHERE WE LIVE IN

In contrast to other trees in the region, these Ontario sugar maples have not been damaged noticeably by air pollution.

ROLES OF SPECIES IN ECOSYSTEMS

TYPES OF SPECIES IN ECOSYSTEMS

From a human perspective, the species in an ecosystem may be categorized into four types: native or endemic, immigrant or exotic, indicator or bellwether, and keystone species. In a particular ecosystem, a given species may be more than one of these types. **Endemic species** are those that normally live and thrive in a particular ecosystem, while **immigrant** or **exotic species** are those that migrate into or are introduced into an ecosystem, deliberately or accidentally, by humans. Some alien species are beneficial to humans while others eliminate many native species. **Indicator species** such as neotropical migratory songbirds provide early warnings of environmental damage to communities or ecosystems. The current decline in numbers of neotropical songbirds in North America indicates that their summer habitats here and their winter habitats in Latin American and Caribbean tropical forests are disappearing. In a similar way, many of the world's amphibians (frogs, toads, and salamanders) are declining, possibly due to increased ultraviolet radiation or chemical contamination (see Chapter 12).

While all species play important roles in their ecosystems, some scientists consider certain species more important than others in helping to maintain the ecosystems of which they are a part. **Keystone species** such as bees, bats, and hummingbirds play crucial roles in tropical forests by pollinating flowering plants, dispersing seeds, or both. Other top predators such as alligators, wolves, and giant anteaters exert a stabilizing influence on their

conditions, **acclimation,** is a protective device, but it has limits. Each adjustment brings a species closer to its absolute limit until, without warning, the next small change triggers a **threshold effect.** This is a harmful or even fatal reaction to exceeding the tolerance limit (similar to adding the straw that broke the camel's back). This threshold effect explains why many environmental problems seem to arise so suddenly. Maple trees in Quebec and Ontario may suddenly seem to have begun dying in droves, but part of the cause may be exposure to numerous air pollutants, including acid precipitation, for decades. The concern about exceeding thresholds also explains why efforts must be made to prevent pollution.

Limiting Factors in Ecosystems

An ecological principle, related to the law of tolerance, is the **limiting factor principle,** which states that too much or too little of any abiotic factor can limit or prevent growth of a population even if all other factors are at or near the optimum range of tolerance. Limiting factors in land ecosystems include temperature, precipitation, humidity, wind, light, shade, fire, salinity, available space, and soil nutrients. If one of these factors, such as the amount of nitrogen in the soil, is insufficient, even though all other factors are at optimum levels, a crop such as corn will not grow once it has used up the available phosphorus. Just as nitrogen levels determine how much corn will grow in a field, growth can be limited by an excess of an abiotic factor such as too much water or too much fertilizer. In aquatic ecosystems, **salinity** (the amounts of various salts dissolved in a given volume of water) is a limiting factor, as is the **dissolved oxygen content** (the amount of oxygen gas dissolved in a given volume of water at a particular temperature and pressure), and availability of nutrients.

Introduction of the zebra mussel to some North American aquatic environments has had devastating impacts on crayfish endemic to the Great Lakes.

ecosystems by feeding on and regulating the populations of certain species. Sea otters of the Pacific Ocean feed on sea urchins and other shellfish, helping to reduce the sea urchins' destruction of kelp beds, thereby providing a larger habitat for many other species and indirectly increasing species diversity (Figure 3–10). Given that the balance of the entire system is keyed to the activities of this species, if the sea otter is removed or its keystone role within the ecosystem changes, the basic nature of the community changes (with more sea urchins there is less kelp and fewer species). On the Canadian prairies, the gopher also is considered a keystone species (Box 3–1). Population crashes and extinctions of other species that depend on the keystone species can send ripple effects through the entire ecosystem.

Ecological Niche

Each species meets the challenge of survival in its own unique fashion. The way an organism interacts with other living things and with its physical environment defines that organism's **ecological niche** or role within the structure and functions of an ecosystem. An ecological niche includes all the environmental (physical, chemical, and biological) conditions an organism or species needs to live, interact, reproduce, and adapt in an ecosystem. **Specialist species** have narrow niches, meaning a species may be able to live only in one type of habitat, eat a few types of food only, or tolerate a narrow range of climatic or other environmental conditions (Enviro-Focus 3).

In tropical and Canadian temperate (see Chapter 9) rain forests, diverse plant and animal species occupy specialized ecological niches within the distinct layers of the forest. These specialized niches enable species to minimize or avoid competition for resources with other species, thus preserving species diversity. Canadian examples include salamanders that depend on habitat found in old-growth forests, and the insectivorous pitcher and sundew plants found only in sphagnum moss/peat bogs. **Generalist species** have broad niches and are able to live in many different places while tolerating a wide range of environmental conditions. Humans are considered a generalist species, as are flies, mice, raccoons, and white-tail deer.

Interactions between Species

Different species in an ecosystem often interact and develop close associations with one another. The major types of species interactions are interspecific competition, predation, parasitism, mutualism, and commensalism.

If commonly used resources are abundant, different species are able to share them and to come closer to occupying their **fundamental niches.** A fundamental niche is the full range of physical, chemical, and biological factors each species could use if there were no competition from other species. In most ecosystems, however, each species faces competition from other species for one or more of the same limited resources of food, sunlight, water, soil nutrients, or space. This is **interspecific competition,** where parts of the fundamental niches of different species overlap significantly. Since no two species can occupy the same niche in the same community indefinitely, one species may occupy more of its fundamental niche than the other species as a result of competition between them. This **competitive exclusion principle** means that one of the competing species must migrate to another area if possible, shift its feeding habits or behaviour, suffer a sharp decline in population numbers, or become extinct.

The degree of fundamental niche overlap may be reduced by **resource partitioning.** Dividing up of scarce resources occurs in order that species with similar requirements can use the resources in different ways, in different places, and at different times. Resource partitioning occurs between owls and hawks that feed on similar prey; owls hunt at night while hawks hunt during the day. Similarly, some species of warblers hunt for insects in different parts of the same coniferous tree (Figure 3–11). Sharing the wealth among competing species results in each species occupying a **realized niche** (that portion of the fundamental niche actually occupied by a species).

Predation, where members of a **predator** species feed on parts or all of an organism of a **prey** species, is the most obvious form of species interaction. A turtle eating a fish in a freshwater pond ecosystem, a fox feeding on a rabbit in a field ecosystem, and a killer whale culling a sick seal in a marine ecosystem are all examples of **predator–prey relationships.** Another type of

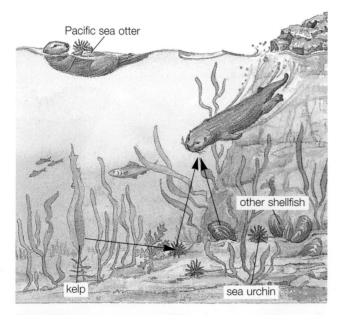

Figure 3–10
Pacific Ocean sea otters: a keystone role

The golden rodent with the impressive name is a keystone species in the Canadian prairies. "Eliminating gophers would wipe out a whole suite of wildlife on the prairies," says biologist Cliff Wallis (Barnett, 1996, p. A4). A long list of wildlife depends on the ground squirrel (gopher) for survival, from wild tomatoes that grow on ground squirrel mounds to salamanders who use gopher burrows as shady shelters on their treks between wetlands. Without ground squirrels, many birds of prey and mammals such as swift foxes and badgers would disappear for lack of food. According to Alberta provincial biologist Steve Brechtel, rare ferruginous hawks depend on gophers for 90 percent of their diet and eat up to 480 annually when raising their young. He suggests that prairie falcons and the endangered burrowing owl (which needs gopher burrows for its home) are in decline in part because the gopher population is in decline.

Gophers have long been targets of eradication efforts by prairie farmers who claim the rodents cause millions of dollars in damage to their fields, grain, and other crops. Highly toxic strychnine is the poison of choice: it takes a mere 0.7 milligrams to kill a gopher, the equivalent of a couple of grains of sand. Once the gopher dies, the poison remains active and kills animals that eat the gopher carcass. Since 1994, the federal government has restricted the amount of strychnine used to kill gophers because of fears of contaminating groundwater and poisoning other animals.

Cliff Wallis points out that poor land management practices are a major contributor to farmers' problems with gophers. People allow overgrazing to occur, clear all the trees that provide

Richardson's ground squirrel: *Spermaphilous richardsonii*

nesting sites for birds of prey, and cultivate right to the edges of fields so there is no room for coyote dens (gophers are a staple of coyote diets). Clearly, many of the problems with gophers have their origin in human actions.

University of Lethbridge biologist Gail Michener, the Jane Goodall of gophers, notes that gophers have survived for tens of thousands of years, far longer than humans have been commercially cultivating the prairies. They are "definitely part of the prairies" and will not be driven easily from their homeland (Dempster, 1996, p. A4). Nor should gophers be eradicated because, in addition to providing food to predators, gophers "balance the grazing pressure by eating species of plants that cows are less interested in" (Holyrood, cited in Barnett, 1996, p. A4). Given the principle of connectedness and the unknown or unanticipated effects people encounter when they simplify ecosystems, gophers deserve greater respect for their role as a keystone prairie species.

SOURCES: Barnett, V. (1996, April 27). Biologist rises to defence of gopher. *Calgary Herald*, p. A4.

Dempster, L. (1996, April 17). Gopher guru says critters here to stay. *Calgary Herald*, p. A4.

predator–prey interaction is **parasitism,** a symbiotic relationship in which the parasite benefits by obtaining nourishment from the host and the host is weakened or perhaps killed by the parasite preying on it. Parasites such as ticks, mosquitoes, and mistletoe plants live outside the host's body, while other parasites such as tapeworms and disease-causing organisms (pathogens) live within the host.

Symbiosis is any intimate relationship between individuals of two or more different species. Sometimes symbiosis can take an extreme form. In the case of three-toed sloths, their fur often is occupied by green algae and pyralid moths that feed on the algae, as well as by house mites, a number of beetle species, and several other kinds of arthropods. A single sloth can be home to over 900 beetles (Perry, 1986).

Mutualism is another symbiotic relationship in which interacting species, such as honeybees and certain flowers, both benefit. In the process of feeding on a flower's nectar, honeybees also are picking up pollen and pollinating the female flowers. Sometimes, mutualistic partners can be completely dependent on one another. In the case of the yucca plant and yucca moth, for instance, the moth transfers pollen between plants and the plants provide both food and a safe habitat for the moth larvae, which hatch from eggs laid inside the flower. Without the yucca moth, pollination (successful reproduction) would not occur in the yucca and, without the yucca plant, the moth would be unable to reproduce successfully because it lays its eggs only inside yucca flowers.

Another type of symbiotic species interaction, **commensalism,** occurs when one species benefits while the other is neither helped nor harmed. On land, a good example of commensalism is the relationship between a tropical tree and its epiphytes (air plants) that live attached to the bark of the tree's branches. Epiphytes do not obtain nutrients or water directly from the tree to which they are anchored, but their position on the tree

Pacific Yew: Trash Tree Now Coveted as Cancer Treatment

For decades, the Pacific yew (a small shrub-like tree) was considered worthless in comparison to the highly profitable Douglas fir. The two species coexist in forested areas in western North America. To accommodate clearcutting of Douglas fir, however, massive cutting and burning of the Pacific yew took place. Impacts on Pacific yew populations as a whole were particularly severe during the 1970s and 1980s when Douglas fir timber production was high. It was not until the mid-1980s and the discovery of taxol that the Pacific yew became a product valued by society.

Taxol is a successful cancer-fighting agent and is particularly useful in treating ovarian cancer. Since the Pacific yew is the only known source of taxol, harvesting of the species is now widespread. This harvesting pressure may decline as new synthetic sources of taxol are developed, but until then, careful management and harvesting of the species is essential. Unfortunately, the Pacific yew is a very slow-growing tree; research has shown that even in undisturbed populations, these trees show little change in size and structure over periods of several decades. The United States Department of

Agriculture forest service (Busing & Spies, 1995) estimated that disturbed populations may require centuries to recover the population size and structure characteristic of old-growth forest stands.

In 1992, the United States introduced management guidelines for Pacific yew conservation (Busing & Spies, 1995). These guidelines require the establishment of genetic reserves for yew, replanting after harvest, and retention of some live yew trees in harvesting areas. Although the Pacific yew is but one of the millions of species sharing planet Earth, its transition from trash tree to valued resource underscores the need to preserve and protect even the most seemingly insignificant species.

Pacific yew bark: one person's treatment requires the bark from six to 100 trees.

SOURCE: Busing, R.T., & Spies, T.A. (1995). *Modeling the population dynamics of the Pacific yew.* United States Department of Agriculture, Forest Service, Research Note PNW-RN-515.

INTERESTING INTERNET SITE: Sierra Club. Endangered species and their habitats: Protecting the "web of life." http://www.sierraclub.org/ecoregions/endangered.html

allows them to receive adequate light, water (by rainfall dripping down the branches), and minerals (washed out of the tree's leaves by rainfall). The epiphytes benefit from the association while the tree remains generally unaffected.

Recent research in old-growth forest canopies of the Pacific Northwest has revealed that epiphytes (lichens, mosses, and liverworts) contribute to creation of treetop soil (from decaying remains of leaves, epiphytes, and needles). Since soils in temperate rain forests tend to be

nutrient poor because of leaching by heavy rains, tree roots actually tap soil up in their own canopies. When they are wet, nitrogen-fixing lichens are particularly important in canopies because they release excess nitrogen that may be absorbed by other epiphytes or the tree itself. This critical source of forest nutrition is declining as logging of old-growth forests (colonized most heavily by nitrogen-fixing lichens) is causing these lichens to decline (Moffett, 1997).

In a marine environment, commensalism occurs between various species of clownfish and sea anemones.

Figure 3–11
Resource partitioning and niches among *Dendroica* species (wood warblers). Each species spends most of its feeding time in a distinct portion of the trees it frequents. The shaded regions identify where each species spends at least half its foraging time.

The stinging tentacles of the anemones paralyze most fish that touch them, but clownfish gain protection by living unharmed among the tentacles and feeding on the detritus left from the meals of their host anemones. The sea anemones seem neither to be harmed by this relationship nor to benefit from it.

ENERGY FLOW IN ECOSYSTEMS

FOOD CHAINS AND FOOD WEBS

One way in which individuals in a community interact is by feeding on one another. Through feeding, energy, chemical elements, and some compounds are transferred from organism to organism along **food chains** (the sequence of who feeds on or decomposes whom in an ecosystem). Ecologists have assigned every organism in an ecosystem to a feeding or **trophic level** depending on whether it's a producer or a consumer and on what it eats or decomposes (see Figure 3–8). Producers (plants) start the food chain by capturing the sun's energy through photosynthesis and they constitute the first trophic level. Primary consumers (and omnivores) eat the plants and make up the second trophic level; secondary consumers (and omnivores) eat the herbivores and form the third trophic level; and tertiary consumers (and omnivores) belong to the fourth trophic level. Detrivores or decomposers process detritus from all trophic levels.

Simple food chains such as described above occur rarely in nature because few organisms eat just one other kind of organism. Typically, the flow of energy and materials through terrestrial, aquatic, and oceanic ecosystems occurs on the basis of a range of food choices on the part of each organism involved. These organisms form a complex network of feeding relationships called a **food web.** In a simplified Great Lakes example, the food web shows relationships between some of the better-known species including lake trout, salmon, herring gulls, bald eagles, and humans (Figure 3–12).

An important feature of energy flow in ecosystems is that it is linear or one way. Energy can move along the food chain until it is used; at that point, it is unavailable

The meeting of two links in the food chain.

BOX 3-2
TOXINS AND THE GREAT LAKES ECOSYSTEM

In 1971, a biologist at Scotch Bonnet Island in Lake Ontario found only 12 herring gull chicks where there should have been 100. That disturbing discovery of the reproductive problems of the ubiquitous herring gull became a symbol of the problems afflicting wildlife in the Great Lakes ecosystem.

In the early 1970s, a program designed to monitor persistent toxic chemicals in the eggs of herring gulls soon showed that water birds in the Great Lakes were among the most heavily contaminated in the world. High levels of chlorinated organic contaminants in the gulls' eggs coincided with high embryonic mortality and behavioural changes in adults (such as inattentiveness) that resulted in lower hatching success and physiological abnormalities in embryos and chicks.

Contaminants in herring gull eggs declined through the 1970s as a result of regulations implemented to control use and production of chlorinated organic compounds. However, in 1981

Eaglet hatched with twisted beak.

and 1982, levels increased briefly again, indicating that persistent contaminants continued to cycle through the ecosystem. The less easily controlled sources of these contaminants included leaching from landfill sites, disturbance of lake sediments, and deposition from the atmosphere. As herring gulls are sentinels for the presence of biologically significant concentrations of chemicals in the Great Lakes, monitoring of contaminant levels continues (Government of Canada, 1991).

Bald eagles also are extremely sensitive monitors of ecosystem quality. The fact that nesting pairs reintroduced to both the north and south shores of Lake Erie continue to survive confirms that ecosystem quality in those parts of the Great Lakes has improved. The fact that many of their eggs are fertile also is evidence of improvements in environmental quality. In 1991, however, 8 of 12 hatchlings died of wasting by the age of four weeks—wasting is a syndrome linked with persistent toxic substances. In 1993, bald eagles were hatched with twisted beaks and deformed talons, a problem caused by persistent toxic substances. These events indicate that efforts made since the late 1970s to reduce some contaminant levels have made substantial progress, but not sufficient progress to restore the viability of bald eagle chicks in the populations of bald eagles nesting near the shoreline of the Great Lakes. By implication, there is potential danger to the dense human population around the Great Lakes.

Since it is not yet possible to retrieve or remove completely a persistent toxic substance once it has entered the environment, the focus must be on preventing the generation of such substances in the first place, rather than on trying to control their use, release, and disposal after they are produced. For those substances that persist and bioaccumulate in the environment, there is no safe level. The challenge is to implement the goal of zero discharge for persistent toxic substances, that is, to stop their generation, use, and release into the environment.

SOURCES: Government of Canada. (1991). *The state of Canada's environment—1991.* Ottawa: Supply and Services Canada, p. 18-16.

International Joint Commission. (1992). *Sixth biennial report under the Great Lakes Water Quality Agreement of 1978 to the governments of the United States and Canada and the state and provincial governments of the Great Lakes basin.* Ottawa: International Joint Commission.

Muldoon, P., & Jackson, J. (1994). Keeping the zero in zero discharge. *Alternatives,* 20(4), pp. 14–20.

---

alfalfa. Lightning discharges also transform (fix) atmospheric nitrogen into usable nitrates that enter the soil in rain.

In the second step of the nitrogen cycle, the ammonia (NH_3) from Step 1 is converted to nitrate (NO_3-) through the action of nitrifying bacteria. In the third step of the cycle, plant roots absorb nitrates and/or ammonia to produce proteins and nucleic acids that, in turn, are consumed by animals and converted into animal proteins.

In the fourth, or ammonification, stage of the nitrogen cycle, the nitrogen compounds in waste products from living oraganisms as well as dead plants and animals

are decomposed by ammonifying bacteria. Ammonia produced by ammonifying bacteria enters the nitrogen cycle and is available again for nitrification and assimilation. Denitrification, the final stage in the process, occurs when denitrifying bacteria reduce NO_3- to gaseous nitrogen (N_2), and return it to the atmosphere.

Humans have intervened in the nitrogen cycle in several ways. One important intervention occurs when burning fuels release large quantities of nitric oxide (NO) into the atmosphere. When nitric oxide combines with oxygen to form nitrogen dioxide (NO_2) gas, it can then react with water vapour to form nitric acid (HNO_3), a

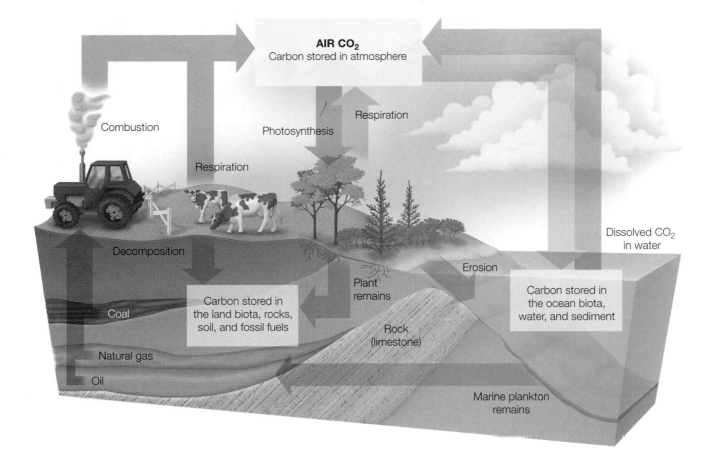

Figure 3–13

A simplified diagram of the carbon cycle

component of acid deposition (acid rain) that can damage trees and aquatic systems. Water pollution is another significant impact of human intervention in the nitrogen cycle, particularly as it relates to the use of nitrogen fertilizers. Overuse of commercial fertilizers on land can lead to excess nitrogen compounds in agricultural runoff and in the discharge of municipal sewage. Nitrogen-based fertilizers stimulate the growth of algae and aquatic plants that, when they subsequently decompose, deplete the water of dissolved oxygen and cause other aquatic organisms, including fish, to die of suffocation. Nitrates from fertilizers also can leach or filter down through the soil and contaminate groundwater, causing concern about the quality of drinking water.

Phosphorus Cycle

Phosphorus does not exist in a gaseous state and does not circulate in the atmosphere. Instead, phosphorus slowly cycles from phosphate deposits on land to shallow sediments in the oceans to living organisms and then back to the land and oceans (Figure 3–15). As water runs over

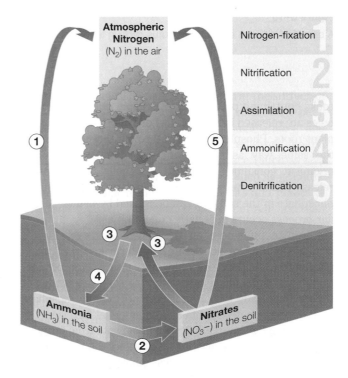

Figure 3–14

A simplified diagram of the nitrogen cycle

can break rock apart by repeated expansion and contraction, and rocks may be dissolved by weak acids that form in the presence of carbon dioxide, organic material, and water; such actions produce sediments that may be transported by wind, water, or ice. The interaction of all processes that change rocks from one type to another is the rock cycle, which is responsible for concentrating mineral resources on which humans depend.

TERRESTRIAL AND AQUATIC ECOSYSTEMS

THE GEOGRAPHY OF LIFE

For centuries, people have been fascinated by geographic variations in the kinds and numbers of species found in various parts of the world. Unless they are in zoos, polar bears do not inhabit southwestern British Columbia, nor do arbutus trees grow in the Northwest Territories. Geographic variations occur, in part, because the distributions of plant and animal species are governed by the ability of each species to tolerate the environmental conditions of its surroundings. On a global scale, distribution patterns of species have been recognized for centuries; in each major kind of climate a distinctive type of vegetation develops, and certain animals and other kinds of organisms are associated with each major type of vegetation. Similarly, certain aquatic organisms assemble in each of the Earth's major aquatic ecosystems.

LIFE ON LAND: MAJOR TERRESTRIAL BIOMES

A biome is a kind of ecosystem—a large, relatively distinct region such as a desert, tropical rain forest, tundra, or grassland characterized by certain climatic conditions, soil characteristics, and plant and animal inhabitants regardless of where on Earth it occurs. More than any other factor, the climate—particularly average temperature and precipitation differences—determines the boundaries of Earth's major biomes (see Figure 3–5) or Canada's ecozones (see Figure 3–6).

For plants, precipitation generally determines whether a land area is forest, desert, or grassland. In terms of precipitation, for instance, we find generally that desert areas receive less than 25 centimetres annually, grasslands receive 25 to 75 centimetres, and forests receive more than 100 centimetres per year. When temperature and precipitation factors are combined, we find hot areas that receive 100 or more centimetres of rainfall per year sustain tropical savannas whereas temperate

Arctic tundra in the Yukon.

areas support deciduous forests. If temperate forest soil types are added as a limiting factor, we find that maples and beeches are more successful on high-nutrient soils while oaks and hickories are more successful on low-nutrient soils. Acting together, these and other factors lead to deserts, grasslands, and forests in tropical, temperate, and polar areas.

Tundra is the northernmost biome, characterized by **permafrost** (a permanently frozen layer of subsoil) and low-growing vegetation adapted to extreme cold and a very short growing season. The taiga, or boreal forest, is found south of the tundra and is dominated by coniferous trees. Temperate forests occur where precipitation is relatively high. Temperate rain forests, such as those found on the northwest coast of North America, also are dominated by conifers, whereas temperate deciduous forests are dominated by broad-leaved trees that seasonally lose their leaves.

In areas of moderate precipitation, temperate grasslands (and grain crops) thrive on deep, mineral-rich soil. Tropical grasslands or savannas often are similar to open woodland with scattered trees interspersed with grassy areas. Characterized by a climate of mild, wet winters and very dry summers, dry woodlands and shrublands (chaparral) display thickets of trees and small-leafed shrubs. Deserts occur in both temperate and tropical areas where there is little precipitation and high evaporation. Communities and organisms in deserts possess specialized water-conserving adaptations. Tropical rain forests, characterized by very high precipitation that is evenly distributed during the year, have mineral-poor soils and yet support at least three stories of forest foliage and a high species diversity, including many epiphytes.

Climate and vegetation vary with latitude (distance from the equator) and altitude (height above sea level). If we were to travel from the equator to the North or South poles or from low to high altitudes, parallel changes in

76

vegetation would occur (Figure 3–17). That is, changes in the type and distribution of vegetation seen while hiking up a mountain (gaining altitude) would be similar to the changes in vegetation seen while travelling toward the North Pole (increasing latitude). Hiking some of the trails in the Canadian Rockies, for example, we would be able to see the temperate deciduous forest at the base of the mountain give way to subalpine coniferous species that, with increasing elevation gain, in turn would give way to alpine tundra below the permanent ice and snow of the peak.

LIFE ON EARTH: MAJOR AQUATIC BIOMES

Oceans

Oceans cover about 71 percent of the Earth's surface, serving as a huge reservoir for carbon dioxide, helping to regulate the temperature of the troposphere, and providing habitats for about 250 000 species of marine animals and plants (many of which are eaten by humans and other organisms). Oceans contain many valuable resources, including sand and gravel, oil and natural gas, iron, phosphates, and magnesium. Also, as long as they

Rivers carry nutrients to the ocean, where those nutrients support many coastal and marine species.

are not overloaded, their size and currents enable oceans to mix and dilute many human-produced wastes that flow or are dumped into them, rendering the wastes less harmful or even harmless.

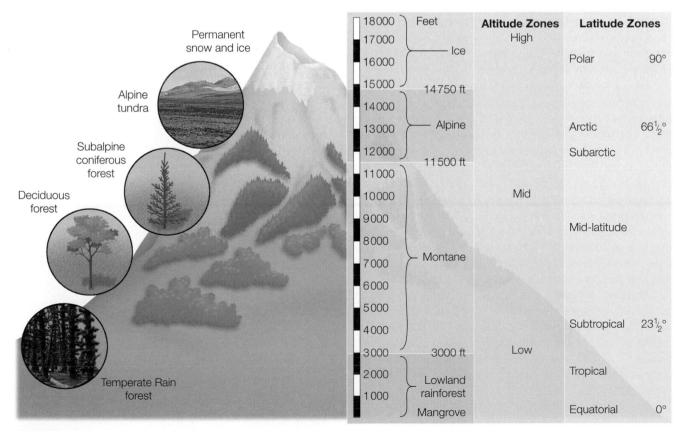

Figure 3–17
Generalized effects of altitude and latitude on climate and biomes

The coastal zone and the open sea are the two major life zones of the oceans. Although it constitutes less than 10 percent of the ocean's area, the **coastal zone** contains about 90 percent of all marine species and is where most of the large commercial marine fisheries are located. Coastal zones also are among the most densely populated and most intensely used and polluted ecosystems on Earth. Coral reefs, estuaries, coastal wetlands, and barrier islands are among the most highly productive ecosystems within the coastal zone. Their very high net primary productivity per unit of area is due to the ample sunlight and nutrients deposited from land and stirred up by wind and ocean currents.

Found in warm tropical and subtropical oceans, slow-growing **coral reefs** are as rich in species as tropical rain forests; a single reef may contain more than 3000 species of corals, fish, and shellfish. Not only do almost one-third of all the world's fish live on coral reefs, providing critical fishing grounds for many countries, but also coral reefs reduce the energy of incoming waves, thus protecting about 15 percent of the world's shorelines from storms. In spite of their importance, coral reef formations are being degraded and destroyed by pollution, siltation from clear-cutting operations inland, land-reclamation efforts, tourism, and mining of coral formations for building materials.

As bodies of coastal water partly surrounded by land, **estuaries** have access to the open sea and a large supply of fresh water from rivers. The combination of several factors—nutrients from the land transported into the estuary by rivers and streams, ocean current action that rapidly circulates the nutrients and filters out waste products, and the presence of many plants whose roots and stems mechanically trap food material—provides important nursery conditions for the larval stages of most commercially important shellfish and fin fish species. **Coastal wetlands** and **mangrove swamps** also are breeding grounds and habitats for marine organisms (oysters, crabs), waterfowl, shorebirds, and other wildlife. Here, too, human ignorance has caused the loss of estuarine environments as people have used coastal wetlands and tidal marshes as dumps or have filled them with dredged material to form artificial land for residential and industrial developments. Mangrove swamps often are destroyed to provide firewood and agricultural land.

Barrier islands, the long, low, narrow offshore islands of sediment that run parallel to much of North America's Atlantic and Gulf coasts, help protect coastal wetlands, lagoons, estuaries, and the mainland from storm damage by dispersing wave energy. These islands also come under stress from human recreational and developmental activities.

The marine environment has two main divisions: the **benthic** environment (ocean floor) and the **pelagic** environment (ocean water). The pelagic environment is divided, in turn, in two different ways—across its surface and through its depths. Its three vertical zones—the euphotic, bathyl, and abyssal zones—are based chiefly on the penetration of sunlight (Figure 3–18). The euphotic region (the upper 100 to 200 metres of ocean water) allows enough sunlight to penetrate for photosynthesis to take place. Beyond that depth, light penetrates weakly or not at all, and those few organisms living in the abyssal zone are adapted to darkness and scarcity of food. Except at deep-sea thermal vents, the average net primary productivity per unit of area in the open sea is quite low.

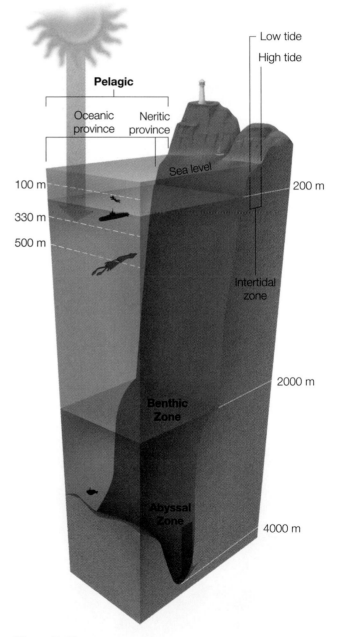

Figure 3–18
Zonation in the marine environment

Freshwater Ecosystems

Freshwater ecosystems include the standing water in lakes and ponds, flowing water in rivers and streams, and freshwater wetlands (marshes and swamps). Lakes are (large) bodies of standing water formed when precipitation, overland runoff, or groundwater flowing from springs fills depressions on the earth's surface. Typically, the water in large lakes would have three basic life zones—littoral, limnetic, and profundal—while small lakes would lack a profundal zone. Each of these zones provides habitats and niches for different species.

The **littoral zone** is the shallow-water and vegetated area along the shore of a lake or pond (Figure 3–19). Nutrient availability and photosynthesis being greatest here, this is the most productive zone of the lake. Frogs and tadpoles, turtles, worms, crustaceans, insect larvae, and many fish as well as insects are found in this zone. Extending downward as far as sunlight penetrates, the **limnetic zone** is the open-water area away from the shore. Here the main organisms are phytoplankton (photosynthetic cyanobacteria and algae) and zooplankton (nonphotosynthetic organisms including protozoa—animal-like protists—and small animals including the larval stages of many animals that are large as adults).

Aquatic vegetation provides cover and nursery conditions for fish and shellfish.

Larger fish spend most of their time in the limnetic zone, although they may feed and breed in the littoral zone. There is less vegetation in this zone due to its depth.

The deepest zone of a lake is its **profundal zone** where lack of light means no producers live. Considerable food drifts into the profundal zone from the other two

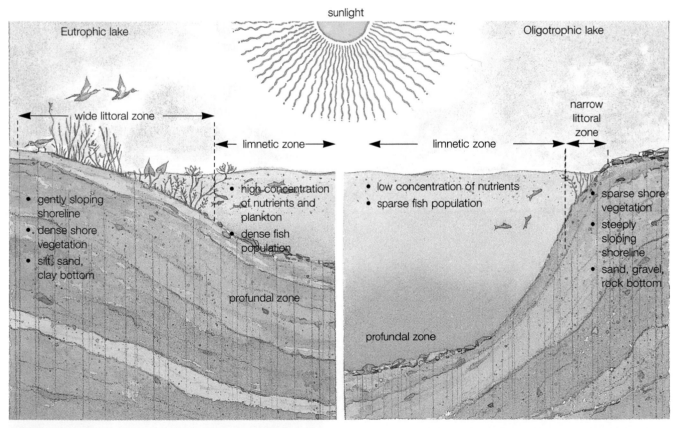

Figure 3–19
Basic life zones in eutrophic and oligotrophic lakes

zones and decay bacteria decompose the dead plants and animals, freeing the minerals from their bodies. With no producers to absorb and incorporate these minerals into the food chain, however, the profundal zone habitat becomes rich in minerals and anaerobic, and few organisms live there.

Normal lakes that have minimal levels of nutrients are unenriched or **oligotrophic,** whereas a lake that is enriched (with nitrates and phosphates) in excess of what producers need is termed **eutrophic.** Many lakes fall somewhere between the two extremes of nutrient enrichment and are called **mesotrophic** lakes.

Freshwater Rivers and Streams

Movement of water from the mountains to the seas gives rise to different environmental conditions throughout a river system and from stream to stream. Headwater streams (the sources of a river) usually are shallow, swiftly flowing, highly oxygenated, and cold. Organisms here frequently exhibit adaptations such as suckers to avoid being swept away by the current, or flattened bodies to slip under or between rocks. Farther from its headwaters, the river usually widens and becomes deeper, slower flowing, less oxygenated, and not as cold. Although their shapes are streamlined to reduce resistance when moving through water, organisms in these larger, slow-moving water bodies do not need the same adaptations as those in faster waters. In fact, where the current is slow, plants and animals characteristic of lakes and ponds replace those of the headwaters.

Flowing water ecosystems are different from freshwater ecosystems not only because of currents but also in their dependence on the land for much of their energy. Up to 99 percent of the energy input in headwater streams comes from leaves and other detritus (dead organic matter) carried by wind or surface runoff into the stream. Farther downstream, rivers have more producers and are less dependent on detritus as an energy source.

Water moving downhill is associated also with landform creation: over the years, friction of sediment-laden waters can level mountains and cut deep canyons into the landscape. Rocks and sediments removed by the water are deposited in low-lying areas, contributing to salt marshes and building up deltas and other landforms.

Inland Wetlands

Transitional between aquatic and terrestrial ecosystems, **wetlands** usually are covered with fresh water at least part of the year and have characteristic soils and water-tolerant vegetation. Inland wetlands include marshes, dominated by grass-like plants; swamps, dominated by woody plants; bogs, including peat moss bogs; prairie potholes; mud flats; floodplains; fens; wet meadows; and the wet Arctic tundra in summer. While some wetlands are covered with water year round, others are seasonal,

A flowing water ecosystem in the Queen Charlotte Islands.

including prairie potholes (small shallow ponds formed when glacial ice melted at the end of the last ice age) and floodplain wetlands.

Inland wetlands provide habitat for game fish, migratory waterfowl, beaver, otters, muskrats, and other wildlife, and they improve water quality by acting as a sink to filter, dilute, and degrade sediments and pollutants as water flows through them. Wetlands help control flooding by storing excess water during periods of heavy rainfall, or when rivers flood their banks, by slowly releasing the water back into the rivers. Not only do wetlands help to provide a steady flow of water throughout the year, they also reduce riverbank erosion and flood damage. Through infiltration, wetlands serve a very important function as groundwater recharge areas. Freshwater wetlands produce many commercially important products such as wild rice, cranberries, and peat moss. Many people also enjoy fishing, hunting, boating, photography, and nature study in wetland areas.

Cranberry fields are one example of the agricultural use of wetlands.

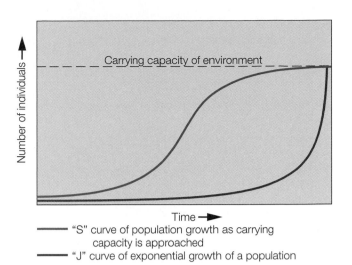

Carrying capacity of environment

Number of individuals ↑

Time →

—— "S" curve of population growth as carrying capacity is approached
—— "J" curve of exponential growth of a population

Figure 3–20
"S" and "J" curves of population growth

[handwritten marginal notes:]
change – constant
births/ deaths
immigration } = pop
emigration
otic potential
J curve – ex potential ESS
m. ting:
vuct
?nviv
carrying capacity
= predation
competition among
species, h₂o,
nesting
seasonal

ables: birth
and immigr
deaths and
bers. A ver
population
+ emigratio
affected by
ronmental
     Popula
Under idea
on its grow
maximum r
conditions,
exponentia
against tir
(Figure 3–
potentials e
span (whe
reproductio
survive to reproductive age. Generally, larger organisms
such as elephants and whales have lower biotic potentials
whereas microorganisms have the greatest biotic potentials. *In nature, however, there are always limits to
growth,* and no population can continue to grow indefinitely at its biotic potential. Instead, a population will
reach a size limit imposed by a shortage of one or more of
the limiting factors of light, water, space, and nutrients.
Essentially, the number of organisms in a population is

of permanent
increasingly
on, dredging
), and urban

thing hap-
caused by
stments to

controlled by the ability of the environment to support
that population.
     The limits set by the environment that prevent organ-
isms from reproducing indefinitely at an exponential rate
are known collectively as **environmental resistance.**
The carrying capacity represents the highest population
that can be maintained for an indefinite period of time by
a particular environment. Many factors determine carrying capacity, including predation, competition among
species, migration, and climate. As well, seasonal or
abnormal changes in the weather or food supplies, water,
nesting or calving sites, and other crucial environmental
resources can alter the carrying capacity for a population.
If tracked over long periods of time, the rate of population
growth for most organisms decreases to about zero; this
levelling out occurs at or near the limit of the environment's ability to support a population. The curve on a
graph of population numbers plotted against time has a
characteristic "S" shape that also shows the population's
initial exponential increase (note the "J" shape at the
start), followed by a levelling out as the carrying capacity
of the environment is approached (Figure 3–20).
     Sometimes, because of a reproductive time lag (the
time required for the birth rate to fall and the death rate
to rise in response to environmental resource limits), a
population temporarily will overshoot the **carrying
capacity** (Figure 3–21a). Unless large numbers of individuals can avoid local environmental degradation by
moving to an area with more favourable conditions, the
population will crash. Often such a population will fall
back to a lower level that fluctuates around the area's carrying capacity. Also during the overshoot period, if degradation and destruction of local environmental resources
occurs, the area's carrying capacity may be lowered.
     In nature, three general types of population change
curves may be observed: relatively stable, irruptive, and
cyclic (Figure 3–21b). If we were to examine many of the

Figure 3–21

Selected population change dynamics

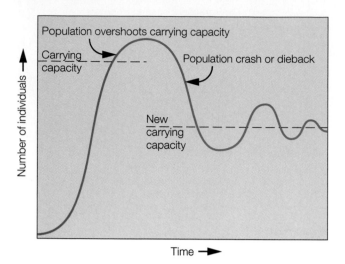

a) A reproductive time lag and population crash

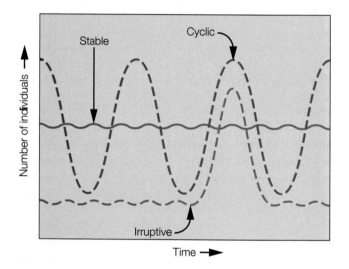

b) Three idealized types of population change curves

species found in undisturbed tropical rain-forest habitats, we would find their population sizes fluctuate slightly above and below their carrying capacities. Assuming no significant changes in those capacities, these species would be exhibiting relatively stable population sizes. If we considered a species such as the raccoon, which normally has a fairly stable population, we would observe an occasional explosion or irruption of the population to a high peak, followed by a crash to a relatively stable lower level. The population explodes in response to factors (such as better weather, more food, or fewer predators) that temporarily increase carrying capacity for the population. In some other instances, species undergo sharp increases and periodic crashes in their numbers; the actual causes of these boom and bust cycles are not well understood, although predators sometimes are blamed.

Species reproduction strategies vary widely. Some, such as algae, bacteria, rodents, many fish, most insects, and annual plants, produce a great many offspring early in their life cycle. The offspring usually are small, mature rapidly, and have short life spans, many dying before they can reproduce. Such species are opportunistic and reproduce rapidly when favourable conditions exist or when a new habitat or a new niche becomes available (a newly plowed field, a recently cleared forest). If environmental conditions are not favourable, however, such populations will tend to go through boom and bust cycles.

At the other end of the reproductive strategy spectrum are species such as humans, elephants, whales, sharks, birds of prey, and long-lived plants whose offspring are few in number, fairly large, and often nurtured for lengthy periods to ensure that most reach reproductive age. Populations of these species exhibit an S-shaped curve as their numbers are maintained near the carrying capacity of their fairly stable habitats.

Human populations, too, are affected by population biology dynamics. If we look back to events such as the 1845 destruction of the Irish potato crop (by a fungus infection), we can see a human population crash in which about one million people died and three million people emigrated. Today, changes in technology, society, and culture appear to have extended Earth's carrying capacity for the human species—we seem to have controlled many diseases, increased food production, and used energy and matter resources at rapid rates in order to make habitable and usable many formerly uninhabitable and unusable parts of the Earth. On a planet that has finite resources and space, a critical question is how long will we be able to keep extending this carrying capacity.

Biosphere II, a US$30-million experiment, was an attempt to develop a self-sustaining ecological system (effectively extending carrying capacity). Occupying more than three acres near Tucson, Arizona, the area was completely enclosed in glass and steel and its occupants were sealed off from the Earth. Powered by solar energy, and theoretically containing everything required to sustain life, Biosphere II housed more than 3800 species of macroscopic plants and animals, including eight human researchers, who spent two years (1991–93) living inside this artificial environment. The simulated earth environments contained within Biosphere II were intended to provide food and the means to recycle water and wastes, and to purify air and water.

Scientists and other observers criticized the project for having a secretly installed carbon dioxide recovery system (to augment Biosphere II's air recycling system), for letting outside air in, and for having a large supply of food hidden inside. While the creators of Biosphere II denied the charges, the experience showed how difficult it is to maintain natural cycles and species diversity even in such a simplified biosphere. This lesson should cause

PART 2:
THE ECOSPHERE WE LIVE IN

natural
forts to

ıral

we are
In this
al evo-
popula-
touted
mental
he evo-
ins the
onflicts
biolo-
evolu-

ıat the
lay of
condi-
vari-
arious
romos-
ms. A
essed
vithin
xactly

same genes. **Mutations,** the random and unpredictable changes in DNA molecules that can be transmitted to offspring, bring about this variability. Every time a cell divides, the DNA is reproduced so that each new cell gets a copy, but sometimes the copying is inaccurate, resulting in a change in the DNA and a subsequent change in inherited characteristics. External environmental agents such as radiation (X-rays, ultraviolet light) or certain toxic organic chemicals also may come in contact with the DNA and alter the molecule. The result of millions of random changes in the DNA molecules of individuals in a population is genetic variability.

Offspring with a mutation frequently fail to survive, but in other cases mutations result in new genetic traits that give individuals and their offspring improved chances for survival and reproduction. Any genetically controlled characteristic—structural, physiological, or behavioural—that enhances the chance for members of a population to survive and reproduce in its environment is called an **adaptation.**

Structural adaptations include coloration (which enables individuals to hide from predators or to sneak up on prey), mimicry (which allows individuals to look like a dangerous or poisonous species), protective cover (shell or thick skin, bark, thorns), and gripping mechanisms (hands with opposable thumbs). Physiological adaptations include the ability to poison predators, to give off chemicals that repel prey, and to hibernate during cold

weather. The ability to fly to a warmer climate during winter is an example of behavioural adaptation, as are resource partitioning and species interactions such as parasitism, mutualism, and commensalism.

Individuals with one or more adaptations that enable them to survive under changed environmental conditions are more likely to produce more offspring with the same favourable adaptations than are individuals without such adaptations; this is known as **differential reproduction. Natural selection** is the process by which organisms whose biological characteristics (beneficial genes) better fit them to the environment are better represented by descendants in future generations than are those organisms whose characteristics are less fit for the environment. Natural selection has four major characteristics that over time demonstrate the combination of factors leading to evolution: genetic variability (inheritance of traits in succeeding generations, with some variation in those traits); environmental variability; differential reproduction that varies with the environment; and the influence of the environment on survival and reproduction.

Limits to adaptation exist in nature. Human lungs and livers, for example, do not quickly become more capable of dealing with air pollutants and other toxins to which we are exposed. Human skin cannot evolve sufficiently rapidly to be more resistant to the harmful effects of ultraviolet radiation. The reasons for our inability to adapt quickly relate chiefly to our reproductive capacity. Unlike mosquitoes, rats, and species of weeds, humans and other large species such as sharks, elephants, and tigers cannot produce large numbers of offspring rapidly, so our ability to adapt quickly to particular environmental changes through natural selection is very limited. In addition, since a population can adapt only for traits that are present in its gene pool, even if a favourable gene were present, most members of the population would have to die or become sterile so that individuals with the trait could become dominant and pass on the trait. This is hardly a desirable solution! We must remember, also, that species adaptations develop in the context of their ecological situation (relationships with other organisms and the environment), and that our knowledge of this complexity is incomplete.

Speciation and Extinction

Two other processes, speciation and extinction, are believed to have affected the millions of species on Earth. **Speciation** is the formation of two or more species from one as the result of divergent natural selection in response to changes in environmental conditions.

One mechanism generating speciation is geographic isolation, a situation in which populations of species become separated for a long time in areas with different environmental conditions. This may occur naturally (as when part of a group migrates for food) or through human-related activities. Highway construction, for example, may quickly separate a small group of individuals from a larger population. If these groups remain geographically separated for a long time and do not interbreed, they may begin to diverge in their genetic makeup because of different selection pressures. Continued reproductive isolation may mean that members of the separated populations become so different that they cannot interbreed and produce fertile offspring. If this occurs, one species has become two as, perhaps, occurred with arctic and grey foxes. It is thought that these two species were once one but separated into northern and southern populations that adapted to different environmental conditions (the arctic fox with its white, heavy fur and short ears, legs, and nose adapted to cold conditions, and the grey fox with its lightweight fur and long ears, legs, and nose adapted to heat).

Extinction is the second process affecting Earth's species. A species is eliminated from existence when it cannot adapt genetically and reproduce successfully under new environmental conditions. The continuous, low-level extinction of species that has occurred throughout much of the history of life is termed **background extinction. Mass extinction,** in contrast, is the disappearance of numerous species over a relatively short period of geological time. Fossil and other geological evidence point to catastrophic global events that eliminated major groups of species simultaneously. While extinction is a crisis for the affected species, extinction provides an opportunity for other species to evolve to fill new or vacant ecological niches in changed environments (a process called adaptive radiation). Biodiversity, one of the Earth's most important resources, may be expressed in an equation: species biodiversity = number of species + speciation − extinction.

Ecological Succession

A community of organisms does not spring into full-blown existence but develops gradually through a series of stages until it reaches maturity. The process of community development over time, in which the composition and function of communities and ecosystems change, is called **succession.** When not disturbed by large-scale natural disasters or human actions, ecological succession is a normal process in nature, resulting in a shift from immature, rapidly changing, unstable communities to more mature, self-sustaining communities. Mature communities exhibit greater complexity in their ecosystem structure and function than do immature communities, and are characterized by large plants, high species diversity, many specialized ecological niches, high numbers of interconnecting links between members of the community, and high efficiency of nutrient recycling and energy use.

Succession usually is described in terms of the species composition of the vegetation of an area, although each successional stage also has its own charac-

teristic animal life. Ecologists recognize primary and secondary types of ecological succession, depending on conditions at a particular site at the outset of the process. **Primary succession** involves the development of biotic communities in a previously uninhabited and barren habitat with no or little soil. A bare rock surface recently formed by volcanic lava or scraped clean by glacial action, or a new sandbar deposited by shifting ocean currents, or a surface-mined area from which all overburden (soil) has been removed, are examples of conditions under which primary succession begins. Usually the first signs of life are the hardy pioneer species such as microbes, lichens, and mosses that are quick to establish large populations in a new area.

Secondary succession begins in an area where the natural vegetation has been removed or destroyed but where soil is present. Burned or cut forests and abandoned farm fields are common sites where secondary succession occurs. The presence of soil permits new vegetation to spring up quickly, often in a matter of weeks, and subsequent successional stages to develop over the next 100 or more years.

Ecological succession is not necessarily an orderly process, with each successional stage leading inevitably to the next more stable stage until the area is occupied by a mature or **climax community.** The exact sequence of species and community types that appear during the course of succession in a given area can be highly variable. Even the climax community is not permanent; it will change as environmental conditions change, once again illustrating the constancy of change in nature.

HUMAN IMPACTS ON ECOSYSTEMS

Over the past century, human use of natural ecosystems usually has simplified them. Subsequent to plowing native prairie grasses, clear-cutting forests, and filling in wetlands, we replaced the complexity of thousands of plant and animal interrelationships in these ecosystems with monocultures of wheat, canola, or commercially valuable trees, or with highways, parking lots, and buildings.

Humans spend a great deal of money defending such monocultures from invasion by pioneer species because weeds (plants), pests (insects or other animals), and pathogens (fungi, viruses, or disease-causing bacteria) can destroy an entire monoculture crop unless it is protected by pesticides or some form of biological control. Given that fast-breeding insect species undergo natural selection and develop genetic resistance to pesticides, people end up using stronger doses or switching to new pesticides. Ultimately, natural selection in the pests increases to the point that these chemicals are ineffective. This danger is seen in the comeback of malaria, principally because of mutant forms of the mosquito-borne microbe that are becoming increasingly resistant to drugs (Nichols, 1997).

These processes highlight the important point that when humans intrude into nature, we can never affect merely one thing, but instead we cause multiple effects, many of which are unpredictable in their outcomes. Our pervasive influence is because of the **principle of con-nect**...

[left column partially obscured by handwritten notes: "Speciation.", "principle of connectedness.", "interdependence / diversity / resilience / adaptability / unpredictability / limits", "participation web net..."]

Maintaining a balance between simplified human ecosystems and the more complex natural ecosystems that surround us is a challenge, particularly given the rate at which we have been altering nature for our purposes.

WORKING WITH NATURE

Living systems have six key features—interdependence, diversity, resilience, adaptability, unpredictability, and limits—that suggest humans could learn to live sustainably if they understood and mimicked how nature perpetuates itself. Learning to live sustainably begins with recognition of the following: humans are a part of, and not separate from, the dynamic web of life on Earth; human economies, lifestyles, and ultimate survival depend totally on the sun and the Earth; and everything is connected to everything else, although some connections are stronger and more important than others.

The law of conservation of matter and the second law of energy tell us that, as each of us uses resources, we add some waste heat and matter to the environment. In recent decades, the rapid economic growth and rising material standards of Canada and other industrialized countries have been supported by accelerating resource consumption and increasing throughput of Earth's materials and energy. In maximizing short-term economic gain, the effluents and pollutants of our high-waste, throwaway society have generated a legacy of degraded water, air, soil, forests, and biological diversity of the planet. "As the world becomes ecologically over-loaded, conventional economic development actually becomes self-destructive and impoverishing. Many scholars believe that continuing on this historical path might even put our very survival at risk" (Wackernagel & Rees, 1996, pp. 2–3).

We can develop more sustainable lifestyles, but one of the first things we must do is acknowledge and accept the reality of ecological limits and the resultant changes that such acceptance will bring to our socioeconomic systems. Even if we were to undertake to recycle many more materials so that economic growth might continue without depleting resources and without producing large volumes of pollutants, we need to remember that recycling matter resources requires high-quality energy, energy that cannot be recycled. If we were to strive to become a recycling society as an interim stage in moving toward achieving a sustainable society, we would need not only an inexhaustible supply of affordable high-quality energy, but also an environment with an infinite capacity to absorb, disperse, dilute, and degrade heat and waste. Since such efforts can be temporary solutions at best, the scientific principles and ecological functioning identified in this chapter help show us that human society, including the human economy, is a subsystem of the ecosphere. If we are to achieve sustainability, we must shift our emphasis "from 'managing resources' to managing *ourselves*" and "learn to live as part of nature": such a shift in emphasis would mean that "[e]conomics ... becomes human ecology." (Wackernagel & Rees, 1996, p. 4).

The implications of such a shift would require that we undertake a range of actions to achieve sustainability, including reduction in use of matter and energy resources through more efficient and appropriate use of energy, a shift to renewable energy sources, less waste of renewable and nonrenewable resources of all types, and an emphasis on pollution prevention and waste reduction. A reduction in human population growth rates and alleviation of poverty are part of the solution to the current unsustainable use of resources and global life-support systems. In essence, achieving a sustainable future requires that Canadians and all Earth's citizens learn to work with nature.

Chapter Questions

1. Using the second law of energy, explain why many poor people in developing countries are vegetarians (primarily).

2. Distinguish between an ecosystem and a biological community.

3. Why is a realized niche usually narrower (more restricted) than a fundamental niche?

4. Explain the difference between a habitat and a niche.

5. Using the second law of energy, explain why there is such a sharp decrease in usable energy as energy flows through a food chain or web. Does the energy loss at each step violate the first law of energy?

6. Why is the cycling of matter essential to the continuance of life on the Earth?

7. Why is an understanding of biogeochemical cycles important in environmental science? Use an example or two to justify your answer.

8. Compare and contrast the geochemical cycles for phosphorus and nitrogen.

9. What climate and soil factors produce each of the major terrestrial biomes?

10. Why are coral reefs and coastal and inland wetlands such important ecosystems? Why have human activities destroyed so many of these vital ecosystems?

11. Is the human species a keystone species? Explain.

12. Why are natural ecosystems less vulnerable to harm from insects, plant diseases, and fungi than simplified ecosystems?

references

Barnett, V. (1996, April 27). Biologist rises to defence of gopher. *Calgary Herald,* p. A4.

Botkin, D., & Keller, E. (1995). *Environmental science: Earth as a living planet.* Toronto: John Wiley and Sons, p. 105.

Busing, R.T., & Spies, T.A. (1995). *Modeling the population dynamics of the Pacific yew.* United States Department of Agriculture, Forest Service, Research Note PNW-RN-515.

Cunningham, W.P., & Saigo, B.W. (1995). *Environmental science: A global concern* (3rd ed.). Dubuque, IA: Wm. C. Brown Publishers, p. 353.

Dambrofsky, G. (1996, April 8). Ranchers bothered by killer coyotes. *Calgary Herald,* p. A3.

Dempster, L. (1996, April 17). Gopher guru says critters here to stay. *Calgary Herald,* p. A4.

Fellman, J., Getis, A., & Getis, J. (1995). *Human geography: Landscapes of human activities.* Dubuque, IA: Wm. C. Brown Publishers, p. 454.

Government of Canada. (1996). *The state of Canada's environment—1996.* Ottawa: Supply and Services Canada. Figure II.2.

Huyghe, P. (1993). New species fever. *Audubon,* 95(2), pp. 88–92, 94–96.

Kaufman, D.G., & Franz, C.M. (1993). *Biosphere 2000: Protecting our global environment.* New York: HarperCollins College Publishers.

International Joint Commision. (1992). *Sixth biennial report under the Great Lakes Water Quality Agreement of 1978 to the governments of the United States and Canada and the state and provincial governments of the Great Lakes basin.* Ottawa: International Joint Commission.

McKnight, T. (1990). *Physical geography: A landscape appreciation* (3rd ed.). Englewood Cliffs, NJ: Prentice Hall, p. 53.

Miller, G.T. (1994). *Sustaining the Earth: An integrated approach.* Belmont, CA: Wadsworth Publishing Company.

Moffett, M.W. (1997). Climbing an ecological frontier: Tree giants of North America. *National Geographic,* 191(1), pp. 44–61.

Muldoon, P., & Jackson, J. (1994). Keeping the zero in zero discharge. *Alternatives,* 20(4), pp. 14–20.

Perry, D. (1986). *Life above the jungle floor.* New York: Simon & Schuster.

Postel, S. (1996). Carrying capacity: Earth's bottom line. In J.L. Allen (Ed.). *Environment 96/97* (pp. 28–36). Guilford, CT: Dushkin Publishing Group/Brown and Benchmark Publishers.

Wackernagel, M., & W. Rees. (1996). *Our ecological footprint: Reducing human impact on the Earth.* Gabriola Island, BC: New Society Publishers.

Sierra Club. Endangered species and their habitats: Protecting the
"web of life."
http://www.sierraclub.org/ecoregions/endangered.html

"Since 1940 world numbers have grown
by 3 billion. By 1960 environmental
stresses were already showing: severe
soil erosion, spreading deserts, and
shrinking forests. By 1970 there were
added the problems of gross-scale pollution and, by 1980, acid rain and mass
extinction of species, plus suspicion of
the greenhouse effect and ozone-layer
depletion. Today it is plain there is
biospheric breakdown of multiple sorts.
If present trends continue until 2025, will
we be looking out on a biosphere needing
centuries or millennia to repair?"

N. Myers (1990, p. 39)

C H A P T E R   4

Human Population Issues and the Environment

Chapter Contents

CHAPTER OBJECTIVES   89
INTRODUCTION   89
BASIC POPULATION CONCEPTS   89
   Population and Technology   89
   Human Demography   91
HUMAN POPULATION GROWTH   91
   Population Dynamics   93
   Exponential Growth   94
PROJECTING FUTURE POPULATION
  GROWTH   95
   Doubling Time   95
     The Logistic Growth Curve   97
DEMOGRAPHIC TRANSITION   97
   The Four-Stage Model   97
   Diseases and Death in Industrial
     Society   99
   Zero Population Growth   99
     Carrying Capacity   100
     Limiting Factors   100
   Age Structure   100
     The Dependency Ratio   105
   Fertility Rates and Lag-Time Effects   105
     Future Population Trends   106
     Cultural Factors   107
     Life Expectancy   108
FACING THE PROBLEMS OF WORLD
  POPULATION GROWTH   108
   Increasing the Marriage Age   108
   Birth Control in Developing Nations   109
   National Birth Rate Reduction
     Programs   110
   Migration   111
POPULATION AND ENVIRONMENTAL
  SUSTAINABILITY   111
Chapter Questions   112
References   112
Additional Information Sources   113

Chapter Objectives

After studying this chapter you should be able to

- explain why some people consider the human population issue to be *the* environmental issue

- understand how population size is affected by rates of birth, death, fertility, and migration

- discuss the importance of exponential growth rates, doubling times, and other measures of population dynamics

- describe the four major phases in the demographic transition

- construct an age structure diagram and use it to predict future population growth rates

- discuss the approaches taken in response to world population growth

INTRODUCTION

The direct link between growth in human population numbers and environmental damages has led to claims that the human population issue is *the* environmental issue. The tremendous increase in human numbers is testament to the biological success of humans as a species. But, when we combine our biological success with our great power to cause environmental change, we realize that humans are using up, depleting, and degrading Earth's limited resources, causing many problems for the sustainability of ourselves and other plant and animal species that share this planet. Pollution of natural environments, declining energy reserves, reduced biodiversity, and wildlife extinctions—all these problems and more are related to human population growth.

This chapter examines fundamental concepts about population growth dynamics, the state of the current human population, and how the human population has changed over time. We consider the consequences of continued human population growth as well as approaches to help solve the human ecological problem.

BASIC POPULATION CONCEPTS

If you are the typical age of most university or college students, you probably were born in the mid- to late 1970s. At that time, the world contained close to 4 billion people. In 1995, the world's population was approximately 5.8 billion people, and it is possible—if the annual growth rate remains at about 1.8 percent—that during your lifetime human numbers will grow to between 8 and 9 billion. At that growth rate, about 90 million people are added to the Earth's population each year, more than three times the entire population in Canada! About 90 percent of these 90 million people are born in the developing nations in Africa, Asia, and Central and South America (Box 4–1). The 1990 average population growth rate in these developing regions was about 1.9 percent, while in developed nations such as Canada, the United States, Japan, and those of Western Europe, the growth rate was less (sometimes much less) than 1 percent (Kent & Crews, 1990).

POPULATION AND TECHNOLOGY

The threats humans pose to the sustainability of the environment are a result of the total number of people on Earth and the impact each person has on the environment. In the past, when there were fewer people on Earth and when their technology was limited, the impacts

Ste. Catherines Street, Montreal, 1901.

Ste. Catherines Street, Montreal, 1952.

Ste. Catherines Street, Montreal, 1996.

humans had on their environment were small scale and confined to local areas. If a local resource were overused, the effects were not large and long-term impacts were almost nonexistent. Now the fundamental problem is that there are so many people with such powerful technologies that human impacts have the potential for important, large-scale, and long-term environmental changes.

As Paul Ehrlich (1971), a well-known American expert in population biology and ecology, has noted, the total impact of the human population on the Earth's environment can be expressed as a simple relationship, known as the "population times technology" equation:

$$
\begin{array}{ccc}
\text{total} & & \text{total} \\
\text{number of} \quad \times & \text{environmental} & = \text{environmental} \\
\text{individuals} & \text{impact per} & \text{effect or impact} \\
& \text{individual} &
\end{array}
$$

Either an increase in the total number of people or an increase in the individual impact each of us has on the environment results in an increase in the total human impact or effect on the environment.

Technology has greatly increased the impacts people have on the environment. Two major impacts are the increased use of Earth's resources, and the new or different kinds of effects that humans have on the environment through use of technology. Whereas earlier peoples lived by hunting and gathering and used simple wooden or stone tools for crop production, today millions of car owners drive fossil-fuelled vehicles, thereby generating significantly increased demands for oil and steel, and releasing increasing volumes of air pollutants. Only many years after the invention of chlorofluorocarbons (CFCs) for use as a coolant in air conditioners and refrigerators, and as a propellant in spray cans, did we realize CFCs caused depletion of the ozone layer in the upper atmosphere. Clearly, the combination of rapid increases in both population and technology has increased our environmental impact.

There is one dimension of the population–technology issue that is particularly important for Canadians and residents of other developed nations to understand. The addition of each new individual in the population of a developed or industrialized country results in a greater effect on the environment than does the addition of each new individual in the population of a developing nation. Canadians often express their concerns about the environmental impacts of developing nations whose populations continue to grow so rapidly compared to the Canadian population. However, we need to be aware that Canadians and residents of other smaller, industrialized nations have greater per-capita effects on the environment because of our higher standards of living and use of technology. Countries such as the United States, Japan, and those of the European Union, which have large populations and high levels of use of technology, cause enormous environmental effects.

For Canadians and others who contribute to or otherwise value international aid, this aspect of the population–technology issue poses a troubling dilemma. Various aid agencies commonly strive to achieve two fundamental objectives: an improvement in the standard of living and a decline in overall human population growth. However, in supporting efforts to improve standards of living, we could be contributing to increases in the total environmental impact, a result counterproductive to the environmental benefits of a reduction in population growth. This does not mean we should not support international aid, but it does indicate a need to better understand the dynamics of human population growth so that our aid efforts are effective.

HUMAN DEMOGRAPHY

To improve our understanding of human population impacts on the biosphere and its resources, we need to study some basic human demography. **Demography** is the scientific study of the characteristics and changes in the size and structure of human populations (as well as nonhuman populations such as wildlife, fish, and trees). Demographers use a variety of tools, terms, and concepts to understand important population dynamics. One such tool is the national census (Box 4–2). Some of the terms and concepts we consider here include birth and death rates, age structure, the demographic transition, and total fertility.

HUMAN POPULATION GROWTH

Historical growth of the human population is often described in terms of four major periods or stages (Table 4–1). The first stage represents the early period of hunters and gatherers when total world population, population density, and average rate of growth were very low. Stage 2, beginning about the time of agricultural settlement, was characterized by the first major increase in the total world population and a much greater density of people. Stage 3 began about the time of the Industrial Revolution and saw a rapid increase in the human population as a result of improvements in health care and food supplies. Stage 4 represents today's increasingly urbanized world where the rate of population growth has declined in wealthy, industrialized nations but has continued to rise rapidly (until recently) in poorer, developing countries.

Although the total human population has increased with each succeeding stage, the modern era is unprecedented in terms of population growth (Table 4–2). The

Population growth leads to increased energy consumption.

BOX 4-2:
NATIONAL CENSUSES

A census is an official count of the people in a country, including information about their ages, gender, and livelihood. In western civilization, the first estimates of population were attempted in the Roman era (particularly for taxation purposes), and there were occasional efforts to estimate numbers of people during the Middle Ages and the Renaissance. The first modern census was taken in 1655 in the Canadian colonies by the French and English.

Sweden began to undertake the first series of regular censuses in 1750 and the United States began in 1790 to undertake a census every ten years. However, many countries do not undertake censuses or conduct them only irregularly. For much of the developing world, for example, census coverage has been sporadic or inaccurate because of the cost and effort involved in conducting a national census. Several other factors contributed to censuses being infrequent, incomplete, and inaccurate, including insufficient funds; lack of trained census personnel; high rates of illiteracy as well as widespread suspicion of governmental activities that limit the questions census takers are able to ask; isolated populations; and poor transportation.

While this situation has been improving, it is wise to remember that the limitations noted above cause various types of errors to be present in census data. When using census data, one should acknowledge such potential for error.

TABLE 4-1
A BRIEF HISTORICAL OVERVIEW OF HUMAN POPULATION GROWTH STAGES

Stage	Time Period	Population Density	Total Human Population	Average Rate of Growth
1. Hunters and gatherers	• From first humans on Earth to beginning of agriculture	• About 1 person per 130–260 km² in the most habitable areas	• As low as 250 000 to less than a few million	• At this time, the average annual rate of increase over the entire history of human population is less than 0.00011% per year.
2. Early, preindustrial agriculture	• Beginning between 9000 B.C. and 6000 B.C. and lasting until about the 16th century A.D.	• Domestication of plants and animals and the rise of settled villages increased human population density to 1 or 2 people per km²	• About 100 million by A.D. 1 and 500 million by A.D. 1600	• The growth rate was perhaps 0.03%, large enough to increase the human population from 5 million in 10 000 B.C. to about 100 million in A.D. 1 (the Roman Empire accounted for about 54 million). • From A.D. 1 to A.D. 1000, the population increased to between 200 and 300 million.
3. The machine age (Industrial Revolution)	• Beginning about 1600 with the Renaissance in Europe • The transition from agricultural to literate societies; better medical care and sanitation reduced the death rate.		• About 900 million in 1800, almost doubling in the next century, and doubling again to about 3 billion by 1960	• By 1600, the growth rate was about 0.1% per year, increasing about 0.01% every 50 years until 1950. • Growth resulted from the discovery of the causes of diseases, invention of vaccines, sanitation improvements, medical and health advances; advances in agriculture led to a rapid increase in production of food, clothing, and shelter.
4. The modern era	• From the 1950s onward	• Increasing urbanization of population	• About 5.8 billion in 1995	• Growth rate reached 2.1% between 1965 and 1970, declining slightly to between 1.7 and 1.8% in the 1980s and 1990s.

SOURCE: Adapted from Botkin, D.B., and Keller, E.A. (1995). *Environmental science: Earth as a living planet.* New York: John Wiley & Sons, p. 87. Used by permission.

TABLE 4–2
WORLD POPULATION MILESTONES

World Population Reached:			Predicted World Population:		
1 billion in	1804		6 billion in	1998	(11 years later)
2 billion in	1927	(123 years later)	7 billion in	2009	(11 years later)
3 billion in	1960	(33 years later)	8 billion in	2021	(12 years later)
4 billion in	1974	(14 years later)	9 billion in	2035	(14 years later)
5 billion in	1987	(13 years later)	10 billion in	2054	(19 years later)
			11 billion in	2093	(39 years later)

SOURCE: United Nations, Population Division, Department for Economic and Social Information and Policy Analysis. (1994). *World population growth from year 0 to stabilization.* New York: United Nations.
Also at: gopher://gopher/undp.org:70/00/ungophers/popin/wdtrends/mileston

dramatic increase in the total human population since 1950 and the contribution of developing regions to that growth are evident in Figure 4–1. Although there was little or no change in the maximum length of a human lifetime during the second and third stages in the history of human population growth, there were changes in birth, death and population growth rates, in age structure, and *average* life expectancy. To ensure we understand these changes in population sizes and the causes of these changes, let's consider some population dynamics.

POPULATION DYNAMICS

As discussed in Chapter 3, changes in population sizes occur through births, deaths, immigration (arrivals from elsewhere), and emigration (individuals leaving to go elsewhere). How rapidly a population grows depends on the difference between the **crude birth rate** (CBR) and **the crude death rate** (CDR). This difference is known as the **crude growth rate** (CGR), and may be expressed as

$$CGR = CBR - CDR$$

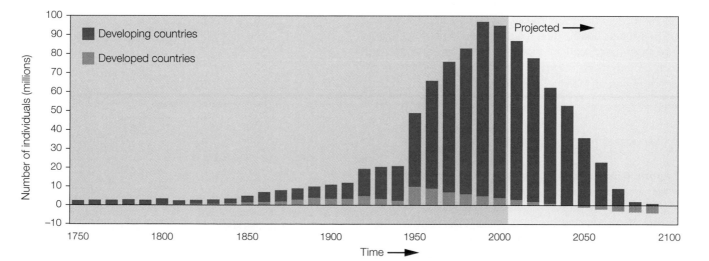

Figure 4–1

World population growth, 1750–2000

NOTE: For each decade it is possible to identify how many million people were added each year (for example: for the 1980–90 decade, about 82 million people were added each year for a total increase of 820 million people in that time). Note also that from about 2040, it is predicted that developed regions will experience a negative growth rate and their absolute numbers will decline.

In this simple equation, the crude birth rate (or, more simply, the birth rate) is the annual number of live births per 1000 population. It is "crude" because it relates births to total population without regard to the age or sex composition of that population (which means we cannot make accurate predictions about the future dynamics of the population based on such data). Using the formula above, a country with a population of 4 million and with 80 000 births per year would have a crude birth rate of 20 per 1000.

The crude death rate, also called the mortality or death rate, is calculated the same way as the crude birth rate: the annual number of deaths per 1000 population. The crude growth rate of a population is the net change, or simply the difference between the crude birth rate and the crude death rate.

Death rates can be calculated for specific age groups. For instance, the **infant mortality rate** is the ratio of deaths of infants under 12 months of age per 1000 live births. The 1995 infant mortality rate in the developing world was 66.2 per 1000 live births; in contrast, in the developed countries it was 6.9 per 1000. Even though worldwide infant mortality has fallen 37 percent since 1970, 8.4 million infants died in 1995 before reaching their first birthday (World Health Organization, 1996).

National birth and death rates vary widely. In 1991, for instance, Malawi recorded 52 births per 1000 population, while Italy recorded only 10 births per 1000. In 1990, infant mortality rates for all of Africa reached 109 per 1000, but were over 150 for individual nations such as Ethiopia. Even within nations, there can be variations in these rates. The former Soviet Union, for example, had a national infant mortality rate of 29 (1990), but in parts of its Central Asian region, infant death rates climbed to above 110. In contrast, infant mortality rates in Canada, the United States, and Western Europe ranged from 6 to 10. Note that these low rates can obscure locally higher rates of infant deaths due, for example, to prenatal exposure to mercury, lead, or dioxins from industrial pollution, such as may have occurred recently in the Peace River health region of Alberta (Pederson, 1997).

EXPONENTIAL GROWTH

Exponential growth in numbers of any species occurs when growth takes place at a constant rate per time period (see Chapter 3 discussion and Figure 3–20). During the first half of the 20th century, the modern stage of human population history, population actually increased at a rate faster than an exponential rate (this occurred when the population growth rate peaked at 2.1 percent between 1965 and 1970). This increased rate reflected gains in health and medical care, in sanitation

practices, and improvements in food production. Since then, the human growth rate has declined globally to between 1.7 and 1.8 percent (World Bank, 1992). Table 4–3 illustrates average annual growth rates for the world from 1950 to 2050.

TABLE 4-3
SELECTED AVERAGE ANNUAL GROWTH RATES FOR THE WORLD (1950–2050)

Year	Population	Average Annual Growth Rate (%)
1950	2 555 898 461	1.44
1954	2 728 297 382	1.87
1956	2 832 536 024	1.95
1960	3 038 930 391	1.33
1961	3 079 552 761	1.80
1962	3 135 560 616	2.19
1963	3 204 953 986	2.19
1964	3 275 941 217	2.08
1965	3 344 855 925	2.07
1966	3 414 981 586	2.02
1967	3 484 617 262	2.04
1968	3 556 354 911	2.07
1969	3 630 875 051	2.05
1970	3 705 987 692	2.07
1975	4 087 382 478	1.76
1980	4 457 593 483	1.71
1985	4 854 659 097	1.68
1990	5 281 672 973	1.58
1995	5 691 012 889	1.41
2000	6 090 912 914	1.28
2010	6 862 796 548	1.10
2020	7 601 785 909	0.92
2030	8 276 375 737	0.77
2040	8 877 430 755	0.61
2050	9 368 223 050	

CAUTION: Given the difficulties that may be encountered in conducting a national census (Box 4–2), the accuracy implied by these precise statistics may be inappropriate. Consider these data as illustrative rather than definitive.

SOURCE: U.S. Census Bureau, International Data Base. Total midyear population for the world: 1950–2050. http://www.census.gov/ipc/www/worldpop.html

PART 2:
THE ECOSPHERE WE LIVE IN

PROJECTING FUTURE POPULATION GROWTH

If human population growth is such an important environmental issue, we need to know what will happen to our population in the future. Projections of future population growth are "what if" exercises to forecast how quickly the world's population might increase, and whether or when it might stop increasing. Given certain assumptions about future tendencies in birth and death rates as well as migration, an area's population can be calculated for a given number of years into the future. While such calculations indicate population changes that may be upcoming, they must be interpreted carefully because they vary according to the assumptions made. One of the simplest approaches to population projections is to calculate doubling time.

DOUBLING TIME

Doubling time is, as the term suggests, the length of time required for a population to double in size. Figure 4–2 shows that it would take 70 years for a population with a rate of increase of 1 percent to double, and only 35 years to double if the rate of increase were 2 percent. A

general rule is that the doubling time is approximately equal to 70 divided by the annual percentage growth rate (the "magic number" 70 is derived from a logarithmic equation). Thus, doubling time (T) can be estimated by the formula

$$T = 70/\text{annual growth rate (\%)}$$

In populations that are growing exponentially, doubling times change very quickly as the growth rate changes. The following examples highlight the effect that small changes in population growth rates have on doubling times. In 1993, the Canadian population grew by approximately 0.8 percent; its doubling time (70 ÷ 0.8) was about 87 years. In other European nations, annual rates of population growth are about 0.1 percent; at this rate, their doubling times are about 700 years. China, the most populous nation on earth, is growing at a rate of about 1.2 percent and will double its population in about 60 years. The Jamaican population grew at a rate of 1.9 percent in 1993; at that rate its population would double in about 37 years. Also in 1993, the population in Sudan grew at 3.1 percent rate, doubling in under 23 years, while the population in Jordan grew at a rate of 3.6 percent, leading to a doubling time of approximately 19.4 years.

The effect of doubling times on the environment, its resources, and their sustainability depends on the absolute size of the initial population. For instance, the doubling of a population of 1000 will have less impact than

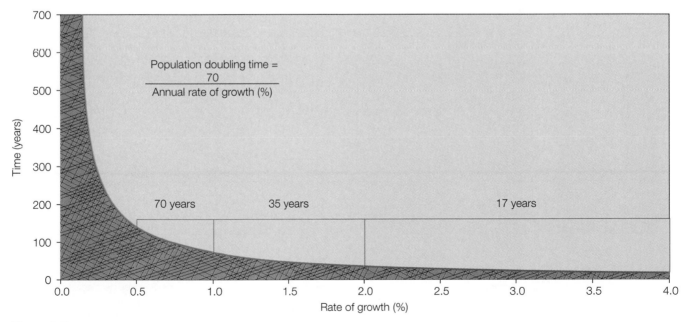

Figure 4–2

Doubling times and population growth rates

SOURCE: Adapted from Kaufman, D.G., & Franz, C.M. (1993). *Biosphere 2000: Protecting our global environment.* New York: HarperCollins College Publishers, p.134.

the doubling of a population of 10 000 or 100 000. Even though growth rates do not remain constant, and doubling times do not predict accurately the real growth of a population, the doubling time is a valuable measure because it allows us to visualize what future social and environmental conditions would be like if present growth rates were to continue. See Box 4–3 for information on use of computer models to project population futures.

BOX 4-3
USING COMPUTER MODELS TO PROJECT POPULATION FUTURES

Computer models that project what might happen if the world's population, resource use, and economic growth continue to expand are one tool we can use to help reach a sustainable future. An early set of projections, contained in *The Limits to Growth,* helped policy and decision makers understand that, if the 1970s trends in economic, resource use, and population trends were to continue unchecked, within 100 years the limits to human growth would be reached. The models also identified what policy changes might prevent this collapse. *The Limits to Growth* was influential in challenging society's thinking about planetary limits, and in generating much debate and subsequent research in this field.

In 1992, in *Beyond the Limits,* the same group of authors updated their original study by manipulating information about policy decisions on population, resource use, pollution control, and industrial and food output per capita. These newer projections indicated that the world already has overshot some of its limits. If current trends continue unchanged, the models predicted global economic and environmental collapse sometime in the next century. However, these models also projected outcomes of economic and environmental sustainability (see graphs below).

Computer scenarios projected possible ways to avoid overshooting limits and the collapse that would follow. Some of the assumptions built into this model were that, starting in 1995, the following would occur:

- technological improvement continues at 1990 levels
- 100 percent effective birth control is available to everyone
- no couple has more than two children
- industrial output is stabilized at US$350 per capita (equivalent to average 1990 standard of living in Europe)

If we view these kinds of projections as challenges and opportunities, achieving economically and environmentally sustainable futures can be achieved by using nonrenewable materials and energy resources at much lower rates; using renewable resources no faster than they can regenerate; and reducing waste and pollution dramatically (using all resources at maximum efficiency). In particular, emphasis on sufficiency, equity, and quality of life, and the cooperation that is required to acheive these goals, will be important, positive directions for sustainable futures.

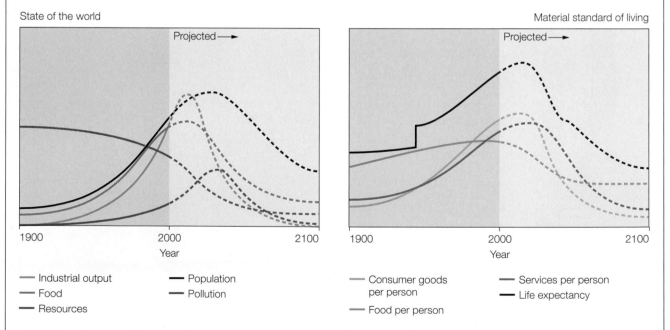

SOURCES: Meadows, D.H., et al. (1972). *The limits to growth: A report for the Club of Rome's project on the predicament of mankind.* New York: Universe.

Adapted from Meadows, D.H., et al. (1992). *Beyond the limits: Confronting global collapse, envisioning a sustainable future.* Post Mills, VT: Chelsea Green Publishing.

PART 2:
THE ECOSPHERE WE LIVE IN

In countries such as Canada, where there is low population growth (because both birth and death rates are low), the effects of immigration and emigration can play a role in changing the national growth rate and doubling time. The nature of immigration policies, such as those intended to attract wealthier immigrants who can promote economic growth and development, also have important implications for future population growth rates.

The Logistic Growth Curve

As was noted in Chapter 3, no population can continue to grow indefinitely at an exponential rate and be able to sustain itself. Eventually it will run out of food and space. Unchecked human population growth also would stress the country's social, economic, and political systems. If exponential rates of growth do not occur, what will the changes in a population be like as time passes?

One long-standing idea is that over longer periods of time the human population would follow a smooth S-shaped curve known as the **logistic growth curve** (Figure 4–3). In this case, the population increases exponentially at the outset (note the "J" shape at the start) and then levels out as the carrying capacity of the environment is reached. Once a population reaches the limits of its envi-

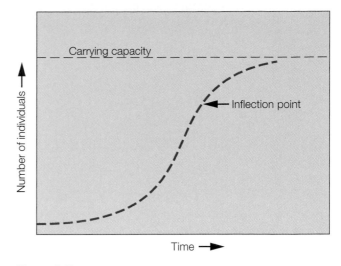

Figure 4–3
Logistic growth curve

This S-shaped (logistic growth) curve shows the population increasing exponentially at the outset (note the J shape) and then levelling out as the carrying capacity of the environment is reached. The inflection point is where the S curve changes slope and curves toward the horizontal.

ronment, the population tends to remain at or near the carrying capacity with a rate of population growth around zero. Although the logistic growth or "S" curve simplifies actual population changes over time, it does seem to describe population growth patterns observed in animal populations (in nature and the laboratory).

If death rates continue to decline owing to continuing improvements in food supplies, health, and medicine, it is unlikely that the logistic growth curve will be useful in projecting the maximum future human population size. Instead, if a human population is to achieve zero population growth (a stabilized or nongrowing population where birth and death rates are equal), it must pass through the demographic transition. Demographic transition is the subject of the following section.

DEMOGRAPHIC TRANSITION

THE FOUR-STAGE MODEL

Based on their observations of what happened to the birth and death rates of the European population as it urbanized and industrialized during the 19th century, demographers have derived a four-stage model of population change (Figure 4–4). Since all of the highly developed nations with advanced economies have gone through this **demographic transition,** and have reduced their population growth rates, demographers suggest this model is a key to understanding how far a nation has moved toward

Many developing nations are confronted with problems providing adequate housing and sanitation for their growing populations.

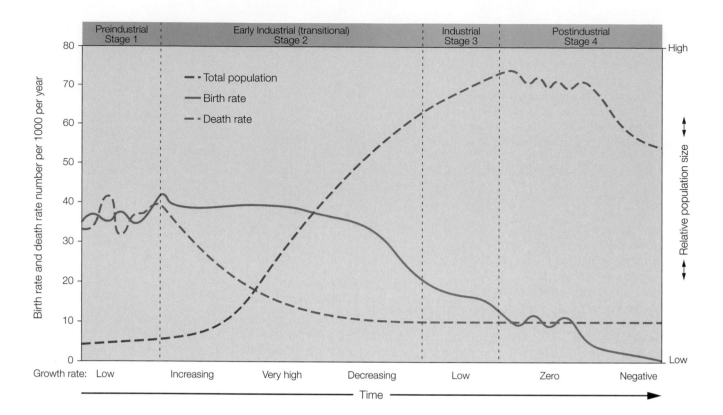

Figure 4–4

Demographic transition

This generalized model of demographic transition identifies its four stages and the changes in birth and death rates over time that result in changes in the population growth rate.

zero population growth. The model also may point to a nation's ability to consider and achieve sustainability within its economy.

In the preindustrial stage, harsh living conditions gave rise to a high birth rate (to compensate for high infant mortality) and a high death rate; there was little population growth. Although no countries are in the first stage today, Finland in the late 1700s would have been in the first demographic stage. As a result of more reliable food and water supplies as well as improved health care, the second or transitional stage is characterized by a decline in the death rate. However, because the birth rate is still high, the population grows rapidly (by about 2.5 to 3 percent per year). By the mid-1800s, Finland was in the second stage of the demographic transition, as are much of Latin America, Asia, and Africa today.

Some of these countries seem to be caught in a **demographic trap,** unable to break out of the second stage. Their rapidly expanding populations—resulting in part from a parental desire for large families—virtually ensure continued human suffering and continued damage to an already degraded resource base. Whether some of

In postindustrial nations the aging of the population is evident.

PART 2:
THE ECOSPHERE WE LIVE IN

these nations will be able to achieve a lower birth rate before reaching disastrously high population levels that will be subject to catastrophic mortality is unknown. If the demographic transition is to be achieved, educational and family-planning efforts are required to help parents realize that a small family size is to their benefit.

The industrial or third demographic stage is characterized by a declining birth rate that eventually approaches the death rate. (As it declines, population growth may fluctuate depending on economic conditions.) The relatively low death rate, combined with a lower birth rate, slows population growth in the third stage. Reasons for the decline in births include better access to birth control, declines in infant mortality, improved job opportunities for women, and the high cost of raising children. By the early 1900s, Finland had reached this stage.

In the fourth or postindustrial phase of the demographic transition, birth rates decline further to equal (or fall below) the low death rates. Zero population growth (or even population decrease) is achieved partly because parents understand the benefits of small family size. It is at this point that emphasis can shift from unsustainable to sustainable forms of economic development.

DISEASES AND DEATH IN INDUSTRIAL SOCIETY

One of the key reasons why economically developed societies have been able to complete the demographic transition is because modern medicine has been able to reduce greatly the number of deaths due to epidemic diseases. Typically when an epidemic disease occurs in a population, a large percentage of people are affected by it—consider the number of people who contract cholera, measles, mumps, or influenza during an outbreak.

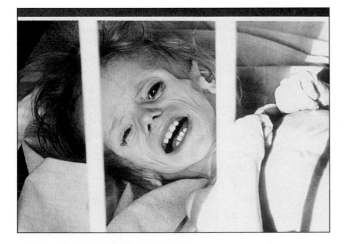

A young AIDS victim in Romania.

Although the past 100 years have brought a decrease in epidemics in industrialized nations, there is mounting concern that overuse of antibiotics (among other things) is leading to resistant strains of disease organisms and an increase in the incidence of these diseases. In part, the spread of resistant forms of diseases such as tuberculosis, malaria, and cholera also reflects the high density of populations of poor people. Acquired Immune Deficiency Syndrome (AIDS) also is a factor in the increasing incidence of deaths due to epidemics (because individuals with AIDS lack resistance to these diseases).

Animal populations also are susceptible to disease epidemics. In early 1997, at least 50 000 pigs in Taiwan were slaughtered in an attempt to control hoof and mouth disease. Humans can carry this disease (but don't die from it), so Taiwan's largest zoo and all national parks were closed to protect animals there from potential human carriers (Kohlenberg, 1997). Bovine spongiform encephalopathy (BSE), or mad cow disease, also led to the killing of thousands of British, Swiss, and German cattle. Linked to the human brain-wasting disorder Creutzfeldt-Jakob disease, BSE is spread by feed containing ground parts of cows, sheep, and other mammals. Ottawa indicated it would ban domestic cattle food that contains such material. Though the link has not been established definitively, microbiologists warned that BSE could cross the species barrier from cows to humans (Drohan, 1997).

ZERO POPULATION GROWTH

The logistic growth curve has been used in many projections of the eventual maximum population size in specific nations as well as the world. Despite the fact that the logistic curve permits simple calculations of a future carrying capacity, its use is unrealistic—it ignores potential changes in the environment and possible technological changes that may affect human population growth in the future, including zero population growth.

A number of social and economic consequences have resulted from population stability in Europe. In a zero population growth situation, when births plus immigration exactly equal deaths plus emigration, there are fewer young people, an increasing proportion of older citizens, and a rise in the median age of the population. If there is actual population decline, as is now common in Europe, reduced demand for facilities such as schools and universities is resulting in their permanent reduction. Instead of providing schools, governments have to provide pensions and various social services for the roughly 25 percent of their citizens who are aged 60 and over, through the taxation of a diminishing work force. In 1991, for instance, for every 10 workers in Germany there were 4 pensioners; by 2030, the numbers are expected to be equal. Canada's political leaders and social planners have noted the potential for a similar zero population growth situation to arise in Canada, and are aware of the need for futures planning including pension reform.

Carrying Capacity

When we talk about the carrying capacity of the environment for humans, we are talking about the maximum number of the human species that a particular habitat (or the planet) can support sustainably (long term). If a population exceeds that carrying capacity, it changes the environment in ways that decrease the future population size. If we want to avoid human and environmental degradation, it is important to be able to estimate carrying capacity.

What is the carrying capacity of a nation or the planet for humans? No one knows for sure how many humans can be supported by the Earth, and calculations vary widely depending on the assumptions that have been made. Almost 200 years ago, the English clergyman, historian, and political economist Thomas Malthus (1766–1834) made the earliest—and perhaps some of the most famous—statements about the threat of uncontrolled human population growth (Box 4–4). In his 1798 "Essay on the Principles of Population," Malthus indicated his belief that the human ability to multiply far exceeded our ability to increase food production. His pessimistic conclusion was that unless people found a more humane solution, famine, disease, and warfare were inevitable because they act to curb population growth.

Critics of Malthus point out that his predictions have not come true, that technology has enabled humans to live at increasing densities, and that technology will continue to provide a way out of a Malthusian fate. Ultimately, however, Malthus is correct about the final outcome of unchecked population growth in a finite world. Even though Malthus did not anticipate the capability of technological advances to delay the inevitable population collapse that occurs when carrying capacity is exceeded, and even though some people believe that the Earth can support many more people than it does now, in the long run there is an upper limit to the number of people the Earth can support.

Given this reality, among the challenging questions that face us now are how to achieve a constant world population, or at least stop the population increase, in ways that are most beneficial to most people. The search for an answer requires that we apply our knowledge of environmental science, in combination with arguments about rights, values, and ethics, all within a global perspective. For example, to calculate a carrying capacity we would need to determine and agree on what the average standard of living and quality of life should be. At least to some extent, these are questions about values and how we define a sustainable future.

Limiting Factors

The factors that eventually will limit human populations can be categorized as short term (1 year), intermediate term (greater than 1 year and less than 10 years), and long term (10 or more years). Some factors might fit more than one category, such as by having both short- and intermediate-term effects, for instance.

Short-term factors that limit human populations include those events that disrupt a country's food supply and distribution. Political events such as civil wars, or a local crop loss, or a shortage of energy to transport foodstuffs, or weather changes such as drought or heavy rains, could lead to food disruptions. On the global level, major disasters such as the outbreak of a new disease, or a new strain of a disease that previously was under control (Enviro-Focus 4), or the spread of a toxic chemical world wide, also are examples of short-term effects on availability of food and, ultimately, the human population.

Intermediate-term factors that could limit human populations include declines in the supply of firewood or other cooking and heating fuels; some climate changes; a systemwide dispersion of toxic pollutants into fresh water bodies, oceans, and fisheries; desertification; and energy shortages that affect food production and distribution. Long-term factors include soil erosion; declines in the quantity and quality of groundwater supplies; global warming; and widespread pollution and pollutants such as acid precipitation.

Many people believe that the quality of human life will continue to improve into the future as our technology improves. However, if one of the limiting factors is the amount of biological resources available per person, some data indicate we already have passed the peak of resource availability (Table 4–4) and have approached the limits of productive capacity with our existing technology. This suggests we have exceeded the long-term carrying capacity of the Earth for people (and, in so doing, complements the findings of computer-model projections noted previously).

AGE STRUCTURE

Since it is difficult to forecast the future of population growth through use of doubling times, exponential growth, and logistic curves, we can consider the **population age structure,** which identifies the distribution of the population by age. A useful tool, analysis of the population age structure provides information about current and future birth, death, and growth rates; about current and future social and economic status; and about our likely impact on the environment.

For any population, the number of males and the number of females at each age, from birth to death, can be

Long before most scholars were concerned about overpopulation, Malthus was writing his warning about it. In 1798 his famous "Essay on the Principles of Population" was published and read by Darwin, Marx, and many others. In that essay, Malthus clearly noted the potential of geometric growth in the human population to outstrip the arithmetical increase in food supply. To prevent this, Malthus felt population control was necessary. If people failed to control their own numbers, Malthus believed that "natural controls" of warfare, famine, and disease would solve the problem.

The premises on which Malthus based his arguments are included among the following excerpts from his essay.

Thomas Robert Malthus (1766–1834)

> I think I may fairly make two postulata.
> First, that food is necessary to the existence of man.
> Secondly, that the passion between the sexes is necessary, and will remain nearly in its present state. ... Assuming, then, my postulata as granted, I say, that the power of population is indefinitely greater than the power in the earth to produce subsistence for man.
> Population, when unchecked, increases in a geometrical ratio. Subsistence only increases in an arithmetical ratio. A slight acquaintance with numbers will show the immensity of the first power in comparison of the second.
> By that law of our nature which makes food necessary to the life of Man, the effects of these two unequal powers must be kept equal.

This implies a strong and constantly operating check on population ...

> [The power of population growth is so great] that premature death must in some shape or other visit the human race. The vices of mankind are active and able ministers of depopulation, but should they fail, sickly seasons, epidemics, pestilence and plague, advance in terrific array, and sweep off their thousands and ten thousands. [Should these fail,] gigantic famine stalks in the rear, and with one mighty blow, levels the population with the food of the world.

Born in the shire of Surrey, England, Malthus studied theology at Cambridge and became an ordained minister. While still a minister, he began writing his essay on population. Gradually, writing and lecturing became his major interest. In 1805 he was appointed a professor of modern history and political economy at Laileybury College; he held this position until his death.

For more on Malthus, see Dupaquier, J., & Fauve-Chamoux, A. (Eds.) (1983). *Malthus past and present.* New York: Academic Press.

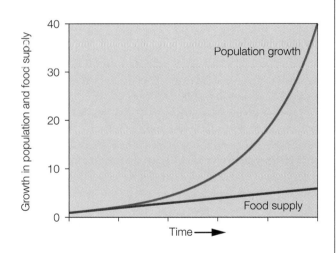

SOURCE: Jordan, T.G., and Rowntree, L. (1990). *The human mosaic: A thematic introduction to cultural geography.* New York: Harper & Row, p. 43.

represented in a generalized age structure (or population pyramid) diagram (Figure 4–5). The diagram is divided vertically in half; typically the right side represents the females in a population, and the left side represents the males. The bottom one-third of the diagram represents prereproductive humans (from birth to 14 years of age); the middle one-third represents humans in their reproductive years (15 to 44), and the top one-third represents postreproductive humans (45 years and older). The width of each

of these segments is proportional to the population size, so that the greater the width, the larger the population.

We can use population age structure diagrams to predict population. The overall shape of the diagram reveals whether the population is expanding, stable, or declining. The age structure diagram of a country with a very high growth rate, such as Kenya or Nigeria, is shaped like a pyramid. In contrast, the age structure diagrams of countries with stable or declining populations,

'The Cell from Hell' and Other Epidemics

"The Cell from Hell"

Toxic dinoflagellates *(Pfiesteria piscicida)* have been keeping humans company from ancient times. Unicellular parasites belonging to both animal and plant kingdoms, and able to live in both salt and fresh water—the more polluted the better—dinoflagellates have been responsible for red tides (algal blooms) since biblical times. During the past five years, dinoflagellates have killed billions of fish on the eastern seaboard of the United States, and afflicted hundreds of divers, fishers, sailors, and swimmers with festering skin sores, faulty memories, immune failure, and even personality changes. Able to take on 24 different shapes (from hibernating cyst to two-tailed flagellates that stun prey with neurotoxins), the airborne vapours from dinoflagellates have caused scientists to black out. Dinoflagellates deserve their biohazard level three status!

As much like the latest *X Files* threat as dinoflagellates seem to be, their emergence off the coast of North Carolina appears to be in response to nutrient-rich human and animal wastes that have been spilled into coastal rivers and flowed to the sea. North Carolina's booming hog industry (15 million pigs concentrated on clay-based soils) produces more waste than the people of New York City. When nitrogen-rich pig manure escapes into water courses (through leaching, or following collapse of a holding pond wall, for example), it becomes food for plankton, which in turn attract the voracious fish-flesh-eating dinoflagellates.

In spite of warnings from scientists about the unpleasant microbial consequences of and need to clean up the waste created by corporate pig-farming practices, North Carolina's health department denied there were any water quality problems, and dismissed the toxic hangovers of fishers as hearsay. In what appeared to be an effort to protect the billion-dollar pig industry and other polluters, scientific findings were denigrated regularly. Human arrogance, poor government, and irresponsible economics are the chief reasons why dinoflagellates are flourishing in the ocean off North Carolina's coast (Barker, 1997).

Malaria

Most endemic in sub-Saharan Africa, where often more than 50 percent of the population in rural areas is infected, malaria puts about 40 percent of the world's population at risk. Of the estimated one million deaths annually from malaria, about 800 000 are children under five years of age. In spite of massive efforts to eradicate it, malaria is making a comeback. There seems to be an upward trend in the number of cases in the Americas and some Asian countries. The increase is due partly to the growing resistance of malaria-carrying mosquitoes to insecticides and of the *Plasmodium* parasites to anti-malarial drugs (World Resources Institute, 1992).

A growing number of Canadian travellers are bringing malaria home with them; in 1995, 637 cases of malaria were reported in Canada (Nichols, 1997). Infectious disease specialists are alarmed that too many travellers go into malaria-infected regions of Africa, Asia, and Latin America without accurate information or proper antimalarial medication. Chloroquinine is the least costly and most widely used drug against malaria. Very effective when used in conjunction with a good primary health-care system, the administration of chloroquinine outside of health-care systems actually has contributed to the resurgence of malaria. People who were unknowingly affected by malaria and who stop taking their antimalarial drugs too soon have low doses of the drugs in their system. This provides an ideal breeding ground for the development of mutations. Mefloquine, one of the main replacements for chloroquinine, is more costly and may have side effects.

Family members attend to a malaria victim.

Cholera

In other parts of the world, the threats to human health posed by environmental deterioration were evident in early 1991, when for the first time in the 20th century, a cholera epidemic struck six Latin American countries. More than 300 000 cases of cholera and 3200 deaths were reported by September 1991, mostly in Peru, but also in Ecuador, Colombia, Mexico, Guatemala, and Brazil.

Cholera is an acute intestinal infection caused by *Vibrio cholerae* bacterium and transmitted principally through contaminated water and food, particularly raw vegetables and seafood. Children are highly susceptible to this disease, which spreads rapidly in overpopulated communities with poor sanitation and unsafe drinking water. The outbreak in Peru appeared almost simultaneously in communities along a 1200-kilometre stretch of coastline. Cholera was felt to be a side effect of the rapid urbanization of that country. The growth of crowded slums and the lack of safe water and sanitation facilities have been prime factors in these outbreaks. While cholera is treatable with rehydration salts, the ultimate solution requires improvements in water, sanitation, health and education, and food safety (World Resources Institute, 1992).

SOURCES: Barker, R. (1997). *And the waters turned to blood: The ultimate biological threat.* New York: Simon and Schuster.

Nichols, M. (1997, May 19). Malaria's comeback. *Maclean's,* p. 57.

World Resources Institute. (1992). *World resources 1992–93.* New York: Oxford University Press.

OTHER READING: Nikiforuk, A. (1991). *The fourth horseman: A short history of plagues, emerging viruses and other scourges.* Toronto: Viking.

TABLE 4–4
PER CAPITA AVAILABILITY OF RESOURCES

Resource	Peak Per Capita Production	Year of Peak Production
wool	0.86 kg/person (1.9 lb/person)	1960
wood	0.67 m³/person (0.88 yd³/person)	1967
fish	5.5 kg/person (12.1 lb/person)	1970
mutton	1.92 kg/person (4.21 lb/person)	1972
beef	11.81 kg/person (26.0 lb/person)	1977
cereal crops	342 kg/person (754.1 lb/person)	1977

SOURCE: Adapted from World Bank. (1985). *World development report.* New York: Oxford University Press.

such as Italy and Germany, respectively, have narrower bases (Figure 4–6).

In countries that have rapidly expanding populations, the largest proportion of the population is in the prereproductive age group. It is estimated that about one-third of the population worldwide is under 15 years of age. This means that the probability of future population growth is great; when all these children mature, they will become the parents of the next generation. Even if the birth rate does not increase, and even if these parents were to have only two children (to just replace themselves), the population growth rate would continue to increase simply because there are more people reproducing.

In contrast, the narrower bases of the age structure diagrams of countries with stable or declining populations indicate that a smaller proportion of children will become the parents of the next generation. The age structure diagrams of countries with stable populations (neither growing nor shrinking) illustrate that the numbers of people at prereproductive and reproductive ages are approximately the same. In stable populations, also, a larger percentage of the population is in the postreproductive age group than in countries with rapidly increasing populations. Many nations in Europe have stable populations. Other European nations, such as Germany and Hungary, have populations that are shrinking in size. In these countries, the prereproductive age group is smaller than either the reproductive or postreproductive age groups.

As is evident in Figure 4–1, most of the worldwide population increase since 1950 has occurred in the developing countries, reflecting the younger age structure as well as the higher-than-replacement-level fertility rates of their populations. (Fertility rates are considered in a following

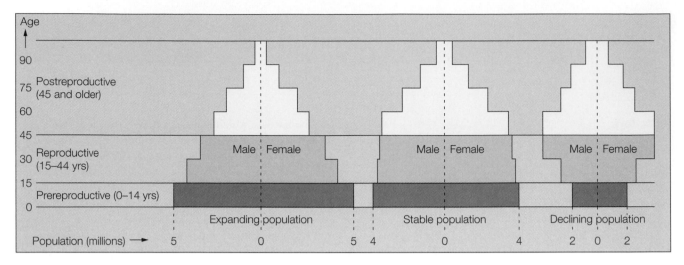

Figure 4–5

Generalized age structure diagrams for expanding, stable, and declining populations

NOTE: These generalized age structure diagrams represent an expanding population, a stable population, and a population that is decreasing in size. In each diagram, the left half represents the males in that population while the right half represents the females. The horizontal divisions in the diagram separate the prereproductive, reproductive, and postreproductive age groups, while the width of each segment represents the population size of each group.

section). In 1950, about 66.8 percent of the world's population was in developing countries in Africa, Asia (excluding Japan), and Latin America; the remaining 33.2 percent was in developed nations in Europe, the former U.S.S.R., Japan, Australia, and North America. As the world's population more than doubled between 1950 and 1994, the number of people in developing countries had risen to 79.2 percent of the worldwide population in 1994 (Raven, Berg & Johnson,

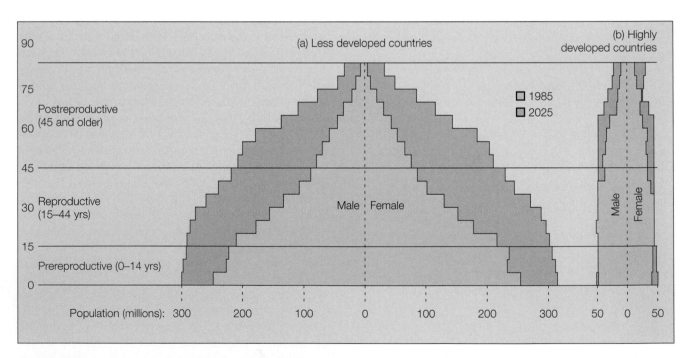

Figure 4–6

Age structure diagrams for less developed and highly developed countries

NOTE: The green region represents the actual age distribution in 1985. The orange region represents the projected increase in population and age distribution in 2025. Clearly there is a much higher percentage of young people in less developed countries than in highly developed countries. A much greater population growth is projected for less developed countries when their large numbers of young people enter their reproductive years.

1993). Most of the anticipated population increase during the next century also will take place in developing nations.

The proportion of a country's population in each age group influences strongly the demand for certain types of goods and services within that national economy. For instance, a country with a high proportion of young people has a high demand for educational facilities and certain types of health delivery services, whereas a population with a high percentage of elderly people also requires medical goods and services specific to that age group.

The Dependency Ratio

The **dependency ratio** is another useful measure (based on age structure) to forecast the condition of the future human population. The dependency ratio is a simple measure of the number of dependants, young and old, that each 100 people in their economically productive years (usually 15 to 64) must support. The ratio is calculated as

$$\frac{\text{sum of the number of people under 15}}{\text{and over 65 years of age}}$$
$$\frac{}{\text{number of people between ages 15 and 65}}$$

Statistics Canada (1996) indicated that in 1996, an estimated 6 063 600 Canadians were between the ages of 0 and 15 years, and 3 657 900 were aged 65 years and up, for a total of 9 727 500 dependent-age people. There were 20 242 000 working-age people, so the dependency ratio was 0.48 (9 721 500 divided by 20 242 000) or 48 dependent-age people for every 100 working-age people.

The dependency ratio affects the economic conditions of a population: the larger the ratio, the lower the present and near-future living standards. In preindustrial societies, where average lifetimes are short, younger persons care for the elderly within the same family. In modern technological societies, however, family size is reduced and the elderly are supported through the collection and distribution of taxes (that is, those who work provide funds to care for those who cannot work). Provision for the elderly is a necessary factor in achieving zero population growth because, without it, parents will rely on a large number of children to ensure their future well-being. But the shift from an age structure like that of Kenya (where about 50 percent of the population was under 15 years of age in 1991) to that of Austria (which is experiencing a decline in population growth) results in a decrease in the tax base for care of the elderly because of the smaller percentage of the population that is working.

These situations pose problems for national governments, particularly with regard to attempting to promote sustainability. Governments often are overwhelmed by the need to provide hospitals, clinics, health care, schools, housing, roads, and employment opportunities for their rapidly growing populations. One way to increase tax income to support these ventures is to increase the percentage of young people in the population; in turn, this promotes rapid population growth. Short-term economic pressures facing national governments can lead to political policies supporting rapid population growth that is not in the long-term interest of the nation. Yet, if governments are unable to raise the finances to support their population needs, the cycle of poverty, illiteracy, and unemployment continues and strengthens, and the potential to achieve sustainability declines.

A large proportion of seniors also can strain a nation's social services network. Health care, nursing homes, transportation infrastructure, and social security systems are all stressed by an increasing proportion of older citizens. In the future, if fertility and growth rates remain low, care of the aging baby boomers (people born between 1946 and 1964) will fall to a declining number of younger workers. This situation, too, may generate economic and political policies that may not be appropriate in the long term.

FERTILITY RATES AND LAG-TIME EFFECTS

Another set of measures useful in understanding changes in growth of the human population are fertility rates and lag-time effects. In general, measures of fertility, or the actual bearing of offspring, are a reasonably accurate indicator of the potential for future population growth. The **general fertility rate** is the number of live births per 1000 women of childbearing age per year. Ages 15 to 49 are commonly cited as the childbearing years. A more helpful indicator, from the perspective of predicting potential future population growth, is the **age-specific fertility rate,** the number of live births per 1000 women of a specific age group per year.

One of the most important lag effects is the **total fertility rate (TFR),** which is the average number of children expected to be born to a woman during her lifetime

Current responses to aging populations in developed countries include the establishment of gated retirement communities.

(TFR is based on the current age-specific fertility rate and assumes that current birth rates remain constant throughout the woman's lifetime). A TFR of 2.1 children generally is considered to be the replacement level fertility for the moderately developed countries.

Replacement fertility is the fertility rate needed to ensure that the population remains constant as each set of parents is replaced by their offspring. A fertility rate of 2.1 births per woman enables each woman to replace herself and her mate and allows for the death of some female children before they reach their reproductive years. However, from the day that a population achieves replacement fertility, that population will continue to grow for several generations—a phenomenon known as **population momentum** or **population lag effect.**

Population momentum occurs because a population that has had a very high fertility in the years before reaching replacement level will have a much younger age structure than a population that has had lower fertility before reaching the replacement threshold. In a population that is approaching replacement-level fertility, the proportion of young people is important, because the size of the largest recently born generation as well as the size of the parent generation determine the ultimate size of the total population when births and deaths finally are balanced. Even after reaching replacement-level fertility, as long as the generation that's producing births is disproportionately larger than the older generation (where most deaths occur), births will continue to outstrip deaths, and the population will continue to grow (Merrick, cited in Fellman, Getis & Getis, 1995). Clearly, this time lag is very important to human populations as it has tremendous implications for resource use, environmental impacts, and sustainability.

In many less developed countries, the average replacement fertility is 2.5 or more, reflecting the greater risk of death faced by children in those countries. Table 4–5 illustrates TFRs for a number of developing and developed nations. In 1995, for example, the total fertility rate in Ethiopia was 7.1; this means that a woman in her childbearing years would be expected to have about 7 children by the time she reached 49 years of age. If Ethiopia were to maintain a TFR of 7.1, its population would be expected to grow very rapidly, whereas if Canada maintained its TFR of 1.8 over a long time, the population would decline. The trend to continued population growth in Ethiopia (at least to the year 2000) and the downward trend in growth of the Canadian population are both visible in Table 4–5.

A comparison of developed and developing nations suggests that the TFR declines as income increases. In countries such as Bangladesh, Nigeria, and Nepal, where the average income per person is a few hundred dollars per year, total fertility rates are high. In developed nations such as Canada, Japan, and Denmark, where per-capita annual incomes are above US$10 000, total fertility rates are at or below replacement level. Table 4–5 also illustrates the predicted decrease in the TFR from 1995 to 2000; this trend continues that observed from about 1950, and is reflected also in the declining rates of population growth worldwide (although the world's population is still growing). Figure 4–7 illustrates the current and projected future decline in the world's total fertility rate from 1950 to 2020 as the world's population increases. Figure 4–7 notes that by the year 2020, a woman would have about two children during her lifetime, a major decline from an average of greater than three in the 1990s (Kent & Crews, 1990).

Future Population Trends

The human population has reached a turning point; although our numbers continue to increase, the global rate of population growth has declined during the past few decades and is predicted to continue to decline (see Table 4–5). Even if replacement fertility is reached rapidly on a global basis, it will take many years for the world population to stabilize (because of the momentum of the world's present age structure).

Experts at the World Bank and the United Nations have projected that the rate of population growth will continue to decrease slowly until zero population growth is attained by the end of the 21st century. Even if replacement fertility is achieved quickly, the world's population is projected to stabilize at between 10.1 and 12.5 billion, double what we know today. The population in developed countries is expected to increase from 1.3 to 1.9 billion, while population numbers in developing nations are expected to increase from 4.1 to 9.6 billion. In these kinds of projections, developing countries will account for up to 95 percent of the total increase.

Traditionally, large families have played an important social, cultural, and economic role in developing nations.

PART 2:
THE ECOSPHERE WE LIVE IN

TABLE 4-5

TOTAL FERTILITY RATES AND POPULATION GROWTH RATES: SELECTED COUNTRIES AND YEARS

Country	Total Fertility Rate (%)		Annual Rate of Growth (%)		Population Growth Rates (%)			
	1995	2000	1995	2000	1950–60	1960–70	1990–2000	2040–50
Developing Countries								
Afghanistan	6.2	5.9	5.1	2.5	1.9	2.3	5.9	1.7
Argentina	2.7	2.5	1.1	1.1	1.8	1.5	1.1	0.3
Bangladesh	3.7	3.1	1.9	1.7	1.8	2.1	1.8	0.5
Chile	2.3	2.0	1.3	1.0	2.2	2.1	1.3	−0.1
China (Mainland)	1.8	1.8	1.0	0.8	1.5	2.3	1.0	−0.3
Egypt	3.7	3.2	1.9	1.8	2.4	2.2	2.0	0.6
Ethiopia	7.1	6.8	2.9	2.5	1.8	2.0	2.8	1.7
Guatemala	4.6	4.0	2.5	2.3	2.9	2.9	2.5	0.8
India	3.3	2.9	1.7	1.5	1.9	2.2	1.7	0.5
Jamaica	2.5	2.2	0.9	0.6	1.6	1.7	0.8	0.2
Kenya	4.6	3.7	1.7	1.7	2.9	3.2	2.4	1.0
Laos	6.0	5.4	2.8	2.7	2.0	2.1	2.8	1.2
Mexico	3.1	2.8	1.9	1.7	3.0	3.0	1.9	0.5
Nepal	5.2	4.7	2.4	2.4	1.1	1.7	2.4	1.2
Nigeria	6.3	6.0	3.1	3.0	2.1	2.3	3.0	1.8
Peru	3.1	2.7	1.8	1.5	2.6	2.8	1.8	0.2
Rwanda	6.1	5.7	9.0	1.5	2.4	2.1	2.2	1.9
Thailand	1.9	1.8	1.1	0.9	3.2	3.0	1.1	−0.2
Venezuela	3.0	2.5	2.0	1.6	4.1	3.5	2.0	0.4
Zimbabwe	4.2	3.5	0.6	0.8	3.4	3.2	1.5	1.2
Developed Countries								
Canada	1.8	1.8	1.1	0.9	2.7	1.7	1.2	0.0
Denmark	1.7	1.6	0.4	0.3	0.7	0.7	0.3	-0.6
Finland	1.7	1.6	0.1	0.1	1.0	0.4	0.3	-0.7
Germany	1.3	1.6	0.7	0.7	0.6	0.7	0.8	-0.8
Iceland	2.2	2.2	0.8	0.9	2.1	1.5	0.9	0.1
Japan	1.5	1.5	0.2	0.2	1.2	1.0	0.2	0.8
Luxembourg	1.8	1.6	1.6	1.5	0.6	0.8	1.5	-0.7
Norway	1.7	1.6	0.5	0.4	0.9	0.8	0.5	-0.6
Sweden	1.8	1.6	0.7	0.3	0.6	0.7	0.6	-0.6
United Kingdom	1.8	1.8	0.2	0.1	0.4	0.6	0.3	-0.5
United States	2.1	2.1	0.9	0.8	1.7	1.3	1.0	0.6

SOURCE: U.S. Census Bureau. (1996). *International data base summary demographic data.*
http://www.census.gov/ipc/www/idbsum.html

Cultural Factors

In the developed world, a decrease in family size is recognized as an important step toward reduction in the global population growth rate. Most cultures of the world, however, put a strongly positive value on large families and high birth rates. Their reasoning is pragmatic: a large family provides such benefits as protection from enemies, a greater chance of leaving descendants, and a type of insurance for retirement. In societies without life and disability insurance schemes, and without retirement programs, family members provide care for the elderly.

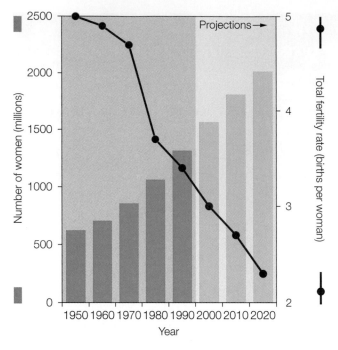

Figure 4–7

World decline in total fertility rate, 1950–2020

SOURCE: Adapted from Kent, M.M., & Crews, K.A. (1990). *World population: Fundamentals of growth.* Washington, DC: Population Reference Bureau.

Other cultural arguments are offered for large families. In Africa, for example, cultural beliefs link men's virility with the number of offspring they produce. Additional reasons for high birth rates and large families in Africa include the formerly high rates of infant and childhood mortality, low education levels (particularly for women), young age at marriage, and lack of access to family planning services and safe, reliable means of birth control. Religious and moral arguments are also part of the discussion of why large families are considered valuable. The influence of these arguments is noted briefly in the following section on birth control in developing nations.

Life Expectancy

As noted previously, life expectancy is the estimated average number of years a person of a specific age can expect to live. Although life expectancy varies by nation, gender, age, and other factors, life expectancy for the human population has not increased since ancient times.

Reconstructions of life expectancies in other periods in history suggest that death rates among young people in Rome and medieval Europe were much higher than they are now. Conversely, life expectancy values appear higher for ancient Romans aged 55 and above than for modern British people of the same age. This may mean that hazards, such as pollution-induced diseases associated with modern life, may concentrate more on the aged in industrialized nations.

FACING THE PROBLEMS OF WORLD POPULATION GROWTH

Even though rapid growth in world population is not the only reason for environmental problems, the rate of growth in numbers of the human species inhabiting Earth has exacerbated issues relating to food supply, land and soil resources, water resources, and the net primary production of the world's lands and oceans (such as forests and fish). If population growth is slowed, and resource consumption per person is decreased, the world will be in a better position to tackle many of its most serious environmental problems. Even though the relationships among population growth, utilization of natural resources, and environmental degradation are complex, one challenging question is how to slow or stop population growth. If we have not already exceeded the Earth's carrying capacity, slowing the rate of population growth should give us more time to find solutions to these problems.

INCREASING THE MARRIAGE AGE

One simple and effective way of slowing population growth is to delay the age of marriage and of first childbearing by women. This tends to occur naturally as more women enter the work force and as education levels and standards of living increase. Sometimes, social pressures that lead to deferred marriage and childbearing are very effective also.

The average age at which women marry varies widely among all countries, but there is always a correlation between marriage age and a nation's fertility rate. The difference between Sri Lanka and Bangladesh, two developing nations in Asia, illustrates this relationship. In Sri Lanka, the average marriage age is 25 and the average number of children born per woman is 2.5. In Bangladesh, in contrast, the average age at marriage is 16, and the average number of children born per woman is 4.9. Increases in the marriage age could help achieve the 40- to 50-percent drop in fertility that many countries require to reach zero population growth.

In developing countries there exists, also, a strong correlation between the fertility rate and the amount of education a woman receives. Typically, women with more education tend to marry later and have fewer children. In part, education provides women with greater knowledge of ways to control their fertility and the means to improve the health of their families, thereby decreasing infant mortality. Education also opens doors to new careers and ways of attaining status for women besides motherhood. As family incomes of educated people have increased

PART 2:
THE ECOSPHERE WE LIVE IN

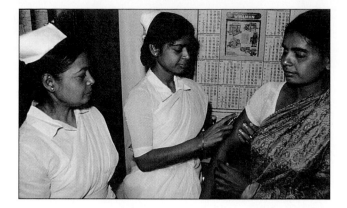

Improved levels of health care are increasing life expectancy in many developing nations.

(because of their ability to earn more money), their standards of living also have increased and smaller family sizes have resulted.

In 1950, China first set laws for minimum marriage ages; men could marry at 20 and women at 18. In 1980 these were revised upward so that the minimum marriage age was 22 for men and 20 for women. As a result of this and other population control programs that promote a national goal of reaching zero population growth by the year 2000, China's birth rate dropped from 32 to 18 per thousand people, and the average fertility rate dropped from 5.7 to 2.1 children during the period 1972–85.

BIRTH CONTROL IN DEVELOPING NATIONS

Considerable emphasis is placed on family planning centres and their programs to provide birth control services in the developing world. Both traditional methods (such as abstinence, breast-feeding, and induction of sterility with natural agents) and modern methods (including oral contraceptives, the Norplant arm implant, surgical sterilization, mechanical devices, and medically provided abortions) have been used to decrease birth rates. Interestingly, the World Bank noted that traditional practices such as breast-feeding (because they delay the resumption of ovulation) sometimes have provided more protection against conception in developing countries than have family planning programs (Guz & Hobcraft, 1991). Abortion is one of the most controversial methods of birth control from a moral perspective, even though it is one of the most important birth control methods because of its effect on birth rates (between 30 and 50 million abortions are performed annually).

The use of contraceptives and contraceptive devices is widespread in many parts of the world. For example, in eastern Asia, about two-thirds of women use contracep-

tive devices, and in Central and South America about 40 percent of the women use them. In Africa, the rate of use is less than 10 percent. This low rate of use results from factors such as cultural barriers to family planning, and the low social status and educational levels of women, including the inability to afford contraceptives.

In many developing African nations, women and children grow the subsistence crops, graze animals, gather wood and water, use most of the household's energy in cooking, and care for the immediate environment of the household (World Resources Institute, 1992). Women are the primary resource and environmental managers in the household, and yet their health and education often are neglected in comparison to those of men. Women's education helps in improving the health of children and also enables women to plan their families and increase birth spacing (thus reducing maternal mortality risk).

Aside from the difficulty of achieving widespread social acceptance of the idea of fewer children and smaller families, many women need assurance that the children they do have will survive. Improved access to affordable family planning services is important in this context. In addition, in many male-dominated African societies, family planning centres provide information primarily to women. These centres might be more effective as *family* planning centres if both women and men were counselled on birth control alternatives.

A common problem in many male-dominated societies is that even if women want no more children, they often do not use contraceptives because their husbands want more children, particularly sons. Many men in developing nations exhibit chauvinistic attitudes toward birth control. Condom use is avoided (except with prostitutes, out of concern for AIDS) as it runs counter to cultural expressions of manhood and the desire to build up their ethnic group (Stock, 1995).

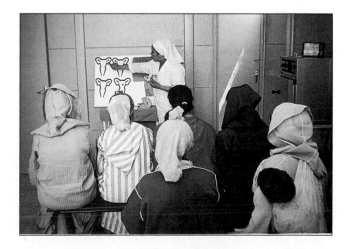

Family planning education helps women to control family size and the interval between births.

In various parts of the world, religion has an important influence on forms of birth control used. Many Roman Catholics in developing countries consider rhythm the only acceptable form of birth control, but this does not hold true in more developed countries where sterilization, the pill, and even abortion (Italy) are among the most popular methods. Political influences also are important; in 1984, for instance, when developing nations appeared ready to benefit from family planning, the U.S. administration under Ronald Reagan denied funding to the International Planned Parenthood Federation, one of the largest nongovernmental organizations providing family planning assistance to LDCs. The Americans prohibited funding for organizations involved in abortion-related activities or for countries where family planning activities were considered to be coercive (such as payment for undergoing sterilization).

NATIONAL BIRTH RATE REDUCTION PROGRAMS

If efforts to reduce birth rates are to be successful, people must be willing to change their attitudes and to gain knowledge of the means to control births, and they must be able to afford these means. As noted above, changes in attitudes can arise simply as a response to increased standards of living. More frequently, however, formal family planning programs have been necessary to (1) help people understand both the problems that arise from rapid population growth as well as the benefits of reduced population growth, and (2) provide information about birth control methods as well as access to them.

Because the choice of population control methods involves social, moral, and religious beliefs, which vary widely between nations and individuals, it is difficult to generalize about a world approach to reduce birth rates. In 1974, however, representatives to the World Population Conference approved a plan that recognized the right of individuals to decide freely the number and spacing of their children, and their right of access to information to help them achieve their goals. The 1994 Program of Action of the United Nations International Conference on Population and Development (ICPD) reaffirmed these basic rights. The ICPD also directed attention to the need to increase people's—especially women's—access to information, education, skill development, employment, and high-quality health services. Empowerment of women, elimination of inequality between men and women, and education are three important factors in attaining sustainable futures throughout the world.

In 1952, India became the first nation to establish a government-sponsored family planning program. In part because of the diversity of cultures, languages, religions,

and customs in different regions of the country, India did not experience immediate results from population control efforts. However, India's action was a stimulus to the introduction of family planning programs in almost every other nation worldwide. In 1976, the Indian government moved more aggressively to introduce new incentives to control population growth and to force compulsory sterilization on any man with three or more living children. Compulsory sterilization failed to affect the birth rate significantly and was very unpopular.

More recently, efforts to integrate development and family planning projects have been undertaken; for instance, adult literacy and population education programs have been combined. Voluntary birth control has been promoted through multimedia advertisements and educational channels. As well, emphasis on lowering the infant mortality rate, on improving the status of women, and on increasing the spacing between births has been successful. India's total fertility rate has declined from about 5.3 in 1980, to 3.3 in 1995 (see Table 4–5).

In 1978, recognizing that its rate of population growth had to decline or the quality of life for everyone in China would decrease, the Chinese government implemented a plan to push China into the third demographic stage (characterized by a decline in the birth rate and a relatively low death rate). Incentives to promote later marriages and one-child families were prominent in this aggressive plan, as were penalties (such as fines, surrender of privileges) for the second and any succeeding child.

While these measures compromised individual freedom of choice, they did bring about a drastic reduction in China's fertility from about 5.8 births per woman in 1970 to 2.1 births per woman in 1981. In thousands of suspected cases, however, parents killed newborn baby girls

China's one-child policy is an example of an official government response to the need for population control.

in preference for male babies (keeping alive the tradition that sons provide old-age security for their parents). Even if these actions were not reported, evidence of the practice of female infanticide can be seen in demographic data. For example, the 1990 census of China found just 93.8 females for every 100 males (the usual ratio was 105 to 106 females for every 100 males). This translates into at least 30 to 40 million females (3 to 4 percent of the population) missing from the Chinese population. More recently, education and publicity campaigns (rather than coercion and penalties) have been applied in population control programs. For instance, teachers have been taught how to integrate population education into the curriculum.

From simple provision of information, to promotion and provision of some of the means of birth control, to offering rewards and implementing penalties, a wide variety of approaches has been used to reduce the rate of population increase (overpopulation) in the developing world. In the developed world, too, there is a need to confront "consumption overpopulation" and to formulate policies that encourage recycling of resources and elimination of needless production, and discourage overconsumption and the throwaway mentality.

MIGRATION

In the past, migration was an important way by which people could escape their overuse of local resources. While migration is still important, particularly when political situations, natural disasters, or other such events warrant moving, migration represents only temporary and finite relief—today there are no new territories on Earth. Even if our technologies permitted us to colonize previously unused areas such as the Antarctic or the deep sea, these ventures would be limited and likely short lived. If commercial space travel and colonization were possible, they could take care of only a few of the more than 90 million people added each year to the human population. It is important, then, to realize that both developing and developed nations need to face their own population problems. They also need to understand the impacts of these population problems on environmental sustainability.

POPULATION AND ENVIRONMENTAL SUSTAINABILITY

Canadians need to be concerned about population growth here and in other parts of the world because population growth anywhere ultimately has some impact on the Earth's ecosystems. Many environmental problems, including air and water pollution and global climate change, transcend national boundaries—as population grows, demands for resources increase, resulting in pollution and waste being added to the biosphere. Increased resource use also has an effect on population: environmental pollutants that mimic human hormones may be one cause of the declining ratio of boys to girls born in Canada since 1970 (Pollutants may be linked, 1997).

More population means more energy is used, and there is a resultant escalation of problems such as global warming, acid precipitation, oil spills, and nuclear waste. More population means more land is required for agriculture, housing, industrial sites, and transportation links, leading to deforestation, soil erosion, and less land for agriculture and habitat for other species (contributing to their extinction, perhaps). As lands are cultivated, they become less productive than naturally vegetated areas. More population means a greater demand on water resources for drinking, irrigation, waste disposal, and industrial processes. Often there is a concomitant decline in quantity or quality of the body of water used for these purposes.

As we shall see in Part 3 of this book, human demands on the resources for Canada's future are numerous and multifaceted. If Canadians and other inhabitants of this planet are to experience a reasonable quality of life, steps need to be taken to protect human and environmental health, to prevent resource abuse through conservation, and to preserve living systems. The following chapters outline what's happening to natural resources in Canada, what is being done (or has been done) about the various issues, and what needs to be done to ensure sustainability of Canada's part of the global environment.

Chapter Questions

1. How do the crude birth rate and the fertility rate differ? Which measure is a more accurate statement of the amount of reproduction occurring in a population?

2. The world population in 1995 was 5.6 billion and the growth rate was 1.4 percent. Calculate the doubling time of this population. If the doubling time of the human population is decreasing, can the human population be growing strictly according to an exponential curve? Explain why or why not.

3. Why is it important to consider the age structure of a human population?

4. Why is demographic momentum a matter of interest in population projections?

5. What is meant by the demographic transition? When would one expect replacement fertility to be achieved—before, during, or after the demographic transition?

6. Debate the following statement: Canada must increase immigration in order to avoid a collapse in our population.

7. What population size do you believe would allow the world's people to have a good quality of life? Justify your response.

references

Barker, R. (1997). *And the waters turned to blood: The ultimate biological threat.* New York: Simon and Schuster.

Botkin, D.B., & Keller, E.A. (1995). *Environmental science: Earth as a living planet.* New York: John Wiley & Sons.

Drohan, M. (1997, June 27). British beef returns to McDonald's menu. *The Globe and Mail* (Toronto), p. A11.

Dupaquier, J., & Fauve-Chamoux, A. (Eds.) (1983). *Malthus past and present.* New York: Academic Press.

Ehrlich, P. (1971). *The population bomb* (rev. ed.). New York: Ballantine Books.

Guz, D., & Hobcraft, J. (1991). Breastfeeding and fertility: A comparative analysis. *Population Studies,* 45, pp. 91–108.

Kaufman, D.G., & Franz, C.M. (1996). *Biosphere 2000: Protecting our global environment.* (2nd ed.). Dubuque, IA: Kendall/Hunt.

Kent, M.M., & Crews, K.A. (1990). *World population: Fundamentals of growth.* Washington, DC: Population Reference Bureau.

Kohlenberg, L. (1997, April 7). And this little piggy went ... *Time,* p. 12.

Meadows, D.H., et al. (1972). *The limits to growth: A report for the Club of Rome's project on the predicament of mankind.* New York: Universe.

Meadows, D.H., et al. (1972). *Beyond the limits: Confronting global collapse, envisioning a sustainable future.* Post Mills, VT: Chelsea Green Publishing.

Miller, G.T. (1994). *Living in the environment* (8th ed.). Belmont, CA: Wadsworth Publishing Company, p. 221.

Miller, G.T. (1994b). *Sustaining the Earth: An integrated approach.* Belmont, CA: Wadsworth Publishing Company.

Myers, N. (1990). *The Gaia atlas of future worlds: Challenge and opportunity in an age of change.* London: Gaia Books.

Nichols, M. (1997, May 19). Malaria's comeback. *Maclean's,* p. 57.

Pedersen, R. (1997, July 14). High birth defects probed. *Calgary Herald,* p. A1.

Pollutants may be linked to declining male births. (1997, January 8). *Calgary Herald,* p. A9.

Raven, P.H., Berg, L.R., and Johnson, G.B. (1993). *Environment: 1995 version.* Orlando, FL: Saunders College Publishing/Harcourt Brace College Publishing.

Statistics Canada. (1996). *Population projections by age groups and sex.*
http://www.statcan.ca/Documents/English/Pgbd/People/Population/demo23a.htm

Stock, R. (1995). *Africa south of the Sahara.* New York: Guilford Press.

U.S. Census Bureau. International Data Base. Total midyear population for the world: 1959–2050.
http://www.census.gov/ipc/www/worldpop.html

U.S. Census Bureau. (1996). International Data Base.
http://www.census.gov/ipc/www/idbsum.html

United Nations, Population Division, Department for Economic and Social Information and Policy Analysis. (1994). World population growth from year 0 to stabilization. New York: United Nations. Also at:
gopher://gopher/undp.org:70/00/ungophers/popin/wdtrends/milestone

World Bank. (1985). *World development report.* New York: Oxford University Press.

World Health Organization. (1996). The World Health report 1996: Fighting disease, fostering development. Geneva, Switzerland: World Health Organization.
http://www.un.org./Pubs/CyberSchoolBus/special/globo/glotrend/morworl.htm

World Resources Institute. (1992). *World resources 1992–93: A guide to the global environment.* New York: Oxford University Press.

additional information sources

Nikiforuk, A. (1991). *The fourth horseman: A short history of plagues, emerging viruses and other scourges.* Toronto: Viking.

Population Reference Bureau:
http://www.igc.apc.org/pub/media.htm

Statistics Canada:
http://www.statcan.ca/Documents/English/Pgdb/People/Population/

United Nations: The State of World Population 1996:
http://www.unfpa.org/swp96.html

United Nations Population Fund: http://www.unfpa.org/

United States Census Bureau:
http://www.census.gov/ipc/www/idbsum.html

United States Census Bureau: http://www.census.gov/cgi-bin/ipc/popclockw

World Population Count: http://sunsite.unc.edu/lunarbin/worldpop

Zero Population Growth: http://www.zpg.org/zpg/

Resources for Canada's Future

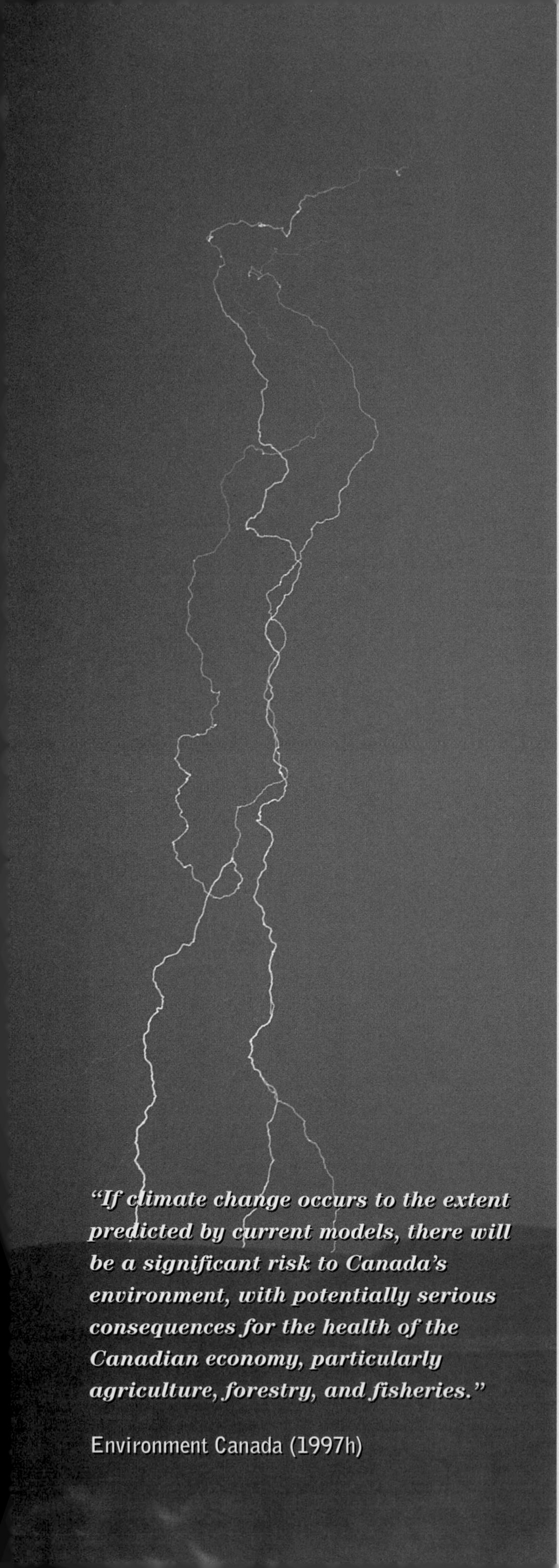

CHAPTER 5

Our Changing Atmosphere

Chapter Contents

CHAPTER OBJECTIVES 117
INTRODUCTION 117
HUMAN ACTIVITIES AND IMPACTS ON THE
ATMOSPHERE 121
  Stratospheric Ozone Depletion 121
    The Ozone Layer 121
    Depletion of the Ozone Layer 121
      Ozone-Depleting Substances 122
      Volcanoes and Ozone
        Depletion 123
    Antarctic Ozone Depletion 124
    Tropical and Mid-Latitude Ozone
      Depletion 124
    Ozone Depletion Impacts on the
      Atmosphere 124
    Ultraviolet Radiation and Its
      Impacts 125
  Climate Change 126
    Greenhouse Gases and Climate 126
    Human Activities and the Greenhouse
      Effect 127
      Carbon Dioxide 127
      Methane 127
      Nitrous Oxide 128
      Chlorofluorocarbons 128
    Predicting Climate Change 128
      Impacts of an Enhanced
        Greenhouse Effect 130
    Indicators and Effects of Climate
      Change 130
    Some Other Influences on
      Climate 134
      El Niño and the Southern
        Oscillation 134
    The Greenhouse Effect in the
      Future 135
  Other Atmospheric Changes 137

"If climate change occurs to the extent predicted by current models, there will be a significant risk to Canada's environment, with potentially serious consequences for the health of the Canadian economy, particularly agriculture, forestry, and fisheries."

Environment Canada (1997h)

Acidic Deposition   137
   What Is Acid Rain?   137
   Sources of Acidic Pollutants   138
   Effects of Acidic Deposition   138
   Signs of Progress   140
  Airborne Contaminants   142
RESPONSES TO ATMOSPHERIC
  CHANGES   143
  International Actions   143
   Protecting the Ozone Layer   143
   Controlling Greenhouse Gas
    Emissions   143
  Canadian Law, Policy, and Practice   145
  Canadian Partnerships and Local
   Actions   148
FUTURE CHALLENGES   149
Chapter Questions   151
References   151
Additional Information Sources   153

Chapter Objectives

After studying this chapter you should be
able to

- understand the main issues and concerns
  relating to Canada's atmosphere
- identify a range of human uses of the
  atmosphere
- describe the impacts of human activities on
  the atmosphere around us
- appreciate the complexity and interrelatedness of issues relating to the atmosphere
- outline Canadian and international
  responses to the need for protection of the
  atmosphere
- discuss challenges to a sustainable future
  for the atmosphere

INTRODUCTION

Finally, summer is here! For many Canadians, that means it's time to head for the outdoors and all our favourite activities—swimming, fishing, mountain biking, hiking, beachcombing, softball, and many others. It's great to get some exercise and fresh air; too bad we forgot the sunscreen and got a sunburn, though—that peeling skin is so ugly! And we even checked the UV Index before we left; we should just leave a container of sunscreen in our bags and packs so we can't forget it next time.

For others of us, sun tanning is what summer's all about. In fact, the darker the tan, the better. Those tanning salons are great, especially early in the season, because we can get a head start on our tans and look good at the beach or the pool right away. And power tanning, now that really works—the products have no sunscreen at all!

Given what is known about the potential impacts of ultraviolet (UV) radiation on our skin and health, however, we realize that too much sun (UV radiation) is dangerous. But how do we know when we should be cautious about being in the sun? Sunburned skin is damaged skin, but how long does it take our skin to burn when exposed?

Excessive exposure to the sun and ultraviolet radiation damages
skin and may result in serious problems such as skin cancer.

Does it make a difference if we're at the beach or in the mountains?

One tool we have to help us make decisions about our exposure to UV radiation is the UV Index. The UV Index was a Canadian first; in 1992, Canadian scientists devised a method to predict the strength of the sun's UV rays, based on daily changes in the ozone layer. That same year, they developed the UV Index and Canada became the first nation in the world to issue countrywide daily forecasts of tomorrow's UV. Now, Environment Canada's UV Index is produced twice daily for at least 48 locations across Canada, as well as holiday destinations, and is available on radio and TV, in the newspaper, and through our local weather offices. (You can find the latest UV Indices for selected Canadian cities at Environment Canada's Weather Forecast Web site listed in the Additional Information Sources section of this chapter.)

The Index measures UV radiation on a scale of 0 to 10, with 10 being a typical midday value for a summer day in the tropics (where the UV is at its highest on Earth). As Table 5–1a indicates, the higher the number on the UV Index, the more UV radiation you receive, and the faster your skin burns. Depending on where you live in Canada, your exposure to UV rays will vary. In summer, you'll receive roughly three times more UV radiation if you live in southern Canada than if you live in the Northwest Territories (Mills & Jackson, 1995). Table 5–1b indicates some typical summer midday UV Index values for places in Canada (and two others for comparison).

Among the other knowledge we have of UV radiation is that it varies with altitude; at 1000 metres, UV radiation is 7 percent stronger, and at 3000 metres it is 20 percent stronger, than at sea level. Although UV intensity is low during winter, it may be enhanced significantly by reflection: up to 85 percent of UV radiation will be reflected off fresh snow (skiers beware!). Water reflects less than 10 percent of the incoming UV radiation; roughly 40 percent passes through the first 30 centimeters of fresh water and over 80 percent through the same depth in a swimming pool (swimmers take note!). Clouds reduce (but do not eliminate) UV exposure: variable or light cloud cover reduces UV radiation by 10 to 20 percent, whereas heavy, dark, overcast decks of cloud reduce UV by 50 to 80 percent. Also, clear sky radiation reaches a daily maximum at solar noon. During the summer, this usually occurs between 1:00 and 1:45 p.m. local time, depending on location (Mills & Jackson, 1995).

All of this information helps us make informed choices and take actions (or change our behaviour) to reduce our exposure to UV radiation (Table 5–1a). The UV Index helps us plan our outdoor activities so we can prevent overexposure to the sun's rays. Not only can excessive sun exposure result in painful sunburn, it can lead to other serious health problems including melanoma, a life-threatening form of skin cancer. In addition to melanoma, exces-sive UV exposure can lead to premature aging of the skin, cataracts, nonmelanoma skin cancers, and immune system suppression (possibly including an increase in some types of infectious diseases and a reduction in the effectiveness of some vaccination programs).

The majority of most people's sun exposure occurs before age 20; research indicates that cumulative effects of excessive sun exposure, especially sunburn in young children, can produce skin cancer in later years. Even one or two blistering sunburns during childhood may double the risk of melanoma later in life (United States Environmental Protection Agency, 1995). According to the Canadian Dermatology Association, over 60 000 Canadians develop skin cancer annually (Canadian Safety Council, n.d.). Melanoma is the fastest-rising form of cancer in men and the third-fastest in women. Today, about one in seven Canadians can expect to get some form of skin cancer in his or her lifetime (Enviro-Focus 5). Because skin cancer takes between 10 and 20 years to develop, we have not yet seen the full impact of post-1980 ozone depletion on Canadian skin cancer rates.

While the incidence of skin cancers in Canada has increased rapidly during the past two decades, perhaps partly as a result of greater awareness and improved diagnostics, it is difficult to link ozone-related impacts directly to human health effects. For instance, the increase in skin cancers could reflect lifestyle choices, such as growth in popularity of tropical vacations, rather than an increase in UV-B intensity due to thinning of the ozone layer (Government of Canada, 1996). (See page 125 for more on ultraviolet radiation.) Nevertheless, a sustained 10 percent thinning of the ozone layer globally is expected to result in nearly two million new cases of cataracts per year and a 26 percent increase in the incidence of nonmelanoma skin cancer (Environment Canada, 1997b). The Australian slogan "Slip, Slap, Slop"—slip on a T-shirt, slap on a hat, and slop on the sunscreen—is good advice for Canadians, too. Other ways to be sun wise are identified in Table 5–1a.

The amount of incoming UV radiation is determined partly by the angle of the sun above the horizon and the amount of ozone in the atmosphere. Due to the release into the atmosphere of ozone-depleting chemicals, the Earth's ozone layer has thinned during the past 15 to 20 years. The ozone layer over Canada, for example, is 5 to 10 percent thinner than before 1980. As a result, there has been a slight increase in UV-B radiation at ground level. Destruction of stratospheric ozone, the Earth's natural shield from harmful UV radiation, is the first of two major issues associated with atmospheric change we examine in this chapter. The second major issue considered is the production of gases (such as carbon dioxide, methane, and nitrous oxide) that enhance the Earth's natural greenhouse effect and are strongly suspected of leading to global climate change.

TABLE 5–1
LIVING WITH ULTRAVIOLET

a. The UV Index: Strategies to Reduce UV Exposure

UV Index	Category	Sunburn Time
Over 9	Extreme	< 15 minutes
7–9	High	About 20 minutes
4–7	Medium	About 30 minutes
0–4	Low	> 1 hour

- Sunburn times are for light, untanned skin; the times would be somewhat longer for those with darker skin.

Strategies to Reduce UV Exposure

Minimize sun exposure

- Plan outdoor activities before 11 a.m. or after 4 p.m., and consult UV Index for daily forecasts of UV intensity.
- Practise sun protection behaviours when outdoors between April and September, between 11 a.m. and 4 p.m. every day.
- In winter, practise sun protection behaviours during periods of extended exposure and/or when you are near fresh/bright snow.
- When visiting warmer climates, remember that UV radiation is more intense there; sun protection is particularly important.
- There is no such thing as a healthy tan; UV radiation from sun and tanning lamps is a major contributor to skin cancer.

Seek shade

- Seek shade, particularly during the 11 a.m. to 4 p.m. period.
- Work toward creating shade in the form of shelters, canopies, and trees.

Cover up

- Wear tightly woven, loose-fitting clothing to cover your arms and legs.
- Wear a hat with a wide brim to shade your face and neck.
- Wear sunglasses that absorb or block 99 to 100 percent of UV radiation.

Use sunscreen

- Use sunscreen in conjunction with shade, clothing, hats, and sunglasses, not instead of them (and reapply every two hours).
- Sunscreens are not intended to increase length of time spent in the sun but to reduce exposure and provide some protection from sunburn when people need to be in the sun.
- Use a sunscreen with sun protection factor (SPF) #15 or higher.

b. The UV Index: Typical Summer Midday Values

Location	UV Index	
Tropics	10.0	Extreme
Washington, DC	8.8	High
Toronto	8.0	High
Halifax	7.5	High
Edmonton	7.0	High
Yellowknife	6.0	Moderate
Iqaluit, NWT	4.8	Moderate
North Pole	2.3	Low

SOURCES: Environment Canada. (n.d.). UV and you. http://www.ns.ec.gc.ca/udo/uv/uvandyou.html

Mills, C., & Jackson, S. (1995). Workshop report: Public education messages for reducing health risks from UV radiation. http://alep.unibase.com/sunconf/papers/cmills/cmills.html

United States Environmental Protection Agency. (1995). Sun protection for children. http://www.epa.gov/ozone/uvindex/uvwhat.html

ENVIRO-FOCUS 5

A Sun Sensitivity Test and 'Spot Check'

Your risk of skin cancer is related to your skin type and the amount of time you spend in the sun. How vulnerable are you? Try the Canadian Dermatology Association's Sun Sensitivity Test to determine your chances of getting skin cancer and whether you need to act differently with regard to UV exposure.

Yes No

- ☐ ☐ I have red or blond hair.
- ☐ ☐ I have light-coloured eyes—blue, green, or grey.
- ☐ ☐ I always burn before I tan.
- ☐ ☐ I freckle easily.
- ☐ ☐ I had two or more blistering sunburns before I turned 18.
- ☐ ☐ I lived or had long vacations in a tropical climate as a child.
- ☐ ☐ My family has a history of skin cancer.
- ☐ ☐ I work outdoors.
- ☐ ☐ I spend a lot of time in outdoor activities.
- ☐ ☐ I am an indoor worker, but I like to get out in the sun as much as possible when I am able.

- Score yourself 10 points for each each "YES."
- Add an additional 10 points if you use tanning devices, tanning booths, or sun lamps.

(80–100) You are in the high-risk zone. Read on to find out how you can protect your skin from the sun.
(40–70) You are at risk. Take all precautions possible.
(10–30) You're still at risk. Carry on being careful.

The Canadian Dermatology Association also produces "Spot Check," a quick reference guide to moles and pigmented spots on our skin (see sidebar). Checking your moles and spots for changes could help catch skin cancer early when it is most easily treated. Most skin cancers are not life threatening, but they can cause extensive disfigurement if left untreated.

For further information, contact the Canadian Dermatology Association at the address given in the Additional Information Sources section at the end of this chapter.

SOURCE: Canadian Dermatology Association. Reproduced courtesy of the CDA.

spot check

Normal mole: round or oval, even colour. **Many** moles–*increased* risk of melanoma skin cancer.

Atypical mole: mix of browns, smudged border, often bigger than 5 mm. *Increased* rick of melanoma skin cancer.

Melanoma skin cancer: potentially deadly. **Look for *changes* in: Colour:** new colour, black, brown, red, blue, or white.

Shape: irregular, border scalloped but well defined.

Size: enlarges.

Acinic Keratoses: not skin cancer. Indicates excess sun exposure over many years. Red, rough, scaly spots, may itch or sting. *Increased* risk of skin cancer.

Basal cell skin cancer: Can cause disfigurement. Flesh-coloured, red, or black round bump with a pearly border, develops into ulcerating sore.

Squamous cell skin cancer: Can be life threatening. Thickened, red, scaly bump or wart-like growth, develops into a raised crusted sore.

Common skin cancers usually appear on sun-exposed areas.

See your dermatologist if you note any of the above.

HUMAN ACTIVITIES AND IMPACTS ON THE ATMOSPHERE

As noted in Chapter 3, the Earth's atmosphere is that thin film of gases that is crucial to the sustainability of life on this planet. With the coming of the Industrial Revolution nearly 250 years ago, human productivity and technological creativity augmented the geological, biological, and other natural forces of atmospheric change. Excluding water vapour and particulates, the atmosphere still consists of 99.9 percent nitrogen, oxygen, and argon, but the remaining 0.1 percent of atmospheric trace gases that are being altered substantially by human activities are of great concern. In the sections that follow, we explore the issues of stratospheric ozone depletion and climate change with a view to understanding both the ways in which human activities have caused atmospheric change and the implications of such changes.

STRATOSPHERIC OZONE DEPLETION

The Ozone Layer

Although ozone (O_3) is found throughout the atmosphere, about 90 percent of it occurs in the stratosphere at altitudes of 18 to 35 kilometres (Figure 5–1). The maximum ozone concentration within this band or ozone layer occurs between 20 and 25 kilometres above the Earth's surface (World Meteorological Organization, 1994). Even here, ozone molecules are scattered so thinly (about 300 parts per billion at peak concentrations) that, if compressed to ground level pressure, they would form a band of pure ozone only 3 millimetres thick at sea level. This is equivalent to 300 Dobson units (DU), the unit usually used to measure the thickness of the ozone layer in the atmosphere (Box 5–1).

Ozone is produced in largest quantities near the equator where sunlight is most direct and intense. However, varying stratospheric pressures and stratospheric winds cause ozone to move toward the poles with the result that ozone may be 50 percent thicker at mid and higher latitudes than in the tropics. Ozone thickness also varies seasonally: most poleward transport of ozone occurs in winter. With little or no ozone-destroying sunlight available at that time of year, stratospheric ozone increases over the winter and peaks near the end of the cold season (February in the northern hemisphere). As sunshine intensifies with the coming of spring, ozone depletion resumes and continues through the summer. In Canada this means lowest ozone thicknesses usually are recorded in the summer and fall. In the tropics, where solar energy input is more constant over the seasons, ozone variations are much smaller.

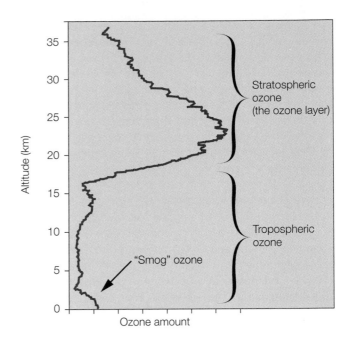

Figure 5–1
Distribution of ozone in the atmosphere

SOURCE: Government of Canada. (1996). *The state of Canada's environment—1996.* Ottawa: Supply and Services Canada.

Depletion of the Ozone Layer

The human role in ozone layer depletion has been suspected since the late 1960s, when it was argued that water vapour and oxides of nitrogen from proposed subsonic and supersonic aircraft might deplete stratospheric ozone. Although effects of aircraft (and later, space shuttles) were determined to be negligible, the issue of chemical contamination from our industrialized society began to be investigated.

BOX 5–1
NEW CANADIAN TECHNOLOGY: THE BREWER OZONE SPECTROPHOTOMETER

Canada is recognized as a world leader among countries involved in research and development of new or improved environmental technologies, including those related to atmospheric science.

The Brewer Ozone Spectrophotometer, a ground-based ozone monitoring instrument that was patented in 1991 by Environment Canada's Atmospheric Environment Service, is a case in point. Considered to be the world's most accurate ozone-measuring device, the Brewer is produced in Canada by Sci-Tech, a Saskatchewan company. About 80 units were in use in more than 25 countries around the world in 1997.

In 1974, two American scientists (Drs. F.S. Rowland and M. Molina) hypothesized that chlorofluorocarbons (CFCs) could persist in the atmosphere long enough to diffuse upward into the stratosphere, be broken up by intense solar radiation, and release active chlorine atoms that, in turn, would destroy ozone. Initially people treated this theory with skepticism. However, growing evidence and the discovery of the "ozone hole" over the Antarctic in 1985 focused attention on CFCs and other synthetic compounds.

Ozone-Depleting Substances We now know that emissions of chlorofluorocarbons alone account for more than 80 percent of total stratospheric ozone depletion. Together, CFC-11 and CFC-12 account for about half of the ozone-depleting chlorine entering the stratosphere (World Meteorological Organization, 1994). Other synthetic compounds also contribute to ozone depletion, including carbon tetrachloride, halons, hydrochlorofluorocarbons (HCFCs), methyl bromide, and methyl chloroform. All these chemicals are members of a large class of chlorine- and bromine-containing compounds known as industrial halocarbons.

The most widely used of all the ozone-depleting substances (ODSs), CFCs were researched intensively in the early 1930s as a safe and efficient refrigerant to replace toxic ammonia. The characteristics of CFCs—nontoxic, nonflammable, chemically stable—quickly made them the prime choice as refrigerants. From the late 1950s to the late 1960s, the uses of CFCs multiplied: they were used as blowing agents in plastic foam production (for cushioning, insulation, packaging), as propellants in aerosol spray cans, and as solvents to clean electronic equipment and microchips. Today, CFCs continue to be used widely as coolants in refrigeration and air conditioners, as solvents in degreasers and cleaners, as a blowing agent in foam production, and as an ingredient in sterilant gas mixtures. Canada's 20 million household refrigerators alone contain about 5 million kilograms of CFC-12 (each compressor contains an average charge of 0.25 kilograms of CFC-12).

Their chemical stability allows CFCs to survive in the atmosphere for several decades to a few centuries. During this period they diffuse gradually from the troposphere into the stratosphere where they eventually are broken down by intense UV radiation. This process—which is more complex than described here—releases chlorine atoms that react easily with ozone, producing chlorine monoxide and oxygen (Figure 5–2). In turn, the chlorine monoxide breaks down quickly, freeing its chlorine atom to combine again with another molecule of ozone. This property (actually a catalytic chain reaction) enables a single atom of chlorine to destroy approximately 100 000 ozone molecules over a one-to-two-year period before it forms a more stable combination with another substance (Rowland, 1989). During the past 100 years, the abundance of chlorine in the stratosphere has increased from a natural background level of about 0.6 parts per billion to about 3.6 parts per billion in 1994.

In 1986, Canadian companies used 19 100 metric tonnes of CFCs, or about 2 percent of the world's total. By 1991, that had been reduced by 45 percent, to 11 000 metric tonnes. In 1980, Canada became one of only four countries to ban the major propellant uses of CFCs, and by 1990, almost all aerosol uses of CFCs were prohibited in Canada. Worldwide, however, between 800 000 and 900 000 metric tonnes of CFCs continue to be released into the atmosphere annually (Forester, 1991). This level of CFC emissions is significant when we realize that the ozone depletion it may trigger could be 100 times larger than the original emissions.

Other industrial halons contribute to ozone depletion. For example, carbon tetrachloride (used to make CFCs, in drycleaning, as an industrial solvent, and as an agricultural fumigant) contributes slightly less than 8 percent to global ozone depletion. Introduced in the 1950s, methyl chloroform is an all-purpose industrial solvent used to clean metal and electronic parts. A substitute for toxic carbon tetrachloride, methyl chloroform is used in large quantities, and much of it is vented directly to the atmosphere during metal cleaning. It was recognized as an important ODS in 1989, and is estimated to contribute about 5 percent to total global ozone depletion.

Hydrofluorocarbons (HCFCs) contain chlorine, but because they contain hydrogen also, they break down in the lower atmosphere and result in a lower ozone depletion effect. HCFCs are known as transitional chemicals because they represent an interim step between strong ODSs and ozone-friendly replacement chemicals; they account for about 0.5 percent of global ozone depletion, but their use is increasing.

Halons are used primarily as fire suppressants for delicate equipment, computer and electronic equipment facilities, museums, ships, and tanks, and they are in general use in industries, homes, and offices. Produced in large quantities in the 1980s, levels in the atmosphere have not risen rapidly because most halons have not been vented yet, but remain stored in fire extinguishers. Currently, halons contribute about 5 percent to global ozone depletion, although their concentrations are increasing (along with concerns for future impacts of these long-lived ODSs).

Methyl bromide has been used as a pesticide since the 1960s but has been recognized as an important ODS only since 1991. Farmers use it to sterilize soil in fields and greenhouses, and to kill pests on fruit, vegetables, and grain before export. Approximately 90 percent of the methyl bromide use in Canada occurs in Ontario and Quebec. Scientists estimate that human sources of methyl bromide are responsible for 5 to 10 percent of global ozone depletion. Although it has a relatively short lifetime, bromine removes ozone very effectively; consequently, methyl bromide is considered a significant

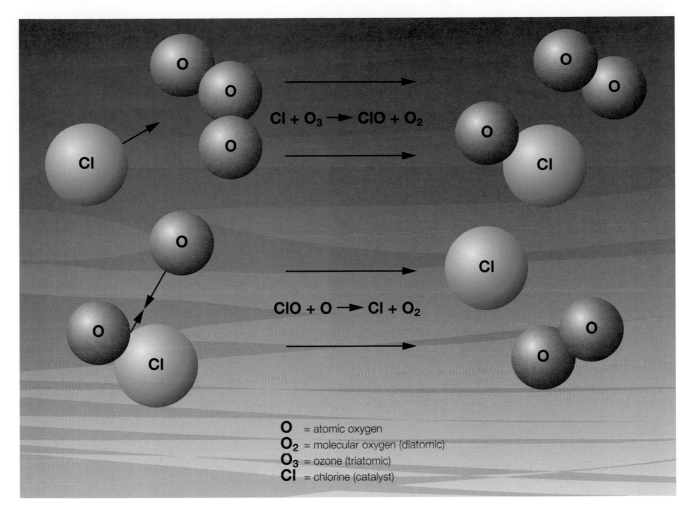

$$Cl + O_3 \rightarrow ClO + O_2$$

$$ClO + O \rightarrow Cl + O_2$$

O = atomic oxygen
O$_2$ = molecular oxygen (diatomic)
O$_3$ = ozone (triatomic)
Cl = chlorine (catalyst)

Figure 5–2
How ozone-depleting substances destroy stratospheric ozone

NOTE: Chemical reactions in the stratosphere are considerably more complex than the two equations shown here. However, these equations demonstrate the basic form of a chemical change reaction as occurs in depletion of ozone in the stratosphere.

SOURCE: Adapted from Hengeveld, H. (1995). *Understanding atmospheric change: A survey of the background science and implications of climate change and ozone depletion* (2nd ed.). SOE Report No. 95-2. Ottawa: Environment Canada.

contributor to ozone depletion. This short lifetime characteristic suggests that an immediate reduction in consumption of methyl bromide could have a more immediate effect on reducing ozone depletion than would be the case if we were to reduce consumption of longer-lived substances (but at the same time, this does not imply we should not act on the longer-lived ODSs!).

Our use of industrial halocarbons, including CFCs, will continue to have far-reaching effects on the atmosphere. While the chemical interactions and effects of these substances are extremely complex and are not yet understood fully, we do know that they portend potentially severe atmospheric changes.

Volcanoes and Ozone Depletion In addition to the human role in ozone-layer depletion, volcanoes can erupt

with sufficient force that they inject dust particles and gases into the stratosphere. If that happens, volcanic particles (aerosols) can affect ozone levels because they speed up the chemical reactions that destroy ozone directly. They also can block incoming UV radiation and affect weather patterns that indirectly influence ozone formation and destruction. For the first six months following the eruption of Mount Pinatubo in the Philippines in June 1991, local stratospheric ozone concentrations were as much as 20 percent below previous levels (Environment Canada, 1997d). The severe Antarctic ozone depletion in 1993 has been attributed partly to the presence of aerosols from this eruption (Manney, Zurek, Gelman, Miller & Nagatani, 1994). However, the impact of volcanic particles is short-lived: in a few years, particulates settle out of the atmosphere, thus posing a reduced threat to the ozone layer.

Antarctic Ozone Depletion

The British Antarctic Survey began measuring stratospheric ozone in 1957. In 1985 members of the survey published data showing clearly that ozone concentrations remained at about 300 Dobson units from 1957 to 1970 but, following 1970, there was a sharp drop to about 200 DU in 1984 (Farman, Gardiner & Shanklin, 1985). Since then, ozone concentrations have been quite variable, hitting a high of about 250 DU in 1988 and a low of about 90 DU in 1993 (Hamill & Toon, 1991; Stolarski, 1988). Satellite data on ozone concentrations prior to 1985 confirmed the British Antarctic Survey findings, and the depletion in ozone was dubbed the ozone hole. (Note that there is not an actual hole in the ozone shield around the Earth, but there is a decrease in the concentration of ozone that occurs during the Antarctic spring—September to November—each year.)

The most dramatic depletion of the ozone layer occurs over the Antarctic during the southern spring. Two events that occur in the southern polar region during winter are important to the severity of this ozone depletion. One event, known as the **polar vortex,** occurs during the polar winter (night) when the Antarctic air mass is partially isolated from the rest of the atmosphere and circulates around the pole. The second event is the formation of **polar stratospheric clouds** (PSC); these form in the extremely low temperatures (below - 78°C) that develop within the polar vortex as it matures, cools (in the absence of heating by sunlight or by the influx of warmer air from lower latitudes), and descends. Ice crystals in these clouds provide the medium for a complex variety of chemical reactions that lead to rapid depletion of ozone when sunlight returns in the spring (see Toon & Turco, 1991).

In the Antarctic, ozone depletion has become more pronounced over time. In 1989, the area of serious depletion (where total ozone thickness was less than 220 DU) covered about 7.5 percent of the southern hemisphere. In October 1993, ozone thicknesses of 91 DU were recorded and in 1993–94, the area of reduced ozone thickness covered about 10.7 percent of the southern hemisphere (an area about the size of North America). Since then, ozone losses often have started earlier and the affected areas have expanded more rapidly than previously (cited in Government of Canada, 1996). In September–October 1996, the ozone hole over Antarctica grew to its largest size in history.

Tropical and Mid-Latitude Ozone Depletion

Because the natural replenishment rate of ozone at low latitudes is high, ozone-depleting chemicals have had the least effect on tropical ozone levels. However, ice particles do occur in the stratosphere over the tropics and, at times, there is an abundance of aerosols in the stratosphere from volcanic eruptions. As yet, however, there is

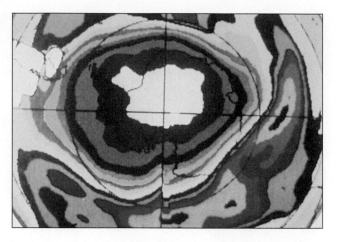

A computer-enhanced image of the ozone "hole" over the South Pole region.

no substantial evidence to support the theory that these particles cause ozone depletion in the tropics.

Satellite measurements show that average ozone concentrations over the mid-latitudes of the northern hemisphere have declined by about 7 percent since 1978 (Figure 5–3). However, because the Arctic vortex is much less stable than the southern polar vortex and breaks up sooner, and because the Arctic stratosphere is slightly warmer and less conducive to PSC formation, it is anticipated that ozone depletion on the scale experienced in the Antarctic will not occur in the Arctic. Nevertheless, if an enhanced greenhouse effect cools the atmosphere as predicted, the conditions for PSC would improve and increase the possibility of more pronounced Arctic ozone depletion. As if to confirm this threat, in March 1997 ozone values over the Canadian Arctic reached their lowest values since monitoring began in the 1960s. We need to appreciate that ozone depletion remains a global concern, from the poles to the tropics.

Ozone Depletion Impacts on the Atmosphere

When ozone depletion occurs in the stratosphere as a result of the use of CFCs and other industrial halons, that area of the upper atmosphere is cooled. Normally, when ozone absorbs incoming UV radiation, it warms the surrounding atmosphere. But, as ozone levels decline as a result of ODSs, the stratosphere cools. In addition, carbon dioxide in the atmosphere (on the rise because of burning of fossil fuels) may contribute indirectly to stratospheric cooling and could accelerate onset of Arctic ozone depletion.

Ozone depletion also may affect global climate indirectly through the loss of phytoplankton. Threatened by increased levels of UV radiation (see the following section), productivity of oceanic phytoplankton may be reduced. If their productivity is reduced, their ability to store approximately 80 percent of the CO_2 released into

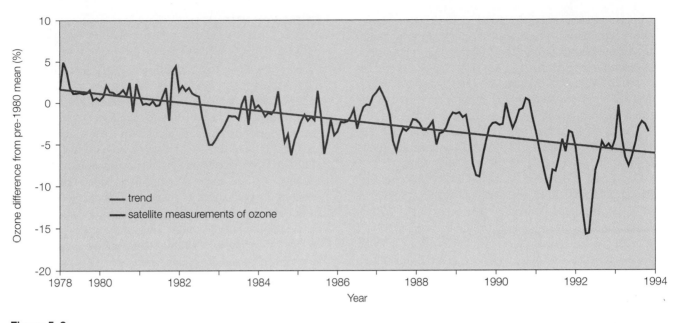

Figure 5–3

Total ozone trend, 30–65°N

SOURCE: Government of Canada. (1996). *The state of Canada's environment—1996.* Ottawa: Supply and Services Canada.

the atmosphere by human activities will be reduced. That means atmospheric concentrations of CO_2 may rise, enhancing the greenhouse effect and changing global climate. Phytoplankton also produce dimethyl sulphoxide, a chemical important in the creation of clouds above the oceans. Phytoplankton losses may affect cloud patterns and global climate.

As increased levels of UV radiation reach the lower atmosphere, it is anticipated that the reactivity of chemicals such as ground-level ozone, hydrogen peroxide, and acids will increase. Such changes could exacerbate human health problems and could mean more difficulty and expense in achieving current air pollution reduction goals (Government of Canada, 1996). As we saw at the outset of this chapter, ozone depletion also results in an increase in UV radiation reaching the earth: this is the subject of the following section.

Environment Canada maintains excellent Web sites, Stratospheric Ozone and State of the Ozone Layer over Canada, listed in the Additional Information Sources section of this chapter.

Ultraviolet Radiation and Its Impacts

When it is sufficiently intense, UV radiation can break stable chemical bonds and damage deoxyribonucleic acid (DNA), the genetic coding material that all living things carry in their cells. Of the three wavelength regions of UV radiation, the longest and least powerful wavelengths are known as UV-A (between 320 and 400 nanometres; 1 nanometre is 1 millionth of a millimetre). These wave-

lengths pass through the atmosphere almost as easily as visible light and are relatively harmless to most organisms within the normal range of intensity. In contrast, UV-C rays are the shortest (between 200 and 280 nanometres) and most biologically harmful, but they are absorbed almost completely in the upper atmosphere and do not reach Earth's surface.

A small proportion of the more powerful middle wavelengths (UV-B, between 280 and 320 nanometres) reaches the Earth's surface and may cause biological damage to people, plants, and animals. Note that UV-B radiation always has affected people, but, as Canadians increasingly spend more time outdoors (and expose more of their skin while doing so), the effects on human health have become more prevalent. And, as more UV-B reaches Earth as a result of ozone depletion, it may compound the effects of our sunworshipping habits.

How much UV radiation reaches the Earth's surface depends on the angle of the sun, the presence of atmospheric aerosols, the amount and type of cloud, and the thickness of the ozone layer. Ozone, because it absorbs almost all of the most harmful UV-C and most UV-B radiation, is one of the most important determinants of how much UV-B radiation reaches the Earth. It has been calculated that, under clear skies in the mid-latitudes, every 1 percent decrease in the thickness of the stratospheric ozone layer results in an increase in UV-B radiation of about 1.1 to 1.4 percent (McElroy, Kerr, McArthur & Wardle, 1994).

Anticipated UV-B radiation increases during the next decade (at least) will continue to affect public health, and will impact on terrestrial, freshwater, and marine plants; animals; agricultural crops and livestock; forests; freshwater resources; fisheries; and building materials. While there are widely varying responses from species to species and within different varieties of a single species, many plants will show reduced photosynthesis and growth. For instance, important global food supply crops such as wheat, rice, barley, peas, oats, sweet corn, and soybeans are particularly sensitive to UV-B radiation, as are tomatoes, cucumbers, broccoli, cauliflower, and carrots.

For every 1-percent increase in UV-B radiation reaching the Earth, food production could drop by 1 percent (Environment Canada, 1997e). Both British Columbia and Ontario vegetable production regions could be affected as UV-B disrupts the way plants use nitrogen. Some livestock species would require protective shelters to avoid reduction in their productivity; other livestock, such as free-range species, would require more land to compensate for the reduced productivity of the plants on which they graze.

While only a few species of Canadian trees have been tested for UV-B sensitivity, increased radiation adversely affected over 45 percent of them, particularly young seedlings. This has important implications for the ability of sensitive replacement species to survive in clear-cut logged areas, and means that if young trees fail to survive, forest sector productivity will decline. Practices such as selective cutting (see Chapter 9) could help reduce potential losses.

Since more than 30 percent of the world's animal protein for human consumption comes from the sea, possible losses caused by ozone depletion would further stress many commercial fish species. Phytoplankton losses, described below, could disrupt fresh- and saltwater food chains and lead to a species shift in Canadian waters. In turn, loss of biodiversity could result in reduced fish yields for sport and commercial fisheries. Even farmed fish raised in shallow ponds with no shade provided could suffer cataracts and lesions (Environment Canada, 1997e).

Organisms such as phytoplankton and zooplankton, living in the surface layers of lakes and oceans, may provide clear evidence of UV radiation damage related to ozone depletion because of their relatively direct exposure to the sun. The blooms of Antarctic phytoplankton, for instance, begin to develop just as ozone thinning is occurring; a 1990 estimate suggested that phytoplankton productivity was 6 to 12 percent lower within the zone of ozone depletion than beyond it (Prézelin, Boucher & Schofield, 1994). Increased UV-B intensity also may be contributing to global declines in frog and toad populations (see Chapter 12). These examples illustrate the complexity of determining increased UV radiation impacts on natural populations, and of predicting its effects on different ecosystems.

CLIMATE CHANGE

Greenhouse Gases and Climate

Carbon dioxide (CO_2), methane (CH_4), ozone (O_3), nitrous oxide (N_2), and water vapour are the five most important greenhouse gases. These gases perform ecologically critical functions including regulation of air temperature. Serious consequences for the stability of ecosystems and the well-being of human societies can arise from even small changes in the atmospheric concentrations of these gases. Furthermore, since climate is a result of the exchanges of energy and moisture within the Earth–ocean–atmosphere system, anything that alters the distribution of energy within the system or the amount of energy entering or leaving the Earth's atmosphere inevitably changes the planet's climate.

This simple fact identifies the importance of greenhouse gases but also belies the complexity of greenhouse warming. Although some parts of our understanding about the changing atmosphere are theoretical or uncertain (see Hare, 1995), the reality is that atmospheric changes carry immense potential consequences for life and life-support systems on Earth. As such, climate change issues claim our immediate attention and action.

If you refer back to Figure 3–3, you will remember that the Earth–ocean–atmosphere system is warmed by absorption of shortwave radiation from the sun and cooled when longwave infrared radiation is released back toward space. The role greenhouse gases play in this energy exchange is a critical one; they retard the loss of heat from Earth to space, raising the temperature of the Earth's surface and surrounding air. By keeping the planet's mean surface temperature at about 15°C (about 33°C warmer than it would be otherwise), this natural greenhouse effect makes the difference between a living and a lifeless planet (Government of Canada, 1996).

Greenhouse gases enter the atmosphere through several natural processes. Water vapour, for example, enters the atmosphere via evaporation and transpiration processes. Ozone is produced through various chemical reactions within the atmosphere, and carbon dioxide comes mainly from plant and animal respiration, combustion, and the decay of organic matter in soils. Most of the naturally occurring methane is produced from the decay of organic matter in wetlands, while most of the naturally produced nitrous oxide enters the atmosphere from chemical reactions in soil.

Eventually, natural processes also remove greenhouse gases from the atmosphere. When carbon dioxide is absorbed into the oceans, or when forests and agricultural crops remove carbon dioxide as they grow, or when water vapour returns to the Earth as precipitation, these gases are said to have reached their destinations or "sinks." When sources and sinks are in balance, atmospheric concentrations of greenhouse gases remain stable, but if the balance is upset, concentrations will change until a new balance is reached.

Assuming all other factors remain constant, when greenhouse gas concentrations change, temperatures at the Earth's surface also change. Evidence of this is found through analyses of ancient air bubbles trapped inside ice cores taken from the polar ice caps. These air bubbles revealed that greenhouse gases had an important role in the onset and decline of ice ages in the past (Government of Canada, 1996; Intergovernmental Panel on Climate Change, 1995).

Human Activities and the Greenhouse Effect

Since the Industrial Revolution began in 1750, concentrations of greenhouse gases have increased substantially. For instance, concentrations of carbon dioxide have increased by more than 25 percent, methane concentrations have more than doubled, and nitrous oxide concentrations have increased by nearly 13 percent. In addition, particularly since the 1970s, significant quantities of synthetic greenhouse gases (mainly CFCs and halons) have been added to the atmosphere for the first time. However, there are many uncertainties in our understanding of linkages and flows, and sources and sinks, of all these gases.

Carbon Dioxide Carbon dioxide releases constitute the largest of all greenhouse gas emissions resulting from human activities. Between 1980 and 1989, human activities resulted in annual releases of an estimated 7.1 billion tonnes of carbon into the atmosphere. An average of 5.5 million tonnes came from burning fossil fuels, cement production contributed a small amount, and most of the remaining 1.6 billion tonnes was attributed to the clearing and burning of tropical forests. Although these amounts may seem small when compared with the 150 billion tonnes of carbon released to and removed from the atmosphere each year by natural sources and sinks, they have been sufficient to disrupt the natural balance between carbon sources and carbon sinks.

Part of the evidence supporting the contention that human activities have caused the increase in atmospheric concentrations of CO_2 is the timing of the increases—about 60 percent of the increase in CO_2 has occurred since 1958, when fossil fuels powered a rapid growth in the postwar global economy (Figure 5–4). Since burning 1 kilogram of pure carbon releases 3.6 kilograms of CO_2, it is not difficult to appreciate why CO_2 levels have increased rapidly. Another part of the evidence is that analyses of Antarctic ice cores show present concentrations of CO_2 are higher than any known natural values in recent geological history. Still another piece of evidence comes from carbon isotopes in the atmosphere; changes in their relative mix point to an increase in carbon isotopes that originate from burning fossil fuels and forests (Intergovernmental Panel on Climate Change, 1995).

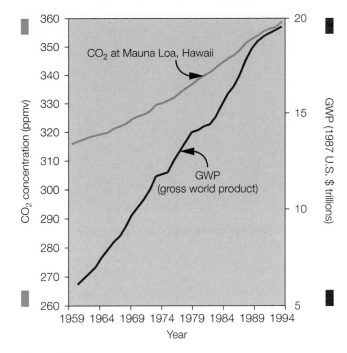

Figure 5–4

Atmospheric concentration of carbon dioxide since 1959, and gross world product since 1960

NOTE: Measurements of CO_2 are taken at Mauna Loa Observatory, HI, far from urban areas and the direct effects of human and other biological activity (where CO_2 levels would be elevated because of factories, power plants, and motor vehicles).

SOURCE: Government of Canada. (1996). *The state of Canada's environment—1996*. Ottawa: Supply and Services Canada. Figure 15.3.

At the beginning of the Industrial Revolution, the concentration of CO_2 in the atmosphere was about 280 parts per million (a level that appears to have been constant for the preceding 700 years). In 1994, the average atmospheric CO_2 concentration reached 358 parts per million (Hengeveld, 1997), and the rate of increase is about 0.5 percent annually. While this seems small, if CO_2 continues to grow at this rate, there could be a doubling of the concentration in about 140 years (this is known as *enhanced greenhouse effect*).

Methane It is estimated that natural sources (such as wetlands, termites, and oceans) discharge 160 million tonnes of methane annually. Human-related methane emissions (of between 300 and 450 million tonnes annually) are more than double the amount of natural emissions. Among the largest anthropogenic sources of methane are rice paddies (methane is released by anaerobic activity in flooded rice lands), livestock-related enteric fermentation (which occurs in the digestive tracts of cattle and sheep), and biomass burning. Fossil fuel production (natural gas, coal) constitutes another important

Rice paddies and livestock are major human-related sources of methane gas emissions. Canada contributes about one percent of the world's methane to global warming.

source of methane emissions (Intergovernmental Panel on Climate Change, 1995; Rodhe, 1990).

Methane emissions had been increasing at a rate of about one percent per year until 1991. For reasons that are unknown, but possibly related to control of leaks in Russian natural gas systems (Kerr, 1994), or reduced biomass burning in the southern hemisphere (Hengeveld, 1997), the increase stopped in 1991 and 1992.

Nitrous Oxide Although the total amounts of natural and anthropogenic emissions of nitrous oxide are unclear, estimates suggest that up to 40 percent are human related, derived principally through cultivated soils, landfill sites, and other industrial sources (Government of Canada, 1996; Hengeveld, 1997). Nitrous oxides may contribute up to 5 percent of the anthropogenic greenhouse effect.

Chlorofluorocarbons As noted earlier in this chapter, because they are synthetic and their production is well documented, estimates of CFC and halon emissions are much more precise. While these chemicals will continue to enter the atmosphere for some time after their production has stopped, CFC emissions are declining because of production phase-outs established through the 1987 Montreal Protocol on Substances that Deplete the Ozone Layer (and later amendments).

Some fluorine compounds, known as perfluorocarbons (PFCs), are byproducts of aluminum and magnesium smelting. These gases are present in the atmosphere at concentrations in the low parts per trillion, but because they absorb radiation in a highly efficient manner, and have molecular life times of thousands of years, they contribute to the additional warming created by increased concentrations of greenhouse gases.

The ultimate impact of higher concentrations of greenhouse gases on climate depends on their radiative characteristics (types and amounts of energy they absorb) and their residence time in the atmosphere. Carbon

dioxide, the least efficient absorber of infrared radiation, has had the greatest climatic impact of all the human-related greenhouse gases, not only because emissions of CO_2 are much greater than those of other gases, but also because additional quantities of CO_2 may take from 50 to 200 years to return to sinks in the oceans and forests.

In contrast, methane absorbs 15 to 27 times as much infrared radiation over a 100-year time frame as does CO_2, but methane has a much smaller, direct impact on global warming. This is because methane emissions are about 20 times smaller than CO_2 emissions and methane remains in the atmosphere for between 9 and 15 years only. Nitrous oxide emissions are about 1000 times lower than carbon dioxide emissions, but nitrous oxide absorbs 310 times as much infrared radiation as an equal mass of CO_2 over a 100-year time frame and remains in the atmosphere for 120 years (Government of Canada, 1996). CFCs and PFCs are the most powerful greenhouse gases: over a 100-year time frame, a tonne of CFC-12 (with an estimated atmospheric lifetime of 102 years) would absorb 8500 times as much infrared radiation as a tonne of CO_2.

When we take absorptive capacity, atmospheric lifetime, and other factors into consideration, carbon dioxide has been estimated to account for 64 percent of the additional greenhouse warming that has occurred since preindustrial times, methane for 19 percent, nitrous oxide for 6 percent, and CFCs and halons for 11 percent (Shine, Fouquart, Ramaswamy, Solomon & Srinivasan, 1995). We may find, as we attempt to reduce CO_2 emissions and find substitutes for other greenhouse gases, that rates of increase of emissions other than CO_2 may change, too, requiring different responses and adaptations from us.

Predicting Climate Change

In their efforts to analyze climatic effects of increasing concentrations of greenhouse and other gases in our atmosphere, scientists are using computer models to predict future climates. These models are based on the physical laws that govern behaviour of the earth–ocean–atmosphere system, and scientists use mathematical equations describing these laws to conduct experiments on the climate system that would be impossible (or unwise) to carry out in the real world. For instance, much of our understanding of potential climatic impacts of greenhouse warming comes from experiments on enhanced greenhouse or "doubled carbon dioxide" climates (where the models simulate the climate that results when CO_2 concentrations are about 560 parts per million by volume, or twice the preindustrial concentration).

The most elaborate of these models are the general circulation models (GCMs). In three dimensions and over time, these models simulate the workings and interactions of the sun, atmosphere, oceans, land surfaces, soils, vegetation, and ice. Like any model, these GCMs have their strengths and limitations; they can represent some physical processes with precision but others with much less accuracy. So far, the models have been unable to predict realistically the effects of global changes in climate on the subcontinental and regional characteristics of future climate and weather (Hengeveld, 1997). However, the various models agree that, with a doubling of CO_2 over preindustrial levels, several major changes are likely (Table 5–2).

An example of the simplified output of a GCM for Canada illustrates some of the findings, such as temperatures in southern regions nearly 5°C warmer throughout the year and in northern regions as much as 8 to 12°C warmer in winter (Figure 5–5). This particular model also

indicated seasonal increases in water supply for the West Coast, Yukon, and much of the Arctic, but a decrease of more than 20 percent in soil moisture of the rich farmlands of the south-central region. The implications for farmers if Canada's bread basket experiences further drying are serious; moving agricultural activity northward

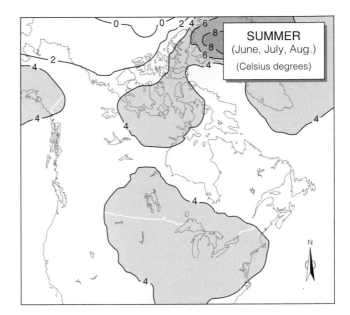

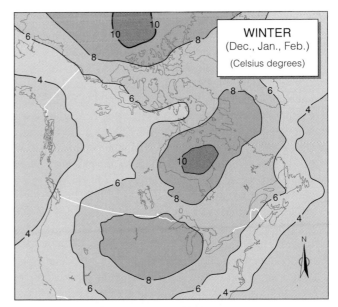

Figure 5–5

A simplified general circulation model for Canada: Temperature projections for winter and summer seasons (doubled carbon dioxide concentrations)

NOTE: For a doubling of CO_2 concentrations, the GCM projects an increase of 3.5°C in the Earth's average temperature but shows more substantial warming over much of Canada, particularly in winter.

SOURCE: Environment Canada. (1994). *Modelling the global climate system*. Ottawa: Atmospheric Environment Service, p. 12.

TABLE 5 – 2
GENERAL CIRCULATION MODELS AND PREDICTED CLIMATIC CHANGES

With a doubling of carbon dioxide over preindustrial levels:

- average global surface temperature eventually would increase by 1.5 to 4.5°C (best estimates suggest about 2.5°C)

- warming would not be distributed uniformly over the globe: greatest warming would occur in higher latitudes in winter and the least in the tropics; continental interiors would warm more than the oceans

- the stratosphere would become cooler

- average global precipitation and evaporation would increase by 3 to 15 percent—most models predict that soil moisture in northern mid-latitudes would decrease during summer in the continental interiors

- sea ice cover and seasonal snow cover in the northern hemisphere would decrease

- globally, sea level would rise at an increasing rate

SOURCE: Government of Canada. (1996). *The state of Canada's environment—1996*. Ottawa: Supply and Services Canada. Chapter 15.

is not a fully satisfactory alternative as northern soils are less fertile than those used currently.

The Intergovernmental Panel on Climate Change (IPCC) is a group of leading scientists from over 30 countries, organized jointly by the World Meteorological Organization and the United Nations Environment Programme in 1988, to study global climate change. Faced with these kinds of results from GCMs, the IPCC predicted that if actions were not taken to stabilize or reduce emissions of greenhouse gases, global mean surface air temperatures would increase during the next century by between 0.1°C and 0.5°C per decade, the fastest rate of temperature change in human history (Intergovernmental Panel on Climate Change, 1996).

Impacts of an Enhanced Greenhouse Effect

Although many Canadians might relish the prospect of a warmer climate in this high-latitude country—especially warmer winters—the kinds of climate changes predicted by global circulation models might not necessarily be positive ones. For instance, average global temperatures would be higher than at any time during the past 100 000 years, and climatic changes could occur very quickly, providing ecosystems with little time to adapt to the new conditions and humans with little time to develop measures to counter such changes.

The impacts that an enhanced greenhouse effect would have on human societies and natural ecosystems depend on how regional climates respond. In turn, regional climate responses will depend not only on how local factors such as evaporation and soil moisture change, but also on how the circulation patterns of the oceans and the atmosphere evolve. Changing oceanic and atmospheric circulation patterns would cause some regions to warm dramatically, others to warm only moderately, and still others (possibly the North Atlantic region off the coast of Labrador) to cool. As storm tracks could shift at the same time, some areas would receive more precipitation and others less.

With an enhanced greenhouse effect, changes in the size or frequency of extreme events such as heat waves, droughts, hurricanes, and thunderstorms could occur. Small changes in climate variability can produce large changes in the frequency of extreme events. For example, a general warming would tend to lead to an increase in the number of days with extremely high temperatures during summer and a decrease in the number of days with extremely low temperatures in winter. Some climate models suggest precipitation will increase in intensity in some areas, leading to the possibility of more extreme precipitation events, while other areas could experience more frequent or severe drought (Intergovernmental Panel on Climate Change, 1996).

Studies of the impacts of climate change on recreation in Nahanni National Park Reserve (Staple & Wall, 1996), on the Bathurst caribou herd (Brotton & Wall,

It is predicted that global warming will cause greater climatic variability, damaging crops through more severe droughts and more intensive precipitation.

1997), and on the Mackenzie Basin (Cohen, 1995) are among efforts being made to understand the economic, social, and environmental effects of climate change. Table 5–3 presents a summary of the range of possible impacts of an enhanced greenhouse effect (and also highlights the uncertainty associated with these changes).

Indicators and Effects of Climate Change

Atmospheric scientists are confident that human activities are increasing greenhouse gas concentrations and that this will affect future climate. Their evidence of climate change and the role of greenhouse gases in that change comes from several sources, including global weather and ocean temperature records from the past century. When these temperature records from land areas and oceans are analyzed, they suggest that the average air temperatures over land areas have increased by slightly more than 0.5°C and average sea surface temperatures have increased by about 0.4°C (Folland & Parker, 1995). As the climate models predicted, this warming has been stronger in the middle and high latitudes than in the

TABLE 5-3

SELECTED IMPACTS OF AN ENHANCED GREENHOUSE EFFECT

Area of Change	Description or Comment
Air temperature	• Average global temperatures would be higher than at any time in past 100 000 years. • Temperature changes could occur very quickly, allowing little time to adapt to new conditions or develop countermeasures to slow or reverse the course of events.
Sea-level rise	• Increase in average global temperature will increase the rate at which global sea level is rising (because seawater expands when warmed). • An influx of fresh water from melting glacial ice also would increase ocean volume. • Mean sea level could rise at a rate of 1 to 11 centimetres per decade over the next century. • Since 25 percent of the world's population lives in coastal areas, such increases would expose coastal communities to more frequent, damaging storms and flooding; salination of freshwater supplies; and the need to relocate sewer outfalls and freshwater intakes, as well as to construct or extend defensive barriers. Canada's east coast and Fraser Delta, where land is subsiding, would experience aggravated flooding. • In some coastal areas of central Canada (Hudson Bay) and Scandinavia, where postglacial rebound is occurring, only minimal (if any) sea-level rise would occur.
Natural ecosystems	• Boundaries of natural ecosystems would change. • Species trapped outside their normal climatic range would be forced to adapt or migrate in order to survive.
Forests	• Productivity of some forests would increase, and others would be vulnerable. • Increased drought would result in increased loss of forests to wild fires. • Because trees migrate through a slow process of spreading seeds, rapid climate changes could mean large areas of forest dieback before new species could advance. With dieback, more CO_2 would be released and enhance the cycle of warming, dryness, fire, and further release of CO_2. • Trees would be exposed to new insect pests and diseases.
Agriculture	• Agriculture would face similar problems to those in natural ecosystems but would be less vulnerable because of human interventions in plant adaptation. • Uneven distribution of global precipitation would mean major droughts could be problematic in many areas, particularly the continental interiors in the northern hemisphere. • Because plants become more efficient at capturing and using moisture when carbon dioxide concentrations increase (called carbon dioxide fertilization), yields of some food crops would increase, although corn, sugarcane, and some other plants do not respond to carbon dioxide fertilization; weeds would experience a similar positive response. (Note: CO_2 fertilization applies when plants are receiving adequate moisture, temperatures, and nutrients, and are not limited by pests or diseases.) • Crop selection would be key to successful adaptation; traditional crops might be abandoned in favour of new varieties more suited to new climatic conditions. • In Canada, warmer temperatures would increase the area of land with appropriate climatic conditions for agriculture, but much of this land would have soils only marginally suited to agriculture.
Other economic activities	• Hydroelectric power generation, recreational activities such as skiing, and transportation (shipping and snow removal) would all be affected by changes in the precipitation regime. • In the Canadian Arctic and subarctic, land transportation would be affected adversely by decay of permafrost and shorter winter roads season. • Aboriginal and traditional hunting patterns would be disrupted. • Different cooling and heating costs would be experienced under different climate change conditions.

TABLE 5-3
(CONTINUED)

Area of Change	Description or Comment
Human health	• Tropical diseases and insect pests might extend their range into the mid-latitudes; in southern Canada, malaria could become a concern. • Warmer weather would intensify formation of ground-level ozone in smog.

SOURCE: Government of Canada. (1996). *The state of Canada's environment—1996*. Ottawa: Supply and Services Canada. Chapter 15.

tropics, and strongest in the continental interiors of the northern hemisphere. In Canada, temperature records show the northwestern interior has warmed by as much as 1.8°C while the eastern Arctic has cooled over the past 50 years (Government of Canada, 1996). The effects of these predicted temperature changes, as well as other climate change effects, are illustrated in Figure 5–6.

Long-term temperature data is scarce for deep ocean waters, but a cooling of over 1°C in the Labrador Sea between the early 1970s and 1990 has been observed (Lazier, 1996). While this may seem to be a small change, it is important to note that the top three metres of the ocean store as much heat as the entire atmosphere. Small changes in heat storage in the oceans can affect global climate (as well as ecosystems) significantly.

Other sources of evidence of widespread warming are the following: long-term sea-level records as well as recent satellite measurements that show increases in sea levels; the worldwide retreat (melting) of mountain glaciers during the past 100 years; a modest reduction in the percentage of land covered by snow in the northern hemisphere since the 1970s; and increased precipitation in the mid-latitudes of the northern hemisphere and throughout most of the southern hemisphere.

Even though most of these observations are consistent with the changes projected by the GCM experiments, they do not prove that an enhanced greenhouse effect is the cause. The reason they fail to do so is that since the end of the last ice age (10 000 years ago), the world's average surface temperature has varied over a range of almost 2°C from purely natural causes. Given this evidence, recent temperature changes could be the effect of natural fluctuations in the climate system.

Even in the absence of absolute proof, however, scientific consensus is that the correspondence between trends in climate of the past century, and their observed and modelled geographical distribution patterns, point toward a discernible human influence on global climate (Hengeveld, 1997; Intergovernmental Panel on Climate Change, 1996). If average global temperatures continue to rise a further 0.5 to 1.0°C beyond current values, the greenhouse warming hypothesis likely would be confirmed as it would be the only explanation that could reasonably account for such an increase (Kerr, 1995). In the meantime, the precautionary principle indicates that action should be taken to prevent atmospheric deterioration. Later in the chapter we review some international and national efforts taken to deal with atmospheric issues.

Global warming has resulted in the retreat of Angel Glacier in Jasper National Park. Compare the 1935 photo (left) with the 1991 photo and notice how much the "wings" and "trunk" of the glacier have melted.

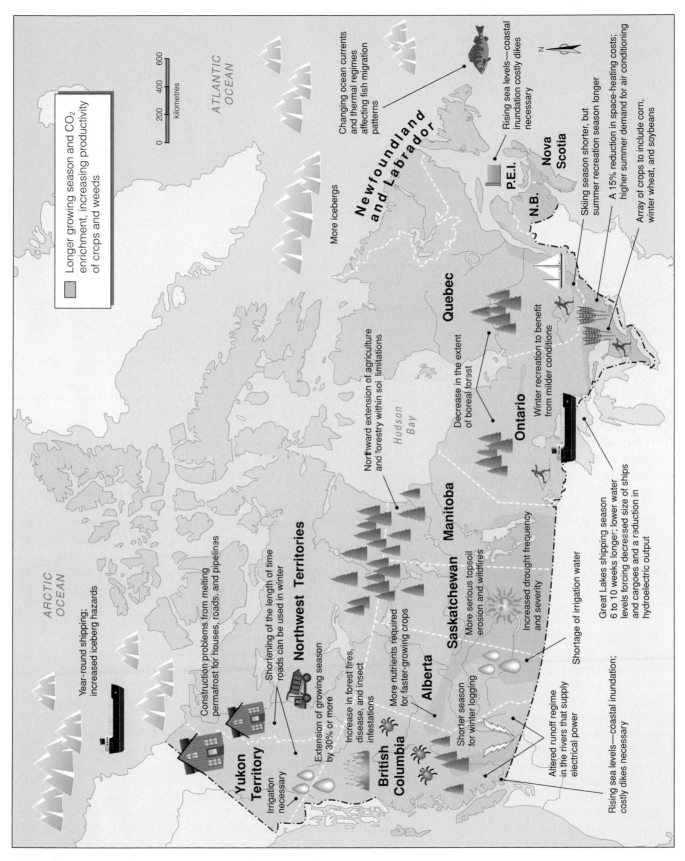

Figure 5–6

Effects of climate change

SOURCE: Environment Canada, Atmospheric Environment Services. (1995). *Global climate change fact sheet.* Ottawa.

(Further information on climate change is available on the Internet; refer to Environment Canada's 1996 National Environmental Indicator Series on climate change, available at the Green Lane Web site listed in the Additional Information Sources section of this chapter.)

Some Other Influences on Climate

Other human-related factors that affect global warming include sulphates that form in the atmosphere when sulphur dioxide and other sulphurous gases combine with oxygen. Sulphur emissions from human sources (mostly burning fossil fuels) have increased since the 1860s from less than 3 million tonnes annually to approximately 80 million tonnes in 1980. Generated principally in the industrialized regions of North America and Europe, and more recently in China, sulphur emissions are of concern because of their contribution to acid precipitation (see the acidic deposition section later in this chapter).

In conjunction with fine aerosols from the burning of forests, one of the direct effects of sulphates is to produce a cooling effect that may have moderated the warming from greenhouse gases (Taylor & Penner, 1994). Sulphate aerosols may promote cooler surface temperatures by providing condensation surfaces to aid cloud formation, thereby increasing reflection of solar radiation back to space (but this process is complex and not understood fully). Some regions that are within a few thousand kilometres downwind of industrialized areas actually show cooling as a result of the substantial effects sulphate aerosols have on incoming solar energy (Kerr, 1995).

Human-produced aerosols are not a practical solution to increased greenhouse gas concentrations, however, because the complexity of their effects and influence are not well understood. It is inappropriate to consider their climate effects as simple offsets to the much more uniform effects of greenhouse gases (Hengeveld, 1997). Also, aerosols are not a solution to greenhouse warming because of the costly effects that acid deposition incurs, as well as air quality impacts from burning fossil fuels.

For instance, in China, the world's number one producer and consumer of coal, acid precipitation (resulting from sulphur dioxide emissions from industrial and domestic use of coal) destroys hundreds of millions of dollars worth of crops and forest annually (Schoof, 1996). Even in Taiyuan, a city of three million people in the northern province of Shaanxi, where natural gas has replaced coal for most home heating, smog continues to be a human health hazard. Particulate levels, down to 540 micrograms from 1200 micrograms per cubic metre 10 years ago, remain at a level at least six times the maximum recommended by the World Health Organization (Schoof, 1996). While industrialized North American and European emitters continue to reduce their sulphur emissions, it is possible their reductions will be offset by increases in sulphur emissions from developing countries

Inadequate control of emissions from Beijing's Capitol Iron and Steel factory means residents contend with smog and other health hazards.

such as China, which relies on its large reserves of coal to meet its increasing energy demands.

El Niño and the Southern Oscillation   Global climate patterns also can be disrupted by the ocean–atmosphere system called El Niño and the Southern Oscillation (ENSO). The El Niño is the invasion of warm surface water from the western equatorial Pacific to the eastern equatorial region and along the coasts of Peru, Ecuador, and northern Chile. Normally along these coasts, the cold Peruvian current moves northward, and southerly winds blowing offshore promote the upwelling of cold, nutrient-rich water that supports large populations of fish, particularly anchovies.

Each year, around Christmas time, a warm current of nutrient-poor tropical water moves south, displacing the cold water. In most years, El Niño is not very warm and lasts perhaps as long as a month. However, about every three to seven years, this phenomenon becomes very strong, persisting for several months. The Japanese Meteorological Agency considers an El Niño to be underway when the tropical Pacific Ocean is a minimum 0.5°C above normal for at least six consecutive months (Nkemdirim & Budikova, 1996).

El Niño changes the sea surface temperature and causes the pressure and wind patterns to change and perhaps reverse. That is, pressure and wind at opposite ends of the South Pacific oscillate with El Niño; El Niño affects the atmosphere and global temperature by pumping heat energy into the atmosphere. What is strictly a local South American phenomenon is turned into an Earth event with global implications (Figure 5–7).

Along the Peruvian coast, major El Niños cause high mortality in fish and marine plant populations. In the tropics, El Niño events disrupt every aspect of the weather and impact physical and human environments through monsoons and droughts; crops fail, forests burn, terrestrial and marine habitats are compromised. In western North America and southern Canada, the northward extension of warm tropical waters provides greater than normal water vapour, which is associated with flooding in the west and mid-west and unseasonably warm, dry winters in the foothills of the Rockies and western prairies. Floods and droughts both negatively affect agricultural production (Nkemdirim & Budikova, 1996). Research on El Niño events is important to understanding the potential perturbations that affect global climate.

(For a review of recent developments relating to the science of climate change, see the Spring 1997 issue of *CO₂/Climate Report* newsletter, listed under Environment Canada [1997], and check the Web site for the Canadian Global Change Program, listed in the Additional Information sources section of this chapter.)

The Greenhouse Effect in the Future

The most powerful of the forces of change that have been acting on the Earth's climate system during the past 150 to 250 years are anthropogenic greenhouse gas emissions. At the end of 1993, for instance, average global carbon dioxide concentrations were about 28 percent above the preindustrial level. In order to evaluate the potential climate effects of equal emissions of each of the greenhouse gases, the concept of relative **Global Warming Potential** (GWP) has been developed to take into account the differing times that gases remain in the atmosphere. This index defines the warming effect due to an instantaneous release of one kilogram of a given greenhouse gas in today's atmosphere, relative to that of carbon dioxide (Intergovernmental Panel on Climate Change, 1990).

Table 5–4 illustrates the effect over 100 years of emissions of greenhouse gases relative to carbon dioxide. Although CO_2 is the least effective greenhouse gas per kilogram emitted, its contribution to global warming, which depends on the product of the GWP and the amount of gas emitted, is largest. Given a number of difficulties in

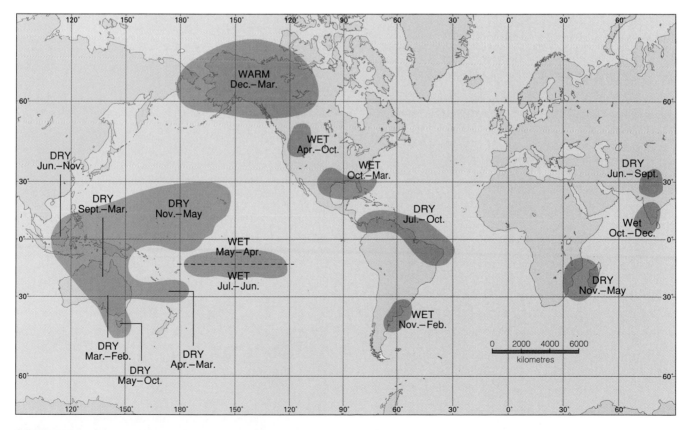

Figure 5–7

Spatial and seasonal distribution of precipitation anomalies associated with the El Niño–Southern Oscillation

SOURCE: Adapted from Nkemdirim, L., & Budikova, D. (1996). The El Niño–Southern Oscillation has a truly global impact: A preliminary report on the ENSO Project of the Commission on Climatology. *International Geographical Union Bulletin,* 46, p. 30. Reprinted by permission.

Greenhouse Gas	Global Warming Potentials	1990 Emissions (Tg)[a]	Relative Contribution Over 100 Years
carbon dioxide	1	26 000.00+	61.0%
methane	21	300.0	15.0%
nitrous oxide	310[b]	6.0	4.0%
hydrofluoro-carbons	140 to 11 700[b]	0.9	11.0%
eg., HCFC-22	1500	0.1	0.5%
perfluorocarbons	6500 to 9200[b]		
sulphurhexa-fluoride	23 900[b]		

NOTES: [a] Tg: 26 000 TG (teragrams) of carbon dioxide = 7000 Tg of carbon

[b] 1995 data

SOURCES: Hengeveld, H. (1997). 1994–95 in review: An assessment of new developments relevant to the science of climate change. CO_2/Climate Report, 97–1, p. 6.

Intergovernmental Panel on Climate Change. (1990). *Scientific assessment of climate change.* Geneva: World Meteorological Organization and United Nations Environment Programme, p. 12.

devising and calculating the values of GWPs, including inadequate inclusion of feedbacks such as changing atmospheric composition, these values should be considered estimates and subject to change. The GWPs, however, help us understand more about the significance of each greenhouse gas and where to direct remedial actions.

Clearly, future levels of greenhouse gas emissions will reflect the influence and interplay of factors such as population growth, economic growth, and deforestation rates on the one hand, and higher energy prices, improvements in energy efficiency, the availability of practical alternatives to fossil fuels, the development of policies and controls for regulating greenhouse gas emissions, and preserving reservoirs of carbon on the other hand (Government of Canada, 1996). Even if it were possible to hold carbon dioxide emissions at 1990 levels, given current trends, atmospheric concentrations would continue to rise to a level about 60 percent higher than preindustrial levels by 2050 (450 parts per million by volume), and about 85 percent higher by 2100 (520 parts per million by volume) (Intergovernmental Panel on Climate Change, 1995).

These trends suggest that, without significant progress in controlling emissions, a doubled carbon dioxide atmosphere appears inevitable. With about 90 million people being added to the world population every year, and potential growth in the economies of India and China (fuelled largely by coal), the world community must be vigilant in controlling the upward pressure on greenhouse gas emissions. At the same time, there needs to be full and careful consideration of social, economic, and environmental dimensions of this issue.

As well, uncertainties exist regarding the future size and behaviour of some of the natural sinks that remove greenhouse gases from the atmosphere. There are concerns about the ability of oceans and terrestrial ecosystems to continue to absorb nearly half the carbon dioxide emitted by human activities. Climate change could be affected by unexpected feedbacks as well. For instance,

As the top producer and consumer of coal in the world, China experiences high levels of acid precipitation, smog, and particulate pollution.

the polar regions are estimated to have very large quantities of methane locked away in frozen hydrates. If large areas of permafrost were to thaw, some of this gas would be released and could result in a marked intensification of the greenhouse effect (Bubier, Moore & Bellisario, 1995; Government of Canada, 1996).

OTHER ATMOSPHERIC CHANGES

Numerous human activities, including the burning of fossil fuels for transportation, heat, and other energy needs, smelting and refining of metals, pulp and paper processing, and pesticide and fertilizer applications in agricultural operations, introduce both gaseous and particulate contaminants into the air. Whether they are common or more exotic substances, the atmosphere can transport these contaminants long distances from their place of origin. No part of Canada is immune to atmospheric contamination.

Acidic Deposition

In the late 1970s and during the 1980s, acid rain became a very worrisome environmental issue for a great many Canadians. As early as the 1950s, scientists had detected abnormal acidity in precipitation and in the waters of Nova Scotia lakes and, in the 1960s, severe losses among fish populations in acidified lakes southwest of Sudbury had

been noted. In 1976, prompted by Canadian and international research findings, Environment Canada established a scientific program to study the occurrence and effects of long-range transport of airborne pollutants (LRTAP).

Scientists reported that meteorological conditions in Canada were conducive to long-distance transport of acidic pollutants and that sensitive soils, waters, fish, and forests were susceptible to damage. Long-term research by David Schindler and other scientists at the Experimental Lakes Area in northwestern Ontario was instrumental in demonstrating convincingly that acid rain killed trout at acidic levels that (American) politicians had said were harmless. The immediacy of the issue, and realization that acid rain could affect everyone, helped ensure that scientists, the media, legislators, environmentalists, and the general public made acid rain a major focus.

What Is Acid Rain? Acid rain occurs when pollutants such as sulphur dioxide (SO_2) and nitrogen oxides (NO_x) are converted chemically to sulphuric acid and nitric acid in the atmosphere, transported, and eventually deposited. Since diluted forms of these acids fall to Earth as rain, hail, drizzle, freezing rain, or snow (wet deposition), or are deposited as acid gas or dust (dry deposition), they are referred to as *acidic deposition.*

The strength of an acid is described using the logarithmic pH scale, where 0 is highly acidic, 7 is neutral, and 14 is basic or alkaline (Figure 5–8). On this scale, normal rain has a pH value between 5.6 and 5.0, and acid rain is

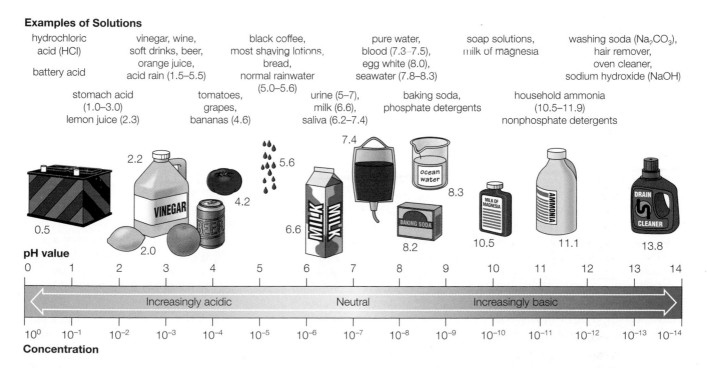

Examples of Solutions

| hydrochloric acid (HCl) | vinegar, wine, soft drinks, beer, orange juice, acid rain (1.5–5.5) | black coffee, most shaving lotions, bread, normal rainwater (5.0–5.6) | pure water, blood (7.3–7.5), egg white (8.0), seawater (7.8–8.3) | soap solutions, milk of magnesia | washing soda (Na_2CO_3), hair remover, oven cleaner, sodium hydroxide (NaOH) |

| battery acid | | | | | |

stomach acid (1.0–3.0) lemon juice (2.3)   tomatoes, grapes, bananas (4.6)   urine (5–7), milk (6.6), saliva (6.2–7.4)   baking soda, phosphate detergents   household ammonia (10.5–11.9) nonphosphate detergents

Figure 5–8

The pH scale

NOTE: Values shown are approximate.

precipitation that has a pH below 5.6. Because the pH scale is logarithmic, a pH value of 3 is 10 times more acidic than a pH value of 4, and 100 times more acidic than a pH value of 5. Much of the precipitation that falls over eastern North America and Europe can be 10 to 100 times more acidic than natural rainfall.

Sources of Acidic Pollutants More than 90 percent of the SO_2 and NO_x emissions occurring in eastern North America are from human activities. In 1994, 50 percent of the total eastern Canadian SO_2 came from the smelting or refining of sulphur-bearing metal ores and 20 percent from the burning of fossil fuels for energy. In contrast, in 1993 in the United States, about 72 percent of SO_2 emissions came from coal- or oil-fired electrical generating stations. In Canada in 1990, 35 percent of NO_x pollutants were formed during the burning of fossil fuels for on-road transportation, 23 percent in industrial processes, 12 percent in power generation, and the remaining 30 percent from various other sources (Environment Canada, 1996b). In 1980, which has served as the reference year for tracking emissions, SO_2 emissions were estimated to be 4.6 million tonnes in Canada, and 24 million tonnes in the United States, while emissions of NO_x were 1.8 million tonnes in Canada and 20 million tonnes in the United States.

Acid rain is not confined to eastern Canada, but is continental in distribution. A variety of point-source emissions of acidic pollutants associated with local smelters, hydrothermal plants, pulp and paper mills, and oil-and-gas processing facilities occur in the prairies, for example, and southwestern British Columbia is exposed to point sources of local and foreign origin. Also, in spite of the lack of any significant emission sources, the Yukon and Northwest Territories are exposed to acid deposition originating in Eurasian and eastern North American locations.

As the media and public concern about acid rain increased through the 1960s and 1970s, and governments responded with new emission standards, power plants, smelters, and industries began using smokestacks up to 300 metres high. These stacks enabled users to reduce local concentrations of air pollutants, and to meet government standards without adding expensive air pollution control devices. Once released into the atmosphere, however, acidic pollutants could be carried up to 1000 kilometres by prevailing wind and weather systems, across national and international borders, before being deposited.

Downwind of these tall stacks, regional pollution levels began to rise. In eastern North America, prevailing winds push pollutants to the northwest and northeast; through computer modelling, it was estimated that more than 50 percent of the acid rain in eastern Canada came from American sources, mainly in Ohio, Indiana, Pennsylvania, Illinois, Missouri, West Virginia, and Tennessee. Until the Clean Air Act of 1990 called for a significant reduction in American emissions of SO_2 and a modest

reduction of NO_x by the year 2000 (and comparable reductions in Canadian emissions), the large flow of acid deposition from the United States to Canada was the source of political tension between these two countries during the 1980s (see McMillan, 1991).

Throughout this period, environmental groups did a great deal to educate the media and the public about acid rain (and other pollution issues) and to encourage politicians to act against it. While political lobbying about acid rain was unsuccessful during President Reagan's administration, it did help achieve significant acid rain amendments to the 1990 American Clean Air Act during the Bush administration.

Effects of Acidic Deposition In addition to exposure to emissions from thermal generating stations in the United States, areas in the southern Canadian Shield, southern Nova Scotia and New Brunswick, and much of Newfoundland have been exposed to acidic deposition from smelters in Manitoba, Ontario, and Quebec. Because much of the region has little ability to buffer or neutralize acidic pollutants (due to thin, coarsely textured soils and granitic bedrock), many of the more than 700 000 lakes are expected to continue to lose populations of fish and other freshwater species. For example, salmon populations in 31 Nova Scotia rivers have been lost or depleted because acidic precipitation has resulted in the loss of one-third of available Atlantic salmon habitat (Government of Canada, 1996). (See Table 5–5 for an overview of acid deposition effects.)

About 43 percent of Canada's land area is highly sensitive to acid precipitation (Figure 5–9). Not only are bodies of fresh water and aquatic life affected by acid precipitation, but other species such as trees can be impacted also. In eastern Canadian forests, for example, 96 percent of the land with high capability for forestry is subject to sulphate deposition in excess of the target of 20 kilograms per hectare annually (although it should be noted that the area receiving 20 kilograms per hectare declined by nearly 59 percent from 1980 to 1993). White birch in southeastern New Brunswick have died or deteriorated as a result of acid fog, as have white birch stands on the shores of Lake Superior (where acid fog occurs frequently) and in the Bay of Fundy region. (For further examples of recent research on the links between acidic deposition, climate change, and ozone depletion, see the articles by Likens, Driscoll & Buso [1996] and Yan, Keller, Scully, Lean & Dillon [1996] listed in the Additional Information Sources section of this chapter.)

Between 1985 and 1987, a survey of more than 2 million hectares of sugar maple stands in Quebec revealed that 3 percent of the area was severely damaged, 47 percent showed moderate damage, and the remaining 50 percent had marginal symptoms of acidic deposition. Canada's Acid Rain National Early Warning System (ARNEWS) has been assessing and monitoring forest health at 150 sites

TABLE 5–5
EFFECTS OF ACIDIC DEPOSITION

Aspect Affected	Nature of Effects
Aquatic ecosystems	• Interactions between living organisms and the chemistry of aquatic habitats are extremely complex; as one species changes in response to acidification, the entire ecosystem is likely affected through predator–prey relationships of the food web.
	• As water pH approaches 6.0, crustaceans, insects, and some plankton species begin to disappear.
	• As pH approaches 5.0, major plankton community changes occur; less desirable species of mosses and plankton may invade, and progressive loss of some fish populations is likely (most highly valued species generally are least tolerant of acidity).
	• Below pH of 5.0, water is mostly devoid of fish; bottom is covered with undecayed material; nearshore areas may be dominated by mosses.
	• Terrestrial animals dependent on aquatic ecosystems also are affected; for waterfowl dependent on aquatic organisms for nourishment and nutrients, loss of food sources reduces habitat quality and reproductive success declines.
Terrestrial plant life	• Natural vegetation and crops are affected.
	• Protective waxy surfaces of leaves are affected, lowering disease resistance.
	• Plant germination and reproduction may be inhibited.
	• Soil weathering and removal of nutrients are accelerated.
	• Some toxic elements such as aluminum become more soluble; high aluminum concentrations in soil can prevent plant uptake and use of nutrients.
Animal life	• Effects are hard to assess.
	• As a result of pollution-induced alteration of habitat or food resources, acid deposition may cause population decline through stress (fewer available resources), and lower reproductive success.
Socioeconomic consequences	• Lower productivity in fisheries, forestry, and agriculture results in lower profits and fewer jobs for some of Canada's important industries.
	• Acid deposition causes accelerated corrosion, fracturing, and discoloration of buildings, structures, and monuments.
Human health	• We eat food, drink water, and breathe air that has come in contact with acid deposition.
	• Research shows there is a link between this pollution and respiratory problems in sensitive populations (see Box 5–2).
	• Acid deposition can increase the levels of toxic metals such as aluminum, copper, and mercury in untreated drinking-water supplies.

SOURCE: Environment Canada. (1997g). *A primer on environmental citizenship*. Ottawa.

across the country. Scientists at the Laurentian Forestry Centre, one of 32 ARNEWS sites in Quebec, have been able to assess damage to trees caused by insects, diseases, acid deposition, pollutants, and climatic extremes. They determined the effects of drought and soil freezing on the health of maples following the 1981 decline, for instance (Natural Resources Canada, 1997).

In addition to impacting sensitive ecosystems such as forests, acid deposition affects farmlands, wildlife, and freshwater species. For instance, high levels of acidic deposition may cause metals to leach into the water system from soils surrounding acid-sensitive bodies of fresh water. High acidity and elevated levels of metals such as aluminum can seriously impair the ability of water bodies to support aquatic life, and result in a decline in species diversity. Such effects impact negatively on related water uses such as sport fishing and recreation. In addition, there has been speculation about the role of aluminum in Alzheimer's disease.

Other human health responses to acidic pollutants may lead to aggravation of respiratory ailments such as bronchitis and asthma (Box 5–2). Since more than 80 percent of all Canadians live in areas with high acid deposition–pollution levels, susceptible individuals may experience

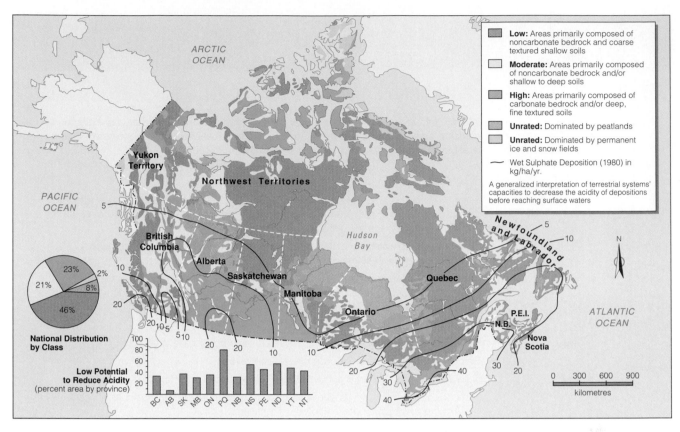

Figure 5–9

Potential of soils and bedrock to reduce acidity of atmospheric deposition in Canada

NOTE: Values shown are approximate.

SOURCE: Environment Canada, Inland Waters/Lands Directorate. (1988). *Environmental fact sheet: Acid rain: A national sensitivity assessment.*

increased respiratory problems. For example, research has shown a relationship between decreased lung function, increased cardiorespiratory mortality, and long-term exposure to acidic aerosols (Environment Canada, 1996b).

Acid precipitation causes about $1 billion damage in Canada annually (Environment Canada, 1997g). In addition to damage to lakes, fish habitat, and forests, some of Canada's heritage buildings, including the Parliament Buildings in Ottawa, are being eroded slowly by acidic precipitation.

Signs of Progress To deal with acid deposition impacts, a variety of control strategies were implemented, from international agreements to reduce and prevent long-range transboundary air pollution to extensive research and assessment programs on acidic deposition. Much of this assessment work was carried out during the 1980s by the federal–provincial Research and Monitoring Coordinating Committee. Monitoring of acid levels in more than 200 lakes in Ontario, Quebec, and the Atlantic region (between 1981 and 1994) revealed that 33 percent showed

Acid precipitation damages both natural and human environments, including important heritage structures such as statues and buildings.

PART 3:
RESOURCES FOR CANADA'S FUTURE

BOX 5-2
AIR QUALITY AND YOUR HEALTH

Acid air pollution, smog, and ground-level ozone—alone or in combination—can be major human health hazards in both urban and rural areas. Major health effects of various forms of air pollution are related to impacts on the human respiratory system. For instance, research indicates that ground-level ozone increases the susceptibility of asthmatics to common allergens such as dust mites and moulds that thrive in ordinary buildings. Similarly, people with respiratory problems may suffer more symptoms during periods of high ozone levels. In Ontario, more people are admitted to hospitals for respiratory problems when elevated levels of ozone and/or sulphates occur (however, it is not clear that these pollutants are the only ones responsible for higher hospital admissions; particulates and climate also may play a role).

Research is continuing into the effects of low-level, long-term exposure to ground-level ozone and the decreased ability of people's lungs to ward off disease, particularly if the inhaled ozone has penetrated deeply into the lungs and damaged some of the alveoli (individual air sacs in the lungs where the exchange of oxygen and carbon dioxide takes place). After years of exposure, these small lesions in the lungs of experimental animals have been shown to result in connective tissue damage (scar tissue formation deep in the lungs); the implications of this accelerated aging of lung tissue for humans are being investigated.

While the impacts of acid deposition on the environment have been discussed widely, the effects of acid air pollution on human health have tended to go unrecognized. The suspended acidic particles of compounds such as sulphuric and nitric acids are small enough to penetrate deeply into our lungs when we breathe. There they may cause such effects as coughing, congestion, and constriction of the airways; increased mucus production in the respiratory system; and reduced ability to clear foreign matter from the lungs. Recent studies show that more people are hospitalized with respiratory problems on days when acid air pollution is relatively high.

Health Canada has compared children living in Portage la Prairie, Manitoba, where acid air pollution is low, with children in Tillsonburg, Ontario, where the pollution level is relatively high. On average, the Ontario children had a two percent lower lung function and more chest colds, coughs, allergies, and stuffy noses than their prairie counterparts. While not dramatic, this measurable difference was followed up in studies of five Saskatchewan and five Ontario communities, where virtually the same results were found.

Other health problems derive from motor vehicle exhaust and combustion processes. Eye irritation, for example, is a result of two pollutants, peroxyacetyl nitrate and aldehydes. Particulates, originating from diesel exhaust and industrial activities, are of concern for human health for two reasons: they are small enough to be inhaled deeply into the lungs, and they act as a transport medium for compounds such as acids or metals that may adhere to them. Particulates and what is attached to them are known to cause short-term respiratory irritation.

People who exercise in a smoggy environment, such as running along a main thoroughfare during rush hour, may find a decrease in their performance due to carbon monoxide. Emitted from all motor vehicle exhaust, carbon monoxide binds with red blood cells much more readily than oxygen does. In this way, if some red blood cells bind with carbon monoxide, less oxygen may be available to the body's muscles and organs during the exposure to air pollution. Other groups at risk are pregnant women, infants, and people with cardiovascular or respiratory disease, including chronic angina. Smokers may be at particular risk because they have higher levels of carbon monoxide from smoking.

Indoor air quality can be affected as a result of energy conservation measures (more tightly sealed houses), and may present even greater health risks than does exposure to outdoor air pollution in our largest cities. As a result, attention has been given to the design and construction of "healthy houses" that substantially reduce human exposure to a wide range of indoor air pollutants. Healthy house construction involves planning to achieve energy efficiency and healthy indoor air quality through insulation, specialized windows, and landscaping that captures natural energy. Construction materials are recycled, environmentally benign, and nonallergenic where possible. Although tightly sealed for energy efficiency, a healthy house is well ventilated through efficient air-exchange systems.

In the work environment, a variety of illnesses are attributed to "sick buildings." People report such maladies as minor eye irritation and tearing, nasal congestion and headaches, lethargy, sore throats, and coughs. Often these symptoms may be associated with building renovations, including painting, plastering, and carpeting; when combined with inadequate ventilation, the emissions associated with these activities frequently have an adverse impact on employees and workers.

Little is known about how much pollution we actually are exposed to, and how much really affects our health. Increasingly, researchers have people carry pollution-measuring devices so that "personal exposure monitoring" can be undertaken and relationships between regional air pollution monitoring data and personal exposure levels established. Such data is expected to help in assessment and development of air quality guidelines to protect human health.

---

some improvement in acidity, acid levels were stable in 56 percent, and 11 percent (in the Atlantic region) were becoming worse (Environment Canada, 1996b).

In the Sudbury region, the majority of monitored lakes showed an improvement in acidity, due mainly to control of SO_2 emissions from Sudbury's nickel smelters. Long acknowledged as the largest industrial producer of SO_2 emissions in Canada, Inco Limited's plant at Copper Cliff released SO_2 at a rate of 5500 tonnes per day (2 million tonnes annually) in 1969. Since then, company initiatives and government emission control regulations reduced annual emissions to about 685 000 tonnes in 1992 and efforts were underway to reduce them further to 265 000 tonnes by 1994 and even lower in subsequent years. Similarly, the 550 000 tonnes of SO_2 released in 1980 at the Noranda Minerals copper smelter at Rouyn-Noranda, Quebec, are projected to be reduced 90 percent by the year 2000 through efforts such as use of new smelting technologies and extraction of sulphuric acid (Elder, 1991).

By 1985, a Canadian Acid Rain Control Program was formalized; the seven provinces east of Saskatchewan agreed to reduce their combined SO_2 emissions to 2.3 million tonnes per year by 1994. This target was exceeded in 1993, principally because of industrial process changes, installation of scrubbers, and switching away from high-sulphur fuels. In 1994, total eastern Canadian SO_2 emissions were 1.7 million tonnes (a 56 percent reduction from 1980 levels).

In 1991, an agreement with the United States obliged Canada to establish a permanent national limit on SO_2 of 3.2 million tonnes and a 10 percent reduction in projected NO_x emissions from stationary sources, both by the year 2000. Canada met this goal in 1993 and, by 1994, national SO_2 emissions were down to approximately 2.7 million tonnes. Beginning in 1995, the United States committed to reduce its annual SO_2 emissions to 14.4 million tonnes (9.1 million tonnes below 1980 levels), and its NO_x emissions by approximately 1.8 million tonnes, by the year 2000.

In 1995, Canada began to develop a national strategy on acidifying emissions for beyond the year 2000. This strategy aims to protect acid-sensitive ecosystems, human health, and air visibility in Canada, as well as to ensure Canada achieves its international commitments.

Airborne Contaminants

In the Canadian High Arctic, where there are few known local anthropogenic sources of contaminants, PCBs and other organochlorines, polycyclic aromatic hydrocarbons (PAHs), mercury, lead, cadmium, and radionuclides have been found in lakes and rivers. Air currents brought these substances from all industrial regions of the northern hemisphere. Studies have shown that atmospheric inputs of mercury (and other contaminants) have increased by a factor of three since 1900 (cited in Government of Canada, 1996). Water bodies collect the contaminants deposited within their drainage basins and, in turn, aquatic biota bioaccumulate these substances (see Chapter 8). In the Arctic, hexachlorocyclohexane (HCH) is the organochlorine found at highest concentration in fresh waters, while toxaphene, PCBs, and chlordane are the compounds found at highest concentrations in fish. This is one source of the PCBs found in breast milk of Aboriginal women in the Arctic.

Many Canadian cities continue to experience unacceptable air quality, particularly during summer. Ground-

Smog obscures the Toronto skyline on a summer day in 1996. Airborne pollutants, including ground-level ozone and particulates, contribute to this air quality problem.

level ozone, formed by the action of sunlight on pollutants such as nitrogen oxides, can combine with airborne particles and other types of pollution to form smog. People with respiratory problems, children, the elderly, and people who exercise vigorously outdoors during the summer are at risk, particularly if they live in the lower Fraser Valley of British Columbia, the Windsor–Quebec City corridor (where two-thirds of the Canadian population reside), and southern New Brunswick and southwestern Nova Scotia. These areas are subject to Canadian and American emissions of **volatile organic compounds** and nitrogen oxides, and experience serious episodes of ground-level ozone pollution (Environment Canada, 1996a; Government of Canada, 1996). National parks such as Kejimkujik and Fundy have recorded high levels of pollutants drifting up from the northeastern United States. If climate change causes average air temperatures in these areas to continue to rise, this situation could be aggravated.

In addition to human health concerns, ground-level ozone, sulphur dioxide, and nitrogen dioxide injure plants and damage rubber, paint, plastic, and other materials. Fine airborne particles (with diameters less than one-millionth of a metre) are increasingly subject to study as it is believed these particles can adsorb toxic organic compounds and carry them deep into our lungs. Little is known about the effects on human health of trace amounts of the toxic hydrocarbon benzene (found in city air from unburned gasoline in vehicle exhaust). Because it is known to cause a specific form of leukemia in humans, levels of benzene in gasoline are to be regulated by the federal government (Environment Canada, 1996a). (See Chapter 13 for further details on urban air quality issues.)

RESPONSES TO ATMOSPHERIC CHANGES

INTERNATIONAL ACTIONS

Protecting the Ozone Layer

For more than a decade, Canada has been at the forefront of international efforts to protect the ozone layer. Since the early 1980s, Canada has supported strongly the need for international controls on ozone-depleting substances (ODSs). On June 4, 1986, Canada became the first country to sign the Vienna Convention, a framework for controls on the production and consumption of ODSs. Canada played a leading role in developing the Montreal Protocol on Substances That Deplete the Ozone Layer, signed by 24 nations on September 16, 1987. The Montreal Protocol was the first truly international effort to cooperate on protecting the environment, and was the first international mechanism designed to address an arising global environmental problem (Environment Canada, 1997a). The protocol was the result of unprecedented cooperation between all levels of government, the scientific community, industry, and the Canadian public (Environment Canada, 1996c).

The complex Montreal Protocol came into effect on January 1, 1989, and required each party to the protocol to freeze its production and consumption of CFCs at 1986 levels by July 1, 1989, to reduce them by 20 percent by 1993, and to further reduce them to 50 percent of 1986 levels by 1998. Also, each nation was required to limit its production and consumption of halons at 1986 levels by 1992. Recognizing that developing nations would need more than the specified time to control their emissions of ODSs, the Montreal Protocol permitted these countries a 10-year grace period in which to comply, and established a fund to provide financial and technological support to developing country parties. Canada contributes about $5 million per year to this fund, and has provided technical assistance to Chile, China, Brazil, India, and Venezuela (Environment Canada, 1997a).

As of December 1996, 161 countries have signed the twice-amended Montreal Protocol; Box 5–3 provides details on the phase-out schedule for ODSs included in the Montreal Protocol as well as Canadian targets. In 1996, an important milestone was reached when all developed countries eliminated the production and banned the importation of most new supplies of the most damaging ODSs, such as CFCs. The United Nations has designated September 16 as the International Day for the Preservation of the Ozone Layer (Environment Canada, 1996c).

The 10th anniversary of the Montreal Protocol was celebrated in September 1997, when the annual meeting of the parties was held in Montreal.

While there has been progress in fighting ozone depletion, the battle is far from over. Reductions in ODSs take years to be reflected in the stratosphere and, because we still use ozone-depleting chemicals, ODSs are continuing to build up in the stratosphere. Even with the Montreal Protocol's global schedule to eliminate ODSs, and even if all nations meet their international commitments to phase out ODSs, the ozone layer is not expected to return to normal (that is, pre-1980 levels) until at least the year 2050. Given that the ozone layer is not expected to repair itself for more than 50 years, Canadians (and others) face a significant challenge in continuing to choose ozone-friendly practices. Already some Canadians have engaged in, and been convicted of, smuggling CFCs to the U.S. These actions work against efforts to recover and recycle CFCs. Adhering to the schedule of the Montreal Protocol is important because living without an ozone layer is not desirable.

Controlling Greenhouse Gas Emissions

The world community largely has recognized that anthropogenic greenhouse gases represent a real risk of climate change. At the 1992 Earth Summit, more than 150 nations signed the United Nations Framework Convention on Climate Change (FCCC). Although it does not set any specific goals for achieving its objectives, the FCCC calls for nations to stabilize greenhouse gas concentrations in the atmosphere at a level that would prevent anthropogenic interference with the climate system. In order that food production not be threatened, and to enable economic development to proceed in a sustainable manner, the FCCC suggested that action should occur within a time frame that would allow ecosystems to adapt naturally to climate change.

As a first step toward achieving these broad objectives, most industrialized nations have committed to stabilize net greenhouse gas emissions (other than those covered by the Montreal Protocol) at 1990 levels by the year 2000. A variety of measures have been considered, but many countries are emphasizing moderation of energy demand through increased efficiency of energy use. Also, replacement of high-carbon fuels such as coal and gasoline with alternatives such as propane, natural gas, and gasohol (or ethanol- or methanol-blended) gasoline is being encouraged. France and Japan plan to increase their reliance on nuclear energy, while Germany and Denmark intend to increase use of renewable, wind-generated and solar power sources. Some countries have used economic incentives or carbon taxes to influence consumer behaviour, and there are calls for international emissions

The Montreal Protocol is science based and relies on assessment panels of the United Nations Environment Programme to guide its revisions. As noted in the text, the Montreal Protocol has been amended on two occasions, in London in 1990 and in Copenhagen in 1992. At these meetings, several changes were made to the original agreement:

London:

- Tighter control measures for CFCs and halons were agreed on.
- Carbon tetrachloride and methyl chloroform were added to the list of controlled substances.
- The Interim Multilateral Fund was created to help developing countries (whose annual per-capita consumption of controlled substances did not exceed 0.3 kg) to meet the control measures of the Protocol.

Copenhagen (not yet ratified):

- Phase-out deadlines for several ozone-depleting substances (ODSs) were accelerated.
- Resolutions were adopted to encourage recovery, recycling, leakage control, and destruction of ODSs.

- Methyl bromide, HCFCs, and HBFCs (hydrobromofluorocarbons) were added to the list of substances subject to control.
- A definition of "essential use" was agreed on.

In 1995, in Vienna, the parties to the Montreal Protocol made some additional adjustments, agreeing to add a phase-out schedule for methyl bromide and a reduction of the cap for the base level of HCFC consumption. In the following table, the original Montreal Protocol terms are noted, as are the London and Copenhagen amendments and the Vienna adjustments. As well, Canada's timetable for elimination of ODSs established under the Ozone Layer Protection Program is identified.

This table clearly illustrates the increasing number of ODSs that must be controlled and ultimately eliminated. The table also shows that despite progress in controlling ODSs, depletion of the ozone layer is not a fully resolved problem. It is to be hoped, however, that advancements in the schedule will continue to occur as our understanding of the dynamics of ozone-depleting processes continues to progress.

	Montreal Protocol	London Amendments	Copenhagen Amendments	Vienna Adjustments	Canadian Targets as of January 1, 1996
CFCs	50% reduction from 1986 levels by 1999	100% elimination by 2000	100% elimination by 1996		100% elimination by 1996
Halons	Freeze at 1986 levels by 1992	100% elimination by 2000	100% elimination by 1994		100% elimination by January 1, 1994
Carbon tetrachloride		100% elimination by 2000	100% elimination by 1996		100% elimination by January 1, 1995
Methyl chloroform		100% elimination by 2005	100% elimination by 1996		100% elimination by 1996
HCFCs		Phased out between 2020 and 2040	Freeze consumption at base level[a] in 1996; 100% elimination by 2030	Phase out consumption in 2020; exemption of up to 0.5% of base-year levels until 2030 for servicing existing equipment	Limit to uses where more acceptable alternatives do not exist beginning January 1, 1996; 100% elimination by 2020
HBFCs			100% elimination by 1996		100% elimination by 1996
Methyl bromide			Freeze production and consumption at 1991 levels in 1995	Reduce production and consumption by 25% by 2001, by 50% by 2005, and by 100% by 2010, with exemption for preshipment and quarantine applications	Freeze production and consumption at 1991 levels in 1995, and reduce by 25% by January 1, 1998; 100% elimination by 2001 (except quarantine and preshipment applications in both cases)

NOTE: The 100% elimination targets are subject to the Essential Use Provision, which may allow for continued use if it is essential for the health, safety, or functioning of society and if there are no technically and economically feasible alternatives or substitutes available.

[a] Base level is defined as the 1989 consumption of HCFCs plus 2.8% of 1989 consumption of CFCs.

SOURCES: Environment Canada. (1997f). Canada's ozone layer protection program: A summary. http://www.ec.gc.ca/ozone/protect/index.html

Government of Canada. (1996). *The state of Canada's environment—1996.* Ottawa: Supply and Services Canada.

trading agreements (Economists' statement, 1997). Earth Summit +5 reviewed international progress toward greenhouse gas reduction (Box 5–4).

A number of international structures also have been developed over the past few decades to help determine the causes and appropriate responses to global environmental change, including climate change. Probably the best known of these structures is the Intergovernmental Panel on Climate Change (IPCC), but other international scientific inquiry and decision-making programs include the International Geosphere Biosphere Program (IGBP), the International Human Dimensions Program (IHDP), the Scientific Committee on Problems of the Environment (SCOPE), and the International Geographical Union's Commission on Climatology (IGU).

CANADIAN LAW, POLICY, AND PRACTICE

After signing the Montreal Protocol in 1987, Canada worked on putting a control program in place that would meet its international commitments. By 1995, when consultation meetings were held across Canada, the national Ozone Layer Protection Program was strengthened and target dates for phase out of ODSs were accelerated. For example, nonrecoverable uses of HCFCs are to be eliminated by 2010, and the consumption of methyl bromide is to be reduced by 25 percent by 1998 and eliminated completely by 2001.

One set of regulations under the Canadian Environmental Protection Act (CEPA), the Ozone-Depleting Sub-

---

BOX 5-4
EARTH SUMMIT +5

In 1992, the first international Earth Summit convened to address urgent problems of environmental protection and socioeconomic development. More than 100 heads of state signed the Convention on Climate Change, the Convention on Biological Diversity, endorsed the Rio Declaration and the Forest Principles, and adopted Agenda 21. At that time, the Commission on Sustainable Development was created to monitor and report on implementation of the Earth Summit agreements. It was agreed that, from June 23 to 27, 1997, a special session of the United Nations General Assembly would take stock of how well countries, international organizations, and sectors of civil society had responded to the challenge of the Earth Summit (United Nations, 1997a).

The Earth Summit +5 session ended with the chairman's general verdict: "Our words have not been matched by deeds" (Leopold, 1997). In terms of the atmosphere, a similar reality emerged from Earth Summit +5: despite the adoption of the Convention on Climate Change, "the emission and concentration of greenhouse gases (GHGs) continue to rise, even as scientific evidence … points ever more strongly to the severe risk of global climate change" (United Nations, 1997b). Significantly, the General Assembly agreed that "insufficient progress has been made by many developed countries in meeting their aim to return GHG emissions to 1990 levels by the year 2000."

Canada is among the majority of developed nations that will exceed its greenhouse gas targets (by at least 8 percent) as will the United States (target exceeded by 13 percent). At the General Assembly, Prime Minister Chrétien indicated that Canada's cold climate and resource-based economy hinder our ability to meet the emissions goal because it requires a reduction in the use of fossil fuels. This failure to meet set goals may be explained partly by the failure of provincial authorities to set goals for energy efficiency, fuel switching, cleaner cars, and increasing public transit (Beaulieu, 1997).

The international community represented at Earth Summit +5 confirmed that the problem of climate change is one of the biggest challenges facing the world in the next century. They agreed that the ultimate goal is to achieve stabilization of greenhouse gas concentrations in the atmosphere at a level that would prevent dangerous anthropogenic interference with the climate system. Agreement was also widespread regarding the need to consider legally binding, realistic, and equitable targets that would result in significant reductions in greenhouse gas emissions within specified time frames (such as 2005, 2010, and 2020). These legally binding targets for developed countries are scheduled to be adopted in Kyoto, Japan, in December 1997.

International cooperation will be important in attaining reductions in greenhouse gas emissions (particularly technology transfer to, and building capacity in, developing nations). In addition, strengthening of systematic observational networks will be important in enabling identification of climate changes and assessment of potential impacts of change. As sobering as the Earth Summit +5 was, and as insufficient as the action has been to date, the lessons and challenges are clear as the international community prepares for the next comprehensive review of Agenda 21 in the year 2002.

SOURCES: Beaulieu, P. (1997). Province has no excuse. *Alternatives*, 23(3), p. 3.

Earth Summit leaves nations deeply divided. (1997, June 28). *Globe and Mail* (Toronto), p. A11.

Leopold, E. (1997, June 28). Summit ends on sour note. *Calgary Herald*, p. A17.

United Nations. (1997a). Earth Summit +5: General information. http://www.un.org/dpcsd/earthsummit/gn97info.htm

United Nations. (1997b). Programme for further implementation of Agenda 21.
http://gopher.un.org/00/ga/docs/S-19/plenary/ES5.TXT

---

stances Regulations, deals with control of ODS production, import, and export. A second set of regulations, the Ozone-Depleting Substances Products Regulations, deals with control of manufactured products (such as aerosols and plastic foam packaging) that contain ODSs (for a related issue, see Box 5–5). Also under the CEPA, two environmental codes of practice have been developed for use in both public and private sectors. These codes recommend practices for pollution prevention, emission reduction, environmental management, and preventive maintenance regarding halon and fluorocarbon emissions.

The National Action Plan for the Recovery, Recycling and Reclamation of CFCs was endorsed by the Canadian Council of Ministers of the Environment (CCME) (Box 5–6) in October 1992. The plan, originally set mainly on the recovery, recycling, and reclamation of CFCs from refrigeration and air conditioning systems,

Planting seedlings for new forests is one way to help remove carbon dioxide from the atmosphere.

BOX 5–5

BEAUTIFUL BRITISH COLUMBIA MAGAZINE MAKES THE SWITCH TO POLY BAGS

Environmental benefits can be achieved in multiple ways through business decisions attuned to reducing waste, air, and water pollution. The case of the *Beautiful British Columbia* switch to poly bags provides such an example.

Founded in 1959, *Beautiful British Columbia* is a magazine dedicated to publishing well-researched articles and captivating photography of British Columbia's scenery, parks, wilderness, wildlife, geography, ecology, and heritage. With a paid circulation of over 250 000, *Beautiful British Columbia* is mailed to 173 countries worldwide. In 1995, the magazine discontinued mailing their issues in paper sleeves, opting instead for poly bags. The company's decision to switch was based on a number of factors, including reduced mailing costs, improved customer service, and environmental considerations.

The magazine is produced entirely in British Columbia and efforts are made to print and distribute each issue with concern for the environment. The magazine is printed with soya-based ink on recycled fibres made from lumber chips and sawdust. *Beautiful British Columbia* sponsors tree-planting programs to replace more fibre than the magazine uses each year. (In 1995, for example, about 40 Grade 7 and Grade 12 students from Ucluelet schools planted 2600 western red cedar on a 2-hectare clearcut, next to a salmon-spawning stream.)

The photographs for *Beautiful British Columbia* are processed by a Vancouver company that cleans and reuses all its photo-processing chemicals. In addition, the company's offices have reduced waste by 75 percent through an in-house recycling program. The switch to sealable poly bags has allowed the company to deliver its magazine in an improved format while reducing stress on the environment.

The use of poly bags has reduced postal expenses by more than $2000 per issue. The previous paper wrapper weighed approximately 10 grams whereas each poly bag weighs 5 grams. With four issues per year, $8000 in mailing expense is

saved annually. The poly bag also has allowed the magazine to be delivered in a format more appealing to the customer. Market research conducted for *Beautiful British Columbia* concluded that advertising was the least appealing feature of the magazine. As the paper bagging machine could place only one item in the wrapper, advertising inserts were stapled into the magazine. With the poly bag, advertising is included in the bag, not in the magazine itself. In addition, the poly bag is waterproof and more durable than the paper alternative.

The company based its environmental decision to change to poly bags on research obtained by the Plastic Bag Information Clearinghouse, a program of the Plastic Bag Association. The following information was passed along to magazine subscribers in a letter explaining the switch from paper to plastic:

- Manufacturing plastic bags requires 30 to 40 percent less energy, creates 63 to 73 percent fewer air emissions, and 90 percent less water pollution than comparable paper bags.

- Equivalent strength and size plastic wrappers weigh much less than paper and are less bulky; less weight and volume means less fuel is required to transport the magazines.

- Per kilogram, it takes 85 times more energy to recycle paper than it does to recycle plastic.

The plastic bag manufacturer selected by *Beautiful British Columbia* uses recycled plastic material, 60 percent of which is recycled industrial poly film scrap. Of course, the magazine encourages its customers to recycle both the magazine and the poly bag.

For more information, contact *Beautiful British Columbia* or the Plastic Bag Information Clearinghouse. Both addresses are given in the Additional Information Sources section at the end of this chapter.

Made up of environment ministers from the federal, provincial, and territorial governments, the Canadian Council of Ministers of the Environment (CCME) is the major intergovernmental forum in Canada for discussion and joint action on environmental issues of national and international concern. Generally, the 13 environment ministers meet twice per year to discuss national environmental priorities and determine work to be carried out under the auspices of CCME.

CCME promotes cooperation on and coordination of interjurisdictional issues such as air pollution, waste management, and toxic chemicals. In efforts to achieve a high level of environmental quality across the country, members of the CCME propose nationally consistent environmental standards and objectives. However, the CCME cannot impose its proposals as it has no authority to implement or enforce legislation.

In order to achieve specific goals, and to reach consensus on proposed national policies, CCME members work through task groups. In 1997, there were 10 task groups that reflect CCME's current priorities:

- *Harmonization Working Group:* works to minimize overlap and duplication between federal and provincial/territorial programs

- *National Task Force on Packaging:* aims to reduce packing waste by 50 percent by the year 2000 (compared to 1998 levels)

- *Water Quality Guidelines Task Group:* works to develop, approve, and publish national water quality guidelines as well as ecosystem health indicators

- *Environmental Education and Communications Task Group:* serves as a forum for information exchange among its members and encourages sharing of environmental education materials

- *State of the Environment Reporting Task Group:* focuses on promoting more harmonized state of the environment reporting across Canada, including database support for other CCME task groups

- *Economic Integration Task Group:* examines issues related to integrating the environment and the economy

- *National Air Issues Coordination Committee:* provides advice to ministers and deputy ministers on how best to address national air quality problems; develops coordinated air issue management plans and strategies; tracks progress in achieving targets to reduce air pollutants

- *Hazardous Waste Task Group:* identifies significant national issues in hazardous waste management; provides guidance on these issues and/or national guidelines or codes of practice

- *Contaminated Sites Advisory Group:* advised on implementing site remediation of high-risk abandoned, contaminated sites; was dissolved in 1995 when the National Contaminated Sites Remediation Program was completed; same functions of the contaminated Sites Advisory Group are carried out by the Soil Quality Guidelines Task Group

- *Soil Quality Guidelines Task Group:* develops, recommends, and publishes national soil quality guidelines

A recent effort of the CCME is its Pollution Prevention Awards program that gives national recognition to companies and organizations showing cutting-edge accomplishments or leadership in pollution prevention. For more information, see the CCME Web site listed in the Additional Information Sources section of this chapter.

---

now encompasses all aspects of pollution prevention and all industry sectors that use ODSs.

Canada's 1995 National Action Program on Climate Change (NAPCC) presents a range of detailed, sector-specific, mostly voluntary measures for achieving stabilization of greenhouse gas emissions. Among the program's options are development of incentives, regulations, and technical training to improve energy efficiency in residential and commercial sectors; altered subsidies in energy, transportation, agriculture, and forestry industries; and measures to encourage the use of more fuel-efficient cars (Canadian Council of Ministers of the Environment, 1995; Government of Canada, 1996).

Examples of the agricultural measures that the NAPCC promotes to reduce soil carbon loss (and greenhouse gas emissions) are increased use of conservation tillage practices, and reduced use of summer fallow. Similarly, increased cultivation of forage crops and actions to gain additional improvements in crop yields are intended to help increase carbon sequestration. The program also promotes the development of new forests to increase the removal of carbon dioxide from the atmosphere.

Another part of the NAPCC is the Voluntary Challenge and Registry Program that invites Canadian companies and organizations to develop action plans to limit their net greenhouse gas emissions. By the spring of 1996, about 70 percent of business and industrial emitters had signed letters of intent to develop action plans (Environment Canada, 1996d). However, a major question remains concerning how effective these voluntary measures will be in achieving the necessary reductions in greenhouse gases.

Even though the precautionary principle underlies this National Action Program on climate change, without significant action under the Voluntary Challenge and Registry Program as well as additional government measures under the NAPCC it will be difficult to stabilize Canada's greenhouse gas emissions at 1990 levels. Projections are that with normal population and economic growth alone, energy-related emissions likely will increase by 13 percent over 1990 levels by the year 2000 (Canadian Council of Ministers of the Environment, 1995). This gives added importance to the adaptation strategies that are part of the NAPCC.

Adaptation strategies offer returns that make them worth doing even if greenhouse gas concentrations continue to increase. For example, in agriculture, reduced vulnerability to climate change can be attained by avoiding monocropping and selecting crops or species that demand less water. Similarly, in forestry, strengthening fire and pest monitoring and intensifying fire fighting may be considered. Other sectors such as fisheries, construction, and energy supply could undertake adaptation strategies that would produce environmental and economic benefits in addition to reductions in greenhouse gas emissions.

(For detailed information on Canada's situation and responses to meet commitments under the United Nations Framework Convention on Climate Change, see

Traffic lanes reserved for buses, car pool vehicles, and cyclists are becoming more common in Canadian cities.

Canada's first and second national reports on climate change [Environment Canada, 1994; 1997]. Both reports are listed in the Additional Information Sources section at the end of this chapter, and so is the URL for the second climate change report.)

The federal government also has an Efficiency and Alternative Energy Program underway, encompassing dozens of initiatives to reduce greenhouse gas emissions by improving energy efficiency through improvements to equipment, appliances, buildings, industrial processes and machinery, and motor vehicles and transportation systems. Use of alternative energy sources such as low-carbon transportation fuels, noncarbon fuels such as hydrogen (see Chapter 11), and renewable energy sources such as biomass, wind, and solar power also are promoted. Communities and public utilities are being encouraged to place greater emphasis on demand management, co-generation (use of a fuel for both electricity and useful heat), and district heating.

Provincial and territorial jurisdictions have developed their own climate change action plans, and some Canadian municipalities have formed the "Twenty Percent Club" in their efforts to share cost-effective strategies to reduce greenhouse gas emissions by 20 percent of 1988 baseline levels by 2005 (see Chapter 13).

CANADIAN PARTNERSHIPS AND LOCAL ACTIONS

Information transfer and education programs have been part of Canada's efforts to reduce consumption of ODSs. For instance, in partnership with the Knowledge of the Environment for Youth (KEY) Foundation, Environment Canada undertook an education initiative to develop and implement curriculum materials on protection of the ozone layer for schools across Canada. In order to make environmentally responsible decisions, people need to know the purpose and function of the ozone layer and understand how human activities contribute to the ozone-depletion problem. This initiative recognized the important role that education has in encouraging appropriate actions and discouraging damaging behaviours. The KEY Foundation—itself an educational partnership among people who work in the environment, school system, government, and industry—is recognized as a credible source of accurate, balanced, and current education resources on the environment.

As part of the National Action Plan for the Recovery, Recycling and Reclamation of CFCs, more than 65 000 people have been trained in the recovery and recycling of ODSs in servicing refrigerator and air conditioning units. The cooperation of industry has been critical in success of these ventures and in taking up the challenge of protecting the ozone layer, achieving reductions specified under the Montreal Protocol faster than required.

Northern Telecom, for instance, formerly the single largest Canadian user of solvents containing ODSs, pledged to eliminate use of CFC solvents from all its operations by the end of 1991. Working with chemical manufacturers, Northern Telecom spent about $1 million on research and development between 1988 and 1991, and saved about $4 million during the same period on the costs to purchase new and dispose of used solvent. In 1989, Northern Telecom cofounded what is now called the International Co-operative for Environmental Leadership, made up of multinational companies that share information on alternatives to ozone-depleting solvents (Environment Canada, 1997c).

The Great Lakes–St. Lawrence Basin Project is a joint, Canadian–American research initiative of the Atmospheric Environment Service's Environmental Adaptation Research Group and the National Oceanic and Atmospheric Administration's Great Lakes Environmental Research Laboratory. The project was established to improve understanding of the complex interactions between climate and society so that informed regional adaptation strategies could be developed in response to potential climate change and variability. In May 1997, a binational symposium was held in Toronto to consider issues involved in adapting to climate change and variability in the basin (Great Lakes Commission, 1997).

At the community level, cities have taken action on climate change. In 1992, for example, Ottawa City Council committed to reduce citywide emissions of carbon dioxide by 20 percent of 1990 levels by the year 2005. The city's task force on the atmosphere includes energy utilities, commercial building owners, local home builders, community and environmental groups, as well as city staff and elected officials. Together, the city and Environment Canada are developing a monitoring system to chart the city's progress toward the 20 percent reduction target.

By 1996, the city of Calgary had a climate change action plan in place, in support of Canada's Climate Change Voluntary Challenge Registry program. Even though the greenhouse gases generated by the Corporation of the City of Calgary are small provincially (and infinitesimally small on a global scale), the city's position is that even a small reduction in greenhouse gases by its operations is one step in the larger goal of benefiting the global community.

As of 1992, in a move to reduce air pollution and the health problems that result from smog and other contaminants, British Columbia began to conduct inspections of the exhaust emissions of its cars and light trucks. Reducing vehicle exhaust was expected to help prevent 3600 deaths, 23 000 cases of chronic bronchitis, 123 000 emergency room visits, and save up to $30 billion in medical bills by the year 2020 (Joyce, 1995). Since older vehicles pollute more than newer ones, the province, along with several private partners, instituted the SCRAP-IT program, whereby owners of fully operational vehicles made prior to 1982 were offered cash or transit passes to get their cars off the road. A similar effort is due to begin in Ontario in the summer of 1998.

In 1995 at Winnipeg city hall, the Sierra Club of Canada launched the Zer-O-Zone project to foster public awareness of and support for Manitoba's ozone protection regulation. Other environmental advocacy groups and consumer groups continue to be active in programs to protect the ozone layer and to control greenhouse emissions on the local level.

FUTURE CHALLENGES

In light of the potential that stratospheric ozone depletion and an enhanced greenhouse effect have to jeopardize Earth's life-support systems, the level of international cooperation that has developed to control ozone-destroying substances is a major success. Actions for controlling greenhouse gases, however, are much less advanced than those for ozone depletion, perhaps partly because, until very recently, there was less scientific certainty surrounding the warming issue. Perhaps, also, the lack of an ozone hole to draw attention to the problem of global warming has been a factor.

Compared to eliminating ODSs, the social and economic challenges involved in controlling and reducing greenhouse gas emissions are formidable. Eliminating CFCs and other ODSs affects only a small part of the global economy, but their elimination has been difficult despite the availability of practical alternatives. Greenhouse gases, however, derive principally from fossil fuels;

Testing motor vehicle emissions, in both voluntary and required programs, can be done quickly and efficiently.

fossil fuel energy is the basis of our industrial economy. "Reducing greenhouse gas emissions to the level necessary to stabilize their atmospheric concentrations will require a massive reorientation of the world's energy use away from carbon-based fuels and towards more benign alternatives and greater energy efficiency" (Government of Canada, 1996). Such adjustments could have enormous political, social, and economic costs if they are undertaken too quickly, particularly since economically practical fossil fuel alternatives remain scarce. At the same time, without decisive action greenhouse gas concentrations could rise to levels that pose serious consequences for human societies as well as the natural world.

If the public as well as policymakers are to respond to atmospheric changes now, then stewardship provides an important springboard from which to react. What actions will help reduce the risks of climate change? Individually, for example, we can buy ozone-friendly products, and ensure that the technicians who service our refrigerators or air conditioners recover and recycle the CFC coolants. Collectively, if meaningful change is intended, millions of Canadian households will need to examine their attitudes and change the way they use their cars and public transit systems. If communities can be designed with sustainability in mind, walking and bicycling could reduce reliance on vehicles and fossil fuels. Sustainable agricultural methods (see Chapter 6) as well as energy efficient housing and transportation alternatives (see Chapter 13) are part of the suite of actions required if the ozone layer is to recover fully and greenhouse gas emissions are to be reduced significantly.

In addition, improved communication between the scientific community and the public is necessary. If research findings are to be applied to reduce the risks of atmospheric change, awareness and understanding must be increased. One way to accomplish this is to restore, maintain, and enhance both national and local state-of-the-environment monitoring and reporting operations. As well, it will be important to disseminate more broadly the findings of these operations. Wider exposure of results from monitoring studies, presented through school, college, and university curricula, and with accurate commentary in the media, will be important in ensuring that all members of Canadian society are aware of the nature of choices facing them as far as their individual behaviour toward the environment is concerned, as well as the substantial amount of work ahead if the rate of atmospheric change is to be influenced by individual actions.

Knowledge building has been ongoing for decades in the scientific communities associated with atmospheric change, but there is a need for clear and effective translation of scientific information into lay persons' terms. Just as the international community rallied to undertake significant measures to stop the depletion of the ozone layer once they understood the implications of ozone depletion, so too might more members of Canadian society act in more environmentally responsible and sustainable ways if they possessed a better understanding of how their actions affect the atmosphere and, more broadly, the environment in which they live.

Promotional materials from Toronto's 1997 Bike Week campaign.

Chapter Questions

1. Why is acidic deposition a problem of continuing importance to Canadians? In what ways is your region affected by acidic depostion? What effort has been made to overcome the problem?

2. Discuss the major causes and effects of ozone depletion (both for the world and for Canada).

3. Discuss the different anthropogenic greenhouse gases in terms of their contributions to global warming.

4. What consumption patterns and other lifestyle choices do you make that directly and indirectly add greenhouse gases to the atmosphere? What actions might you take to reduce your contribution to this problem?

5. What do you think are the most important initiatives to combat ozone depletion and greenhouse gas emissions on an international scale? Within Canada? Justify your choices.

6. In highly technological societies, is 100 percent clean air possible? Is it a feasible air quality standard? Why or why not?

references

Bealieu. P. (1997). Province has no excuse. *Alternatives,* 23(3), p. 3.

Brotton, J., & Wall, G. (1997). The Bathurst caribou herd in a changing climate. *Climate Change Digest,* 97-01. Ottawa.

Bubier, J.L., Moore, T.R., & Bellisario, L. (1995). Ecological controls on methane emissions from a northern peatland complex in the zone of discontinuous permafrost, Manitoba, Canada. *Global Biogeochemical Cycles,* 9, pp. 455–70.

Canadian Council of Ministers of the Environment. http://www.mbnet.mb.ca/ccme/

Canadian Council of Ministers of the Environment. (1995). *Canada's National Action Program on Climate Change 1995.* Ottawa.

Canadian Global Change Program. http://www.cgcp.rsc.ca/

Canadian Safety Council. (n.d.). *National Summer Safety Week (May 1–7).* http://www.safety-council.org/SUN.HTM

Cohen, S.J. (1995). Mackenzie Basin impact study: Summary of interim report #2. *Climate Change Digest,* pp. 95-01. Ottawa.

Earth Summit leaves the nation deeply divided. (1997, June 28). *Globe and Mail* (Toronto), p. A11.

Economists' statement on climate change. (1997). *Delta,* 8(1), p. 6.

Elder, F. (1991). Acidic deposition: Acid test for the environment. In Government of Canada. *The state of Canada's environment—1991.* (pp. 24-1–24-24). Ottawa: Supply and Services Canada.

Environment Canada. (1996a). Urban air quality. *SOE Bulletin,* No. 96-1 (Spring). Ottawa.

Environment Canada. (1996b). Acid rain. *SOE Bulletin,* No. 96-2 (Spring). Ottawa.

Environment Canada. (1996c) International day for the preservation of the ozone layer: Recognizing human achievement. http://www.ec.gc.ca/minister/speeches/ozone_s_e.htm

Environment Canada. (1996d). Climate change. *SOE Bulletin,* No. 96-4 (Spring). Ottawa.

Environment Canada. (1997a). The Montreal Protocol. http://www.ec.gc.ca/ozone/protect/sect8e.html

Environment Canada. (1997b). Countdown to Montreal. http://www.ec.gc.ca/ozone/Brochure.eng.html

Environment Canada. (1997c). The business of ozone. http://www.ec.gc.ca/ozone/protect/sect11e.html

Environment Canada. (1997d). A primer on ozone depletion. http://www.ec.gc.ca/ozone/primer/primeroz.html#life

Environment Canada. (1997e). Stratospheric ozone. http://www.ec.gc.ca/ozone/

Environment Canada. (1997f). Canada's ozone layer protection program: A summary. http://www.ec.gc.ca/ozone/protect/index.html

Environment Canada. (1997g). A primer on environmental *citizenship.* Ottawa.

Environment Canada. (1997h). *Canada's second national report on climate change: Actions to meet commitments under the United Nations Framework Convention on Climate Change.* Ottawa.

Environment Canada. (n.d.). UV and you. http://www.ns.ec.gc.ca/udo/uv/uvandyou.html

Environment Canada Weather Forecast. Ultraviolet Indices. http://www.tor.ec.gc.ca/text/fpcn48.wao.htm

Environment Canada. The Green Lane. http://www.ec.ga.ca/

Farman, J.C., Gardiner, B.G., & Shanklin, J.D. (1985). Large losses of total ozone in Antarctica reveal seasonal ClO_x/NO_x interactions. *Nature, 315*, pp. 207–10

Folland, C.K., & Parker, D. (1995). Correction of instrumental biases in historical sea surface temperature data. *Quarterly Journal of the Royal Meteorological Society, 121*, pp. 319–67.

Forester, A. (1991). Stratospheric ozone: Wearing thin. In Government of Canada. *The state of Canada's environment—1991.* (pp. 23-1-23-24). Ottawa: Supply and Services Canada.

Government of Canada. (1996). *The state of Canada's environment—1996.* Ottawa: Supply and Services Canada.

Great Lakes Commission. (1997). Adapting to climate change and variability in the Great Lakes–St. Lawrence Basin. http://www.glc.org/announce/97/climate/climate.html

Hamill, P., & Toon, O. (1991). Polar stratospheric clouds and the ozone hole. *Physics Today, 44* (12), pp. 34–42.

Hengeveld, H. (1995). Understanding atmospheric change: A survey of the background of science and implications of climate change and ozone depletion. 2nd ed. SOE Report No. 95-2. Ottawa: Environment Canada.

Hengeveld, H. (1997). 1994–95 in review: An assessment of new developments relevant to the science of climate change. *CO_2/Climate Report*, 97-1, 52 pp.

Intergovernmental Panel on Climate Change. (1990). *Scientific assessment of climate change.* Geneva: World Meteorological Organization and United Nations Environment Programme.

Intergovernmental Panel on Climate Change. (1995). *Climate change 1995. Summary for policymakers: radiative forcing of climate change.* In J.T. Houghton, L.G.M. Filho, J. Bruce, H. Lee, B.A. Callander, E. Haites, N. Harris, A. Kaltenberg & K. Maskell (Eds). *Climate change 1994—radiative forcing of climate change and an evaluation of the IPCC 1992 emission scenarios.* (pp. 7–34). Cambridge: Cambridge University Press.

Intergovernmental Panel on Climate Change. (1996). *Climate change 1995: IPCC second assessment report. Vol. 1. The science of climate change.* In J.T. Houghton, L.G.M. Filho, B.A. Callander, N. Harris, A. Kaltenberg & K. Maskell (Eds.). Cambridge: Cambridge University Press.

Joyce, G. (1995, October 17). B.C. pushes tough standards. *Calgary Herald*, p. A2.

Kerr, R.A. (1994). Methane increases put on pause. *Science, 263*, p. 751.

Kerr, R.A. (1995). Studies say—tentatively—that greenhouse warming is here. *Science, 268*, 1567–68.

Lazier, J.R.N. (1996). The salinity decrease in the Labrador Sea over the past thirty years. In D.G. Martinson et al. (Eds). *Natural climate variability on decade to century time scales.* Washington, DC: National Research Council, National Academy Press.

Leopold, E. (1997, June 28). Summit ends on sour note. *Calgary Herald*, p. A17.

Manney, G.L., Zurek, R.W., Gelman, M.E., Miller, A.J., & Nagatani, R. (1994). The anomalous Arctic lower stratosphere polar vortex of 1992–1993. *Geophysical Research Letters, 21*, 2405–8.

McElroy, C.T., Kerr, J.B., McArthur, L.J.B., & Wardle, D.I. (1994). Ground-based monitoring of UV-B radiation in Canada. In R.H. Biggs & M.E.B. Joyner (Eds). *Stratospheric ozone depletion/UV-B radiation in the biosphere.* (pp. 271–82). Berlin, Germany: Springer-Verlag.

Miller, G.T. (1994). *Living in the environment* (8th ed.). Belmont, CA: Wadsworth Publishing Company.

Mills, C., & Jackson, S. (1995). Workshop report: Public education messages for reducing health risks from UV radiation. http://alep.unibase.com/sunconf/papers/cmills/cmills.html

Natural Resources Canada. (1997). Laurentian Forestry Centre. http://www.cfl.forestry.ca/75a.htm

Nkemdirim, L., & Budikova, D. (1996). The El Niño–Southern Oscillation has a truly global impact: A preliminary report on the ENSO Project of the Commission on Climatology. *International Geographical Union Bulletin, 46*, pp. 27–37.

Prézelin, B.B., Boucher, N.P., & Schofield, O. (1994). Evaluation of field studies of UV-B radiation effects on Antarctic marine primary productivity. In R.H. Biggs & M.E.B. Joyner (Eds.). *Stratospheric ozone depletion/UV-B radiation in the biosphere.* (pp. 181–94). Berlin, Germany: Springer-Verlag.

Raven, P.H., Berg, L.R., & Johnson, G.B. (1993). *Environment, 1995 version.* Orlando, FL: Saunders College Publishing/Harcourt Brace College Publishing.

Rhode, H. (1990). A comparison of the contributions of various gases to the greenhouse effect. *Science, 263*, p. 271.

Rowland, F.S. (1989). Chlorofluorocarbons and the depletion of stratospheric ozone. *American Scientist, 77*, pp. 36–45.

Schoof, R. (1996, November 4). "A sea of coal": Chinese struggle to wipe out throat-stinging smog. *Victoria Times Colonist,* p. D10.

Shine, K.P., Fouquart, Y., Ramaswamy, V., Solomon, S., & Srinivasan, J. (1995). Radiative forcing. In J.T. Houghton, L.G.M. Filho, J. Bruce, H. Lee, B.A. Callander, E. Haites, N. Harris, A. Kaltenberg & K. Maskell (Eds). *Climate change 1994—radiative forcing of climate change and an evaluation of the IPCC 1992 emission scenarios.* (pp. 163–203). Cambridge: Cambridge University Press.

Staple, T., & Wall, G. (1996). Climate change and recreation in Nahanni National Park Reserve. *Canadian Geographer, 40*(2), pp. 109–20.

Stolarski, R.S. (1988). The Antarctic ozone hole. *Scientific American, 258*(1), pp. 30–36.

Taylor, K.E., & Penner, J.E. (1994). Response of the climate system to atmospheric aerosols and greenhouse gases. *Nature, 369*, pp. 734–37.

United Nations. (1997a). Earth Summit +5: General information. http://www.un.org/dpcsd/earthsummit/gn97info.htm

United Nations. (1997b). Programme for further implementation of Agenda 21. http://gopher.un.org/00/ga/docs/S-19/plenary/ES5.TXT

United Nations. (1997c). Second National Reports on Climate Change. http://www1.ec.gc.ca/cgi-bin/foliocgi.exe/climate_e/toc?

United States Environmental Protection Agency. (1995). Sun protection for children. http://www.epa.gov/ozone/uvindex/uvwhat.html

World Meteorological Organization (WMO). (1994). *Scientific assessment of ozone depletion 1994.* WMO Global Ozone Research and Monitoring Project, Report No. 37. Geneva.

Beautiful British Columbia
929 Ellery Street
Victoria, BC V9A 6B4
(604) 384-5456
(604) 384-2812 fax
http://www.beautifulbc.com/bbc/index/htm

Canadian Council of Ministers of the Environment. Home page.
http://www.mbnet.mb.ca/ccme/

Canadian Dermatology Association
774 Echo Drive, Suite 521
Ottawa, ON K1S 5N8

Canadian Global Change Program. http://www.cgcp.rsc.ca

Environment Canada. (1994). *Canada's national report on climate change: Actions to meet commitments under the United Nations Framework Convention on climate change.* Ottawa.

Environment Canada. (1996). Green Lane: National Environmental Indicator Series on climate change. http://www.ec.gc.ca

Environment Canada. (1997). Weather forecast: ultraviolet (UV) Indicies [sic]. http://www.tor.ec.gc.ca/text/fpcn48.wao.htm

Environment Canada. (1997). State of the ozone layer over Canada. http://www.cmc.doe.ca/cmc/htmls/A-ozone.html

Environment Canada. (1997). *CO$_2$/climate report* (May). Downsview, ON.

Environment Canada. (1997). Canada's second national report on climate change: Actions to meet commitments under the United Nations Framework Conventions on climate change. Ottawa. http://www1.ec.gc.ca/cgi-bin/foliocgi.exe/climate_e/toc?

Hare, F.K. (1995). Contemporary climatic change. In Mitchell, B. (Ed). *Resource and environmental management in Canada.* (pp. 10–28). Toronto: Oxford University Press.

Likens, G.E., Driscoll, C.T., & Buso, D.C. (1996). Long-term effects of acid rain: Response and recovery of a forest ecosyatem. *Science,* 272, pp. 244–46.

McMillan, T. (1991). *The real story about Canada's acid rain campaign in the United States.* Notes from remarks by the Honourable Tom McMillan, Canadian Consul General to New England, to the National Conference on Government Relations, Ottawa.

Plastic Bag Information Clearinghouse
1817 E. Carson Street
Pittsburgh, PA 15203 USA
1-800-438-5856

Toon, O.B., & Turco, R.P. (1991). Polar stratospheric clouds and ozone depletion. *Scientific American,* 264(6), pp. 68–74.

Yan, N.D., Keller, W., Scully, N.M., Lean, D.R.S., & Dillon, P. (1996). Increased UV-B penetration in a lake owing to drought-induced acidification. *Nature,* 388, pp. 457–59.

Agroecosystems and Land Resources

Chapter Contents

CHAPTER OBJECTIVES 155
INTRODUCTION 155
CANADA'S AGRICULTURAL LAND BASE 156
   Socioeconomic Changes in Canadian
     Agriculture 157
   Jurisdiction and Tenure 159
HUMAN ACTIVITIES AND IMPACTS ON
   AGRICULTURAL LANDS 159
   Soil Quality 161
     Soil Organic Matter Levels 161
     Wind, Water, and Tillage Erosion 161
     Soil Structure 162
     Soil Salinization 163
     Chemical Contamination 163
   Water Quality 163
   Agriculture and Biodiversity 164
   Greenhouse Gases 166
   Energy Use 168
RESPONSES TO ENVIRONMENTAL IMPACTS
   AND CHANGE 168
   International Initiatives 169
     Desertification 169
   Canadian Efforts to Achieve Sustainable
     Agriculture 172
     An Illustration: Sustainable Agriculture
       in Manitoba 172
     Nontraditional Agricultural
       Activities 176
       Organic Farming 176
       Game Farming and Ranching 176
       Agricultural Biotechnology 177
     Partnerships 178
FUTURE CHALLENGES 180
Chapter Questions 182
References 182
Additional Information Sources 183

"In the last decade there has been much discussion on creating a more stable, more sustainable agricultural industry ... that would be less polluting, would maintain (even enhance) our healthy and attractive landscape, and would be less stressful on farm operators.... even a brief scan should convince anyone that 'sustainable agriculture' ... is quite different from the present pattern, and that even moving in the direction of achieving [sustainability] objectives requires major changes in much of our present society."

I. McQuarrie, in Fleming (1997), pp. 54–55

Chapter Objectives

After studying this chapter you should be able to

- understand the main issues and concerns relating to Canada's land resources and their agricultural use
- identify a range of agricultural uses of our land resources
- describe the impacts of agricultural activities on the land around us
- appreciate the complexity and interrelatedness of issues relating to land, and agroecosystems
- outline Canadian and international responses to the need for sustainable agriculture and agroecosystems
- discuss challenges to a sustainable future for land resources, agroecosystems, and agriculture

INTRODUCTION

Global warming sometimes is blamed on cattle because they produce methane during digestion. But how much gas does a cow really pass? Scientists already know that the cow probably has been unfairly victimized—driving your car 3.2 kilometres discharges as much methane as a cow produces all day, and one landfill in the Vancouver area produces more greenhouse gas than all the cattle in British Columbia! On a worldwide scale, Canadian cattle are responsible for only 0.15 percent of the methane produced.

Scientists also know that Canadian cattle can be made to release less methane if they are well fed with grain (poor-quality hay diets result in higher levels of methane). A more difficult issue to resolve is the 25 percent increase in methane emissions from cows during winter compared to summer (the cause may be decreased digestive efficiency in colder temperatures). Research into cow methane has shown that a commercial feed additive, monesin, sold with the promise of reducing methane, is not effective—individual cows still produce between 200 and 400 litres of methane daily.

Millions of cattle occupy Canadian agricultural lands, contributing in important ways to the economy. Perhaps more than any other industrialized nation, Canada depends on the land for its economic well-being. Directly or indirectly, one in three workers is employed in agriculture, forestry, mining, energy, or other land-based activity sectors. Each year these activities account for approximately half of the value of Canada's exports; valued at $15.3 billion, agricultural exports were 6.8 percent of the nation's exports in 1994. Beyond the significance of Canada's lands to the economy, their diversity and quality are linked closely to our sense of national identity.

In this chapter, the main focus is on agricultural uses of land resources and on the impacts that food production activities have on sustainability of land resources. As the environmental archaeology of many ancient societies demonstrates, all civilizations depend on the ecological availability of their agricultural base (Taylor, 1994). In Canada, there is "mounting evidence that economic sustainability is jeopardized by the neglect of the physical and biological resource on which agriculture depends" (Science Council of Canada, 1992, p. 13). We examine the nature of these concerns and consider efforts undertaken and required to move toward environmental as well as economic sustainability of Canadian agricultural lands.

CANADA'S AGRICULTURAL LAND BASE

With a total area of 9 970 610 square kilometres, Canada's surface area (both land and freshwater bodies included) occupies 7 percent of the world's land mass and supports about 0.5 percent of the world's people. A wide range of landscapes and ecological zones across Canada (see Chapter 3) results in great diversity of climate, landform, vegetation, mineral, and hydrocarbon resources, as well as a variety of economic activities. In terms of agricultural activities, environmental concerns include soil fertility, water quality, loss of wildlife habitat and wetlands, pesticide and herbicide use, biotechnology and biodiversity, globalization of the food system, and food security. (Some of these concerns are discussed in other chapters.)

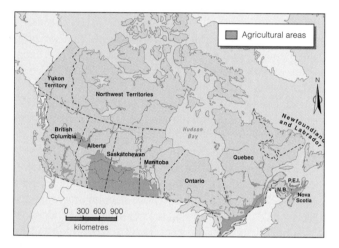

Figure 6–1

Agricultural areas within Canada

SOURCE: Government of Canada. (1996). *The state of Canada's environment—1996.* Ottawa. Figure 11.1.

It is important to have reliable information about the quality and suitability of land resources for particular uses if Canada's lands are to be used and managed wisely and sustainably for agricultural production (as well as other activities). One of the largest land inventories undertaken in the world, the Canada Land Inventory (CLI) focused on information about the most productive lands, mostly in the southern, heavily populated portions of the country. Completed in the 1970s, the CLI provides information regarding the long-term capabilities of about 2.6 million kilometers of land to support agriculture, forestry, waterfowl, ungulates, and outdoor recreation.

Only 11 percent of Canada's land is capable of supporting any form of agriculture, and less than 5 percent is capable of producing crops (Government of Canada, 1996). Far more limited than most Canadians appreciate, class 1 agricultural capability lands occupy less than 0.5 percent (about 42 000 kilometres) of Canada's total land area. Fifty-one percent of that class 1 agricultural capacity land is located in southern Ontario (Statistics Canada, 1994a). It is worth noting that Canada does not have any vast agricultural reserves; virtually all the land that is amenable to agricultural production and that has not been built on or paved over is in agricultural use. Figure 6–1 illustrates the location of agricultural areas within Canada, while the amount of agricultural land (in CLI classes 1 to 3) in each province is identified in Table 6–1.

In spite of the preceding statement, there is limited data about how much land suitable for agriculture is actually being farmed, and there is no current national database identifying how much land really is available for agricultural use. This is an important gap in knowledge, given that expanding human needs and economic activities have been increasing pressures on land. For instance, the Royal Commission on the Economic Union and Development Prospects for Canada (1985) noted that agricultural lands were being lost to suburbs and shopping centres, among other things.

Canada depends on a small percentage of good-quality land to support agriculture. Balancing competing demands for land is a necessity if both a healthy environment and a prosperous economy are to exist.

TABLE 6–1
LAND CAPABILITY FOR AGRICULTURE, BY PROVINCE

Hectares of Canada Land Inventory Lands, by Province[1]

Agricultural Land Capability Class[2]	Nfld.	P.E.I.	N.S.	N.B.	Que.	Ont.	Man.	Sask.	Alta.	B.C.	Canada	% of total area
1	0	0	0	0	19 533	2 156 776	162 508	999 727	786 555	69 948	4 195 047	0.45
2	0	261 352	166 259	160 792	909 671	2 217 771	2 530 258	5 873 285	3 838 965	397 688	16 356 041	1.77
3	5 504	141 524	982 457	1 152 089	1 281 043	2 909 460	2 440 485	9 420 057	6 110 044	999 778	25 442 441	2.76
Total	5 504	402 876	1 148 716	1 312 881	2 210 247	7 284 007	5 133 251	16 293 069	10 735 564	1 467 414	45 993 529	4.98

NOTES: 1. Yukon and the Northwest Territories are not covered by the CLI.

2. Land capability classes 1, 2, and 3 (out of 7 classes) are Canada's prime agricultural lands containing the best soils with the highest potential to produce varied crops now and in the future. Saskatchewan possesses the largest amount of prime agricultural land, followed by Alberta, Ontario, and Manitoba. In general, prime agricultural lands also are located where climatic conditions are favourable for farming.

SOURCE: Government of Canada. (1996). *The state of Canada's environment—1996.* Ottawa: Supply and Services Canada. Table 10.6.

The competition and conflict over land uses that occur have caused many Canadians to recognize the necessity of balancing competing demands on our limited land if we are to maintain both a healthy environment and a prosperous economy. The resulting challenge for sustainable agriculture is to maintain and enhance the quality of Canada's finite agricultural soils as well as the air, water, and biodiversity resources that are part of agroecosystems.

Agroecosystems are communities of living organisms, together with the physical resources that sustain them (such as biotic and abiotic elements of the underlying soils and drainage networks), that are managed for the purpose of producing food, fibre, and other agricultural products. These are complex and dynamic systems, with many interrelationships; any action in one component of an agroecosystem affects other components and ecosystems. For example, a farmer's decision to use management practices such as fertilizers or pesticides is influenced by his or her access to technology as well as by the economics of the marketplace and government policy. Such management practices affect the health of agroecosystems and, ultimately, the productivity and sustainability of agriculture in Canada.

SOCIOECONOMIC CHANGES IN CANADIAN AGRICULTURE

Changes in the social, economic, and technological conditions associated with agriculture in Canada have been reflected in a decrease in the number of, and a growth in the size of, farms in Canada. While more than 98 percent of all farms in Canada are family owned and operated, Figure 6–2 illustrates that the number of farms declined by about half, while their size increased about two and one-half times, during the 1941–91 period (Statistics Canada, 1994b). This shift, reflecting a move from mixed farming to specialized systems, led to increased productivity and efficiency. For example, 97 percent of Canada's wheat is grown on the Prairies, and 75 percent of Canada's corn grows in Ontario. Currently, 8 percent of farms occupy about 43 percent of all farmland. This means that a small proportion of farmers actually determines whether sustainable practices are applied on almost half of Canada's finite agricultural lands (Government of Canada, 1996).

Although the total area of farmland remained relatively constant between 1971 and 1991, there were some important changes in agricultural land use. The first major change was that some farmlands near urban centres were converted to nonagricultural uses; land that was brought into agricultural production tended to be of lower quality. The second important change was that cropland increased by 20 percent, indicating more intensive use of agricultural land and resulting in greater production per unit of land area. The third major change was that the area devoted to **summerfallow** (land not sown for at least one year, to conserve soil moisture and to enhance nitrogen accumulation) declined by 27 percent. Figure 6–3 indicates these changes.

The Canadian agriculture and agri-food industry—farmers, suppliers, processors, transporters, grocers, and restaurant workers—is the third largest employer in Canada, generating about $82 billion in domestic retail and

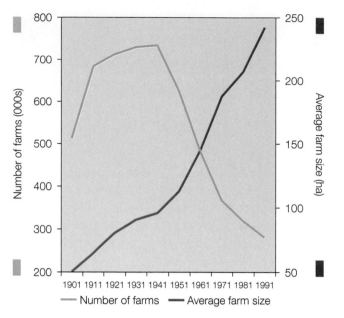

Figure 6–2

Change in number and size of farms in Canada, 1901–1991

SOURCE: Government of Canada. (1996). *The state of Canada's environment—1996*. Ottawa: Supply and Services Canada.

food service sales annually. An average Canadian farm produces enough food for 120 people, but about 1.8 million Canadians are involved in bringing the food from all farms to our tables. Agri-food is one of the top 5 industries in Canada, and accounts for about 8 percent of the gross domestic product.

Grains, oilseeds, and meats are the prime commodities in Canadian agriculture: in 1994, meats (cattle, hogs, veal, and lamb) contributed 27 percent to farm cash receipts, while grains and oilseeds (wheat, oats, barley, flax seed, canola, soybeans, and corn) contributed 30 percent. The largest proportion of farm cash receipts comes from eggs, dairy, poultry, and other livestock in all regions except the Prairie provinces, where grains and oilseeds account for more than 50 percent of farm cash receipts.

In 1993, 48 percent of Canada's agricultural production was exported; the Prairie provinces remain more dependent on exports and interprovincial trade than eastern provinces, where the majority of food produced is consumed domestically (Government of Canada, 1996). This means prairie farmers are the most susceptible to changes in international prices and food consumption trends. Accordingly, international trade agreements such as the North American Free Trade Agreement and the

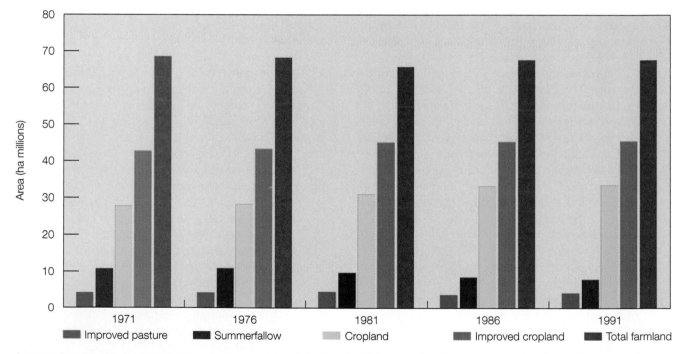

Improved pasture is area improved by seeding, draining, irrigating, fertilizing, and brush or weed control, not including areas where hay, silage, or seeds are harvested.
Summerfallow is area that has been left idle (not worked) for at least one year.
Cropland is the total area on which field crops, fruits, vegetables, nursery products, and sod are grown; improved pasture and summerfallow are excluded.
Improved cropland is the sum of cropland, summerfallow, and improved pasture.
Total farmland is the total area of land operated, including improved cropland and unimproved land.

Figure 6–3

The use of farmland in Canada, 1971–1991

SOURCE: Government of Canada. (1996). *The state of Canada's environment—1996*. Ottawa: Supply and Services Canada.

PART 3:
RESOURCES FOR CANADA'S FUTURE

World Trade Organization Agreement have important influences on Prairie (and Canadian) agriculture. These agreements also have resource management and environmental implications that are not yet understood fully.

JURISDICTION AND TENURE

Although the Canadian Constitution gives provincial governments jurisdiction over management and control of land use within their boundaries, federal policies, programs, and ownership still influence the ways in which provinces implement their land use strategies and plans. For instance, federal energy, agricultural, transportation, and other policies have implications for land use. Furthermore, Parliament can directly regulate land use for specific purposes (such as for the safe operation of airports), and the research and information produced by the federal government can greatly impact on policies and programs of all orders of government and on decision making in the private sector as it relates to land use. Parliament has legislative jurisdiction over land in Yukon and the Northwest Territories, and is responsible for land for national parks, migratory bird sanctuaries, and Native reserves.

About 90 percent of the land in Canada is owned by federal and provincial governments (Crown land). The federal government is the country's single largest landowner, with just over 40 percent of all Crown land; its largest land holdings are in Yukon and the Northwest Territories. Together provincial governments own 50 percent of the Crown land, and most Canadians live on the 9.7 percent that is privately owned. Given their land ownership, governmental ministers at various levels have important responsibilities in land use decision making.

In taking action to achieve sustainability in land use, governments can support research that will improve knowledge of the land and its uses, can undertake inventories, and can promote citizen awareness and action

Almost half of Canada's agricultural production is exported, some of it through the port of Vancouver.

through provision of appropriate information. In addition, the challenge of Aboriginal rights and land claims requires consideration of the issues of social justice and fair access to Canada's land resources in determination of sustainable land use (Box 6–1).

HUMAN ACTIVITIES AND IMPACTS ON AGRICULTURAL LANDS

Agriculture and land management practices affect the environmental sustainability of agroecosystems. This section identifies some of these management practices and their impacts on soil and water quality, biodiversity, and greenhouse gases.

BOX 6 – 1
ABORIGINAL PEOPLE, LAND CLAIM AGREEMENTS, AND ENVIRONMENTAL PROTECTION

Historically, Aboriginal peoples did not believe they could own the land any more than they could own the sky; rather, people shared the land with other living organisms. Hunting, fishing, trapping, and other harvesting of the land's living resources was the basis of their economy, cultural distinctiveness, and way of life. In recognition of the special relationship Inuit and First Nations peoples have maintained with the land, Canadian governments have made some efforts to settle claims based on Aboriginal title. Land claim agreements and treaties are intended

to assure First Nations and Inuit peoples of certain rights to natural resources, including land.

For many Aboriginal communities today, resource development is an important means of attaining economic progress and a reasonable standard of living. Reserves and areas covered by land claims agreements provide Inuit and First Nations people with control over agriculture and a wide range of other resource-related activities such as hunting, trapping, fishing, logging, and tourism. Sometimes hydrocarbon extraction, and

CHAPTER 6:
AGROECOSYSTEMS AND LAND RESOURCES

mining of surface and underground materials, are included in agreements. The Canadian Aboriginal Economic Development Strategy helps ensure that Aboriginal communities benefit from these opportunities, but underlying such efforts is the knowledge that ownership of land is fundamental to achieving their desired economic, cultural, and environmental objectives. The equity implied in ownership also is a fundamental principle in sustainability of land resources.

There are two basic types of Aboriginal land claims: comprehensive and specific. In 1991, the federal government established a Specific Claims Initiative to deal with cases of alleged nonfulfillment of Indian treaties or alleged improper administration of lands or other assets under the Indian Act or other formal agreements. Both federal and provincial governments are involved in negotiations to resolve these situations; settlements have involved millions of dollars in financial compensation.

Comprehensive claims are based on Aboriginal title to land arising from First Nations and Inuit traditional use and occupancy of land. In those parts of Canada where Aboriginal title has not been dealt with by treaty or other lawful means—Yukon, Labrador, most of British Columbia, and parts of Quebec and the Northwest Territories—Aboriginal tribal councils, bands, or communities assert their title to specific geographic areas. Settlements are agreed on, and include such features as establishment of ownership of land and resources, measures to stimulate

economic development, commitment to negotiate self-government, acknowledgment of the continuing interest of Aboriginal groups in management of renewable resources and environmental protection, as well as measures to ensure that developmental benefits are shared by Inuit and First Nations people (Department of Indian Affairs and Northern Development, 1995; Government of Canada, 1996). Examples of recent comprehensive claims agreements and their features are provided in the accompanying table.

Most Canadians benefit from a number of regulations that deal with environmental problems such as water supply and treatment, solid waste disposal, and industrial emissions. First Nations people who live on the 2261 reserves across the country, however, are not afforded that same level of environmental protection. Provincial statutes, regulations, and permits that govern the use of land and activities on land often have no legal force on reserves or First Nations land. This means that governmental ability to respond to concerns about drinking water, waste disposal, contaminated soil, control of industrial emissions and effluents, as well as environmental emergencies (such as spills, leaks, and explosions) is curtailed greatly. One solution through the Canadian Environmental Protection Act would be to give authority to the Minister of the Environment to enter into agreements with First Nations and Inuit peoples to administer any necessary regulations.

Examples of Comprehensive Claims Agreements

Agreement/Royal Assent	Elements
Gwich'in Comprehensive Land Claim Agreement December 22, 1992	• Gwich'in receive approximately 24 000 km² of land in the NWT and Yukon • mineral rights included on 4299 km² land • tax-free payment of $75 million over 15 years • resource royalties from Mackenzie Valley shared • guaranteed wildlife harvesting rights • participation in decision-making bodies
Final Agreements with the Council for Yukon Indians and Four First Nations May 29, 1993	• four Yukon First Nations receive 17 235 km² land settlement including mines and minerals (as of April 1997, settlements with other Yukon First Nations not finalized) • financial benefits of $79.9 million • rights in management of national parks and wildlife areas • specific rights for fish/wildlife harvesting • special economic employment opportunities
Final Agreement on the Tunngavik Federation of Nunavut July 9, 1993	• Inuit of Nunavut receive approximately 350 000 km² of land (36 000 km² includes mineral rights) • financial compensation: $1.148 billion over 14 years • share of resource royalties • guaranteed wildlife harvesting rights • participation in decision making re: land/environmental management • political accord to create a new territorial government of Nunavut in the eastern Arctic by 1999
Land Claim Agreement of the Sahtu Dene and Métis June 23, 1994	• Sahtu Dene and Métis given ownership of nearly 40 000 km² of land in the NWT (1813 km² includes subsurface rights) • financial settlement of $75 million over 15 years • a continuing share of resource royalties • guaranteed wildlife harvesting rights • participation in decision-making bodies

SOURCE: Government of Canada. (1996). *The state of Canada's environment—1996.* Ottawa: Supply and Services Canada. Chapter 10.

SOIL QUALITY

In an agricultural context, soil quality refers to the ability of the soil to support crop growth without resulting in soil degradation or other harm to the environment (Acton & Gregorich, 1995). Soil quality is affected by land use and by land management practices. Monoculture cropping, fallowing, intensive row cropping, and up-and-down slope cultivation are among the methods that cause the soil to be susceptible to processes that reduce its quality. These processes result in loss of organic matter; erosion by wind, water, and tillage; changes in soil structure; salinization; and chemical contamination.

Soil Organic Matter Levels

Organic matter (plant, animal, or microorganism matter, either living or dead) is an essential component of soil because organic matter stores and supplies plant nutrients, retains carbon, helps water infiltrate into soil, and stabilizes soil. The amount of organic matter in agricultural soils varies between 1 and 10 percent; how much is optimal depends on local climate, the amount of clay in the soil, and the intended use of the land (Government of Canada, 1996).

Although there is a lack of comprehensive data regarding soil organic matter across Canada, it is known that during the decade following the cultivation of crops on previously undisturbed forest or grassland soils, organic matter levels usually decline. Research has shown that since initial cultivation, Canada's uneroded agricultural soils have lost between 15 and 30 percent of their organic matter. However, trends in some regions indicate that levels of organic matter are holding steady or are increasing because of improved management practices. In the Prairie provinces, for example, more farmers are replenishing organic matter taken out of the soil through cropping by adding crop residues, manure, and commercial fertilizers (Gregorich et al., 1995).

Wind, Water, and Tillage Erosion

Natural processes such as **erosion** can be accelerated by farming activities; in fact, erosion of soil by wind and water is the most widespread soil degradation problem in Canada (Government of Canada, 1991). **Tillage erosion** on rolling or hummocky land, where soil moves downhill during plowing operations, for example, also contributes to loss of topsoil. The topsoil is the soil layer best able to support life; if topsoil is blown or washed away, the remaining soil not only has a reduced ability to provide the fertility required for crops, but also a lowered capacity to accept and store water. If topsoil or other products of soil erosion are introduced into water bodies, they can have detrimental effects there also.

Canada's agricultural lands have been classified in terms of their susceptibility to erosion. Almost all regions

of the country are concerned about **wind erosion,** but the Prairies in particular experience extensive, damaging wind erosion. About 36 percent of cultivated land in the Prairies is subject to high to severe risk of wind erosion, particularly in parts of southern Manitoba and Alberta and in a large part of Saskatchewan (Figure 6–4) (Wall, Pringle & Padbury, 1995). Soil losses to wind erosion not only lead to reduced productivity and loss of economic returns, but also cause abrasion damage to buildings, machinery, and vegetation. Airborne nutrients and pesticides eventually may degrade water quality and aggravate health problems in downwind areas.

All of Canada's agricultural regions are at risk of soil erosion by water, but the risk is greatest on land under intensive cultivation; overall, about 20 percent of Canada's agricultural areas have a moderate- to high-level risk of **water erosion.** While the Prairie provinces have a low inherent risk of soil erosion by water, the same cannot be said for other regions. Eighty percent of cultivated lands in the Maritimes, 75 percent of British Columbia lands, and 50 percent of lands in Ontario have been identified as having high to severe risk of soil erosion by water (see Figure 6–4) (Wall, Pringle & Padbury, 1995). In British Columbia's Peace River area, erosion on summerfallow lands has been as high as 14 tonnes per hectare per year, and in the Fraser Valley, erosion rates under row crops have been as high as 30 tonnes per hectare annually. In southwestern Ontario, water erosion may reduce yields by as much as 40 percent. Even though DDT is not used anymore, it can still be detected in soil eroding from agricultural areas in the Great Lakes basin. In Atlantic Canada, potato lands have some of the worst water erosion problems, such as in Prince Edward Island, where losses of up to 20 tonnes of soil per hectare per year have occurred in the past.

Depending on the cropping and land management practices used, the risk of soil erosion can be exacerbated or minimized. In Canada, between 1981 and 1991, risks of wind and water erosion were reduced through changes in

Water erosion is a major factor in the decline of soil quality, particularly on land under intensive cultivation.

Figure 6–4

Risk of wind and water erosion in Canada

SOURCE: Government of Canada. (1996). *The state of Canada's environment—1996.* Ottawa: Supply and Services Canada. Figures 11.9 and 11.10.

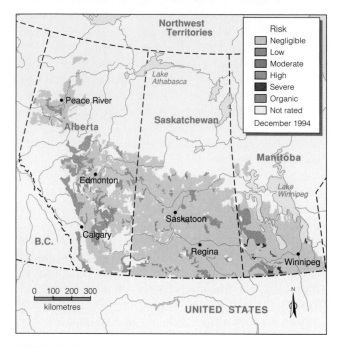

a) Risk of wind erosion in the Prairie provinces under 1991 management practices

NOTE: Management practices based on 1991 Census of Agriculture.

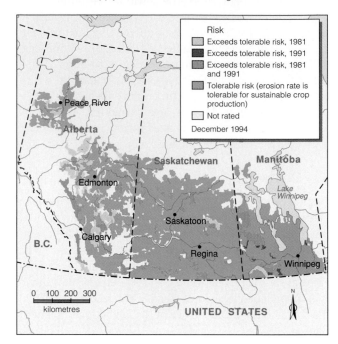

b) Risk of water erosion in the Prairie provinces, 1981 and 1991

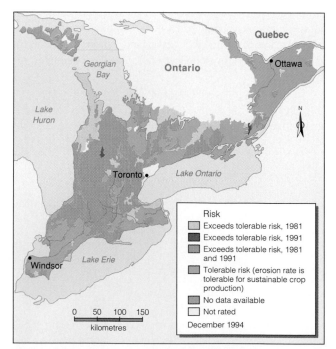

c) Risk of water erosion in southern Ontario, 1981 and 1991

NOTE: "Tolerable risk" refers to soils that are at risk of erosion at a rate that is tolerable for sustainable crop production under the most common management practices.

land tillage practices including reductions in summerfallow, changes in cropping patterns, and use of erosion control measures.

Soil Structure

Soils that are low in organic matter content, wet, and finely textured are most vulnerable to structural degradation, particularly if land management practices such as intensive tillage, row cropping, and short rotation periods are employed. One of the most recognized forms of structural degradation, **soil compaction,** results mainly from repeated passes of heavy machinery over wet soil during tillage and harvesting, causing what was a well-aerated soil to restrict air and water movement and thus reducing the ability of plant roots to penetrate the soil and derive sufficient moisture and nutrients.

Certain crops, such as potatoes, corn, soybeans, and sugar beets, often are associated with compaction because they require long growing seasons—they are planted in the early spring and harvested in the fall when the soil is frequently moist. One study estimated that soil compaction not only reduced crop yields by 10 percent but also cost Canadian producers more than $130 million annually (Science Council of Canada, 1986).

Another study reported that economic losses due to soil compaction were greatest in Quebec, where it was

PART 3:
RESOURCES FOR CANADA'S FUTURE

An example of soil salinization in an agricultural area of southern Alberta.

estimated that 20 percent of the best farmland was compacted. In British Columbia, soil compaction was widespread, and in Ontario, 50 to 70 percent of clay soils were adversely affected by compaction. In Atlantic Canada, there are naturally compacted subsoils and hardpans (hardened soil layers with greatly reduced porosity); farming on moist soils in this region causes additional compaction. Soil compaction is not a serious problem on the Prairies (Topp et al., 1995).

Soil Salinization

Salinization, an excess of salts in soils, is another factor that can reduce soil capacity to produce crops. Reduced crop production occurs because saline soils restrict the amount of water plants can withdraw from the soil. Unlike soil erosion, which usually occurs on the surface, salinization generally affects soils at depth. In dryland soils, such as occur on the Prairies, salinization is a natural process that takes place when a high water table, high rate of evaporation, and soluble salts all occur together (Government of Canada, 1996).

If water moves from areas of saline soils to streams, lakes, or underground aquifers, salts can degrade the quality of water available for domestic use, livestock, and irrigation. Salt water draining from saline soils may degrade the quality of neighbouring, downslope areas also, suggesting that controls on drainage may help efforts to reclaim saline areas.

Prairie saline soils existed long before settlement and cultivation occurred, but land management processes that affect the soil–water balance (such as replacing natural vegetation with crops and summerfallow) may modify the extent and degree of soil salinity. It was commonly thought that summerfallow was a major cause of soil salin-ization, but recent research has not corroborated that observation (Harker, Penner, Harron & Wood, 1995).

Other recent research has shown that while soil salinity is a continuing problem in some prairie soils, only about 2 percent of prairie agricultural land has more than 15 percent of its area affected by salinity. Most (62 percent) prairie agricultural land has less than 1 percent of its area affected by salinity, while of the remaining 36 percent of land, between 1 and 15 percent is affected (Eilers, Eilers, Pettapiece & Lelyk, 1995). Nevertheless, losses to farmers in southern and central regions of Alberta, Saskatchewan, and scattered parts of Manitoba were estimated to have ranged between $104 and $257 million per year during the 1980s.

Chemical Contamination

The suitability of soil for various uses, including food production, can be affected by **chemical contamination.** While some research shows that the contamination of agricultural soils with pesticide and nonpesticide contaminants is not a serious problem, other research shows that Canadian agricultural soil is contaminated by heavy metals such as cadmium, lead, and zinc. These metals are persistent and affect the health of plants, animals, and humans (Webber & Singh, 1995). Heavy metals enter agricultural soils mostly through atmospheric deposition as well as through fertilizers, animal manures, and sewage sludge that is applied to agricultural land as a source of organic matter and nutrients.

WATER QUALITY

Both surface water and groundwater resources can be impacted directly by agricultural use of land. **Surface runoff** can carry sediment, nutrients, pesticides, and bacteria from agricultural lands and contaminate surface water bodies. Groundwater resources can be contaminated by nutrients or pesticides when rainwater, irrigation water, and snowmelt percolate through the soil.

The nutrients that plants need for growth are obtained from soil, water, and air. If a farmer is to attain economic yields and sustain soil fertility, often it is necessary to replace the nutrients removed when crops are harvested by adding extra nitrogen, phosphorus, and potassium in the form of manure or commercial fertilizers. Depending on the type and intensity of crop and land management practices, soil characteristics, weather, and the type and amount of chemicals applied, that portion not used by crops or absorbed or retained in the soil can move into surface water or leach into groundwater.

If phosphorus enters surface water bodies, it can lead to accelerated **eutrophication** (nutrient pollution), whereas nitrates can make water unfit for human consumption. Given that about 26 percent of Canadians rely on groundwater for domestic purposes, and that more than 85 percent of livestock consumes water from underground sources, protecting water resources from agricultural contamination is essential (Government of Canada, 1996; Reynolds et al., 1995).

The water quality surveys and monitoring efforts that have been conducted reveal that pesticides usually are found in concentrations below the safe limits specified in the Canadian Water Quality Guidelines. Concentrations of nutrients and bacteriological contaminants sometimes exceed acceptable limits (Government of Canada, 1996; Reynolds et al., 1995). In terms of groundwater, there is insufficient long-term, detailed monitoring data to provide a comprehensive understanding of the current status and trends of agrochemicals entering Canada's groundwater. However, there are numerous examples across the country demonstrating that the main impact of agricultural activities on water quality is contamination by nitrates (Table 6–2).

Compared to 20 to 30 years ago, pesticides are said to be less of a problem because current pesticides are less persistent and more specialized. Nevertheless, public concerns remain about potential health hazards associated with water contamination; it is expected that such concerns will encourage increased use of nonchemical pest controls and decreased use of pesticides (Gregorich & Acton, 1995). Public concern also is one of the reasons why water quality has emerged in the 1990s as one of the key environmental issues facing agriculture.

AGRICULTURE AND BIODIVERSITY

Agricultural impacts on genetic, species, and ecosystem biodiversity of native wild species has become an important environmental issue. "Generally speaking, the quantity and quality of wildlife habitat in Canada have been degraded by settlement and agricultural development. Although farmlands and rangelands do provide enhanced habitat for certain species (a number of which cause extensive damage to orchards and standing crops), others have declined as a direct result of agricultural expansion and production practices. Many species of native plants, amphibians, reptiles, fish, birds, and mammals are endangered or threatened as a consequence of habitat loss to agriculture" (Government of Canada, 1991, p. 9-9).

On the prairies, for example, much of the original habitat has been altered significantly, largely through agriculture. Less than 1 percent of the original tallgrass prairie, 18 percent of the shortgrass prairie, 24 percent of the mixed-grass prairie, and 25 percent of the aspen parkland remain (Gauthier & Henry, 1989). This level of modification of original ecosystems has led to a concern for their continued viability and for the survival of the species that inhabit these areas, on the prairies and beyond (Government of Canada, 1991; Van Tighem, 1996).

A farmer spreads manure on a field to replace nutrients lost through harvesting.

There are several ways in which current agricultural land management practices continue to modify biodiversity. Biodiversity is reduced when agricultural production systems with little crop rotation provide large areas of uniform habitat. Also, aquatic biodiversity can be affected by water draining from agricultural fields, carrying nutrients, eroded sediments, and pesticides. Similarly, wild species composition and abundance can be affected through selective grazing of preferred forage plants that alters the vegetation composition (Mineau et al., 1994; Government of Canada, 1996).

Eighty-five percent of the decline in Canada's original wetland area is attributed to drainage for agriculture (Figure 6–5) (Rubec, 1994). Severe effects such as this result in marked shifts in vegetation and animal species composition, including that of migratory species. Changes

The burrowing owl is just one prairie species whose existence has been endangered by the agricultural alteration of its habitat.

TABLE 6–2
SELECTED EXAMPLES OF AGRICULTURE-RELATED WATER QUALITY ISSUES IN CANADA

Region	Water Quality Issues
British Columbia Fraser Valley	• Several aquifers show significant amounts of agrochemicals, mainly nitrates. • Abbotsford aquifer is highly susceptible to contamination from extensive use of high-nitrogen poultry manure on raspberry and forage crops in combination with climatic (heavy winter rainfall) and soil conditions that promote leaching. Monitoring of nitrate concentrations since 1995 suggests annual increases of 0.7 mg/L, and about 60 percent of samples collected from a highly sensitive region of the aquifer exceeded the Canadian Water Quality Guidelines safe limit of 10 mg/L. Twelve different pesticides have been detected in the aquifer, four at levels exceeding the Canadian Freshwater Aquatic Guidelines, and four (for which there are no Canadian guidelines) that exceed Washington State water quality standards for groundwater.
Okanagan Valley	• Significant leaching of nitrates has been reported in an important aquifer near Osoyoos. Septic effluent and fertilizer use in orchards are the major suspected sources of nitrate.
Dry Prairie Region Southern Alberta and Saskatchewan	• Non–point-source contamination of groundwater is rare because of the low intensity of agriculture (grain farming and low-density cattle grazing) and the dry climate. • Under certain conditions, agrochemical entry into the subsoil and groundwater can be significant. At some Alberta locations, application of maximum recommended rates of feedlot cattle manure has resulted in nitrate contamination of soil and groundwater.
Southern Manitoba	• Since about 1975, intensive agriculture and increased use of fertilizer and manure have caused a buildup of certain agrochemicals in some areas. For instance, elevated levels of nitrates have been found in the subsoils of fields heavily fertilized or manured (or both), and in cereal grains or horticultural crops. Although nitrate levels found in groundwater were not significant, the potential for future contamination is high.
Ontario and Quebec	• In southern Ontario and Quebec, the main agricultural contaminants are nitrate, bacteria, and the herbicide atrazine. Nitrate contamination occurs from a combination of fertilizer use, natural nitrate in the soil, and nitrogen compounds in rainwater. Bacterial contamination results from the high rate of application of liquid manure. Atrazine contamination is mostly a result of intensive, continuous corn cropping in the past. • In the early 1990s, an Ontario-wide survey found that 37 percent of 1300 farm wells tested contained coliform bacteria, fecal coliform, or nitrate in amounts exceeding those recommended in Ontario Drinking Water Objectives. Nitrates at levels above the maximum acceptable concentration were found in 13 percent of the wells, and 7 percent contained unacceptable concentrations of both coliform bacteria and nitrate-nitrogen. • A 1990–91 study of 70 wells in a sensitive region of Portneuf County, Quebec, showed that 29 wells had nitrate-nitrogen levels in excess of 10 mg/L, and 18 wells showed bacteriological contamination. Except for the pesticide aldicarb (used for insect control in potato production), low levels of pesticides were detected in half of the wells. In the case of aldicarb contamination, levels exceeded the Canadian drinking water standard of 9 micrograms/L in three wells.
Atlantic Canada New Brunswick	• Two studies (1973–76, 1988) of private groundwater wells in three intensive potato production areas showed that a substantial proportion of wells in two of the three regions sampled had nitrate concentrations above the Canadian drinking water standard and that nitrate levels were correlated with the intensity of potato production. Thirty-nine percent of the wells in the most intensive production area had nitrate levels above the standard. The cause appeared to be nitrogen from both soil and fertilizers.
Nova Scotia	• A survey of farm wells in Kings County, where most of the province's potatoes and corn are grown, showed that 41 percent had detectable levels of pesticides (none exceeded safe limits). Nine percent of the samples showed bacteria above the guideline levels and 13 percent exceeded the safe limit for nitrate.

SOURCE: Government of Canada. (1996). *The state of Canada's environment—1996*. Ottawa: Supply and Services Canada. Chapter 11.

in habitat have direct effects on populations and life cycles of ducks, geese, swans, shorebirds, songbirds, and butterflies that inhabit North, Central, and parts of South, America. The risk to biodiversity through habitat change is epitomized in the example of migratory songbirds and the shift from traditional shade-loving coffee plants to high-yield, sun-loving plants in modern Latin American coffee plantations (Box 6–2).

In spite of their historical effects in Canada, some agricultural practices can enhance wildlife habitat and promote biodiversity. That is, some farmers may strive to maintain populations of pollinator species, pest predators, and soil fauna, as well as to preserve wetland habitats (which also conserves groundwater and helps protect against drought). Planting of shelter belts, planting forage crops on marginal croplands, and planned grazing systems are other means by which farmers may provide habitat for many forms of wildlife (Government of Canada, 1996). Taking steps to ensure that soil organic matter is retained (thereby providing habitat for microorganisms), and employing integrated pest management techniques (Box 6–3) can reduce the risks from pesticides to nontarget species. Furthermore, farmers who are taking part in

habitat conservation programs such as the North American Waterfowl Management Plan (NAWMP) (see Chapters 7 and 12), have helped secure more than 260 000 hectares of habitat on the Prairies.

GREENHOUSE GASES

Agriculture may act both as a sink and as a source for several atmospheric greenhouse gases thought to be responsible for climate change. There are four main ways that agricultural activities relate to greenhouse gas concentrations: (1) soils are an important natural source of and reservoir for carbon, (2) methane is emitted from livestock and liquid manure, (3) nitrous oxide is released from nitrogen fertilizers, and (4) carbon dioxide is released from the burning of fossil fuels in farming activities (Government of Canada, 1994).

In 1994, agriculture contributed about 6.4 percent of Canada's total greenhouse gas emissions, equivalent to about 39 million tonnes of carbon dioxide. Of that total, about 60 percent (23.6 million tonnes) was methane from domestic animals and manure, about 29 percent (11.2 mil-

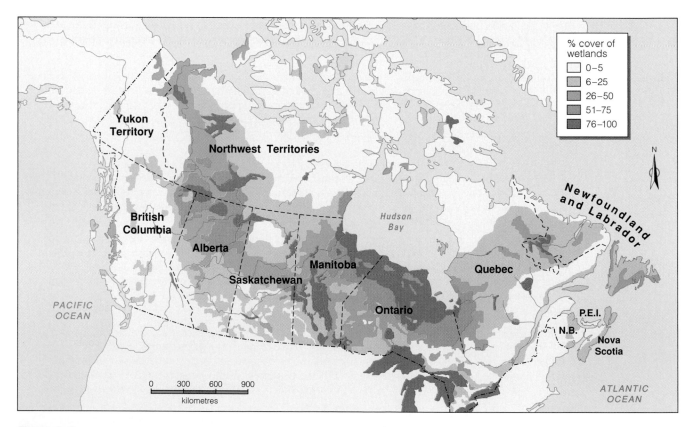

Figure 6–5
Distribution of wetlands in Canada

SOURCE: Government of Canada. (1996). *The state of Canada's environment—1996.* Ottawa. Figure 10.12.

PART 3:
RESOURCES FOR CANADA'S FUTURE

of Canada's cultivated soil is near equilibrium (because losses during the first few years are most rapid), small fluxes of carbon into or out of soils can translate into large quantities of carbon dioxide when totalled across Canada (Government of Canada, 1996).

Soil carbon fluxes influence the overall greenhouse gas balance for agriculture. This means that an individual farmer's actions to retain and increase levels of organic matter in soils can assist the soil to sequester carbon and offset carbon dioxide emissions from agriculture. Increasing **conservation tillage** and zero tillage are among the practices that are useful from both climate change and soil

lion tonnes) was carbon dioxide from fossil fuel use, and about 11 percent (4.2 million tonnes) was nitrous oxide from nitrogen fertilizer (cited in Government of Canada, 1996). These statistics should be used cautiously as they contain known omissions (for example, neither nitrous oxide emissions from soil or manure, nor carbon dioxide emissions from soil are included).

Interestingly, although fertilizer use has remained relatively constant since 1985, the amount of nitrogen in the total fertilizer mix increased from about 10 percent in 1960 to about 30 percent in 1985 (Government of Canada, 1994). In addition to emissions from use of nitrogen fertilizers, nitrous oxides are generated also from nutrient cycling in agricultural soils (this is poorly understood, even though it may be the largest source of nitrous oxide from agriculture).

Since cultivation began, estimates are that Canada has lost about 25 percent of its total agricultural soil carbon. Even though it is believed that the carbon content

Given the risks of wind and water erosion of prairie lands, many farmers employ conservation tillage practices, including the use of implements such as the seed wheel.

RESPONSES TO ENVIRONMENTAL IMPACTS AND CHANGE

If Canadians are going to achieve sustainable (agricultural) land use, then careful planning must be undertaken to maintain the prosperity and diversity of our economy simultaneously with environmental integrity and ability of the land to replenish renewable resources (such as the quality of the soil), as well as the preservation and enhancement of the social fabric. In other words, agricultural sustainability needs to emphasize integration of economic, social, and environmental concerns.

From its perspective, Agriculture and Agri-Food Canada expects that, when agriculture and agri-food production is carried out in a sustainable manner, the natural resource base will be protected; degradation of soil, water, and air quality will be prevented; the economic and social well-being of Canadians will be enhanced; a safe and high-quality supply of agricultural products will be assured; and the livelihood and well-being of agricultural workers and their families will be safeguarded (Environment Bureau, n.d.).

One way in which this perspective has been promoted has been through development of market opportunities for Canadian agricultural and agri-food products. To that end, in 1993, Canada's agricultural industry and the federal and provincial governments set a goal to achieve $20 billion in agri-food exports by the year 2000. World trade in unprocessed grains (such as wheat), oilseeds (mostly canola), meat and meat products, and live animals enabled the agriculture sector to reach a record $19.9 billion in exports in 1996. (More than 50 percent of the sales were to the United States, followed by 12 percent to Japan, and 10 percent to the European Union.) A new goal has now been set: to win a minimum 4-percent share of the world market (about $40 billion worth) by the year 2005.

Some people might criticize this approach for its apparent emphasis on sustainable (economic) growth rather than on environmental sustainability. This example highlights the different views people may bring to the quest to achieve sustainability of agricultural lands. Different perspectives often generate conflict; resolution of the conflict requires responses that incorporate understanding about the cultural, economic, and ecological roles of land.

Throughout the world, many people believe that an efficient food production system exists when crops are grown where costs are least (often in developing countries) and the food shipped to markets around the world. The trend toward globalization means that food in our

quality perspectives. Additional agricultural practices that may help reduce greenhouse gas emissions include reduced summerfallow area, increased forage production, improved crop yields, reduced methane emissions from farm animals (through improved feed additives and feeding technology), improved efficiency of manure use, decreased fossil fuel use, and increased use of renewable fuels such as ethanol (Government of Canada, 1996).

ENERGY USE

Agricultural activities consume energy directly in tilling, harvesting, heating, and ventilation. The pattern of agricultural energy use in 1990 was 28 percent in primary production, 22 percent in processing and packaging, 18 percent in distribution, and 32 percent for storage and preparation. Fuels for transportation account for 57 percent of the energy used in primary production on the farm, while a further 25 percent is accounted for by fertilizers. Approximately 3 percent of Canada's total energy consumption is used on farms to support primary agricultural production (Government of Canada, 1996).

The main environmental concern regarding energy use in agriculture is consumption of fossil fuels and the resultant emission of greenhouse gases. If production and use of renewable fuels such as ethanol could be expanded, environmental benefits could include lower net carbon dioxide emissions. (Research at Agriculture and Agri-Food Canada in Sainte-Foy, Quebec, continues on plants such as the Jerusalem artichoke that yields up to 18 tonnes per hectare of ethanol-producing biomass.) Other practices, including reduced tillage, new herbicides with lower application rates, and genetic improvements in plants such as greater resistance to disease and lower fertilizer needs, point the way toward reduction in energy use and achieving sustainability of agroecosystems.

stores is said to travel an average of 2000 kilometres (Olson, 1997). This model of food production is supported by international agreements such as the North American Free Trade Agreement (NAFTA) and the General Agreement on Tariffs and Trade (GATT).

Efficiency, however, does not always consider social and environmental effects, especially in developing nations. For instance, when officials in developing countries emphasize **cash crops** (crops grown for export) over food production for local people, and when people do not have access to land to grow their own food or have enough money to buy it, one result is increasing migration to cities. Few jobs are available in the cities, so poverty increases (and poor people continue to be exploited as cheap sources of labour). In the name of efficiency, too, pesticides that are banned in Canada are used in developing nations. Other environmental degradation occurs due to nonexistent or weak legislation and regulations, and lack of enforcement.

Alternatives to the globalization of the current food system include **regional sustainability.** In this system, developing countries would be encouraged to first grow food for themselves and then crops for export. Such a shift would require either debt reduction or debt forgiveness by the developed world, however (Olson, 1997). Canada provides at least $300 million worth of food annually to countries in need. The following section briefly considers some of the international initiatives that have been taken toward agricultural sustainability. National, local, and partnership initiatives undertaken to work toward sustainability of agriculture and the land base on which it depends also are examined.

INTERNATIONAL INITIATIVES

In 1992, Agenda 21 noted that world food production must more than double in the next 40 years to meet the needs of a growing population, more than 80 percent of which will live in the developing world. The challenge is to increase agricultural production without further degrading the environment.

In this regard, Canada's International Development Research Centre (IDRC) has promoted sustainable agriculture for many years. Its projects have included research on farming systems designed to maximize use of the marginal lands that many small-scale farmers in developing countries are obliged to cultivate, while doing the least environmental damage. IDRC also has investigated using alternative farming practices such as integrated pest management, which reduces the need for costly chemical fertilizers (see Box 6–4 for a brief discussion of rice–fish farming in Indonesia) and agroforestry, which incorporates the use of trees for multiple purposes such as forage, fire-

wood, windbreaks, and soil enrichment. In addition to this work, IDRC has sponsored research on the preservation of Indigenous knowledge systems (International Development Research Centre, 1993). (See also the short article by Roach, listed in Additional Information Sources.)

In many developing nations, women bear the major burden in agriculture and food production. They have extensive knowledge of local ecosystems and can help in conserving biodiversity and protecting the environment if given an opportunity to be involved equally in decision making relating to sustainable agriculture (Enviro-Focus 6). (For further examples of the role of women in agriculture, see the articles by Jowkar and by Seck, listed in the Additional Information Sources at the end of this chapter.)

Desertification

During the 1970s and again in the 1980s, devastating droughts affected the West African Sahel; thousands of people and millions of animals died. Satellite images clearly showed altered vegetation patterns, and people began to talk about expanding deserts and sand dunes on the march. Closer scientific examination revealed that much of the vegetation change reflected water shortage and not permanent loss of soil fertility or land degradation. However, the loss of soil productivity, crop failures, scarcity of fuelwood, and reduced availability of grazing lands for livestock forced many people to abandon their land and become environmental refugees. Although many African nations made plans to address the problem, little serious action was taken to combat **desertification** (Canadian International Development Agency, 1995; Cardy, 1994).

Desertification is land degradation that occurs in arid, semiarid, and dry subhumid areas as a result of complex

Desertification is particularly problematic in Africa, where a combination of unsustainable land use practices and climatic variations have resulted in overexploitation of the land.

BOX 6–4

SUSTAINABLE AGRICULTURE IN INDONESIA: RICE–FISH FARMING

An excellent example of how food production and environmental benefits can be combined is found in a project in Indonesia. There, rice-growing and fish culture, carried out in the same field, demonstrate an integrated approach to farming that will sustain productivity into the future.

In rice–fish farming, fish are raised in flooded fields of rice. The practice has a long history: Asian farmers have been raising fish in their rice fields for 2000 years or longer, providing farm families with important sources of carbohydrates and animal protein at the same time.

Originally, wild fish bred naturally in the fields and were harvested whenever possible. Fish husbandry techniques evolved over time in many countries. But the advent of high-yielding rice varieties changed all that, because they demanded high inputs of pesticides and herbicides that were toxic to the fish. The result was that many farm families were deprived of an important source of nutrition.

Within the past decade, as the need for more efficient and sustainable farming systems increased, rice–fish farming enjoyed a renewed interest in almost all Asian countries. A project that began in 1987 with the Sukamandi Research Institute for Food Crops and the Indonesian Research Institute for Freshwater Fisheries aimed to raise the visibility of rice–fish farming to Indonesian farmers and government policymakers.

In this project, farmers dig a small pond or trench surrounded by a protective bank of soil in a low-lying area of the rice field and introduce small fish fingerlings—carp, tilapia, catfish, or other species—into it. When the field is flooded rice is planted as usual. The fish are let out of their pond and allowed to forage through the rice field.

What happens is that rice and fish benefit each other. Pests of the rice provide food for the fish, which in being eaten protect

the rice: the fish feed on insects such as leafhoppers, stem borers, and aphids, plus possibly other invertebrates such as crabs and snail larvae. The fish also recycle nutrients through feeding and depositing feces in the submerged soil, which fertilize the rice. Initial research has indicated that uptake by the rice plants of important nutrients like phosphorous and nitrogen is significantly improved. Dr. Achmad Fagi, the leader of the Indonesian project, found that "rice–fish culture with common carp actually increased the yields of commonly used rice varieties." Farmers can get increased family nutrition from eating the fish, or they can increase their cash income by selling the fish.

Pesticides, herbicides, and to a lesser degree, chemical fertilizers, continue to create problems for rice–fish farmers, but the Indonesian government has recognized the problem by reducing many of the import subsidies on pesticides.

SOURCE: International Development Research Centre (IDRC). (1993). *Agenda 21: Green paths to the future.* Ottawa: IDRC, p. 7. Reprinted by permission.

interactions between unpredictable climatic variations and unsustainable land use practices by people who, in their struggle for survival, overexploit agricultural, forest, and water resources (Canadian International Development Agency, 1995). Desertification is more than just desert encroachment; it refers to degradation of dry land to the point where it is difficult to restore its former level of productivity (partly because of the loss in biological diversity).

Desertification is a worldwide problem, affecting about one-sixth of the world's population, most of whom live in the poorer regions of the world. African nations are the most vulnerable and the least able to combat the problem without international assistance. Desertification affects the livelihoods of an estimated 900 million people, and costs (in terms of income loss) about US$42

billion annually (Canadian International Development Agency, 1995). While the West African Sahel is the most seriously affected region in the world, vast areas in Asia as well as North, Central, and South America are affected (Figure 6–6). Technically, with dry lands in the three Prairie provinces, Canada is an affected country. Should climate changes occur as predicted, and currently dry regions become drier, Canada might well need the lessons learned in other countries to formulate a Canadian response to this issue.

During UNCED (the Earth Summit) in 1992, the African countries felt that inadequate attention was being paid to desertification, one of their most pressing concerns. A major achievement of the Rio conference was the adoption of a special chapter in *Agenda 21* on combatting desertification and drought. This chapter recommended

Women and Sustainable Agriculture in Africa

Shimwaayi Muntemba, the executive director of the Environment Liaison Centre in Nairobi, Kenya, says the search for strategies to halt environmental degradation and introduce sustainable development into Africa must begin by recognizing and legitimizing women's knowledge.

Muntemba, who coordinated much of the research of the Brundtland Commission on food security, agriculture, environment and women, works with WEDNET, a multinational and multidisciplinary project on women and natural resource management in Africa.

WEDNET's main purpose is to strengthen the role of indigenous knowledge in international development. It has involved research by women in Senegal, Burkina Faso, Mali, Ghana, Nigeria, Tanzania and Zambia, most of it concentrated on activities such as management and conservation of livestock, water, harvest, soil, food security, nutrition, health, and technology.

A computerized information-sharing network is being established between ELC and its Canadian counterpart at York University. Muntemba hopes that the system will allow African researchers to share their knowledge with Canadians. She notes that if this had happened in the colonial past, the story of Zambia's agricultural development would be different.

For many years, she says, the farmers of Zambia logged trees, burned the branches, and used the ash as fertilizer for the soil. That system of soil conservation was known as "Citemene," and it symbolized the effective, indigenous use of soil by the African people.

"Crops rarely failed in this part of the country," Muntemba says. "Land could be used for five years before being left to rest."

But when colonial farmers came they dismissed the Citemene method as backward and destructive. They promoted the use of chemical fertilizers which acidified the soil.

"Now they have left we must try and regenerate the soil," says Muntemba. She says that tropical soils are very fragile and require a variety of agricultural techniques.

Muntemba uses WEDNET and her position at ELC to heighten the awareness of women's indigenous knowledge in Africa.

"We have come a long way since the 1970s when women began to be discussed as central to agriculture," she says. "Now there is an actual appreciation of the fact that women's economic and agricultural activities are located within the context of environmental sustainability."

SOURCE: International Development Research Centre (IDRC). (1993). *Agenda 21: Green paths to the future.* Ottawa: IDRC, p. 29. Reprinted by permission.

that further political effort be made to negotiate an intergovernmental convention on desertification within two years. Paralleling the Convention on Climate Change and the Convention on Biological Diversity, the Convention to Combat Desertification was signed on October 14, 1994.

CIDA was Canada's lead agency in negotiations for this latter convention. The potential for partnerships among communities, NGOs, international organizations, and governments was emphasized as a way to find lasting solutions to desertification. Donor countries such as Canada provided financial and technical support to combat desertification—CIDA earmarked $100 million

over five years to address West African desertification and degraded natural resources, particularly water (Canadian International Development Agency, 1994).

Like IDRC, CIDA has been involved in innovative approaches to desertification control for more than 20 years. Projects have varied from sand dune control and land stabilization in West Africa, to establishment of a regional network of national tree centres in Southern Africa, to community-based agroforestry programs in India, and to teaching community environmental awareness in the Andean highlands of Peru (Canadian International Development Agency, 1995).

Figure 6–6
World drylands and desertification

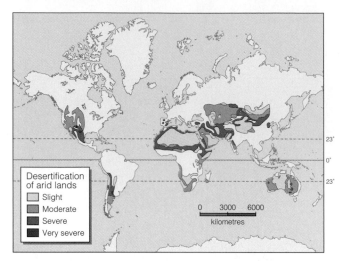

a) World status of desertification of arid lands

SOURCE: Dregne, H.E. (1983). *Desertification of arid lands*. Char, Switzerland: Harwood Academic Publishers. Figure 1.2, p. 16. Reprinted by permission.

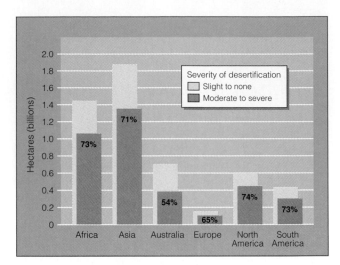

b) Drylands by continent

SOURCE: Cardy, F. (1994). Desertification. *Our Planet,* 6(5), p. 4.

CANADIAN EFFORTS TO ACHIEVE SUSTAINABLE AGRICULTURE

Chapter 10 of *Agenda 21* presents an integrated approach to land planning and management designed to lead toward sustainability. Based on *Agenda 21,* Canada identified seven priorities as being relevant to our domestic land issues. Briefly these priorities emphasize provincial land use functions; increased use of information systems; strengthening of federal, provincial, and territorial relations; consultations and partnerships; support of Aboriginal land use initiatives; coordinated state-of-the-environment monitoring; and application of an ecosystem approach to land use planning and management (Government of Canada, 1996).

To demonstrate some of these priorities, let's take a closer look at sustainable agriculture in Manitoba.

An Illustration: Sustainable Agriculture in Manitoba

Agriculture is a key component of the Manitoba economy and its successful continuation is dependent on sustaining the province's land and water resources. The government of Manitoba recognized the economic and social importance of farming in the province and illustrated this concern in its 1995 State of the Environment Report (Manitoba Environment, 1995).

Farming has a long history in Manitoba with settlement patterns determined largely by the availability of productive agricultural lands. Migration to the province was rapid in the early 1900s due to the export potential of and high prices garnered by agricultural commodities, notably wheat. In 1995, agriculture in Manitoba was a $4-billion industry, accounting for one in seven jobs and 11 percent of provincial gross domestic product. Farmland comprises close to 14 percent of the total land area of Manitoba, or 7.7 million hectares. Improved farmland accounts for 5.4 million hectares, while the remainder is used in its natural state for hay and grazing. For the most part, agriculture is concentrated in the southern one-third of the province, in the prairie and boreal plains ecozones. Typical of developed world agriculture, there has been a significant expansion in the size of farms in Manitoba, but fewer farmers are working the land.

Early Manitoba settlers initially were attracted to the better drained areas. Given the large extent of permanent and semipermanent wetlands in the province (e.g., the Red River Valley was 60 percent wetlands), drainage efforts were underway before the turn of the century. Large-scale drainage work in Manitoba began after the Land Drainage Act was passed in 1895. Under this Act, 24 drainage districts were formed and fostered the construction of 5794 kilometres of drains. By the 1930s, approximately 810 000 hectares of land had been drained for agriculture. High costs associated with maintaining the drains led to their deterioration in many areas; eventually the Manitoba government assumed responsibility for most of the major drainage systems.

Productive agriculture would not be possible in Manitoba without the widespread use of drainage systems. In addition to the potential benefits provided by drainage (increased yields, improved crop quality, increased fertilizer efficiency, and reduced farm labour), a number of drawbacks often result from draining the land. These drawbacks include loss of wetlands and wildlife habitat (the Red River Valley is now 1 percent wetlands), reduced availability of natural water storage areas, increased river flooding, and lower groundwater recharge capability. Drainage channels also lead to increased sedimentation levels in lakes and rivers. For example, millions of tonnes of sediment deposited into Dauphin Lake through erosion of the Edwards Creek drainage channel has created a 100-hectare delta. Mitigating the problems associated with drainage requires ecologically sound land use planning strategies. In fact, construction of new drainage systems is no longer supported by the Manitoba government. Existing systems will be maintained or reconstructed only to increase crop yields or to reduce erosion or deposition. Further, provincial policy requires that drainage improvement in one area cannot adversely affect another area.

The Manitoba government recognizes that the survival of the agricultural sector can be secured only by sustaining productivity of the land: "[n]ot every acre of land in southern Manitoba can be cultivated. Furthermore, thousands of acres already cultivated should never have been cleared in the first place" (Manitoba Environment, 1995, p. 30).

In 1989, Manitoba and the federal government cooperated in establishing a multiyear, multiprogram, soil conservation agreement. Farming for Tomorrow, the on-farm component of the agreement, encouraged farmers to use the land more efficiently by improving eroded, saline, and marginal lands. Specific initiatives under this program included the Conservation Cover Program (which provided forage to 16 200 hectares of farmland in 48 municipalities) and a rotational grazing program (which assisted farmers in preparing a forage plan to better manage their pastureland). Although the Farming for Tomorrow program was completed in 1994, similar initiatives are continuing under the Canada–Manitoba Agreement for Agricultural Sustainability (CMAAS). CMAAS is a $20.8–million cost-shared program between the province and federal government. Under the agreement, 66 local conservation groups participate in seven major resource management programs relating to soil and water, integrated resource management, integrated pest management, forage and cover crop utilization, livestock management, innovative partnership initiatives, and consumer and urban awareness programs. In 1994, these local conservation groups initiated more than 300 on-farm projects with funding of over $21 million.

A number of other efforts are taking place to ensure a sustainable future for the agricultural sector in Manitoba. Accompanying the rise of local land stewardship is the practice of conservation farming. An important method of conservation farming involves directly seeding the land

In the early 1900s, thousands of kilometres of drainage systems were constructed in southern Manitoba.

without tillage. By directly seeding into standing stubble (crop residues, straw, etc.), soil is protected from erosion and moisture is conserved near the surface, fostering quicker crop emergence. Reduced tillage has a negative side as the use of herbicides may be required to control weeds. Through the Farming for Tomorrow program, the province purchased or leased conservation seeding equipment and made it available to farmers for a nominal fee. Over a 4-year period, 134 000 hectares of cropland were seeded using conservation seeding equipment. (For further information on conservation tillage see Box 6–5.)

In response to growing concern over chemical pesticides, the Manitoba government, industry, and nonprofit groups initiated a number of programs to encourage safe and responsible pesticide use. A certification program to license agricultural chemical dealers under the Pesticide and Fertilizers Control Act was established in 1993. The course-based program, cosponsored by the Western Fertilizer and Chemical Dealers Association, spans the three Prairie provinces and is more comprehensive than previous licensing programs.

A further safeguard related to the licensing of pesticide dealers is the development of warehousing standards by the Crop Protection Institute. Chemical manufacturers have agreed that dealerships not meeting the industry warehousing standards will not be sold pesticide products. Manitoba Environment uses the standards as a license control condition for new chemical and fertilizer dealerships. In addition, a 50 percent reduction in the

BOX 6-5
CONSERVATION TILLAGE AND ZERO TILLAGE

During the past decade or so, producers, industry, and government have made concerted efforts to reduce the extent of wind and water erosion on Canada's agricultural lands through the use of soil conservation practices. An appropriate mixture of land management practices tailored to the conditions and needs of individual farms can provide multiple benefits for preserving soil health and productivity, minimizing water contamination, conserving wildlife habitat, and maintaining farm nutrient balances.

Examples of such management practices include growing forage crops in rotations or as permanent cover, growing winter cover crops, planting shelter belts, strip cropping, using buffer strips, and using conservation tillage techniques and contour cultivation. As shown in the graph below, significant proportions of Canadian farmers were using one or more erosion control practices on their farms in 1991 (note that not all farms require erosion control, and that some practices are applicable in some areas and not others).

Conservation tillage, including zero or no tillage, was used on 31 percent of the land seeded (Box Figure 6–2). This form of tillage leaves a portion or all of the crop residue on the soil surface and special equipment sows seeds for the new crop through the standing stubble from the previous crop (see photo next page). This practice provides protection against erosion, reduces soil crusting, helps retain moisture by trapping snow, allows rain and snowmelt water to soak directly into the ground, and increases soil organic matter content. In addition, continuous ground cover provides better habitat for ground-nesting birds and a wide array of other wildlife. Studies in Alberta and

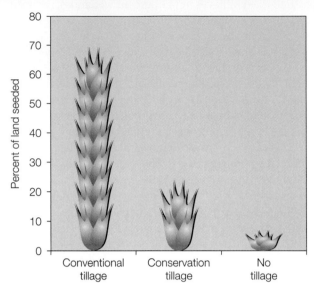

Box Figure 6–2

Tillage practices in Canada

Conventional tillage: most of the crop residue (plant material remaining after harvest) is incorporated into the soil.
Conservation tillage: most of the crop residue is left on the soil surface to provide protection against erosion, reduce soil crusting, and increase the organic matter content of soils; also known as mulch tillage, minimum tillage, and reduced tillage.
No tillage: any system where soil is not disturbed between harvesting one crop and planting the next; includes direct seeding into stubble or sod; also known as zero till.

SOURCE: Government of Canada. (1996). *The state of Canada's environment—1996.* Ottawa. Figure 11.7.

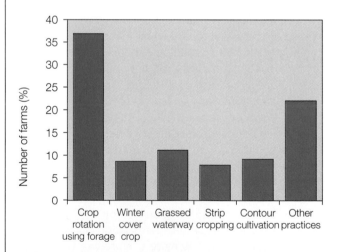

Box Figure 6–1

Erosion control practices used in Canada

NOTE: 1991 was the first time that this type of information had been collected in the Census of Agriculture; therefore, there are no trends. A farm may use more than one erosion control practice or none at all.

SOURCE: Government of Canada. (1996). *The state of Canada's environment—1996.* Ottawa: Supply and Services Canada. Figure 11.6.

Manitoba demonstrated that using conservation farming practices improved farmers' incomes by $6.42 per hectare per year in Alberta and by $32.78 per hectare per year in Manitoba (Government of Canada, 1996). "These systems appear to be the most cost-effective soil practice for general use across the country" (Government of Canada, 1996).

Since the 1970s, Ducks Unlimited has worked in partnership with farmers to assist them conserve their soil and water resources while improving the environment for wildlife and people. By 1995, Ducks Unlimited had invested $1.6 million in research and demonstration on zero tillage. Increased funding through Prairie CARE, a major component of the North American Waterfowl Management Plan, allowed Ducks Unlimited to expand its role in zero tillage in all three Prairie provinces as well as Ontario and British Columbia.

A Saskatchewan farmer began his first moves toward zero tillage in 1985 because he saw the depletion of his soil resources and wanted his farm to remain viable for his children. "Zero till addresses the long-term sustainability of the land and my family, as well as providing a better home for wildlife" (Lyseng, 1995, p. 15). An important benefit of zero tillage was that fall-seeded

BOX 6-5
(CONTINUED)

Ducks Unlimited agrologist Lee Moats, himself a zero till farmer, inspects a winter wheat field he seeded August 28, 1994. He displays viable plants ready to spring to life in April. The old straw cover and the new wheat plants provide good duck nesting cover.

crops were more likely to survive over winter with the protection of straw and crop residue. For example, this farmer would plant fall rye or winter wheat following a harvest and watch the new crop grow for a month or two until freeze-up. With the spring melt the crop would be waiting for returning ducks. The cover from fall-seeded crops means ground nesting birds of all species have a better chance to avoid predation. Also, no spring field operations means nest successes are higher compared to conventional farming methods (Lyseng, 1995).

Ontario Land CARE (Conservation of Agriculture, Resources and Environment) is a Ducks Unlimited program. One element of this program is the establishment of conservation tillage clubs where Ducks Unlimited financially assists groups of farmers to purchase and share no-till equipment. Conservation tillage clubs are designed to be demonstration sites for neighbouring farmers interested in learning about the practice (Kinkel & Werner, 1997).

Five farm operators from Meaford, Ontario, recently formed Bighead Conservation Tillage Club. One of the members, who carries on a tradition of conservation started by his father, has added the no-till drill to his arsenal of management techniques for growing corn silage crops. In addition to his revised tillage practices, this farmer has gained a new mindset on farm planning and land use on his property. The club agreement resulted in securement of a 20-acre wetland on his property, and the adjacent idled and no-till fields provide habitat for waterfowl and other wildlife (Kinkel & Werner, 1997).

The Bighead Club president indicated that some of his land suffered severe erosion as a result of intense row cropping. Now, having taken many years of careful management to restore the land to its full cropping potential, and with use of the no-till drill and planned crop rotation, some of his fields do not need to be plowed for seven years. Such savings in time, soil, and money are lessons that many farmers in the erosion-prone area are interested in learning. By demonstrating conservation and no-till techniques, members of the Bighead Conservation Tillage Club may impact the agricultural operations of the surrounding farming community in significant ways. At the same time, the aims of Ducks Unlimited to ensure quality wetland and wildlife habitat are being met.

For more detailed information about zero tillage, see Agriculture Canada's Web site No-till: Making it work, listed in the Additional Information Sources section of this chapter.

SOURCE: Lyseng, R. (1995). Why zero till? *Conservator,* 16(1), p. 14.

number of rural pesticide dealers is forecast because of the revised standards.

Since its creation in 1990, an innovative, nonprofit corporation known as the Association for a Clean Rural Environment (ACRE) has helped to reclaim over 2.5 million pesticide containers. Across Canada, a voluntary fee of one dollar for each pesticide container sold goes into a fund used to ensure proper collection, decontamination, and recycling of the containers. ACRE reimburses municipalities for managing the collection sites, provided the sites meet strict environmental guidelines. There are 125 municipal collection sites in Manitoba, almost all of which follow environmental guidelines set out by Manitoba Environment. The rate of return for both metal and plastic pesticide containers increased from 33 percent in 1990 to 80 percent in 1994. In 1995, ACRE received a Sustainable Development Award of Excellence for its efforts in collecting pesticide containers.

The success of programs such as these can be attributed to the cooperative efforts of governments, industry, nongovernment groups, and particularly the members of the farming community themselves. The 1995 State of the

Canadian farmers have been pivotal in the successful collection and recycling of empty agrichemical containers.

Environment Report also was a useful way to publicize the progress and concerns of provincial agriculture to the residents of Manitoba. (For more information on state-of-the-environment reporting in Manitoba, contact Manitoba Environment at the address listed in the Additional Information Sources section at the end of this chapter.)

Nontraditional Agricultural Activities

In Canada, efforts to sustain agroecosystems historically have focused on stewardship of land and soil resources on individual farms. Individually, farmers have been searching for new ways to diversify and to achieve sustainability within their agroecosystems. Nontraditional agricultural activities have been gaining in popularity, including **organic farming** (reliance on a management system using natural soil-forming processes and crop rotation schemes rather than synthetic inputs), **alternative livestock** production (raising non-native species and domesticated native species), and **agroforestry** (combining production of trees, shrubs, agricultural plants and/or animals in the same land area). Agricultural biotechnology efforts have resulted in biofertilizers, biofeeds, and plants with novel traits. Organic farming, game ranching, and biotechnology are discussed briefly below.

Organic Farming Founded in 1975, Canadian Organic Growers (COG) is a national information network for organic farmers, gardeners, and consumers. Their objectives include conducting research into alternatives to traditional chemical- and energy-intensive food production practices, and endorsing practices that promote and maintain long-term soil fertility, reduce fossil fuel use, reduce pollution, recycle waste, and conserve nonrenewable resources. In addition, COG assists in educational and demonstration projects to help people understand the value and integrity of organic foods.

Organic farming is one way to promote the goals of a decentralized, bioregionally based food system that sees food produced by local farmers and consumed by local people. Reducing transportation costs, bolstering local marketing systems and economies, and promoting greater regional food self-reliance are other benefits of consuming (organic) foods within the region where they are produced.

Community shared agriculture (CSA) farms are a related development, where local people share the risk of (organic) food production with farmers by buying a share in the produce prior to the growing season. Sometimes, depending on the individual farmer, a share in the produce involves a commitment on the part of the shareholder to work in the CSA garden for a day or more. CSA farms promote local production and consumption with associated reduction in transportation needs, thus contributing in small ways toward reduced air quality problems. CSA farms also may provide opportunities for urban residents to get their hands dirty, and perhaps help people to appreciate directly the value of agricultural land. (In Chapter 13 we consider urban agriculture and some of the benefits it brings to people and the planet.)

Game Farming and Ranching One type of alternative livestock production is the raising of game species. Farmers and ranchers have discovered that the pleasant-tasting, low-cholesterol and low-fat meat of the North American elk, or wapiti, makes it an attractive ranching species. The velvet (nonhardened antler) is an annual crop and is valued highly in the marketplace. Although elk have been part of the ranching scene for 30 to 40 years, the industry has grown greatly from about the mid-1980s. In 1990, 32 prominent elk ranchers formed the North American Elk Breeders Association (NAEBA) to promote elk ranching as an agricultural pursuit. In 1996, almost 750 NAEBA members (including Canadians) were farming or ranching about 30 000 elk.

The opportunity to socialize with the farmer and other shareholders is just one of the benefits of community shared agriculture farming.

Wild elk are the basis of initial herds for game ranching and captive breeding purposes.

Capture of elk from the wild is illegal, and reputable elk ranchers do not take part in these activities. However, the first captive elk herd in any area is based on wild animals. In Manitoba, as the conservation co-chair of the Sierra Club's Prairie chapter wrote, the province's natural resource officers used elk baiting, particularly around Riding Mountain National Park, to attract and then capture wild elk (Chambers, n.d.). These captured elk were to form the basis of a new provincial game ranching industry.

In 1986, public consultation in Manitoba had revealed intense opposition to game ranching. In 1995, without public consultation or review, the province introduced new legislation (Livestock Industry Diversification Act and the Elk Game Production Regulation) and began an elk roundup. Opposition by conservation groups, wildlife groups, animal rights groups, the Winnipeg Humane Society, and individuals had no impact on the government's decision to proceed.

Opposition was expressed not only about wild animals being kept in captivity, but also about the threat of the spread of disease among the unique subspecies of elk in the area. Like many other provinces, Manitoba already had difficulties with poaching and the trade in animal parts. Harvesting of antler velvet "to sell to the lucrative Asian folk medicine market" (Chambers, 1996) was of great concern as a stimulus to increased poaching for velvet. The NAEBA indicated that "[t]ypically, the velvet profits are enough to pay for feeding the entire herd year round"; in 1996, annual revenues from velveting just one mature bull elk were US$1495 (Elk On Line, 1996).

Agricultural Biotechnology Although it is not a new discipline, **biotechnology** is an umbrella term that covers a broad spectrum of scientific tools. Biotechnology takes advantage of living organisms, or their parts, to produce products; making yogurt, making cheese, and making bread are traditional biotechnological activities. More advanced activities include the production of antibiotics, vaccines, and enzymes. One new aspect of biotechnology is genetic engineering to remove or precisely transfer specific characteristics or genetic information from one organism to another, thus altering the characteristics of these organisms. When combined with traditional techniques, biotechnology provides a way to develop plants, animals, and foods with novel attributes (Agriculture and Agri-Food Canada, 1996).

Some of the benefits of biotechnology to Canadians are the production of newer and better products that may be lower in price than their traditional counterparts; more rapid diagnosis and treatment of certain diseases; and, in agriculture, superior food products and healthier agricultural plants and animals (Agriculture and Agri-Food Canada, 1996). There are a number of potential environmental risks associated with genetically engineered agricultural products, however. These concerns relate to the potential for organisms such as plants to spread and transfer their genetically altered material (known as outcrossing) and increase harm to nontarget species from the release of modified plants or microorganisms. This could disrupt the balance in natural ecosystems through the replacement of a few or large numbers of species. Also, there is the potential for loss of biodiversity (Agriculture and Agri-Food Canada, 1996). (For one NGO's view on the dangers of biotechnology, see the reference to Lycett in the Additional Information Sources section; for more information on outcrossing, see Agriculture and Agri-Food Canada, 1997b, also in Additional Information Sources.)

Given these concerns, on April 1, 1997, the new Canadian Food Inspection Agency (CFIA) took over responsibility for regulating agricultural products to see whether they are safe for humans, animals, and the environment. New regulatory requirements have been developed to address the safety of novel organisms in the environment. Before the agricultural products of biotechnology may be used, they undergo a preregulatory review to determine if a new product is "substantially equivalent" to a product already approved (in which case it will be approved for release), or if a risk assessment will be required. If a risk assessment is necessary, let's say for plants with unique traits, a series of guidelines outline the criteria that must be considered in assessing risk (Agriculture and Agri-Food Canada, 1997a). Table 6–3 outlines the series of issues that would be considered in an environmental safety assessment of a plant with genetically altered characteristics.

Sometimes, potential risks can be managed by imposing conditions that reduce risks, such as limiting the release of a bioengineered product to a confined area. In the case of plants with novel traits, an environmental assessment is required for confined field trials, a second

Issues considered include:

- Does the plant have the potential to become a weed of agriculture or to be invasive of natural habitats?
- Is there potential for gene flow to wild relatives whose hybrid offspring may become more weedy or invasive?
- Does the plant have the potential to become a plant pest?
- Is there a potential impact on nontarget organisms?
- Is there a potential to impact on biodiversity?
- Is there a potential for the development of resistance as a result of the release of this plant?

SOURCE: Agriculture and Agri-Food Canada. (1997). Information Bulletin ... Regulating agricultural biotechnology in Canada: Environmental questions.
http://www.aceis.agr.ca/fpi/agbiotec/enviroe.html

The spuds have a new family member with unparalleled resistance to insects.

The hairy potato, developed from a wild tuber with thin, insect-resistant spines, secretes a sticky substance that kills insects by trapping them.

Experts from the International Potato Center in Lima, Peru, say the nontoxic substance on the potato's hair will control 50 to 95 percent of aphids, leaf hoppers, mealy bugs, mites, thrips, and tuber moths. The large Colorado beetle, a common potato pest, is controlled by having its reproductive capabilities impaired. After the sticky substance is eaten by the bug, its stomach bloats, crushing the ovaries.

Potatoes, the world's fourth most important food crop, typically require heavy applications of agricultural insecticides, some of them highly toxic. Scientists hope the tuber will help cut the $370 million annual insecticide bill in the developing world.

Scientists from Cornell University who developed the fuzzy new hybrid say it tastes like a normal potato and has the same nutritional value with similar yields and growing characteristics.

The tuber will be introduced in 30 to 40 countries next year. Tests have already been conducted in the U.S., Asia, Africa, Latin America, and Europe.

SOURCE: Bugs hate hairy potato. (1993). *Alternatives*, 19(4), p. 3. Reprinted by permission.

assessment is required for unconfined release, and if a plant is to be used as a food or feed, then it must undergo further safety assessments by Health Canada or CFIA before it is used in commercial production (Agriculture and Agri-Food Canada, 1997a).

Potatoes are one crop that has been genetically modified through biotechnology in Canada (Box 6–6). The first specific application of biotechnology, to improve resistance to the Colorado potato beetle, is expected to be available to consumers in 1997. In order to address consumer acceptance of potatoes that have been genetically altered, the International Centre for Agricultural Science and Technology (ICAST) coordinated a study involving interviews with opinion leaders, preconsumer stakeholders, media, educators, religious leaders, and provincial potato marketing agencies; a nationwide telephone survey of potato producers; and consumer focus groups (International Centre for Agricultural Science and Technology, 1995). Among other things, the findings identified a weak but growing consumer awareness of biotechnology applications in foods. (For a review of key findings, see the Web site for ICAST listed in the Additional Information Sources section.)

Partnerships

Environmental issues related to agricultural use of land can be national in scope or can exhibit regional distinctiveness. National agricultural issues pertaining to the environment include greenhouse gas emissions and climate impacts, energy use, and genetic resources. Regional concerns include soil quality, water quality, and wildlife issues. Through the agricultural component of

Canada's Green Plan (which ended March 31, 1997), federal–provincial–territorial agreements were established to support a number of activities aimed at ensuring long-term sustainability of the resources agriculture shares and on which it depends, as well as to assist the transition to more sustainable farming practices (Government of Canada, 1996). Activities under the Green Plan also contributed to meeting some of Canada's national and international environmental commitments, such as the Conventions on Climate Change and the Convention on Biological Diversity.

With funding from the sustainable agriculture component of Canada's Green Plan, and by building on the National Soil Conservation Program (see below), stakeholders were involved as partners in program design, delivery, and funding. Environmental farm planning was one idea developed by Ontario farmers; each farmer assesses his or her own farm to highlight its environmental strengths, identify areas of concern, and set realistic goals to improve environmental conditions. Up to 12 000 individual farm plans were expected to be completed by 1997, and similar programs were initiated in other parts of the country (Government of Canada, 1996). In addition, many farmers voluntarily have organized themselves into various associations and societies aimed specifically at environmental objectives. (Further information on two governmental partnership agreements, the Canada–Saskatchewan Agriculture Green Plan Agreement and the Canada–Ontario Agriculture Green Plan, may be found through the Web site addresses listed in the Additional Information Sources section. The URL for a volunteer organization, the Ecological Farmer's Association of Ontario, is provided also.)

The National Soil Conservation Program was jointly funded (from 1989 to 1993) by federal and provincial governments to encourage appropriate soil use and management to sustain long-term soil productivity and, in western Canada, to encourage economic diversification where applicable. This program was effective in increasing awareness of soil conservation issues and solutions within the agricultural sector, largely as a result of the involvement of producers and producer groups (Government of Canada, 1996). On the prairies, the Prairie Farm Rehabilitation Act (PFRA) (1935) helped implement the National Soil Conservation Program. (For further information, see the Web site for the PFRA listed in the Additional Information Sources section.)

The Permanent Cover Program was a five-year program (1989–94) offered to farmers in the Prairie provinces and the Peace River region of British Columbia. The main objective of this program was to convert marginal lands under cultivation (CLI classes 4, 5, and 6) to permanent forage or tree cover. About 15 000 farmers agreed to convert approximately 522 000 hectares of erosion-prone marginal land from annual crops to permanent

cover for periods of 10 to 21 years. In areas of the Prairies where there is high waterfowl potential, the Permanent Cover Program has been integrated with the NAWMP's habitat conservation program. Farmers have helped to secure about 261 000 hectares of waterfowl land, including 71 000 hectares of wetlands and 190 000 hectares of grassed land (Government of Canada, 1996).

Agricultural producers were the main force behind the establishment of the National Agriculture Environment Committee in 1994. This committee continues to work to establish national proactive strategies on environmentally sustainable agriculture issues and provides a forum through which regional and local producer groups can share knowledge, identify courses of action, and work toward solutions in a coordinated fashion.

The Federal/Provincial Committee on Land Use initiated a program called the Perspective on Land Issues in Canada Process. This effort was intended to identify the major land issues that Canada will face heading into the 21st century, some broad options for resolving the issues, and the role that land use planning does and should play in sustainability. In the summer of 1995, the committee held a national forum to seek input from different sectors of Canadian society. In its efforts to progress toward the goals of Chapter 10 of *Agenda 21*, the committee identified the need for improved coordination among land resource data systems as well as the need to enhance Canada's capacity to gather and assess national data.

Statistics Canada is developing a set of land accounts as part of the environmental accounting being done under the Canadian System of National Accounts. These accounts present integrated statistics on land use, cover, capability, and value, and some of them are linked to socioeconomic information from agriculture and population censuses. In the long run, such linkages should help minimize land use conflicts, and relate agricultural planning and management activities to the capabilities and

The Prairie Care Project helps conserve and restore wetland habitat for waterfowl and other species.

The Canadian government supports research at its Agriculture Research Stations across the country.

limitations of different landscapes to support various land uses (Government of Canada, 1996).

Various efforts have been undertaken at the provincial level to integrate land use planning and management. For example, the former Commission on Resources and Environment (CORE) in British Columbia had legal responsibility under the 1992 CORE Act to develop a provincial strategy for land use and related resources and environmental management. Community-based participatory processes and dispute resolution systems were used in defining land uses for different parts of the province. (For a brief outline of the CORE mandate, see the Web site for CORE listed in the Additional Information Sources section.) Increasingly, ecosystem frameworks are being used to assess current land use practices across Canada (Government of Canada, 1996).

Cooperative research into sustainability of agroecosystems also continues, some of it in partnerships with industry. Examples of these efforts include developing disease- and pest-resistant crop varieties; reducing pesticide use; developing integrated approaches to pest management; improving the efficiency of animals (through breeding and nutrition), resulting in less manure and better use of forage and grains; and developing more efficient fertilizer application technology and innovative approaches to manure management, especially because these affect water quality.

FUTURE CHALLENGES

Even though there has been progress toward managing land in a sustainable manner, difficulties remain. Economic, environmental, and social issues that characterize contemporary agriculture are identified in Table 6–4. The message of this table is that although we have achieved dramatic

increases in short-term food production, conventional agricultural technologies have done so by increasing long-term social and environmental costs in soil degradation, loss of arable land, use of an increasingly controlled and select number of species, an increasing reliance on chemicals, and increased financial debt (Taylor, 1994).

The methods that have been used in farming have not always encouraged agriculture to be dependent on the natural system's heterogeneous characteristics but rather have forced farmers to standardize procedures and technology to achieve uniform results in mass quantities (industrial agriculture). As a result, the call for alternative agricultural practices—ones that are sustainable and maintain agricultural resources as renewable resources—often results in more individualistic and less capital-intensive operations. Regardless, there is a growing realization that the status quo is not sustainable, which means that new and creative alternatives are now required (Taylor, 1994). Stewardship, protection, and monitoring, as well as knowledge building, are part of the new alternatives.

Some of the changes in Canadian agriculture since the mid-1980s have increased the pressure to remain competitive in national and international markets. These pressures also bring opportunities to respond in innovative ways, particularly as reductions in financial assistance from governmental programs will require increased self-reliance and response to market signals on the part of individual, or groups of, farmers. Since some of the most effective innovations have been farmer driven, including developments in conservation farming techniques and systems, the ability of farmers to respond to both stewardship interests and economic changes and to adopt new management systems and technologies is not in question.

The health and productivity of agroecosystems clearly are fundamental necessities in sustainability of agricultural land resources. However, it is difficult to monitor trends or changes in agroecosystem quality because the information base is lacking. This also makes it difficult to determine if public and private investments in sustainability activities—maintaining life-support systems, preserving biological diversity, and maintaining the productive capacity of species and ecosystems—are achieving the desired ends (Government of Canada, 1996).

Knowledge building is required, and among the most promising tools to monitor agroecosystems and to enhance the database are remote sensing and Geographic Information Systems (GIS). In conjunction with Statistics Canada's Census of Agriculture, Agriculture and Agri-Food Canada's research station experimental data, and data from farmers, GIS can link together the databases to improve the baseline for assessing changes. Specifically, indicators of agroecosystem health may be manipulated within a GIS, including soil degradation, soil quality, crop yield, soil cover and management, conservation practices adopted, land conversions, and nutrient balance. (For a brief note on ecological monitoring, including agroecosystems, see

TABLE 6-4

ECONOMIC, ENVIRONMENTAL, AND SOCIAL ISSUES THAT CHARACTERIZE CONTEMPORARY NORTH AMERICAN AGRICULTURE

Economic	Environmental	Social
• technologically efficient crop production • increased reliance on monocultures • increased dependence on fossil fuels, chemical fertilizers and pesticides, and borrowed capital • reduced profitability • increasingly mechanized approach to food production • reliance on canola oil, durum wheat, and a few others as major export crops • security of food supply and of Canada's agricultural economy being put at risk • crop specialization • export markets subject to foreign protectionism • increased reliance on imports (often of foods that could be grown here) • dramatic increases in input costs but low farm produce prices contribute to financial stress • production of food almost totally dependent on oil and gas (to provide chemicals and machinery, and to process and distribute farm products)	• decline in soil productivity • growing dangers to animal and human health (chemicals) • increased vulnerability of plants to climatic changes and new diseases • ongoing requirement by corporate-based seed banks to use custom-designed fertilizers and pesticides • reduced long-term resilience due to genetic diversity in plants • surface and groundwater contamination by pesticides • loss of wildlife habitat • combined effects of soil erosion, acidification, compaction, salinization, and irrigation costing taxpayers almost $1.4 billion per year • use of farm chemicals and runoff resulting in sediment damage to inland lakes and waterways, loss of recreational fishing, increased water treatment and dredging costs • loss of land to urbanization (e.g., 80% of wetlands in Fraser River Basin taken over by agriculture)	• crushing debt burden • rapid disappearance of family farm, rural life • loss of agricultural land to encroaching urban development, transportation networks, airports, and industrial parks • effects of decades of government policies • almost 60% of land converted to urban use was prime agricultural land formerly • growing concern about pesticide safety and soil degradation • concern about long-term effects of agricultural chemicals on human health and the environment • growth of alternative farming techniques in part due to increase in public demand for organic products • goal of long-term stewardship of land for future generations

SOURCE: Taylor, D.M. (1994). *Off course: Restoring balance between Canadian society and the environment.* Ottawa: International Development Research Centre. Reprinted by permission.

the Web site for the Canada Centre for Inland Waters listed in the Additional Information Sources section.)

Progress has been made toward preserving biological diversity and maintaining the productive capacity of species and ecosystems through the increased use of sustainable land management practices. The challenge is to continue, as appropriate, to increase conservation tillage, to decrease summer fallow, to reduce use of herbicides and pesticides, to remove more marginal land from crop production into forage or other uses, and to continue to restore and enhance wildlife habitat. Stewardship remains an important impetus for continued protection of agro-ecosystems, given that wind and water erosion, salinization, soil compaction, organic matter loss, and contamination of groundwater by nitrates, pesticides, and bacteria, continue to occur.

Resolving these challenges to the sustainability of Canadian agroecosystems and land resources requires long-term commitment. As has been demonstrated during the past decade or so, given the right care, the health of agricultural soils and agroecosystems can be maintained and even improved. As our understanding of environmental and other impacts on Canadian agriculture increases, and as sustainable and conservation methods continue to improve, it will become easier to avoid adverse impacts from farming operations. Achieving the goal of sustainable agriculture is a responsibility shared among farmers, the agri-food industry, government, and consumers—cooperation and partnerships between these groups is an important key to ensuring both agriculture and the environment (land) are sustained.

Chapter Questions

1. Identify and discuss the main ways in which soil quality of agricultural lands may be degraded. What are the sources and impacts of other human activities on agricultural lands?

2. Why should soil conservation be a concern of every Canadian, not just farmers?

3. Why are Integrated Pest Management approaches better for the environment than earlier approaches? How could you employ IPM principles in a small vegetable garden behind a house in a city?

4. Could farming lead to the spread of deserts and another Dirty Thirties dust bowl experience in Canada? How might it be prevented?

5. Describe the various efforts Canada has made in attempting to achieve sustainable agriculture at international and national levels.

6. What are some of the advantages and disadvantages of nontraditional agricultural activities (such as organic farming) in achieving economic and environmental sustainability of Canadian agricultural lands?

references

Acton, D.F., & Gregorich, L.J. (1995). Understanding soil health. In D.F. Acton & L.J. Gregorich (Eds.). *The health of our soils—toward sustainable agriculture in Canada.* (pp. 5–10). Ottawa: Agriculture and Agri-Food Canada.

Agriculture and Agri-Food Canada. (1996). Biotechnology, agriculture and regulation. http://www.aceis.agr.ca/fpi/agbiotec/geninfo.html

Agriculture and Agri-Food Canada. (1997a). Information Bulletin ... Regulating agricultural biotechnology in Canada: Environmental questions. http://www.aceis.agr.ca/fpi/agbiotec/enviroe.html

Birds lose out in modern coffee plantations. (1997). *Encompass,* 1(2), p. 24.

Bugs hate hairy potato. *Alternatives,* 19(4), p. 24.

Canadian International Development Agency (CIDA). (1994). Canada signs International Convention on Desertification. News Release 94-41, Hull, QC: CIDA.

Canadian International Development Agency (CIDA). (1995). *CIDA and desertification: working to preserve our common future.* Hull, QC: CIDA.

Canadian Organic Growers. (1997). About Canadian organic growers. http://www.gks.com/cog/cogab.htm

Cardy, F. (1994). Desertification. *Our Planet,* 6(5), p. 4.

Chambers, A. (n.d.). Manitoba's elk—just another farm animal? http://www.sierraclub.ca/prairie/elk.html

Department of Indian Affairs and Northern Development. (1995). *Comprehensive claims or modern treaties.* Information Sheet No. 9. Ottawa.

Dregne, H.E. (1983). Desertification of arid lands. Char, Switzerland: Harwood Academic Publishers. Fig. 1.2, p.16.

Eilers, R.G., Eilers, W.D., Pettapiece, W.W., & Lelyk, G. (1995). Salinization of soil. In D.F. Acton & L.J. Gregorich (Eds.). *The health of our soils—Toward sustainable agriculture in Canada.* (pp. 77–86). Ottawa: Agriculture and Agri-Food Canada.

Elk On Line. (1996). Elk Breeders Home Page. http://www.wapiti.net/

Environment Bureau. (n.d.). Agriculture in harmony with nature: Strategy for environmentally sustainable agriculture and agri-food development in Canada. http://aceis.agr.ca/policy/envharmon/indexe.htm

Gauthier, D.A., & Henry, J.D. (1989). Misunderstanding the prairies. In M. Hummel (Ed.). *Endangered spaces: The future for Canada's wilderness.* (pp. 183–95). Toronto: Key Porter Books.

Government of Canada. (1991). *The state of Canada's environment—1991.* Ottawa: Supply and Services Canada.

Government of Canada. (1994). *Canada's national report on climate change: Actions to meet commitments under the United Nations Framework Convention on Climate Change.* Ottawa.

Government of Canada. (1996). *The state of Canada's environment—1996.* Ottawa: Supply and Services Canada.

Gregorich, E.G., Angers, D.A., Campbell, C.A., Carter, M.R., Drury, D.F., Ellert, B.H., Groenevelt, P., Hallstrom, D.A., Monreal, C.M., Rees, H.W., Voroney, R.P., & Vyn, T.J. (1995). Changes in soil organic matter. In D.F. Acton & L.J. Gregorich (Eds.). *The health of our soils—Toward sustainable agriculture in Canada.* (pp. 41–50). Ottawa: Agriculture and Agri-Food Canada.

Gregorich, L.J., & Acton, D.F. (1995). Summary. In D.F. Acton & L.J. Gregorich (Eds.). *The health of our soils—Toward sustainable agriculture in Canada.* (pp. 111–20). Ottawa: Agriculture and Agri-Food Canada.

Harker, D.B., Penner, L.A., Harron, W.R., & Wood, R.C. (1995). *For now we see through a glass darkly, historical trends in dryland salinity point to future expectations under irrigation.* Saskatoon: Canadian Symposium on Remote Sensing.

International Centre for Agricultural Science and Technology (ICAST). (1995). *Consumer acceptance of potatoes that have been genetically modified through biotechnology.* Saskatoon: ICAST.

International Centre for Agriculture Sciences and Technology (ICAST). http://www.aceis.agr.ca/misb/potato/epotato.html

International Development Research Centre (IDRC). (1993). *Agenda 21: Green paths to the future.* Ottawa: IDRC.

Kinkel, N., & Wemer, K. (1997). Conservation tillage ... spread the word! *Conservator,* 18(1), p. 24.

Koala, S. In *IDRC Reports,* 22(2), p. 4.

Lyseng, R. (1995). Why zero till? *Conservator,* 16(1), pp. 14–15.

Manitoba Environment. (1995). *State of the environment report for Manitoba.* Winnipeg.

McQuarrie, I. (1997). Agriculture and ecology. In T. Fleming (Ed.). *The environment and Canadian society.* Toronto: ITP Nelson, pp. 54–55.

Mineau, P., McLaughlin, A., Boutin, C., Evenden, M., Freemark, K., Kevan, P., McLeod, G., & Tomlin, A. (1994). Effects of agriculture on biodiversity in Canada. In Environment Canada, Biodiversity Science Assessment Team. *Biodiversity in Canada: A science assessment for Environment Canada.* (pp. 59–113). Ottawa.

Olson, K. Agriculture and the environment. *Environment Views and Network News,* 1(1), p. 22.

Reynolds, W.D., Campbell, C.A., Chang, C., Cho, C.M., Ewanek, J., Kachanoski, R.G., McLeod, J.A., Milburn, P.H., Simard, R., Webster, G.R.B., & Zebarth, B.J. (1995). Agrochemical entry into groundwater. In D.F. Acton & L.J. Gregorich (Eds.). *The health of our soils—Toward sustainable agriculture in Canada.* (pp. 97–109). Ottawa: Agriculture and Agri-Food Canada.

Royal Commission on the Economic Union and Development Prospects for Canada. (1985). *Report: Royal Commission on the Economic Union and Development Prospects for Canada.* Vol. 2. Ottawa.

Rubec, C.D.A. (1994). Canada's federal policy on wetland conservation: A global model. In W.J. Mitsch (Ed.). *Global wetlands: Old world and new.* (pp. 909–17). Amsterdam: Elsevier Science B.V.

Science Council of Canada. (1986). *A growing concern: Soil degradation in Canada.* Ottawa.

Science Council of Canada. (1992). *Sustainable agriculture: The research challenge.* Report No. 43. Ottawa: Science Council of Canada.

Statistics Canada. (1994a). *Canadian agriculture at a glance.* Ottawa.

Statistics Canada. (1994b). *Human activity and the environment 1994.* Ottawa.

Taylor, D.M. (1994). *Off course: Restoring balance between Canadian society and the environment.* Ottawa: International Development Research Centre.

Topp, G.C., Carter, M.R., Culley, J.L.B., Holmstrom, D.A., Kay, B.D., Lafond, G.P., Langille, D.R., McBride, R.A., Patterson, G.T., Perfect, E., Rasiah, V., Rodd, A.V., Webb. K.T., & Wires, K.C. (1995). Changes in soil structure. In D.F. Acton & L.J. Gregorich (Eds.). *The health of our soils—Toward sustainable agriculture in Canada.* (pp. 51–60). Ottawa: Agriculture and Agri-Food Canada.

Van Tighem, K. (1996). From wilds to weeds: Alberta's changing ecosystems. *Environment Views,* 19(5), pp. 5–8.

Wall, G.J., Pringle, E.A., & Padbury, G.A. (1995). Erosion. In D.F. Acton & L.J. Gregorich (Eds.). *The health of our soils—Toward sustainable agriculture in Canada.* (pp. 61–76). Ottawa: Agriculture and Agri-Food Canada.

Webber, M.D., & Singh, S.S. (1995). Contamination of agricultural soils. In D.F. Acton & L.J. Gregorich (Eds.). *The health of our soils—Toward sustainable agriculture in Canada.* (pp. 86–96). Ottawa: Agriculture and Agri-Food Canada.

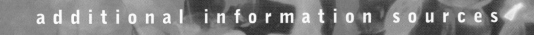

additional information sources

Agriculture and Agri-Food Canada. (1997b). Information Bulletin ... Biotechnology and environmental concerns: Outcrossing. http://www.aceis.agr.ca/fpi/agbiotec/crosse.html

Agriculture Canada. No-till: Making it work. http://www.res.agr.ca/long/ap/bmp/notillbmp.html

Canada–Ontario Agriculture Green Plan. (1997). Canada–Ontario Agriculture Green Plan, 1992–1997. http://res.agr.ca/lond/gp/gphompag.html

Canada–Saskatchewan Agriculture Green Plan Agreement. (n.d.). Farm-based program: Canada–Saskatchewan Agriculture Green Plan Agreement. http://www.wetland.sk.ca/landsprg/funding/fund02.htm

Canadian Centre for Inland Waters. Ecological Monitoring and Assessment Network. (1995). Use of remote sensing for ecological monitoring in Canada. http://www.cciw.ca/eman-temp/reports/publications/remote-sens/main.html

Commission on Resources and Environment (CORE). (n.d.). *Mandate.* http://www.com/core/about.html

Ecological Farmer's Association of Ontario. http://www.gks.com/efao/

Jowkar, F. (1994). Women bear the brunt. *Our Planet,* 6(5), pp. 16–17.

Lycett, P. Life at the edge of the abyss. http://www.gks.com/wwwcof/biotech/index.html

Manitoba Environment. Building 2, 139 Tuxedo Avenue, Winnipeg, MB R3N 0H6.

Prairie Farm Rehabilitation Act. (1997). PFRA: Serving prairie people since 1935. http://aceis.agr.ca/pfra/

Roach, T. (1994). Ancient ways guide modern methods. *IDRC Reports,* 22(2), pp. 9–10.

Seck, M. (1994). Unearthing the impacts of tenure. *IDRC Reports,* 22(2), pp. 11–12.

"Water is a precious and finite natural
resource, one which is essential to all
life and vital to ecological, economic
and social well-being. Yet, water is
often wasted and degraded. Therefore
we face both individual and collective
responsibilities to use and manage
water resources wisely. This will only
be accomplished as we recognize the
intrinsic value of water and practice
conscious and committed stewardship,
recognizing that this precious heritage
must be safeguarded for future
generations."

Canadian Water Resources Association (1994)

C H A P T E R 7

Fresh Water

Chapter Contents

CHAPTER OBJECTIVES   185
INTRODUCTION   185
WATER SUPPLY AND DISTRIBUTION   186
    Earth's Freshwater Resources   186
    Canada's Freshwater Resources   186
WATER USES AND PRESSURES ON
    WATER QUALITY   188
    Water Uses   188
    Pressures on Water Quality   190
    The Importance of Water   192
        Water as a Common Link   192
        Water as a Source of Conflict   192
        Water as a Hazard   193
HUMAN ACTIVITIES AND IMPACTS ON
    FRESHWATER ENVIRONMENTS   194
    Domestic and Urban Uses and Impacts   194
        Safe Drinking Water and Sanitation
            Facilities   194
        Demand for Water   196
        The Great Lakes and St. Lawrence
            River Basin: A Case Study   197
    Agricultural Uses and Impacts   200
    Industrial Uses and Impacts   202
        Groundwater Contamination   202
        Impacts on Beluga Whales   204
        Acidic Deposition   204
    Hydroelectric Generation and Impacts 204
    Recreational Uses and Impacts   207
RESPONSES TO ENVIRONMENTAL IMPACTS
    AND CHANGE   208
    International Initiatives   208
        Agenda 21   208
        The Ramsar Convention   208
    Agreements between Canada and the
        United States   209
        The Great Lakes Water Quality
            Agreements   209
        Remedial Action Plans   210
    Canadian Law, Policy, and Practice   210
        Water Legislation and Policy
         Responses   210

Inquiry on Federal Water
Policy 211
Shared Jurisdiction 211
Financial Constraints 212
Research and Application 212
Ecological Monitoring and
Assessment Network 212
Environmental and Water Quality
Guidelines 212
Great Lakes Cleanup Fund and
Great Lakes 2000 213
Northern River Basins Study 213
Canadian Partnerships and Local
Action 214
Flood Damage Reduction
Program 214
Watershed Planning 214
Fraser River Action Plan 215
North American Waterfowl
Management Plan 216
Making a Difference Locally 216
FUTURE CHALLENGES 218
Chapter Questions 219
References 219
Additional Information Sources 221

Chapter Objectives

After studying this chapter you should be able to
- understand the nature and distribution of Canada's freshwater resources
- identify a range of human uses of freshwater resources
- describe the impacts of human activities on freshwater and freshwater environments
- appreciate the complexity and interrelatedness of freshwater environment issues
- outline Canadian and international responses to freshwater issues
- discuss challenges to a sustainable future for freshwater resources in Canada

INTRODUCTION

Fresh water is the lifeblood of the ecosphere and it's Canada's lifeblood, too. Water is vital for ecosystems. It is a key element in Canadians' economic and recreational activities and in the quality of our lives. However, Canada's generous endowment of water, about 9 percent of the world's renewable supply, is being stressed by the demands we are putting on it. Per capita, Canadians' water use is the second highest in the world. While about 80 litres of water daily is sufficient to sustain a reasonable quality of life, Canadians' daily indoor household use in 1994 averaged about 340 litres per person (Government of Canada, 1996). The average African uses only 20 litres of water every day (WaterCan takes the lead, 1994). The Canadian rate of consumption is more than twice that of European countries and may be due, in part, to the common perception that Canada has an unlimited supply of fresh water, as well as to the low prices we pay for water (which encourages waste rather than conservation).

Other stressors on water include the growth of large urban centres, increased industrial activity, and use of agricultural chemicals, all of which are overloading the natural ability of the hydrological cycle to renew and purify water. Over 15 000 lakes in eastern Canada are dead because of acidic pollutants generated both within and beyond Canadian borders (Government of Canada, 1996). Literally hundreds of chemical substances used in Canada and around the world are found in Canadian waters, including groundwater, and some are in our food chains.

In many parts of Canada, water quality has been degraded. For years we have contaminated the Fraser River with incompletely treated sewage, landfill leachates, chemicals from wood treatment and pulp and paper mills, and runoff from forestry and agricultural activities. Prairie rivers have been impaired due to agricultural runoff; the Great Lakes and St. Lawrence River have suffered from industrial and municipal pollution, urban and agricultural runoff, and atmospheric deposition; and Prince Edward Island's groundwater supplies have been threatened by agricultural pesticides (Government of Canada, 1991).

In some parts of the country such as the southern Prairies, high demand for water already has caused shortages; if future climate changes alter precipitation patterns and affect the water cycle, current water supply problems may be exacerbated. It also is possible that pressures to divert Canadian waters southward will increase as continental economic unions (such as the North American Free Trade Agreement) bring pressures to share resources, particularly water resources (Bruce & Mitchell, 1995). Although Canadian governments repeatedly have stated

Water is a valuable part of Canada's natural heritage.

100 000 glaciers alone are estimated to contain 1.5 times the volume of surface waters (Government of Canada, 1991).

During long droughts, little infiltration or percolation occurs to recharge groundwater storage, and there is little runoff to maintain river flows and lake levels. As a result, plants and trees become parched and water bodies may shrink in size. Conversely, during long periods of heavy rainfall, there is little absorption into saturated ground and runoff increases, sometimes causing lakes and rivers to flood. Major floods in June 1995 on the Oldman and South Saskatchewan Rivers in southern Alberta, and in July 1996 in the Saguenay River–Lac Saint-Jean area in Quebec, have been attributed to intense rainfall. Higher than normal winter precipitation helped set the stage for the 1997 spring floods on the Red River in Manitoba.

In addition to variations in supply, water quality is a concern in different parts of Canada. Concentrations of naturally occurring impurities (minerals), such as calcium, magnesium, sodium, potassium, sulphate, and chloride, can affect the use of surface water for drinking, swimming, or supporting diverse aquatic life. Ground-

water, too, can be affected by quality problems. In parts of the Prairie provinces, the Niagara Escarpment, New Brunswick, and Nova Scotia, the groundwater is so salty that most plant species are unable to tolerate it. Groundwater in other parts of Canada contains toxic chemical constituents (such as arsenic, fluoride, and uranium) derived from mineral deposits, while other substances (such as iron) create taste and colour problems.

Water quality also can decline when low flow levels reduce a river's capacity to dilute, dissolve, or absorb pollutants, salts, and other solids. In low flow situations, a higher proportion of the flow comes from groundwater, which generally contains more minerals. The quality of fish habitat suffers under low flow conditions also, because the water warms as air temperatures rise. High flow conditions can be problematic as heavy rain, snowmelt, or runoff carry dissolved and suspended material into rivers, reducing water quality. The water medium (the global hydrological cycle) provides for "free trade" of pollutants as well as movement of essential nutrients, and that's one of the reasons why levels of contamination in Arctic mammals and fish are so high (see Chapter 8).

WATER USES AND PRESSURES ON WATER QUALITY

WATER USES

Every day, at home and at work, we use water in so many situations—cooking, washing, bathing, watering lawns, carrying away unwanted byproducts of our lives—that we are inclined to take it for granted. The two basic ways in which we use water are **instream uses** and **withdrawal uses.** Instream uses, including hydroelectric power generation, transportation, waste disposal, fisheries, wildlife, heritage conservation, and recreation, occur "in the stream" (water remains in its natural setting). Withdrawal uses, such as municipal use, manufacturing, irrigation, mineral extraction, and thermal power generation, remove water from its natural setting for a period of time and for a particular use. Eventually, all or part of the water is returned to its source. The difference between the amount of water withdrawn and water returned to the source is water "consumed."

It is important to note that even in situations where little water is consumed, the aquatic environment may be altered because of a change in quality of water returned to the water body, or because of a disruption in supply. Though many Canadians now understand that pollution cannot be solved by diluting wastes in rivers and lakes, many water bodies still receive direct discharges from a variety of municipal and industrial point sources and from

On-farm and commercial feedlots are potential sources of water contamination.

have a better understanding of how much water is needed for withdrawal and consumptive uses.

Statistics (1991) show that thermal power production is the largest withdrawal use in Canada, followed by manufacturing, municipal, agriculture, and mining withdrawals. (See Figure 7–2.) Note that while manufacturing and mining have increased their water technology efficiency and have reduced their withdrawals, increased use of water for cooling in thermal power production plants accounted for most of the national increase in water withdrawals since 1986 (Government of Canada, 1996).

More than 45 billion cubic metres of water were withdrawn from Canadian sources in 1991, an 88 percent increase since 1972. This averages out to 4500 litres of water withdrawn per person per day for all uses (and to 340 litres per person per day for residential use). Because of this high consumption, and a correspondingly high volume of wastewater, Canadians experience high costs for municipal water infrastructure. About 26 percent of Canadians rely on groundwater sources for their domestic supply (Government of Canada, 1996; Pearse et al., 1985). For instance, 100 percent of Prince Edward Island's population relies on groundwater, as does over 60 percent of the population of New Brunswick and Yukon. In fact, with the exception of British Columbia, groundwater provides 90 percent or more of total water supplies in rural areas of all provinces.

nonpoint sources such as urban and agricultural runoff and atmospheric deposition. From an ecosystem support perspective, it is vital to know how much water is required to meet instream needs. In Canada, this knowledge has been growing, but is still incomplete. We do, however,

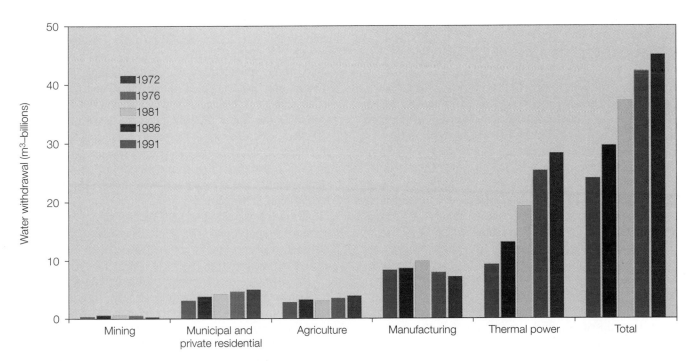

Figure 7–2

Water withdrawal in Canada, 1972–1991

NOTE: For municipal and private residential uses: (a) private residential uses are estimates only; and (b) water supplied to industries from municipal water supplies is excluded.

SOURCE: Government of Canada. (1996). *The state of Canada's environment—1996.* Ottawa: Supply and Services Canada. Figure 10.18.

At the same time that water is becoming increasingly important as an international environmental issue and is of increasing importance to Canada's economic, social, and environmental agendas, the decline in budgets and staff at Environment Canada has required an internal reorientation and reorganization. Beginning in 1993, the federal capacity to deal with water was reduced: the Inland Waters Directorate (the lead federal agency for water) was eliminated; federal water policy lost much of its momentum to other initiatives such as the Green Plan; the Canada Water Act funding for collaborative activity was reduced drastically; and Environment Canada's ability to provide other services such as hydrometric data collection and analysis declined (Bruce & Mitchell, 1995).

Water experts from across the country have provided input to Environment Canada in its efforts to identify new roles and responsibilities and have stressed the importance of an ecosystem approach that pays attention to the entire system and the linkages among its components. However, because "an ecosystem approach is founded on strong sectoral competency," the loss of expertise to deal in depth with the water component of the ecosystem actually may have weakened Canada's ability to deliver an ecosystem approach (Bruce & Mitchell, 1995, p. 3). As resource and environmental managers all over the world are grappling with this same fundamental issue (of balancing the breadth inherent in an ecosystem approach with the depth of a sectoral approach), Canada's review of water programs is important and appropriate.

PRESSURES ON WATER QUALITY

Virtually all water uses lead to pressures on water quality. For example, quality issues relating to municipal use of water include pollution, increased **biological oxygen demand** (BOD), and disease-causing bacteria in the discharge of (untreated) wastewater. In the past, a large proportion of Quebec's urban population was without sewage treatment services, but noticeable progress has been made in constructing treatment plants for municipalities with populations of over 5000 (Government of Canada, 1991, 1996). Progress has been made also in providing First Nations people with potable water and sewage disposal services, but about 17 percent of reserve dwellings are still without sewage disposal facilities (Government of Canada, 1996). In July 1996, the federal government announced a new $98.5-million program to address the most pressing water and sewage problems that posed potential health risks to community members on reserve lands. This money, in addition to the $125 million allocated for water and sewer projects on reserves in 1995, provides an indication of the magnitude, as well as the cost, of rectifying water supply and treatment problems on reserves (Barnett, 1996).

Agricultural uses raise many questions, including the public cost of irrigation works, fertilizer- and pesticide-laden runoff, and soil salinization and erosion problems. Since most crop irrigation takes place in the west, principally in Alberta, these issues are of particular importance there. In the South Saskatchewan River basin, for example, water returning to the rivers via irrigation channels and field runoff carries with it not only fertilizers, pesticides, salts, and sulphates, but also dissolved solids at levels up to double what they were before irrigation (Hamilton & Wright, 1985). Clearly, these contaminants reduce the overall quality of water for aquatic life. Leaky drainage pipes, evaporation, and seepage from irrigation canals and ditches result in inefficient use of water. There have been instances where less than one-third of the water withdrawn from a stream reached the intended crops (Government of Canada, 1991). In the Great Lakes–St. Lawrence region, most water withdrawals for agricultural purposes are used in stock watering.

Discharge of water used in mining (for cooling, drilling, and for operating equipment) and in recovering oil from tar sands (for deep well injection) may degrade water quality by adding suspended solids, heavy metals, acids, and other dissolved substances. Tailings ponds may leak, discharging contaminated water into groundwater or surface bodies. Arctic residents, for example, are concerned about water quality deterioration from abandoned metal mines, as well as from oil and gas developments.

Industrial pollutants in wastewater from the manufacturing sector range from biodegradable wastes to substances (such as PCBs and PAHs) toxic to fish, wildlife, and humans. Effluent from pulp and paper mills includes solid waste and chlorinated organic chemicals such as dioxins and furans, all of which may have detrimental effects on aquatic ecosystems. Residents in British Columbia, northern Alberta, northern Ontario, and the Atlantic provinces have expressed concerns about such discharges. Most thermoelectric plants use water as a coolant, returning water to the source in essentially the same quantity but at a higher temperature. This "heat pollution" can harm aquatic species, such as trout that require cool water. Increased water temperature can increase evaporation rates, which may raise salt concentrations to unacceptable levels (Government of Canada, 1991; Pearse et al., 1985).

Instream uses also impact water quality. Hydroelectric turbines do not consume water, but significant amounts evaporate from storage reservoirs. Damming rivers not only converts wild rivers into regulated ones but also results in loss of habitat for wildlife and fish, barriers to fish movement, and changes in downstream river flow regimes. Hydro dams have inundated valuable agricultural land in the Columbia, Kootenay, and Peace River valleys in British Columbia, and have destroyed some salmon runs. In the dry Okanagan valley, irrigation sometimes has reduced tributary flows late in the season and affected fish propagation (Pearse et al., 1985).

Commercial navigation requires high water levels, which may cause bank erosion, disturb bottom sediments, and threaten beaches, while dredging to maintain depth degrades water quality. Shore property owners in the Great Lakes–St. Lawrence basin prefer lower water levels than do the navigation and power interests, chiefly because lower water levels minimize erosion and protect the owners' beaches, dock facilities, and other property. Shipping may facilitate the introduction of exotic species (such as the zebra mussel—see Box 7–1—introduced into Lake St. Clair via the ballast water of a European ship) and cause pollution, including spills of hazardous materials that may pose threats to municipal water supplies and recreation. Ice-breaking operations also pose a threat to fish and wildlife (Government of Canada, 1991; Pearse et al., 1985).

Discharging municipal and industrial wastes into water bodies has become increasingly less feasible, not only because growth in industrial production and population generates more wastes for discharge (often exceeding the water bodies' assimilative capacity) but because industrial wastes in particular contain persistent and toxic contaminants that remain in the environment. These contaminants affect fish and wildlife and their particular habitat requirements—many species are highly sensitive to changes imposed by pollutants as well as by dams, diversions, and wetland drainage. In northern and coastal areas, fish and wildlife provide the major source of income and are valued as food, as integral to a way of life, and as recreational and aesthetic resources. Water-based recreational pursuits usually do not involve withdrawing or consuming water, but are affected by water body features such as surface area, depth, rate of flow, quality, temperature, and accessibility.

On a national basis, Canadians withdraw only about 2 percent of our water resources from their natural settings. We consume less than 1 percent. This level of consumption suggests that, in general, our instream resource needs are protected. However, there are important regional and local exceptions, including the southern Prairies and individual tributary watersheds to the Great Lakes. Most of Canada's serious water use problems are related to degraded water quality and to disrupted flow regimes, not to inadequate supply. First Nations people are among those whose traditional water-based activities have been most affected by deterioration from pollution and by water storage and diversion projects that manipulate lake levels and river flows: "There is hardly a major drainage system anywhere south of the Arctic which has not been affected by these pressures" (Pearse et al., 1985, p. 48). Furthermore, growing uncertainty about the future and about human influence on climate, land use, and water distribution means that water management policies must support, protect, and promote a high-quality, sustainable water supply.

BOX 7-1
ZEBRA MUSSELS AND LAKE ERIE

Historically, pollution loading in the Lake Erie basin was mitigated through sedimentation from the productive algae and fine soil particles from farmland erosion (these particulates absorbed or adsorbed pollutants). As a result, Lake Erie organisms showed relatively low concentrations of toxic contaminants compared to the other Great Lakes. This may change, however, as eroded soil and nutrient levels decline and as zebra mussels deplete algal populations, thus increasing rates of bioaccumulation of contaminants.

The original aquatic community of Lake Erie was devastated by the almost total removal of native vegetation from the basin and by the exotic (non-native) fish species that invaded after commercial fisheries severely exploited the native species. Along with carp, zebra mussels have impacted heavily on the recovering aquatic community. Voracious filter feeders, zebra mussels are not strongly affected by natural predators or diseases; the zebra mussel population has exploded and caused rapid changes in water quality and clarity as well as in the food web.

Zebra mussels consume large amounts of phytoplankton; their feeding caused a 77-percent increase in water transparency (clarity) between 1988 and 1991. Increased clarity of water permitted sunlight to penetrate deeper, in turn allowing rooted aquatic plants to spread into deeper water. Many organisms benefitted ecologically from this change, but in some areas plant growth interfered with swimming and boating.

The mussels' eating habits, which both deplete the phytoplankton food source also used by other filter feeders and assimilate toxic contaminants, have impacted the food web and may result in major changes in the future abundance of various species of fish. Mussels remove large amounts of particulates, which means that more contaminants remain in the water. The result could be higher contaminant concentrations in the remaining phytoplankton and zooplankton, as well as higher concentrations in fish and wildlife species feeding on the plankton or directly on the mussels and other bottom dwellers.

When zebra mussels arrived, they created physical problems such as clogged intake pipes and jammed machinery. We now know, however, that the invasion by this exotic species has far more complex results. Chemical and biological methods have been proposed to control the mussels, but, mindful of other biocontrols that have proved disastrous, most of the scientific community is reluctant to take these measures. This situation highlights the point that restoring and protecting the Great Lakes ecosystem requires a commitment to achieving sustainability, fostering cooperation and coordination, and preventing (pollution) problems before they arise.

SOURCES: The Governments of the United States of America and Canada. (1995). *State of the Great Lakes: 1995.* Ottawa: Supply and Services Canada.

Zebra mussels: Holding back the tide. (1997). *Coastal Heritage,* 11(4), pp. 10–12.

THE IMPORTANCE OF WATER

Water as a Common Link

When we stop to think about our water systems, we realize how important water is to the Canadian economy and the Canadian identity—how water is a common link between citizens from every part of this nation and, indeed, the world. Although water is absolutely essential in all spheres of life, western societies have not always accorded water its full significance and have permitted its waste and degradation. This contrasts clearly with First Nations peoples' view of the natural world and water's place in it (Box 7–2). Recently, however, more and more Canadians have been demanding protection of their natural heritage, including water resources and aquatic ecosystems.

One of the ways in which rivers are being protected for future generations is through the Canadian Heritage Rivers System (CHRS). The goal is to establish a system of Canadian Heritage Rivers that reflects the diversity of Canada's river environments and celebrates the role of rivers in Canada's history and society. As well, the public is encouraged to learn about, enjoy, and appreciate Canada's rivers. On January 18, 1984, the Canadian Heritage Rivers Board was established to administer the Canadian Heritage Rivers System and to review river nominations for inclusion in the program. As a cooperative program of the federal, provincial, and territorial governments, CHRS objectives include ensuring long-term management that will conserve and protect the natural, historical, and recreational values of the best examples of Canada's river heritage.

The French River in Ontario was the first Canadian Heritage River named, in 1986. Since then, sections of at least 27 rivers, with a total length of more than 5700 kilometres, have been added to the system. Although only participating governments may nominate rivers to the CHRS, private citizens or goups may suggest rivers to the responsible provincial or territorial parks agencies. (For more information on nominating a river, or on the Canadian Heritage River System itself, contact the board at the address given in the Additional Information Sources section at the end of this chapter. Also see the Environment Canada [n.d.c] and Van Tighem [1990] references in Additional Information Sources.)

Water as a Source of Conflict

As fundamental as water is to life on Earth and to the sociocultural dimensions of Canadian lifestyles, climate change has the potential to disrupt such water-dependent activities as agriculture and forestry. If precipitation amounts or distribution patterns change, or if temperature regimes are altered, a variety of both positive and negative impacts would be felt in these two sectors and throughout the Canadian economy.

BOX 7–2
A FIRST NATIONS VIEW OF THE NATURAL WORLD

The earth is central to our values. We consider ourselves part of a family that includes all of creation. We refer to the earth as Mother Earth, the giver of all life. We refer to the sun as our eldest brother and the moon as our grandmother. We consider the animal and plant life our brothers and sisters. We consider the waters of the world to be the bloodlines of Mother Earth.... We must make sure that those are always clean so that there will not be a heart attack some day to our mother.

We believe that all of creation has been given instructions by the creator. These instructions are meant to ensure that all of creation can live in harmony and peace.... The waters of the world have been instructed to quench the thirst of all life. It is said that when we drink each cold glass of water, when our throat is so dry, that there isn't a more wonderful feeling of peace and [tranquillity] than what that fresh cold glass of water can do ...

Our philosophies are based on the circle of life. To us, all life is seen as revolving in a circle and interrelated. Because movement is circular, any activity or decision made in the present will be felt in the future. In this circle, we do not see ourselves as separate or above the rest of the natural world, but an integral part of it.

Our lifestyles reflect our closeness to the natural world. We are fishers, trappers, hunters, gatherers, and farmers. These lifestyles keep us in touch with the natural world, spiritually, mentally, and physically, on a daily basis. Our close dependence on the natural world means that we must be thankful that the different parts of the natural world are fulfilling the instructions given to them by the creator. It also reminds us that we must also fulfill our instructions as well.

Because of the close relationship we have with the natural world, we cannot have healthy communities unless we have a healthy environment. Our ancestors have always understood this.... We have always recognized the importance of water. The rivers and lakes are used to transport our people from one community to the next. Fish and waterfowl have long been the major source of food for our people. The plants along its shores are the source of our medicines.

We have always followed the natural laws of the world. These laws are rooted in common sense. They say that if something you plan to do could be detrimental to the natural world, [then] don't do it. If we look at all of creation as part of our family, [then] the decisions we make must ensure that our family will come to no harm either today or in the future. Our dependence on the natural world requires us to follow these laws....

... When the Europeans first came to North America, they could not understand why First Nation people would not sell their land. For us, it was an issue of would you sell your mother? Today we cannot understand why it is okay to discharge pollutants into the waters of the world. It is akin to allowing drugs to be injected into [your] mother's blood and [then] saying it is okay because the blood will dilute it.

SOURCE: Ransom, J.W. (1995, September). Water is life. *Technical Bureau Supplement to Water News*. Canadian Water Resources Association. Reprinted by permission.

While scientists are not all in agreement about what the specific consequences of global warming may be for various parts of the world or for Canada, the nature of Canadian society would change in relation to changes in water resource characteristics. Also, since Canada shares many water bodies with the United States, there would be increased pressure to negotiate water management agreements that satisfy both countries. Depending on the scarcity or abundance and distribution of water, this could raise the issue of large-scale water exports again (Simpson, 1993/1994). Such situations mean that the goal of water sustainability needs to be addressed on both immediate and longer-term time scales and needs to employ policies and programs that achieve not only ecological sustainability but also desired sociocultural outcomes.

In the global context, almost 150 of the world's 214 major river systems are shared by two countries, and another 50 are shared by three to ten nations. Many nations already have seen conflict over access to shared water resources, and the future is likely to bring more conflict, especially if global warming occurs as predicted and severe droughts become more frequent.

In the Middle East, where water disputes already have arisen, the 1967 Arab–Israeli war was fought partly over access to water from the Jordan River basin. In the future, the issue of sharing water between countries will become even more contentious as demands grow in response to increasing population as well as continuing agricultural and industrial development. Currently, for example, Turkey's $20-billion Southeast Anatolian Project, "the biggest engineering feat in history," is using about 2 percent of the annual flow of the Euphrates River for irrigation and has plans to use about one-third of the Euphrates' total flow. Unless the principal states of the Tigris–Euphrates basin (Turkey, Syria, and Iraq) cooperate in determining optimal use of water, a crisis is inevitable because all three countries' plans for irrigation and hydroelectric projects would consume about one-third more than the total flow of the Euphrates (Pope, 1996; Frederick, 1996).

More recently, "water terror" has been an effective weapon in civil wars around the world. During the Bosnian conflict, Serbs discovered how "to hit their enemies where it really hurt: in the water supply." By shutting off Sarajevo's electricity, and with it the city's water pumps, city residents, including dozens of Muslims, were forced to line up at wells, making them easy targets for snipers and mortar shells (Serril, 1997).

In the Mekong River basin, Thailand's demand for water is growing by more than 12 percent per year, Laos is considering major hydroelectric developments, Vietnam is seeking water for irrigation and industrial needs, and Cambodia is concerned about maintaining its fishing industry in light of the major dam and water diversion schemes proposed. If a series of major dams were constructed on the Mekong's main section, critics warn that rare marine species could be threatened, downstream fertility could decrease, flooding and saltwater incursions could increase, and the delta area could be threatened because of reduced silt flow (Pope, 1996).

Water as a Hazard

Sufficient water of appropriate quality is essential to a productive economy. From Canada's early days, surface and groundwater resources have supplied the demand for domestic consumption, transportation, (irrigated) agriculture, food processing operations, power generation, and industrial cooling. The presence of abundant, inexpensive water and hydro-generated power has been attractive to industry. As well, the presence of water has motivated individuals to locate their homes, cottages, and other facilities on the shores of Canada's many lakes, streams, and rivers.

While communities and industries choose to locate on or close to water bodies for transportation, water supply, and aesthetic reasons, the hazardous nature of water is not always appreciated fully. Dangers associated with floods and storms may compromise the safety of people and their property, and damages may entail the loss of lives and property, as well as high cleanup and repair costs. In the case of the Saguenay–Lac Saint-Jean region floods in Quebec in July 1996, about 12 000 people were evacuated from their homes as more than 50 towns and villages were inundated by flood waters that resulted from more than 270 millimetres of rain. At least 7 people died, 100 homes were washed away, and about 1000 homes and 20 major bridges were heavily damaged. In addition, more than 100 tonnes of toxic waste and chemicals spilled into the Saguenay River when floods damaged or destroyed industrial facilities such as pulp and paper mills. Although chemicals such as phosphoric acid, urea, and ferric chloride were dispersed in the heavy river flow, there was concern for toxic hot spots in river sediments. A $450-million relief fund was established to compensate flood victims, and many Canadians contributed to the relief effort.

The 877-kilometre Red River regularly floods the valley of silty loam left behind following the retreat of Lake Agassiz about 7700 years ago. Some years the floods are more memorable than others—in terms of crest levels, the 1826 flood remains the worst; it reached 36.5 feet above the river bed when it crossed the forks of the Red and Assiniboine rivers in the heart of Winnipeg. Manitobans still measure the Red River floods in feet above the river bottom, relative to the 1826 flood (Pindera, 1997).

Following severe floods in 1948 and 1950—the river crest reached 30.3 feet, 80 000 people fled from Winnipeg, 20 000 residents were evacuated from rural areas, 13 000 homes and farms were flooded, and damage estimates totalled $606 million in 1997 dollars—a plan to "tame the Red" was implemented. Massive clay dikes and diversion

Some Manitoba communities were inundated by the 1997 Red River flood despite sandbagging.

dams were built in the Winnipeg area and the $63-million Red River Floodway was opened in 1968. A 47-kilometre-long channel that diverts the Red River around Winnipeg, the floodway was one of many permanent structures erected to control the flow of water through the city. By the 1970s, eight towns between the American border and Winnipeg were protected with permanent dikes also. In 1979, a flood similar to the 1950 flood tested these defence systems; most held back the flood waters and only 7000 people fled their homes.

The history of flooding in the Red River valley reveals that floods commonly occur when the winter snowpack in the southern headwaters of the river thaws before the northern Manitoba reaches of the river are free from ice. From November 1, 1996, to April 20, 1997, record levels of snow fell on ground that had been saturated through a wet autumn. Areas south and east of Winnipeg received winter precipitation amounts that were 175 percent of the annual average, and parts of the Red River drainage basin in North Dakota received precipitation amounts of more than 200 percent of the annual average. Just days after the runoff began in early April, a major storm dumped another 50 to 70 centimetres of snow and freezing rain on top of the near-record snowpack of 250 centimetres.

The 1997 spring flood extended over 205 000 hectares, or about 5 percent of Manitoba's farmland, creating a 2000-square-kilometre "Red Sea." Had the floodway, dams, and dikes not been built, it is estimated that the crest of the flood, the second highest in Manitoba history, would have measured 34.3 feet. Instead, the floodway kept the water level at 24.5 feet. Still, 28 000 Manitobans were evacuated (6000 from Winnipeg), and 2500 properties between Winnipeg and the U.S. border were damaged. Even though 45 000 laying hens and 2000 cattle were moved to safety, dairy farmers' losses have been estimated at $1.3 to $2 billion. Total damages tally more than $150 million, mostly for repairs to roads,

bridges, farms, and homes. The toll on wildlife would not be known until the waters receded completely in late summer. While no one knows when the Red River will flood seriously again, discussions are under way with U.S. authorities to seek joint solutions, and include the question of whether dams or diversions south of the border (where most of the Red River's drainage basin lies) would help reduce damages.

Given the importance of ecologically healthy water bodies for habitat and ecosystem support (for all flora and fauna), and given human dependence on quality water supplies for life and for economic and recreational activities, sustainability must apply to the full range of water elements. That is, the value of wetlands and estuaries, of aquifers and groundwater recharge areas, and of precipitation regimes must be accounted for in the planning and management of water resources.

HUMAN ACTIVITIES AND IMPACTS ON FRESHWATER ENVIRONMENTS

As previously noted, human use of water resources—for domestic, urban, agricultural, industrial, power generation, and recreational purposes—results in a range of variable impacts on fresh water and freshwater environments. This section covers in more detail examples of the kinds of impacts that result from each of these five types of water use.

DOMESTIC AND URBAN USES AND IMPACTS

Safe Drinking Water and Sanitation Facilities

In developing countries, 80 percent of illnesses are water related; globally, about 34 000 deaths occur daily from contaminated water and water-borne diseases (Environment Canada, 1990). These statistics reflect the fact that more than 1.5 billion people lack safe drinking water supplies, and about 1.7 billion have inadequate sanitation facilities. In Canada, municipalities have the responsibility to provide their citizens with safe drinking water. The Guidelines for Canadian Drinking Water Quality indicate that good quality drinking water is free from disease-causing organisms, harmful chemical substances, and radioactive material. Good-quality drinking water also tastes good, is aesthetically appealing, and free from objectionable odour or colour. While these guidelines are not legally binding, they specify limits for substances and describe conditions that affect drinking water quality in Canada.

Even with these guidelines in place, Environment Canada (1995a) has noted that media reports about communities with contaminated drinking water are increasing in frequency from one end of Canada to the other. Reasons for contaminated drinking water in Canada are variable, but in some instances have to do with levels of treatment of municipal wastewater. Since most of the water withdrawn for domestic, industrial, and commercial use re-enters the natural system (river, lake, or aquifer), that used water must, in order to protect human health, be treated to remove a portion of the impurities it contains.

Municipalities may offer one of three levels of sewage treatment. **Primary treatment,** the lowest degree of treatment, is a mechanical process involving removal of large solids, sediment, and some organic matter. As raw sewage enters a treatment plant, it flows through a metal grating (which removes branches and dead animals, for example) and through screens that remove diapers, bottles, and objects of similar size. Sand and gravel settle out in a grit tank. From that point, even though it contains many pathogens, the fluid may be discharged to a receiving water body (thus the danger of contamination) or may enter a secondary treatment process. The sludge is removed and taken to a digester for further processing.

Secondary treatment employs biological processes in which bacteria and other microorganisms degrade most of the dissolved organics, as well as about 30 percent of phosphates and about 50 percent of nitrates remaining in the suspended solids (Wells & Rolston, 1991). Effluent from the primary process may be pumped into trickle filters, aeration tanks, or sewage lagoons. A trickle filter consists of a bed of stones (or other medium) through which water drips; bacteria and other microorganisms in the bed catch organic matter as it trickles past and aerobically decompose it.

In aeration tank digestion (activated sludge process), effluent from the primary process is mixed with a bacteria-rich slurry, air or oxygen is pumped through the mixture, and bacterial growth decomposes the organic matter. Water siphoned off the top of the tank typically is disinfected, usually by chlorination, before it is released into the environment. Sludge is removed from the bottom of the tank; some of it may be used to inoculate the incoming primary effluent, but because of its toxic content (metals, chemicals, pathogens), most of the sludge is dried and landfilled.

If a municipality has space, it may construct a sewage lagoon where exposure of the effluent to sunlight, algae, aquatic organisms, and air slowly degrades the organic matter (with lower energy costs). Natural or constructed wetlands also act effectively to absorb nutrients and other pollutants at low cost. Even in Canada's cold climate, wetlands are proving to be important components of municipal treatment systems.

Tertiary treatment is a chemical process that removes phosphates, nitrates, and additional contaminants such as salts, acids, metals, and toxic organic and organochlorine compounds from the secondary effluent. Sand filters or carbon filters also may be used in advanced wastewater treatment. The treated effluent may be discharged into natural water bodies or used to irrigate agricultural lands and municipal properties such as parks and golf courses. Because tertiary treatment greatly reduces nutrients in the treated wastewater, algal blooms and eutrophication are reduced.

Depending on the municipality, not all water returned to natural systems will have been treated. Municipal storm drains carry rainwater and melting snow—along with pollutants such as garden chemicals, oil from gas stations and driveways, and animal feces—often run directly (and untreated) into oceans, lakes, and rivers. Even if municipal storm drainage is treated, heavy rain or spring runoff can generate sufficient flow to overload a treatment plant and cause both storm and sanitary sewage flows to be discharged in an untreated state.

In general, municipal wastewater treatment levels have been rising steadily in Canada. Both the number of people served by sewage collection and sewage treatment systems has increased (from 18.2 million in 1983 to 21.1 million in 1994), and the level of treatment has increased (In 1983, 27.7 percent of the population was served by tertiary treatment; by 1994 that percentage had risen to 38.7). Similarly, the proportion of the population whose wastewater was discharged untreated dropped from 28.3 percent in 1983 to 7.4 percent in 1994 (Government of Canada, 1996). This issue is discussed further in Chapter 13,

Water treated to a level that will protect human health may still stress aquatic ecosystems when discharged. The lower the degree of sewage treatment provided, the greater the biological oxygen demand of the effluent and the greater its impact on aquatic life. Also, unless wastewater receives secondary treatment, disease-causing bacteria may be present in the effluent. None of these levels of treatment has a proven ability to remove toxic substances, however, and persistent chemicals such as DDT, PCBs, or mirex are removed only by very advanced treatment such as that employing activated carbon. Drinking water supplies may be affected severely by inadequately treated municipal wastewater discharges, industrial and agricultural pollution of water bodies, and leaking landfill sites (see also Chapter 8).

Concern about what constitutes appropriate levels of municipal wastewater treatment is not confined to local residents. In Victoria, British Columbia, the capital city of the province and an international tourist destination, sewage is discharged with only primary treatment to the coastal waters surrounding the community. Some American visitors, who make up a very large proportion of Victoria's tourists, caused considerable consternation among city tourism officials and businesses when, after learning of the sewage issue, the visitors threatened not to visit Victoria. Partly in response to the economic threat that such a tourist boycott of the city would have, and partly because of the desirability of enhancing the level of municipal wastewater treatment, the city has been studying the problem.

Demand for Water

Another urban water issue relates to domestic consumption of, or our demand for, water. At the same time as the safety and security of our water supply are declining due to pollution, dropping water tables, and prolonged drought conditions in some areas, our demand for water is rising (Environment Canada, 1995a). Because of increasing demand, municipal water supply is becoming one of the most critical water issues in Canada. Residential water use accounts for nearly one-half of all the water used in Canadian municipalities. Although each Canadian uses approximately 340 litres of water per day inside the home, and the ways we use that water are similar (Figure 7–4), consumption varies by region (Figure 7–5).

Sometimes we don't realize how much water we consume in our everyday activities. For instance, 65 percent of all residential water use takes place in the bathroom; if your toilet is more than 10 years old, and you flush 4.5 times per day, over the course of one year you will have

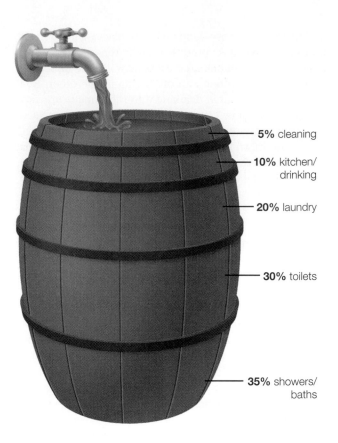

Figure 7–4
Use of water in Canadian homes

SOURCE: Environment Canada. (1995a). *Water: No time to waste: A consumer's guide to water conservation.* Ottawa: Supply and Services Canada.

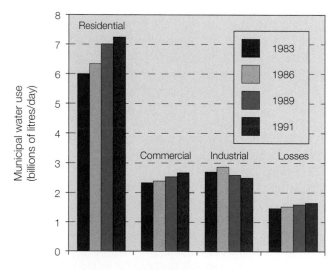

Figure 7–3
Daily municipal water use in Canada, by sector, for selected years 1983–1991

NOTE: Losses also include unaccounted water use such as water used in firefighting.

SOURCE: Environment Canada. (1994). *Urban water: Environmental Indicator Bulletin.* SOE Bulletin No. 94–1. Ottawa: Supply and Services Canada. This graph is taken from the Web site at http://199.212.18.12/~ind/, but the same graph (different configuration) is available in the *Environmental Indicator Bulletin.*

used about 30 000 litres of water to dispose of about 650 litres of body waste. If your toilet is one of the 25 percent that leaks after flushing, you could be losing up to 200 000 litres of water in one year. If you water your lawn in summer, it could need about 100 000 litres of water during the growing season.

In 1991, 20 percent of Canadian municipalities with water supply systems reported problems with water availability (Environment Canada, 1994). About 10 percent of Canadians on municipal water systems rely exclusively on groundwater for drinking water and other domestic uses. Larger municipalities that depend exclusively on groundwater are highly susceptible to water availability problems, particularly if the population in the municipality is growing, if the municipality permits unrestricted use of water, and if water prices are low. Because increasing water demand and use require the construction of new (or expansion of existing) facilities, all of which consume land, energy, and other resources, water conservation and reduction of our demand for water can be important factors in improving the quality and in protecting the quantity of water resources.

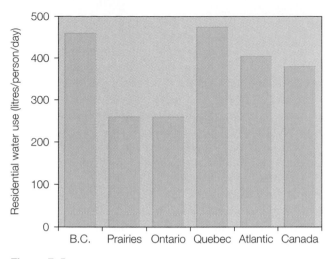

Figure 7–5
Residential water use per person by region, 1991

NOTE: There are insufficient data to include the Northwest Territories and Yukon.

SOURCE: Environment Canada. (1994). *Urban water: Environmental Indicator Bulletin.* SOE Bulletin No. 94–1. Ottawa: Supply and Services Canada, p. 2.

The Great Lakes and St. Lawrence River Basin: A Case Study

Straddling the Canada–United States border, the Great Lakes–St. Lawrence River basin contains about 18 percent of the world's fresh surface water, accounts for about 4 percent of the total length of Canada's shoreline, and is home to over 35 percent (about 9 million) of the Canadian population. About 33 million Americans also live in the Great Lakes basin. One of out every 3 Canadians and 1 out of every 7 U.S. residents depend on the Great Lakes for their drinking water, which amounts to about 140 000 litres of water per second (Environment Canada, 1990). The Great Lakes also have played a major role in the development of both Canada and the United States. The Great Lakes form part of the inland waterway for shipment of goods into and out of the heart of the continent; are the site of industrial, commercial, agricultural, and urban development; and are a source of hydroelectricity and recreation.

Broad, long-standing issues affecting the Great Lakes–St. Lawrence River basin include deteriorating water quality through industrial and municipal uses, fluctuating water levels, flooding, and shoreline erosion. Acid precipitation, airborne toxins, depletion of wetland areas, the sale and diversion of water from the system, increased demand on shoreline recreational facilities, and climate change are among the concerns affecting the basin (see Hodge & Bubelis, 1991, in Additional Information Sources).

Since early in this century, significant changes in land use have occurred in the Great Lakes–St. Lawrence

basin, including deforestation, drainage of wetlands, and urbanization. These changes have altered the runoff characteristics of the drainage basin, as have the navigational and other structures built to regulate the outflows of lakes Superior and Ontario. Other human activities have affected lake levels and the lakes themselves: examples include the Long Lac and Ogoki diversions built to bring water into Lake Superior for hydropower generation and logging; the diversion at Chicago that takes water out of Lake Michigan to support domestic, navigation, hydroelectric, and sanitation uses; and the Welland ship canal, built to bypass Niagara Falls and to provide water for power generation (Environment Canada, 1990). Dredging and channel modifications have affected lake levels and flows as well.

Compared to natural factors, human effects on lake levels are small. Nevertheless, changing Great Lakes water levels are of great concern because of their impact on the multiple and often conflicting uses of the lakes. Shore owners prefer low lake levels because low levels mean less risk to their properties, while shipping and hydroelectric companies prefer high lake levels because high levels

Built to overcome a height difference of 99 metres between Lake Erie and Lake Ontario, the Welland Canal affected lake levels and flows profoundly.

permit them to carry more cargo and to generate more electricity (Sanderson, 1993). Depending on the lake and climate change scenario employed, predictions are that lake levels may drop by 0.5 to 2.5 metres. This is a significant threat, not only to shipping and other economic concerns but also to the ecology of the Great Lakes and the lower St. Lawrence where increases in tidal effects and saltwater intrusion could occur (Government of Canada, 1996).

Since there is an annual cycle of levels on the Great Lakes (high in summer and low in winter), as well as periodic effects from the passage of storms (on Lake Erie, for example, a major storm can cause short-term water level changes of as much as 5 metres), damage due to wave action can be extensive (Environment Canada, 1990; Sanderson, 1993). Along the Canadian shore of the Great Lakes, annual flooding and erosion damage averages about $2 million. However, for every 1-centimetre decline in Great Lakes water levels, 93 metric tonnes must be subtracted from the total load a Great Lakes boat can carry (Environment Canada, 1990). Balancing such competing interests, and improving shoreline management to achieve sustainability of water resources and related habitats, are among the challenging responsibilities of international agencies such as the International Joint Commission, provincial governments, and municipal planners. Later in this chapter, some efforts undertaken to restore the Great Lakes ecosystem are noted.

Eutrophication and persistent toxic chemicals have been the focus of water quality issues in the Great Lakes basin for many years. By the late 1960s, scientists, policymakers, and the general public were aware that high levels of nutrients such as phosphorus and nitrogen were causing eutrophication of the Great Lakes. Lake Erie in particular was "dying" from uncontrolled growth of aquatic plants, lowered levels of oxygen, and conditions unfavourable to fish survival. During the same period, "the Cuyahoga River running through Cleveland was so clogged with oils and greases that it caught fire in 1969. The city had to build a fire wall and declare the river a fire hazard" (cited in Royal Commission on the Future of the Toronto Waterfront, 1992).

By the late 1970s, more complex problems relating to synthetic toxic chemicals were the focus of attention. Over 360 compounds have been found in Great Lakes waters, more than one-third of which have been shown to be toxic to humans and wildlife. By 1985, 11 compounds had been identified as critical pollutants in the Great Lakes basin ecosystem (Table 7–1) because of their persistence, recycling, wide dispersal, bioaccumulation, and biomagnification in the food web (Royal Commission on the Future of the Toronto Waterfront, 1992; International Joint Commission, 1992). While levels of some critical contaminants in the Great Lakes ecosystem have been reduced, two factors combine to suggest that future improvement may be slow.

The first of these factors is that contaminants are released continuously from sediment as the ecosystem slowly purges itself. The second factor is that inputs of toxic substances continue; for example, PCB inputs continue because more than half the PCBs produced are still in use or are in storage and disposal sites and thus have the potential to enter the Great Lakes environment (International Joint Commission, 1992).

In the 1970s, 1980s, and early 1990s, considerable research was undertaken, some of which established direct links between environmental concentrations of persistent toxic substances and damage in a living species (International Joint Commission, 1992). Studies on concentrations of toxins in herring gull eggs in the Great Lakes (see Box 3–2) (Bishop and Weseloh, 1990), in coho salmon from the Credit River in Ontario (cited in Government of Canada, 1991), on bald eagle hatchlings (International Joint Commission, 1992), and of other toxins in other wildlife species, demonstrated the need to stop the input of persistent toxic substances into Great Lakes waters. Among other actions, efforts to reduce the discharges to zero are considered later in this chapter.

Human health also is threatened by exposure to persistent toxins from municipal sewage and industrial and agricultural chemicals. A study of Michigan women who consumed more than 0.5 kilograms of Lake Michigan fish per month during their pregnancies demonstrated that their newborns showed a significantly higher percentage of decreased birth weight, head circumference, and neurobehavioural development. Psychological tests administered to these same children when they were four years old indicated they were suffering from learning deficits (Government of Canada, 1991).

The Trent–Severn Waterway between Lake Ontario and Georgian Bay in Ontario was conceived as a military defence route in the 1780s, but was built for commerce in the 1800s (and completed in 1920). Today, nearly 200 000 recreational boats use its locks and channels. Communities that once needed the waterway as a means of bringing logs to their lumber mills now depend on tourism dollars from the boaters and tourists who patronize their marinas, stores, hotels, and restaurants. Water quality problems are among the environmental challenges that face the waterway. Phosphate pollution from agricultural lands and from lawns is causing algae and weed problems, and the growing population of cottagers has led to increased pollution from septic tanks. If these are not well maintained, they can leak disease-causing bacteria into lakes and rivers and contaminate shallow groundwater supplies. Also, as the number of residents and cottagers has grown, development has encroached into wetlands, threatening some rare plant species (Cayer, 1996). These kinds of problems exist in various locations throughout the Great Lakes–St. Lawrence basin and the rest of the country as well.

CRITICAL POLLUTANTS IN THE GREAT LAKES BASIN ECOSYSTEM (1991)

Pollutant	Use	Method of entry into Great Lakes Basin
all polychlorinated biphenyls (PCBs)[a]	• insulating fluid in electrical transformers and in production of hydraulic fluids, lubricants, and inks • previously used as a vehicle for pesticide dispersal • includes 209 related chemicals of varying toxicity	• from air or in sediments • through leakage, spills, and waste storage and disposal
DDT and its breakdown products (including DDE)[b]	• insecticide • most uses stopped in Canada in 1970 • still used heavily for mosquito control in tropical areas on other continents	• from air or in sediments
dieldrin[b]	• insecticide once used extensively on fruits • use no longer permitted for termite control in Canada	• from air or in sediments
toxaphene[b]	• insecticide developed as a substitute for DDT • used on cotton • Canadian use virtually ceased in early 1980s	• from air or in sediments
2,3,7,8-tetrachlorodibenzo-p-dioxin (TCDD) and 2,3,7,8-tetrachlorodibenzo-furan (TCDF)	• chemicals created in manufacture of herbicides used in agriculture and for prairie (range) and forest management • byproduct of burning fossil fuels with chlorinated additives, wastes containing chlorine, and in pulp and paper production processes that use chlorine bleach • created in production of pentachlorophenol (PCP) • contaminant in Agent Orange herbicide used in Vietnam • most toxic of 75 forms of dioxin (polychlorinated dibenzodioxins)	• from air or in water or in sediments
mirex[c]	• fire retardant • pesticide to control fire ants • breaks down to more potent chemical, photomirex, in presence of sunlight	• from air or in sediments • residuals from manufacturing sites, spills, and landfills
mercury	• used in metallurgy • byproduct of paint, chlor-alkali, and electrical equipment manufacturing processes	• occurs naturally in soils and sediments • releases into aquatic environment may be accelerated by acidic deposition
alkylated-lead	• fuel additive • used in solder, pipes, and paint	• released when burning leaded fuel, waste, cigarettes, and from pipes, cans, and paint chips
benzo(a)pyrene	• produced when fossil fuels, wood, wastes, and charcoal are burned, including in forest fires • from automobile exhausts • one of many forms of polycyclic aromatic hydrocarbons (PAHs)	• product of incomplete combustion of fossil fuels and wood
hexachlorobenzene (HCB)	• byproduct of burning fossil fuels and wastes that contain chlorinated additives • found in manufacturing processes using chlorine • contaminant in chlorinated pesticides	• byproduct of combustion of fuels and incineration of waste

[a] manufacture and new uses prohibited in Canada and the United States
[b] use restricted in Canada and the United States
[c] banned for use in Canada and the United States

SOURCES: After the Royal Commission on the Future of the Toronto Waterfront. (1992). *Regeneration: Toronto's waterfront and the sustainable city: Final report.* Toronto: Supply and Services Canada and Queen's Printer of Ontario, p. 105; and after Government of Canada. (1991). *The state of Canada's environment—1991.* Ottawa: Minister of Supply and Services Canada, p. 18-15.

AGRICULTURAL USES AND IMPACTS

Significant changes to Canada's agricultural practices during the past century have included new crop varieties, management practices, and increased productivity. These changes sometimes have been accompanied by increased environmental impacts including degraded soils, contaminated water bodies, and altered biodiversity. Wetland habitat reduction in Ontario and the Prairies, fertilizer and pesticide runoff into aquatic systems, erosion, and increasing levels of water withdrawal and consumption are among the major effects of agriculture on water resources in Canada (see Chapter 6).

Wetlands, along with their ecologically productive and purifying functions and their contributions to the socioeconomic well-being of Canadians, have been disappearing since settlement began. In the Great Lakes basin, for example, wetlands continued to be lost to agricultural and residential development at a rate of 8100 hectares per year (Environment Canada, 1990). Despite the massive loss of wetlands, they continue to contribute between $5 and $10 billion annually to the Canadian economy through support of commercial and sports fishing, waterfowl hunting, trapping, recreation, peatland forestry, water purification, groundwater discharge, and flood peak modification (Environment Canada, 1990).

There is potential danger to wetlands from the pesticides and nutrients used in intense agricultural activities as well. Shoreline wetlands on the Canadian side of Lake Erie are a case in point. From 1992 to 1994, researchers studying the problem showed that pesticides were transported in water and in sediments from streams and creeks surrounding the wetlands into the wetlands and downstream into Lake Erie. Alachlor, a pesticide banned in 1989, was detected at one of the sampling stations. The highest pesticide concentrations occurred between May and July, immediately after pesticides were applied to the fields and following spring precipitation. Research continues into the impacts and cumulative effects of chronic exposure of Lake Erie's marsh and lake biota to these concentrations of pesticides (Government of Canada, n.d.). (For further information on wetlands and their ecology, significance, and conservation, see the Web site for the Wetland Resource Centre listed in the Additional Information Sources section at the end of this chapter.)

Groundwater, too, is subject to contamination from non-point sources such as fertilizers and pesticides applied to agricultural lands. In the lower Fraser Valley and southern Ontario, for example, high nitrate levels and fecal coliform bacteria in wells used for drinking water have been traced to the application of fertilizers and manure to fields, as well as to leakage from septic tanks. Given the large areas involved in agriculture, and the concentrations of dairy cattle, poultry, and other livestock in these areas, heavy applications of manure may exceed the assimilative capacities of the soils and lead to declines in

Irrigation water is applied to the land using a variety of methods, including central pivot and oscillating sprinklers and irrigation canals.

water quality. The cumulative effects of septic systems may result also in widespread contamination of shallow groundwater. (For information on pesticide contamination of groundwater, see the Crowe and Milburn reference in Additional Information Sources for this chapter.)

Soil erosion by water varies widely across Canada, with the most severe losses of soil occurring in the Peace

200

River area and Fraser Valley of British Columbia, parts of Saskatchewan, southwestern Ontario, the Eastern Townships of Quebec, and Prince Edward Island (Government of Canada, 1991). Not only is soil loss by water erosion costly in terms of reduced crop productivity and higher production costs, but also sediment damages occur. These damages include reductions in channel capacity; alteration and destruction of fish habitats; accelerated plant and algal growth from excess nutrients; buildup and transportation of heavy metals, pesticides, and other toxic substances; lower recreational values; and increased costs to ensure water is fit for human consumption (Government of Canada, 1991). Estimates of the annual on-farm economic impacts of water ersosion are (in 1986 dollars) $266–424 million for Canada as a whole; $155–197 million of that total occurs in the Prairie provinces (Government of Canada, 1991).

While irrigation is the fourth largest withdrawal use in Canada, it is the largest consumer of water (see Figure 7–2). In the west, irrigation is used to increase the productive capacity of land for forage, cereal, and oilseed crops, while in eastern Canada, irrigation traditionally has been applied to fruit, tobacco, and vegetable crops. Irrigated crops come with a price tag: reservoir construction floods scenic river valleys, destroys historically and culturally important sites, reduces or eliminates habitat for fish and wildlife, and alters the flow and water quality of a river, often disadvantaging downstream users. Sediments accumulate in reservoirs, reducing their capacity, and below a dam there may be streambed erosion. These impacts associated with major infrastructure for irrigation can change flooding patterns to the detriment of some adapted species such as cottonwood trees (Box 7–3), reduce water quality, harm fish populations, and, because

---

BOX 7-3
SOUTHERN ALBERTA'S COTTONWOODS AND THE 1995 OLDMAN RIVER FLOOD

Within a 26-hour span on June 5–0, 1995, more than 140 millimetres of rain fell on the headwater region of the Oldman River in southwestern Alberta. The intense rainfall caused unusually high streamflow peaks that surged downstream and spread across the entire floodplain. As damaging as this flood was— $39 million was paid out from the Flood Recovery Program—this event may have played a very important role in securing the long-term future of the cottonwood (a poplar species) forest.

In an area of low regional rainfall (less than 200 millimetres falls annually), southern Alberta's cottonwoods are found in river valleys where streams maintain sufficient groundwater for their growth. Along the rivers the trees provide important wildlife habitat, are a valuable recreational amenity, and the shallow root systems help reduce streambank erosion during high flows. The life cycle of river valley cottonwoods is linked intimately with the flow of the streams and rivers, particularly high flow conditions that not only provide water essential for the survival of established trees, but also help seedlings become established. Floods that overflow the river banks saturate the seedbeds and recharge the floodplain water table so that when the seeds are released (normally from mid-June to mid-July), they land on wet soil and may be able to survive until their roots reach a deeper and more dependable water supply.

In spite of the fact that a mature cottonwood tree can produce more than 20 million seeds annually, the seeds must germinate quickly to be successful. Even if the seedlings establish themselves during favourable conditions, seedling survival past midsummer is uncertain due to high levels of drought stress. Their survival appears to be enhanced during years when flooding occurs. Given the dams, reservoirs, and other struc-

tures that regulate the Oldman River (and most other rivers in southern Alberta), and the consequent changes in flooding regimes, the cottonwoods have been aging and dying, and few young trees have been growing to replace them.

The 1995 flood may have been a critical opportunity for regeneration of the riparian cottonwood stands. Surveys following the flood showed that many seedlings survived their first critical year,

although it would take three to four years to determine whether the saplings would be able to withstand the usual drought and flood conditions and grow to maturity. Engineers and water managers are studying whether it would be possible to benefit downstream cottonwood forests and enhance the survival of the cottonwood seedlings by fine-tuning the flow regime afforded by the control structures on the Oldman River. If those managers can assist seedling survival through the next year or two, that would be a "significant step in ensuring the long term survival of the riparian [cottonwood] forests in southern Alberta. The start of a new generation of river valley cottonwoods is a benefit from a once in a lifetime flood that can last and be enjoyed for many years to come."

SOURCES: Abbott, E. (1996, June). The magnitude of the June 1995 southern Alberta flood. *Technical Bureau Supplement to Water News,* 15(2), pp. 1–3.

Mahoney, J. (1996, June). The effect of the 1995 Oldman River flood on riparian cottonwood forests. *Technical Bureau Supplement to Water News,* 15(2), pp. 3–8.

of water fluctuation from reservoir operation, destroy waterfowl nests and homes of water-dwelling mammals such as beaver and muskrat.

In parts of the Prairies where surface waters are scarce, not all impacts of water storage areas such as impoundments and canals are negative. In addition to the water they provide for irrigation, water impoundments can be used for recreation and fishing, and may provide new types of habitat for wildlife. In the past, the brush and weeds that grew beside canals and fence lines provided excellent cover for birds and small mammals (see Box 3–1). More recently, increased chemical control of brush and weeds and the attempts to reduce water losses through canal lining and use of water pipelines have diminished the positive effects of irrigation works on wildlife.

In the Prairie provinces, irrigation water is applied to over 635 000 hectares. While the area to be irrigated has not enlarged significantly during the past decade, there has been an increase in the amount of water applied per hectare since 1981. This trend, combined with regional climate change scenarios that point to more frequent and prolonged droughts on the Prairies, with increased drying up of wetlands, suggests the need for improved efficiency in water use. With modern methods and technology, estimated water savings range from a reduction of up to 10 percent on irrigation needs for extensive grain and oilseed production, to up to 50 percent savings on intensive fruit and vegetable production (Government of Canada, 1996).

Other environmental concerns related to irrigated land result from the increased use of pesticides and fertilizers compared to amounts farmers would usually employ under dryland conditions. When irrigation water runs off the fields, residues from these substances may enter streams or be leached into groundwater, contaminating those water bodies. Irrigation may exacerbate dryland salinization of soils by altering shallow groundwater conditions that, in turn, accelerate surface evaporation. Replacing natural vegetation with short-season cereal grains is one action that can trigger salinization. Salts can leach from irrigated lands also, sometimes as a result of unlined canals causing water tables to rise in areas where salts are present in the subsoil. About six to eight million hectares of land in western Canada contain soils that may be affected by salinization; in 1989, costs attributable to salinity ranged from $104 to $257 million annually (Government of Canada, 1991).

INDUSTRIAL USES AND IMPACTS

Industrial sites have been located near water bodies not only for the water they supply, but also for the transportation, cooling, and effluent discharge roles they fulfill. Historically, ignorance about the cumulative impacts of industrial activities on the environment led to groundwater and soil contamination and other downstream effects. Today, greater awareness has reduced the severity of impacts, but human and wildlife health-related concerns from previous activity continue to surface.

Industrial activities, ranging from food processing to manufacturing, rely on large amounts of clean water to produce their goods and large amounts of water to carry away the waste and byproducts of these processes. While manufacturing withdraws the second highest volume of water in the country (see Figure 7–2), use of more efficient water technologies has enabled this sector to withdraw significantly less water since 1981. With continued emphasis on efficiency and conservation, further reductions in withdrawal rates (perhaps as much as 40 to 50 percent) are expected to continue, with no sacrifice of economic output or quality of life.

Groundwater Contamination

Toxic industrial byproducts enter aquatic environments, including groundwater, as point sources of waste disposal or through leaks and spills. Point sources related to waste disposal sites for industrial chemicals, underground injection wells for industrial waste, waste rock and mill tailings in mining ares, and coal tar at old gasification sites. Point sources related to leaks and spills include leaky tanks or pipelines containing petroleum products, wood preservation facilities, and road salt storage areas. In terms of groundwater contamination, the potential is greatest if disposal occurs in or near sand and gravel aquifers. Over many years in Ville Mercier, Quebec, industrial wastes had been placed in lagoons in an old gravel pit. Predictably, water supplies of thousands of residents in the region were rendered unusable, and a replacement supply had to be pumped from a well 10 miles away (Environment Canada, 1996a).

The overall extent of groundwater contamination from industrial sources in Canada is not known, although hundreds of individual cases have been investigated. Such cases include contamination by the pesticide aldicarb in Prince Edward Island, industrial effluents in Elmira, Ontario, and various pesticides in the Prairies, as well as creosote contamination in Calgary and other communities and industrial contamination in Vancouver. Frequently, recognition of the contamination occurs only after water users have been exposed to potential health risks and the cost of cleaning the water supply is extremely high (Environment Canada, 1996a). Cleanup is often impossible, and groundwater aquifers may remain contaminated for decades.

In addition, contaminated groundwater migrates via the hydrological cycle to nearby rivers and lakes, creating surface water pollution that can be as serious as contamination of groundwater supplies. Given that groundwater moves slowly, it may take decades before contamination is detected; scientists expect the discovery of more contaminated groundwater aquifers and new contaminants during the next few decades. Experience suggests prevention of contamination in the first place is by far the most practical solution to this problem.

Among the wide variety of industrial chemicals in commercial use world wide, dense nonaqueous phase liquids (DNAPLs) are particularly troublesome. DNAPLs include dry-cleaning solvents (such as trichloroethylene and tetrachloroethylene), wood preservatives (Box 7–4), and chemicals used in asphalt operations, automobile production and repair, aviation equipment, munitions, and electrical equipment. DNAPLs can be generated and released in accidents such as the Hagersville tire fire. Heavier than water, these substances sink quickly and deeply into the ground where they dissolve very slowly and then may move with the groundwater flow. These sources of contamination are very difficult to find and almost impossible to clean up (Environment Canada, 1996b). Except in large cities, drinking water is tested rarely for these contaminants, yet in 1995 a study of more than 480 municipal and communal groundwater supplies

determined that almost 12 percent of them contained detectable concentrations of either trichloroethylene or tetrachloroethylene (Government of Canada, 1996).

Leaking underground storage tanks and piping constitute another widespread impact of industrial activities on water resources. During the past two decades there has been an increasing number of leaks of petroleum products because the 30- to 40-year-old tanks in which these products were stored had inadequate corrosion protection. (Before 1980, most tanks were made of steel and up to half of them leaked by the time they were 15 years old.) Most petroleum products have the potential to contaminate large quantities of water: for example, one litre of gasoline can contaminate one million litres of groundwater. In the Atlantic provinces, where groundwater usage is high, the problem of leaking underground storage tanks is particularly severe. Very often the problem is detected only when people start smelling or tasting gasoline in their water (Environment Canada, 1996c).

BOX 7-4
CREOSOTE WASTE PRODUCTS AND CONTAMINATED SITES

In Canada, creosote is used as a wood preservative on railway ties, bridge timbers, pilings, and large-sized lumber. Creosote itself is composed of hundreds of compounds, the largest group being the polycyclic aromatic hydrocarbons (PAHs).

Areas of contaminated soil, water, or materials result from the application, manufacture, storage, transportation, or spillage of creosote. While the total amount of waste creosote entering the Canadian environment is not known, it is estimated that 256 000 cubic metres of moderately and highly contaminated soil is associated with 11 abandoned or operating creosote-application facilities in Canada. In all provinces except Prince Edward Island, waste creosote is known to be entering soils, groundwater, and surface waters at 24 sites.

In Calgary, creosote pooled beneath the Bow River near the site of a former Canada Creosote wood-preservative plant has entered the river and reduced the number of benthic invertebrates (caddisflies and stoneflies) within about one kilometre downstream from the site. These species, important to the fish on which the Bow River's world-class fly fishery is based, were replaced by less sensitive snails and crane flies. Waste creosote and the PAHs found in it were detected at levels higher than those known to cause severe effects to freshwater and marine organisms.

Given that some residents downstream of Calgary drink water taken directly from the Bow River, and given that the Siksika Nation people have noticed irregularities in the fish caught along their section of the river, a gravel berm was constructed as a tem-

porary measure to stop creosote from mixing with the flow of the river. The berm was not watertight but reduced creosote seepage to the riverbed surface by up to 80 percent in the short term.

Alberta Environment and Environment Canada officials determined that a permanent, 635-metre-long, subsurface, impervious containment wall and treatment system were necessary. Costing close to $4 million, the containment project includes a pumping system to take the dirty water containing the lighter creosote oils (which float to the top of the water table in the ground) into an on-site water treatment plant prior to their discharge into Calgary's sanitary sewer system. Contaminated residues from the water treatment plant are transported off-site to an approved facility for re-use or disposal. Annual costs to operate the pumping wells and water treatment are about $100 000. Since some of the creosote that soaked into the soil and rock was heavier than water, it is impossible to clean up the site totally with current technology.

Under the National Contaminated Sites Remediation Program, the Alberta and federal governments shared the cost of this project. Even though the company that owned and operated the plant from the 1920s until 1964 is known and is responsible for the contamination, the company is not paying for the cleanup because practices at the site then were standard for the time and the company probably was not contravening any legislation.

Associated with the containment project are plans for increased river and on-site monitoring of the atmosphere, land, and water to ensure public safety.

SOURCES: Environment Canada & Health Canada. (1993). Creosote-impregnated waste materials. http://www.ec.gc.ca/library/elias/bibrec/302071B.html

Alberta Environmental Protection. (1995). *Summary material from November 17, 1994, Canada Creosote Stakeholder Workshop.*

Impacts on Beluga Whales

Industrial (and agricultural) pollution also poses an insidious threat to the small population of threatened beluga whales (estimated at 525 members in 1992) that inhabits the St. Lawrence estuary (Beluga habitat in St. Lawrence, 1996). Research scientists are trying to confirm why the health of the whales is not improving. It is known that beluga calves are being poisoned by their mothers' milk, and that older beluga are dying from cancerous tumors (Béland, 1996). Pollution is one possible culprit, as the blubber and bodies of nearly all of the 15 beluga that wash ashore in an average year are heavily contaminated with more than 25 potentially toxic contaminants. These include heavy metals such as mercury and lead, PCBs, DDT, and pesticides such as mirex and chlordane. Beluga carcasses are so contaminated they could qualify as hazardous waste. Other possibilities are being examined also, including in-breeding problems and marine traffic from tourists that hampers reproduction (McIlroy, 1995).

The possibility that industrial and agricultural pollution, along with habitat degradation, are major contributors to ill health among beluga remains a prime target of investigation. For instance, the pesticide mirex, once manufactured upstream of the St. Lawrence near Niagara Falls, has been banned in Canada and the United States since 1970. There appear to be few traces of mirex in the St. Lawrence, but it is still found in Great Lakes sediments. It seems that eels migrating from the Great Lakes carry the pesticide to the St. Lawrence, where the beluga eat the eels (Norris, 1994). An aluminum smelter that once dumped waste containing a powerful carcinogen, benzo(a)pyrene, into the Saguenay River (which feeds the St. Lawrence), also is a possible cause of beluga deaths. This, in conjunction with the fact that discharges of PCBs have been eliminated and that levels of PAHs and lead have been reduced by 97 and 92 percent, respectively, may suggest that residual contamination of the river is a problem (Beluga habitat in St. Lawrence, 1996). (Industrial pollution of rivers is discussed in Chapter 8.)

Researchers at the University of Montreal have examined 73 of the 175 beluga cadavers found on the shores of the lower St. Lawrence since 1983. They discovered an enormous number of whales—almost 20 percent (14 of 73)—suffered from cancer. This number accounts for more than half the cancer cases found among all the dead whales in the world. Only 1 of the 1800 whales that washed ashore and were examined in the United States, for example, was found to have cancer, and there were no cases at all among Arctic beluga (Smelters suspected, 1995).

Acidic Deposition

Atmospheric changes, some of which result from industrial activities, are impacting freshwater systems. Acidic deposition continues to be a severe stress on freshwater ecosystems in eastern Canada. Water chemistry models predicted that up to 20 000 of the lakes in these areas would become acidic (pH under 5) under 1980 emissions levels. Sulphate deposition has declined from a high of 40 kilograms per hectare per year to an average of 10 to 15 kilograms per hectare per year, but since the critical value is thought to be less than 8 kilograms per hectare per year, the current reduction programs in Canada and the United States (targeted at an objective of 20 kilograms per hectare per year) mean that as many as 25 percent of Atlantic Canada's lakes likely will not recover, even if reduction programs were implemented fully (Government of Canada, 1996).

It is clear that in spite of improvements in industrial emissions and reduced deposition loads, many lakes are continuing to lose populations of fish and other freshwater species. The variable levels of improvement in lake acidity seen in monitoring studies of 202 lakes throughout southeastern Canada showed that in Ontario, 60 percent of lakes tested were improving, 7 percent were worse, the rest were stable; in Quebec, 11 percent were improving, 7 percent were worse, the rest were stable; and in the Atlantic region, 12 percent were improving, 9 percent were worse, the rest were stable (Government of Canada, 1996). (For further information on acidification research as well as other factors affecting lake water quality and ecosystem health in the Experimental Lakes Area, see the Schindler and Bayley, and the Millard references listed in the Additional Information Sources section of this chapter.)

HYDROELECTRIC GENERATION AND IMPACTS

Historically, Canada has been one of the world's major builders of dams and diversions. By 1991, 650 major dams had been built or were under construction in Canada; over

Compared to those in the St. Lawrence River estuary, Arctic beluga remain healthy.

80 percent of the dams are for electric power generation and many of the diversions are used to concentrate flows for hydroelectric development. While substantial economic benefits result from damming and altering rivers, these activities also incur wide-ranging, long-term ecological consequences related to the effects of impounding water in reservoirs and of altering natural patterns of streamflow (Table 7–2). Social disadvantages also occur, such as when communities are flooded out or people are forced to modify their traditional ways of life and livelihood.

From an ecological perspective, the Peace–Athabasca delta area in northern Alberta is an example of how the balance of an ecosystem that depends on flooding can be altered by construction of dams and reservoirs. The delta is a key staging and nesting area for waterfowl and is important habitat for bison, moose, and various fish species. Since the late 1960s, when the Bennett Dam was constructed on the Peace River in British Columbia 1200 kilometres upstream from the delta, the dam has been lowering the annual flood peak levels of the Peace River. Effects on the ecosystem have been significant, particularly

the successional trend from wetlands to less productive land habitats and decreased biodiversity (Environment Canada, 1993a; Government of Canada, 1991, 1996). As a remedial effort, weir construction has been undertaken to try to offset the effects of the upstream river regulation.

Other wetlands in the Saskatchewan River delta and the Atlantic provinces have been affected by the operation of upstream dams. Since the late 1960s in Atlantic Canada, hydroelectric developments have eliminated or modified extensive areas of freshwater wetlands, flooded property and wildlife habitat, altered summer water temperatures, and reduced downstream water quality during low flow periods, a factor that is particularly important for watercourses receiving pollutants (Environment Canada, n.d.a). Impassable dams on the Indian (Halifax County), Mersey, Sissiboo, and Meteghan rivers in Nova Scotia have rendered most of their Atlantic salmon habitat inaccessible, and inadequate flows for fish downstream of the Annapolis River dam presented serious problems in 1991.

In the late 1970s, the Smallwood Reservoir of the Churchill Falls hydroelectric project in Labrador was

TABLE 7-2
SELECTED ECOLOGICAL AND SOCIAL IMPACTS OF DAMS AND DIVERSIONS

Agent	Process/Comment	Impacts

Impounding water in reservoir	• Reservoirs enlarge existing lakes or create new lakes in former terrestrial or wetland ecosystems.
	• In Canada, hydroelectric reservoirs cover an area of 20 000 square kilometres.
	
	• Dams can lead to local and regional problems but alternatives have environmental consequences: e.g., coal-fired thermal power plants emit more greenhouse gases and toxic substances such as mercury.
		• Displaces people
		• Disrupts wildlife habitat
		• Influences local climate
		• May cause small earthquakes
		• Affects water quality and quantity:
		  – increased evaporation, reduced flow downstream
		  – change in water temperatures
		  – decrease in dissolved oxygen level
		  – increase in nutrient loadings and eutrophication potential
		  – degradation or enhancement of fish habitat
		• Converts organic matter flooded by reservoir to toxic methylmercury that accumulates and magnifies in food webs, making fish unsafe for human consumption
		• Causes shoreline problems due to fluctuating water levels: shoreline biological communities unable to establish, erosion and turbidity increase

Altering natural streamflow patterns	• Efforts to control flooding by building dykes, hardening shorelines, or regulating streamflow with dams and diversions must be balanced with the preservation of fish and wildlife habitats, ecosystem functioning, and the way of life of Aboriginal peoples.	• Reduces natural flooding and annual flood peak levels • Causes loss of waterfowl and wildlife habitat • Causes successional trends from wetlands to less productive terrestrial habitats, with consequent reduction in biodiversity
Interbasin diversions	• Diversions involve the transfer of water from one river basin to another.	• May result in transfer of fish, plants, parasites, bacteria, and viruses

SOURCE: Government of Canada. (1996). *The state of Canada's environment—1996.* Ottawa: Supply and Services Canada. Chapter 10.

experiencing problems with high levels of methylmercury accumulation in fish downstream, but 16 years after the flooding, mercury levels dropped back to normal levels (Environment Canada, n.d.a). Concerns about the transfer of foreign species from one basin to another halted the Garrison Diversion project in North Dakota. This project could have introduced biota from the Missouri River system into the Hudson Bay watershed (Government of Canada, 1996). Cancellation of Phase 2 of the James Bay hydro project reflected concern about ecological, social, and economic aspects of the megaproject (Enviro-Focus 7).

It appears that the era of big dams and diversions is coming to an end in Canada. Between 1984 and 1991, only six large dams were constructed (e.g., Rafferty–Alameda, Oldman, and Laforge), some only after lengthy public discussions. Long-standing plans for the Kemano River (B.C.), Conawapa–Nelson rivers (Manitoba), and Phase 2 of the James Bay project (Quebec) have been shelved indefinitely. Combined, the changes in economics, priorities, and political influence (particularly of Aboriginal people) have made the construction of large dams and diversions less desirable and feasible (Government of Canada, 1996).

ENVIRO-FOCUS 7

Hydroelectric Dams in Northern Quebec: Environmental and Human Issues

On April 30, 1971, then Quebec premier Robert Bourassa unveiled plans created by Hydro-Québec to dam several rivers in the northern part of the province, thereby creating tens of thousands of jobs, a new export product (power), an enticement to investment in extractive industries, and an opportunity to increase the economic autonomy of the province. Two months later construction of roads into the James Bay area began, though the feasibility study being conducted by Hydro-Québec had not been completed and the Cree and Inuit residents had not been informed of the plans to flood their territory. Daniel Coon Come, grand chief of the Cree, and others such as Billy Diamond, chief of the Rupert House Cree, organized quickly to protect their territory and way of life

In May 1972, lawyers for the Indians of Quebec Association, through whom the Cree brought their protest, sought a court injunction to halt the project. On November 15, 1973, Judge Malouf granted the injunction, announcing his decision that work on the James Bay project should cease immediately because the development would damage the environment and destroy the Cree and Inuit ways of life.

The developers immediately appealed. One week later, on November 22, Judge Turgeon reversed Judge

Malouf's decision, indicating that because of the investment in the development to date, the inconvenience to the James Bay Energy Corporation and the James Bay Development Corporation would be greater than the damage to the Cree if the project proceeded. Feeling powerless to stop the first phase of the James Bay Project, the Cree entered into negotiations concerning Aboriginal rights, which culminated in the 1975 James Bay and Northern Quebec Agreement, giving the Cree millions of dollars in compensation and Quebec sovereign rights to the region. Ultimately, the completed Phase 1 of the James Bay project (the La Grande River hydroelectric complex) flooded more than 10 000 square kilometres of land to generate more than 10 000 megawatts of power, and cost an estimated $16 billion. Work was scheduled to begin in 1992 on the addition of 5000 megawatts of power to the James Bay complex via Phase 2 in the Great Whale (La Grande Baleine) River area. This portion was expected to be completed in 1995.

The scale of Phase 2 of the James Bay project stimulated worldwide debate. Proponents of the development argued that Canadians and Americans needed large amounts of electricity for their homes and businesses, and that hydroelectric power was environmentally sound (as it was renewable and did not contribute to global warming). Opponents noted that the Great Whale project would flood over 5000 square kilometres in an area where 12 000 Cree and 5000 Inuit lived, and that caribou, snow geese, marten, beaver, black bear, polar bear, and elk were at risk of losing their habitat. Other concerns were raised about methylmercury accumulation and poisoning of the food supply for local inhabitants, and about disrupting the balance of an

ENVIRO-FOCUS 7
(CONTINUED)

incompletely understood complex hydrological cycle in the area. More legal wrangling occurred, and in 1990 the National Energy Board granted Hydro-Québec a licence to export electricity to New York and Vermont, provided that there was no conflict with relevant environmental standards and that the federal government conducted an environmental impact assessment.

Groups began forming networks to lobby against Phase 2 of the project, including the James Bay Defense Coalition, the New England Energy Efficiency Coalition, coal-mining interests in the United States, and political and environmental activists such as the Sierra Club. More legal and political action followed. Activists in Maine and Vermont succeeded in convincing their state governments to refuse power from the Great Whale project. In 1992, the New York Power Authority cancelled a $12.6-billion contract with Hydro-Québec when the state legislature passed a law requiring the state to explore conservation and alternative energy sources before importing power. Several other states followed

suit in response to pressure from environmental groups and because of a diminished need for electricity.

On August 31, 1993, Hydro-Québec released its 5000-page environmental impact statement (EIS) for the Great Whale project. This EIS indicated that the project would have impacts that were moderate and localized, that could be mitigated, and that would displace no Aboriginal communities. A joint panel of federal, provincial, and Indigenous representatives reviewed the EIA, and on November 17, 1994, ordered Hydro-Québec to rework the study. The following day, Quebec premier Jacques Parizeau announced that the Great Whale project was no longer a priority of the provincial government and would not be constructed.

Environmental nongovernmental organizations that had worked with the Cree in their efforts to halt the project continued to work to replace megaprojects such as the Great Whale with energy efficiency and conservation. These kinds of action may have contributed to the decline in major dam construction projects in Canada.

SOURCES: Arragitainaq, L., & Fleming, B. (1991). Community-based observations on sustainable development in southern Hudson Bay. *Alternatives*, 18(2), pp. 9–11.

Bennett, A.A. (1993). Hydro Quebec released their environmental impact statement. http://bioc09.uthscsa.edu/natnet/archive/nl/9309/0001.html

Deocampo, D. (1993). Background on Hydro-Québec in James Bay. http://bioc09.uthscsa.edu/natnet/archive/nl/9303/0043.html

Grégoire, P., Schetagne, R., & Laperle, M. The environmental and human issues raised by large hydroelectric dams in northern Québec. (1995). *Technical Bureau Supplement to Water News*, 14(1).

James Bay dam, electricity and impacts. (n.d.). http://gurukul.ucc.american.edu/TED/JAMES.HTM

Wilson, A. (1994). Feature: Victory over Hydro-Québec at James Bay. http://www.mv.com/dan/nhsc/planet/planet1294/ftr-canada.html

RELATED SOURCE: For a summary of major environmental modifications brought about by the project, see Berkes, F. (1990). The James Bay hydroelectric project. *Alternatives*, 17(3), p. 20.

This same trend is not evident in the developing world, where dam construction is proceeding quickly. However, as the example of the cancellation of the Arun River dam in Nepal points out, there is hope that changes in public and political thinking about the values of water resources will help protect the natural, cultural, and recreational values of rivers there in the future.

RECREATIONAL USES AND IMPACTS

Boating, fishing, swimming, skiing, and golf are among the recreational activities that many Canadians enjoy. The effects of these activities, including engine discharges,

fecal coliform contamination, contamination from artificial snow making, and nutrient enhancement through fertilizer and pesticide runoff, impact water resources in different ways. Second homes and seasonal residences also introduce developmental impacts such as faulty or poorly maintained septic tanks, construction of facilities on the foreshore, and higher peak demand for water.

Growing demands from ski resorts to tap nearby water bodies for snow-making purposes are likely to continue and to increase if climate change occurs. Golf courses also require water for irrigation purposes. In light of the potential for decreased snowfall and reduced stream flow under changing climatic conditions, the use of other sources of water increases in importance. One possibility, applied on

CHAPTER 7:
FRESH WATER

How much water is required to keep this desert golf couse green?

RESPONSES TO ENVIRONMENTAL IMPACTS AND CHANGE

How sustainable are Canada's freshwater resources? What is needed to maintain the health of freshwater systems? How do we balance the social, environmental, and economic interests of freshwater resource users? These and many other questions highlight the importance of planning for a sustainable future, one that includes fresh water. As the following examples demonstrate, international as well as individual and cooperative efforts make a difference when it comes to achieving sustainability of freshwater resources.

INTERNATIONAL INITIATIVES

Agenda 21

Canadian representatives to the United Nations Conference on Environment and Development (UNCED) signed Agenda 21 in recognition of our international obligations to protect the quality and supply of freshwater resources, and to manage them in an integrated fashion. Upon signing, Canada was committed as well to help developing countries and local communities link the knowledge, people, and organizations that would enhance their decisions and policies about water (International Development Research Centre, 1993).

An example of Canada's involvement in the transfer of water quality technology took place in the communities of Split Lake, Manitoba, and Maquehue and Chol-Chol, Chile (International Development Research Centre, 1993). In the first phase of the project, Cree people from Split Lake learned how to monitor water quality and were trained to conduct appropriate tests on water samples. The intention was that these skills be useful to the Split Lake community as well as to other Aboriginal communities in the area. In a later phase of the project, the Cree and Mapuche people from Maquehue and Chol-Chol collaborated in transferring the water-testing technology to Chile. Cree technicians, for instance, were involved in the laboratory setup in Chile. This project illustrates how collaboration to build the human capacity within each community can result in gains for all parties involved. As such, capacity building is an important component of the Agenda 21 plan of action to achieve environmentally sound and sustainable development throughout the world.

The Ramsar Convention

Other international efforts to sustain freshwater resources and related environments are based on conventions and agreements that establish the objectives and obligations of

a trial basis in ski resorts in Canada, turns ski resort or household effluent into snow. Golf course irrigation technology now employs state-of-the-art systems to control the timing and amount of water applied to greens and to apply only an appropriate amount of fertilizer or pesticide to help reduce nutrient-laden runoff.

Over the past two to three decades, popular recreational areas such as the Gulf Islands in British Columbia, Georgian Bay in Ontario, and Minnedosa in Manitoba have experienced increased population growth and related development of recreational housing and facilities. Where water is in high demand, relevant authorities in some instances have taken action to institute water restrictions during summer drought periods and to encourage water conservation efforts by offering subsidized rates on low-flush toilets, for example. Water costs (prices) to consumers also have been increased to help pay for improved supply and treatment systems.

The impacts recreational development may have on community water supply and treatment facilities are seen clearly in the town of Banff, located in Banff National Park, Alberta. With a resident population of about 7000, the town of Banff provides the water infrastructure to accommodate up to 25 000 visitors per night and close to 5 million visitors per year. Obviously, there is a large difference in the nature and cost of facilities required to service 7000 residents versus 25 000 visitors. The town bears the cost of operating and maintaining water facilities for their own and for visitors' use, and levies taxes on residents and businesses to help raise funds required to do so. Up to 1997, the town had not instituted a direct water service charge to visitors (such as a toilet tax included in the price of a hotel room). In the interests of resident–visitor equity as well as the sustainability of Banff's water supply, it may be appropriate for the town's water managers to charge visitors directly for their water use and to educate all water users on the need for water conservation.

those countries that signed the agreement. In 1981, Canada became a contracting party to the Convention on Wetlands of International Importance, an intergovernmental treaty that provides the framework for international cooperation for the conservation of the world's wetland habitats.

Known also as the Ramsar Convention, this agreement was first adopted in 1971 in Ramsar, Iran. There, representatives of 18 nations had gathered to determine how wetlands could be protected from drainage, land reclamation, pollution, and overuse by competing land uses, and how the economic benefits, hydrological and ecological functions, and critical habitat values of wetlands could be preserved. In 1995, with 84 contracting members, the objectives of the convention focused on stemming the loss of wetlands and ensuring their conservation and sustainable use for future generations (WetNet Project, n.d.). Canada has designated over 13 million hectares of wetlands and associated uplands in its 33 Ramsar sites.

International cooperation and partnerships are important elements in attaining conservation and sustainable management of wetland resources. In North America, international and cooperative partnerships proved to be valuable in the establishment of the North American Waterfowl Management Plan (Canada, the United States, and Mexico) and in the operation of other wetland conservation efforts including the Western Hemisphere Shorebird Reserves Network. The Canadian Wildlife Service, the lead agency in implementing the Ramsar Convention in Canada, also promotes Latin American wetland habitat initiatives.

The Canadian Ramsar Network coordinates Ramsar activities within Canada. For more information on this network and Ramsar publications, contact the North American Wetland Conservation Council (Canada) at the address given in Additional Information Sources at the end of this chapter. For further information on Ramsar sites of the world, see the Web site for WetNet: The Wetlands Network listed in the Additional Information Sources section of this chapter.

AGREEMENTS BETWEEN CANADA AND THE UNITED STATES

Another international initiative designed to deal with human impacts on freshwater resources and environments involves transboundary agreements between Canada and the United States. The Great Lakes Water Quality Agreements and Remedial Action Plans undertaken to restore the Great Lakes ecosystem are considered briefly here.

The Great Lakes Water Quality Agreements In 1909, the United States and Canada signed the Boundary Waters Treaty to establish the International Joint Commission

(IJC). The IJC was assigned three basic responsibilities: to arbitrate disputes related to boundary waters, to conduct feasibility studies for both federal governments, and to approve applications for water diversion projects that would affect flow on either side of the border.

The first formal recognition of basin-wide water quality occurred in 1912 when the IJC was requested to investigate pollution problems in the Great Lakes. After several years of study, the IJC recommended that a new treaty between the United States and Canada was necessary to control pollution (Environment Canada, United States Environmental Protection Agency, Brock University, and Northwestern University, 1987). No agreement was reached at that time. In fact, it was not until water quality concerns escalated in the 1950s and 1960s that the signing of the first Great Lakes Water Quality Agreements (GLWQA) took place in 1972.

In addition to setting common water quality objectives, the GLWQA established cooperative research programs and called for surveillance and monitoring to identify problems and measure progress. The main objective of the original agreement was to control eutrophication by reducing

Two issues associated with water contamination are diseased fish, such as this walleye with lymphosarcoma, and public health concerns.

phosphorus discharges by industry and sewage treatment plants. The second GLWQA, signed in 1978, strengthened pollution standards and reinforced earlier water quality objectives. This agreement represented a move toward more holistic planning of the entire basin by calling for restoration and maintenance of the chemical, physical, and biological integrity of the Great Lakes ecosystem.

A significant step toward achieving this objective took place in 1985 when the IJC's Great Lakes Water Quality Board identified 42 Areas of Concern (AOC). An AOC is a geographic area where the "beneficial use" of water or biota fails to meet the objectives of the GLWQA. In 1987, the GLWQA was revised to incorporate Remedial Action Plans as the formal process for restoring beneficial use to all the Great Lakes AOC. Of the 43 Areas of Concern identified, 17 were in Canada.

Remedial Action Plans A Remedial Action Plan (RAP) is a strategy that identifies the types of pollution that are present in a waterway, the geographic extent of the affected area, how water quality will be restored, and who will ensure that restoration is carried out. "RAPs are a breakthrough in cleanup programs in that they formally bring governments, businesses, industry, educators, environment groups, and individual citizens to the table on a long-term basis to discuss how to restore degraded areas in their regions to a healthy state. The aim is to focus local attention on defining problems and finding solutions, based on what residents want for the future of their harbours, bays and rivers" (Environment Canada, 1995b).

RAPs in Canada are carried out under the 1994 Canada–Ontario Agreement Respecting the Great Lakes Basin Ecosystem. This agreement sets firm targets for environmental priorities in the Great Lakes and serves as a coordinating mechanism between the federal and Ontario governments. However, involvement in the RAP process extends far beyond governments. For a RAP to be successful, local citizens, scientists, educators, the business community, and even children must be involved in cooperative learning about the specific area, and in all the stages of restoring and maintaining integrity of the Great Lakes.

Once it has been demonstrated that beneficial uses have been restored to an AOC, the AOC may be delisted. Beneficial uses are considered restored when the effectiveness of the RAP measures is confirmed by the surveillance and monitoring process. The final RAP document includes conclusions by the scientific and technical participants, the Public Advisory Committee, and the federal and provincial governments. The minister of foreign affairs is responsible for forwarding the final document to the IJC for delisting approval. In November 1994, Collingwood Harbour, a Canadian site on Lake Huron's Georgian Bay, became the first AOC officially delisted. For a brief discussion of how the local community restored beneficial uses, see the section on Great Lakes Cleanup Fund and Great Lakes 2000 later in the chapter.

(For further information on Great Lakes Water Quality Agreements, see the IJC's magazine *Focus,* or contact the IJC at the address identified in the Additional Information Sources section at the end of this chapter. Also, see the Web site for Environment Canada's Canada Centre for Inland Waters and for GLIMR, the Great Lakes Information Management Resource, listed in the Additional Information Sources section of this chapter.)

The recognition that Canada's environment must be viewed as an integrated system of ecosystems means that the 1991 Canada–United States Air Quality Agreement may be viewed partly as a response to human impacts on water. That is, because the atmosphere is an important medium for the exchange of matter and energy within and among ecosystems, actions affecting air quality are important in a water quality context also. In this instance, the focus of the Canada–United States Air Quality Agreement is on reducing emissions of sulphur dioxide and nitrogen oxides; the linkage between air and water via acid deposition is clear.

CANADIAN LAW, POLICY, AND PRACTICE

If Canadians are going to achieve sustainability of the nation's water resources, ecosystem-level understanding must be incorporated into decision making about water. It is no longer sufficient to include only the quantity or quality of rivers, lakes, and streams in decisions. Now, water resource managers must collect, assess, blend, and synthesize data on biotic and abiotic characteristics of water resources so that the health and productivity of whole aquatic ecosystems can be maintained. New tools, techniques, and methods are needed to understand and manage Canada's water resources. The following sections illustrate briefly some of the responses that have been undertaken to move toward sustainability.

Water Legislation and Policy Responses

There is a considerable volume of Canadian legislation that pertains to water (Table 7–3). While the International Boundary Waters Treaty Act dates from early this century, most of the water-related legislation dates from (or was revised during) the 1980s. The Canada Water Act, dating from 1970, provides for comprehensive and cooperative management of Canada's water resources, including water quality issues. The establishment in 1971 of the Department of the Environment and of the Inland Waters Directorate (now defunct) was in recognition of the need for better environmental management in general and water resources in particular.

As the agency charged wholly with the responsibility to administer the Canada Water Act, Environment Canada tries to ensure that Canada's freshwater management is

TABLE 7-3

SELECTED CANADIAN WATER LEGISLATION AND RELATED POLICIES, PROGRAMS, AND PLANS

Date	Water legislation and related policies, programs, and plans
1909	International Boundary Waters Treaty Act (International Joint Commission established)
1970	Canada Water Act
1970	International Rivers Improvement Act
1971	Department of the Environment Act (DOE and Inland Waters Directorate established)
1972	Great Lakes Water Quality Agreement
1978	Revised Great Lakes Water Quality Agreement of 1978
1979	Government Organization Act
1984–85	Inquiry on Federal Water Policy
1985	Arctic Waters Pollution Protection Act
1985	Canada Shipping Act
1985	Canada Wildlife Act
1985	Dominion Water Power Act
1985	Fisheries Act
1985	Navigable Waters Act
1987	Federal Water Policy
1987	Federal Wetlands Policy
1987	Great Lakes Health Effects Program
1987	Protocol to the Great Lakes Water Quality Agreement
1988	Canadian Environmental Protection Act
1988	St. Lawrence Action Plan
1988	Water 2020: Sustainable Use for Water in the 21st Century (Science Council of Canada)
1989	Great Lakes Action Plan (Preservation Program; Health Effects Program; Cleanup Fund)
1990	The Green Plan
1992	Canadian Environmental Assessment Act
1992	Northwest Territories Waters Act
1992	Yukon Waters Act
1993	National Roundtable on the Environment and the Economy Act
1993	St. Lawrence Vision 2000
1994	Department of Natural Resources Act
1994	Migratory Birds Convention Act
1994	Split Lake Cree First Nation Flooded Land Act

undertaken in the best national interest, and promotes a partnership approach among the various levels of government and private sector interests that contribute to and benefit from sustainable water resources.

Inquiry on Federal Water Policy The 1984–85 Inquiry on Federal Water Policy conducted Canada-wide hearings as it worked toward development of a federal water policy. Released in 1987, the policy has the overall objective of encouraging efficient and equitable use of fresh water in a manner consistent with social, economic, and environmental needs of present and future generations. To achieve this broad objective, governments and individual Canadians need to become aware of the true

value of water in order to use it wisely. In the years since the federal water policy was established, the concept of sustainability has become prominent, prompting the Canadian Water Resources Association to develop a set of sustainability principles for water management in Canada in 1994. These principles are to practise integrated water resource management, to encourage water conservation and the protection of water quality, and to resolve water management issues.

Shared Jurisdiction In Canada the division of responsibilities for water is complex and often is shared. Under the Constitution Act of Canada, provinces have primary responsibility for both surface and groundwater resources and legislate flow regulation and most areas of water use. The federal government has responsibility for the northern territories, national parks, First Nations reserves, and navigation and fisheries, and in areas of trade, treaty relations, taxation, and statistics. The shared responsibilities are health, agriculture, significant national water issues, and interprovincial water issues.

Financial Constraints

Significant federal budget reductions to Environment Canada and other government agencies are resulting in major changes in personnel and programs affecting water. Clearly, Environment Canada faces a challenge in managing water resources with fewer financial and personnel resources while at the same time responding to increasing public expectations regarding human health and water quality. These budget constraints have generated scientific and public unease about how much priority the federal government attaches to water resources.

Budget constraints also affect the provinces' ability to contribute to water research and management. In Ontario, for example, the provincial government is considering self-regulation of industry and is likely to make other cuts that will affect the health of the Great Lakes. These changes include reduced funding for municipal water and sewage projects that have been critical in the cleanup so far. It is possible, also, that targets under the 1994 Canada–Ontario Agreement Respecting the Great Lakes Basin Ecosystem, including wetland rehabilitation and upgrading of municipal sewage treatment plants, might be scaled back because funding available through the Great Lakes Cleanup Fund is being reduced (Silcoff, 1996). A generation of successful Great Lakes cleanup efforts may be threatened by these cuts. Similar effects and concerns for the future of water resources occur in other provinces as environmental budgets are reduced.

Research and Application

In spite of financial constraints, research efforts to respond to impacts of human activities on water resources and environments continue. The Canada Centre for Inland Waters (CCIW) "is one of the world's leading centres for water research, generating environmental information and knowledge about the Great Lakes" (Beal, 1995). Headquartered at the CCIW, the National Water Research Institute (NWRI) is Canada's largest freshwater establishment. Scientists there conduct multidisciplinary programs of aquatic research in partnership with Canadian and international researchers. For example, the NWRI conducts studies on the sustainability and remediation of groundwater resources in Canada, including how contaminants are transported in groundwater and how to restore contaminated groundwater. The new knowledge from these projects is used to support regional activities within Environment Canada

such as the Great Lakes Cleanup Fund and the federal water policy (Canada Centre for Inland Waters, n.d.).

Ecological Monitoring and Assessment Network The Ecological Monitoring and Assessment Network (EMAN) was established by Environment Canada in 1994 in an effort to improve communication and cooperation among scientists conducting ecological monitoring activities. By encouraging independent scientists and those from different jurisdictions to concentrate their work at the Ecological Science Cooperatives across Canada, to share information from their ecological experimentation and research, and to synthesize and integrate results, EMAN's overall objective is to understand what is changing in the environment and why.

If scientists can collect data and exchange information on environmental trends and the health of the Canadian environment with regard to climate change, water quality, air quality, and biodiversity, then a monitoring network can be used to share information and identify problems. Early identification of problems should enable scientists to establish possible consequences of environmental change, bring this to public attention, and communicate it to decisionmakers and policymakers for action. Effectively, EMAN provides a framework for improving Canadians' understanding of ecosystem function and change at national and ecozone levels.

Scientists associated with each Ecological Science Cooperative (ESC) undertake research covering all facets of ecological inquiry, including water resources. EMAN is a national coordinating network that provides the means for these scientists to link with national hydrological, weather, wildlife, forest, and agricultural networks as well as other North American and global monitoring and research networks. In addition, EMAN promotes broad distribution of results in both scientific and popular literature.

ESCs are ecozone based and consist of a number of research and monitoring sites that, in time, will cover all the characteristic ecosystems within each ecozone. Eventually, it is intended that each of Canada's ecozones will have its own ESC, but in the meantime, some ESCs are concerned with more than one ecozone, some ESCs have sites in more than one province or territory, and most provinces and territories (will) have ESC sites in more than one ecozone. (For further information about EMAN, see the Web site listed in the Additional Information Sources section of this chapter.)

Environmental and Water Quality Guidelines Canada's environmental quality guidelines have been developed to provide basic scientific information about the effects of organic, inorganic, radiological, physical, and microbiological parameters on aquatic resources. Promulgated by the Canadian Council of Ministers of the Environment (CCME), these guidelines are required under Part 1, Section 8, of the Canadian Environmental Protection Act.

In the Canadian environmental quality guidelines, water managers are provided with the most current scientific and technical information concerning the effects of priority parameters on water uses in Canada. These parameters act as "environmental yardsticks" to assess water quality issues and concerns, establish water quality objectives at specified sites, provide targets for control and remediation programs, and provide information for state-of-the-environment reporting.

Although they are nonregulatory, the Guidelines for Canadian Drinking Water Quality specify the conditions that affect drinking water quality, and the Guidelines for Canadian Recreational Water Quality specify conditions for primary and secondary recreational uses including swimming, boating, and fishing. Environment Canada and Health Canada worked closely with the provinces and territories to develop these guidelines. For additional information on the Canadian Water Quality Guidelines, contact the address listed in the Additional Information Sources section at the end of this chapter.

Great Lakes Cleanup Fund and Great Lakes 2000

To meet its obligations under the 1987 Protocol to the Canada–United States Great Lakes Water Quality Agreement, the federal government announced its $125-million Great Lakes Action Plan in 1989. One component of the action plan was the Great Lakes Cleanup Fund, which provided funding to implement cleanup activities in the 17 Canadian Areas of Concern.

During the first term of the Great Lakes Cleanup Fund (1989–94), more than 50 ecosystem-based projects were undertaken, directly involving community members in remediation of local water quality problems. Partnerships developed among all levels of government, conservation authorities, private industry, service clubs, and public interest groups; these partnerships contributed money, skills, and services totalling about $70 million in addition to the $35 million provided by the Great Lakes Cleanup Fund. Ultimately, the fund enabled cost-effective remediation techniques to be tested and applied to other sites throughout the Great Lakes. These results demonstrated practical solutions to environmental problems, and provided Canadian companies with opportunities to market their environmental technologies on a global basis.

Collingwood Harbour, the first Area of Concern to be delisted, was a recipient of Great Lakes Cleanup Fund support. Fifteen partners contributed their expertise and support in upgrading Collingwood's sewage treatment plant to reduce high levels of phosphorus entering the harbour; this resulted in millions of dollars in savings for the municipality. The amount of water pumped dropped by 35 percent as a result of an environmental education program and water conservation measures (Boundary Waters a Shared Resource, 1995). Contaminated sediment in the harbour was removed also. Town residents were involved through the design and construction of

In Collingwood, Ont., Enviropark reflects cooperative efforts among industry, governments, and local groups.

Enviropark, "an active learning opportunity or children's park with a difference. Play structures imitate the town's sewage network, and an obstacle course illustrates the food chain" (Environment Canada, 1993b).

In 1994 the federal government renewed its commitment to the Great Lakes Action Plan with the announcement of the seven-year, ecosystem-based Great Lakes 2000 program. The main objectives of this program are to restore degraded sites, prevent and control pollution, and conserve and protect human and ecosystem health. Drawing on experience gained through the Great Lakes Cleanup Fund, we know that the principles of sustainability, shared responsibility and partnerships, and pollution prevention will be important for the continued success of the plan. (For further information about the Great Lakes Cleanup Fund and Great Lakes 2000 program, see the Web site for the GLIMR listed in the Additional Information Sources section of this chapter.)

Northern River Basins Study

The Northern River Basins Study (NRBS) was established in September 1991 by the governments of Canada, Alberta, and the Northwest Territories to examine how development affects the Peace, Slave, and Athabasca river basins in Alberta and the N.W.T. These river basins contain two national parks and a large number of Aboriginal residents who live traditional lifestyles; the river basins are also under considerable pressure from pulp and paper, oil sand, agriculture, and municipal growth interests.

The NRBS was aimed at providing a scientifically sound information base on contaminants, nutrients, area food chains, drinking water, aquatic uses, hydrology and sediments, and traditional knowledge, as well as a synthesis or modelling of results. An important element of the study was the incorporation of members of the public, particularly those with traditional ecological knowledge. Governments will need to incorporate the new knowledge generated from the study into policies, regulations, monitoring, and research programs. It was suggested (Halliday, 1996) that there is a potential role for EMAN in the long-term management of northern river basins. (For a brief review of key findings and recommendations, see the reference to Northern River Basins Study and the Web site for the NRBS listed in the Additional Information Sources section at the end of this chapter.)

CANADIAN PARTNERSHIPS AND LOCAL ACTION

Achieving sustainability in any resource context requires an integration of effort and cooperation among nations, organizations, and individuals. Canadians have been developing the means to achieve the necessary cooperation and partnerships; the following examples demonstrate a variety of forms that actions toward sustainability have taken.

Flood Damage Reduction Program

On the national level, the Canadian government and various provinces have signed agreements regarding flood damage reduction and flood risk mapping in an effort to discourage inappropriate development and reduce flood loss and damage in flood risk areas. (Flood risk areas consist of the floodway and floodplain: see Figure 7–6.) These agreements generally sought to identify, map, and designate flood risk areas in urban communities and, through public information programs, to increase awareness of flood risk among the general public, industry, and government agencies.

Once the flood risk areas were mapped, municipalities were encouraged to adopt land use regulations that would promote only open space uses (such as golf courses) and would prohibit construction of new buildings or other structures in the floodway. Development in the floodplain would be permitted only if certain structural controls were incorporated. No federal or provincial buildings or other structures that would be vulnerable to flood damage were to be located in the flood risk area.

After implementing appropriate land use regulations, each community formally would designate its flood risk areas under the Flood Damage Reduction Program. In the event of a flood, a community would not receive financial assistance from federal and provincial government sources for new buildings or other new structures damaged by the flood if they were located in flood risk areas. These new policies did not affect existing development in the floodway and floodplain areas. Existing property and development, however, might be flood-proofed (any

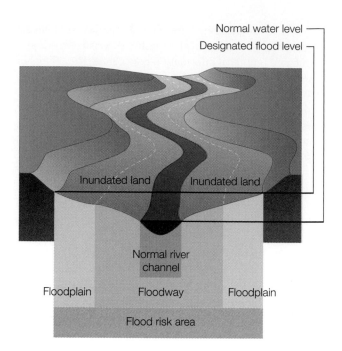

Figure 7–6
Schematic example of flood risk areas

SOURCE: Adapted from Environment Canada. (n.d.c). *Information sheet: Calgary, Alberta.* Ottawa: Canada–Alberta Flood Damage Reduction Program.

action or permanent protection applied to prevent flood damage, such as use of elevated pads to build above flood levels) or acquired by government.

This major policy initiative of the 1970s not only restricted building in the mapped floodplains, but also succeeded in reducing flood losses and in preserving many river valleys in high population regions for wildlife and recreational activities.

Watershed Planning

Planning and management of water and other resources on a **watershed** basis is an example of an ecosystem-based approach to achieving sustainability. In Ontario, conservation authorities have existed since the 1940s. The Conservation Authorities Act gives these authorities the power to study their watersheds in order to determine how the natural resources of the watershed may be conserved, restored, developed, and managed. Unfortunately, the act limits conservation authorities' powers to use water, to alter watercourses, and to fill and construct in floodplains.

Planning for areas defined on an ecosystem basis, such as a watershed, is not possible under Ontario's Planning Act, neither does the province require that watershed strategies be incorporated into municipal planning and development control processes (Royal Commission on the Future of the Toronto Waterfront, 1992).

Some special arrangements exist, such as the legislation that protects the Niagara Escarpment and nearby lands as a continuous natural environment, and the province recognizes the need for and value of planning based on ecological systems, but the necessary changes to encourage watershed planning have not been implemented. (This does not imply that conservation authorities do not undertake ecosystem-based planning, merely that the institutional basis for it on the provincial level is lacking.) Furthermore, fiscal restraint in the public sector in the 1990s has resulted in reduced support for Conservation Authority programs. Development of a comprehensive water and land policy now seems more difficult to achieve, even though it is as essential as it ever was (Anderson, 1997).

In other jurisdictions, for instance in Saskatchewan and Alberta, some holistic river basin planning is being undertaken. Saskatchewan's Meewasin Valley Authority, for example, is a conservation agency for the Meewasin Valley, part of the South Saskatchewan River valley flowing through Saskatoon and the rural municipality of Corman Park. An 80-kilometre section of the river is the subject of a 100-year master plan that recognizes the need to preserve and enhance the valley for future generations. The plan focuses on the integrity of the natural system and employs an open decision-making process that accommodates changing ideas and needs. The river and its natural system are the basis of the plan that also addresses concerns about health, urban and rural areas, access to the river, and the past, present, and future.

A 1993 initiative, Partners FOR the Saskatchewan River Basin, has applied its mission—"to promote awareness, linkages, stewardship, knowledge and respect for the basin ecosystem and heritage that will encourage sustainable use of the basin's natural resources and nurture cultural values"—to the entire river basin. Partners FOR the Saskatchewan River Basin uses an ecosystem approach that integrates economics, environment, and society in its efforts to cooperate in managing the basin for a sustainable future.

Over 120 partners (representing education, environmental nongovernmental organizations [ENGOs], First Nations, industrial users, Métis Nations, natural and cultural heritage, tourism, and water management sectors) are participating in developing and implementing stewardship projects ranging from an eco-canoe tour project to a workshop to discuss management issues of the Saskatchewan River delta (one of only five inland deltas in the world). Their goal is to increase environmental stewardship of the basin's natural and cultural resources by developing and implementing education, information, and demonstration projects. (For further information on Partners FOR the Saskatchewan River Basin, see the Web site and the mailing addresss listed in the Additional Information Sources section at the end of this chapter.)

Fraser River Action Plan

The Fraser River produces more salmon than any other single river system in the world. The vast network of lakes and tributaries in the Fraser River basin provides spawning and rearing habitat for six salmon and 29 other fish species, as well as 87 more species of fish in the estuary. Fraser River salmon, especially sockeye, form the backbone of British Columbia's commercial fishery as well as sport and Aboriginal fisheries. Many social and cultural benefits derive from the Fraser's fisheries through recreation, tourism, and enhancement of people's way of life. (Fisheries issues are discussed in more detail in Chapter 8.)

Fraser River fish, however, are under intense pressure, mainly from degraded water quality and habitat losses due to urban and industrial development, logging impacts, water use conflicts, and overfishing of some stocks. The Fraser River Action Plan (FRAP), announced June 1, 1991, by the federal ministries of Environment and Fisheries and Oceans, aims to improve the long-term health and productivity of the Fraser River. Specifically, the objectives of the $100-million program include assessment of the health of the river; reduction of pollution entering the river; and improvement of fish and wildlife productivity in the basin. In addition, creation of partnerships with provincial and local governments, Aboriginal and community groups, environmental organizations, industry and labour, and other stakeholders is necessary to develop a cooperative management program for the Fraser River basin based on the principles of sustainability. Fisheries and Ocean's role in FRAP ended in March 1997, but Environment Canada will continue to implement the FRAP mandate through March 1998.

With regard to enhancing fish and wildlife habitat, dozens of FRAP projects have been undertaken to improve conditions for rearing and spawning fish, encourage protection of wetlands and streams, and increase the amount of available habitat. To rebuild fish stocks, FRAP work included development of a comprehensive management plan for all Fraser River salmon species, and collection and analysis of scientific data on which sound management decisions can be made. This information is complemented by data on pollution point sources in the basin, and a wastewater database.

The Fraser River Action Plan alone cannot clean up pollution and restore habitats in the Fraser basin—the job simply is too large. That's why partnerships are crucial to keeping the basin healthy after the program ends. To ensure that the basin's rich water (and other) resources would be maintained for future generations, the Fraser Basin Management Board (FBMB) developed a Charter for Sustainability. When the FBMB was succeeded by the new Fraser Basin Council on April 1, 1997, the council's mandate was to promote and monitor the implementation of the charter. The Charter for Sustainability is to serve as a blueprint for people of differing opinions and experiences to work together toward the goal of long-term sustainability of the Fraser basin.

North American Waterfowl Management Plan

The Canadian prairies have been bountiful producers of cereal grains and rich grazing grasses for almost a century. They also have supported abundant wildlife—almost half the North American continent's waterfowl breed in this region. After World War II, however, a combination of drought and rapid agricultural expansion involving wetland conversion from a natural state to agricultural and other uses resulted in the loss of thousands of acres of wildlife habitat and a progressive decline in waterfowl populations. Without habitat, there is no wildlife; compared to base levels of the 1970s, by the mid-1980s the number of ducks breeding on the prairies had reached alarmingly low levels. Mallard ducks, for example, decreased from 8.7 to 5.5 million, pintail from 6.3 to 2.9 million, and blue-winged teal from 5.3 to 3.8 million (Environment Canada, n.d.b).

In light of this severe decline, the North American Waterfowl Management Plan (NAWMP) was established. The plan emphasizes the importance of the health of the land over the long term and uses massive cooperative funding of land conservation programs as a method of restoring waterfowl and other wildlife habitat. A 15-year agreement, signed originally in 1986 by Canada and the United States, became a continent-wide program to conserve North America's waterbirds when Mexico signed the agreement in 1988. In 1994, an update and 10-year extension renewed the commitment of these three partners to cooperate in a fully continental effort in wetlands conservation (Environment Canada, n.d.b). The updated plan promotes the objectives of the international Convention on Biological Diversity, a key to sustainability.

Across North America, 32 regional habitat joint ventures are identified as priorities under the NAWMP agreement. The largest and most important joint venture region includes Canada's prairie potholes (so named because of the millions of wetlands dotting the prairie landscape). Most of the original grasslands in this area, as well as 40 to 70 percent of the original wetlands, have been lost to agricultural development. Because this region provides the breeding area for half of North America's waterfowl population, it is ranked as the highest priority under the NAWMP. The Prairie Habitat Joint Venture guides conservation of the Canadian prairie pothole region under the NAWMP, and aims to restore waterfowl populations to 1970 spring breeding levels of between 17 and 20 million (Environment Canada, 1995c).

The NAWMP is not an isolated program. Provincial and federal wildlife agencies work directly with landowners on habitat retention programs that offer a wide range of wildlife benefits. The Quill Lakes project in southern Saskatchewan, the Buffalo Lake project near Stettler, Alberta, and HELP in the Minnedosa region of Manitoba are examples of the commitments to prairie land and habitat conservation. The Western Hemisphere Shorebird Reserve Network is another example of cooperation among the three federal governments that, in turn, cooperate with nongovernmental organizations such as Wetlands for the Americas and Ducks Unlimited.

Ducks Unlimited is an important partner in implementing elements of the NAWMP. Established in 1937 in the United States, Ducks Unlimited, Inc. began to raise funds to protect Canadian breeding grounds where the majority of North American ducks are produced. The ultimate goal was (and is) to ensure that hunters from the United States would have ducks to hunt. Ducks Unlimited Canada was incorporated in 1938 as the biological and engineering branch to develop habitat projects.

Ducks Unlimited Canada works as a partner to implement NAWMP's continental conservation program, but also has delivered important wetland and wildlife habitat programs across Canada for 60 years. In Alberta, home to 20 percent of all the ducks surveyed each spring in North America, Ducks Unlimited Canada has spent more than $100 million to complete over 2800 individual habitat management projects, and restore, enhance, or preserve more than 725 000 hectares of critical waterfowl habitat. (For an example of their efforts to rehabilitate one large marsh using treated waste water from a meat-packing plant, see the Haworth-Brockman and Smallwood article in the Additional Information Sources section at the end of this chapter.)

Making a Difference Locally

The Swan Lake Christmas Hill Nature Sanctuary, located just a few minutes from downtown Victoria, British Columbia, provides one example of the importance of dedicated volunteers and the differences they make to the environmental health of a community and its water resources. While the issues and events described in Box 7–5 are specific to this nature sanctuary, they are repeated—with local differences—in many parts of Canada, demonstrating the significance of local stewardship in the movement toward environmental sustainability.

The preceding examples have demonstrated a range of international as well as individual and cooperative stewardship efforts that have focused on achieving balance among social, environmental, and economic interests in freshwater resource use, and in moving toward sustainability of freshwater resources. There are challenges ahead; they are the subject of the final section of this chapter.

The transformation of Swan Lake, British Columbia, from a smelly, murky, polluted pond to a quiet nature sanctuary bordered by walking and cycling trails is a tribute to community vision and cooperation and many hours of work by local volunteers. While this story reflects events in one location, there are countless other examples of Canadians' dedication to improving local water bodies and environmental quality in general.

By the mid-1850s, the area surrounding what is now the Swan Lake Christmas Hill Nature Sanctuary had been cleared of most trees and native vegetation for agriculture. About 1860, the area's first year-round recreational resort was built. Although Swan Lake Hotel guests and local residents used the 94-hectare lake for swimming, fishing, boating, and ice-skating, it was never used for drinking water (humic and tannic acids leached from the soil gave the water a yellow-brown colour). After being destroyed by fire in 1894 and again in 1897, the hotel was not rebuilt.

In succeeding years, the water quality of Swan Lake deteriorated due to nutrient enrichment from the sulfides and yeast in effluent from two wineries; coliform bacteria contamination from sewage plant effluent discharged into waterways draining into the small lake; and biological oxygen demand problems resulting from past use of agricultural fertilizers, from cattle and waterfowl wastes, and from garden chemicals. Swan Lake became a smelly, eutriphying lake no one wanted to visit.

In the 1960s, the local municipality of Saanich began acquiring land around the lake, and, to protect the natural environment, the area was designated a nature sanctuary in 1975. Since then, the municipality has spent more than $2 million to develop facilities, and the nonprofit Swan Lake Christmas Hill Nature Sanctuary Society has raised and invested an equal amount. Provincial and federal agencies have ensured that projects meet public safety standards and habitat improvement criteria.

An interpretive centre has been built, about four kilometres of trails and boardwalks have been constructed, and a demonstration garden of native plants has been started with volunteer assistance from local contractors. In 1995, more than 15 000 school children, community group members, and casual visitors took part in the nature sanctuary's educational programs or enjoyed a quiet walk.

The society's mission is to foster understanding and appreciation of nature and to develop personal responsibility for the care of the natural environment. School programs are the main vehicle by which the society fulfils this mission, but volunteers also help maintain the sanctuary for other users. A growing appreciation of the value of this oasis in the midst of the city has contributed to growth in volunteer hours, as well as cooperation and partnerships among citizens, community businesses, and governments.

Though no longer ugly, Swan Lake remains threatened by use of fertilizers, pesticides, and herbicides in the watershed. Chemicals enter storm drains that run into the lake, leading to algae growth and associated problems. Education programs are needed to inform homeowners and residents about the consequences of excessive fertilizer use, to promote the benefits of gardening with native plants, and to conserve water. In the future, continued funding must be established for community-based environmental education and partnership activities, including the addition of some small parcels of private land around the lake to help meet the growing public demand for meaningful natural history and outdoor experiences.

As examples of effective stewards of land and water resources, the Swan Lake Christmas Hill Nature Sanctuary Society and its governmental, industry, and citizen partners deserve recognition. They are part of the movement toward ecological sustainability and public accountability that is changing our approach to managing our shared environment.

SOURCES: Curtis, M. (1995, September 27). Back to nature. *Victoria Times Colonist,* p. B1.

Gardening chemicals causing the algae growth in Swan Lake. (1995, July 5). *Saanich News,* p. 24.

Partners in stream restoration. (1995, Winter). *Swan Lake Christmas Hill Nature Sanctuary Newsletter,* p. 2.

Roberts, T., & Morrison, T. (1995). *Swan Lake Christmas Hill Nature Sanctuary: A place to explore; a world to discover.* Victoria, BC: Swan Lake Christmas Hill Nature Sanctuary Society.

Swan Lake Christmas Hill Nature Sanctuary. (1995). *Information on finances and use, 1975–1995.* Victoria, BC: Swan Lake Christmas Hill Nature Sanctuary Society.

Swan Lake Christmas Hill Nature Sanctuary. (1996). *1995 Annual Report.* Victoria, BC: Swan Lake Christmas Hill Nature Sanctuary Society.

Zaccarelli, W. (1975). *An inventory of the biota of Swan Lake with some basic limnological spects* [sic] *and recommendations.* Victoria, BC: Swan Lake Christmas Hill Nature Centre Society.

FUTURE CHALLENGES

Fresh water is essential to humanity and to all life. As the fundamental basis of aquatic and related ecosystems, sustainability of water is vital. Achieving sustainability of fresh water involves finding a proper balance in meeting all the competing needs for water, that is, in balancing human needs, and the needs of natural ecosystems. Although Canada contains a wealth of fresh water underground and in its lakes, rivers, and wetlands, regional differences exist in the distribution of water, its quality, the human environments it supports, and the wildlife that depends on it.

In the Prairies and interior of British Columbia, there is competition for limited water supplies between agricultural irrigation interests, growing urban demands, energy production, and the desire of residents to preserve natural ecosystems. In the most heavily populated and industrialized regions of the country, including the Windsor–Quebec corridor and parts of the Pacific and Atlantic coasts, water is plentiful, but impaired water quality and physical alterations to aquatic habitats are problematic. Persistent toxins such as PCBs in Great Lakes and St. Lawrence River sediments and the presence of DNAPLs and other contaminants in groundwater are among the unintended and poisonous byproducts of past industrial development.

In the north and other sparsely populated regions of the country, transport of contaminants (acid precipitation, toxic metals, and persistent organic compounds) from distant sites, and acid drainage from closed mines, threaten water quality. In addition, the health of certain populations, such as Aboriginal people, may be at particular risk from bacteria and pathogens in well water. While progress has been made in slowing the degradation of freshwater resources in Canada, uncertainties such as future climate change and its potential impacts on water supply and distribution remain as challenges for water resource managers.

As changing economic conditions have resulted in declines in government supported programs such as water monitoring, local stewardship will become an even more important element in reaching sustainability objectives. In order to protect and conserve water resources for future generations, communities and regions will need to identify ways in which they can monitor threats to freshwater supplies and ecosystems, and judge the effectiveness of prevention and remediation measures. Just as the concerted effort of individuals associated with Prairie Habitat Joint Venture programs successfully demonstrated the value of healthy ecosystems, so too the ability of people to organize their desires for protection of a wide range of water values should empower them to devise and implement alternative systems of monitoring. While government resources must remain available to collect basic data on water quality and quantity (to support drinking water guidelines, for instance), it is not unreasonable for the community of water users to accept some increased responsibility for its sustainability.

Establishing an appropriate framework for economic, ecological, and social sustainability of water resources is a complex and difficult task. Although integrated approaches and regional plans have been implemented in major drainage basins such as the Fraser River and the Great Lakes–St. Lawrence basin, to what degree do they succeed in maintaining resilient, biologically diverse ecosystems? Do we understand, yet, what all the principles are on which Canada's water resources ought to be governed for the next century and beyond? Knowledge building—about the physical nature of freshwater resources, about how to protect water quality and aquatic ecosystems, and about human demand for water—is clearly an important dimension in achieving sustainability.

Knowledge building, too, is affected by shrinking government support; therefore new cooperative and partnership approaches to research and understanding should be examined and applied. If we agree that a long-run approach is appropriate in attaining sustainability of water resources in Canada, then perhaps the following quotation expresses something of what Canadian water policy should be like for the future:

> Ecology requires that watercourses, as living ecosystems, be given specific and meaningful protection. The principles of conservation and ecology merge into the overarching idea of sustainability: water policies should include hard-edged guarantees so that water use will allow both living watersheds and economies to be sustainable indefinitely for the good of future members of the community. (Bates, Getches, MacDonnell & Wilkinson, 1993, 181)

Chapter Questions

1. With Canada's abundant water supply, should we be concerned about water availability in the future? Why or why not?

2. Discuss the range of pressures that humans place on water resources that lead to water quality concerns.

3. Compare and contrast the important environmental problems related to domestic and industrial uses of water.

4. We often take our water supply for granted. These questions may challenge us to think more carefully about water in our communities.

   a. What are the major sources of the water supply?

   b. How is water use divided among residential, commercial, industrial, and other uses? Which sector consumes the largest volume of water?

   c. How have water prices changed in the past 20 years? Do water prices encourage conservation? Where is water being wasted?

   d. What water supply and quality problems does your community experience?

   e. What plans does your community have in place to ensure an adequate supply of safe drinking water for the future?

5. Why is it important to incorporate ecosystem understanding in the responses that Canadians make to water resource issues (at international, national, and local levels)?

6. What can you do to demonstrate stewardship with regard to water resources?

references

Abbott, E. (1996, June). The magnitude of the June 1995 southern Alberta flood. *Technical Bureau Supplement to Water News,* 15(2), pp. 1–3.

Alberta Environmental Protection. (1995). *Summary material from November 17, 1994 Canada Creosote Stakeholder Workshop.*

Anderson, J.S. (1997). Ontario's Conservation Authorities—pioneer watershed managers. *Water News,* 16(1), pp. 4–7.

Arragitainaq, L., & Fleming, B. (1991). Community-based observations on sustainable development in southern Hudson Bay. *Alternatives,* 18(2), pp. 9–11.

Barnett, V. (1996, July 11). Water, sewer funding on tap. *Calgary Herald,* p. A5.

Bates, S.F., Getches, D.H., MacDonnell, L.J., & Wilkinson, C.F. (1993). *Searching out the headwaters: Change and rediscovery in western water policy.* Washington, DC: Island Press.

Beal, S. (1995). The Canada Centre for Inland Waters. http://www.cciw.ca.

Béland, P. (1996). The book of the dead. *Canadian Geographic,* 116(3), pp. 46–47.

Beluga habitat in St. Lawrence improving, but still 12 years from full recovery. *Environment Policy and Law,* 6(12), p. 352.

Bennett, A.A. (1993). Hydro Quebec released their environmental impact statement. http://bioc09.uthscsa.edu/natnet/archive/nl/9309/0001.html

Bishop, C., & Weseloh, D.V. (1990). *Contaminants in herring gull eggs from the Great Lakes.* Burlington, ON: Environment Canada, Canadian Wildlife Service. SOE Fact Sheet No. 90-2.

Boundary Waters a Shared Resource. (1995). Global Agenda, 3(1). http://www.dfait-maeci.gc.ca/english/news/newsletr/global/

Bruce, J., & Mitchell, B. (1995). *Broadening perspectives on water issues.* Canadian Global Change Program Incidental Report Series No. IR95-1. Ottawa: The Royal Society of Canada.

Canada–Alberta Flood Damage Reduction Program. (n.d.). *Information sheet: Calgary, Alberta.* Ottawa.

Canada Centre for Inland Waters. Groundwater remediation project, Aquatic Ecosystem Restoration Branch, National Water Research Institute. http://gwrp.cciw.ca/gwrp/

Canadian Water Resources Association. (1994). *Sustainability principles for water management in Canada.* Cambridge, ON: Canadian Water Resources Association.

Cayer, S. (1996). Lakes and ladders: Up and down the locks and channels of Ontario's Trent–Severn Waterway. *Canadian Geographic,* 116(4), pp. 32–47.

Curtis, M. (1995, September 27). Back to nature. *Victoria Times Colonist,* p. B1.

Deocampo, D. (1993). Background on Hydro-Québec in James Bay. http://bioc09.uthscsa.edu/natnet/archive/nl/9303/0043.html

Environment Canada. (1990). *A primer on water: Questions and answers.* Ottawa: Supply and Services Canada.

Environment Canada. (1993a). *Water works!* Freshwater Series A-4. Ottawa: Supply and Services Canada.

Environment Canada. (1993b). *Project highlights: Great Lakes Cleanup Fund.* Ottawa: Supply and Services Canada.

Environment Canada. (1994). *Urban water: Environmental Indicator Bulletin.* SOE Bulletin No. 94-1. Ottawa: Supply and Services Canada.

Environment Canada. (1995a). *Water: No time to waste: A consumer's guide to water conservation.* Ottawa: Supply and Services Canada.

Environment Canada. (1995b). Canadian Great Lakes Remedial Action Plan Update. http://www.cciw.ca.glimr/rep-test/overview.html

Environment Canada. (1995c). Prairie Habitat Joint Venture: Conserving an international resource. http://www.mb.doe.ca/ENGLISH/LIFE/WHP/PHJV/phjv.home.html

Environment Canada. (1996a). How we contaminate groundwater. http://www.doe.water/water/en/nature/grdwtr/e_howweg.htm

Environment Canada. (1996b). DNAPLs. http://www.cciw.ca/glimr/data/water-fact-sheets/facta5-e.html

Environment Canada. (1996c). Leaking underground storage tanks and piping. http://www.cciw.ca/glimr/data/water-fact-sheets/facta5-e.html.

Environment Canada. (n.d.a). State of the environment in the Atlantic region. http://www.ns.ec.gc.ca/soe/cha4.html

Environment Canada. (n.d.b). The North American waterfowl management plan. http://www.doe.ca/tandi/NAWMP/bkgd_e.html

Environment Canada. (n.d.c). Information sheet: Calgary, Alberta. Ottawa: Canada–Alberta Flood Damage Reduction Program.

Environment Canada & Health Canada. (1993). Creosote-impregnated waste materials. http://www.ec.gc.ca/library/elias/bibrec/302071B.html

Environment Canada, United States Environmental Protection Agency, Brock University, and Northwestern University. (1987). *The Great Lakes: An environmental atlas and resource book.* Toronto: Environment Canada.

Frederick, K.D. (1996). Water as a source of international conflict. *Resources,* Issue 123 (Spring), pp. 9–12.

Gardening chemicals causing the algae growth in Swan Lake. (1995, July 5). *Saanich News,* p. 24.

Government of Canada. (n.d.). Impact of agricultural pesticides on coastal wetlands. http://www.cciw.ca/nwri/data/nwri-digest/digest-21-9.html

Government of Canada. (1991). *The state of Canada's environment—1991.* Ottawa: Supply and Services Canada.

Government of Canada. (1996). *The state of Canada's environment—1996.* Ottawa: Supply and Services Canada.

Grégoire, P., Schetagne, R., & Laperle, M. (1995). The environmental and human issues raised by large hydroelectric dams in northern Quebec. *Technical Bureau Supplement to Water News,* 14(1). 8 pp.

Halliday, R.A. (1996). *Northern river basins study.* Paper presented at the Ecological Monitoring and Assessment Network, Second National Science Meeting, Halifax, Nova Scotia, January 17–20.

Hamilton, H., & Wright, A. (1985). *Water quality and quantity model for irrigation in the South Sasketchewan River Basin.* Paper presented at the 38th Canadian Water Resources Association Conference, Lethbridge, AB.

Inquiry on Federal Water Policy. (1984). *Water is a mainstream issue.* Ottawa.

International Development Research Centre (IDRC). (1993). *Agenda 21: Green paths to the future.* Ottawa: IDRC.

International Joint Commission. (1992). *Sixth biennial report under the Great Lakes Water Quality Agreement of 1978 to the governments of the United States and Canada and the state and provincial governments of the Great Lakes basin.* Ottawa: International Joint Commission.

James Bay dam, electricity and impacts. (n.d.). http://gurukul.ucc.american.edu/TED/JAMES.HTM

Laycock, A. (1987). The amount of Canadian water and its distribution. In M.C. Healey & R.R. Wallace (Eds.). *Canadian Aquatic Resources.* (pp. 13–41). Canadian Bulletin of Fisheries and Aquatic Sciences, 215. Ottawa: Supply and Services Canada.

Mahoney, J. (1996, June). The effect of the 1995 Oldman River flood on riparian cottonwood forests. *Technical Bureau Supplement to Water News,* 15(2), pp. 3–8.

McIlroy, A. (1995, September 9). Beluga behavior beguiles scientists. *Calgary Herald,* p. B4.

Norris, K. S. (1994). Beluga: White whale of the north. *National Geographic,* 185(6), pp. 2–31.

Partners FOR the Saskatchewan River Basin. http://www.saskriverbasin.ca

Partners in stream restoration. (1995, Winter). *Swan Lake Christmas Hill Nature Sanctuary Newsletter,* p. 2.

Pearse, P.H., Bertrand, F., & MacLaren, J.W. (1985). *Currents of change: Final report, inquiry on federal water policy.* Ottawa: Environment Canada.

Pindera, G. (1997). Red River dance. *Canadian Geographic,* 117(4), pp. 52–62.

Pope, H. (1996). Sharing the rivers. *People & the Planet,* p. 5(1), p. 5.

Ransom, J.W. (1995, September). Water is life. *Technical Bureau Supplement to Water News.* Canadian Water Resources Association.

Roberts, T., & Morrison, T. (1995). *Swan Lake Christmas Hill Nature Sanctuary: A place to explore; a world to discover.* Victoria, BC: Swan Lake Christmas Hill Nature Sanctuary Society.

Royal Commission on the Future of the Toronto Waterfront. (1992). *Regeneration: Toronto's waterfront and the sustainable city, final report.* Toronto: Supply and Services Canada and Queen's Printer of Ontario.

Sanderson, M. (1993). Climate change and the Great Lakes. In P.L. Lawrence & J.G. Nelson (Eds.). *Managing the Great Lakes shoreline: Experiences and opportunities.* (pp. 181–93). Waterloo, ON: Heritage Resources Centre, University of Waterloo.

Serrill, M.S. (1997, November). Wells running dry. *TIME,* 150 (17A), pp. 16–21.

Silcoff, S. (1996, July 16). Budget cuts poison Great Lakes forecast. *The Globe and Mail,* p. A1.

Simpson, B. (1993/1994, December/January). Liquid gold: Parts of the United States are drying up, and Americans are looking north for salvation. Will Canada eventually have to sell water south? *Earthkeeper: Canada's Environmental Magazine,* pp. 14–19.

Smelters suspected in belugas' cancers. (1995, June 11). *Calgary Herald,* p. A9.

Swan Lake Christmas Hill Nature Sanctuary. (1995). *Information on finances and use, 1975–1995.* Victoria, BC: Swan Lake Christmas Hill Nature Sanctuary Society.

Swan Lake Christmas Hill Nature Sanctuary. (1996). *1995 Annual Report.* Victoria, BC: Swan Lake Christmas Hill Nature Sanctuary Society.

Wilson, A. (1994). Feature: Victory over Hydro-Québec at James Bay. http://www.mv.com/dan/nhsc/planet/planet1294/ftr-canada.html

Zaccarelli, W. (1975). *An inventory of the biota of Swan Lake with some basic limnological spects* [sic] *and recommendations.* Victoria, BC: Swan Lake Christmas Hill Nature Centre Society.

Zebra mussels: Holding back the tide. (1997). *Coastal Heritage,* 11(4), pp. 10–12.

additional information sources

Berkes, F. (1990). The James Bay hydroelectric project. *Alternatives,* 17(3), p. 20.

Bocking, R.C. (1987). Canadian water: A commodity for export? In M.C. Healy & R.R. Wallace (Eds.). *Canadian Aquatic Resources.* (pp. 105–35). Canadian Bulletins of Fisheries and Aquatic Sciences, p. 215. Ottawa: Supply and Services Canada.

Canadian Heritage Rivers Board
Parks Canada
Ottawa, ON K1A 0M5

Canadian Water Quality Guidelines
Evaluation and Interpretation Branch
Environmental Conservation Service
Environment Canada
Ottawa, ON K1A 0H3

Crowe, A.S., & Milburn, P.M. (Eds.). (1995). The contamination of groundwater by pesticides in Canada. *Water Quality Research Journal of Canada,* 30(3).

Ecological Monitoring and Assessment Network (EMAN). Environment Canada. http://www.cciw.ca/eman/

Environment Canada. (1995). Centre for Inland Waters. http://www.cciw.ca

Environment Canada. (1997). Great Lakes Information Management Resouce (GLIMR). httpl://www.cciw.ca/glimr/intro.html

Environment Canada. (n.d.c). Canadian Heritage Rivers. http://www.mb.doe.ca/ENGLISH/WATER/ISSUES/heritage.html

Gale, R.J.P. (1995). NAFTA and its implications for resource and environmental management. In B. Mitchell (Ed.). *Resource and Environmental Management in Canada: Addressing conflict and uncertainty.* (pp. 99–127). Toronto: Oxford University Press.

Haworth-Brockman, M., & Smallwood, S. (1989). Cool, clear, refreshing ... effluent. *Conservator,* 10(3), pp. 10–14.

Hodge, T., & Bubelis, P. (1991). Great Lakes basin: Pulling back from the brink. In Government of Canada. *The state of Canada's environment—1991.* (pp. 18-1–18-31). Ottawa: Supply and Services Canada.

International Joint Commission
Great Lakes Regional Office
100 Ouellette Avenue, Eighth Floor
Windsor, ON N9A 6T3
(519) 257-6700

Millard, L. (1990). Ecosystem research programme threatened. *Alternatives,* 17(3), pp. 12–13.

North American Wetland Conservation Council (Canada)
Suite 200, 1750 Courtwood Crescent
Ottawa, ON K2C 2B5

Northern River Basins Study: Key findings and recommendations. (1997). *Water News,* 16(1A), pp. 10–15. http://www.gov.ab.ca/~env/nrbs/nrbs.html

Partners FOR the Saskatchewan River Basin
402 Third Avenue
Saskatoon, SK S7K 3G5
(306) 665-6887
(306) 665-6117 fax
http://www.saskriverbasin.ca

Schindler, D.W., & Bayley, S.E. (1991). Fresh waters in cycle. In C. Mungall & D.J. McLaren (Eds.). *Planet under stress: The challenge of global change.* (pp. 149–67). Toronto: Oxford University Press.

Van Tighem, K. (1990). Heritage rivers: Preserving the spirit of Canada. *Canadian Geographic,* 110, p. 2.

Wetland Resource Centre
http://www.wetlands.ca/wetcentre/wetcentre.html

WetNet Project. (n.d.). Canada and the Ramsar Convention. http://www.wetlands.ca/wetcentre/wetcanada/RAMSAR/booklet/booklet.html

CHAPTER 8

Oceans and Fisheries

Chapter Contents

CHAPTER OBJECTIVES   223
INTRODUCTION   223
    The *Irving Whale* Recovery Project   223
CANADA'S MARINE ENVIRONMENTS   225
    Canada's Arctic Ocean Environment   225
        Biophysical Characteristics   225
        Threats to Ecosystem Integrity   227
            Hydroelectric Development   227
            Long-Range Transport of
                Pollutants   227
            Climate Change   229
            Overhunting   229
            Nonrenewable Resource
                Extraction   229
    Canada's Pacific Ocean Environment   229
        Biophysical Characteristics   229
        Threats to Ecosystem Integrity   230
            Global Change   230
            Marine Pollution   230
    Canada's Atlantic Ocean Environment 230
        Biophysical Characteristics   230
        Threats to Ecosystem Integrity   232
            Lack of Knowledge   232
            Anthropogenic Impacts and
                Marine Pollution   232
            Commercial Fishing   232
            Sea-Level Rise   232
        Summary of Concerns Facing Canada's
        Ocean Regions   233
HUMAN ACTIVITIES AND IMPACTS ON
MARINE ENVIRONMENTS   236
    Fisheries   236
        The 1995 Canada–Spain Turbot
        Dispute   236
        The Northern Cod Moratorium   238
        Pacific Herring and Salmon Stocks   242
            Pacific Herring   243
            Coastal Salmon   245
    Pollution   247
        Industrial and Chemical Effluents   247

Municipal Sewage   254
Marine Shipping, Ocean Dumping, and
    Plastics   255
    Marine Shipping   255
    Ocean Dumping   255
    Plastics   255
Coastal Development   256
    Urban Runoff   256
    Physical Alterations   258
Offshore Hydrocarbon Development   259
Atmospheric Change   260
RESPONSES TO ENVIRONMENTAL IMPACTS
AND CHANGE   260
    International Initiatives   261
        United Nations Convention on the
            Law of the Sea   261
        Agenda 21   262
    Canadian Law, Policy, and Practice   262
        Revised Oceans and Fisheries
            Legislation   262
        Coastal Zone Management Efforts   264
    Canadian Partnerships and Local
        Actions   265
FUTURE CHALLENGES   267
Chapter Questions   268
References   268
Additional Information Sources   271

Chapter Objectives

After studying this chapter you should be able to

- identify a range of human activities occurring in the marine environment
- discuss the impacts of human activities on the marine environment
- describe the complexity and interrelatedness of marine environment issues
- specify Canadian and international responses to oceans and fisheries issues
- discuss challenges to a sustainable future for oceans and fisheries resources

INTRODUCTION

THE *IRVING WHALE* RECOVERY PROJECT

During a storm on September 7, 1970, the cargo barge *Irving Whale* sank in the southwestern Gulf of St. Lawrence (Figure 8–1). En route from Halifax, Nova Scotia, to Bathurst, New Brunswick, the *Irving Whale* was carrying 4270 metric tonnes of Bunker C heavy fuel oil when she sank slowly by the stern and settled flat on the sea floor. Between 400 and 600 metric tonnes of Bunker C fuel oil (similar in appearance and smell to asphalt sealing compounds) leaked from the barge for two days following the sinking, creating a slick that covered an estimated 400 square kilometres. Later, about 200 tons of oil fouled 80 kilometres of the shores of Iles-de-la-Madeleine (Magdalen Islands). During the cleanup operation, about 200 000 bags of oil debris were recovered and buried in the dunes of the Iles-de-la-Madeleine.

Following the sinking, the Canadian Coast Guard observed oil leaking from the cargo tank pressure relief valves; divers subsequently secured the barge vents to control leakage. Since the *Irving Whale* sank, the Coast

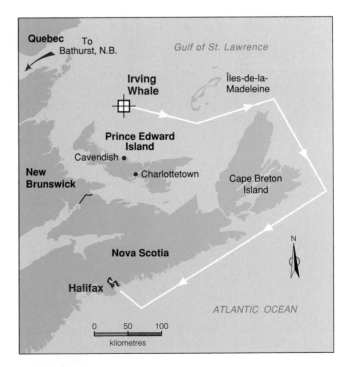

Figure 8–1
Irving Whale Recovery Project: schematic map of barge route to Halifax

SOURCE: Environment Canada. (1997). *Operation Irving Whale.*
http://www.ns.ec.gc.ca/whale2/index.html

Guard maintained regular aircraft and surface surveillance to check for pollution. The barge continued to leak intermittently, losing about 27 percent of its original cargo. Since 1970, most of the oil that escaped had been dispersed by natural processes with little or no damage to seabirds or fisheries. However, in November 1990, oil reached the Rustico–Cavendish Beach area on Prince Edward Island. About 100 sea birds were oiled, and a 3-kilometre-long by 180-metre-wide slick was observed. In 1992, oil was reported on crab trap floats near the *Irving Whale*. By 1996, about 3150 metric tonnes (or 3 214 700 litres) of fuel oil remained on board the sunken vessel.

Resolving the environmental hazard posed by the *Irving Whale* has been a lengthy, complex process. A series of federal government studies assessed the options available for dealing with the leaking barge, including the environmental risks of pumping the oil out or lifting the barge. In 1993, it was confirmed that raising the barge with the oil on board was preferable because it was less risky to the environment. On August 5, 1994, after consultation with the public and stakeholder groups throughout the Gulf of St. Lawrence region, federal Transport and Environment ministers announced that the federal government would proceed with a proposal to lift the sunken barge, recover its Bunker C oil, and clean and sell or dispose of the barge in an environmentally acceptable manner. A contract to lift the *Irving Whale* was awarded in June 1995.

In July 1995, company representatives from Irving Oil informed Environment Canada officials that approximately 9.3 metric tonnes (6800 litres) of a PCB known as Aroclor 1242 had been found within the cargo heating system of their barge. The *Irving Whale* was equipped with a heat exchange unit to ensure that the Bunker C fuel cargo remained at a high enough temperature to ensure easy unloading (at 10°C, Bunker C has the consistency of liquid honey or corn syrup; at 0°C, the temperature of the water around the Irving Whale, Bunker C barely flows).

Although it coats marine birds because it floats at or below the ocean surface, fresh Bunker C fuel generally is not toxic to plants or marine mammals because it contains few volatile organic compounds. The environmental risks of PCBs such as Aroclor 1242 include their high oil solubility (meaning they dissolve readily in the tissues of plants and animals) and their tendency to bioaccumulate. Scientists fear that long-term exposure to PCBs, even at low concentrations, has negative impacts on health, reproduction, and neurological and liver function.

Not surprisingly, considerable concern was expressed when hypothetical worst-case scenarios of major PCB spills from the *Irving Whale* showed immediate, short-term lethal or sublethal local effects on the diverse biological resources of the Gulf of St. Lawrence. Not only could several rare, threatened, and endangered species of migratory birds and marine mammals be affected, but the more than $200 million in annual revenues from the tourism and fishing industries could be jeopardized.

On July 25, 1995, following additional environmental assessment (EA) work by federal scientists, the ministers announced the recovery operation would proceed as planned that summer, with special attention to containment of the PCBs. (As part of the EA, federal officials reported PCBs in samples taken from the bags of debris buried in 1970 in the dunes of the Iles-de-la-Madeleine.) Poor weather caused continuous delays in the recovery operation.

Worried about a PCB spill during the recovery operation, two Quebec environmental nongovernmental groups succeeded in obtaining a legal stay of the decision to raise the barge until September 11. This delayed the project sufficiently that the barge could not be raised safely due to weather concerns. During the fall of 1995, the environment minister ordered additional study of the environmental consequences of raising the *Irving Whale* with its PCBs on board, including alternatives for dealing with PCBs, stresses to which the barge would be subjected during the lift, and potential social, environmental, and economic impacts of various PCB spill scenarios. Also, public consultations were held in the Atlantic provinces and Quebec. On April 16, 1996, the ministers of Environment and of Fisheries and Oceans announced their intention to proceed with the recovery operation commencing mid-June 1996. At this point, the court challenge was dropped.

The *Irving Whale* waits to be lifted onto the floating drydock for transport to Halifax.

PART 3:
RESOURCES FOR CANADA'S FUTURE

On July 30, 1996, the *Irving Whale* was raised, intact and with no apparent environmental damage. Salvage crews loaded the barge onto a floating drydock for the trip to a Halifax shipyard where the barge was cleaned, and the PCBs were shipped to Alberta's Swan Hills disposal facility for destruction. In addition to the legal issue of who owns the barge, the question that remains is who will pay the estimated $30 to $35 million it cost to raise the barge. The federal government's belief in the polluter pays principle suggests the Irving family should pay, but they have not volunteered to do so. (For more details and photos about the *Irving Whale* Recovery Project, see Environment Canada's Operation Irving Whale Web site listed in the References section of this chapter.)

The stated purpose of the joint Fisheries and Oceans and Environment Canada project to recover the *Irving Whale* was to protect the Gulf of St. Lawrence's environment and to remove the environmental hazard that the barge, its fuel oil cargo, and the heating fluid containing PCBs posed to the environmental health and economic well-being of the Gulf of St. Lawrence and surrounding communities. In these respects, the case of the *Irving Whale* demonstrates many of the degradation issues that face Canada's oceans and fisheries—the threats of pollution, habitat destruction, and human ignorance of how marine systems work. In addition to these issues, overharvesting, climate change, and ozone depletion affect the living and nonliving resources of oceans and coasts in Canada and the world over.

A brief overview of selected biophysical characteristics and threats to ecosystem integrity within each of the Arctic, Atlantic, and Pacific oceans is provided in the sections that follow. The discussion identifies various sociocultural, economic, and ecological issues of relevance to oceans and fisheries within Canada, and also internationally.

CANADA'S MARINE ENVIRONMENTS

As a maritime nation, bordered by the Arctic, Atlantic, and Pacific Oceans (Figure 8–2a), Canada has jurisdiction over immense marine holdings including the longest coastline (about 244 000 kilometres), the longest inland waterway, the largest archipelago, and the second largest continental shelf (about 3.7 million square kilometres) of any country in the world.

In spite of the geographical and historical importance of oceans, few Canadians realize how extensive and varied our ocean environments really are; few understand the wealth of natural resources that oceans contribute to the subsistence, social, economic, and cultural needs of the

nation's people; and fewer still appreciate that Canada has international legal obligations and economic incentives to protect oceans from degradation. Many of Canada's legal obligations are enshrined in the 1982 United Nations Convention on the Law of the Sea, which came into force on November 16, 1994, giving Canada jurisdiction over an almost 5 million square kilometre **Exclusive Economic Zone.** The Law of the Sea and other international issues are discussed later in this chapter.

CANADA'S ARCTIC OCEAN ENVIRONMENT

Biophysical Characteristics

Canada's coldest ocean area, the Arctic, contains about 173 000 kilometres of coastline (twice that of the east and west coasts combined) and over 1 million square kilometres of continental shelf waters that provide most of the food for Canadian Inuit. The majority of this area is covered seasonally by ice one to two metres thick. Maximum sunlight enters the water column in July, after the ice breaks up, limiting phytoplankton production to the late summer. As a result, Arctic waters produce only about one-quarter of the organic biomass per unit area compared to that produced over the east and west coast continental shelves.

Major currents influencing Arctic waters include the flow of polar water southeast through the archipelago, the West Baffin Current, and the Hudson Bay gyre, a circular current that creates a small, nearly closed circulation system characterized by nutrient enrichment and high levels of biological productivity (Figure 8–2b). Locally, currents help maintain open water areas called **polynyas** for much or all of the year. The largest of these polynyas, the North Water in north Baffin Bay (Figure 8–2a), allows an early and persistent phytoplankton bloom. A biological hotspot, the North Water and other smaller polynyas serve as vital winter refuges for marine mammals such as polar bears, seals, whales, and sea birds that overwinter in the north (Welch, 1995; National Advisory Board on Science and Technology, 1994). The ice edges that exist at polynyas and along floe edges (between landfast and drifting ice) are very important feeding and staging grounds for marine mammals and sea birds, particularly during spring and early summer migrations.

True polar Canadian waters have only a small commercial fishery potential. The arctic char commercial fishery, for example, is worth about $1.2 million annually; however, most of the major arctic char populations are harvested at or above maximum **sustainable yield** (Welch, 1995). Commercial quantities of turbot (Greenland halibut) support a successful shore-based winter fishery on south Baffin Island, worth $1 million annually. Other species such as redfish, round-nosed grenadier, Greenland

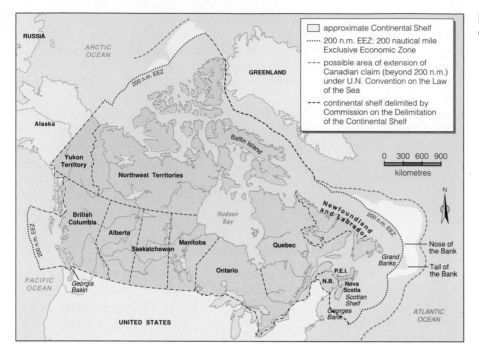

Figure 8–2a
Canada's marine environment

Figure 8–2b
Selected characteristics of Canada's
Arctic Ocean environment

Figure 8–2c
Selected characteristics
of Canada's Pacific
Ocean environment

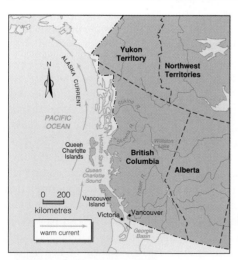

Figure 8–2d
Selected characteristics
of Canada's Atlantic
Ocean environment

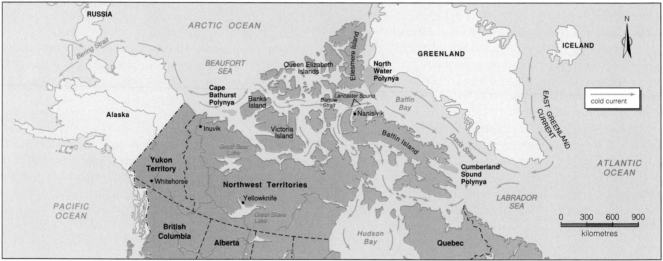

SOURCE: Adapted from Tobin, B. (1994). *A vision for ocean management.*
Ottawa: Fisheries and Oceans, p. 1.

PART 3:
RESOURCES FOR CANADA'S FUTURE

sharks, clams, shrimp, and scallops may support small commercial operations. Although its commercial potential has not been assessed, there is a large biomass of kelp in nearshore shallow waters throughout the eastern Arctic.

Marine mammals and sea birds are the main biological products of the Canadian Arctic Ocean. Generally, both sea bird and marine mammal populations are stable, with some exceptions such as thick-billed murres, which are declining because of mortality through incidental netting, oil fouling, and hunting elsewhere in their range. With regard to marine mammals such as whales, population data are inadequate to detect any but the largest changes. Currently, the scattered, low-density human population that depends on marine mammals for food and cultural continuity takes about 130 beluga from the western Arctic and 300 beluga, 330 narwhal, and 390 walrus from the eastern Arctic (Welch, 1995). The need for careful husbandry of the existing whale populations to at least maintain this level of domestic consumption is evident, given that there are no large sources of marine production left to exploit. A large harvest of High Arctic beluga and narwhal stocks by Greenlanders compounds the management and conservation problem of these species.

The long and complex food web (with five trophic levels) that supports top predators in Arctic marine systems encourages **biomagnification** of pollutants such as chlorinated organic compounds (DDT and PCBs) in the fatty tissues of these animals. PCBs in seawater biomagnify at each link in the food chain so that PCB levels in marine mammal blubber in the Canadian Arctic are a million or more times those in the Arctic Ocean (Figure 8–3) (Welch, 1995). This means that animal tissues eaten by northerners may have relatively high PCB concentrations. The long life spans of species such as polar bears and whales, coupled with a strong dependence on fat reserves within and between species, including humans, means Arctic ecosystems are particularly vulnerable to this type

Narwhals are an important source of country food for indigenous communities in the Canadian Arctic.

of contamination (Government of Canada, 1991). This issue of bioaccumulation is revisited briefly in the pollution section of human impacts on marine environments.

Threats to Ecosystem Integrity

Most of the major threats to Arctic ocean waters impact the higher trophic levels, including marine mammals, sea birds, and polar bears. This is important not only because these species are of the most interest to users (local people as well as tourists) but also because the roles of the top predators may be important in the structure and function of the ecosystem. If top predators are impacted by one or more of the threats described briefly below, feedback may alter the structure and function of the ecosystems.

Hydroelectric Development Hydroelectric dams and developments in Quebec, Ontario, and Manitoba will continue to affect rivers flowing to the Arctic primarily by increasing winter flows and decreasing summer flows. In turn, altered flows may cause changes in ocean currents, nearshore ice conditions, nutrient availability, the timing and magnitude of ice algal and phytoplankton production, the use of estuaries by marine mammals and anadromous fish, and the ways in which coastal residents use the land and the sea (Welch, 1995). Although research programs are continuing, knowledge of many Arctic ecosystems is so poor it is possible only to guess at long-term changes. Caution is necessary, since once put in place, hydroelectric developments are irreversible.

Long-Range Transport of Pollutants Ecosystem integrity is threatened also by the long-range transport of pollutants (LRTP) into the Canadian Arctic from agricultural and industrial activities elsewhere in the northern hemisphere. Persistent organic pollutants (halogenated compounds) and heavy metals are the most important groups of LRTP contaminants. These substances are difficult to metabolize, so they accumulate along the food chain, culminating in top predators such as Arctic marine mammals and sea birds.

PCBs evaporate from cropland, dumpsites, lands, and waters to the south. While they may enter the Arctic via ocean currents, their main pathway is atmospheric transport. Winter air flowing from Europe and Asia over the North Pole deposits thousands of tonnes of soil, flyash particles, and associated pollutants on land and in the sea. When snowmelt occurs in June, these substances enter the oceans, are concentrated by algae and phytoplankton, and passed on up the food chain. At each trophic level, the persistent organic pollutants are not excreted efficiently, resulting in about a 10-fold increase of concentration at each trophic level (Welch, 1995). The long length of Arctic food chains concentrates contaminants to levels that are high enough to constitute potential health hazards for the animals and humans higher up the chain.

Figure 8–3

Biomagnification of PCBs in the Arctic

SOURCE: Government of Canada. (1991). *The state of Canada's environment—1991.* Ottawa: Supply and Services Canada, p. 15-18.

Mercury has always occurred in natural ecosystems and is naturally high in long-lived top predators such as seals, whales, and polar bears. However, research has revealed that concentrations of mercury in the hair of humans and seals currently inhabiting Greenland are three to four times higher than they were in the hair of preindustrial humans and seals. We do not know what physiological and behavioural effects mercury concentration in top marine predators might be, although we can surmise they are at risk (they cannot switch to an alternate food source as humans might do). LRTP contaminants may pose the most important threat to the integrity of the Arctic marine ecosystem; the cultural and economic costs of the loss of polar bears, for example, are almost incalculable. Taking the required global actions to clean up these pollutants is very difficult; Canadians can regulate only what happens within our own boundaries.

Climate Change The scientific consensus is that the effects of climate change will be evident at high latitudes most clearly as increases in winter temperature and snowfall, and as reductions in the extent and thickness of sea ice. Gradually, arctic will be transformed into subarctic; animals, ice edges, and other boundaries will shift northward. Overall productivity might increase and some marine mammals and sea birds may thrive. Increased UV radiation as a result of ozone depletion over the poles may damage phytoplankton at high latitudes, but perhaps not enough to affect ecosystem integrity. Much remains unknown, however, and climate change remains a concern for Arctic seas.

Overhunting Historically, commercial overhunting of marine mammals has caused almost total extirpation of eastern Arctic bowhead whales, severe reduction in the number of western Arctic bowheads, loss of Ungava Bay beluga, and reduction of walrus stocks. At least in part, current low populations of beluga in eastern Hudson Bay and southern Baffin Island are a result of overhunting by Aboriginal peoples. Now that land claims settlements have brought co-management mechanisms to marine mammal management, there are expectations that stocks prone to overhunting will be protected.

Nonrenewable Resource Extraction Specific geographic sites such as the Polaris and Nanisivik base metal mines (see Figure 8–2b) and the Bent Horn oil field in the High Arctic (see Figure 11–3) appear to pose minor threats to local ecological integrity. Oil and gas exploration in the Beaufort Sea has been a source of hydrocarbon contamination (from drilling muds and fuel spills), but greater threats will occur during the production phase (perhaps during the next 20 years). Oil spills from wells, tankers, and pipelines around the world demonstrate that, in spite of stringent regulations, the Arctic will not be exempt from disasters. Depending on the time of year of a massive oil spill, Arctic marine ecosystem integrity would receive moderate to extremely severe damage.

The proposed use of two bulk carriers of liquefied natural gas to move natural gas from the High Arctic islands eastward through the Northwest Passage, up to 60 times per year, would impact negatively on the bird and mammal concentrations of Barrow Strait–Lancaster Sound (and is not likely to be approved). Other proposals to develop ports for shipping Arctic metals to markets would result in heavy ship traffic through summer beluga whale concentrations, and these proposals have not been subject to environmental assessments (Welch, 1995).

CANADA'S PACIFIC OCEAN ENVIRONMENT

Biophysical Characteristics

Of Canada's marine environments, the Pacific shoreline is the shortest (27 000 kilometres) and has the narrowest continental shelf (typically 16 to 32 kilometres wide), as well as the warmest waters (8 to 14°C at the surface). (see Figures 8–2a and c.) Strong currents, including the northward-flowing Alaska Coastal Current, tides, and upwellings help mix the waters, giving the region a very high level of biodiversity.

Hundreds of fish species occur in this region, including shellfish such as shrimp, scallops, crabs, and clams; anadromous species such as Pacific salmon (five species), char, steelhead, and Dolly Varden; catadromous eel family members; and other marine species such as Pacific cod, rockfish, flounder, lingcod, and herring. Millions of sea birds, both coastal and offshore species, and large numbers of marine mammals, such as whales, porpoises, dolphins, sea otters, and sea lions, live and feed in or migrate through British Columbia waters.

The coastline is rocky, and only a few small estuaries exist. Mudflats are found at the head of fjords, especially in the southern part of the province, and deltaic deposits occur at the mouths of major rivers such as the Fraser, Skeena, and Stikine.

British Columbia's commercial fishing sector landed almost 300 000 tonnes of fish and shellfish in 1992, worth close to $1 billion wholesale and about $411 million to fishers. Salmon landings comprised about 23 percent of the total catch but were valued at 47 percent of the landed value (Department of Fisheries and Oceans, 1994). Recreational fishing removed about 1.2 million fish from British Columbia waters in 1992 in exchange for an estimated $800 million in revenue (including expenditures on gear, boats, accommodation, food, gas, and clothing).

First Nations people are active participants in the commercial fisheries. In 1992, through Native-only licences intended to increase their participation, they owned 20 percent of the salmon fleet, 26 percent of the roe herring fleet, and 71 percent of spawn-on-kelp licences. (This does not include percentages of Aboriginal people who own regular licences or who operate company-owned vessels.) In addition, more than one million salmon are harvested annually in their food fishery (Paisley, 1994).

Aquaculture is one of British Columbia's fastest growing industries. In 1992, the farm gate value of aquacultural production was close to $120 million, making aquaculture number four in value behind dairy, beef, and poultry production. Shellfish production is also a major industry; there are over 400 oyster beds and 68 clam-farming sites in the province (Paisley, 1994).

Threats to Ecosystem Integrity

Global Change Not all is well in Canada's Pacific Ocean marine environment. Scientific evidence suggests that ocean surface temperatures are increasing on the Pacific coast, although clear answers as to why this is happening and what effects they will have on marine environments are not available yet. We do know that global environmental changes such as the El Niño–Southern Oscillation (Chapter 5) not only reduce upwelling and lower productivity but influence fish behaviour. In an El Niño year, salmon swim out away from the Alaska coast and closer to the British Columbia coast, resulting in record catches off British Columbia, and a scarcity for Alaska. Since the salmon quotas between British Columbia and Alaska are set annually, the presence of El Niño is a factor in determining how they are allocated (National Advisory Board on Science and Technology, 1994).

Marine Pollution There are growing threats to the sustainability of the natural resource base, particularly in areas such as the Georgia Basin where growing human coastal populations generate increasing waste disposal, municipal wastewater, urban and agricultural runoff, and industrial, oil, and chemical discharges and spills. In part because of immigration, recent population growth rates have reached 25 to 30 percent in Vancouver and Victoria, where more than 50 percent of the 3.2 million B.C. inhabitants (1992) live. Aboriginal peoples account for about 4 percent of the provincial population (Beckmann, 1996). Most communities apart from Victoria and Vancouver are small, with tourism- or resource-based economies. Since 1962, shellfish harvesting has been closed in Boundary Bay, and as of February 1995 over 120 200 hectares of coastal marine habitat were closed to shellfish harvesting due primarily to sewage contamination, as well as contamination by toxic substances such as dioxins and furans (Government of Canada, 1996). Victoria and Vancouver are facing questions about whether upgrading of their sewage treatment facilities will result in measurable environmental improvement. Both the sport and commercial salmon fishery have experienced critical losses of

species, habitat, and biodiversity (Paisley, 1994). Many west coast species are threatened or endangered, including the southern sea otter, grey whale, right whale, short-tailed albatross, spectacled eider, marbled murrelet, and various stocks of Chinook and sockeye salmon and groundfish.

The preceding overview of some of the biophysical characteristics and threats to ecosystem integrity facing each of Canada's three ocean regions has demonstrated a range of biological, geophysical, and economic factors that must be considered in planning for sustainability of Canada's ocean resources. The summary that follows links these and additional issues in the context of sociocultural, economic, and ecological dimensions of sustainability.

CANADA'S ATLANTIC OCEAN ENVIRONMENT

Since John Cabot's small ship arrived off the coast of Newfoundland in 1497, the Grand Banks have been hailed as the world's richest hunting ground for Atlantic (northern) cod. So thick that ships were said to be slowed by them, the cod stocks seemed inexhaustible. But, in 1992, in light of unrestricted exploitation, stock declines, and fish plant closures, the Canadian Department of Fisheries and Oceans placed a two-year moratorium on cod fishing in an attempt to avert ecological disaster. The moratorium provides clear evidence of how a once bountiful resource can be decimated through human ignorance and disregard of precautionary conservation principles.

Biophysical Characteristics

The eastern coastline of Canada is about 40 000 kilometres long, but the dominant physical feature of the east coast marine environment is the large, submerged continental shelf (see Figures 8–2a and d). Characterized by raised offshore areas of the seabed known as banks, with shallow water depths often of 50 metres or less, these

A school of pollock off Nova Scotia.

areas of the continental shelf are associated with high levels of biological productivity and marine life. At 250 000 square kilometres, the Grand Banks are the largest bank in the northwest Atlantic.

Three interconnected ocean currents—the Labrador Current, Gulf Stream, and Nova Scotia Current—mix and exchange coastal and deeper ocean waters, causing upwelling (bringing stored nutrients from the sea bottom up through the water column) and increased biological productivity, particularly along the edge of the Scotian shelf and the southern Grand Banks. The Labrador Current brings cold Arctic waters down to the eastern margin of the Grand Banks, while the warm Gulf Stream flows up the east coast of the United States and over the southern Grand Banks. The Nova Scotia Current is a smaller coastal movement of cool water from the Gulf of St. Lawrence along the Scotian Shelf to the Gulf of Maine. The complex mixing of these major currents, local gyres, eddies, and tides, as well as spring discharge from northern rivers and melting ice from the low Arctic, combine to increase biological productivity and marine life diversity.

Temperature and salinity also have consequences for marine environments and climates. Atlantic Canada's offshore seawater is relatively cold but a slight change in temperature can have great impacts on biological production. For instance, because each fish species has a range of tolerance to water depth and temperature, a change of 1°C can affect the distribution of a species, particularly if the species is living in the extreme limits of their distribution. A recent decline in water temperature may be a contributing factor in the collapse of the groundfish fishery. Similarly, declines in salinity resulting from increases in Arctic snowmelt may have contributed to the decline in cod and other groundfish (Meltzer, 1995). However, scientific knowledge of the effects of changes in temperature and salinity is incomplete, and further research is needed.

For centuries, the spring phytoplankton bloom on the wide Atlantic continental shelf has supported several major fisheries. In 1990, for example, cod and other groundfish such as haddock, plaice, flounder, and halibut accounted for about 80 percent of total Canadian landings in weight and were valued at over $375 million. While catches of pelagic species such as herring, mackerel, tuna, salmon, and capelin were valued at over $77 million in 1990, the invertebrate fisheries for shrimp, lobster, crab, scallops, and clams netted more than $475 million that same year. Combined, the 1990 total catch of 1.2 million tonnes from the Atlantic coast accounted for 78 percent of Canada's total landings by weight and 67 percent by value (Government of Canada, 1991; National Advisory Board on Science and Technology, 1994).

In 1995, then federal Fisheries Minister Brian Tobin announced that cod stocks may have declined to the point of commercial extinction. Currently, the cod fish industry has been virtually shut down, and the Department of Fisheries and Oceans has estimated that the northern cod spawning stock is only 5 percent of its historical average (National Advisory Board on Science and Technology, 1994). Although scientists have been able to indicate possible causes of the dramatic decline in the four-hundred-year abundance of northern cod and other groundfish species, they are unable to explain the decline with certainty, or to determine the relative importance of each causal factor.

Some of the possible causes include fishing power (the continuous increase in harvesting capacity) and overfishing; the Canadian offshore trawler fleet and its destruction of habitat, interruption of spawning, and excessive dumping and discarding of unwanted catches; the impacts of other gear types such as gill nets and cod traps; and the foreign fishery outside the 200-mile limit (Blades, 1995). Scientists are concerned that global warming will increase Arctic ice melt, sending more icebergs south and continuing the drop in water temperature in the northwest Atlantic. Colder seawater is expected to affect the spawning and migratory habits of the living resources, decreasing cod and other fish stocks (Meltzer, 1995).

East coast waters support the feeding and breeding of many marine mammals and sea birds. While whales are not harvested commercially, they are vulnerable to fishing gear entanglement and ship collisions. As whale watching and other, associated nature-based tourism activities have become more popular, the overall need to protect whales has been acknowledged and the Department of Fisheries and Oceans has established three whale conservation areas off New Brunswick and Nova Scotia. Seals, on the other hand, have been a controversial and politicized issue on the east coast for almost 20 years. Landsmen in Newfoundland and residents of the Iles-de-la-Madeleine currently undertake commercial fisheries for harp and hood seals. Many people, including some scientists, believe that rapid growth in seal populations has been a contributing factor to the biomass decline in groundfish.

Millions of seabirds also nest and breed on Canada's east coast. However, changes in oceanic conditions and currents as well as overfishing have affected capelin and herring, important food fish for the sea birds. As capelin populations have declined—capelin are the key link between upper and lower levels of the food web, and are the principal food source for larger fish, sea birds, and marine mammals—scientists have documented declines in sea bird populations (Carscadden, Frank & Miller, 1989).

Productivity of the Atlantic marine ecosystem is a function of diverse geographic and physiographic conditions such as shallow rich estuaries and bays that provide ideal habitat for shellfish, and the oceanic currents, tidal flows, gyres, and upwellings on the continental shelf that influence the interactions of fish, mammalian, invertebrate, and plant communities. There are few comprehensive productivity studies, however, and limits to our knowledge have contributed to overfishing, marine degradation, and other problems.

Although a nonconsumptive use of marine life, whale watching may have a negative impact on some species.

In addition to its biological productivity, sedimentary formations underlying the continental shelf contain a variety of mineral resources including petroleum, sand and gravel, silica sands, and precious metals. Commercial production of crude oil began in June 1992 in the Cohasset-Panuke oil field located 256 kilometres southeast of Halifax. The giant Hibernia project 312 kilometres east of St. John's on the northeast Grand Banks is expected to begin oil production before the end of 1997.

Threats to Ecosystem Integrity

Lack of Knowledge Much remains unknown about the highly variable yet interconnected Atlantic marine environment, and much research is required if scientists are going to be able to predict and prevent the negative consequences of human activities on marine ecosystems. The same is true if scientists are to understand the nature and implications of environmental changes. Fundamentally, this lack of knowledge underscores the importance of a precautionary approach toward use of ocean resources.

Anthropogenic Impacts and Marine Pollution Although the coastal population of the Atlantic provinces is widely dispersed and there are few areas of industrial development, there are some hot spots of pervasive marine pollution including the St. Lawrence River and estuary, Halifax harbour, and St. John's harbour. Such hot spots are likely to grow in number and magnitude with increasing population, economic growth, and industrial development in coastal areas. Increasing competition for ocean space and limited resources also is anticipated, highlighting the need to have a coordinated approach to management of marine resources in the region.

Many productive shellfish areas have been contaminated by municipal or industrial effluents such as sewage, heavy metals, and polycyclic aromatic hydrocarbons. Since 1940 the number of shellfish area closures has increased steadily until, in 1989 for instance, over 39 percent (more than 150 000 hectares) of the area classified as suitable for direct harvesting of shellfish in Atlantic Canada was closed (Government of Canada, 1991). Similar conditions cause closures of recreational beaches, restrictions on siting of aquaculture operations, and limits on development options in general.

Other point sources of pollution occur adjacent to Canada's Atlantic Ocean environment, including effluents from pulp and paper mills, mines, and minerals processing plants; food processing plant discharges; and oil and hazardous chemical spills. Non-point sources of pollution include pesticides and other chemicals from agricultural and urban runoff, and atmospheric acid deposition.

Commercial Fishing Many people believe that the decline in the groundfish biomass was caused by overfishing, but incomplete knowledge of the impacts of fishing and fishing practices on the natural marine ecosystems means the effects of overfishing are not always clearly identifiable. Other factors that may have contributed to the loss include discarded fishing nets and gear that continue to catch fish, marine mammals, and sea birds without human supervision ("ghostfishing"), and the dumping of plastics and other refuse. The possible impacts of commercial dragging/trawling, although still controversial, include damages to critical habitat and the possible removal of complete spawning grounds of some species (Meltzer, 1995).

Sea-Level Rise Some scientists believe that global warming will have serious implications for Atlantic Canada, particularly with regard to sea-level rise. Under current climate change scenarios, much of the coasts of Prince Edward Island, New Brunswick, and Nova Scotia would face increased rates of bluff erosion, beach erosion, and destabilization of coastal dunes. While some parts of the coast would be submerged permanently, in other places new beaches, spits, and barriers could form. The area's largest urban centres would be fine, but many small communities are in sensitive locations and could be damaged (Stokoe, LeBlanc, Larson, Manzer & Manuel, 1990). More research is needed here, also, to identify specific impacts and to design appropriate protection strategies.

PART 3:
RESOURCES FOR CANADA'S FUTURE

SUMMARY OF CONCERNS FACING CANADA'S OCEAN REGIONS

Canada's coat of arms bears the motto *A Mari Usque Ad Mare*—from sea to sea—a clear designation of the significance of Canada's oceans to the life of the country. For centuries, different cultures in Canada have depended on the bounty of the oceans to support their traditional ways of life. From the Inuit groups in the Arctic and the First Nations peoples on the Pacific and Atlantic coasts, to the one thousand or so communities of fishers bordering the Atlantic, the ability to harvest various species of fish and shellfish, marine mammals, and sea birds to support both subsistence needs and commercial opportunities has been fundamental to the continuation of the lifestyles of these people.

Until relatively recently, these lifestyles were supported by generally stable, healthy ocean ecosystems that permitted growth in both fishing and processing industries based on what were thought to be renewable resources. Today, however, as humans have exploited fish stocks and other marine mammal and sea bird populations in order to earn a living, not only has the renewability of these resources come into question, but also their sustainability is suspect. In 1989, 10 countries accounted for about 70 percent of the volume of total world catch (Figure 8–4b), mostly Peruvian anchoveta, Chilean jack mackerel, Alaskan pollock, and Japanese pilchard (Figure 8–4a). However, after increasing steadily for more than 30 years, the world catch of ocean fish dropped sharply in 1990 and appeared to have peaked at between 85 and 90 million tonnes per year (Figure 8–4c). The 1995 catch was about 91 million tonnes (Food and Agriculture Organization, 1997a).

The United Nations Food and Agriculture Organization (FAO) has estimated that catches of 70 percent of marine species have reached or exceeded sustainable levels. Given the need to conserve aquatic resources for the future, the FAO adopted the formal, global code of conduct for responsible fisheries in 1995. This nonmandatory code indicated that the right to fish carried with it the obligation to do so in a responsible manner in order to ensure effective conservation and management of living aquatic resources. Another important principle contained in this code is the admonition to all fisheries management organizations to apply a precautionary approach to conservation, management, and exploitation of aquatic resources and environments (Food and Agriculture Organization, 1997b).

In addition to continuing ecological stresses such as growth in fishing pressure and stock or species collapses, there have been a number of new human stresses as well as climatic and natural uncertainties that have added to the difficulties in managing and protecting marine environmental resources for the future. For instance, the pace of coastal development, including tourism and recreational growth, has exacerbated problems relating to use of environmentally sensitive sites, water pollution, and waste disposal, while industrial growth has added new toxic chemicals such as dioxins and furans to effluent discharges. These stresses have ecological and economic implications such as biomagnification of contaminants in fish, wildlife, and humans, reduced fish reproduction, fish die-offs, shellfishery closures, beach closures, and tourism losses.

Additional human stresses relate to energy supplies; as Canadian land-based supplies of petroleum resources decline, offshore oil and gas finds become more viable economically. Exploration and production activities may alter or contaminate habitats temporarily, whereas operational or accidental releases of toxic substances may degrade habitat for long periods. Marine transport safety and pollution issues continue to affect Canadian as well as international waters. Between 1976 and 1987, 171 significant marine spills (of 1000 tonnes or more each) dumped 52 000 tonnes of contaminants on the Atlantic coast, and 180 significant spills on the Pacific coast added 48 000 tonnes of contamination to ocean waters. Petroleum spills constituted 67 percent (by number) of these spills on the Pacific coast and 88 percent on the Atlantic coast (Government of Canada, 1991).

The volume of marine traffic carrying toxic or harmful substances is a major concern for ports and their approaches. The port of Vancouver, for example, annually ships more than one million tonnes of petrochemicals to offshore markets (Government of Canada, 1991). Shipping accidents are a continuing concern, such as the holing of the barge *Nestucca* off the coast of Washington state on December 23, 1988. This accident caused a spill of 875 tonnes of Bunker C fuel oil that subsequently killed about 46 000 sea birds in British Columbia and

The high volume of traffic carrying toxic cargo through the port of Vancouver is a continuing concern.

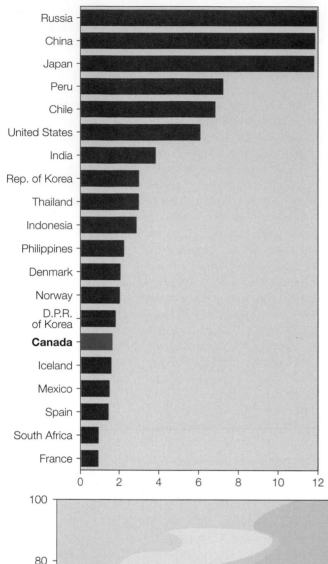

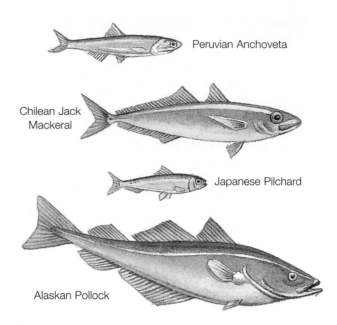

Figure 8–4a

World's most-fished species

SOURCE: Haysom, I. (1997, June 15). Fished out: Centuries of harvesting seas are nearing end, book warns. *Calgary Herald,* p. A2.

Figure 8–4b

National percentage of total world fish catch, 1989

SOURCE: Adapted from Lean, G., & Hinrichsen, D. (1992). *Atlas of the environment.* Oxford: Helicon Publishing, p. 158.

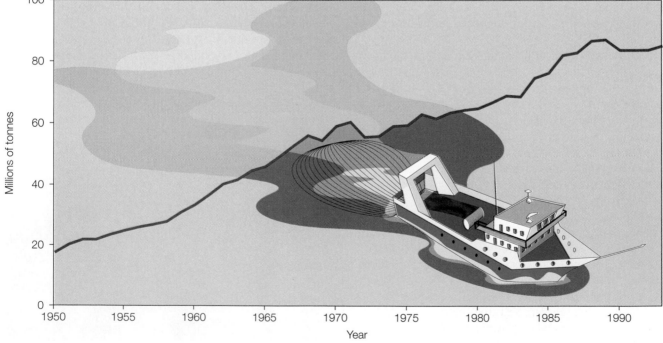

Figure 8–4c

World total fish production in marine waters, 1950–1993

SOURCE: Food and Agriculture Organization of the U.N. (1996). Factfile: Total fish production. http://www.fao.org/news/FACTFILE/Ff9604-e.htm

PART 3:
RESOURCES FOR CANADA'S FUTURE

Washington state, caused mortality and damage to plants within the intertidal zone, and contaminated sandy beaches and salt marshes along the entire length of the west coast of Vancouver Island. While marine accidents can cause spills of large volumes of oil, most of the oil entering the oceans does so by virtue of decisions by ship captains, not by accidents. While on the high seas, many captains deliberately decide to pump out bilge water contaminated with leaked fuel oil or lubricating oil, or to discharge washings from fuel or cargo tanks over the side. These actions, and the perception that oceans have an infinite capacity to absorb waste, need to be changed if long-term sustainability of ocean environments is to be assured.

Global atmospheric, climatic, and sea-level changes are difficult to predict with certainty, but will affect all three Canadian coasts, particularly the Arctic. Inundation of coastal communities and wetland habitats, for example, could displace coastal populations and affect marine species distribution patterns, potentially leading to major economic restructuring.

The impacts of overharvesting both within and beyond Canada's 200-nautical-mile fishing zone have been most evident on the Atlantic coast, where thousands of jobs were lost in Newfoundland and Labrador (National Advisory Board on Science and Technology, 1994). In the Arctic, there is concern about the potential consequences of opening a commercial char fishery when there is a lack of knowledge about the links between arctic char and other species (Beckmann, 1995). And, along with poor monitoring capabilities and management strategies, British Columbia's fishing strategy was blamed in the disappearance of more than two million salmon in 1994 (National Advisory Board on Science and Technology, 1994). In both Atlantic Canada and British Columbia, the issues of excessive fishing capability and the power of fishing technologies compound the fundamental, unresolved problem of too many fishermen chasing too few fish.

Six major interconnected and strikingly similar threats to Canada's marine environmental sustainability exist (to varying degrees) on all three coasts: harvesting practices, urban encroachment, pollution, habitat loss, atmospheric change, and loss of biodiversity (Figure 8–5). Specific examples of aspects of some of these threats are discussed in the following section.

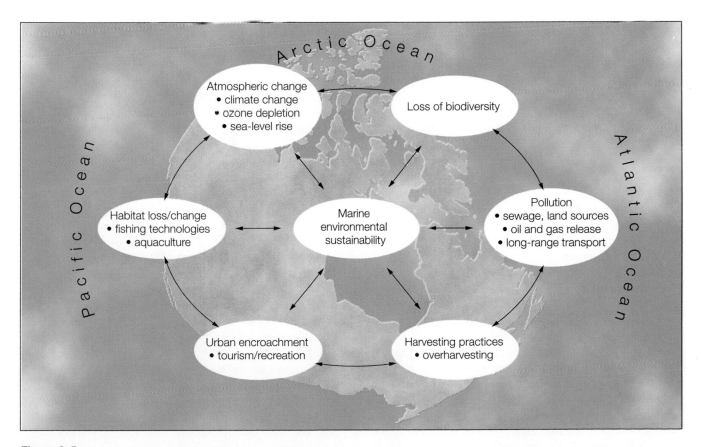

Figure 8–5

Common threats to Canada's marine environmental sustainability

HUMAN ACTIVITIES AND IMPACTS ON MARINE ENVIRONMENTS

FISHERIES

The 1995 Canada–Spain Turbot Dispute

The unthinkable has come to pass: The wealth of oceans, once deemed inexhaustible, has proven finite, and fish, once dubbed "the poor man's protein," have become a resource coveted—and fought over—by nations. (Parfit, 1995, p. 2)

The right of nations to exploit their coastal waters is well established in customary law and formal treaties, but it is only recently that international oceanic law has come to grapple with the question of whether a coastal nation has a right to demand protection of migrating species important to coastal economies even while these species are in international waters. The 1995 Canada–Spain conflict over turbot (or Greenland halibut: *Reinhardtius hippoglossoides*) is a recent incident highlighting this issue of transboundary stock protection.

As the world population continues to grow, global demand for fish continues to increase steadily. For the past 15 years or so, aquacultural products have augmented global fish catches, enabling the demand to be met. However, with more than 70 percent of the world's fisheries already fully exploited, in decline, seriously depleted, or under drastic limits to allow their recovery, competition for remaining stocks is intense (Jandl, n.d.; Food and Agricultural Organization, 1997a).

As commercially valuable stocks of the bigger, slower growing species have declined, commercial fishing fleets have turned to "fishing down the food chain," targeting increasingly large quantities of smaller species of fish with less commercial value. In the case of the Spanish factory trawler fleet, their arrival on the Grand Banks in the mid 1980s was a result of their "fishing down African hake" and being "diverted to the Northwest Atlantic to find new fishing possibilities" (Department of Fisheries and Oceans, 1995c).

Canadian fishers have harvested turbot in our coastal waters for many years, but, in 1986, European Union (EU, previously EC or European Community) vessels, mostly from Spain and Portugal, began to seriously overfish groundfish stocks managed by the Northwest Atlantic Fisheries Organization (NAFO; an agency of the United Nations Food and Agricultural Organization). Some of these stocks were located on the "nose" and "tail" of the Grand Banks just outside Canada's 200-mile limit (Figure

8–6). Turbot catches remained at about 20 000 tonnes from 1985 to 1988, then grew to 47 400 tonnes in 1989 and to 63 000 tonnes in 1992 (Department of Environment, n.d.; Department of Fisheries and Oceans, 1995a; Gomes, 1995; Revel, n.d.).

In September 1994, NAFO adopted a 1995 **Total Allowable Catch** (TAC) for turbot of 27 000 tonnes, less than half of what had been caught in 1993 and 1994. In January 1995, the minister of Fisheries and Oceans (Brian Tobin), attended a special NAFO meeting in Brussels to determine how the turbot that migrated across the 200-mile limit should be shared. At the close of that meeting, Tobin claimed victory for Canada's conservation focus regarding turbot stocks, noting that most of NAFO's 15 major fishing nation members had voted for the allocation of 16 300 tonnes to Canada (a 60 percent share), and 3400 tonnes to the EU (a 12-percent share). The remainder of the TAC was allocated to Russia (3200 tonnes), Japan (2600 tonnes), and others (1500 tonnes) (Department of Fisheries and Oceans, 1995b, 1995c).

Under the provisions of a NAFO objection procedure, however, the EU could reject the NAFO decision, set its own quotas, and allow EU vessels to fish virtually without restriction in the northwest Atlantic. As expected, the EU filed its objection to the turbot allocation in March 1995, and announced that its members would catch 18 000 tonnes of turbot, unilaterally setting the quota at 69 percent of the catch. Essentially, quota allocations sparked the confrontation that evolved into the Canada–Spain "turbot war."

In a move designed to permit Canada to conserve the turbot and other groundfish stocks that straddle the 200-mile limit, coastal fisheries protection regulations were amended in 1994 and in 1995. These regulations allowed Canada to seize Spanish and Portuguese vessels (and other ships flying flags of convenience) if they were caught fishing outside the 200-mile limit in defiance of NAFO quotas. This step was necessary because many European Community vessels registered with non-NAFO countries such as Panama and then fished without quotas, thus exacerbating the effects of EU overfishing. Also, according to the Department of the Environment (n.d.), foreign fisheries on the nose and tail of the Grand Banks outside 200 miles were characterized by the harvest of prespawning juveniles (immature fish), damaging future recruitment of the turbot stocks.

Diplomatic efforts to resolve these problems had continued, but it was under the coastal fisheries protection regulations that on March 9, 1995, Canadian authorities boarded and seized the Spanish fishing trawler *Estai* after a chase at sea ended when warning shots were fired across its bow. The *Estai* captain was arrested and the ship was escorted into St. John's harbour by Fisheries and Coast Guard vessels. Subsequently, Spain accused Canada

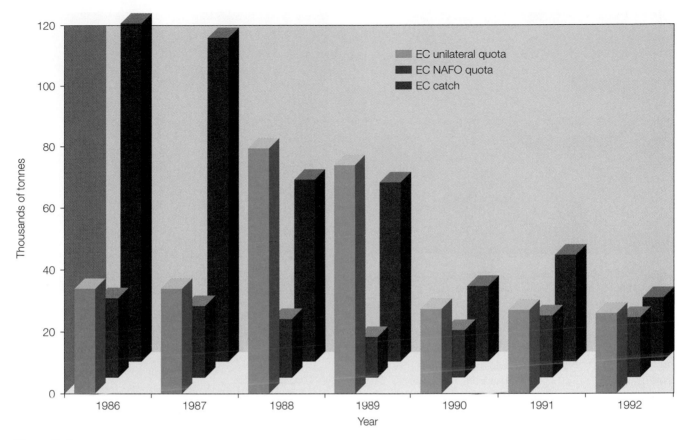

Figure 8–6

Evidence of overfishing of NAFO-managed groundfish stocks by European Union vessels

SOURCE: Environment Canada. (n.d.a.). *State of the environment in the Atlantic region.* http://www.ns.ec.gc.ca/soe/cha4.html

of breaking international law when it seized the *Estai* in international waters. That case is still before the International Court of Justice.

Inspection of the *Estai* revealed that 79 percent of its catch was undersized turbot and that 25 tonnes of American plaice, an endangered species that NAFO had put under moratorium, were stored behind false bulkheads. The *Estai's* net, which its crew had cut deliberately during the chase at sea, was recovered from the Grand Banks—its mesh measured 115 millimetres, although the smallest mesh size mandated for turbot by NAFO was 130 millimetres. Furthermore, the 115-millimetre net had an 80-millimetre mesh liner (net), to take even smaller fish (Bryden, 1995a). International regulations that have been adopted into the United Nations Convention on the Law of the Sea decree that fish cannot be caught before reaching a certain spawning size, to ensure the survival of the species. Canada claimed that this illegal net would account for the undersized turbot catch aboard the *Estai,* and was proof of Spanish overfishing and violation of international rules to preserve endangered fish species.

The *Estai* was released on March 15, 1995, on payment of a $500 000 bond, and discussions with the EU to

settle the dispute resumed. About two weeks later, Fisheries and Oceans Minister Tobin was in New York City on a public relations mission. As diplomats meeting at the UN

The Spanish fishing vessel *Estai* was seized by Canadian authorities and impounded in St. John's harbour.

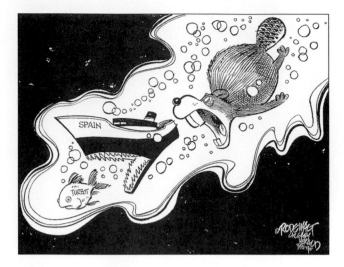

Calgary Herald, March 15, 1995, p. A4. Drawing by Vance Rodewalt.

Fisheries minister Brian Tobin displays an undersized turbot during his public relations mission in New York.

Conference on Straddling Fish Stocks and Highly Migratory Fish Stocks were considering how to enforce fisheries rules on the high seas, Tobin displayed the 5.5-tonne net from the *Estai* on a barge on the East River across from the United Nations buildings. Holding up a tiny turbot in front of the illegal net, Tobin told "an army of international reporters and television crews" that "no baby fish can escape that monstrosity, that ecological madness. That's vacuuming the ocean floor and that's destroying and killing everything there" (Bryden, 1995b, 1995c). This was the day "a clever publicity stunt turned the tide in Canada's favor and the Spanish were ... branded around the world as despoilers of the high seas unscrupulously vacuuming baby fish from the ocean floor" (Gessell, 1995).

On April 15, 1995, Canada and the EU reached an agreement on the conservation and management of transboundary stocks. The Canada–European Union Control and Enforcement agreement was a bilateral commitment to provide better rules, effective enforcement, and more severe penalties governing all Canadian and EU vessels fishing in specific areas regulated by NAFO. Among the major components of the new enforcement agreement were placement of independent, full-time observers on board vessels at all times; increased satellite surveillance and tracking; increased inspections and more rapid reporting of infractions; verification of gear and catch records; significant penalties to deter violations; and new minimum fish size limits. Also under the agreement, new catch quotas for both Canada and the EU were put in place for the remainder of 1995 (Canada and Spain would each receive 10 000 tonnes of the 27 000-tonne quota).

In conjunction with their bilateral negotiations with the European Union, Canadians had been working internationally toward a binding United Nations convention regarding conservation of migratory or straddling fish stocks on the high seas. A draft agreement was finalized and adopted without a vote by the UN General Assembly in August 1995. When legally in force—30 days after at least 30 countries have ratified the treaty—the agreement will provide enforcement measures to prevent depletion of fish in international and national waters.

Turbot hostilities with Spain, from March 3 to April 15, 1995, were estimated to have cost the Canadian taxpayer over $3.24 million. This includes over $954 000 to operate ships that monitored the Spanish fishing boats, $231 000 for air surveillance, more than $752 000 in salaries for the RCMP and other law enforcement officers, and over $89 000 for Fisheries and Oceans Minister Tobin's New York publicity campaign (Gessell, 1995).

Did Canada win the "turbot war"? If the reduction in numbers of major violations (from 25 in 1994 to 1 in 1995) of NAFO regulations is any indication, then it appears that Spain and other members of the EU have been cooperating with NAFO and Canada in regulation of the Grand Banks turbot fishery (Cox, 1996). The ability to cooperate in order to regulate catches and to conserve stocks is an important step toward sustainability of the resource. However, if sustainability is to be achieved, it is critical that all parties act responsibly and look to the best interest not only of all participants but also the fishery resources themselves. Responsible fishing includes reduction in waste, such as that described in Enviro-Focus 8, following.

The Northern Cod Moratorium

The unsustainable harvest of fish stocks is an increasingly important issue in Canada, perhaps nowhere felt more keenly than in outport Newfoundland. The northern cod

50 Million Meals Dumped at Sea

In 1994, a record 340 million kilograms of edible fish were dumped back into the ocean off Alaska because they were too big, too small, or the wrong sex—that's about 50 million meals wasted by discarding fish! The Alaska Department of Fish and Game reported that among the seafood estimated to have been dumped by large factory trawlers were 7.7 million kilograms of halibut, 1.8 million kilograms of herring, 200 000 salmon, 360 000 king crabs, and 15 million tanner crabs. Fifteen percent of the total bottomfish catch of 2.2 billion kilograms, including pollock, cod, and sole, was wasted. Some of the discarded fish originated in B.C. streams flowing through the Alaska Panhandle.

The U.S. National Marine Fisheries Service calculates these volumes of waste based on observational data, which means that the actual amount of wasted fish could be much higher. If the statistics below represent the waste occurring off Alaskan coasts alone, how much fish is wasted worldwide?

Volume of Fish Wasted (Alaska)

1992	227 million kilograms
1993	336 million kilograms
1994	340 million kilograms

Factory trawlers routinely haul in 10 to 30 tonnes of fish in a single net. If the fish are not of the right species or size to process aboard ship, or if only female fish are required in order to harvest their eggs (a delicacy in Japan that fetches top prices), they are simply thrown back in the water. Usually dead or dying, these fish are a deplorable display of waste. Alaska state officials want the North Pacific Fishery Management Council to endorse a plan requiring offshore fishermen to keep everything they catch. Fisheries Minister Fred Mifflin could impose a similar rule on ships fishing in Canadian waters.

Responsible behaviour in the fishing industry, including controls on waste, is a necessity for sustainability in global fisheries, particularly in light of depleted stocks and declining catches around the world. Unless stocks are conserved, fish could become a luxury only the wealthy could afford.

SOURCES: Canadian Press and Associated Press. (1995, December 3). Millions of kilos of seafood dumped in sea. *Victoria Times Colonist*, p. D8.

Stop high seas plunder. (1995, December 12). *Victoria Times Colonist*, p. A4.

(*Gadus morhua*) was the focal point of the distinctive culture of the small, once isolated communities scattered around the coast adjacent to fishing grounds. Peopled mostly by those of English and Irish descent, Newfoundland outports have persisted for over 300 years based on small-scale, seasonal fisheries production. Although historical records indicate that northern cod have experienced general and localized cycles of abundance and severe decline (Harris, 1993), the fish always came back, and outport people adapted to these fish failures "in a variety of idiosyncratic, cultural, social and political ways ranging from diversified gear types and occupational strategies to the costly and problematic relationships between fishers, local merchants, and governments" (McCay, 1978; McCay & Finlayson, 1995).

All that changed in the 1960s when foreign trawlers, built to withstand the icy winter storms of the North Atlantic, arrived on the Grand Banks. By 1968 their size and fishing power had boosted northern cod catches to over 800 000 metric tons, or four times their historical average of 200 000 metric tons. This increase in catch clearly was the result of actions of the offshore foreign fleet and it came at the expense of the inshore Newfoundland fishers (Figure 8–7). The 1968 catch, labelled "the killer spike," had two very important impacts on the fishing industry in Newfoundland. Not only did the huge harvest in 1968 remove a very large number of the northern cod population, it also is thought to have reduced the resiliency of the stock to rebound from fishing mortality and the challenges of changing environmental conditions, including reductions in seawater and Labrador Current temperatures (McCay & Finlayson, 1995; Department of Environment, n.d.). Also—and highly significant from a sustainability perspective—by the 1980s expectations

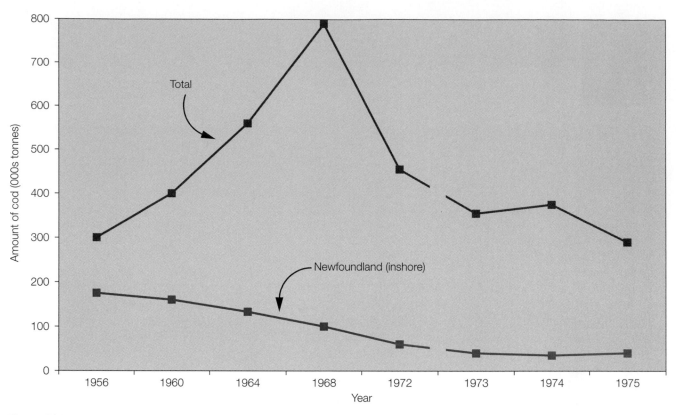

Figure 8–7

Newfoundland cod harvests showing the 1968 "killer spike" and impact on inshore fishers' catches

NOTE: These cod harvests took place in non-NAFO areas.

SOURCE: Adapted from McCay, B.J., & Finlayson, A.C. (1995). The political ecology of crisis and institutional change: The case of the northern cod. Paper presented at the Annual Meeting of the American Anthropological Association, Washington, DC. http://www.lib.unconn.edu/ArcticCircle/NatResources/cod/mckay.html

were that the northern cod stocks could sustain annual catches of at least 400 000 metric tons, double historical averages (McCay & Finlayson, 1995).

In 1977, in the context of negotiations at the UN Convention on the Law of the Sea, Canada declared a 200-mile exclusive fisheries zone (see Figure 8–2). That zone excluded about 10 percent of the Grand Banks—the nose and tail—where important stocks of cod, flounder, and redfish moved between Canadian and international waters and were fished commercially, outside Canada's control. In 1979, NAFO assumed responsibility for conservation of 10 northwest Atlantic fish stocks (including cod) outside Canada's 200-mile limit. Within the exclusive fisheries zone, Canada imposed strict controls: foreign fishing was phased out, the offshore fishery became a Canadian fishery, and the federal government developed a science-based system of fisheries management (McCay & Finlayson, 1995; Department of Fisheries and Oceans, 1995d).

As a consequence of the extension of fisheries jurisdiction to 200 miles, there was a perception of increased resource abundance and economic opportunity. Canadian fish catching and fish processing capacity expanded rapidly

(Table 8–1 lists selected events leading up to the 1992 moratorium). After an initial period of increased catches in the late 1970s and early 1980s, however, groundfish stocks within and outside the exclusive fisheries zone declined

Many of Atlantic Canada's fishing communities were affected economically and socially by the decline in fish stocks.

PART 3:
RESOURCES FOR CANADA'S FUTURE

TABLE 8-1

SELECTED EVENTS LEADING TO THE 1992 NORTHERN COD MORATORIUM IN NEWFOUNDLAND

Settlement (1600s)	• Many coastal communities settled because of the abundance of cod.
	• Early boats (known as shallops) were 9 to 12 metres in length and carried up to five men fishing with hooks and lines.
Late 1800s	• Trawler fishing off the Grand Banks began to replace traditional methods.
	• Dragging in rich spawning areas of the Grand Banks signalled a potential for a resource collapse.
	• Calls to stop trawling were ignored due to the push for competitiveness.
	• Opponents of trawling were forced to adopt the practice to remain competitive.
	• The division between inshore and offshore fishers became firmly entrenched.
1955	• The town of Grand Bank opened a fish plant with three company-owned trawlers.
1963	• Northern offshore cod stocks were estimated at 1.6 million tonnes.
1977	• Canada extended its fishing boundary from 12 to 200 nautical miles with the expectation of rebuilding the resource to provide increased catch rates for Canadian fishers.
	• Fishing companies expanded rapidly.
1983	• The east coast fishery was restructured to rescue five financially troubled fish companies (National Sea Products, H.B. Nickersons, Fishery Products Ltd., Lake Group, and Connors Bros.).
	• Two large companies emerged: Fishery Products International and National Sea Products.
	• The result was a further rift between inshore and offshore fishers: inshore continued to be fished by small, independently owned boats, while the offshore fishery was dominated by corporate-owned, large-volume fishing trawlers.
Mid-1980s	• To gain a competitive edge, National Sea Products introduced *The Cape North*, a factory freezer trawler that could stay at sea for up to three months.
1988	• The Total Allowable Catch (TAC) of northern cod was 266 000 tonnes.
	• 95% of fishermen worked the inshore waters; they were allotted 15% of the TAC.
1990	• The TAC of northern cod was 197 000 tonnes.
	• The actual catch of northern cod was 127 000 tonnes.
March 1992	• The TAC for 1992 was reduced from 180 000 tonnes to 120 000 tonnes.
July 1992	• A two-year moratorium on the northern cod fishery was announced by federal Fisheries Minister John Crosbie.
1994	• The moratorium was extended "indefinitely."
September 1996	• A limited recreational fishery was announced (cod could be caught for personal use).
1997	• A small commercial fishery was permitted on the south and west coasts.

SOURCES: Demont, J. (1992, July 13). When the future died. *Maclean's,* 105(28), pp. 15–16.

Frazer, S. (1992, May). When all the fish were gone. *Canadian Forum,* 71(809), pp. 14–17.

Gillmor, D. (1990, July/August). A fine kettle of fish. *Equinox,* pp. 66–75.

---

drastically (see Figure 8–6). By the mid-1980s, excess capacity and overcapitalization were evident. For example, vessel length restrictions that had been implemented to help bring Canadian catches within legal limits were undermined by development of jumbo draggers with larger hold capacities, bigger nets (a capacity of 164 tonnes compared with 23 tonnes), more powerful engines, and higher price tags ($750 000 compared with $200 000) than conventional draggers.

About this time, the Department of Fisheries and Oceans discovered there had been "serious and systematic errors in stock assessments of northern cod" (McCay & Finlayson, 1995). In response, quotas were lowered, but it was not until the late winter stock survey in 1992 that the magnitude of the problem was recognized—the fish had not come back, and maybe never would. By July 1992 it was estimated that the biomass of northern cod, Atlantic Canada's most important commercial fish stock, was about one-third the average since 1962 and on the verge of commercial extinction. On this basis the Canadian government declared a two-year moratorium on the entire $700-million northern cod fishery: the intent of the moratorium was to allow the stock to rebuild.

About 35 000 fishers and fish plant workers were affected by this closure, as were their families, businesses, and community organizations dependent on their work. Government assistance for the planned two-year closure was provided through the Northern Cod Adjustment and Recovery Program. In 1994 the northern cod stock was reassessed and results indicated a continued decline and concern for biological extinction of the stock. The moratorium remains in place, with talk that it will last for another 10 to 15 years perhaps. As well, with the closure of the food fishery in the summer of 1994, it became illegal for Newfoundlanders to jig for cod to feed their families (see Welbourn, 1995, in Additional Information Sources). The recreational (food) fishery reopened on a limited basis in 1996. Fishery-dependent workers and families in Atlantic Canada and Quebec were promised $1.9 million in income replacement and retraining assistance until the end of May 1999 (Department of Environment, n.d.; McCay & Finlayson, 1995; Sinclair & Page, n.d.). However, the support program will end one year early because it has run out of money.

The collapse of the groundfish fishery is a crisis of historic proportions for Newfoundland and the rest of Atlantic Canada as the displaced fishers and plant workers have lost their traditional livelihoods, independence, and way of life, and all levels of society and the economy have suffered (Blades, 1995). This issue demonstrates the difficulty in achieving the sustainability goal of intergenerational equity. While policies designed to promote sustainability have identified the need to preserve the Earth's natural resources for future generations, current policies to deal with the loss of fish stocks place a heavy, perhaps even unfair, share of costs on the present generation of fishers (Leith, 1995).

While the socioeconomic impacts of the northern cod closure are not fully understood yet, it is clear how difficult it is to find a balance between protecting fish stocks and their habitat and providing fish and fishing opportunities for Canadians now and in the future. The causes of the crisis are many, complex, and interrelated, and include domestic and foreign fishing pressure, overfishing, predation by seals, **ghostfishing** and **driftnetting,** government policies, corporate interests, the failures of international management, environmental and climatic factors, and the errors and uncertainties of science. It is clear, also, that the knowledge base for decision making must be improved (Conservation Council of New Brunswick, 1995; Department of Environment, n.d.; McCay & Finlayson, 1995; Sinclair & Page, n.d.).

Critical gaps in knowledge and their role in the collapse of the northern cod stock were recognized by a broad spectrum of fishery stakeholders. For instance, some inshore fishers were among the first to perceive the inaccuracy of the Department of Fisheries and Ocean's science-based stock estimates, but the fishers' warnings went unheeded. Academics and other analysts were among those who called for an internal reevaluation of scientific stock assessment and its methods. Scientists, too, who reassessed their estimates of stock sizes and showed that their earlier claims had overestimated the stock's abundance by as much as 100 percent and underestimated fishing mortality by about 50 percent, concurred that lack of knowledge had played a role in overfishing and, ultimately, the moratorium. In addition, it was recognized that the scientific side of fisheries decision making often was subject to considerable political pressure and intervention. Thus, when changes in the process of assessing and allocating the resource were initiated, there was agreement that it was necessary to open up the decision-making process and to decentre science (McCay & Finlayson, 1995; Department of Environment, n.d.).

The value of a more participatory and inclusive decision-making process was reflected in the 1993 decision of the minister of Fisheries and Oceans to create the Fisheries Resources Conservation Council (FRCC) (for FRCC's Internet address, see the Additional Information Sources section at the end of this chapter). Comprising 14 members, including scientists, academics, fishing industry groups, and other experts outside of the Department of Fisheries and Oceans, the FRCC now has the final authority for resource assessments and for recommendations to the minister regarding quotas and other conservation strategies. The broad spectrum of interests and expertise represented on the FRCC should help ensure that important dimensions of decision making are not overlooked in the future and that efforts toward sustainability are directed appropriately.

Pacific Herring and Salmon Stocks

The "turbot war" and the northern cod moratorium are two of many examples of human impacts on fisheries in the northwest Atlantic where harvesting practices have had critical ecological impacts on fish stocks, their habitat, and biodiversity, as well as significant social and economic effects on fishing communities and regions. If we shift our attention to the west coast fisheries, we find similar, long-standing issues: overfishing Pacific stocks such as salmon and (roe) herring; managers attempting to use such measures as quota restrictions, gear restrictions, and area closures to protect the stock, reduce dumping, and ensure economic returns to Aboriginal, commercial, and recreational fishers; and scientists grappling with their ability to assess stocks accurately, set TACs appropriately, model ecosystem interrelationships, and understand the impacts of fishing gear on species and habitats.

Pacific Herring Harvested and managed solely by Canadians, Pacific herring are not only the most abundant fish species on Canada's west coast but also are a regional indicator of marine resource sustainability. Providing four to five months' employment for up to 6000 people, and contributing millions of dollars ($180 million in 1993) to the provincial and national economies, herring are central to the marine food web. Pacific herring are a key fish in the summer diets of Chinook salmon, Pacific cod, lingcod, and harbour seals, and herring eggs are important in the diet of migrating sea birds and grey whales (Environment Canada, 1994).

Pacific herring require abundant algal beds and uncontaminated waters in which to spawn, but herring spawning habitat is threatened by coastal development (Box 8–1). In

Herring spawning off the west coast of Vancouver Island.

BOX 8–1
THREATS TO HERRING SPAWNING HABITAT

Pollution and other coastal human stresses, particularly near coves, inlets, and estuaries, can destroy, contaminate, or alter algal beds used by spawning herring and thereby affect herring survival and growth. In British Columbia, the evidence for such local impacts on a herring stock and its spawning grounds is, in part, circumstantial, because the herring return to spawn in the same general, but not specific, location each year.

Some significant losses of herring spawning habitat have been recorded within the Strait of Georgia, a region of the province's greatest human settlement, industrial development, and marine transport. For example, herring spawned repeatedly in Nanaimo Harbour, nearby Newcastle Channel, and Ladysmith Harbour until 1950, but not since. The Nanaimo Harbour foreshore has been completely altered by urban development, and Ladysmith Harbour has become an important site for log storage over the last several decades. Herring have not returned to spawn in Pender Harbour, 70 kilometres north of Vancouver, since 1977; this locale has experienced waterfront residential growth over the past two decades.

Fisheries and Oceans Canada scientists currently are assessing this and other evidence of herring habitat losses along the B.C. coast. Their analyses may show trends that can be reported as new environmental indicators.

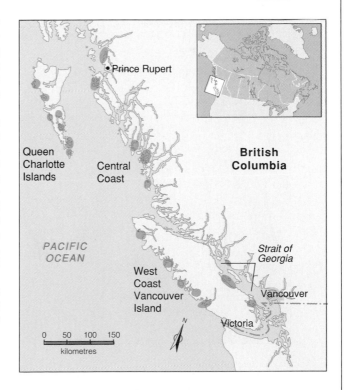

SOURCE: Environment Canada. (1994). Sustaining marine resources: Pacific herring fish stocks. *SOE Bulletin* No. 94–5. Ottawa, p. 5.

addition, Pacific herring are sensitive to natural fluctuations in ocean climate and ecology, including ocean temperature and predators such as the Pacific hake. Waters off the west coast of Vancouver Island undergo alternating periods of cool and warm water that, since 1976, have been intensified by strong El Niño events (Figure 8–8). Young herring survival is reduced during warm events because Pacific hake are abundant and also because large numbers of Pacific mackerel migrate north into B.C. waters and feed on herring and other species during the summer. On average, the eight most abundant predatory fish off Vancouver Island's west coast consume an estimated 45 000 tonnes of herring annually (six times more than is harvested there each year). The spawning biomass declines because fewer young herring survive to join the spawning stock. Conversely, survival and growth are relatively strong when the summer biomass of hake is low and the annual water temperature is cool, about 10°C (Environment Canada, 1994).

Until the late 1960s, herring were harvested and reduced into low-value products such as fish meal and oil. Very large quantities of herring—up to 250 000 tonnes in 1962—were caught in this reduction fishery, exceeding the biomass that was left alive to spawn (Figure 8–9). By

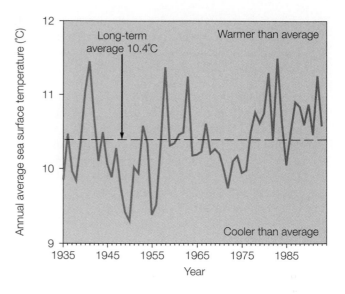

Figure 8–8

Variations in sea surface temperature off the west coast of Vancouver Island, 1951–1993

SOURCE: Environment Canada. (1994). Sustaining marine resources: Pacific herring fish stocks. *SOE Bulletin* No. 94–5. Ottawa: Environment Canada, p. 6.

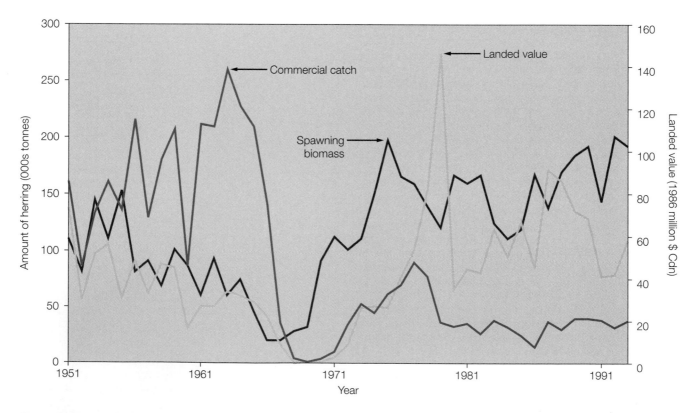

Figure 8–9

Spawning biomass, commercial catch, and economic value of Pacific herring, 1951–1993

SOURCE: Environment Canada. (1994). Sustaining marine resources: Pacific herring fish stocks. *SOE Bulletin* No. 94–5. Ottawa: Environment Canada, pp. 3, 4.

the mid-1960s, the commercial herring fishery could not be sustained as most of the older spawning fish had been removed from the populations. Coast-wide, only 15 000 tonnes of herring were left to spawn in 1965 and, in 1967, the federal government closed all herring fishing, except traditional food and bait fisheries, for four years.

Fortunately, Pacific herring are among a group of fish species that can recover dramatically from a reduced population size, and by 1993 the stocks had rebuilt to 100 000 to 200 000 tonnes. Since 1983, catches have not been permitted to exceed 20 percent of each stock's spawning biomass and, should stock abundance drop, the fishery can be closed (Environment Canada, 1994). One-year closures have occurred in 1985 and 1986 for west coast Vancouver Island stocks, and in 1988 and 1994 for the Queen Charlotte Islands roe fishery, all because of low biomass caused by natural factors. (Of note is that in 1990, the Supreme Court of Canada issued a landmark ruling in the Sparrow decision that outlined First Nations/Aboriginal people's right to fish for food, social, and ceremonial purposes. This right takes priority over all other uses of the fishery, subject to certain overriding considerations such as conservation of the resource.)

In 1972, a new fishery began to harvest B.C. herring for its high-quality roe. Known as *kazunoko* to the Japanese, herring roe is a traditional delicacy that sells for $120 to $150 per kilogram in Japan. The highly controlled roe fishery removes about 35 000 tonnes per year and, even though only about one-tenth the amount of herring is taken compared to the 1960s reduction fishery, the value of the roe fishery has been above $40 million annually since 1982, peaking at about $150 million in 1979 (see Figure 8–9). First Nations people, for whom herring has been a traditional food, have been active participants in the food and commercial roe fishery. In 1991, for instance, they owned about 25 percent of the herring roe fleet vessels and almost 75 percent of the licences to harvest roe spawned on kelp (Environment Canada, 1994).

About 1200 boats participate in the lucrative roe fishery; in 1991, herring contributed $214 500 to the gross income earned on each boat (in comparison, salmon accounted for $146 500 per boat) (Environment Canada, 1994). A combination of high financial stakes and stringent control efforts by the Department of Fisheries and Oceans to ensure that quotas are not exceeded means the roe fishery is "an aggressive event where fishermen attempt to net as much herring as they can in the few minutes an opening is declared" (Meissner, 1995). In 1994, for example, the Strait of Georgia roe herring fishery for seine vessels was open for only 30 minutes. In 1995 herring roe openings on different parts of the coast ranged from five minutes to 24 hours, 50 minutes. In the latter case, in Barkeley Sound (on the west coast of Vancouver Island), a pool system was set up to take the low quota of 1394 tons. Because of limited stocks, only 3 of the 23 seine boats were permitted to set their nets for the

Herring punts used by First Nations fishers in the herring roe fishery.

herring, but the value of the catch was to be split evenly among the 23 vessels. This decision to fish on a pool basis was made in an effort to come as close as possible to meeting the Department of Fisheries and Oceans quota. If all vessels participated, there was a greater chance of exceeding the quota.

While knowledge of Pacific herring is not complete, and their habitat is threatened by a variety of coastal developments, understanding and taking into account the interplay between such factors as herring stocks, fishing pressure, climate and seawater temperatures, and pollution, help ensure these fish will be productive in the future and continue to contribute to ecological diversity on the Pacific coast.

Coastal Salmon Salmon stocks pose different kinds of problems, ranging from the need for conservation of stocks through enhancement programs, and improvement of environmental conditions through installation of sewage treatment systems, to political negotiations to apportion catch levels between Canadian and American fishers. Due to a combination of factors—ocean conditions related to El Niño events, harvesting practices, and habitat destruction due to past industrial practices—wild Chinook salmon stocks on the west coast of Vancouver Island have been severely depressed, some risking extinction. In 1992 and 1993, for example, young salmon migrating out to sea suffered devastating predation by major increases in mackerel and Pacific hake (related to El Niño–induced changes in ocean water temperature). These events meant that, in 1995 and 1996, numbers of Chinook returning to spawn in the 68 wild Chinook streams where they were hatched on Vancouver Island were forecast to be as low as one-tenth of recent averages. That is, a wild stock that would usually have 100 spawners could have as few as 10. If this were to occur, many Chinook stocks could suffer a major loss of genetic diversity which would hinder stock rebuilding (Saving the wild Chinook, 1995).

To enable as many spawning adults as possible to get back to their streams, the Department of Fisheries and Oceans reduced harvest rates by up to 50 percent and also took eggs from wild Chinook stocks to be raised in Vancouver Island hatcheries for later release into their home streams. In 1996, in order to reduce the harvest rate by over 90 percent, commercial catch restrictions planned for west coast Vancouver Island Chinook included closure of some area fisheries, time limits on others, and strict enforcement measures. Recreational and Aboriginal fisheries also were constrained in efforts to contribute to conservation of threatened stocks (Department of Fisheries and Oceans, 1996).

Predictably, reaction was not all positive, particularly among recreational fishing industry operators who were affected by the closure of Chinook fisheries on the west coast of Vancouver Island and off the Queen Charlotte Islands. When the Department of Fisheries and Oceans closed the fisheries, many of these operators' clients demanded refunds for fishing trips they had booked months in advance (Masterman, 1996).

Recognizing that "Pacific fisheries of the future must be based on real conservation and a sustainable fishery," conservation has become the Department of Fisheries and Ocean's top priority (Pacific fisheries for tomorrow, 1995). In light of recent research that shows that salmon are a keystone species as a food resource for such wilderness icons as bears and bald eagles, and that healthy salmon runs, especially those genetically distinct salmon in smaller streams, are linked intimately to the well-being and survival of everything from small Aboriginal coastal communities whose entire existence depends on salmon to whole forest systems and the provincial economy, conservation of salmon is vital to preserving ecologically significant links between oceanic, freshwater, and terrestrial ecosystems (cited in Robinson, 1995).

Fisheries and Oceans Minister Brian Tobin took up the political and legal challenges of Chinook conservation in 1995 when Alaskan officials unilaterally announced increased harvest rates on Chinook salmon, outside the bilateral procedures provided in the 1985 Pacific Salmon Treaty. Among other things, the Pacific Salmon Treaty promotes shared Canadian–U.S. responsibility for conservation of salmon stocks and provides for equitable distribution of catch between Americans and Canadians. When Alaskan officials refused to stop the commercial catch of Chinook salmon returning through Alaskan waters to spawn in B.C. and U.S. streams, U.S. Pacific Northwest tribal groups along with Washington and Oregon state officials initiated legal proceedings to halt the Alaskan fishery. Canada joined the action as an "amicus curiae" (friend of the court), pointing out that Canada had imposed severe restrictions on domestic harvest in the name of conservation and rebuilding of Chinook stocks. Also, Canadian fishers felt there was an imbalance in the number of Canadian-spawned salmon caught by U.S. fishers and the number of U.S.-spawned salmon caught by Canadians (which translated into a $60 to $70 million loss for Canadian fishers).

In early September 1995, a U.S. district court judge decided to halt the commercial Chinook harvest. Tobin was pleased, noting that Canadian efforts to conserve and rebuild Chinook stocks would not be frustrated by excessive harvesting in Alaska. Canada and the United States also agreed on the appointment of a mediator to help reach an agreement on the long-standing differences in interpretation of the equity principles of the Pacific Salmon Treaty (Department of Fisheries and Oceans, 1995e; Kenny, 1995).

As is frequently the case, however, it is difficult to obtain agreement: as of June and July 1996, Canadians again were criticizing the United States' Chinook management plans, which proposed catch levels two and one-half times what Canadian scientists were recommending as necessary for conservation. Canada had proposed a 1996 catch limit of 60 000 Chinook for all fisheries in southeast Alaska, where 60 percent of the Chinook caught originate in Canadian waters. Canadian fishers have greatly reduced their catch to achieve conservation including, in 1996, complete closure of all directed commercial fisheries on Chinook and all sport and Aboriginal fisheries of west coast Vancouver Island Chinook stocks.

The inherent ecological difficulty in maintaining the health and sustainability of Chinook stocks is compounded by the economic pull of potential catches. This is one fisheries instance where it might well be said that "the force of economics overpowers conscience" (Parfit, 1995, p. 11). In June 1997, despite year-long consultations, negotiations between the United States and Canada collapsed when the two sides could not agree on how small a quota of endangered United States–bound Coho salmon should be intercepted by Canadian fishers, and how much the United States should compensate Canada by taking fewer Canadian-bound fish entering the Fraser River. For the fourth consecutive year the two nations failed to agree on quotas; each ended up setting its own maximum quotas, almost as if there were no treaty.

Canada's "vigorous but not aggressive" quotas were designed with a specific political component in mind: to demonstrate that U.S. fishers would be better off with a joint management plan and shared quotas (Howard, 1997). Under this plan to take up to 24 million fish, Canadians could intercept up to 78 percent of southbound sockeye salmon before they reached U.S. waters. Americans, in turn, announced quotas similarly favourable to their fishers.

Scientists and others expressed concern that Canada's key conservation objectives could be ignored in retaliatory actions, and that the level of fishing possible under unilateral quotas could signal the demise of some stocks. High-level officials, including federal Fisheries Minister David Anderson, suggested Canada should seek international arbitration (a proposal the United States previously has rejected). The El Niño advisory issued for 1998, and the knowledge that there will be "lots of mackerel munching on the salmon" (Murphy, 1997), highlights the importance of finding long-term solutions to sustainability of living marine resources.

There are many variable perspectives on and interactions among fisheries issues that have not been raised in detail here. For instance, the importance of salmon to the cultures of Aboriginal people; the effects of commercial fishing pressures on biodiversity; the challenges of developing management strategies to achieve intergenerational equity; the ongoing research programs to help protect stocks and achieve sustainable fisheries—all are vitally important in cultivating a healthy, sustainable resource and fishing community for the future. Fortunately, some of the confrontation between stakeholders that has existed in the past is giving way to new ways of dealing with complex and sensitive fisheries management issues. We'll examine some of these initiatives and actions later in the Responses to Environmental Impacts and Change section of this chapter (page 260).

POLLUTION

Coastlines are the primary habitat of the human species, probably because coastal ecosystems possess an extraordinary endowment of natural resources from which everyone can benefit from their renewable wealth and a high quality of life (Olsen, 1996). Unfortunately, the litany of human impacts on the marine environment is lengthy. Bacterial/viral contamination, oxygen depletion, toxicity, bioaccumulation, habitat loss or degradation, depletion of biota, and degradation of aesthetic values are among the notable effects of human-induced change in the coastal zone.

Contamination of Canada's oceans and coastlines is principally the result of human activities, including discharges of municipal wastewater; industrial effluents such as discharges from pulp and paper mills; urban and agricultural runoff; solid waste and litter such as plastics, logs, and nets; ocean dumping; and coastal developments such as housing, harbours, causeways, and marinas (Government of Canada, 1991). Table 8–2 provides an overview of selected characteristics and examples of human activities that have affected Canada's coastal environments.

Industrial and Chemical Effluents

Industrial effluent is an example of a **point source** of pollution, that is, pollution that enters the natural environment from stationary, readily identifiable sources. Other examples of point sources are those from municipal sewage, mining and ore-processing operations, discrete oil and chemical spills, and food processing plants. **Non-point sources** of pollution include urban and agricultural runoff as well as atmospheric deposition of pollutants. Both point-source and non–point-source releases of pollution to inland freshwater receiving bodies can be carried along rivers to the oceans where they can have effects that are just as devastating to the marine environment as they are to the shorelines where they are discharged.

As noted in Table 8–2, the St. Lawrence River channels large quantities of runoff and industrial wastewater past many communities on its way to the Atlantic Ocean. In 1988, when the federal and provincial governments announced cleanup plans for the St. Lawrence River (St. Lawrence Action Plan), 50 of the largest factories in the Montreal area were selected to cut their discharges into the river (Figure 8–10). Measurements at that time showed that every day the 50 companies involved were discharging 572 000 kilograms of suspended solids, 455 000 kilograms of organic matter, 1830 kilograms of oils and greases, 995 kilograms of heavy metals, and 74 100 kilograms of other metals into the St. Lawrence.

Since then, the results of the St. Lawrence Action plan (1988–93) and the St. Lawrence Vision 2000 program (1995–2000) have been evident in declining levels of mercury, PCBs, and other heavy metals, and in improved health of fish. Quebec government tests show large perch caught in 1993 near Maple Grove contained average mercury levels of 0.42 milligrams per kilogram (compared to 1.02 milligrams per kilogram in 1985) and undetectable levels of PCBs (below 0.02 milligrams per kilogram compared to 0.08 milligrams per kilogram in 1985). Emissions from the original 50 factories continue to be measured regularly, and another 56 companies have been targeted to reduce their levels of toxic discharges under the St. Lawrence Vision 2000 plan (Brocklehurst, 1996).

Although lower levels of industrial pollution now reach the St. Lawrence River and Atlantic Ocean, not all companies in Atlantic (or the rest of) Canada comply with current pollution prevention regulations. For instance, on May 14, 1996, a Newfoundland provincial judge ordered Corner Brook Pulp and Paper Limited to pay a $750 000 combined fine and penalty for pollution violations under the 1992 federal Pulp and Paper Effluent Regulations issued under the federal Fisheries Act. (These regulations are designed to control industrial discharges from pulp and paper mills in order to protect fish and their habitat from suspended solids, biochemical oxygen demanding matter, and lethal effluent.) This fine, the largest paid to that date in Canada, was levied because the company had been out of compliance with the Pulp and Paper Effluent Regulations for several months by failing to complete construction of a new effluent treatment system. Corner Brook Pulp and Paper Limited, which was discharging an estimated 31 463 289 cubic metres of untreated effluent per year, was charged with depositing mill effluent into Humber Arm coastal waters (Environment Canada, 1996a; Environment Canada, n.d.a).

Mill effluent has three major types of constituents: dissolved organic compounds, suspended solids, and an inorganic component. Each of these effluents, often lethal to fish, can degrade water quality and aquatic habitat in rivers, estuaries, and coastal waters. Suspended solids such as cellulose fibres, wood particles, small pieces of bark, and lime mud can settle out of suspension near mill outflows, smothering the benthic habitats of species such as shellfish, lobsters, and polychaete worms, and interfere with species such as salmon that use gravel on river bottoms to spawn or feed. Large areas can be affected by suspended solids—wood fibre has been deposited on the bottom of Humber Arm for up to two kilometres north and

---

TABLE 8–2
HUMAN ACTIVITIES IN THE COASTAL ZONE: SELECTED CHARACTERISTICS AND EXAMPLES

Human Activities	Characteristics	Examples
Pollution • Sewage and land-based sources of marine pollution • Municipal sewage	• 80% of marine pollution is from human sources including municipal sewage, industrial effluents, oil and chemical spills, and urban and agricultural runoff. • In 1989, less than 1% of the population living in coastal communities of 1000 or more was serviced by tertiary treatment, while the wastewater of 38% received no treatment. • Decomposition of solid waste in water uses the dissolved oxygen that marine species require (measured as Biological Oxygen Demand—BOD), leaving less available for those marine species. Sewage releases also inject solid matter (measured as Total Suspended Solids—TSS) including sand, grit, human organic waste, and nonbiodegradable matter into marine environments. • Even when sewage is treated fully, sewage purification systems do not completely eliminate inorganic pollutants such as heavy metals. • The Canadian Environmental Assessment Act (CEPA) does not regulate municipal sewage system discharges.	• Halifax harbour receives about 200 million litres of untreated wastewater daily (1990). • About half of Atlantic and Pacific coast shellfish area closures are due to contamination with bacteria from municipal wastewater. • On the Atlantic coast, BOD and TSS loadings remained fairly constant between 1983 and 1989 but increased on the Pacific coast due to the growth of Victoria and Vancouver. In 1989, BOD levels on the Pacific coast averaged 227 000 kg/day compared with 142 000 kg/day on the Atlantic coast. TSS loadings were similar on both coasts.
• Pulp and paper mill discharges	• Pulp and paper production releases wood fibres, dioxins, and furans. • Chlorine, used in bleaching processes, and pentachlorophenol, used for wood preservation, are known contaminants affecting crabs, prawns, shrimp, and oysters. Bioaccumulations have been found in finfish and sea bird eggs. • CEPA and regulations under the Fisheries Act implemented more stringent regulations. CEPA, for example, requires direct discharges from pulp and paper mills to be free of detectable levels of dioxins and furans, but not all mills comply.	• By 1991 in B.C., approximately 3400 ha of the sea floor were affected by wood fibre from pulp mills; gases that accumulate are toxic to oxygen-breathing organisms. • In Alberni Inlet (Vancouver Island), oxygen depletion in deeper waters has reduced the sockeye salmon run. • In 1987, a heron colony at Crafton (on the east coast of Vancouver Island) near a pulp mill failed to produce young; levels of 2,3,7,8-TCDD, the most toxic form of dioxin, in heron eggs had increased to 210 ppt from 66 ppt one year earlier.

TABLE 8 – 2
(CONTINUED)

Human Activities	Characteristics	Examples
• Industrial and chemical effluents and spills	• Petroleum spills and industrial wastes occur most frequently in harbours; PCBs and pesticides are the most common substances spilled. • Polycyclic aromatic hydrocarbons (PAHs) enter marine environments via petroleum spills and leaks, and runoff, leaching, and disposal of refinery effluents. PAHs can accumulate in fatty tissues of marine organisms causing liver enlargement and cancer in fish. • Heavy metals in estuarine environments may become biologically available; invertebrates living in close association with organic sediments containing high levels of trace metals may incorporate them into their tissues, which subsequently may pass through the food chain to top predators, including commercial fish species. • Synthetic chlorinated organic compounds DDT, PCBs, and toxaphene usually are most prevalent in marine environments. Dioxins and furans, and the pesticides mirex, dieldrin, chlordane, and tributylin also are present. These compounds affect marine life through growth retardation, reduced reproduction, and diminished resistance to disease. Along the Atlantic coast, extensive spraying of forests with pesticides in the 1950s and 1960s is one source of chlorinated organic compounds.	• Annually, about 200 oil slicks are reported in the St. Lawrence River and estuary (between Cornwall and the western tip of Anticosti Island). • In Vancouver and Tuktoyaktuk harbours, levels of PAHs are implicated in cancerous liver lesions in English sole and Arctic flounder. • The endangered population of beluga whales in the St. Lawrence River is heavily contaminated with dozens of toxic chemicals including PCBs, DDT, dieldrin, and mirex (banned since the 1970s). Beluga milk also is toxic, nursing mothers passing on chemicals to their calves. • Mine tailings in B.C. have smothered benthic communities. Cape Breton coal mines discharge acidic wastewater and runoff directly into the ocean, which may lead to bioaccumulation of metals in benthic fauna. High levels of mercury have persisted in the St. Lawrence estuary. Mine sites on Baffin Island show elevated levels of zinc and lead near outfalls and loading docks. • A number of spent nuclear reactor cores dumped in the Kara Sea by the former Soviet Union may threaten the Arctic marine environment in the future (they were not leaking in 1994).
• Long-range transport of pollutants	• The Atlantic coast receives chlorinated organic compounds and other contaminants through long-range atmospheric transport from main industrial and agricultural areas of the U.S.A. and Canada. The St. Lawrence River accumulates large quantities of runoff and industrial wastewater and carries it to the Atlantic Ocean. In the Arctic food web, there are more opportunities for pollutants to concentrate (bioaccumulate) because there are more levels in the food web.	• The Inuit, who depend heavily on marine species for food, are concerned particularly about consumption of mercury and PCBs by pregnant women, which can lead to lower birth rates, smaller infant head circumference, and poor brain and nervous system development.
• Litter and debris	• Plastics are a growing problem: nylon nets, garbage bags, and six-pack yokes entangle marine organisms, killing an estimated two million sea birds and 100 000 marine mammals world wide, each year.	• On Sable Island 160 km off the coast of N.S., plastics comprised almost 94% of the total volume of litter accumulated. • Damage caused by debris blocking cooling systems and entangling propellers costs about $70 million to repair annually (in 1989).

Human Activities	Characteristics	Examples
Coastal Development		
• Urban encroachment and habitat loss	• Roughly 20% of Canada's population lives within 50 km of the coast, and almost all Inuit and Inuvialuit communities in the Arctic are on the coast. Coastal populations are growing: from 1971 to 1986 Vancouver's population grew by 28% and Victoria's grew by 32%. East coast growth rates are slower, with some areas experiencing population decreases, but from 1971 to 1986, Halifax's population grew by 18% and St. John's by 22%.	• Damming in the Hudson Bay–James Bay bioregion changes water flow regimes (releasing less river water in summer and more in winter), which may affect water temperature, salinity, ice floes, ice algae productivity, and phytoplankton production. Also, complex processes may increase concentration of toxic organic mercury in some reservoirs (e.g., organic mercury, if released from a reservoir, can concentrate in the flesh of marine species).
	• Community growth increases pollution and pressure to alter the landscape to build homes and roads, fill wetlands for agricultural land, and build dams to generate power or collect water for urban, agricultural, and industrial use.	• Since 1879, 70% of the shoreline and 50% of the delta wetlands in B.C.'s Fraser River estuary have been altered; in the Maritimes, where agriculture has been practised since the 1700s, figures are even higher. Such modifications have had profound effects on anadromous species such as salmon and catadromous species such as eel, which spend part of their life-cycle in fresh water.
	• Urban encroachment increases BOD and TSS, which can damage breeding, spawning, hatching, and calving areas; interrupt migration patterns; alter species composition; and reduce habitat available to marine species.	
• Structural changes	• The building of causeways, breakwaters, and piers, including those for recreational use, can alter water and sediment flows and affect larval transport of fish and invertebrates.	• Construction of the Annapolis Tidal Power Station in N.S. changed currents, caused upstream erosion, and affected human, fish, and bird populations dependent on the river and associated coastal ecosystems.
	• Expansion of industrial activities, as in Arctic offshore exploration, involves construction of artificial islands and loading docks, causing an increase in suspended sediments and turbidity, generally for short periods.	• Monitoring is continuing to assess effects of structural changes from Confederation Bridge on marine environment in P.E.I.
• Aquaculture	• Because of depletion of wild stocks, both shellfish and finfish are being cultured. Salmon is currently the most lucrative (about $289 million in 1994). Enclosed finfish culturing can be controlled carefully, but farming anadromous and migratory fish in the open ocean can cause problems, including escape of non-native cultured species, penned fish predation on native species, disease transmission, farm waste and chemical releases, habitat loss, and acoustic harassment of marine mammals (to keep them away from pens).	

Human Activities	Characteristics	Examples
Marine Shipping	• Shipping activities can affect the environment through the exchange of ballast water (when water used as ballast is discharged, it may be contaminated with the previous cargo—oil, ore, wine) and release of bilge water, sewage (black water), chemicals, garbage, and other pollutants. • There is concern about the risk to the Canadian marine environment from exotic organisms contained in ballast water that is taken on in a foreign port and discharged into a Canadian port. • Shipping accidents such as that of the *Exxon Valdez* and the *Nestucca* can release large volumes of oil or other cargo.	• Zebra mussels introduced into the Great Lakes ecosystem are thought to have been present in ballast water discharged from a European vessel about 1985. Sea lampreys and lake trout also have altered parts of the Great Lakes ecosystem. • Accidental pollution in the Arctic is of great concern: low temperatures and limited species diversity make the Arctic especially sensitive to pollution and effective cleanup may be impossible. Neither the long-term impact of oil pollution nor the effect of oil on the Arctic system is known.
Atmospheric Change	• Oceans and the atmosphere are inextricably linked through heat and gas exchange. Oceans absorb CO_2 from the atmosphere, and are the largest reservoir of carbon in the global carbon cycle. Atmospheric changes such as increases in greenhouse gas concentrations (CO_2 especially), general warming of atmosphere near Earth's surface, and decline in concentrations of stratospheric ozone have implications for the world's and Canada's oceans. • Detailed knowledge of all processes involved in carbon recycling in oceans is lacking. • Temperature increases are expected to be greatest at high latitudes (but knowledge remains limited). • Sea-level rise (caused by thermal expansion of water and melting of glacier ice) would increase flooding and coastal erosion in low-lying areas such as P.E.I. and the Mackenzie River delta, inundate wetland habitats, and alter marine species distribution patterns. • Stratospheric ozone depletion concerns include increased ultraviolet radiation, which causes skin cancer, reduces crop yields, and damages aquatic life, especially marine microbes, phytoplankton, and zooplankton—the foundation of food chains.	• If warm ocean water shifted north, Fraser River stocks of sockeye salmon would retreat north (currently they are at the southern limit of their geographical distribution). East coast continental shelf waters would warm and freshen, shifting geographic distribution of groundfish stocks. In the north, ice and permafrost could melt, changing species diversity and reducing access to food and habitat. If the Northwest Passage could be used as a shipping route, increased threat of accidental spills and economic opportunity would occur.

SOURCES: Beckmann, L. (1996). *Seas the day: Towards a national marine conservation strategy for Canada.* Ottawa: Canadian Arctic Resources Committee/Canadian Nature Federation.

Government of Canada. (1991). *The state of Canada's environment—1991.* Ottawa: Supply and Services Canada.

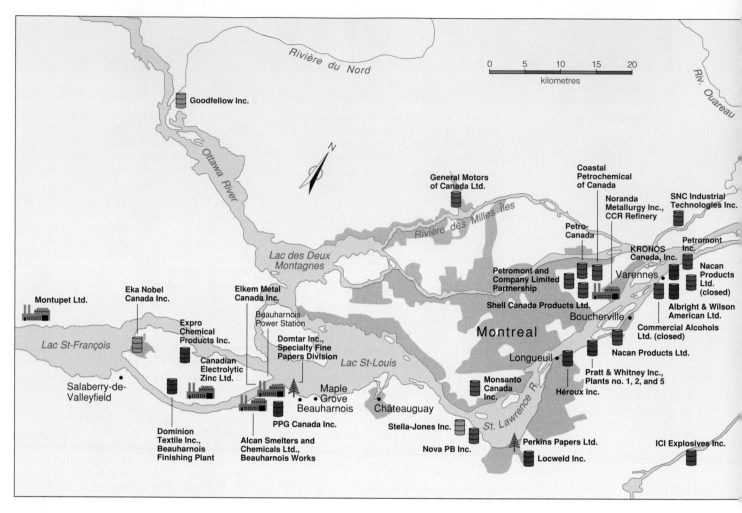

Figure 8–10
Montreal area factories involved in the St. Lawrence River cleanup plans

SOURCE: Brocklehurst, A. (1996). It's not easy being green. *Canadian Geographic,* 116(3), pp. 40–41.

northeast of the outfall of the Corner Brook Pulp and Paper Limited mill (Environment Canada, n.d.a).

A $500 000 fine was imposed for Corner Brook Pulp and Paper Limited's violations of the regulations, and a $250 000 penalty was imposed to ensure compliance with those same regulations. If the company's new treatment system was not fully operational and treating mill effluent by July 1, 1996, a further fine of $500 000 would be imposed. The $250 000 penalty was distributed among three local organizations with environmental interests. Scholarship funds were set up for environmental programs at the local West Viking College and Sir Wilfred Grenfell College, and funding was given to the Corner Brook Stream Development Corporation for its efforts to conserve the Corner Brook stream area (Environment Canada, 1996a).

Less than two weeks later, another pulp and paper company, this time in Ontario, was charged with violations of the Pulp and Paper Effluent Regulations. On May 23, 1996, Domtar Specialty Fine Papers and a mill manager

faced seven charges in the criminal division of the Ontario provincial court relating to the company's mill at St. Catharines. During the period March 1995 to February 1996, it was alleged that the company exceeded release limits for effluent on five occasions and twice failed to meet release reporting requirements contained in the Pulp and Paper Effluent Regulations.

Other industrial activities in Canada such as mining and manufacturing are monitored for their environmental effects. In New Brunswick, for example, the No. 12 lead–zinc mine of the Brunswick Mining and Smelting Company began production in the mid-1960s and, until about 1982, discharged acidic, heavy-metal–contaminated wastewater into the Little River, which empties into Bathurst Basin. Great improvement in the effluent quality was achieved in the early 1980s when the company built a separate wastewater treatment system for mine water. However, this created a new and more difficult problem: partially oxidized sulphur compounds (thiosalts) generated in the milling process at

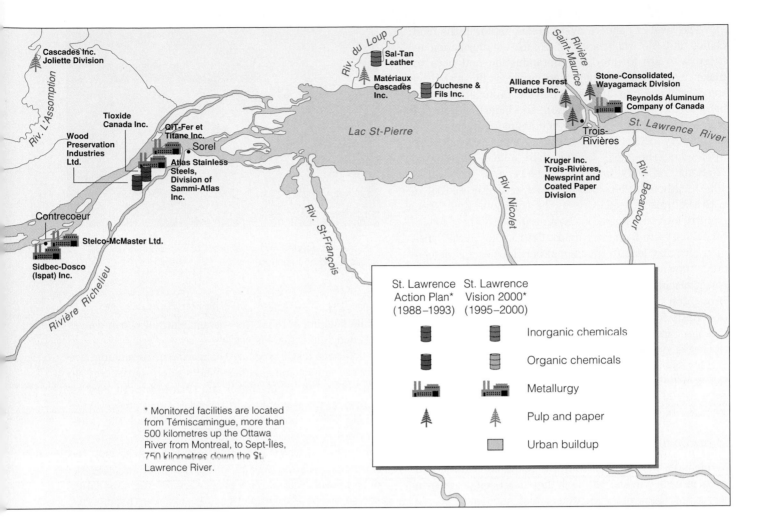

Cascades Inc.
Joliette Division

Riv. L'Assomption

Riv. du Loup

Sal-Tan
Leather

Matériaux
Cascades
Inc.

Duchesne &
Fils Inc.

Lac St-Pierre

Rivière Saint-Maurice

Alliance Forest
Products Inc.

Stone-Consolidated,
Wayagamack Division

Reynolds Aluminum
Company of Canada

St. Lawrence River

Trois-
Rivières

Kruger Inc.
Trois-Rivières,
Newsprint and
Coated Paper
Division

Riv. Becancour

Riv. Nicolet

Riv. St-François

Tioxide
Canada Inc.

QIT-Fer et
Titane Inc.

Wood
Preservation
Industries
Ltd.

Sorel

Atlas Stainless
Steels,
Division of
Sammi-Atlas
Inc.

Contrecoeur

Stelco-McMaster Ltd.

Sidbec-Dosco
(Ispat) Inc.

Rivière Richelieu

* Monitored facilities are located
from Témiscamingue, more than
500 kilometres up the Ottawa
River from Montreal, to Sept-Îles,
750 kilometres down the St.
Lawrence River.

St. Lawrence Action Plan* (1988–1993)	St. Lawrence Vision 2000* (1995–2000)	
		Inorganic chemicals
		Organic chemicals
		Metallurgy
		Pulp and paper
		Urban buildup

the mine were chemically and biologically oxidized when released to the environment, and generated large quantities of sulphuric acid. This acid depressed the pH of Little River, making it uninhabitable to fish and other aquatic organisms; now, only the bacteria that oxidize the thiosalts remain alive in the river. Efforts to treat and remove the thiosalts from the mine water have proved expensive and not very effective (Environment Canada, n.d.a).

Abandoned mines also cause environmental problems; hundreds of derelict mines in Nova Scotia, New Brunswick, and Newfoundland continue to release contaminants such as arsenic, mercury, lead, and zinc for many years after their closure. In Elsa, Yukon, the United Keno Hill Mine (which operated from 1946 until 1989 when economic reasons forced it to close) has been the subject of considerable attention from Environment Canada. Environmental impact assessments have been conducted on the hardrock mining operation every five years since 1974–75 to ensure compliance with the Fisheries Act and to ensure adequate measures are in place to protect the receiving waters. The 1995 impact assessment report noted a significant increase since 1985 in heavy metals in

stream sediments, as well as a reduction in the diversity of the benthic invertebrate community downstream (Environment Canada, 1995). While the mine was not operational as of early 1996, should the owners of the property decide to reopen the mine, the series of environmental impact assessments will provide valuable information on which to develop sound advice for its future development.

As noted previously, Arctic marine systems encourage biomagnification of pollutants such as PCBs and DDTs (see Figure 8–3). From 1985 to 1987, research on Broughton Island, N.W.T., that assessed the possible risk to the health of Arctic residents consuming country foods (seal, caribou, narwhal, fish, walrus) found that 15.4 percent of male and 8.8 percent of female residents ingested more than the Canadian conditional tolerable daily intake of PCBs. Also, PCB concentrations in blood samples exceeded tolerable guidelines in 63 percent of children under 15 years of age, 39 percent of females aged 15 to 44 years, 6 percent of males 15 years and older, and 29 percent of women 45 years and older. One-quarter of the breast milk samples analyzed also exceeded the tolerable PCB level (Kinloch, Kuhnlein & Muir, 1988).

The level of concern over contamination in the food chain, and the importance of complete information to those who are affected by contamination and have to make decisions about their food intake, is illustrated by the case of one Inuk mother. When she brought her sickly baby to the local nursing station, she indicated concern that her breast milk might be contaminated because she ate country foods. She had attempted to protect her baby by feeding the child Coffee Mate mixed with water (National Advisory Board on Science and Technology, 1994). Although there may be risks to health associated with the presence of PCBs in the traditional Inuit diet, country foods are nutritionally superior to southern foods. Switching from a country foods diet to a southern Canadian diet may lead to nutritional deficiencies and associated known risks to health such as obesity, diabetes, cardiovascular disease, and cancer. The research on Broughton Island revealed that the benefits to residents of country foods and of breast feeding were greater than the risks from the PCBs present. Clearly, however, an excessive degree of contamination must be controlled, and levels of contamination monitored so local communities can be assured that country foods are safe to eat (Minister of Supply and Services Canada, 1991; National Advisory Board on Science and Technology, 1994).

Municipal Sewage

Municipal sewage, a point source of pollution, continues to be an issue in Canada. Although there has been progress in increasing the level of treatment and number of people serviced by wastewater treatment systems, concerns remain about environmental and human health effects of municipal sewage. Among the concerns are continuing eutrophication of lakes and rivers, contamination of domestic water supplies, shellfish harvesting closures due to fecal coliform contamination, heavy-metal contamination of sediments, risks associated with swimming in water contaminated with human fecal material, and aesthetic objections to the visible signs of sewage discharge (Environment Canada, n.d.a; Government of Canada, 1996).

In the Arctic, the extremely cold climate severely restricts the rate at which wastes break down in the environment. With local populations growing rapidly, it is not clear that traditional methods of sewage waste disposal alone will be sufficient to avoid contamination of coastal waters in the long term.

Population pressures also affect municipal sewage discharges in the lower Fraser River basin. Currently, municipalities release half of the wastewater entering the lower Fraser River, much of it untreated or primary-treated sewage. If current trends continue, the population of Vancouver and its suburbs will rise from about 1.7 million to about 3 million in the next 25 years (Population: A growing problem, n.d.). Knowing this in advance, it should be possible to plan population and city growth

Hypodermic needles and other medical waste are among the debris found on beaches.

while keeping in mind the sustainability of ocean waters receiving municipal discharges.

Sewage discharges into the marine environment have adverse impacts on shellfish fisheries and tourism but do not pollute the groundwater and surface waters used for domestic water supplies. In the past, since protection of public health (and not the environment) was the prime motivation for treating municipal wastewater, discharges to marine environments were considered as not too serious. In Atlantic Canada, where many communities are near marine waters, the proportion of the population served by waste treatment facilities is lower (by about 50 percent) than in the rest of Canada. Prince Edward Island is the exception where, to protect its important coastal-oriented tourism industry and shellfish resources and to avoid groundwater contamination, almost all municipal waste is treated.

In the Atlantic region in 1987, assuming an average per capita wastewater generation of 0.599 cubic metres per day for all uses, approximately 400 000 cubic metres of untreated wastewater (or roughly enough to fill 160 Olympic-size swimming pools) was being discharged daily into marine environments (Environment Canada, n.d.a). This flow was augmented by a number of aging and inadequate municipal sewage treatment plants that were dumping poorly treated effluent into the region's harbours, rivers, and estuaries.

Halifax and Dartmouth, Nova Scotia, have been dumping raw sewage into Halifax harbour for nearly 250 years. By 1992, 40 outfalls from the two cities were discharging between 100 and 200 million litres (or roughly enough to fill 40 to 80 Olympic-size swimming pools) per day of untreated industrial and urban sewage into the harbour. Beaches on the harbour and the Northwest Arm have been closed to swimmers periodically during the summers (and year-round for shellfishing) because of bacterial contamination. Public criticism also has grown regarding aesthetic concerns (odours and floating debris). Sewage treatment had been studied for at least two decades but it was not until 1987 that federal–provincial negotiations established some funding for the cleanup and for construction of a central primary treatment plant (Environment Canada, n.d.a). As in the case of the Fraser River basin, growing awareness of municipal sewage impacts on ocean waters suggests there is opportunity to take corrective action and move toward sustainability.

MARINE SHIPPING, OCEAN DUMPING, AND PLASTICS

Marine Shipping

As noted earlier (see Table 8–2), shipping activity contributes to degradation of marine environments. From contaminated bilge water to major oil spills, most impacts and problems are caused by human error; many may be avoided (Government of Canada, 1991). As low temperatures and limited species diversity make Canada's north exceptionally sensitive to pollution, northern Canadians are concerned about accidental pollution of Arctic waters, which could occur through shipping incidents or during hydrocarbon exploration. Furthermore, effective spill cleanup in ice-covered areas may be impossible, particularly since the effects of oil on the arctic system are largely unknown.

Aquaculture operations also may be particularly vulnerable to marine shipping, as the 1993 stranding of the oil tanker *Braer* on the Shetland Islands demonstrated. Heading to Canada when she grounded on Sumburgh Head, the *Braer* spilled 96 million gallons of light crude oil, threatening salmon farms 80 kilometres away from the accident site. The Shetland Salmon Farmers Association determined that approximately 2.5 million fish at 16 aquacultural sites were tainted by the oil spill, resulting in a loss of $67.5 million (Golden, 1993).

Oil spills may kill farmed fish and shellfish by direct toxicity, or by smothering them, and can damage them by tainting their flesh. Even the hint of oil contamination may cause consumer uncertainty and affect world fish markets. Given that the salmon (aquaculture) industry in the Bay of Fundy is similar in scope to that of the Shetland Islands, fish farmers in both areas were concerned that the environmental quality around their operations could be destroyed by a tanker accident. With about 350 tankers passing through the Bay of Fundy annually, a serious oil spill might be difficult to contain, particularly if the very high tides in the area were combined with high seas. Such a potential threat emphasizes the need for protection of unpolluted environments in which to raise salmon (Golden, 1993).

Ocean Dumping

Ocean dumping is defined under Part VI of the Canadian Environmental Protection Act as deliberate disposal at sea from ships, aircraft, platforms, and other human-made structures. Dredged material, fish waste, scrap metal, decommissioned vessels (Box 8–2), and uncontaminated organic material of natural origin are among those inert, nonhazardous substances permitted to be dumped. Permits for ocean dumping are granted after an evaluation has been conducted regarding the type of material to be dumped, the intended locations for the loading and disposal, potential environmental impacts, and alternatives to ocean disposal. A permit is not issued if practical opportunities are available for recycling, reuse, or treatment of the waste. Furthermore, Canada banned the disposal of industrial and radioactive wastes at sea in September 1994.

During 1994–95, Environment Canada issued 123 permits for disposal of an estimated 7.8 million tonnes of material, an increase from the previous year of about 3 percent in the total quantity of dumpable material. Over 81 percent of the material disposed of at sea is composed of dredgings (Table 8–3), more than 17 percent is excavation material, and less than 1 percent is fish waste (Minister of Supply and Services, 1996). The 38 percent reduction in the quantity of fish wastes permitted for disposal at sea in 1994–95 reflects the drastic decline in catches in the east coast fishery.

Plastics

Plastics in the marine environment constitute an increasing problem. In high demand because of their durability, light weight, and relatively low cost, plastics do not break down readily and tend to remain in the marine environment for three to five years or longer. In 1990, volunteers with the British Columbia Coastal Cleanup Campaign found more than 1000 pieces of debris per kilometre on some beaches; most of the debris they catalogued was plastic and foam. As the amount of plastic released into the environment grows each year, plastic in the marine environment is accumulating faster than it can break down; tides, winds, and storms deposit plastic all over the world's coastline and seabeds. One study on Sable Island, 160 kilometres east of Nova Scotia, estimated eight tonnes of debris washed up on the island each year, 94 percent of which was plastic.

Marine sensitivity to plastic is high: marine birds and other creatures are hurt or killed when they mistakenly eat or become entangled in it. Plastic can kill by blocking a digestive tract, by releasing toxins as a byproduct during digestion, or through starvation by giving a false sense of being full. Entanglements in plastic often lead to starvation, exhaustion, infection from wounds, and drowning. People, too, are affected by plastic debris when it gets

With a loud bang and clouds of brown and white smoke the decommissioned Canadian destroyer escort *Mackenzie* sank 18 metres below the waters off Sidney, B.C., on September 17, 1995, ending a 34-year naval career in just over four minutes. A popular new tradition for old ships, the *Mackenzie* was the third ship sunk in B.C. waters by the Artificial Reef Society of British Columbia. Within two years of settling on the bottom, over 120 species of marine life were expected to be found in and on the new artificial reef and diving attraction.

The sinking of the *Mackenzie* had been preceded by the scuttling of HMCS *Chaudière* off Sechelt, B.C., in 1992 as well as by the HMCS *Saguenay* in Nova Scotia in 1994. A special ocean disposal activity permitted by Environment Canada under the Canadian Environmental Protection Act, preparing the *Mackenzie* or any other ship to become an artificial reef requires removal of potentially polluting materials such as PCBs, oil, and gauges containing radioactive materials. In addition, holes are cut between compartments and decks to allow safe access for divers. Prior to sending the ship to the bottom, Environment Canada officials inspect the ship for environmental readiness.

Turning the 2370-tonne destroyer HMCS *Chaudière* into an artificial diving reef north of Vancouver was a proving ground for this activity. Environmentalists and First Nations people objected to its sinking because of potential pollution fears. However, Environment Canada instituted a program to observe any effects at the disposal site and in 1993 data showed the old destroyer was home to a wide variety of marine life. In 1994, further videos showed a rich abundance of marine life completely covering the vessel and no evidence of chemical contamination in the water and nearby sediments has been found.

SOURCES: Bell, J. (1995, September 16). Former destroyer to be sunk off Sidney today. *Victoria Times Colonist,* p. B3.

Eggen, M. (1997). That sinking feeling. *Alternatives,* 23(1), p. 7.

Gidney, N. (1995, September 17). Mackenzie goes below as artificial reef. *Victoria Times Colonist,* p. A7.

Minister of Supply and Services. (1996). *Canadian Environmental Protection Act: Report for the period April 1994 to March 1995.* Ottawa: Minister of Supply and Services.

caught in boat propellers, clogs water intakes, or blocks pumping systems. Repairs, lost fishing opportunities, and rising insurance claims cost individuals and the fishing industry both time and money. Communities also may face increasing costs for litter collection (Environment Canada, n.d.b).

Marine plastic debris comes from many sources including careless boaters, beach users, and tourists; cargo vessels, passenger ships, and commercial fishing vessels discharging garbage or accidentally losing cargo; workers at construction sites or other industrial sites who thoughtlessly dispose of waste into marine waters; and poor management practices at landfills (if uncovered, materials may blow into the ocean), and municipal sewage outlets (people dispose of plastic wastes in sewer systems). Rope, containers, grocery and garbage bags, cups and cup lids, and foam pieces are some of the most prevalent forms of plastic debris encountered in the marine environment. A National Marine Plastic Debris research, information, and education program was established by Environment Canada under the Green Plan to improve efforts to deal with the problem.

COASTAL DEVELOPMENT

Globally, growing human populations in coastal areas are posing increasing problems to marine ecosystems as a result of sewage, municipal and industrial wastes, litter, and urban runoff. As well, habitat loss through construction activities and physical alteration of coastal environments is an issue of concern in several parts of the country (see Table 8–2).

Urban Runoff

The lower Fraser River valley, known for its agricultural production, also is an increasingly urbanized area. When rainwater runs off farm land into ditches or washes city streets and industrial sites before draining away, it picks

TABLE 8-3
OCEAN DISPOSAL 1994-1995

Material	Number of Permits		% of Quantity	Quantity of Material	
	Total	Regional		Regional	Total (in Tonnes)
Dredgings (rocks, gravel, sand, silt, clay, wood wastes) mostly from harbours	57	Atlantic 22 Pacific 16 Quebec 19	81.45	Atlantic Pacific Quebec	2 877 510 3 254 550 201 500 6 333 560
Excavation (land sources of soil, rocks)	4	Pacific 4	17.72	Pacific	1 378 000
Fish waste (offal, shells, herring waste, fish processing wastewater)	60	Atlantic 60	0.79	Atlantic	61 329
Vessels (creation of diving attractions)	1	Atlantic 1	0.04	Atlantic	3 051
Dropsondes (small weather instruments remotely deployed in Beaufort Sea as part of a study—sink automatically after use)	1	northern 1	<0.01	northern	0.05

SOURCE: Minister of Supply and Services. (1996). *Canadian Environmental Protection Act: Report for the period April 1994 to March 1995.* Ottawa: Minister of Supply and Services.

up all kinds of contaminants that eventually end up in the river. Manure is one major potential pollutant in agricultural runoff, especially in the Fraser Valley, which has high livestock densities. If improperly applied on fields, pesticides can be problematic if they get into the drainage systems and reach the river untreated or reach groundwater aquifers. Wastewater from poorly maintained septic systems can have the same potential effects. All of these non-point sources of polluted runoff are diffuse and hard to quantify.

It is known, however, that runoff from urban areas collects sediments and chemical pollutants such as trace metals, PCBs, and hydrocarbons (from cars and trucks). The volume of urban runoff for the Fraser River basin as a whole amounts to 500 million cubic metres per year— enough to fill B.C. Place Stadium 250 times (Fraser River Action Plan, n.d.). That volume is more than the annual discharge from municipal and pulp and paper sources combined (Figure 8–11). Because of its large population and extensive urban areas, the lower Fraser River basin contributes the largest amounts of urban runoff in B.C., including almost 55 000 tonnes of suspended solids that enter the Fraser basin each year.

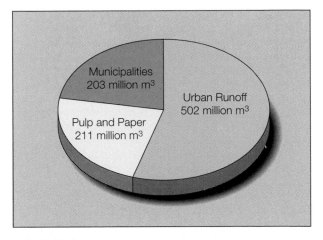

Figure 8–11
Urban runoff in the Fraser River basin

SOURCE: Fraser River Action Plan. (n.d.). *Fact Sheet 2: Pollution in the Fraser.* http://yvrwww1.pwc.bc.doe.ca/ec/frap/fr-fs2.html

The changes that growing urban pressure in the Fraser Valley and expansion of the Roberts Bank Superport area (such as the new high-tech container port,

Deltaport) bring to Fraser delta shore birds are worrisome to researchers. According to current research, environmental changes in the Fraser delta could affect migrating shore birds profoundly. If an oil spill or any other mishap reduced the birds' feeding, many would arrive too late at their Arctic breeding grounds to nest and produce a brood. In other words, habitat degradation on the Fraser River and delta could hinder the shorebirds' success on a breeding ground 3000 kilometres away (cited in Obee, 1996). Such interconnections between human activities and environmental impacts on migrating birds give new meaning to the adage "think globally, act locally."

Urban runoff and other sources of pollution are being studied with a view to cleaning up the Fraser River and restoring its salmon population, among other efforts. Some of these initiatives are considered later in this chapter in the Responses to Environmental Impacts and Change section.

Physical Alterations

Physical restructuring of coastal environments can have impacts on the biotic as well as the abiotic components of an area (see Table 8–2). The construction of a fixed-link bridge between Prince Edward Island and New Brunswick by the consortium Strait Crossing raised numerous such concerns. As noted in Box 8–3, an environmental non-governmental group, Friends of the Island, raised awareness of and concern about the potential harm that ice buildup around the bridge might have on lobster and scallop stocks.

After an unsuccessful court challenge by the Friends of the Island concerning the validity of environmental impact assessments relating to the project, bridge construction commenced (Begley, 1993). The consortium used "proven technology" in its design and construction methods, and built the bridge to carry two lanes of traffic,

---

B O X   8 – 3
CONFEDERATION BRIDGE

When it opened to the public on May 31, 1997, Confederation Bridge was the longest continuous multispan marine bridge in the world. Crossing Northumberland Strait at its narrowest point, the 12.9-kilometre, $840-million bridge has replaced ferry service between Cape Tormentine, New Brunswick, and Borden, Prince Edward Island. The bridge is just over 11 metres wide. The typical bridge elevation off the water is 40 metres, while the navigation span (250 metres wide to accommodate the largest commercial vessel in the region) is 60 metres above the water. All vehicles permitted to travel on the Trans Canada Highway are able to use the two-lane toll bridge, and a shuttle service accommodates pedestrians and cyclists.

Northumberland Strait is a channel of water about 300 kilometres long, between 13 and 55 kilometres wide, and covered with ice from January to April. The strait is one of the richest lobster-fishing areas in Atlantic Canada and lobster provides about 75 percent of the value of shellfish landed in the area. Friends of the Island was a coalition of fishers, ferry workers, farmers, environmentalists, and Islanders who challenged the construction of the fixed-link bridge on environmental grounds. Supported by the Canadian Environmental Defence Fund, the group attempted to overturn a Federal Court ruling that the Government of Canada had conducted a proper assessment of the project's environmental impacts.

The coalition was concerned that the $100-million-a-year Northumberland Strait fishery might be jeopardized by the bridge. The group claimed ice buildup in the strait at the bridge could harm valuable lobster and scallop stocks. Of primary concern to the Friends of the Island was that the potential environmental impacts were determined by consultants retained by the consortium building the bridge.

In June 1995, the Federal Court of Canada ruled that the Government of Canada had taken all the necessary steps before concluding that the megaproject posed no harm to the environment.

Opening celebrations for Confederation Bridge included an opportunity for runners and walkers to cross the bridge unimpeded by vehicular traffic.

PART 3:
RESOURCES FOR CANADA'S FUTURE

24 hours per day, year-round. To prevent any adverse effects of the bridge on the marine environment, the consortium's environmental management and environmental protection plans permit only environmentally safe deicers to be used on the roadway surface during winter. Similar limitations prevail for other seasons and other issues, from wind monitoring to storm drainage systems.

Environmental effects monitoring programs required of Strait Crossing call for repeated measurements of environmental variables over time in order to detect changes caused by external influences, verify impact predictions, and evaluate the effectiveness of mitigation measures. Among the biophysical components studied are terrestrial wildlife areas, physical oceanography (currrents, tides, sediment modelling), fisheries resources, and ice climate and effects of ice scouring in the Northumberland Strait. It will be interesting to see how effective Strait Crossing's lobster enhancement program (which dumped dredged material in nonproductive habitats to establish new lobster terrain) will be, and to determine how accurate environmental impact predictions were.

OFFSHORE HYDROCARBON DEVELOPMENT

Marine ecosystems may be impacted directly or indirectly and for the short or long term by hydrocarbon exploration and production activities. Our still limited abilities to deal with iceberg collisions with production rigs or with spills, well blowouts, and containment in the Atlantic and Arctic ocean environments are key issues related to offshore development. In 1972, the British Columbia government imposed a moratorium on offshore exploration (which has not been lifted), and on the east coast, in response to fishing industry lobbying, exploration activity was banned

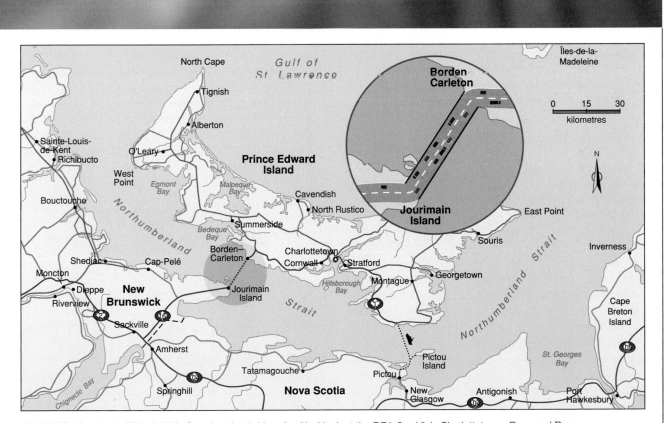

SOURCES: Begley, L. (Ed.). (1993). *Crossing that bridge: A critical look at the P.E.I. fixed link.* Charlottetown: Ragweed Press.

Public Works and Government Services Canada and Strait Crossing Development Inc. (n.d.). *Northumberland Strait Crossing Project: Information package.*

Public Works and Government Services Canada. (1997). *Northumberland Strait crossing project: A link to the future.* http://cycor.ca/nscp/index-e.html

Strait Crossing Team. (n.d.). The Northumberland Strait Bridge. http://wwwpeinet.pe.ca/SCI

Thurston, H. (1997). Steps across the strait. *Canadian Geographic* (March–April), pp. 52–60.

by the federal and Nova Scotia governments in the Georges Bank area until the year 2000.

Exploration for petroleum hydrocarbons began in the Arctic in 1973, and by 1989, 130 wells had been drilled off the Arctic coast; as well, 273 wells were drilled off the Atlantic coast. The Hibernia project off Newfoundland, smaller projects on the Scotian Shelf, and the gas field near Sable Island are, or shortly are expected to be, in production. These projects provide economic development and expansion opportunities for the region, but also pose potentially significant threats to local marine life such as fish on the Grand Banks and grey and harbour seals on Sable Island breeding grounds (Government of Canada, 1991). In the drilling of a well, drilling muds and drill cuttings (typically in the order of 200 to 500 cubic metres) are discharged directly into the ocean. Mud additives used in this process are of particular concern because they may contain a variety of contaminants, including heavy metals, hydrocarbons, and biocides.

Legislation establishing the current drilling moratorium on Georges Bank, due to expire on January 1, 2000, calls for federal and provincial ministers responsible for energy to establish a panel (by no later than January 1, 1996) to conduct a public review of the environmental and socioeconomic impacts of hydrocarbon drilling on the bank. The panel must submit a report to the ministers by no later than July 1, 1999; if the ministers decide to continue the prohibition on drilling on all or part of the bank, they are to issue a written notice on or before January 1, 2000.

An important source of new environmental information that will be considered by the panel is a multidisciplinary research program on the effects of drilling wastes being conducted by researchers at the Bedford Institute of Oceanography in Nova Scotia. Scientists are studying the physical oceanography and sedimentology of Georges Bank, the flocculation behaviour of drilling wastes, drilling waste dispersion around an active rig on Sable Island Bank, and the sublethal effects of drilling wastes on sea scallops, the most important commercial species on Georges Bank. Particular attention is being paid to water circulation so that the horizontal dispersion and transport of particulate drilling wastes can be understood, particularly in the benthic boundary layer. That layer of water, just above the sea floor, is where the scallops filter their food particles. Scientists will use the models they have developed to explore the potential impacts of specific hypothetical drilling scenarios on Georges Bank, and will convey that information to the review panel for their consideration (Drilling on Georges Bank, n.d.).

ATMOSPHERIC CHANGE

Scientists agree that the rate and patterns of climate change over the past century point toward a discernible human influence on global climate (Government of Canada, 1996). As major components of the ecosphere,

oceans and the atmosphere are linked inextricably, primarily through exchange of gases and heat. Oceans absorb CO_2 from the atmosphere, and are the largest reservoir of carbon in the global carbon cycle. Important changes in the properties and composition of the atmosphere are occurring, including changes in greenhouse gas concentrations, general warming of the atmosphere near the Earth's surface, and a decline in stratospheric ozone concentrations. All of these changes have implications for the world's oceans, as do changes in sea level, which threaten loss of wetlands and other fish and wildlife habitat, flooding of property, shoreline erosion, contamination of coastal water supplies, reduced viability of ports, and the further disruption of established fisheries.

Although research is continuing, detailed knowledge of all the processes involved in ocean–atmosphere interactions is lacking. Increases in the amount of CO_2 in solution, changes in the temperature of ocean waters, rising sea levels, and ozone depletion potentially have negative impacts on marine environments and marine life. In anticipation of climate change, Canadian and international scientists have been working independently and collaboratively to improve the knowledge base regarding oceans. A series of research papers on the potential effects of climate change were prepared by the Canadian Climate Centre as part of Canada's state-of-the-environment reporting conducted from the late 1980s to the mid-1990s. Bibliographic information about two of these studies (relating to potential impacts of global warming on fisheries and petroleum industries) may be found under McGillivray, Agnew, McKay, Pilkington & Hill and McBean, Slaymaker, Northcote, LeBlond & Parsons in the Additional Information Sources section of this chapter.

RESPONSES TO ENVIRONMENTAL IMPACTS AND CHANGE

How sustainable are Canada's commercial fisheries? What is needed to maintain the health of major aquatic ecosystems? How do we balance social, environmental, and economic interests in areas that are important for fisheries, shipping, and urban and industrial development? These questions and many others like them reveal the worries that people have regarding the present impacts of human activities and the need to plan and manage resources for a sustainable future. While we know that we need greater ecological knowledge to answer such questions and to move toward sustainability and ecosystem-based approaches to managing ocean resources, there have been efforts at all levels, from international to individual, to make a difference. This section outlines some of these efforts.

INTERNATIONAL INITIATIVES

A variety of international agreements and programs are in place that attempt to safeguard the oceans and their resources for present and future generations. The Organization for Economic Cooperation and Development and the United Nations Environment Programme (UNEP) run oceans and coastal area programs. UNEP's Regional Seas Programme, for example, emphasizes integrated coastal zone management, pollution control measures, and climate change problems. Earlier in the chapter we saw NAFO's difficulties with the lack of enforceable international law to preserve high-seas turbot for future generations (Schram & Polunin, 1995). The United Nations Convention on the Law of the Sea and *Agenda 21,* both described briefly below, are important international initiatives.

United Nations Convention on the Law of the Sea

On November 16, 1994, the United Nations Convention on the Law of the Sea (UNCLOS) came into force, concluding a process that had begun in the mid-1930s. Prior to World War I, it had been recognized that the world needed to develop a legal order for the oceans that would "promote the peaceful uses of the seas and oceans, the equitable and efficient utilization of their resources, the conservation of their living resources, and the study, protection and preservation of the marine environment" (UNCLOS, 1982, cited in Alexandrowicz, 1995).

While the history of the United Nations Convention on the Law of the Sea is both lengthy and complex, the legal regime was developed through international political negotiations during three Law of the Sea (LOS) Conferences. The Third LOS Conference took 10 years (until 1982) to negotiate a final agreement, which, in turn, took 12 years to come into force (in 1994). The resulting United Nations Convention on the Law of the Sea (UNCLOS) is the centrepiece of the international regime for managing the world's oceans (but it is not the only document setting out rules). The widely divergent interests of 150 independent states were reconciled by UNCLOS, which also established the basis for a new equity in use of oceans and their resources.

Among other items in UNCLOS agreements, Exclusive Economic Zones (EEZs) were established that gave coastal states legal power and international obligation to apply sound principles of resource management to

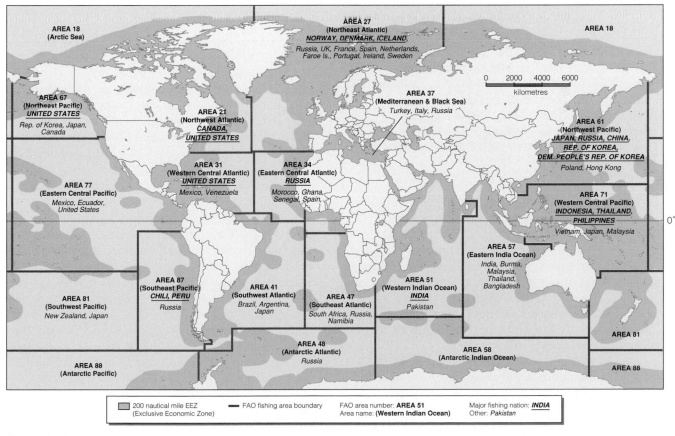

Figure 8–12

FAO fishing area boundaries

SOURCE: Leon, G., Hinrichsen, D., & Markham, A. (1990). *WWF atlas of the environment.* New York: Prentice Hall, pp. 158–59.

Marinas expand as recreational demand grows.

oceans. In addition, UNCLOS declared that more than 45 percent of the seabed area and its resources were "the 'common heritage of mankind,' a concept that represents a milestone in the realm of international cooperation" (Figure 8–12) (World Commission on Environment and Development, 1987, p. 273). This concept means that the world's oceans are inextricably linked and that Canada, as every other maritime nation, has an international responsibility to manage the oceans as a shared global resource.

Even though Canada was a strong supporter of the UNCLOS process and is a major beneficiary of its provisions, Canada is not among the 75 nations that have ratified the convention. Rather, Canada's policy is to enact domestic legislation that complies with international ratification and that specifically supports UNCLOS (National Advisory Board on Science and Technology, 1994). Further discussion relating to UNCLOS is found in the Canadian Law, Policy, and Practice section of this chapter.

Agenda 21

Chapter 17 of *Agenda 21* of the United Nations Conference on Environment and Development (UNCED) deals with the marine environment. Linked directly with UNCLOS, *Agenda 21* sets out the international basis on which to pursue protection and sustainable development of marine and coastal environments and their resources. *Agenda 21* calls for new approaches to marine and coastal area management and development that integrate knowledge from all sources and that are both precautionary and anticipatory (Gerges, 1994).

Agenda 21 focuses on a number of areas such as integrated management and sustainable development of coastal areas, including EEZs, marine environmental protection, climate change, and strengthening regional and international cooperation and coordination in dealing with oceans issues. Given the continued growth of human settlement along the world's coasts, increased coastal recreation, the concentration of industrial development in

coastal areas, and the wealth of exploitable, living marine resources, emphasis is placed on protecting the health of coastal waters. Particular attention is paid to the land-based sources of marine degradation that contribute 70 percent of ocean pollution (International Development Research Centre, n.d.).

CANADIAN LAW, POLICY, AND PRACTICE

Revised Oceans and Fisheries Legislation

Canada's history of governance of marine environments has reflected both federal and provincial responsibilities and jurisdictions. The federal government has responsibility for all matters in waters below the mean high-water mark (except in aquaculture where certain responsibilities have been delegated to provinces through specific memoranda of understanding). Provincial jurisdiction covers provincial lands, shorelines, and freshwater resources (except navigable waters, inland fisheries, and federal lands), and, to some extent, certain areas of the seabed. Federal and provincial jurisdictions overlap in matters of species and habitat conservation, and provincial and municipal jurisdictions include many of the land-based activities that affect the marine environment (Beckmann, 1996; Meltzer, 1995). With the recent conclusion of some major land claims agreements in the Arctic, Aboriginal governments also are involved in the management of human activities in marine environments.

The main federal responsibility for the marine environment and economy lies with the Department of Fisheries and Oceans (DFO), which now includes Coast Guard functions. Primarily, DFO has managed commercially harvestable marine species, but also it is responsible for all marine species (except sea birds) and marine mammals. Other key departments and their major responsibilities are identified in Table 8–4.

The multiple and overlapping jurisdictions that characterize Canadian government in general give rise to fragmentation, duplication, and lack of coordination in marine environmental management and decision making (Beckmann, 1996). Aware that fragmentation tends to cause environmental considerations to be lost among the competing, more powerful economic interests, the federal government has been generating policies and guidelines to deal with that problem. Among the policies developed are the National Marine Conservation Areas Policy and the Canadian Arctic Marine Conservation Strategy.

Despite some excellent plans for marine conservation, pollution control, and species and habitat protection, collapse of numerous fish stocks indicates that Canada has had difficulty managing the commercial fishery in its own waters (Beckmann, 1995). Despite the government's commitment to environmentally sustainable development,

TABLE 8–4
FEDERAL DEPARTMENTS WITH SIGNIFICANT MARINE RESPONSIBILITIES

Department	Selected Major Responsibilities
Fisheries and Oceans	• management of commercially harvestable marine species, and all marine species (except sea birds) and marine mammals; safeguarding of Canada's oceans; Coast Guard functions
National Defence	• border patrol
Natural Resources	• extraction of marine resources such as oil, gas, minerals, and aggregates south of 60°N. latitude
Environment	• protection of marine environmental quality; pollution prevention; sea bird and sea bird habitat protection
Canadian Heritage	• establishment of National Marine Conservation Areas and National Parks through Parks Canada
Indian Affairs and Northern Development	• environmental issues and offshore oil, gas, and mineral development north of 60°N. latitude
Foreign Affairs and International Trade	• marine-related negotiations with other countries (as in the case of turbot negotiations with Spain)
Emergency Preparedness Canada	• response to natural and human-made disasters such as oil spills (on land and at sea)

SOURCES: Beckmann, L. (1996). *Seas the day: Towards a national marine conservation strategy for Canada.* Ottawa: Canadian Arctic Resources Committee/Canadian Nature Federation.

Meltzer, E. (1995). *Overview of the east coast marine environment.* Ottawa: Canadian Arctic Resources Committee/Canadian Nature Federation.

reasons suggested for Canada's failure to prevent degradation of marine waters and species include political inertia, fragmentation of responsibility, and missing legislation (such as a National Marine Conservation Areas Act and an Endangered Species Act) (Beckmann, 1995, 1996; National Advisory Board on Science and Technology, 1994).

In 1994, four key events occurred that looked very promising for the advancement of marine conservation. The first event, in May 1994, was the release by the National Advisory Board on Science and Technology (which reports directly to the prime minister) of its report on oceans and coasts. Recommendations made by the advisory board included a comprehensive marine environment protection system that would safeguard Canada's oceans for the health, enjoyment, and economic welfare of future generations. The second event was Parks Canada's release of its revised "Guiding Principles and Operational Policies," which included a section on establishing marine conservation areas and which recognized the need to design them to accommodate varying levels of human activity within them. Amendments to the Canada Wildlife Act, which enabled the establishment of wildlife areas out to 200 nautical miles, was the third event. This is an important means of extending environmental regulation

to protect marine mammals and their habitat. The fourth event, in November 1994, was DFO's release of "A Vision for Ocean Management," a document that not only outlined the essentials of a new oceans management strategy for Canada but also recommitted DFO to the creation of a Canada Oceans Act.

As Bill C-26, the Canada Oceans Act was passed by the House of Commons on October 21, 1996, and given royal assent in December 1996. The Canada Oceans Act recognizes Canada's jurisdiction over its ocean areas by declaring a contiguous zone and an EEZ, and provides the legislative basis for an oceans management strategy based on the principles of shared stewardship, sustainable development of ocean resources, and the precautionary approach. There are high hopes for the Canada Oceans Act because it is the basis on which cooperative work with the provinces can begin, and through which all Canadians interested in the marine environment and economy can help build an oceans management strategy.

Prior to the passing of the Canada Oceans Act, the provinces had been active. For example, Nova Scotia and New Brunswick had formulated coastal zone management policies and plans. Other cooperative initiatives were undertaken as well, such as the Marine Protected Areas Working Group (Canada–British Columbia) and the Burrard Inlet Environmental Action Plan (Environment Canada–B.C. Ministry of Environment, Lands and Parks) to reduce toxic loadings in the inlet. The Inuvialuit Final Agreement (for the western Arctic) and the Nunavut Final Agreement (for the eastern Arctic) provided for a joint federal–territorial–Aboriginal management system that fosters integrated decision making. (These co-management initiatives are noted briefly in the section on Canadian Partnerships and Local Actions later in this chapter.) Municipalities, with their solid waste and sewage management responsibilities, also have important roles to play in improving the health of Canada's marine systems through careful urban planning and appropriate waste management practices.

On December 11, 1995, Fisheries and Oceans Minister Brian Tobin tabled the first major rewrite of the Fisheries Act since 1868, updating the legal basis for conservation and fisheries management (Department of Fisheries and Oceans, 1995f). In particular, these changes provide greater opportunity for shared management of the resource through partnerships, more effective enforcement, and more flexible regulations—the kinds of changes that have been advocated for a long time by various analysts. Tobin indicated that changes to the Fisheries Act were designed to allow government and industry to move forward into the "fishery of the future."

Six guiding principles inform the "fishery of the future": (1) conservation comes first, (2) industry capacity must be balanced with resource capacity, (3) the fishery must be conducted by professionals, (4) access to the resource should be through multilicensed enterprises, while recognizing the reality of certain specialized fleets, (5) government and industry must operate in partnership, with binding agreements signed by both parties, and (6) Aboriginal rights must be respected (Department of Fisheries and Oceans, 1995f).

Coastal Zone Management Efforts

As the examples above illustrate, even though not all required legislative elements are in place Canada seems to be making progress in revising existing legislation and in creating necessary new legislation pertaining to the marine environment. Efforts to implement coastal zone management in Canada, however, continue to lag.

To mitigate the negative aspects of increasing stress on coastal environments, a number of countries have adopted national coastal zone management (CZM) programs. Coastal zone management may be defined as "the process of implementing a plan designed to resolve conflicts among a variety of coastal users, to determine the most appropriate use of coastal resources, and to allocate uses and resources among legitimate stakeholders" (Hildebrand, 1989, p. 9). Canada does not have a national coastal zone management program; however, regional

---

TABLE 8–5
SHORELINE MANAGEMENT PRINCIPLES FROM THE 1978 CCREM NATIONAL SYMPOSIUM

1. recognize the importance of shore areas
2. employ a cooperative approach to management
3. coordinate policies and programs
4. recognize the role of local governments
5. recognize the contribution of industry
6. recognize the interrelationship of shore activities
7. protect sensitive, unique, and significant areas
8. ensure right of public access
9. make information systems available
10. provide for public education and awareness

SOURCE: Adapted from Hildebrand, L.P. (1989). Canada's experience with coastal zone management. Halifax: Oceans Institute of Canada.

---

efforts exist in parts of the country where resource allocation conflicts and problems of environmental degradation are severe.

In 1978, in an effort to establish a national CZM program, the Canadian Council of Resource and Environment Ministers (CCREM) sponsored a national seminar on coastal zone issues. Although a national strategy did not emerge from this symposium, 10 principles were developed that have helped to guide local and regional coastal management efforts since then (Table 8–5). Beyond establishment of principles, various actions have been taken to improve coastal management, including a variety of regional initiatives such as the Fraser River Estuary Management Program and the Atlantic Coastal Action Program.

The rapidly urbanizing lower Fraser River basin is biologically productive and highly desirable for agriculture, industrialization, and marine transportation. In 1985, intense allocation conflicts among resource users in the area prompted establishment of the Fraser River Estuary Management Program (FREMP) under a federal–provincial agreement. FREMP was developed according to the recommendations of the CCREM symposium and was intended as a model for regional coastal zone management programs (Day and Gamble, 1990).

FREMP administered programs and activities for the estuary by coordinating the efforts of more than 30 agencies including representatives from all levels of government, First Nations, and interest groups. Programs for water quality, waste management, recreation, fish and wildlife habitat, port and industrial development, and navigation and dredging were coordinated successfully under FREMP (Figure 8–13). The experience gained through

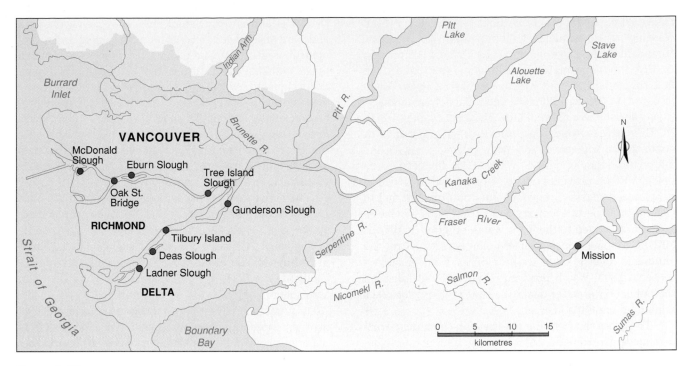

Figure 8–13
FREMP sampling sites in the Lower Fraser River basin.

NOTE: Forty different water quality characteristics were measured, including temperature, dissolved oxygen, salinity, nutrients, metals, and fecal coliforms.

SOURCE: Environment Canada. (1995). *Fraser River Action Plan: Measuring the health of the river.* Vancouver, p. 12.

FREMP was "invaluable to the development of a Canadian approach to CZM" (Hildebrand, 1989, p. 9).

With an improved understanding of the interrelationship of ecosystem components came the realization that, to properly manage the Fraser River estuary, comprehensive planning and management of the entire Fraser River basin was required. In 1991, the Fraser River Action Plan (FRAP) was established under Canada's Green Plan with the objective of developing a management plan for the remainder of the Fraser basin (see Chapter 7). Coordinated initiatives such as FREMP and FRAP offer promise for promoting sound environmental planning and management in other coastal regions of Canada where development and allocation conflicts are intensifying.

Growing demand from the public to become involved in environmental decision making and increasing concern about the quality of Atlantic Canada's waters provided the stimulus for the Atlantic Coastal Action Program (ACAP). Established in 1991 as a 6-year, $10-million project under Canada's Green Plan, ACAP calls upon local community initiative to achieve its central objective of ensuring a sustainable future. Three interdependent key initiatives— planning, education, and local action—were identified at the first ACAP conservation workshop and all 13 ACAP community groups recognized the importance of combining these initiatives in the projects they undertook.

All ACAP projects are community owned and organized with all stakeholders, from governments to interested citizens, participating as equal partners. The federal government provided seed money of up to $50 000 per year to start and maintain each local ACAP community initiative. The enthusiasm of local communities towards the ACAP process was witnessed by the rapid start-up of initiatives, the diverse number of participating stakeholders, and the pace at which plans were developed (Hildebrand, 1993). (For information on how to contact ACAP, see the Additional Information Sources section at the end of this chapter.)

CANADIAN PARTNERSHIPS AND LOCAL ACTIONS

In the early 1990s, the towns of Chatham and Newcastle continued to discharge both treated and untreated sewage into the Miramichi River in northeastern New Brunswick. In addition, the Repap Miramichi Pulp and Paper mill discharged its treated industrial and domestic effluent directly into the river at the mill site. Among other effects, these sewage discharges caused ongoing shellfish harvesting closures in the lower estuary of the river.

Historically, local residents had encountered problems in determining who was responsible for dealing with their environmental concerns about the Miramichi River. Wanting to do something about this situation, the Miramichi River Environmental Assessment Committee (MREAC) became an ACAP community group. One of the first things MREAC did was to establish a River Watch program, which, by 1993, included a public phone-in service called the River Watch Line. By simply calling 1-800-RIVER, the proper government department or organization was contacted, and callers received the information they required. With ACAP financial assistance, MREAC provided this toll-free service to give local people easy access to environmental information and to share their expertise with residents. Water quality assessments were added to the River Watch program in 1994 as MREAC trained and equipped volunteers to patrol the Miramichi River by boat and to monitor water quality. A seasonal Swim Watch program monitored and informed the public of the water quality at key swimming locations (Environment Canada, n.d.c).

These actions from the government–community partnership demonstrate the effort not only to support development of local knowledge and application of environmental, social, and economic information to decision making in the Miramichi watershed, but also to improve health and sustainability of the Miramichi watershed and receiving oceans waters for the benefit of future generations.

The Islands Trust in British Columbia provides another example of the importance of local residents' involvement in planning and development to help achieve sustainability in a marine environment. The islands in the Strait of Georgia and Howe Sound are recognized nationally for their beauty, tranquillity, and unique natural environments. In 1974, the government of British Columbia enacted special protective legislation entitled the Islands Trust Act, which recognized these special qualities. The act states that the objective of the Islands Trust is to "preserve and protect the trust area [of approximately 5178 square kilometres] and its unique amenities and environment for the benefit of the residents of the trust area and of the Province generally, in cooperation with municipalities, and organizations, and the government of the Province" (cited in Islands Trust, 1995). On April 1, 1990, the act was amended to establish the Islands Trust as an autonomous local government agency with land use planning and regulatory authority.

Given its mandate to "preserve and protect ... for the benefit of the residents," the Islands Trust spent more than two years developing its policy statement based on public forums and public comment on drafts of the policy statement. Public forums identified six themes that captured the concerns of Island Trust area residents: fresh water, resources and environment, growth and development, community, local control, and government.

Throughout the policy development and public consultation process used to formulate the policy statement, residents and trust members alike were educated about the social and environmental challenges facing the area and were encouraged to consider environment and development issues simultaneously. This process stimulated public thinking about issues such as marine pollution, about how to encourage stewardship, and about the meaning and use of ecosystem approaches to achieve protection of the Islands Trust area (Crance, 1995). As a coordinating agency that combines regulatory and non-regulatory functions to achieve its objectives, the Islands Trust is a good example of effective agency–community partnership in action at the local level.

Two large land claims agreements in the Arctic have demonstrated a federal–territorial–Aboriginal partnership system that fosters integrated decision making in marine management. Conservation and sustainability are promoted by the use of co-management (cooperative management) in both the Inuvialuit and Nunavut final agreements, which together cover more than half the Arctic coastline. This joint-management approach to marine conservation and sustainable development offers important keys to success in co-management on the east and west coasts, should fishers and managers there agree on its value. (A recognition of the need to move toward cooperative approaches perhaps was seen in the pool system set up in 1995 to limit the catch and share the profit from the Barkeley Sound herring fishery.)

Canadian partnerships have involved governments, agencies, First Nations, coastal communities, and industrial interests. One example is the first fish habitat bank completed in 1992 on the North Fraser River, a joint initiative of the Department of Fisheries and Oceans and the North Fraser Harbour Commission (Fish habitat bank, 1994). The 1988 North Fraser Harbour Environmental Management Plan helps ensure that environmental considerations are an integral part of waterfront development in the harbour. Specifically, construction of compensation habitat is required prior to approval of a project, thus complementing the no net loss principle of the Department of Fisheries and Oceans national habitat policy.

The importance of nutrient-rich marshes for juvenile salmon on their way to sea is well known, and the North Fraser River was lacking in such environments. In this project, almost two kilometres of what was once heavily industrialized foreshore of the Fraser River was reworked to build marsh habitat that would protect fish habitat and river bank vegetation. Development of the Fraser Lands Riverfront Park, which also included boardwalks and a park for people, involved installing a low rock berm parallel to the shore and backfilling with sandy soil to create an intertidal beach to support the growing marsh. About 14 000 plants were planted in the marsh, and native plants and grasses were used in creating the fish habitat and park area.

Even though the working aspect of the Fraser River is giving way to urban uses, the logging industry still floats its logs and log booms down the river; wave action from other boat traffic erodes the river banks, and debris smothers the marshes. Historically, the Department of Fisheries and Oceans did not support storing logs next to marshes because bark settled into the marshes and the logs themselves grounded on the marsh. However, log storage farther away in the river actually helps break the waves down and keeps debris off the marsh. By 1994, two years into its operation, monitoring showed a healthy, successful marsh project (Fish habitat bank, 1994).

Canadian partnerships for marine environmental protection have extended to other nations as well. Ocean Voice International is an Ottawa-based ENGO with international and Canadian activities. Their use of Geographic information Systems (GIS) is an important element in enhancing data collection as well as the effectiveness of marine conservation efforts.

FUTURE CHALLENGES

What would characterize a sustainable future for Canadian oceans and fisheries? A number of points may be identified, including deliberate application of an ecosystem-based approach to management, ethical principles, including interpersonal and intergenerational equity, appropriate technology, and an improved science with clear and objective data. Other features would include achievement of a tolerable level of human pressure on natural resources and ecosystems, an acceptable quality of life (which recognizes the interdependence of humans and their environment), the maintenance of diversity, and people striving cooperatively together toward agreed-on goals that meet environmental, social, and economic objectives.

As the examples in this chapter have illustrated, human developmental activities in and relating to marine environments have resulted in a wide variety of impacts on coastal waters and species. International, national, regional, and local agreements and actions are helping the movement toward resolution of some of these impacts, while work continues on other problems. In general, however, challenges for the future regarding sustainability of Canada's oceans and fisheries resources and environments lie in ongoing efforts to improve our stewardship, protection and monitoring, and knowledge-building activities.

Stewardship, the management of oceans and fisheries resources so that they are conserved for future generations, requires an active, shared awareness of both ethical principles and ecosystem principles on which safeguarding the future of marine environments depends. Equity and respect for all other users of oceans and fisheries resources, and a holistic understanding of ecosystems and their interdependencies at all levels, are among the characteristics required to develop attitudes and practices that

will help achieve a sustainable future. This is as true for professional fishers as it is for recreational users. One related challenge arising here is to educate everyone who uses or impacts marine environments to include care and respect not only for themselves, but also for other people, and the interacting ecosphere, in their decisions.

New ocean agreements, such as Canada's Oceans Act, that are designed to work toward and achieve sustainability, and new fishing management agreements (such as the UNCLOS agreement regarding conservation and management of straddling and highly migratory fish stocks) that are intended to limit overconsumption of particular fish species and stocks, are stewardship practices. Follow-through is required in both instances, however, to ensure the agreements are put in place and enforced. Increasingly—and this applies to all environments, not just oceans and fisheries resources—stewardship implies that the necessary attitudinal characteristics on the part of individuals, agencies, corporations, and governments should include awareness of human impacts, receptivity to change, accountability for decisions taken, and acceptance of responsibility to rectify any negative impacts.

Sustainability depends on many related factors, some of which are little understood or poorly defined, and most of which are very difficult to predict. If Canada's oceans and fisheries resources and environments are going to be protected for the future, monitoring efforts need to be incorporated for measuring the environmental, social, and economic parameters of our development activities. In addition, monitoring effects of variables ranging from effluent discharges to climate change will, over time, help us overcome the problem of inadequate data on which to base management decisions (although this is no guarantee that the acquired knowledge will satisfy the questions that need to be answered). In the meantime, as Canada and other countries present at the 1992 Earth Summit recognized, when the "weight of evidence" suggests that action to protect the environment should be taken to prevent serious or irreversible damage, then the lack of full scientific "proof" is not a reason to postpone measures to prevent that degradation. In light of this precautionary principle, perhaps the Fisheries Minister's actions in regard to protection of turbot stocks were appropriate, if not appreciated by all those ultimately affected by his decisions.

Observer programs for fisheries (as in the case of European Union vessels and others who fish stocks that cross the Canadian 200-mile limit), and the establishment and application of standards for various types of coastal development activity including housing construction, port expansion, and other infrastructural facilities, are means by which marine protection can be promoted. A shared sense of the responsibility for establishing and effectively implementing programs and regulatory mechanisms to ensure continued ecological functioning of marine environments should enable all parties to cooperate and achieve desired common goals, including sustainability. An important part of any cooperative effort is the ability to anticipate what our future needs might be, what impacts climate change might have on marine environments, for instance, and the ability to develop appropriately sensitive environmental protection and monitoring approaches and devices. Protection measures also can be applied to those marine environments that have been restored or rehabilitated.

Given the lack of knowledge of fundamental as well as more sophisticated elements of marine ecosystems and species functions, a key current and future challenge is to enhance research programs and data collection opportunities to build the necessary knowledge. Partnerships at all levels are appropriate here, and are particularly valu-able when they involve First Nations' traditional ecological knowledge (TEK), and the knowledge of fishers and others with long-term experience in marine environments. Opening up the research process to include TEK and the environmental understanding and contributions of people with extensive fishing experience should enable a fuller appreciation of stock status and regeneration methods, for example, as well as an earlier identification of critical gaps in knowledge. Additionally, support for and participation of those affected by decisions will encourage meaningful domestic (and perhaps international) partnerships in identifying alternative economic and employment opportunities.

Chapter Questions

1. Most biological productivity in the oceans occurs near continents, in areas of upwelling currents, on continental shelves, or near river estuaries. For each of the Arctic, Atlantic, and Pacific oceans, identify the kinds of threats that Canadians and their activities (on land and sea) pose to these areas of biological richness.

2. Fish do not respect political or administrative boundaries such as the 200-nautical-mile limit to Canada's Exclusive Economic Zone. What difficulties does this characteristic of fish bring to efforts to protect transboundary fish stocks from overharvesting? What are the implications for sustainability of fish stocks?

3. Discuss the effects that the El Niño phenomenon can have on the west coast fisheries and ocean environment.

4. In what ways can scientific research help us make decisions that will enhance the sustainability of oceans and their resources?

5. Debate the value of the precautionary principle or approach in dealing with international and national oceans and fisheries issues.

6. If you live in a coastal area, identify one or more examples where human activities have impacted or could impact negatively on the sustainability of oceans or fishery resources. What kinds of action were taken (or could be taken) to address the issue(s)? What could you do to make a difference in a current issue?

references

Alexandrowicz, G. (1995). *Law of the Sea: A Canadian practitioner's handbook.* Kingston, ON: Faculty of Law, Queen's University. http://qsilver.queensu.ca/law.seati.htm

Beckmann, L. (1995). Marine conservation—keeping the Arctic Ocean on the agenda. *Northern Perspectives,* 23(1), pp. 1–2.

Beckmann, L. (1996). *Seas the day: Towards a national marine conservation strategy for Canada.* Ottawa: Canadian Arctic Resources Committee/Canadian Nature Federation.

Begley, L. (Ed.). (1993). *Crossing that bridge: A critical look at the P.E.I. fixed link.* Charlottetown: Ragweed Press.

Bell, J. (1995, September 16). Former destroyer to be sunk off Sidney today. *Victoria Times Colonist,* p. B3.

Blades, K. (1995). *Net destruction: The death of Atlantic Canada's fishery.* Halifax: Nimbus Publishing.

Brocklehurst, A. (1996). It's not easy being green. *Canadian Geographic,* 116(3), pp. 40, 41.

PART 3:
RESOURCES FOR CANADA'S FUTURE

Bryden, J. (1995a, March 14). Ship loaded with tiny turbot. *Calgary Herald*, p. A2.

Bryden, J. (1995b, March 29). Canada delivers proof of "ecological madness." *Calgary Herald*, p. A3.

Bryden, J. (1995c, March 29). Lonely, unloved turbot clinging by its fingernails, Tobin says. http://www.southam.com/nmc/waves/depth/fishery/turbot032295.html

Canadian Press and Associated Press. (1995, December 12). Millions of kilos of seafood dumped in sea. *Victoria Times Colonist*, p. D8.

Carscadden, J.E., Frank, K.T., & Miller, D.S. (1989). Capelin (Mallotus villosus) spawning on the southeast shoal: Influence of physical factors past and present. *Canadian Journal of Fisheries and Aquatic Sciences*, 46, pp. 1743–54.

Conservation Council of New Brunswick. (1995). Respecting nature and community: Beyond crisis in the fisheries. *Ecological Fisheries Project Bulletin*, (3). http://www.web.apc.org/~nben/ecofish.htm

Cox, K. (1996, March 16). Who won the great turbot war? http://www.docuweb.ca/~pardos/globe.html

Crance, C. (1995). Government coordinating agencies in Canadian coastal planning and management: The Islands Trust and the Waterfront Regeneration Trust. Unpublished M.A. thesis, Wilfrid Laurier University.

Day, J.C., & Gamble, D.B. (1990). Coastal zone management in British Columbia: An institutional comparison with Washington, Oregon, and California. *Coastal Management*, 18, pp. 115–41.

Demont, J. (1992, July 13). When the future died. *Maclean's*, 105(28), pp. 15–16.

Department of Environment. (n.d.). Sustainability for commercial fisheries. http://www.ns.doe.ca/soe/ch6-43.html

Department of Fisheries and Oceans. (1994). *Fisheries facts: Pacific region (for 1992)*. Vancouver: Department of Fisheries and Oceans.

Department of Fisheries and Oceans. (1995a). Tobin says NAFO must decide equitable sharing arrangement for Greenland halibut. News release, January 27, 1995. http://www.ncr.dfo.ca/communic/newsrel/1995/HQ08E.htm

Department of Fisheries and Oceans. (1995b). Canada wins critical vote on turbot at NAFO. News release, February 2, 1995. http://www.ncr.dfo.ca/communic/newsrel/1995/HQ10E.htm

Department of Fisheries and Oceans. (1995c). Tobin says Canada will not let the EU devastate turbot. News release, February 15, 1995. http://www.ncr.dfo.ca/communic/newsrel/1995/HQ08E.htm

Department of Fisheries and Oceans. (1995d). The fisheries crisis in the northwest Atlantic. *Backgrounder* (July). http://www.ncr.dfo.ca/communic/backgrou/1995/HQ16e.htm

Department of Fisheries and Oceans. (1995e). Tobin comments on U.S. District Court decision on Alaskan chinook fishery. News release, September 12, 1995. http://www.ncr.dfo.ca/communic/newsrel/1995/HQ107E.htm

Department of Fisheries and Oceans. (1995f). Tobin tables Fisheries Act amendments. News release, December 11, 1995. http://www.ncr.dfo.ca/communic/newsrel/1995/HQ140E.htm

Department of Fisheries and Oceans. (1996, May). Commercial catch restrictions and Chinook conservation. *Backgrounder*. http://www.ncr.dfo.ca/communic/backgrou/1966/pr11e.htm

Drilling on Georges Bank. (n.d.) http://biome.bio.dfo.ca/science/drilling.html

Eggen, M. (1997). That sinking feeling. *Alternatives*, 23(1), p. 7.

Environment Canada. (n.d.a). State of the environment in the Atlantic region. http://www.ns.ec.gc.ca/soe/cha4.html

Environment Canada. (n.d.b). Marine plastics debris. http://www.ns.ec.gc.ca/udo/cry.html

Environment Canada. (n.d.c). *ACAP communities in action*. Halifax: Environment Canada.

Environment Canada. (1994). Sustaining marine resources: Pacific herring fish stocks. *SOE Bulletin* No. 94-5. Ottawa: Environment Canada.

Environment Canada. (1995). United Keno Hill Mines impact assessment report (Released). http://yvrwww1.pwc.bc.doe.ca/ep/programs/eppy/yukon/ukhm.html

Environment Canada. (1996a). Corner Brook Pulp and Paper Limited pays $750 000 for pollution violations. http://www.doe.ca/enforce/cor2_p_e.htm

Environment Canada. (1996b). Domtar Specialty Fine Papers charged with alleged violations of the Pulp and Paper Effluent Regulations. http://www.ec.gc.ca/enforce/dom2_p_e.htm

Environment Canada. (1997). Operation Irving Whale. http://www.ns.ec.gc.ca/whale2/index.html

Fish habitat bank completed on the North Fraser. (1994). *Pacific Tidings*, 7(2), pp. 4–5.

Food and Agriculture Organization. (1996). Factfile: Total fish production. http://www.fao.org/news/FACTFILE/Ff9604-e.htm

Food and Agriculture Organization. United Nations. (1997a). The state of world fisheries and aquaculture (Sofia)—1996. Summary. http://www.fao.org/waicent/faoinfo/fishery/publ/sofia/safflye.htm

Food and Agriculture Organization. United Nations. (1997b). Code of conduct for responsible fisheries. http://www.fao.org/waicent/faoinfo/fishing/agreem/codecond/codecon.htm

Fraser River Action Plan. (n.d.). Fact Sheet 2: Pollution in the Fraser. http://yvrwww1.pwc.bc.doe.ca/ec/frap/fr-fs2.html.

Frazer, S. (1992, May). When all the fish were gone. *Canadian Forum*, 71(809), pp. 14–17.

Gerges, M.A. Marine pollution monitoring, assessment and control: UNEPs approach and strategy. *Marine Pollution Bulletin*, 28(4), pp. 199–210.

Gessell, P. (1995, June 22). Turbot war has high net cost for Canada. http://www.southam.com/nmc/waves/depth/fishery/turbot062295.html

Gidney, N. (1995, September 27). Mackenzie goes below as artificial reef. *Victoria Times Colonist,* p. A7.

Gillmor, D. (1990). A fine kettle of fish. *Equinox* (July–August), pp. 66–75.

Golden, S. (1993). Shetland tanker spill worries Canadian fish farmers. *Alternatives,* 19(4), p. 13.

Gomes, M.C. (1995). Turbot affair: The EC vs Canada. Message posted on fish-ecology mailing list of the Bedford Institute of Oceanography, March 20, 1995. http://hed.bio.ns.ca/lists/war/msg00050.html

Government of Canada. (1991). *The state of Canada's environment—1991.* Ottawa: Supply and Services Canada.

Harris, L. (1993). Seeking equilibrium: An historical glance at aspects of the Newfoundland fisheries. In K. Storey (Ed.). *The Newfoundland groundfish fisheries: Defining the reality; Conference Proceedings.* (pp. 1–8). St. John's: Institute of Social and Economic Research, Memorial University of Newfoundland.

Haysom, I. (1997, June 15). Fished out: Centuries of harvesting seas are nearing end, book warns. *Calgary Herald,* p. A2.

Hildebrand, L.P. (1989). *Canada's experience with coastal zone management.* Halifax: Oceans Institute of Canada.

Hildebrand, L.P. (1993). Coastal zone management in Canada—the next generation. In P.L. Lawrence & J.G. Nelson (Eds.). *Managing the Great Lakes shoreline: Experiences and opportunities.* (pp. 13–30). Waterloo, ON: University of Waterloo Heritage Resources Centre.

Howard, R. (1997, June 28). "Vigorous but not aggressive" quotas set for salmon catch. *The Globe and Mail,* p. A5.

International Development Research Centre (IDRC). (n.d.). *Ocean facts: Land-based sources of ocean pollution.* Ottawa: IDRC.

Islands Trust. (1995). An introduction to the Islands Trust. Victoria: Islands Trust. http://www.civicnet.gov.bc.ca/muni/istrust.html

Jandl, T. (n.d.). Turbot dispute between Spain and Canada (turbot case). http://gurukul.ucc.american.edu/TED/TURBOT.HTM

Kenny, E. (1995, July 11). East, west disputes oceans apart. *Victoria Times Colonist,* p. A5.

Kinloch, D., Kuhnlein, H., & Muir, D. (1988). Assessment of PCBs in Arctic foods and diet: A pilot study in Broughton Island, NWT, Canada. *Arctic Medical Research,* 47 (Supplement 1): pp. 159–62.

Lean, G., & Hinrichson, D. (1992). *Atlas of the environment.* Oxford: Helicon Publishing.

Leith, B. (1995). The social cost of sustainability: Distribution and equity in environmental policy. *Alternatives,* 21(1), pp. 18–24.

Masterman, B. (1996, June 3). Rules anger industry. *Victoria Times Colonist,* p. C7.

McCay, B.J. (1978). Systems ecology, people ecology and the anthropology of fishing communities. *Human Ecology,* 6(4), pp. 397–422.

McCay, B.J., & Finlayson, A.C. (1995). The political ecology of crisis and institutional change: The case of the northern cod. Paper presented at the Annual Meeting of the American Anthropological Association, Washington, DC. http://www.lib.uconn.edu/ArcticCircle/NatResources/cod/mckay.html

Meissner, D. (1995, March 1). Boat owners set to throw book at roe protesters. *Victoria Times Colonist,* p. B2.

Meltzer, E. (1995). *Overview of the east coast marine environment.* Ottawa: Canadian Arctic Resources Committee/Canadian Nature Federation.

Minister of Supply and Services. (1996). Canadian Environmental Protection Act: Report for the period April 1994 to March 1995. Ottawa: Minister of Supply and Services. http://www.doe.ca/cepa

Murphy, P. (1997, July 9). El Niño's coming and it's going to be hot. *Victoria Times Colonist,* p. A2.

National Advisory Board on Science and Technology. (1994). *Opportunities from our oceans.* Report of the Committee on Oceans and Coasts. Ottawa: National Advisory Board on Science and Technology.

Obee, B. (1996). Fragile havens for millions of shorebirds. *Beautiful British Columbia,* 38(2), pp. 24–29.

Olsen, S. (1996, February 29). The primary habitat of our species. *Providence Journal-Bulletin.* http://brooktrout.gso.uri.edu/ProJoEd.html

Pacific fisheries for tomorrow. (1995). *Pacific Tidings,* 7(3), pp. 5–6.

Paisley, R.K. (1994). *Regional marine issues overview paper—west coast.* Ottawa: Canadian Arctic Resources Committee/Canadian Nature Federation.

Parfit, M. (1995). Diminishing returns: Exploiting the ocean's bounty. *National Geographic,* 188(5), pp. 2–37.

Population: A growing problem for the Fraser Basin. (n.d.). Fraser River Action Plan Fact Sheet. http://yvrwww1.pwc.bc.doe.ca/ec/frap/fr-fs2.html

Public Works and Government Services Canada and Strait Crossing Development Inc. (n.d.). *Northumberland Strait Crossing Project: Information package.*

Public Works and Government Services Canada. (1997). Northumberland Strait crossing project: A link to the future. http://cycor.ca/nscp/index-e.html

Revel, B. (n.d.). The fish: The Greenland halibut, or turbot. http://www.sfu.ca/~revela/thefish.htm

Robinson, B. (1995, October 15). Healthy ecology rides on the salmon. *Victoria Times Colonist,* p. F2.

Saving the wild chinook. (1995). *Pacific Tidings,* 8(2), pp. 3–4.

Schmelz, A. (1995, November 25). Consortium will build billion-dollar bridge link. *Calgary Herald,* p. A9.

Schram, G.G., & Polunin, N. (1995). The high seas "commons": Imperative regulation of half our planet's surface. *Environment Conservation,* 22(1), p. 3.

Sinclair, M., & Page, F. (n.d.). Cod fishery collapses and North Atlantic GLOBEC. http://www.usglobec.berkeley.edu/usglobec/news/news8/news8sinclair.html

Stokoe, P., LeBlanc, M., Larson, C., Manzer, M., & Manuel, P. (1990). *Implications of climate change small coastal communities in Atlantic Canada.* Ottawa: Environment Canada.

Strait Crossing Team. (n.d.). The Northumberland Strait Bridge. http://www.peinet.pe.ca /SCI

Stop high seas plunder. (1995, December 12). *Victoria Times Colonist,* p. A4.

Thurston, H. (1997). Steps across the strait. *Canadian Geographic* (March–April), pp. 52–60.

Tobin, B. (1994). *A vision for ocean mangement.* Ottawa: Fisheries and Oceans.

Welch, H.E. (1995). Marine conservation in the Canadian Arctic: A regional overview. *Northern Perspectives,* 25(1), pp. 5–17.

World Commission on Environment and Development. (1987). *Our Common Future.* Oxford: Oxford University Press.

additional information sources

Atlantic Coastal Action Program
Environment Canada
4th Floor, Queen Square
45 Aderney Drive
Dartmouth, NS B2Y 2N6

Fisheries Resources Conservation Council.
http://www.ncr.dfo.ca/frcc/index.htm

Government of Canada. (1996). *The state of Canada's environment—1996.* Ottawa: Supply and Services Canada.

McBean, G.A., Slaymaker, O., Northcote, T., LeBlond, P., & Parsons, T.S. (1992). *Review of models for climate change and impacts on hydrology, coastal currents and fisheries in B.C.* Downsview, ON: Canadian Climate Centre.

McGillivray, D.G., Agnew, T.A., McKay, G.A., Pilkington, G.R. & Hill, M.C. (1993). *Impacts of climate change on the Beaufort Sea-ice regime: Implications for the Arctic petroleum industry.* Downsview, ON: Canadian Climate Centre.

Welbourn, K. (1995). Outports and outlaws. *Equinox,* 83 (October), pp. 34–43.

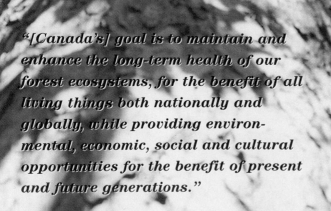

CHAPTER 9

Forests

Chapter Contents

CHAPTER OBJECTIVES   273
INTRODUCTION   273
   Focal Point: Clayoquot Sound   275
THE EARTH'S FORESTS   277
   Global Distribution, Products, and
     Demand   277
   Forests in Canada   278
       Harvesting Systems   282
         Tree Plantations   284
       The Timber Bias   284
       The Falldown Effect   287
THE ECOLOGICAL IMPORTANCE OF
  OLD-GROWTH FORESTS   289
   The Life Cycle in the Old-Growth
     Forest   289
       Standing Live Trees, Snags, and Fallen
        Trees   289
   Carbon Storage   290
   Keys to Diversity   290
       Biological Diversity   291
   The Need for Protection   291
HUMAN ACTIVITIES AND IMPACTS ON
  FOREST ENVIRONMENTS   292
   A Brief Historical Overview of the Forest
     Industry   293
       First Nations and European
        Settlers   293
       Timber Exports and Government
        Ownership   293
       Changing Market Demands, Changing
        Industry   293
       The Shifting Frontier and
        Conservation Concerns   294
       Licensing and Increasing Concen-
        tration of Forest Holdings   294
       Growth in Pulp and Paper   295
       Sustained Yield Focus   295
       Continuing Concentration of Control
        over Harvesting Rights   295
   Timber Production Activities and
     Impacts   295
       Habitat, Wildlife, and Life-Support
        Impacts   296

"[Canada's] goal is to maintain and enhance the long-term health of our forest ecosystems, for the benefit of all living things both nationally and globally, while providing environmental, economic, social and cultural opportunities for the benefit of present and future generations."

Canadian Council of Forest Ministers (1992)

Degradation and Deforestation of
Tropical Forests   300
Pollution   303
Sociocultural Dimensions   304
Tourism and Recreation   304
Other Human Impacts   306
RESPONSES TO ENVIRONMENTAL IMPACTS
AND CHANGE   307
International Initiatives   307
UNCED Forest Principles   307
Agenda 21   308
UNCED Conventions and Other
Responses   308
Canadian Policy, Practice, and
Partnerships   309
Canada's National Forest Strategy   309
Canada's Model Forest Program   313
Criteria and Indicators of Sustainable
Forest Management   313
Local Partnerships and Responses   315
Wildlife and Forestry Activity   315
An Ecoadventure in Clayoquot
Sound   316
FUTURE CHALLENGES   316
Chapter Questions   320
References   321
Additional Information Sources   323

Chapter Objectives

After studying this chapter you should be able to

- understand the nature and distribution of Canada's forest resources
- identify a range of human uses of forest resources
- describe the impacts of human activities on forests and forest environments
- appreciate the complexity and interrelatedness of forest environment issues
- outline Canadian and international responses to forest issues
- discuss challenges to a sustainable future for forest resources in Canada

INTRODUCTION

A s biologically diverse as the people who live here, Canada's forests are a symbol of our national heritage. From the lofty Douglas fir and Sitka spruce in the old-growth temperate rain forests of British Columbia and the rare sassafras and endangered cucumber trees in the Carolinian forests of southern Ontario, to the ground-hugging black spruce, jack pine, and tamarack of the Boreal forest that drapes "like a great green scarf across the shoulders of North America," forests continue to enrich the lives of all Canadians (Natural Resources Canada, 1996a).

More than 330 communities and 880 000 people are supported economically by Canada's forests (Natural Resources Canada, 1996b, c). Yet, employment figures are only part of the story of the values, products, and services associated with forests. Forests are more than trees and a source of timber and fibre for newsprint. Left standing, forests are complex systems that provide many important ecological services such as moderating climate (carbon storage), improving air quality, stabilizing soil, regulating water flow, protecting aquatic ecosystems (in rivers and streams), and providing habitats for plants, fish, and wildlife, including nesting and breeding grounds for many migratory bird species (Environment Canada, 1995a; McKibben, 1996; Sierra Club of Canada, 1996).

Recreation and tourism are increasingly important forest commodities, and the spiritual and cultural values of the forest, long important to First Nations peoples, are of prime interest to Canadians and visitors seeking solitude and sanctuary from urban lifestyles (Davidson, 1996). Specific life forms such as large trees and marbled murrelets also are important forest values. (For more information on forest ecosystem-based values, see Table 9–1.)

If Canadian forests are going to continue to provide jobs, recreation, places of spiritual refuge, and wildlife habitat, then a central concern is to maintain the biological diversity on which the multiple benefits and roles of forests depend. In turn, conserving biodiversity requires forest management to sustain the health and productivity of forest ecosystems. Within the past two to three decades, a major challenge—internationally as well as in Canada—has been to develop an understanding of the complex environmental, economic, social, and political dimensions of forests. Both national and provincial governments in Canada have responded to the growing public concern regarding forests and the environment, and have taken action intended to shift forest management from its historical focus on sustaining output levels for specific forest products toward sustainability of forest ecosystems that protect timber and nontimber values of Canada's forests.

TABLE 9-1
FOREST ECOSYSTEM-BASED VALUES

Forest Value	Comment
Air Quality	Most life on earth depends on a unique chemical reaction—photosynthesis—that happens inside the cells of green plants. The green pigment chlorophyll combines carbon dioxide gas from the air with water from the soil to produce carbohydrates and oxygen. Since plants began to photosynthesize, almost all life has relied on this reaction to produce food, generate oxygen, and remove carbon dioxide. The oxygen people breathe comes from green plants; large forests are major producers of oxygen and also filter pollutants from the air.
Water and Soil	Forests act like massive pumps, helping to recycle water, making it repeatedly available for plant growth. Through this action and their extensive rooting systems, forests also help to maintain a regular pattern of water flow in streams and reduce erosion, thus helping to maintain soils and their nutrients. In doing so they help maintain stream conditions favourable for fish and other species.
Climate	Forests capture carbon dioxide and store vast amounts of carbon which might otherwise accumulate in the atmosphere and contribute to global warming. By producing oxygen and absorbing carbon dioxide forests provide a vital air-conditioning service to the planet.
Biodiversity	Natural (unmanaged) forests are remarkably rich in species. Survival of many species depends on the structural complexity and variety of habitats found in old, natural forests. Managed forests are deliberately simplified to make management easier. This simplification alters resident biodiversity, sometimes dramatically.
Scenic Values	People experience scenery over a large area. Thus, to understand scenic resources, it is necessary to look at broad patterns in the landscape. For residents, scenery provides a backdrop to their lives and reflects on their lifestyles. For tourists, scenic resources often provide the context for a trip or recreational activity. Forests are part of many of the world's most highly valued landscapes. To many people, removal of the forest reduces scenic resource values.
Cultural and Spiritual Values	Forests have values that go beyond specific resource attributes, such as the presence of large trees or deer. They provide traditional foods, materials, and medicinal plants important to indigenous cultures. As systems, they provide a context in which physical and spiritual events take place. Because of their longevity and many values, forests often form part of the cultural identity of the people who inhabit or live near them.
Economic Values	Forests provide many goods, such as wood and its diverse products, fish, wildlife, and water—all of which support human society. The sale of forest products and forest-based experiences generates funds that support health, education, and other social services.
Intergenerational Values	Many forest trees, especially those in the Pacific Northwest, are potentially long-lived, some reaching ages greater than 1000 years. Thus, the values associated with any individual forest can benefit several human generations. Values attributed to forests have changed over human history, and it is reasonable to expect that they will continue to change. The obligation of current generations is to sustain forest systems without damaging their potential value for future generations.

SOURCE: Adapted from Clayoquot Sound Scientific Panel. (1995). *A vision and its context: Global context for forest practices in Clayoquot Sound.* Report 4 of the Scientific Panel for Sustainable Forest Practices in Clayoquot Sound. Victoria: B.C. Ministry of Forests, p. 4. Reprinted by permission.

A researcher examines a 320-year-old Douglas fir in Canada's temperate rain forest.

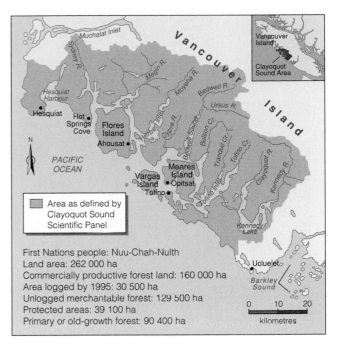

Figure 9–1

Clayoquot Sound area: location and selected statistics, 1995

SOURCE: Clayoquot Sound Scientific Panel. (1995). *A vision and its context: Global context for forest practices in Clayoquot Sound.* Report 4 of the Scientific Panel for Sustainable Forest Practices in Clayoquot Sound. Victoria: B.C. Ministry of Forests, pp. i, 7. Reprinted by permission.

First Nations people: Nuu-Chah-Nulth
Land area: 262 000 ha
Commercially productive forest land: 160 000 ha
Area logged by 1995: 30 500 ha
Unlogged merchantable forest: 129 500 ha
Protected areas: 39 100 ha
Primary or old-growth forest: 90 400 ha

FOCAL POINT: CLAYOQUOT SOUND

In British Columbia, and internationally, the Clayoquot (pronounced *klak-wot*) Sound area became an important focal point in the conflict over forest values and issues of environmental and economic sustainability. Located on the west coast of Vancouver Island, British Columbia (Figure 9–1), the Clayoquot Sound area is rich in forest values, including spectacular natural, unmanaged forests, a long history of First Nations' settlement, world-class scenic and tourism resources, and major commercial fishery and timber industries.

Over 60 percent of the Clayoquot Sound area is assessed as commercially productive forest land and about 20 percent of that has been clear-cut logged. In 1995, about 70 percent (or 90 400 hectares) of the remaining unlogged, merchantable forest was primary or old-growth forest (Clayoquot Sound Scientific Panel, 1995). Old growth is a necessary phase in the life of any forest and is vital to ensure the perpetuation of forests in Canada. (The ecological importance of old-growth forests is explained in a later section.)

In the summer of 1993, thousands of concerned citizens and environmentalists from British Columbia and the world congregated at Clayoquot Sound to protest the British Columbia government's decision to allow major timber companies to clear-cut log more than two-thirds of the sound's rain forests (Box 9–1). "Grandmothers, lawyers, students, politicians, housewives and ex-loggers stood shoulder-to-shoulder to defend this symbol of B.C.'s rapidly disappearing ancient forests and wild places" (Clayoquot Rainforest Coalition, 1995). In their attempts to stop the clear-cutting, over 850 people were arrested (some jailed and later fined) for defying court orders that outlawed the blockading of logging roads (Curtis, 1996; Morell, 1994). "It was the largest expression of civil disobedience in Canadian history" (Western Canada Wilderness Committee, 1994, 1; Devall, 1993).

Since then, the provincial government has accepted the advice of the Scientific Panel for Sustainable Forest Practices in Clayoquot Sound, to "make forest practices in the Clayoquot not only the best in the province, but the best in the world" (cited in Clayoquot Sound Scientific Panel, 1995, p. 1). While this challenge is an appropriate one, it is clear that the panel's mandate did not permit examination of the larger scientific question of whether commercial logging in Clayoquot Sound should take place

BOX 9-1

OVERVIEW OF UNLOGGED FLORES ISLAND, CLAYOQUOT SOUND, CONTRASTED WITH CLEARCUT AREA
ON NORTHWEST COAST OF VANCOUVER ISLAND

These photographs were part of a Clayoquot opinion poll post-card used by the Western Canada Wilderness Committee to encourage people to let Prime Minister Jean Chrétien know how they felt about the clear-cutting of Clayoquot Sound.

SOURCE: Western Canada Wilderness Committee, Vancouver. http://www.wilderness committee.org

at all. Given the significance of the old-growth forests in Clayoquot Sound as a bank for genetic variability, as a wildlife sanctuary, and as a place of cultural and spiritual importance, among other values, this omission is notable.

A large part of the local and international concern about Clayoquot Sound arose because of its significance within the coastal temperate rain forest biome. Although they are found around the world in places such as Chile, Norway, and Tasmania, coastal temperate rain forests are a rare forest type, originally covering less than 0.2 percent of the Earth's land surface. British Columbia forests contain an estimated 18 to 25 percent of the world's coastal temperate rain forests (Kellogg, 1992). About 60 percent of the world's unlogged coastal temperate rain forests and over 95 percent of the unlogged coastal temperate rain forests in the Pacific Northwest occur in British Columbia and Alaska (cited in Clayoquot Sound Scientific Panel, 1995). (The Pacific Northwest is that geographical region including southeast Alaska, British Columbia, Washington, Oregon, Idaho, western Montana, and northern California.)

In North America, the distribution of these globally important, vigorously growing forests is centred on Vancouver Island and "attains its most dramatic expression around Clayoquot Sound" (Clayoquot Sound Scientific Panel, 1995, p. 8). Tall trees are evidence of this "dramatic expression"—for example, the two tallest western red cedars in British Columbia (59.2 and 56.4 metres), the tallest Sitka spruce (95.7 metres), the tallest Douglas fir (82.9 metres), the tallest western hemlock (75.6 metres), and the two tallest yellow cedars (45.4 and 44 metres) are located near Clayoquot Sound (Clayoquot Sound Scientific Panel, 1995). In addition, as scientists have begun to study the complexity of forest ecology, including the canopies of coastal rain forests, they have discovered hundreds of new species that previously were unknown to science (M'Gonigle & Parfitt, 1994; Moffett, 1997).

The controversy over the use and management of forests in Clayoquot Sound reflected the growing international concern for sustainability of forests and their ecosystem-based values. As we shall see in the following sections, awareness of the importance of forests in the global environment has created new obligations for Canada in helping to find solutions to forest issues abroad and at home. This chapter also reviews the state of Canada's forests, identifies the impacts human use and activities have had on forest resources, and notes the efforts of governments, partnerships, and local groups to resolve forest issues. Important new initiatives to broaden the vision of forests and their values are considered also. First, however, we need to appreciate the distribution of the Earth's forests as well as Canada's forests.

Among the tallest trees in Canada's west coast forests are the western red cedar, sitka spruce, Douglas fir, western hemlock, and yellow cedar.

THE EARTH'S FORESTS

GLOBAL DISTRIBUTION, PRODUCTS, AND DEMAND

About 40 percent of the Earth's land surface supports trees or shrub cover. Forests occupy about 3.4 billion hectares (27 percent), and open woodland and mixed vegetation occupy almost 1.7 billion hectares. The former U.S.S.R. contains the largest concentration of forests and wooded areas (942 million hectares), followed by North America (749 million hectares), Europe (195 million hectares), and the Pacific nations of Australia, Japan, and New Zealand (178 million hectares). Combined, the forests of Brazil, Russia, the United States, and Canada contain more than 50 percent of the Earth's forests (Natural Resources Canada, 1996a).

Globally, forests may be classified as temperate, boreal, or tropical (Figure 9–2). Tropical forests, found between the tropics of Cancer and Capricorn, are the most species-diverse ecosystem in the world, containing more than 50 percent of all living species on this planet (cited in Natural Resources Canada, 1996b). During the 1980s, as dramatic satellite imagery showed, the area of tropical forests declined by an average of 15.4 million hectares annually, mainly as a result of the clearing of land for agricultural use in developing nations. In 1990, tropical forests occupied about 1.79 billion hectares, while boreal and temperate forests occupied about 1.67 billion hectares. The predominantly coniferous boreal forests cover 920 million hectares and are located between the Arctic tundra and the Temperate Zone. In contrast to the deforestation of tropical forests, pollution is one of the main human threats to temperate forests.

The estimated value of fuelwood and wood-based products to the world economy is US$400 billion (cited in Natural Resources Canada, 1996b). World wide, the forest sector provides subsistence and wage employment equivalent to 60 million work years, 80 percent of which is in developing countries. In addition, forests provide a wide range of products, including fuel, oils, medicinal plants, and household furniture and building materials. Many forests also are a direct source of food, including fruits, honey, and mushrooms. Increasing awareness of the multiple roles that forests fulfil, and growing scientific knowledge of forests as complex ecosystems, has meant that forest issues have transcended political and sectoral boundaries, becoming a priority in general international debates regarding the future of the Earth's environment and its expanding population (Natural Resources Canada, 1996b).

As the human population continues to expand, global demand for wood and wood products continues to increase. Based on the world's current annual wood consumption of 0.7 cubic metres per person, it has been estimated that the demand for wood could increase by as much as 70 million cubic metres annually (Natural Resources Canada, 1995). This is about as much wood as British Columbia harvests annually. However, there is not enough uncommitted commercial forest in the world today to meet this demand. Does this mean the world will run out of wood? According to the Canadian Forest Service, this is not a likely scenario. If wood becomes scarcer, "[p]rices for wood products will rise, recycling and use of wood waste will increase, more substitutes for wood will be used, technologies will improve, and new wood products will be developed" (Natural Resources Canada, 1996b, p. 42). However, the projected increase in global population is a significant challenge to forest managers throughout the world.

Since the 1970s, the international community has engaged in debates concerning the future of the world's forests, particularly in relation to deforestation in tropical forests. By 1990, deforestation was recognized as symptomatic of a fundamental conflict between human needs and the environment. Subsequently, international discussions

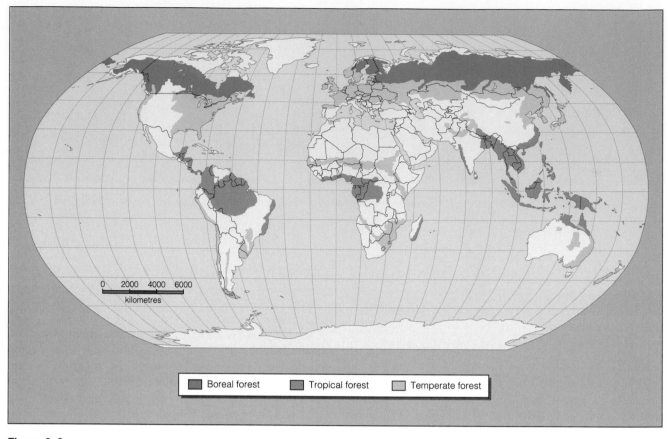

Figure 9–2
Principal forest zones of the world

SOURCE: Natural Resources Canada, Canadian Forest Service. (1996). *The state of Canada's forests 1995–1996: Sustaining forests at home and abroad.* Ottawa, p. 25.

broadened in scope to balance consideration of environmental, social, and economic factors in forest development. Indeed, as is described later in the chapter, efforts to promote sustainable forest management have been part of the focus of the "global forest dialogue" since then (Natural Resources Canada, 1996b).

Because Canada's forests are of benefit to more than Canadians (forests contribute to air quality and biodiversity, for instance), other nations want Canada to nuture our forests wisely so they will continue to provide benefits. And, because Canada relies so heavily on exporting its wood products (see the following section), other countries have powerful means of encouraging good stewardship. Canada is highly sensitive to international actions such as consumer boycotts or "eco-labelling" of wood products (discussed later in the chapter).

FORESTS IN CANADA

There are eight major forest regions in Canada (Figure 9–3) covering approximately 45 percent of our landbase.

Boreal forests occupy more than one-third of Canada, constituting the country's largest biome and providing direct employment for an estimated 165 000 people. British Columbia's temperate forests produce most of Canada's forest products and, because of the large size of the trees, account for about 45 percent of the annual volume cut in Canada. With almost 418 million hectares of forested land, Canada is caretaker of about 10 percent of the world's forests, including about 15 percent of the world's softwood supply (see Table 9–2 for additional Canadian forest facts).

Unlike most nations, the vast majority (94 percent) of Canada's forests are publicly owned. Forests are managed on behalf of each one of us (the public) by provincial governments (71 percent of forests) and federal and territorial governments (23 percent), while the remaining 6 percent of Canada's forest lands are owned privately (Figure 9–4). In some provinces, up to 99 percent of forest land is provincial Crown land, while in Prince Edward Island (88 percent), Nova Scotia (69 percent), and New Brunswick (51 percent), the majority of this land is held privately, often in private wood lots. (For further

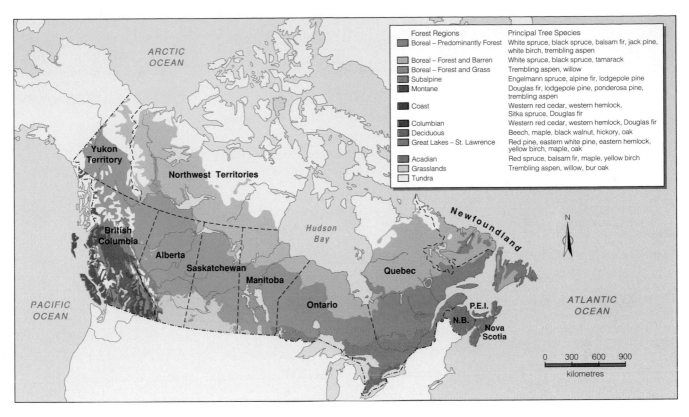

Figure 9–3
Forest regions of Canada

SOURCE: Natural Resources Canada, Canadian Forest Service. (1995). *The state of Canada's forests 1994: A balancing act.* Ottawa. Endpage.

information on private wood lots in the Maritime provinces, see the National Round Table on the Environment and the Economy in the Additional Information Sources section of this chapter.)

Forest management in Canada is a matter of provincial jurisdiction; each province as well as the Northwest Territories has its own set of legislation, policies, and regulations to govern forest activities within its boundaries. In addition to overseeing management of Yukon forest lands, the federal government focuses on trade and investment, national statistics, forest science and technology, Aboriginal affairs, environmental regulations, and international relations (Natural Resources Canada, 1996b).

Forest products continue to be the single largest contributor to Canada's balance of trade. In 1995, for instance, Canada's forest products exports were valued at approximately $41.3 billion; softwood lumber, newsprint, and wood pulp account for most of these exports (Canadian Council of Forest Ministers, 1997; Natural Resources Canada, 1997). In 1995, the forest sector contributed $20.4 billion to Canada's gross domestic product and $34.7 billion to Canada's balance of trade. One in every 15 Canadian jobs is in the wood and paper products or related industries (Canadian Forest Service, 1996).

On a worldwide basis, the amount of forest is decreasing. Most of the loss of forests is recent, 60 percent having occurred since the Industrial Revolution. In North America, 64 million hectares was cleared for settlement and agriculture between 1860 and 1978 (Clayoquot Sound Scientific Panel, 1995). In Canada, between 1979 and 1993, the average area harvested (logged) was 887 000 hectares per year, and the average annual volume of wood harvested was 163 million cubic metres (Natural Resources Canada, 1996). British Columbia's share of this volume of wood produced is about 80 million cubic metres per year, enough wood so that each year a stack of lumber one metre high and one metre wide would circle the equator twice (M'Gonigle & Parfitt, 1994). Overall in British Columbia, 50 percent of the volume logged has been cut since 1972. Coastal old-growth forests are being clear-cut at a rate of about 200 000 hectares per year (M'Gonigle & Parfitt, 1994).

About 200 000 hectares of boreal forests have been opened up for exploitation since the 1980s (doubling the amount of boreal forest harvested in Canada since the 1920s). With little or no public consultation, provincial governments have opened public lands to multinationals from North America, Korea, Hong Kong, Japan, and elsewhere,

TABLE 9-2

SELECTED FACTS ABOUT FORESTS IN CANADA

Forested Lands

- Forests cover 417.6 million hectares (45%) of Canada's land base (921.5 million hectares).
- 57%, or 236.7 million hectares, are considered commercial forests.
- 38%, or 156.2 million hectares, are open forests consisting of muskeg, marshes, and sparse tree cover.
- Most (94%) are publicly owned: provincial governments manage 71%, federal and territorial governments manage 23%, and the remaining 6% is private property of 425 000 landowners

Commercial Forests

- 50.2%, or 118.9 million hectares, are managed for timber production.
- Over 12%, or 50 million hectares, are protected from harvesting by legislation (heritage forests) or policy (protection forests).
- Annually, about 0.8% of the accessible commercial forest is harvested, removing an average of 165 million m^3 of wood and contributing about \$95 per m^3 to Canada's gross domestic product.

Forest Regions (see Figure 9.3)

- Boreal
- Subalpine
- Montane
- Coast
- Columbian
- Deciduous
- Great Lakes–St. Lawrence
- Acadian

Forest Type (1994)

- Softwood (e.g., pine, spruce)   64%
- Hardwood (e.g., poplar, maple)   15%
- Mixed wood   21%

Total Annual Allowable Cut Estimates (millions of cubic metres)

Year	Total	Softwoods	Hardwoods
1990	253	192	61
1991	253	190	63
1992	247	185	62
1993	228	172	56
1994	230	172	58
1995	233	174	59

Tree Species

- approximately 165

SOURCES: Canadian Council of Forest Ministers. (1997). *Compendium of Canadian forestry statistics 1996.* Ottawa.

Environment Canada. (1995b). *Sustaining Canada's forests: Timber harvesting. Overview SOE Bulletin,* No. 95-4 (summer).

Natural Resources Canada, Canadian Forest Service. (1996b). *The state of Canada's forests 1995–1996: Sustaining forests at home and abroad.* Ottawa.

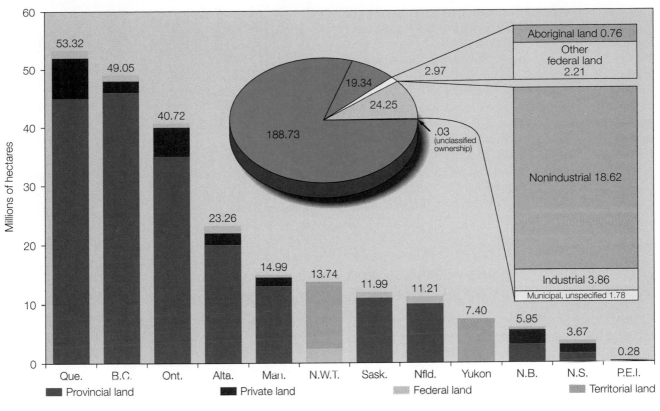

Figure 9–4

Ownership of timber-productive forest lands in Canada

NOTE: Canada's National Forestry Database Program contains information on forestry inventory, allowable annual cuts, forest fires, forest products, and silviculture, and can be viewed on the Web at http://www.nrcan.gc.ca/cfs/proj/iepb/nfdp

SOURCE: Canadian Council of Forest Ministers. (1997). *Compendium of Canadian forestry statistics, 1996.* Ottawa. Figure 1, p. 1.

supporting their plans for pulp, paper, and saw mills, simulated plywood plants, and chopstick factories with subsidies in the order of millions of taxpayer dollars.

Megaprojects in Alberta's boreal forest began in 1986; the Alberta Pacific pulp mill (45 percent owned by the Japanese investor Mitsubishi, 14 percent by Canadian shareholders) consumes 3.2 million cubic metres of timber per year, and the Daishowa-Marubeni bleached kraft pulpmill consumes 1.8 million cubic metres of boreal forest annually (Marchak, 1995). These two multinational firms have leased 15 percent of Alberta's boreal forest land base.

Every day, Saskatchewan's giant Prince Albert pulp and paper complex turns the equivalent of 30 football fields of boreal forest into pulp. The company's 20-year lease covers about 34 000 square kilometres of boreal forest land. In Manitoba, the provincial government has granted the right to about 17 percent of the province (77 percent of its prime boreal forest lands) to one firm, Repap Enterprises Limited.

Ontario and Quebec contain the bulk of Canada's timber-productive boreal forest. Expansion of older mills is occurring throughout these provinces as well, as the

boreal forest is expected to provide 60 years of cutting opportunities (staving off the day when Brazil and Indonesia will dominate pulp markets). In both provinces, as logging has moved north, timber harvesting has conflicted with Indigenous peoples' traditional uses of forest land. In Quebec, for instance, harvesting in the southern fringe of the James Bay region has consumed 600 square kilometres annually, the size of a hunting territory that supported about 30 Cree people (McLaren, 1993). Similarly, in Newfoundland and Labrador, there have been proposals to cut as much as 1.7 million hectares of the sparse, widely separated stands of boreal forests on land claimed by the Innu Nation (Innu Nation, 1995).

Large multinationals also lease much of Nova Scotia and New Brunswick Acadian forest lands. About 80 percent of Nova Scotia's forest production is in pulp, cut by companies such as STORA Forest Industries from Sweden. In New Brunswick, Repap leases about 25 percent of the province's Crown land, mostly for pulp production. Overall, nearly 100 percent of Canada's most productive boreal forest, including several provincial parks and wildlife reserves, is now locked up in 20-year leases and is available for logging (McLaren, 1993).

In light of the globally increasing demands for wood, Canada's important role as a provider of wood products, and the significant contribution of forest products to our nation's economy, questions have been raised about whether Canada can maintain or even increase its supply of timber to provide products for world consumption. Still other questions have been raised about whether current rates of production are too high to permit forests to replenish themselves and to promote forest sustainability (Hammond, 1991; M'Gonigle & Parfitt, 1994; Sierra Club of Canada, 1996). Related to questions about the rate of wood cutting in Canada are concerns about the impacts of harvesting systems and the "timber bias." A brief discussion of these concerns follows.

Harvesting Systems

Clear-cutting remains the dominant method of harvesting in Canada. Typically about 90 percent of Canada's timber has been cut using clear-cutting, and about 7 percent using selection techniques (Table 9–3, Figure 9–5). Recently, however, there has been an increase in selective cutting so that in 1995, 12.7 percent was selectively cut and 85.7 percent was clear-cut. (Other major methods of harvesting trees also are noted in Table 9–3 and Figure 9–5.) Timber companies prefer clear-cutting because, in the short term, it is the most cost-effective way to harvest trees.

Clear-cutting often is defended as a method of logging that mimics natural disturbances. To some degree this may be true in boreal forests, where fire means renewal (for example, seeds in cones of black spruce and lodgepole pine are released by fire), and clear-cutting, like fire, may establish site conditions conducive to regeneration (Hebert, Sklar, Wasel, Ghostkeeper & Daniels, 1995). In ancient temperate rain forests, however, there is no forest-fire dependent cycle and clear-cutting places the whole forest at risk, resulting in landslides, water pollution, loss of plants and animals, and soil degradation. Replanting after clear-cutting can be extremely difficult. After a wind storm or fire, some trees are left standing and all of the tree trunks are left as snags or fallen trees. "No natural disturbance, be it wind, fire, or insects, ever cut all of the trees, loaded them on a truck, and hauled them to a mill" (Hammond, 1991, p. 60).

The practice of **highgrading**—logging the highest quality and most accessible timber first—is an unsound practice associated with selective cutting that debilitates forests (often old-growth forests) in two main ways. Highgrading concentrates logging in small areas that contain the best timber, and progresses through the forest landscape from the best stands and the most readily accessible terrain to areas with less timber and more difficult access.

Standard practice in most British Columbia logging operations, and prevalent previously in boreal forests in Newfoundland and Labrador, highgrading maximizes corporate profits in the short term. In the long term, however,

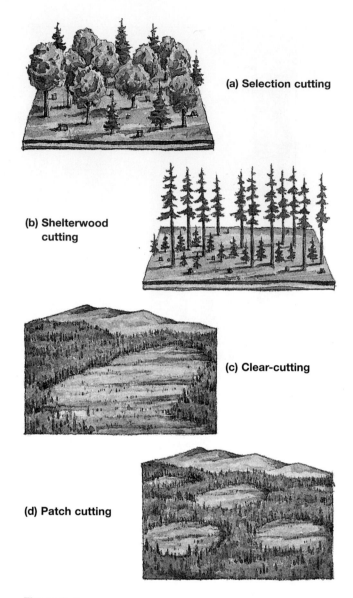

Figure 9–5

Major systems of tree harvesting

SOURCE: Natural Resources Canada, Canadian Forest Service. (1995). *The state of Canada's forest 1994: A balancing act.* Ottawa, pp. 27, 28, 35.

highgrading degrades forest ecosystems in many ways. Where a highgrading operation removes only the best trees, high-quality seed sources (with genetic codes adapted precisely to sites) are lost forever.

Most highgrading does not remove only selected trees, but is actually a form of "progressive clear-cutting," where all trees are removed from large continuous tracts and from entire watersheds. This may occur in a short time (5 years) or over a longer period of 20 or 30 years, but the damage that occurs is similar. Progressive highgrading occurs where logging concentrates first on cutting the best forests, then on the next best forests, followed by the remaining next best forests, and so on.

PART 3:
RESOURCES FOR CANADA'S FUTURE

TABLE 9-3
FOREST HARVESTING METHODS

Method	Characteristics
Selective (or selection) cutting	• The original forest is of varied species and ages. • Only the most valuable species of trees or only trees of prescribed size or quality are cut. • The forest is left to regenerate naturally. • Trees are cut individually or in small clusters. • Almost 7 percent of Canada's timber is cut using selective techniques.
Shelterwood cutting	• The original forest may be evenly or unevenly aged. • All mature trees are removed in a series of cuttings, stretched out over about 10 years. • First cut removes most canopy trees, unwanted tree species, and diseased, defective, and dying trees. • After a decade or so, when enough seedlings have taken hold, a second cut removes more canopy trees but leaves some of the best mature trees to shelter the young trees. • After perhaps another decade, a third cut removes the remaining mature trees and the remaining uniformly aged stand of young trees grows to maturity.
Seed tree cutting	• The original forest is harvested in one cutting, but a few uniformly distributed trees are left to provide seeds for regeneration. • After the new trees have become established, the seed trees may be cut. • About 4 percent of Canada's timber is cut using the shelterwood cutting and seed tree methods.
Clear cutting	• Clear-cutting removes all the trees from an original forest at the same time. • Trees may be cut as whole stands, as strips, or as patches. • After the trees are cut, the forest may be left to regenerate naturally or may be replanted. • Clear-cut areas vary in size (from small patches to thousands of hectares). • Almost 90 percent of Canada's timber is cut using clear-cutting.
Patch (clear) cutting	• Patch clear-cutting leaves small-scale clear-cut areas, perhaps 100 to 200 hectares in size. • Several clear-cut patches adjacent to one another can result in a continuous clear-cut.
Strip cutting	• Strip cutting involves clear-cutting narrow rows of forest, perhaps 80 metres wide, leaving wooded corridors that may serve as seed sources. • After regeneration, another strip is cut above the first, and so on, allowing the forest area to be clear-cut in narrow strips over several decades.
Whole tree harvesting	• Machines harvest entire trees (including roots, leaves, bark, small branches) and cut them into small chips to be used as pulpwood or fuelwood products. • Another variation of clear-cutting, this method deprives soil of plant nutrients and can support replanted trees only if they are fertilized.

Highgrading results in altered climate, removes cover needed by wildlife and new plant growth, degrades the soil, damages fish habitat and water quality, and destroys the forest diversity needed to sustain all forest uses, including future timber supplies (Hammond, 1991). This practice also means that every year both the quality and the value of the remaining forest declines. The timber now standing in many provinces is less valuable per tree and costs more to log per tree than the average quality timber of a few decades ago.

As highgrading depletes high-volume old-growth forests, it also results in a decline in the average volume of timber per hectare in remaining old-growth forests. This means that if timber managers are to "sustain" their cut, they must log a larger forest area each year to produce the same volume of timber. As British Columbia's coastal old-growth forests were clear-cut, for instance, timber companies moved into the interior of the province where the trees are smaller, requiring more land area to be cleared to supply the volume of wood needed to feed local mills. Elsewhere in Canada, after a century or more of clear-cutting, the loss of the Atlantic hardwood forests and almost 90 percent of the Carolinian forests has forced companies in the eastern and central provinces to reach into more remote portions of their provinces to supply industry needs. In New Brunswick, for instance, the remote Christmas Mountains region, the only old-growth forest left in the province, began to be clear-cut in 1992.

Tree Plantations After clear-cutting, in a series of activities designed to simplify the forest, tree plantations devoted to timber production may be developed. The first step is slash burning, where debris (natural supplies of woody material on the ground and in the soil) is removed. Slash burning increases greenhouse gases, increases the likelihood of soil erosion, decreases the availability of soil nutrients, and creates human health problems, particularly respiratory ailments (slash burning smoke contains two carcinogens, namely formaldehyde and polynuclear aromatic hydrocarbons).

The second step is when forest managers plant trees—one or two species only (known as monoculturing)—that are to be grown and cut again in short cycles of 60 to 120 years. Replacement of diverse old-growth forests with monoculture stands brings potential problems, including rapid spread of wildfires in evenly aged stands, blowdown due to poor root formation in planted trees, and loss in the number and variety of mycorrhizal fungi needed for seedling growth (Hammond, 1991).

In the third step, brush is removed, often with chemical pesticides. Forest managers attempt to maximize timber growth by controlling or eliminating competing forms of life from the forest. Brush, however, provides shade for young trees and cover for animals, enriches the soil, and repels unwanted insects. In natural forests, brush plays an important role in sustaining the whole forest (as does every other organism). While economically viable from a forest industry perspective, monoculturing and development of plantation forests potentially reduce both economic and biological diversity (M'Gonigle & Parfitt, 1994; Taylor, 1994). Tree plantations are not forests.

Until recently, **deforestation** was a term applied mostly to tropical rain forests, but deforestation occurs in Canada: in regard to our timber cutting practices, Canada has been referred to as the "Brazil of the North" (Hammond, 1991; McCrory, 1995). The timber industry denies the comparison, pointing out that Amazon rain forests are being cleared for agricultural uses, whereas Canada's forests are being regenerated for timber. However, about 50 percent of the logged area in Canada does not regenerate to productive species within five years of cutting (Hammond, 1991; Diem, 1992). During the period 1979 to 1993, for instance, only 36 percent of the area harvested was replanted or seeded; the remainder was left to "regenerate naturally," in an effort to "help maintain the natural diversity of the forest *and reduce costs*" (Natural Resources Canada, 1996b, p. 88; emphasis added).

The Timber Bias

For many decades, a great number of Canadians and their governments have viewed trees as timber and forests as log supply centres; our institutional approach to forest management has evolved out of that perspective. Typi-

Most tree plantations are characterized by stark rows of one or two species of similar age. Underbrush is absent.

Canadian forests contribute to higher air quality and greater biodiversity and thus are of benefit internationally.

284

PART 3:
RESOURCES FOR CANADA'S FUTURE

cally, politicians legislated for timber cutting and production, and not for forest protection and the stewardship of diverse ecosystems. The "timber bias" prevalent in our use of forests has resulted in a number of ecological, economic, and sociocultural impacts visible on the landscape and in communities.

Early timber industry barons viewed forests as a limitless timber supply. As evidence accumulated that this was not the case, government and industry embraced the idea of **sustained yield** forest management. The idea of sustained yield is that timber should be cut no faster than new trees can grow so that an even flow of timber in perpetuity may be obtained. In effect, this concept means that, if the yield is to be maintained, all the trees cut down should be replaced with new trees that are allowed to mature to a size comparable to the original trees on the site before they are logged. This simple concept becomes obscured in practice, however.

Tree growth data show that the average annual accumulation of wood *volume* (not wood *quality*) peaks before the old-growth stage (Figure 9–6). Timber managers want to grow trees to the point that average timber volume production is greatest (this is called the culmination age), and then clear-cut the trees to produce the greatest timber volume over time. Timber managers consider trees at culmination age—60 to 120 years old—to be "mature"; they rationalize that old growth or "decadent" timber should be cut down because it grows timber volume too slowly.

The word *mature* is used differently by foresters and by scientists. Foresters use the term to mean the *economic maturity* of a tree or forest stand—the youngest age at which the trees can be cut and sold for a profit. On the other hand, scientists call wood mature when it has developed its maximum fibre length; that is, the natural or *ecological maturity* at which trees develop their strongest and highest value wood. A tree is not ecologically mature until it has passed through all forest stages from shrub to old growth. For short-lived tree species this may be 200 to 300 years, but in long-lived species, trees may take up to 1500 years to reach ecological maturity. Trees and forests may live for centuries after reaching maturity, during which time they perform vital ecological functions and accumulate the highest quality wood of their lifetimes (Franklin, 1984). Clearly, economic maturity is reached far sooner than ecological maturity, a convenience that is not lost on those who wish to convert trees to logs.

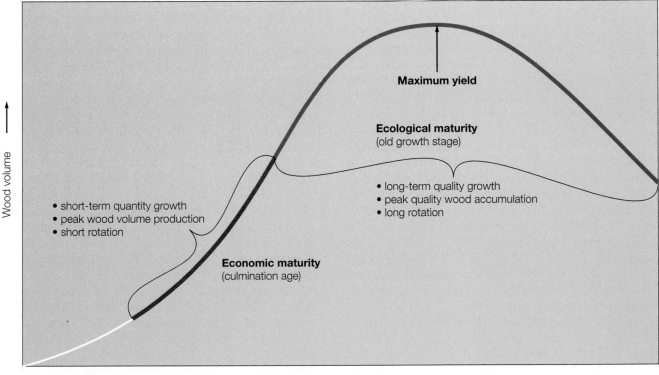

Figure 9–6
Timber volume production

Cutting trees at economic maturity versus ecological maturity, however, is a little like picking green tomatoes instead of waiting for ripe tomatoes. When green, tomatoes have nearly the same volume as red, ripe tomatoes, but the ripe fruit of the tomato is far more desirable and far more valuable. Just as ripe tomatoes sell for a lot more money than green tomatoes, high-quality, old-growth wood can be sold for a lot more than economically mature wood (Hammond, 1991).

It is the old growth or mature wood—clear, fine-grained, and strong—that has made the Canadian timber and pulp and paper industries famous. Timber managers seem to be missing the important point that culmination of value, both ecologically and economically, comes significantly later than culmination of volume. If we were to cut trees at the peak of their ecological and economic value, perhaps both forests and the timber industry could be sustainable.

In order to calculate how much timber should be cut in any one year (called the allowable annual cut, or AAC), current Canadian forestry practice relies on a measure called the rotation period. For any given species, its rotation period is the length of time required to grow a tree to economic maturity. Actual calculations of the annual allowable cut are complicated, however; the rotation period, the total available natural old-growth timber volume, and the annual growth of the forest are the most important factors affecting calculation of the AAC.

The AAC can be manipulated to enable timber managers to cut timber grown in 200 or 500 or 1500 years as though it grew in the rotation period (say, 100 years). The resulting unsustainable cutting rate causes a change from naturally diverse old-growth forests to regulated tree farms containing equal areas of trees from age one to the rotation age. When timber managers finish liquidating the old-growth forests in one rotation period, they subsequently will harvest only trees grown to economic maturity, the equivalent of green tomatoes (Hammond, 1991).

Such decisions do not ensure that timber is being carefully managed to ensure forests for the future. In addition, clear-cutting leaves good wood on the ground after logging, leading to waste of sometimes large quantities of usable wood. In clean logging operations, wood left lying on the ground may amount to one truckload for every three to four truckloads of logs removed. At the other end of the spectrum, wasteful operations may leave behind as much or more usable wood as is hauled away. Good wood may be cut and then left on the ground because provincial government standards for timber use have permitted logging companies to cut (kill) trees that are in their way, or that are not the right species or size, and not remove them. Other "firm wood" standards indicate that if a log contains as little as 15 to 35 percent rot (and is 65 to 85 percent sound wood), it can be left on the site as waste (Hammond, 1991).

The most valuable and nonrenewable wood sources—old-growth trees—often have the most lenient utilization standards. Since it is frequently the case that the highest quality wood fibre is found in the lower logs of old growth trees, and that these old trees tend to contain a significant amount of rotten wood, a firm wood standard of 50 percent or more leads to high amounts of waste. The high quality wood that is in the lower logs can be efficiently and profitably resawn from the shell around the rotten portion and used for finished wood products. For instance, wood made from fine-grained old-growth timber is suitable for guitar tops, and can be worth more than $1000 per board foot. Because this type of wood is not produced by second-growth forests, less waste would occur if the wood were "stored on the stump" rather than felled. Note also that failure to use the wood in old-growth trees increases the pressure to log larger areas of forest to meet the annual allowable cut.

The higher the value added—such as making cabinets, mouldings, panelling, furniture, and guitar tops from lumber—the higher the levels of manufacturing and employment that are generated from each tree cut. Even though British Columbia has the highest quality and highest volume of timber per hectare of any province in Canada, the value added to British Columbia wood products in 1984 was only about half that added in the rest of Canada. The number of people employed per tree cut is a good measure of the timber industry's benefit to society. In spite of its large timber production, for every one job produced in British Columbia in 1984, per 1000 cubic metres of timber (about 33 truckloads of logs), 2.2 jobs were produced from the same amount of timber in the rest of Canada (Hammond, 1991; M'Gonigle & Parfitt, 1994).

These issues are of great interest to many people concerned about the sustainability of British Columbia and Canada's forests. With the increasing global scarcity of old-growth timber (Food and Agriculture Organization, 1997), the province could tap into the economic advantage that exists in the luxury market potential that old-growth trees embody. But, to date it appears as if "corporate, government and union policies remain hooked on a volume economy of mass commodity production.... As if in a process of reverse alchemy, we still convert our old-growth gold into the dull lead of ... two-by-fours" (M'Gonigle & Parfitt, 1994, p. 44).

The pursuit of economic productivity through high-volume, low-labour logging has resulted in declining forests, closure of community mills, and loss of jobs throughout the country (Hammond, 1991; Marchak, 1995; M'Gonigle & Parfitt, 1994; Taylor, 1994). As the most accessible and highest quality (usually old-growth) forests have been highgraded (often with considerable wood waste) to achieve short-term maximum profit, younger and smaller trees have been logged, shortening the rotational period. These practices have contributed to the "falldown effect" and to the potential loss of future economic diversity.

The Falldown Effect

Diversity is the cornerstone of a stable, healthy forest as well as the cornerstone of a stable, healthy economy. Given that forest diversity is achieved through forest protection, and that we do not understand fully how forests work, it would seem reasonable that forest management activities should give priority to, and be consistent with, protection and ecological sustainability. However, timber managers already are aware that their monoculture tree plantations and managed natural stands will never produce the amount of timber provided by the old natural forests they are replacing.

The timber industry calls this reduction in volume of production, caused by the shift from sustainable old-growth forests to nonsustainable monoculture tree plantations, "falldown" (Figure 9–7). Although the amount of

this falldown is unknown, government projections estimate that future harvests will be 20 to 30 percent below allowable annual cuts; other forecasts suggest these figures could double.

Falldown is not a natural process, but one caused by the timber industry's harvesting of old-growth forests, which required 200 to 1000 or more years to grow, at a rate that assumes these forests can be replaced in approximately 60 to 120 years. If falldown were to have been avoided—both biologically and economically—these high-quality forests should have been cut on 200- to 400-year cycles or rotation periods (Hammond, 1991).

Falldown also is a result of timber management practices that damage forest integrity; these practices include nonsustainable logging rates, highgrading, soil and water degradation, and waste (poor timber utilization). Clearcut logging has altered climates such that timber managers may not be able to regrow timber farms with as much volume in as short a period of time as they predict. Monocultures easily could succumb to disease or insect epidemics at any point in their lives, especially if they are increasingly stressed by climate change and acid deposition. These "designed forests" are without the species diversity and genetic diversity needed to balance and buffer a natural ecosystem against large-scale or rapid changes (Hammond, 1991).

Falldown and loss of biological diversity have clear economic impacts. Once the historical diversity of tree species and sizes is gone, employment levels in traditional timber cutting and wood manufacturing will decline, and the wood products industry may be unable to adjust rapidly to local, national, and international demands. In addition to reduced quantities of timber, reductions in quality of timber produced in the second-growth forests are of concern. Old-growth wood from slow-growing trees is clear, soft, fine-grained, strong, and easy to work with. In contrast, second-growth wood is knotty, hard, coarse-grained, weak, and difficult to work with. The reason is that old-growth trees contain about 80 percent mature wood, while 60-year-old second-growth trees contain about 50 percent juvenile wood. Long-fibre, mature wood is not formed on the stem of the tree until branches die (natural pruning), while juvenile, short-fibre wood is produced on the stem as long as wood is growing around green or living branches (Hammond, 1991).

Forintek, a Canadian industry–government research cooperative, analyzed the wood fibre of second-growth Douglas fir and determined that it had low structural strength, that it had problems with warping and workability, and that almost no high-grade lumber could be milled from the short rotation second-growth trees (Kellog, 1989). This decline in quality (strength and workability) is due largely to the shorter length of fibres that make up the second-growth wood. Pulp products such as paper also are stronger when produced from old-growth

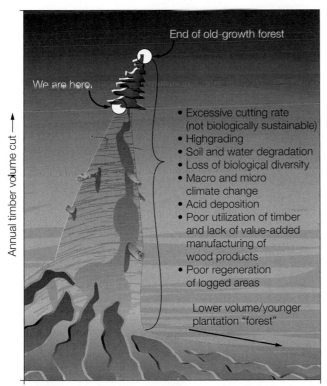

Figure 9–7
The falldown effect

NOTE: Global problems associated with falldown: climate change, ozone depletion, acid deposition

SOURCE: Hammond, H. (1991). *Seeing the forest among the trees: The case for wholistic forest use.* Vancouver: Polestar Press, p. 130. Reprinted by permission.

timber. Forintek's research also revealed that second-growth Douglas fir trees grown on average or better sites needed to reach the age of 90 years and be pruned to increase wood quality in order to have positive dollar value. This finding suggests that annual cutting rates need to be reduced by at least one-third to accommodate a lengthening of rotation ages from 60 to more than 90 years if wood of sufficient value to make a profit is to be grown.

With the falldown—lower volume from younger plantation forests—future timber management in Canada will be based on a "fibre" economy (Figure 9–8). Technology, it is assumed, will provide us with the ability to fabricate construction materials from bonded composites of chips or from pulp obtained from plantation-grown trees or natural regeneration trees grown on short rotations.

The flaws in this plan include the fact that high-quality wood equates to high-value wood, both today and in the future. A study in Washington state, for example, revealed that Douglas fir aged 160 or more years was 56 percent more valuable than wood of the same species aged less than 100 years (Wigg & Boulton, 1989). High-quality wood produced by older trees will always be in demand for manufacture of fine wood products, for quality pulp and paper, and other specialty products.

Much of the high-quality, long-fibre, old-growth timber left in the world is located in western Canada. We can continue to liquidate it and sell it cheaply, or we can cut it on a sustainable basis, make high-quality wood products, and command premium prices. From an economic standpoint, we have scarcity on our side. Because of world demand for high-quality old-growth wood, we could recover the costs of careful stewardship and labour-intensive practices. However, this has not been the agenda of major timber corporations that control forests in Canada (Hammond, 1991).

It has been argued that sustainable cutting of old growth and manufacturing of high-quality wood products can provide more jobs in both the short and long term than can plantation forestry and pulp or wood fibre economies (M'Gonigle & Parfitt, 1994). Selection cutting systems in natural forests require the highest labour per volume logged of all conventional logging systems. Timber products from old-growth forests can feed a diverse sustainable industry including large log sawmills, small log sawmills, pulp mills, paper mills, cabinet shops, millwork plants, furniture factories, beam and truss lamination plants, and so on. Similarly, labour-intensive operations such as commercial thinning in older diverse forests provide growing space for old trees, and furnish intermediate timber products for wood manufacturing. In addition, if planned sensitively, selection logging systems also can protect forest-based recreation (people do not like to hike through clear-cuts but can enjoy hiking through forests from which a few trees have been removed carefully).

Such labour-intensive activity does not have a place in plantation economics where trees of uniform size grow

1900
Solid sawn lumber

1950
Plywood

1960
Laminated beams
Hardboard
Particleboard

1970
Wood trusses
Laminated veneer lumber
Plywood webbed I-beams
Waferboard
Hardboard webbed I-beams
Oriented strand board

1980
Composite lumber
Hardwood lumber

2000

Figure 9–8
Evolution of wood products development

SOURCE: Hammond, H. (1991). *Seeing the forest among the trees: The case of wholistic forest use.* Vancouver: Polestar Press, p. 131. Reprinted by permission.

in straight rows and are logged by machines, reducing employment levels further. In factories, products (such as disposable chopsticks) made from single species trees of a uniform size require much less labour because production systems are highly mechanized and the range of products is very limited. The wood that comes from monoculture forests will be made into pulp and composite products such as fibre boards. In a fibre economy, more and more timber will be required to account for fewer and fewer jobs—as natural forests are reduced to fibre farms, both tree sizes and employment will decline. Corporate profits likely will increase (Hammond, 1991; M'Gonigle & Parfitt, 1994).

Tourism and recreational values and opportunities, largely dependent on outdoor environments including old-growth forests, are reduced or destroyed as clear-cutting and slash burning occur. These social impacts of falldown and loss of biological diversity are in addition to the loss of the forests' function to buffer climate change (because large carbon sinks are gone), the lower quality of water produced (due to possible contamination from pesticides used in the clearing of brush), and the elimination of species.

Destruction of forests and their diversity results, too, in the loss of their spiritual values. Having respect for the forest as a source of physical and spiritual wisdom, First Nations people lived with their forests as integral, contributing community members, and were sustained by them. Often described as traditional stewards of Canada's forests, First Nations practised a philosophy that incorporated love and protection of the forest before any excess bounty was traded or bartered. However, some First Nations people have been affected significantly by logging taking place on lands over which they claim Aboriginal title. While trying to reach just settlement of the land question in court, logging has continued, leaving "empty lands where once there was unimaginable abundance" (Hammond, 1991, p. 135).

We know how to practise sustainable use of our forests and how to stop falldown and loss of diversity. Achieving sustainability requires a reduction in cutting rates, protection of what remains of our old-growth forests, design of timber management systems that perpetuate natural forest diversity, and the implementation and protection of a variety of forest uses. Action is important if we wish to arrest the problem. If we do not act soon, then instead of old, diverse forests that support diverse and sustainable economies, we will see monocultures that produce simplistic and perhaps unstable stands of trees as well as specialized and more unstable economies (Hammond, 1991; Marchak, 1995).

As much as plantations are not forests, there is also the possibility that plantations of hybrid cottonwoods or genetically uniform Douglas fir—if not grown on good forest land and not displacing natural forests or their regeneration—could become sources of significant employment and regional income. That is, some new towns could be based on scientific research related to plantation forestry as well as exploitation of these unnatural forests (Schoonmaker, von Hagen & Wolf, 1997).

The shift away from the old forest economy, based on volume cutting and unsustainable economics of corporate and bureaucratic growth, toward value-based, smaller business and community stewardship brings many opportunities. "If we merge the job benefits from developing an industry around pruning and thinning our second-growth forests, from setting aside our heritage old-growth for new tourism and amenities-based industries, from encouraging selection logging in thousands of new woodlots and community forests ... from harnessing the power of the market so as to return local capital to local communities, from seeking broad new investment strategy for our local capital, then we are talking ... about tens upon tens of thousands of new jobs, jobs that will last, jobs that are healthy ..."—we are talking about a new vision of forests and the forest industry, about "Forestopia" (M'Gonigle & Parfitt, 1991, p. 109).

Part of the challenge in learning to value forests differently and to consider strategies for conservation-based development is to understand why old-growth forests are so important ecologically.

THE ECOLOGICAL IMPORTANCE OF OLD-GROWTH FORESTS

Old-growth or ancient forests share similar characteristics (life cycle, carbon storage, and biological diversity) that make them important legacies for the future of Canadian forests. These characteristics, and the need for their protection, are considered briefly below.

THE LIFE CYCLE IN THE OLD-GROWTH FOREST

Standing Live Trees, Snags, and Fallen Trees

Large, old living trees are virtual forest communities in themselves. For example, the foliage of a single old-growth Douglas fir may have a surface area of over 2800 square metres that, because of the microclimatic differences created by the lean of the tree, may attract epiphytic (aerial) plants such as mosses and lichens to the moist cool portions of the crown and lichens to the drier portions of the canopy. Up to 1500 species of insects have been found in the irregularly shaped branches of a single stand of old-growth forest (Hammond, 1991). Small mammals such as squirrels and tree voles depend on the large accumulations of organic matter in the crowns of individual old-growth trees for their food and shelter. Certain birds such as the northern spotted owl and the marbled murrelet need old-growth canopies for nesting areas and as habitat to rear their young.

No tree lives forever. However, when large, old trees die, their extensive root systems enable them to remain upright for 50 to 75 years in the case of Douglas fir, and up to 125 years in the case of western red cedar. Large snags are a distinct feature of old-growth and unmanaged forests. They provide habitat for many nesting birds and mammals such as woodpeckers, flickers, and marten. Many birds prefer the large, old-tree snags that require centuries of tree growth, growth that is not part of the life cycle in the managed forest. Managed forests and young forests simply do not provide the diversity of habitat options available in old-growth forests over 200 years of age (because snag density increases as forests age). A reduction in the number of snags means a reduction in the numbers of hole-nesting birds that assist in balancing insect populations.

When old snags finally fall to the forest floor, they are perhaps even more valuable in ensuring continuation of tomorrow's forests than they were when they were standing. A fallen tree is literally the soil for future generations of forests. Carpenter ants (which eat insect eggs and larvae, and help keep the defoliating spruce budworm in check), bark beetles, wood borers, and mites invade the wood of the fallen tree, using it as a home and contributing to its decay. As the decaying wood gets wet, it acts like a giant sponge, holding water and slowly releasing water and plant nutrients to the forest. The mycorrhizal fungi that assist forest plants in obtaining the elements needed for growth thrive in this medium.

A healthy, living, large tree in an old-growth forest may have 30 to 40 species of mycorrhizal fungi attached to its roots, providing a rich source of nitrogen to the host tree. European researchers found that in intensely managed forests without old-growth decaying wood in the soil, only three to five mycorrhizal fungi were present. Thus, old-growth decaying wood is an extremely important legacy to future forests. The presence of mycorrhizal fungi enables a fallen tree to become a nurse tree, an ideal place for the germination and growth of the next generation of trees and many other plants. Nurse trees are important for the regeneration of conifers in river or riparian zones; the elevated surface of a fallen tree may offer one of the few places safe from flooding where a young tree may germinate and grow (Hammond, 1991). If a nurse tree is broken or spread apart, its moisture-holding and nutrient-cycling functions are greatly reduced or destroyed.

Over the 250 years it would take a 400-year-old Douglas fir to decompose (or 400 years if the fir were 800 years old), the fallen tree performs other functions, including maintaining the stability of forest slopes. When large living trees or snags fall across the slope, a natural retaining wall is created, holding organic material and soil behind the terrace or barrier, and preventing slumps and erosion. Also, the water and nutrients collected here provide rich conditions for plant growth. Animal habitat is created along the sides of (and often underneath) large fallen trees, providing travel routes for squirrels, mice, and rabbits, and their predators.

Trees that fall into or across streams act as dams or breakwaters to slow the erosive forces of the stream and add diversity to the stream channel. They provide a variety of spawning and rearing habitats for fish, including sites for aquatic plants and insects needed for fish food. Fallen trees that land in streams help stabilize sediment transport by acting as barriers for movement of debris. Over time as the tree decomposes, parts of it may move down the stream and become embedded in a bank, contributing to the formation of a new forest community (Hammond, 1991).

CARBON STORAGE

As we saw in Chapter 3, maintaining the 0.03 percent carbon dioxide in the earth's atmosphere is crucial to maintaining life as we know it. Old-growth forests are the planet's most important land-based storage systems for carbon. Huge amounts of carbon are stored in branches, trunks, roots, fallen trees, and soil organic matter, and the older the tree, the more it can store. For instance, a 450-year-old Douglas fir forest stores more than double the total amount of carbon stored in a 60-year-old Douglas fir forest. There is evidence that the northern hemisphere's land-based carbon sinks are more important for carbon storage than the oceans. This means that Canada's old-growth forests—particularly the vast northern boreal forests—are immensely important in regulating Earth's carbon dioxide levels (Jardine, 1994).

KEYS TO DIVERSITY

The keys to diversity in an old-growth forest are its multiple canopy layers, canopy gaps, and understory patchiness. Just as the diverse canopy provides varied microhabitats for plants and animals, so too do the canopy gaps and understory patches. The Pacific yew, for example, needs the shade, cool temperatures, and high humidity provided by old-growth canopies (see Enviro-Focus 3). Specialized mammals such as the northern flying squirrel and the fisher require the massive spreading branches, deformed tops, hollow trees, and open spaces of the old-growth canopy for their homes. Ungulates such as mule deer, moose, and Roosevelt elk use the dense forest patches for winter shelter and browse the vegetation within the canopy gaps. In fact, of the native mammals on Vancouver Island, 85 percent reproduce in ancient forests (Hammond, 1991).

In contrast, the closed canopies of young forests result in forest simplicity. When a forest is growing, most of the forest's energy is diverted to growing trees, resulting in a uniform, closed canopy that blocks almost all usable light from reaching the ground. Understory trees, shrubs, and herbs are very limited or absent, and populations and species diversity of many life forms decrease during this period of forest development. Natural diversity rebounds when the forest canopy begins to open due to individual tree mortality in the early old-growth phase.

Biological Diversity

"Nature creates forests—we can only watch" (Hammond, 1991, p. 32). Humans have identified only a small number of the organisms in an old-growth forest, and we know even less about plant, animal, fungi, and bacteria functions than we do about the number of species. We do know, however, that the biomass (total amount of living matter) in a Canadian northwest old-growth rain forest is three to eight times as great as the biomass of a tropical rain forest. And, if plants, animals, and microorganisms above, at, and below soil level are included, a northwest old-growth temperate rain forest may be more biologically diverse than a tropical rain forest (Kelly & Braasch, 1988).

Our ignorance of the functioning of Canadian forests is immense, in part because of this diversity. In contrast to tropical rain forests, where the diversity and functioning depend on about 500 different tree species and less than 10 mycorrhizal fungi, the boreal forest contains about a dozen tree species and may depend on as many as 5000 species of mycorrhizal fungi to sustain their integrity. We know that each of these mycorrhizal fungi has a specific role in growth and development of boreal forests, but for the most part we do not know the nature of these functions (Hammond, 1991).

The biological diversity or richness of old-growth forests is critical to the ongoing existence of forests. If measured by numbers of species only, recently disturbed forests have the greatest variety of species. The species that colonize openings created by fire, wind, or the falling of a single tree are called *aggressive generalists* as these species grow in harsh environments. Since disturbances are created constantly by nature and by humans, neither these species nor their habitats are at risk of loss.

In contrast, old-growth species are specialist species that require the ancient forests to survive. Humans cannot create old growth: "[L]ichens which fix nitrogen, small mammals which move mycorrhizal fungi around, and predator insects which eat foliage-consuming insects are some of the gifts of old growth forests which benefit all phases of a forest" (Hammond, 1991, p. 32). While some species require old growth, others may need it only for certain periods in their lives. Grizzly bears need the hiding cover provided by the large crowns of old-growth trees, and they utilize the berry supplies of old-growth canopy gaps. Salmon, required by grizzlies, thrive on the quality of water and habitat supplied only by old-growth forests.

In unmanaged forests, every organism is different genetically, allowing each organism to adapt to its particular environment today and to meet the uncertainties in tomorrow's environments. Maintaining genetic diversity is a natural process in a healthy forest. Just as the complexity and diversity of each individual's contribution within human societies enables societies to continue and thrive, so genetic diversity enables forests to survive. This is why managed forests, such as the genetically identical clones of Douglas fir or white spruce planted to replace logged, old-growth forests, are not forests at all. This is why so many people protested at Clayoquot Sound: if forests are to survive in British Columbia, in Canada, and on this planet, they will survive only with the complexity and diversity found in old-growth, natural (unmanaged) forests. Because of their variety of species and long lives, old-growth forests are a vital storehouse of genetic material, from soil microorganisms to giant trees.

Old-growth forests exhibit extremely large ecosystem diversity in their multilayered canopies and patchy undergrowth. Yet the old-growth soil with its thousands of organisms is the most biologically rich part of the old-growth forest. If this biological legacy of old-growth forests were to be lost, it could lead eventually to critical losses in all forests. Old-growth forests are the climax or zenith of forests. Without them, essential parts required to maintain forests through time are lost. This is perhaps most evident in water and forest relationships. The canopies of standing giant trees catch snow while their root systems and the organic, rich soil filter, purify, and slowly release the water. Fallen trees serve as reservoirs for water and as buffers for stream flows so that most parts of the forest get the water they need, seldom too much or too little. Old growth is a necessary part of any forest ecosystem, a necessary phase in the life of any forest.

THE NEED FOR PROTECTION

Dynamic and enduring, forests are life forms operating on timetables and scales beyond human comprehension. If we understand this, then the necessity of protecting forest ecosystems both during and after any human activities in the forest is clear. Unless we maintain healthy forests we cannot maintain healthy communities (Barnes & Jacobsen, 1997).

One way to maintain healthy forests and healthy communities is to apply the principles of ecological responsibility and balanced use. Ecological responsibility means that all human activities within forest landscapes must be carried out in a way that protects and maintains necessary forest structures and functions. Balanced use means that all forest users, both human and nonhuman, are entitled to a fair and protected land base on which to carry out their various activities. In turn, this means that sufficient natural forest reserves must be protected from all but the gentlest of human uses. Protection of natural areas is required to maintain landscape connections, to maintain a reservoir of species and genetic components, and to provide natural benchmarks so that we can evaluate impacts of forest activities and restore degraded forests.

Part of the controversy over logging in the Temagami region of Ontario (most recently in 1996) derived from concern that not enough of the old-growth white and red pine was being protected. Since 1992, it has been known that less than 1 percent of the old-growth pine forest remains in North America, and less than 1 percent of Ontario's original white pine forest remains. Temagami has the highest concentration of old-growth white and red pine forest ecosystems remaining in the world. It is official Ministry of Environment and Energy policy that old-growth white and red pine forest should be protected. Despite this policy and the knowledge that these are endangered ecosystems, both the Ontario Ministry of Natural Resources (MNR) and the Temagami Comprehensive Planning Council allowed approximately 50 percent of the old-growth pine in Temagami to be logged beginning in 1996. Timber harvests were permitted to supply the needs of people for wood products. Note that in 1996 each old-growth tree was worth approximately $600 in the sawlog market, but the people of Ontario who own the trees received approximately $15 for each tree (Earthroots, 1996).

In the case of the 1400-hectare Owain Lake stand, the third largest old-growth white pine stand in North America, logging was permitted because the MNR assumed that another area containing old-growth white pine (Lake Obabika) was representative of that ecosystem. This assumption was based on a comparison of surficial geology only. Essentially a claim that the stand had no ecological representation value, this assumption permitted the Temagami Planning Council and MNR to indicate the Owain Lake stand did not need protection. To determine accurately if an area is ecologically representative, however, the standard practice is to describe community types (flora and fauna), providing lists of plant species and plant communities as well. Although they had produced such information in the past for other decisions about which stands to protect and which to log, the MNR did not undertake this detailed work for the Owain Lake pine stand (Quinby, 1996).

Independent botanical field studies show that the Owain Lake old-growth pine stand has many ecological features—including 10 plant species, four that are rare regionally and three that are rare locally—that make it different from the other old-growth pine stands (Quinby, 1996). For instance, the rare plant species found at the Owain Lake stand were absent at the Lake Obabika stand. Failure to assess adequately the ecological representation for the Owain Lake stand meant that the value of protecting more than one example of a community type—especially an endangered one—from total loss due to natural disturbances was eliminated. The principles of ecological responsibility and protection of sufficient natural forest reserves from all but the gentlest of human uses were ignored. Users of the area indicate the result: "Where once we hiked in the natural park-like atmosphere of pine, we now walked on a system of all-weather roads.

The visual destruction spoke volumes of disrespect .... [s]mall trees flattened, healthy trunks scarred, pools of black oil, and great wide swaths cut into a once roadless landscape" (McGuffin, 1997).

In effect, acknowledging the importance of all life forms provides impetus to fully protect biological diversity in order to maintain healthy forests and healthy communities. Protecting biological diversity means protecting the integrity of the forest—the biological diversity of forests—at the species, genetic, and ecosystem levels. Because diversity works in interconnected and interdependent ways, biological diversity must be protected in at least two ways. One way is by limiting fragmentation of the forest so that the patterns of and connections between the various clusters or stands that make up a forest landscape can be maintained. Another way involves protecting the structure and composition of the individual parts that make up the forest landscape, including the fallen trees, the soil, the old growth, the riparian and upland corridors, and the natural flows of water, nutrients, and other forms of energy throughout the forest (Hammond, 1991; Noss & Cooperrider, 1994; Quinby, 1996).

Understanding that each forest stand requires old trees, snags, and fallen trees, that brush or competing vegetation is biologically necessary for forest integrity, and that insects and disease are essential parts of a fully functioning forest means that ecologically responsible forestry entails practising timber management as if forests really mattered. If we practised forestry as if forests really mattered, we would ensure that forests always occupied sites where timber was being cut, and we would ensure that "uncommon, declining, and not readily visible species are *not* sacrificed for common species or species desired for human objectives" (Hammond, 1991, p. 210).

HUMAN ACTIVITIES AND IMPACTS ON FOREST ENVIRONMENTS

Canadians depend on their forests for a wide range of services, products, and values. The key to sustaining all of these uses and values—in order that the forest needs of both present and future generations of Canadians may be met—lies in the maintenance of the health, diversity, and productive capacity of forest ecosystems. This means that there is a need for forests in Canada and everywhere to be managed so that their sustainability is assured. However, recognition of this fact is relatively recent, and we continue to see a wide range of problems resulting from practices that did not, or do not, promote sustainability. This section provides a brief historical context of human activities in Canadian forests as well as examples of some of the practices and problems arising from these activities.

A BRIEF HISTORICAL OVERVIEW OF THE FOREST INDUSTRY

First Nations and European Settlers

Before this country became a nation, Canada's Aboriginal peoples derived their basic means of survival—food, clothing, shelter, and tools—from the forests. Forests also were a fundamental dimension in their cultural and spiritual lives. The hunting and gathering peoples of northeastern North America, for example, not only used wood for fuel and shelter but also to produce hunting tools such as arrows and spears. They developed the ability to bend wood without breaking it, and made snowshoes, toboggans, sleds, and canoes. Bowls, baskets, mats, and wooden wedges for splitting logs were all made out of wood. So was string, made from the inner bark of elm, basswood, and other trees. And, long before the disposable diaper (derived from wood pulp, we often forget) arrived on the scene, soft clean mosses from the forest floor provided Indigenous people with an abundant alternative.

Among the wealthiest nonagricultural societies ever known, the First Nations people on the west coast based their lives on use of the abundant cedar trees and the salmon that spawned in the coastal rain forest streams.

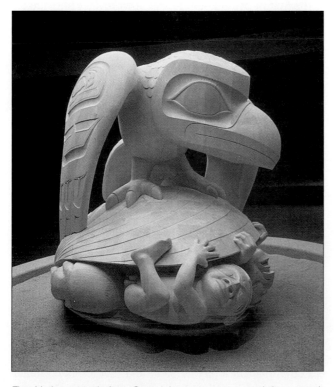

First Nations people from Canada's west coast carved, from wood, artworks in addition to a great number of more utilitarian items.

These people carved wooden totem poles and masks, highly notable elements of their culture, that represented and expressed the integration of the forces of natural and spiritual realms that surrounded them (Knudtson & Suzuki, 1992). The wealth of the coastal forests enabled these First Nations to develop the potlatch economy where masks and other goods were redistributed according to social status.

The European settlers who challenged the original forest inhabitants for possession of lands had a different conception of and relationship with nature and the forest. From the 17th to the 19th centuries, the vast majority of European immigrants wanted to establish farms. The forests of butternut, oak, white pine, walnut, maple, and black cherry trees, as well as the Aboriginal people, were seen as obstacles, something to be conquered and to be driven back to permit homesteading to proceed. Using their muskets, Europeans forcibly removed the Aboriginal people from lands the newcomers wanted to settle; with axes and oxen they slowly began the onslaught against the trees.

Timber Exports and Government Ownership

Not until the beginning of the 19th century, when the Napoleonic wars cut off Britain from its traditional timber supplies in the Baltic, was there much interest in extraction of Canadian forest products for large-scale export. The Royal Navy turned to Canada for the white pine wood required for ship building, and the forests in New Brunswick, Quebec, and the Ottawa Valley were cut and exported as square timber to Britain. The dramatic increase in demand soon attracted English businessmen to Canada, where they established thriving commercial interests based on small operators out in the bush where the trees were being cut. "The prevailing ethic was simple. Cut it down and get it out in as great a quantity and as fast as possible" (Swift, 1983, pp. 34, 35).

By 1826, authorities recognized that forest exploitation could bring in revenues, so they issued licences to cut timber in specific areas. People cutting wood on Crown land had to pay a licence fee as well as duty on the wood actually cut. These actions effectively established the principle of government ownership and control over timberlands that continues to be applied today. In 1849, in response to "poaching [of trees], trespassing and the generalized plunder of the public estate" (Swift, 1983, p. 41), a new timber policy was established that retained government ownership of forest land.

Changing Market Demands, Changing Industry

By the mid-1800s, the Canadian forest industry began to change when sawmills were set up to meet changing market demands for rough-sawn chunks of lumber. The capital required for such facilities led to concentration of control into ever more powerful industrial enterprises. As well as a rush to secure all available supplies of timber, the forest business became more centralized and integrated—the timber barons ran the bush camps, the sawmills, and the plants producing shingles, lath, and doors.

Following Confederation, from 1867 to 1906, the governments of Quebec and Ontario received millions of dollars through the liquidation of their forests, collecting various rents and fees from the timber industry. For instance, between 1867 and 1899, forest-generated income contributed 28 cents out of every dollar collected by the Ontario treasury (Swift, 1983).

The Shifting Frontier and Conservation Concerns

Beginning in the 1840s, the United States began to surpass Britain as the most important market for Canadian forest products. Railroad and city building stimulated increased demand for wood that was met by the spread of logging in Ontario from the Ottawa Valley across the Canadian Shield to Georgian Bay and the Lakehead. These forests helped supply Prairie markets until the British Columbia forest industry hit its stride after 1900. In Quebec, the second half of the 1800s saw exports to the United States steadily gaining ground, while in New Brunswick, the majority of the good pine had been removed from the forests by the 1870s.

As the forest frontier moved increasingly westward, and the lumber boom was ending in the east, a number of eastern timber entrepreneurs moved to British Columbia. There, the timber demands of the 1850s gold rush had stimulated sawmill development, and the easterners were quick to sense an opportunity to diversify their operations into the vast and seemingly limitless coastal forests.

By the late 19th century, the framework for commercial exploitation of Canada's forest resources had been established. There were, however, people who warned that the forests were not infinite. In 1862, for example, even before the peak of the eastern lumber business, John Langton wrote: "We go on practically treating our forests as inexhaustible, and ... we have as yet taken no steps towards preserving what remains to us" (cited in Swift, 1983, p. 47).

Bernhard Fernow, the "Father of Forestry in North America" and founder of the first forestry school in Canada at the University of Toronto, declared in 1914, "As yet the forests are viewed solely as a source of current revenue, not as capital, and the rights of the people and of posterity are sacrificed" (cited in Swift, 1983, p. 48). Fernow's philosophy was based on the idea that forests were renewable natural resources and that trained managers could ensure a supply of forest wood in perpetuity.

Licensing and Increasing Concentration of Forest Holdings

Even though the conservation movement in Canada acknowledged the need for forest conservation, through the decades of the early 1900s the pulp and paper industry was growing, based on the northern expanses of spruce trees too small to be turned into lumber. And in British Columbia, talk was seldom of conservation but rather of the production boom. From 1889, when 43.9 million board feet were cut from provincial land, to 1907, when 566 million board feet of timber were cut (mostly from the rain forest), provincial government coffers benefited greatly. Anxious for even more revenue, in 1905 the British Columbia government abandoned its old system of granting five-year leases to timber companies and established a system of 21-year timber licences that could be bought and sold just as any other commodity. This not only encouraged speculation, it enabled the concentration of forest holdings into fewer and fewer hands.

The large operators wanted their access to the timber to be secure over the longer term and wanted to ensure the renewability of their licences after 21 years. They picked up on the rhetoric of the conservation movement, threatening the government that unless licences (tenures) were renewable, licence holders would high-grade the timber, thereby depleting the province's timber reserves. Even though the operators knew this would result in unrestrained cutting, overproduction, market glut, and low prices, this argument received a sympathetic hearing from the government because of its desire for continuous revenue (Swift, 1983).

In 1909, the British Columbia government appointed a royal commission, chaired by Frederick Fulton (K.C.), to consider all the questions surrounding its forest policy, including licence renewability. In 1910, prior to completion of the Fulton Commission report, the province announced its licence renewability provision. By the time the Fulton Commission reported in 1912, and the Forest Act was passed, one of the key issues facing the forests was defined as fire protection. Prevailing opinion was that, provided the forest were protected adequately from fire, it would regenerate adequately by itself. This would save the government and the companies from spending money on forest management, which would cut into revenues. Even though the Forest Act initiated a Forest Service branch to administer the province's forests, no legislative provision was put in place to ensure long-term supply of timber through intensive forest management. Since the province's goal was for revenue from the forest, and not regulation, the Forest Service was chronically short of funds and staff to carry out even its limited responsibilities.

Nowhere in Canada during the first decades of the 20th century were forests being managed with a view to ensuring future supplies of wood. Still, the idea that big business corporations could most rationally and effectively harvest and manage the "vast, inexhaustible" forest resources was firmly entrenched in the administration of Canadian forest lands. It was this perspective that helped to reshape the eastern Canadian forest industry and that alienated much of the eastern boreal forest regions in Ontario, Quebec, and New Brunswick exclusively for pulp production.

Growth in Pulp and Paper

New pulping technologies (making pulp not from rags but from new tree species such as black spruce) and the new market opportunities that accompanied the growth of literacy, growth in importance of newspapers, and growth in consumer spending in Canada during the early 1900s created the impetus for a new pulp and paper industry.

Because loans for the expensive mills were not forthcoming without security, the large joint-stock paper companies—with the help of friendly politicians—were able to gain large timber concessions that assured access to adequate supplies of pulpwood (and the necessary loans). "Naturally, the biggest companies got the biggest concessions, usually on the basis of having promised to build new mills, use more wood and employ more workers" (Swift, 1983, p. 63).

Sustained Yield Focus

Following the financial crash of the Depression, reduced government expenditures on forestry branches affected protection, regulation, management, and research programs. The concerns of a few, relatively powerless people who understood the progressive depletion that was occurring in the nations' forests, the failure of natural regeneration, and the declines in future values and employment that these issues implied, were ignored by governments and industry.

By the end of World War II, not even an adequate inventory of forest resources existed. Without knowledge of how much timber there was, how fast it was growing or being cut or being depleted by fires and pests, and how well it was being utilized, it was almost impossible to manage the forests. Nevertheless, pressure on timber reserves continued to escalate, particularly for housing for veterans returning to civilian life. Wartime overcutting, with even greater postwar demands, meant high-grade wood was becoming harder to find. Logging moved up from the valley bottoms onto the mountainsides, visible evidence of the decline in timber quality and accessibility.

In 1945 another royal commission, chaired by the Honourable Gordon Sloan, recommended a sustained yield policy for British Columbia forests. In an effort to obtain a perpetual lumber supply, tree farm licences (TFLs) were established in law. Initially granted for perpetual terms, and ultimately for 25 years with virtually automatic replacement provisions, this was the first time a specific policy was established to treat British Columbia forests as renewable resources (Drushka, Nixon & Travers, 1993; Swift, 1983). However, the Forest Service was not guaranteed sufficient funds to adequately undertake the required policing of TFLs. By 1956, 23 TFLs had been awarded, most going to large, integrated forest products firms such as MacMillan Bloedel and Crown Zellerbach. This concerned the small logging and sawmilling businesses who were anxious about their ability to compete with the big companies for access to timber.

Continuing Concentration of Control over Harvesting Rights

Another royal commission on forestry, this one chaired by economist Peter Pearse and completed in 1976, revealed the continuing concentration of control over timber harvesting rights by a few large companies. From 1940 (pre-TFLs), when 58 firms held about 52 percent of the 4 million acres under timber licence, to 1990 when the 10 largest companies held the rights to 69 percent of the harvesting area, the big forest companies have become even bigger multinational forest companies, with integrated forest management operations around the world (Drushka et al. 1993).

Pearse called this concentration of corporate control a matter of "urgent public concern" because it meant, in the communities where these corporations operated, that they eliminated competition from the logging business, did not sell their timber on the open market where it would be available to the most efficient mills, and threatened to overwhelm the smaller resident business community (Drushka et al., 1993). In other words, past experience has shown that the forest tenure system appears not to have provided the long-term security or sustainability required to ensure that forests survive as ecologically functional and productive landscapes.

TIMBER PRODUCTION ACTIVITIES AND IMPACTS

The preceding overview of historical timber production activities in Canada identified the shift from small-scale, low-impact use of forests by Aboriginal people and early settlers to the large-scale, high-impact forest cutting practices adopted by large corporations on Crown land. The thinking and expansive talk about vast, inexhaustible, or limitless forests that characterized the early 20th century, as well as the focus on deriving maximum profit as quickly as possible, led to economically driven decisions about forest management. Thus, clear-cutting became the principal choice and conventional method of harvesting, and both the area of timber as well as the volume and species of timber harvested annually have continued to increase (Figure 9–9). "Once the forest is clearcut, most non-timber uses and values, such as wilderness, tourism, fisheries, wildlife habitat, soil and slope integrity, or water quality, are usually degraded or destroyed, for one or more human generations" (Drushka et al., 1993, p. 100). Conventional harvesting methods also contribute significantly to the large problem of loss of biodiversity.

It has become clear that the nature of harvesting practices and the concentration of harvesting rights in multinational corporations have not always satisfied local socioeconomic sustainability or environmental sustainability concerns. Although the fundamental problem of

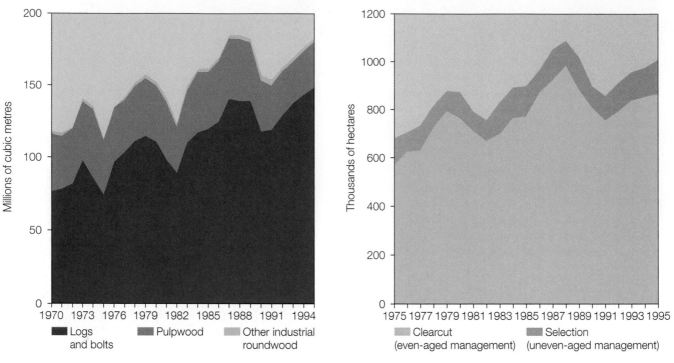

Figure 9–9

Annual area and volume of timber harvest in Canada

NOTES:

• Roundwood is the term applied to the major types of products harvested from Canadian forests. Roundwood includes sections of tree stems (with or without bark), logs, bolts (short logs to be sawn for lumber or peeled for veneer), pulpwood, posts, pilings, and other products "still in the round." Industrial roundwood also includes fuelwood for industrial or institutional needs, and firewood for household or recreational needs.

• Regional harvest trends vary substantially from this national picture.

SOURCE: Canadian Council of Forest Ministers. (1997). *Compendium of Canadian forestry statistics 1996.* Ottawa.

failure to protect forests for the future was recognized more than a century ago, it is only more recently that actions toward sustainability have begun to be developed. These actions and efforts are examined in more detail in the section dealing with responses to environmental impacts and change. Following, however, are a number of examples of the impacts of timber production on selected forest elements as well as other impacts of human activities on forest ecosystems.

Habitat, Wildlife, and Life-Support Impacts

Timber cutting, especially clear-cutting, can have significant negative effects on habitats for all species, on wildlife, and on humans, as well as on ecological life-support systems. From their place in the world's carbon storage system to their reservoir of genetic diversity, old-growth forests across Canada provide a range of immensely important global functions. After having clearcut, or committed to log, so much of the country's old-growth timber, it is only recently that the search for appropriate levels of forest use has begun. It is only

recently, also, that increased levels of knowledge have provided some basic premises on which to make more informed choices about management efforts.

Canada's forest regions are home to more than two-thirds of all species found in Canada, including about 76 percent of our land-dwelling mammals and 60 percent of breeding bird species (Natural Resources Canada, 1996b). Of the roughly 200 000 species that are dependent on forest habitats (two-thirds of the total species estimated to exist in Canada), 76 have been identified as species at risk (Table 9–4). The decline in numbers of many of these forest-dwelling species may be attributed partly to habitat loss due to timber harvesting.

The very rare Queen Charlotte goshawk, for example, was assigned "vulnerable" status in 1995 by COSEWIC— the Committee on the Status of Endangered Wildlife in Canada (Box 9–2). Only three nests have been reported on the Queen Charlotte Islands and six have been reported on Vancouver Island. The goshawk prefers to nest in large, unfragmented stands of mature forests with closed canopy cover. The dense vegetation provides ideal breeding habitat, with cover and protection from preda-

TABLE 9–4
FOREST-DWELLING SPECIES AT RISK IN CANADA (1995)

	Mammals	Birds	Plants
Endangered	wolverine eastern cougar Vancouver Island marmot	northern bobwhite northern spotted owl Acadian flycatcher whooping crane Kirtland's warbler	large whorled pogonia wood poppy small whorled pogonia cucumber tree heart-leaved plantain pink milkwort spotted wintergreen hoary mountain-mint small white lady's slipper Furbish's lousewort southern maidenhair fern

Threatened	woodland caribou
	  (Gaspé population)
	wood bison
	Newfoundland pine marten
		marbled murrelet
		hooded warbler
		yellow-breasted chat
		  (Okanagan population)
		white-headed woodpecker
			red mulberry
			purple twayblade
			Kentucky coffee tree
			nodding pogonia
			bird's-foot violet
			blunt-lobed woodsia
			sweet pepperbush
			ginseng
			golden seal
			round-leaved greenbrier
			deerberry
			mosquito fern
			American chestnut
			van Brunt's Jacob's ladder
			blue ash
			white wood aster

Vulnerable	fringed myotis bat
	spotted bat
	Keen's long-eared bat
	pallid bat
	southern flying squirrel
	Nuttall's cottontail rabbit
	  (Okanagan population)
	Gaspé shrew
	eastern mole
	grey fox
	grizzly bear
	woodland caribou
	  (western population)
		cerulean warbler
		prairie warbler
		ancient murrelet
		flammulated owl
		prothonotary warbler
		Cooper's hawk
		Louisiana waterthrush
		great grey owl
		yellow-breasted chat
		  (Eastern population)
		Queen Charlotte goshawk
			phantom orchid
			wild hyacinth
			shumard oak
			western silver-leaf aster
			swamp rose mallow
			broad beech-fern
			false rue-anemone
			few-flowered club-rush
			green dragon
			hop tree
			American columbo
			cryptic paw lichen

SOURCE: Natural Resources Canada, Canadian Forest Service. (1996b). *The state of Canada's forests 1994–1996: Sustaining forests at home and abroad.* Ottawa, p. 77.

tors. In addition to threats from poaching and pesticides, the Queen Charlotte goshawk has lost suitable nesting trees and foraging habitat due to timber harvesting (Natural Resources Canada, 1996b).

As trees disappear through logging, so do a wide range of other living things. The woodland caribou, for instance, is dying out as its boreal habitat in northwestern Ontario is logged. In British Columbia, the mountain caribou population is declining as logging in old-growth forests destroys an important food source—the lichen that grow on mature timber (Natural Resources Canada, 1995). (For additional information on caribou, see Pruitt,

The Committee on the Status of Endangered Wildlife in Canada (COSEWIC) assesses the rarity of Canada's flora and fauna. To determine the status of a species, experts must collect information about the past and present geographical distribution of that species. To get an idea of how much change there has been in a species, its current range is compared to its historical range.

COSEWIC representatives include people from federal and provincial wildlife agencies, universities, scientific institutions, and non-governmental organizations across Canada. The committee meets annually to consider candidate species for which experts have prepared status reports. By 1994, COSEWIC had evaluated 351 species or populations. Of these, 10 had insufficient information to permit classification, and 86 did not require designation as rare, vulnerable, threatened, or endangered. The 1994 status of Canada's wildlife (excluding invertebrates, fungi, algae, bacteria, and other wild organisms about which relatively little is known) is shown below.

Although COSEWIC and other national programs monitor and assess species at risk, there is no comprehensive program in Canada to assess the status of wildlife in general, or of forest species in particular.

	Known Species	Status of Species and Subspecies at Risk				
Species Group	Total	Endangered	Threatened	Vulnerable	Total	% of Species Group
Mammals	193	11	8	22	41	21.2
Birds	578	14	9	22	45	7.8
Fish	1 091	3	12	38	53	4.8
Plants	4 328	23	30	29	82	1.9
Amphibians and reptiles	83	4	3	7	14	16.8
Total	6 273	55	62	118	235	3.7

SOURCES: Eagles, P.F.J. (1995). Environmental management in parks. In P. Dearden & R. Rollins (Eds). *Parks and protected areas in Canada.* (pp. 154–84). Toronto: Oxford University Press.

Natural Resources Canada, Canadian Forest Service. (1995). *The state of Canada's forests 1994: A balancing act.* Ottawa, p. 23.

1997, as well as the Web sites for the Government of the Northwest Territories, and for the woodland caribou, listed in the Additional Information Sources section of this chapter).

Migratory birds such as the Cape May warbler, whose summer range includes Ontario's boreal forests, are affected by the loss of habitat caused by logging. As recent research findings have shown, loss of Neotropical migratory birds from forests has important implications for control of insect outbreaks (Box 9–3). In other parts of the world, similar wild species losses occur. Australia has lost 18 of its native mammals in the recent past, many from Western Australia where 95 percent of the natural woodland has been cleared (Pimm, 1996).

Other habitat losses occur as soil and debris from clear-cut slopes erode into rivers and streams, suffocating aquatic species. Rainfall can exacerbate erosion problems: in the Clayoquot Sound area in January 1996, for instance, heavy rain generated over 250 landslides, mostly in clearcut logged areas (Rainforest Action Network, 1996). Companies responsible for other damage to British Columbia streams and fish habitat allegedly caused by logging roads and operations have been difficult to prosecute (Friends of Clayoquot Sound, 1996).

Such effects are found world wide; for instance, in the northern Philippines, logging roads were found to have caused erosion more than 200 times greater than on undisturbed sites (Ryan, 1990). Millions of dollars of damage to fisheries and coral reefs caused by logging-induced sedimentation has been documented. Near Palawan in the Philippines, fisheries in Bacuit Bay were depleted after logging began on surrounding hillsides. Sediment entering the bay smothered up to half of the living coral that supported the fishery, depriving local people of their source of protein (Ryan, 1990). In the mid-1960s, harvesting $14 million worth of timber from the watershed of the South Fork of the Salmon River in central Idaho caused an estimated $100 million damage to the river's Chinook salmon fishery. That industry still has not recovered.

A variety of plants are threatened by timber operations, too. The white wood aster, a perennial herb that is known to grow in only five sites in Quebec and three in the Carolinian forests of Ontario, has declined and was

Neotropical migratory birds such as the rufous hummingbird, the western tanager, or the several warbler species that inhabit the Pacific Northwest and boreal forests, spend only one-third of their lives in Canada or the United States. The remainder of their time is spent in tropical regions such as Mexico, the Caribbean, and Central and South America (or areas in between their summer and winter homes). Of the nearly 200 species of Neotropical birds, some travel thousands of miles twice a year.

These Neotropical birds, as well as resident birds such as juncos, thrushes, pine siskins, chickadees, nuthatches, and some woodpeckers, play an incredible role in helping to keep forest trees healthy. While not all birds eat insects, the majority do, as many as 300 insects per day during the summer months. A pair of breeding evening grosbeaks, for example, can devour 25 000 to 50 000 caterpillars just in the period it takes them to raise their brood.

Recently, United States Forest Service biologists in the Pacific Northwest learned that 35 species of birds, including 24 Neotropical migrants, feed on the western spruce budworm and the Douglas fir tussock moth, which are the two most destructive defoliating insects there. When the caterpillars (or larvae) of the western spruce budworm and Douglas fir tussock moth eat the needles of these trees, they weaken them, making them vulnerable to attack by other insects or to diseases that ultimately kill the trees. Severe outbreaks of these insects can result in the loss of millions of trees over thousands of hectares of forested land.

One of the responses to these insect outbreaks has been to spray insecticides to kill the budworm and tussock moth. However, this partially effective action kills beneficial insects and spiders along with the pests. Killing the beneficial insects affects forest birds and animals that depend on all types of invertebrates for food.

Knowing that both Neotropical and resident birds feed on budworm and tussock moth larvae, the Forest Service scientists planned an experiment to see just how effective the birds were in eating budworms off fir trees. The scientists enclosed entire,

30-foot-tall fir trees in cages of PVC pipe and plastic netting to prevent birds from feeding on the caterpillars on those trees. The results showed that six times more budworms survived on the caged trees than on uncaged trees. This means that the birds were eating five of every six caterpillars, and were making a tremendous difference to the health of the forests.

Unfortunately, the populations of dozens of species of Neotropical migratory birds that spend their summers in the forests of the Pacific Northwest and the boreal forests of northern Canada have declined during the past two decades. Biologists believe these declines are the result of changes in nesting or wintering habitat (or both). Activities such as logging and land clearing result in less available food, fewer nesting sites, and less protection from natural enemies for these birds. Logging and land clearing also affect streamside (or riparian) habitats, which are favourite nesting or foraging sites for many birds species. Building roads and allowing grazing near streams also have caused problems for birds.

If healthy forests are to be maintained, responsible managers need to realize that essential forest-dwelling birds need suitable nesting and foraging areas. This implies that managers need to plan for forest diversity with a variety of tree species of different ages, including standing snags and fallen logs. One international effort to help stem the decline in populations of Neotropical birds, is the Partners in Flight—Aves de las Americas Neotropical Migratory Bird Conservation Program.

Initiated in 1990, the Partners in Flight program brings public and private partners, including Canadian, American, Mexican, Caribbean, and Latin American conservation organizations, together in efforts to conserve migratory songbirds. The basic principles of their strategy, known as the Flight Plan, include promotion of conservation of habitats in breeding, migration, and wintering areas when it should be done—before species and ecosystems become endangered. Conservation based on sound science, such as that described here, is also an important principle of the Flight Plan. Saving our birds is indeed a way to save our forests.

SOURCES: Environment Canada. (1996). *Partners in Flight—Canada.* http://www.ec.gc.ca/cws-scf/canbird/pif/p_title.htm

National Fish and Wildlife Foundation. (n.d.). *Neotropical Migratory Bird Conservation.* http://www.nfwf.org/nfwfne.htm

National Fish and Wildlife Foundation. (1996). *National Fish and Wildlife Foundation.* http://www.bev.net/education/SeaWorld/conservation/nfw.html

Torgersen, T.R., & Torgersen, A.S. (1995). *Save our birds—save our forests.* Portland, OR: United States Department of Agriculture, Forest Service.

United States Geological Survey. (n.d.). *Partners in Flight home page.* http://www.pwrc.nbs.gov/pif/

designated by COSEWIC as a threatened species in 1995 (Table 9–4). This aster is threatened largely because of habitat loss resulting from human and natural changes in the forest ecosystem (Natural Resources Canada, 1996a). In Alberta's boreal forests alone, about 100 plant species

are known to grow only in the boreal forest and about half of these are rare already (Acharya, 1995).

In the Pacific Northwest, wild mushroom harvests likely would be destroyed should logging occur in the old-growth forests where the fungi grow (Box 9–4). The case

The central Swan Hills area, 35 kilometres north of Whitecourt, Alta., September 27, 1949 (9.1 × 9.1 km). North is to the top of the image, as it is in the two accompanying photos.

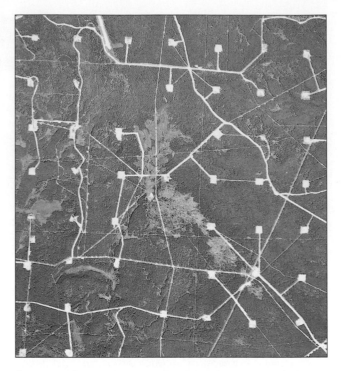

The central Swan Hills area, July 2, 1964 (7.2 × 7.2 km). The grey lines are roads, pipelines, and transmission lines; small squares are well sites; large patches are clear-cuts.

The central Swan Hills area, October 7, 1991 (13.6 × 13.6 km). In just 42 years a wilderness area is transformed into an intensely fragmented, ecologically dysfunctional landscape.

of the "worthless" Pacific yew tree (see Enviro-Focus 3) also highlights the need for enhanced awareness of the importance and protection of what may appear to be insignificant species in our forests. If people are to gain a

full range of benefits from forest products and avoid the irrecoverable losses of biodiversity and ecological function that can occur under certain harvesting regimes, the precautionary principle (see Chapter 1) is applicable.

Degradation and Deforestation of Tropical Forests

Although tropical rain forests occupy only about 6 percent of the world's land area near the equator in Latin America, Africa, and Asia, they provide habitat for at least one-half of the Earth's plant and animal species, and homes and livelihoods for about 100 million people. The global importance of tropical forests relates to their ecological functions as well as to the products produced from their plants—nuts, fruits, chocolate, gums, coffee, wood, rubber, pesticides, fibres, and dyes. In particular, people with high blood pressure, Parkinson's or Hodgkin's disease, multiple sclerosis, and leukemia have been treated with drugs made from tropical plants. Scientists believe many more plants with medicinal values remain to be discovered. For these and other reasons, the issue of tropical deforestation must be included in this discussion of human activities and impacts on forests.

In the developing parts of the world, population growth and chronic poverty are among the reasons there have been massive destruction and degradation of tropical forests. Reasons for the deforestation of tropical forests vary regionally: in Latin America, rain forests often are converted to pastureland, in sub-Saharan Africa, they

BOX 9-4
FORESTS AND WILD MUSHROOMS

The Pacific Northwest has been recognized for a long time for its rich mycota—such as mushrooms, truffles, conks, puffballs, and cup fungi—that are found in conjunction with old-growth forests. The richness of the mycota is related directly to the region's expansive forest communities, diversity of tree species, and weather patterns. Under these conditions, forest tree species form beneficial root symbioses (mycorrhizae) with specialized fungi that obtain their carbohydrate nutrition via the roots of the host trees. The wood of both live and dead trees and the abundance of other organic debris on the forest floor provide rich resources for numerous fungi. In turn, these fungi are very important contributors to the dynamic functioning of forest ecosystems, providing food for organisms from microbes to mammals and contributing to the overall resiliency and diversity of forest ecosystems. "If we are to succeed at managing forest ecosystems in their entirety, we must integrate the biological and functional diversity of forest fungi into future management plans" (Pilz & Molina, 1996, p. 1).

Pushing through the mossy floor surrounding 100- to 200-year-old lodgepole pine, Douglas fir, and western hemlock, the firm, white to pale brown pine mushrooms (Tricholoma magnivelare) are found along the coast and interior mountain ranges of western North America. In Canada, pine mushrooms also are found in the eastern Maritimes, and throughout the boreal forests of Manitoba and Saskatchewan. Under ideal conditions pine mushrooms can grow to more than five pounds each!

Of the more than 30 species of wild edible mushrooms that are harvested in British Columbia, the pine mushroom is one of the few that is picked commercially on a large scale. Pickers who harvest top-grade pine mushrooms can command anywhere from $8 to $300 per pound for these fungi.

The pine fungi is closely related to the very popular Japanese Tricholoma matsutake mushroom, which, because of the medicinal qualities it is believed to contain, has been an integral part of the Japanese diet for centuries. In the 1980s, however, Japanese matsutake crops declined as a result of "the ailing health of its red pine forests, the symbiotic partner of the matsutake" (Welland, 1997, p. 66). (Of note are similar declines in European fungi that have been linked to pollution such as acid precipitation and sulphur dioxide [Amaranthus & Pilz, 1996]). At the same time as supplies of the pine mushroom declined, the demand for it grew; by the early 1990s, Canada was the world's fourth leading exporter of pine mushrooms to Japan.

The pine mushroom is a "fussy fungi, needing an undisturbed forest floor to propagate; any pawing or raking of the moss covering can set future growth back for years" (Welland, 1997, p. 64). Extensive harvesting of several species of edible forest mushrooms during the past decade has heightened awareness and concern for forest fungi on the part of the public and resource managers. While economic benefits are sizable—such as the $40 million that wild mushroom picking contributed to the economies of Oregon, Washington, and Idaho in 1992, or the almost $4 million harvesters earned in 1994 in the Nass Valley in northern British Columbia—so are the concerns about the potential overharvesting of wild mushrooms and the impact of mushroom harvesting on forest ecosystems. Clear-cut logging, scheduled to occur in the Nass Valley soon, also is a concern.

In the United States, legislation and permit systems to regulate the commercial harvest of wild mushrooms on public lands have been instituted. As well, President Clinton's 1993 Forest Ecosystem Management Assessment Team report identified the need to study and protect fungi throughout Pacific Northwest forests and to integrate these forest fungi into ecosystem management plans.

In British Columbia, regulation of the mushroom harvesting industry has been resisted. The Nisga'a First Nation's recent land claims settlement may signal a change, however. As they now own all forest resources within some 2000 square kilometres of the Nass Valley, the Nisga'a patrolled the valley in 1996 to contain the harvesters within main camping centres. As well, through their company, Nass Valley Resources, Inc., they hope to develop a food processing facility in the area for mushrooms, fish, and other local foods. Obviously, none of these actions will result in the opportunity to study or protect the pine mushroom should logging occur. Thus, an adaptive management process is recommended in which, as new information is acquired, it may be incorporated continuously into revised management plans.

SOURCES: Amaranthus, M., & Pilz, D. (1996). Productivity and sustainable harvest of wild mushrooms. In D. Pilz & R. Molina (Eds.). Managing forest ecosystems to conserve fungus diversity and sustain wild mushroom harvests. (pp. 42–61). Portland, OR: United States Department of Agriculture, Forest Service, Pacific Northwest Research Station: General Technical Report PNW-GTR-371.

Pilz, D., & Molina, R. (Eds.). (1996). Introduction. Managing forest ecosystems to conserve fungus diversity and sustain wild mushroom harvests (pp. 1–4). Portland, OR: United States Department of Agriculture, Forest Service, Pacific Northwest Research Station: General Technical Report PNW-GTR-371.

Welland, F. (1997). Mushroom madness. Canadian Geographic, 117(1), pp. 62–68.

Caribou *(Rangifer caribou)* foraging on the tundra vegetation.

are cleared to meet increasing demands for farmland and firewood; and in Southeast Asia, rain forests provide hardwood products for export to industrialized countries.

The high rate of removal of trees in the Brazilian rain forest in the 1980s—the catalyst for much of the global concern regarding loss of tropical rain forests—was based mostly on changes occurring in the state of Rondonia as the World Bank–financed highway (BR 364) was constructed. Undertaken without environmental impact assessments, the highway served to funnel urban migrants (who were looking for ways to improve their quality of life) into the forests. In clearing plots in the forest on which to build their homes and grow crops, these inexperienced newcomers cut and burned too much forest and did not allow depleted soils to recover. This unsustainable small-scale farming, combined with the expansion of livestock ranching operations, ultimately destroyed large tracts of forest. In other regions such as Central America, about two-thirds of tropical rain forests have been lost to livestock raising (Bequette, 1994).

Cash crops displace forests in many parts of the world. The African nation of Ethiopia, for example, once 40 percent forest covered, now uses about 60 percent of its land to grow cotton and a further 22 percent to grow sugar cane. Only about 3 percent remains in forests (Bequette, 1994; Mungall & McLaren, 1990). In other countries, trees are cut to provide land for large plantations on which to grow banana, tea, and coffee crops, mostly destined for the more developed countries. Cacao and rubber planters, as well as growers of marijuana and cocaine-yielding coca, contribute to destruction of tropical forests.

Firewood consumption adds to the problem of tree loss in developing countries. Half of the world's wood is used as fuel for cooking and heating, and yet in 1985, about one in three persons on Earth was not able to get enough fuelwood to meet basic needs or was forced to meet those needs by consuming wood faster than it was being replenished. Wood scarcity creates considerable

hardship for poor families as buying fuelwood or charcoal can take 40 percent of a family's small income. Women, especially, often have to walk long distances to gather fuel. If they cannot get enough fuelwood, poor families often burn dried animal dung and crop residues. This means that these natural fertilizers are not returned to the soil, and, as cropland productivity declines, hunger and malnutrition increase. In addition, cutting trees for fuelwood often results in increased erosion and may even lead to permanent lowering of water tables.

The timber industry is another factor in deforestation. Since 1950, the consumption of tropical hardwoods has increased by a factor of 15, satisfying markets in Japan (which consumes about 60 percent of annual tropical timber production), the United States, and Great Britain. Developing countries often sell off their forests to pay their debts and to create jobs. Ninety percent covered by virgin rain forest, Surinam (on the northeast coast of South America), granted large timber concessions to an Indonesian logging company in 1994. This decision was based on the fact that children in Surinam were dying of hunger and cutting forests would provide much needed jobs and an improved ability to purchase required foodstuffs (Bequette, 1994). The Bahinemos of Papua New Guinea, whose ancestral home is the Hunstein forest, faced similar pressures to gain cash for the education of

People in developing nations rely heavily on fuel-wood cutting, which threatens renewability of forests and associated resources.

their children and to acquire Western goods. However, foreign logging activities, no matter how careful, would cause the loss of large birds such as cassowaries and impact dramatically on the Bahinemos culture and landscape (Bakker, 1994).

Impacts of such decisions can be extreme: countries that once exported timber—Nigeria and the Philippines, for example—now import it. Other Southeast Asian and Central American nations have almost totally deforested their lands: Haiti has lost 98 percent of its original forest cover, the Philippines 97 percent, and Madagascar 84 percent. Most cleared tropical forests are not replanted because timber companies are held responsible for few of the costs of environmental degradation. It is expected that timber in Southeast Asia will be depleted in the 1990s, and that cutting will shift to Latin America and Africa. African mahogany often is logged selectively, perhaps one tree per hectare but, to reach logging sites, trails as much as 100 kilometres long must be cut, opening the way for land-hungry farmers and subsequent degradation of forest lands (Bequette, 1994).

POLLUTION

Pollution is a widespread problem in boreal forests. Pulping operations release toxic organochlorines, such as dioxins, and other substances into water bodies. Sometimes disastrous effects on aquatic life occur, and often damaging effects on the health of First Nations people are observed. Examples abound; in Ontario, long-term discharge of mill effluent threatened local people with Minimata disease (mercury poisoning) from eating contaminated fish from the Wabigoon River system. In the case of the largest bleached kraft mill in the world, Mitsubishi's Alberta-Pacific mill located on the Athabasca River, chlorine is used to bleach 1500 metric tons of pulp per day (Acharya, 1995). Completed in 1993, this mill

Acid rain has had a detrimental effect on the world's forests.

releases dioxins and other toxins that require long-term monitoring to prevent cumulative toxic damage. Throughout British Columbia, too, the health of Indigenous people has been threatened for many years by the eating of fish and shellfish contaminated by pulp mill effluents.

Some of the world's most serious cases of air pollution causing damage to forests are found in Russia. Russian mining and smelting operations produce among the world's highest sulphur emissions that, in turn, have killed off entire Russian forests and damaged forests outside of Russia. During the 1950s and 1960s, huge smelters were built on the mineral-rich Kola Peninsula bordering Norway and Finland. These plants continue to use obsolete technology, and produce nearly as many tons of sulphur emissions as they do metals and minerals. In 1988, for instance, the Severo-Nickel smelter on the Kola Peninsula produced 243 000 tons of nickel, copper, and cobalt, and 212 000 tons of sulphur dioxide (Acharya, 1995).

These sulphur emissions have outright killed forests on 40 000 to 100 000 hectares and damaged 3 million hectares of forest in Russia alone. The damage extends into Norway and Finland; both countries regarded the pollution as a major foreign policy problem and offered help in upgrading the plants. However, because Russia uses its metals to bring in hard currency, the plants continued to operate using imported ores that contained even higher sulphur content than the exhausted local ores.

Elsewhere in Russia, such as at Krasnoyarsk in the south-central part of the country, fluorine emissions from aluminum smelters are identified as the prime cause of 3.2 million hectares of dead and dying forests. Southern Sweden and Norway are impacted by the long-range transport of acid precipitation and other forms of air pollution from this area. Deposition of sulphur dioxide and nitrous oxides has affected soils so radically that some of them may not be able to support another generation of trees. Radioactive pollution is another problem affecting forests in parts of the former Soviet Union, including about 1 million hectares around Chernobyl. As fires in contaminated forests release dust and smoke, radioactive pollution drifts on air currents for hundreds of kilometres (Acharya, 1995).

In Germany, the word *Waldsterben* (meaning "forest death") describes the forest decline that has affected more than one-third of the country's forests, as well as up to 25 percent of the fir and spruce trees in Switzerland and more than 1.2 million acres of forest in Poland and Czechoslovakia (Hammond, 1991). The primary cause of this forest decline is the long-range transport of airborne pollutants (LRTAP) from combustion of fossil fuels in vehicles and from many industrial processes, including thermal power generation and smelting.

The acid deposition that results from this LRTAP causes direct damage and loss of foliage and needles to trees by leaching out nutrients, causing thinning and perhaps fatal damage to the tree's crown. As well, indirect damage through soil acidification (in which heavy metals are released in forms taken up by tree roots) occurs. In Canada, acid precipitation contributes to, and may well be the major cause of, forest decline in southwestern British Columbia as well as the loss of sugar maple trees in Quebec. Slash burning and the pulp manufacturing process also contribute to the problem of forest decline in Canada.

Slowing the rate at which boreal, temperate, and tropical forests are being destroyed requires changes in governmental policies as well as in consumer and corporate awareness, attitudes, and behaviour. Evidence that some of these changes are occurring is presented in the Responses to Environmental Impacts and Change section of this chapter.

SOCIOCULTURAL DIMENSIONS

There are many groups in Canadian society whose interests in the forest are based more on long-term (rather than short-term) economic considerations. Included among such groups are Aboriginal people, nature-based tourism operators, rural water users, ranchers, trappers, small business owners in forest-based communities, wilderness users, scientists, artists, educators, and future generations of Canadians. Governments are expected to manage public forests and forest lands for the long-term benefit of all these people. These same people have been challenging governments to change the ways forests are used, to move away from the old volume economy and to develop a new forest economy, one based on value-added industries and on community, rather than corporate, control of forests.

Indigenous peoples lived as part of the North American forests for centuries before Europeans arrived in this land. Their sovereignty "has never been diminished through conquest, prior discovery, purchase, or fair treaties by the various governments of European descendants which have controlled Canada for the last two centuries" (Hammond, 1991, p. 134). Canadians with a sense of social justice have recognized that, with some exceptions recently, the land question remains largely unresolved. Displacement of indigenous peoples from their traditional homelands by European settlers and the subsequent suppression and sometimes abuse of Aboriginal cultures have diminished the opportunity to learn about sustaining the forests from those people who once were part of them. (For more information on forests and indigenous people, see Barsch, 1997.)

For Aboriginal peoples, the land claims process embodies an enigma: why must something be claimed that was never given up? While struggles are ongoing to address Aboriginal title adequately and to settle land questions justly, the timber industry is said to be "swiftly foreclosing on the options that Indigenous people will

have following any agreement" (Hammond, 1991, p. 135). As noted previously, by the time the land claims process is concluded, forest lands are likely to have been heavily logged. Logging means not only that these people will be denied timber sale royalties, but also that they will lose traditional hunting and gathering territories.

A case in point is that of the Innu living in Nitassinan (Labrador and Quebec); in the summer of 1994, they were involved in land rights negotiations with Canada and Newfoundland when the Newfoundland Forest Service constructed new access roads in Forestry Management District 20, despite legislation requiring an approved forestry management plan before any new activity took place (Innu Nation, 1995). While the forests were not exploited actively by large-scale industrial forest operations at that time, the wood deficit forecast for the island of Newfoundland meant that large pulp interests were looking toward Nitassinan to fill the gap.

Indigenous people are not the only ones attempting to gain more control over timber operations so that forestry-based lifestyles may continue. In many communities, people are working toward environmentally sustainable, socially acceptable, and economically feasible community forestry-based futures (see Hammond, 1997, in the Additional Information Sources section of this chapter). Some of the results of their efforts are noted later in the chapter.

TOURISM AND RECREATION

Natural forest landscapes are an important factor in the health of the tourism industry across Canada. Valued at billions of dollars per year, forest-related tourism occurs in national and provincial parks and in provincial forests through activities such as hunting and fishing, wilderness hiking, river rafting and canoe tripping, skiing, and camping and picnicking. Of considerable economic and social importance is the fact that tourism tends to leave the revenues from these activities in the communities where the tourism occurs (rather than leak revenues to foreign-owned corporations or major urban centres).

Wildlife viewing—from waterways, forest trails, and viewing stations—is a multimillion-dollar, nonconsumptive forest use and activity in Canada. Provided that forest-based tourism occurs in forest areas that are protected and used wisely, long-term annual benefits will accrue to many communities. In contrast, revenues from consumptive use of forests such as clear-cutting are periodic; once the trees are cut and profits taken, there is no more revenue until trees regrow to a merchantable size—in about 100 years in most Canadian forests.

Old-growth forests are prime wildlife habitat and provide superb scenic backdrops for visitors who have been brought to the forest by their interest in birds, mammals, fish, and plants. Even the trees themselves are visitor

Canada's forests provide economic returns through recreation and tourism as well as commercial forestry.

attractions. Cutting old-growth forests for their timber values precludes the economic benefits that come from sustainable, nontimber values such as wildlife viewing. Even though it is difficult to calculate a precise dollar value, trees are worth a lot to the tourism industry. So are intact forest landscapes and forest-dependent wildlife populations such as occur in the Stein, Khutzeymateen, or Kitlope watersheds of British Columbia. Each of these is an area that was slated for logging but was later protected, in part through public demand, because of their undeniably great nontimber values (Robinson, 1994).

A tree containing half a cubic metre of wood—a typical size tree for Canada—can be cut down in less than 30 seconds by machine and sold as a log delivered to the mill for less than $30. What is that tree worth to a rural community that will draw its water supply from a forested watershed for generations to come? What is it worth to a vacationing family, seeking to be refreshed by unspoiled natural beauty (and spending $150 to $250 per day while doing so)? What is it worth to a photographer focusing on a flying squirrel or a grizzly bear? What is it worth to the flying squirrel or the grizzly? If the timber industry takes the trees, then the community, the tourists, the photographer, the flying squirrel, and the bear cannot use the forest. To protect the future economic value of the forest, and of our communities, we need to think beyond the timber (Hammond, 1991; Rowe, 1997).

As a growth industry in Canada, tourism and recreational services will continue to depend on healthy, natural amenities, including unmanaged forests. Thinking beyond the timber means that potential impacts of logging on tourism operations need to be considered in land use decisions.

In 1995, foresters and environmentalists clashed over plans to clear-cut much of the 700 square kilometres of the Algoma Highlands, 150 kilometres northeast of Sault Ste. Marie, Ontario. A 60-square-kilometre conservation reserve was excluded from harvesting, as was a large (temporary) area around Megasin Lake in the centre of the Highlands. Wilderness outfitters in that area argued that logging was incompatible with their successful remote tourism operations, and forced the provincial government to undertake its first ever environmental assessment of a forest management plan. The environmental assessment, however, focused only on the impacts of logging on tourism, and did not consider other environmental impacts (Leahy, 1995).

A proposed "view-scape cut," where narrow bands of trees would be left to ring the major lakes and streams used by tourists, may hide clear-cut slopes beyond the tree ring, but does not provide the healthy, natural forest amenities that are part of the expected quality experience for wilderness visitors. Outfitters worry that this lack of a quality experience could lead to a lack of repeat customers that, in the longer term, could cause a reversal in the economic viability of their operations.

A similar situation exists near Powell River, British Columbia. Fiddlehead Farm is surrounded by extensive tree farm licences and could close because of logging slated for adjacent Giovanno Valley. Visitors to the 32-hectare wilderness hostel arrive by boat and then walk in through two kilometres of forest. The forest company's five-year logging plan includes eight clear-cuts in the valley adjacent to the farm and a mainline logging road across the walk-in access route. The owner of the farm believes the noise and visual impact of summer logging will force her to close the hostel, where not even a generator disturbs the peace now (the farm uses a creek-powered turbine).

The manager of the forestry company, which annually puts about $30 million into Powell River's economy, indicated that because the industry has to exist somewhere, the option of leaving the valley untouched was not negotiable. However, the manner in which the logging was conducted was negotiable: selective logging or smaller clear-cuts could be undertaken, but partial cuts would take twice as long and require twice as many roads. In early 1997, proposed cuts in this area were under review by the British Columbia Ministry of Forests (McPhedran, 1997).

When people involved in tourism and recreational activities access public or private forests for nonconsumptive uses, a number of risks may arise. For instance, more human-started fires may occur, and demands for improved infrastructure (such as toilets and parking lots) may be encountered. In addition, governments and private land owners may face increased liability if natural forest events such as wildfires or falling trees damage equipment or injure or kill visitors. These realities do not diminish the value of natural forests, however, but add a cautionary note to the optimism expressed regarding tourism development in forests.

OTHER HUMAN IMPACTS

Clearing of forest lands for agriculture and grazing, and to accommodate community and urban development, has been ongoing in Canada almost since settlement began. Perhaps nowhere are the impacts of these human activities seen more clearly than in the Carolinian forest in Ontario. Located on the fertile plain north of Lake Erie, less than 10 percent of the area remains in forest cover, the remainder having been cleared since the time of the European settlers. More than 95 percent of the Carolinian forest is privately owned, and less than 1 percent is contained in national and provincial parks. The nature of this forest, its importance, and an indication of efforts being undertaken to conserve what remains of it are discussed in Box 9–5.

BOX 9–5
CANADA'S CAROLINIAN LIFE ZONE

Canada's Carolinian forest covers the southernmost part of Ontario, stretching from the Rouge River Valley in Toronto along the shore of Lake Erie. The forest represents the northern extreme of the eastern deciduous forest region that covers a vast area south of the Great Lakes. The Carolinian forest supports natural habitats and species found nowhere else in Canada. Sixteen endangered plants and animals are native to the Carolinian region, and at least one-third of our country's rare, threatened, or endangered species depend on its natural habitats. More than half of Canada's bird species are found in the Carolinian forest; so is the highest representation of reptiles in Canada. The Carolinian forest is home to the opossum, North America's only marsupial. The forest area is one of the few places in North America where the American chestnut has not been eradicated by chestnut blight. Other Carolinian tree species include the tulip, Kentucky coffee, black gum, cucumber, sycamore, and sassafras.

Early settlers were attracted to the region's relatively warm climate and highly productive agricultural lands. Today more than 20 percent of Canada's population lives in the Carolinian zone. As a result of extensive urbanization in the Toronto to Windsor corridor, less than 10 percent of the land has any forest cover. In fact, all of the counties within the Carolinian zone have less than 20 percent natural forest cover remaining, while some townships are approaching zero percent cover. Clearly, Southern Ontario's Carolinian forests have been and are influenced greatly by human activities.

Although large tracts of Carolinian forest containing similar habitats and range of species remain in the United States,

Cucumber tree.

Canada's Carolinian zone is particularly worthy of conservation. Ontario's small patch is considered crucial because species living near the limit of their range have unique characteristics—such as exceptional hardiness—that can be passed on to and strengthen those species over their entire range.

Protecting Carolinian habitat is especially challenging because most forest remaining in Ontario is fragmented. A variety of complex issues, such as understanding the problem of natural succession, must be considered when managing fragmented natural areas. As a forest matures, new species take over from older ones in a cycle of replacement. In large wilderness areas, most plant species normally survive because occasional natural disturbances, such as fires, storms, and insect infestations, merely slow or reduce the natural succession of the area. While an isolated forest fire may be healthy to a large forest, the same size fire could be devastating to a forest remnant. Conversely, if the remnant is left alone, succession by new species may replace existing ones. The possibility of Carolinian species being replaced by more northerly species is a significant threat in Ontario's Carolinian forests.

One of the best remaining examples of mature Carolinian forest in Canada is the 265-hectare Backus Woods located a few kilometres from Lake Erie. The site was owned by the Backus family, operators of a flour mill and sawmill beginning in 1798. Backus Woods remained largely intact because the family

Tulip tree.

recognized the value of preserving their forest to protect the watershed for the creek that powered their mills. Backus Woods presently is owned by the Long Point Region Conservation Authority and managed by an advisory committee. In the Backus Woods management plan, half the forest is designated as a natural zone, where no human interference is allowed. The remaining half is a conservation zone where action may be taken to stop natural succession if Carolinian species are threatened.

Both conservationists and forest managers agree that Carolinian forests must be further protected and expanded in Ontario. By expanding Carolinian forests, genetic exchange between adjacent forest remnants can be encouraged. Genetic exchange is important to ensure that plants can build up the tolerance needed to respond to environmental changes such as global warming. Organizations such as the World Wildlife Fund and Long Point Region Conservation Authority are working towards enlarging the woods by buying adjacent properties and encouraging voluntary stewardship initiatives.

Stewardship initiatives in Canada's Carolinian zone began in 1983 with the Carolinian Canada project. The initiative was conceived by the Natural Heritage League (a network of 38 private organizations and public agencies linked by mutual interest and involvement in the identification, protection, and management of Ontario's natural heritage), the Nature Conservancy of Canada, and the World Wildlife Fund.

During the 1984 to 1985 period, 36 priority unprotected Carolinian forest sites were identified, two-thirds (9800 hectares) of which were privately owned. A landowner contact program was established to target these owners of our natural heritage and encourage their willingness to enter into stewardship agreements. Voluntary agreements were then negotiated by the league's Natural Heritage Stewardship Program based at the University of Guelph. By 1988, 347 verbal agreements had been negotiated in Carolinian Canada sites, and as of 1996, more than 1000 land owners had been contacted by members of the Natural Heritage Stewardship Program.

For more information about Carolinian Canada, write to the Natural Heritage League at the address given in the Additional Information Sources section at the end of this chapter.

SOURCES: Federation of Ontario Naturalists. (n.d.). *What is Carolinian Canada?* (Brochure).

Gorrie, P. (1994). The enchanted woodland. *Canadian Geographic,* 114(2), pp. 32–42.

Natural Resources Canada, Canadian Forest Service. (1994). *The state of Canada's forests 1993: Forests, a global resource.* Ottawa.

Van Patter, M., & Hilts, S. (1990). Natural heritage protection: Voluntary stewardship or planning control? *Plan Canada,* 30(5), pp. 20–28.

RESPONSES TO ENVIRONMENTAL IMPACTS AND CHANGE

Many countries that produce and consume forest products are trying to come to grips with the need to balance economic and environmental requirements in order to ensure healthy, vigorous forests that can meet the needs of today as well as tomorrow. Over time there has been a continued focus on balancing economic development and conservation, although the relative emphasis placed on development and conservation has varied. A relatively early example is the 1983 International Tropical Timber Agreement (ITTA). In this agreement, most attention was focused on promoting economic expansion, increasing timber processing, and diversifying international trade in tropical timber in order to promote industrialization and improve export earnings. The concept of sustainable use and conservation of tropical forests and their genetic resources was included as the final objective of the ITTA.

Much of the recent international dialogue on the future of the world's forests took place during the two-year process of preparing for the 1992 United Nations Conference on Environment and Development (UNCED). The Canadian delegation "played a lead role in structuring the debate and engaging the world forest community in the deliberations" (Forestry Canada, 1993, p. 68). The following sections identify some important international and Canadian initiatives that have been taken in response to the challenges relating to forest sustainability.

INTERNATIONAL INITIATIVES

UNCED Forest Principles

In recognizing that environmental considerations were becoming increasingly important in the international forest trade, one of Canada's priorities prior to the Earth Summit (UNCED) was to establish an internationally accepted definition and measurement of sustainable forest development. The thinking was that scientifically based international criteria for sustainable forest development would create a level playing field for competitors in forest products markets and would encourage more producers to practise sustainable forest management (Forestry Canada, 1993).

Initially, Canada was aiming to develop criteria for sustainable forest development within a legally binding international agreement. That did not happen, partly because of the different perspectives that nations hold regarding the social, economic, and environmental importance of forests. For instance, developed nations were concerned about protecting tropical rain forests as storehouses of biodiversity and as greenhouse gas sinks, while developing nations felt their tropical forests could be exploited for their timber as well as for potential farmland and as a free source of fuel (Taylor, 1994). By the end of the meetings, however, consensus was achieved and expressed as the UNCED Forest Principles (Table 9–5).

Even though they are not legally binding, these First Principles represent an important international breakthrough in agreement about what constitutes sound forest management. Attaining a legally binding agreement will be challenging, however, as the Forest Principles document contains contradictory elements. On the one hand, for instance, the document indicates that forests should be managed sustainably to meet the social, economic, ecological, cultural, and spiritual human needs of present and future generations. On the other hand, the document underscores the sovereign rights of nations to exploit their forests in ways that continue to endanger the world's forests (see United Nations Conference on Environment and Development, 1992, in the Additional Information Sources section at the end of this chapter). Whether Canada's efforts to change international policy will be successful remains to be seen.

In the absence of a binding agreement, Canada began to implement these Forest Principles through action plans established under the national forest strategy (discussed more fully in the section on Canadian law, policy, and practice).

Agenda 21

The 1992 Earth Summit produced a second document of relevance to forests, *Agenda 21*. The massive (but not legally binding) *Agenda 21* document set an international agenda for development and the environment in the 21st century, focusing particularly on the needs of developing nations. *Agenda 21* recognized the impacts human activities have had on forests: "Forests worldwide have been and are being threatened by uncontrolled degradation and conversion to other types of lands uses ... and environmentally harmful mismanagement including ... unsustainable commercial logging ... and the impacts of loss and degradation of forests are in the form of soil erosion, loss of biological diversity, damage to wildlife habitats and degradation of watershed areas" (cited in Taylor, 1994, p. 104).

TABLE 9–5
UNCED FOREST PRINCIPLES

The Non-Legally Binding Authoritative Statement of Principles for a Global Consensus on the Management, Conservation, and Sustainable Development of All Types of Forests

- Establish national guidelines and scientifically based international criteria for the conservation, management, and sustainable development of forests

- Perceive forests as integrated ecosystems with a whole range of diverse values (such as timber, culture, wildlife, and soil conservation)

- Promote public participation in decision making, and, in particular, ensure the participation of women and Aboriginal peoples

- Develop the skills, education, knowledge, and institutions needed to support forest conservation and sustainable development

- Strengthen international cooperation and assistance for forests in developing countries

- Identify and deal with pressures placed on forest ecosystems from outside the forest sector

- Develop policies to ensure the conservation and sustainable development of forests

- Encourage fair international trade in forest products

SOURCE: Adapted from Forestry Canada. (1993). *The state of Canada's forests 1992: Third Report to Parliament.* Ottawa, p. 69.

While *Agenda 21* called for national action and international cooperation to achieve sustainable development, it exhibited serious weaknesses. For instance, the chapter on forestry contained no recommended policy for sustainable forest management. However, Canada viewed *Agenda 21* as a basis for cooperation with, and assistance to, developing nations. Canada's Official Development Assistance Program, managed primarily by the Canadian International Development Research Centre (IDRC), was chosen to implement *Agenda 21*. Established in 1970, IDRC—which already was one of the world's largest donors of development assistance in forestry—provided increased funding for forest research programs.

UNCED Conventions and Other Responses

Global conventions on biodiversity and climate change also were signed by heads of state at the Earth Summit. The Convention on Biological Diversity, a legally binding

Road construction through rugged terrain often increases the risk of landslide.

as the Montreal Process (for boreal and temperate forests) and the Helsinki Process (for forests in Europe). Both are working to establish internationally accepted principles and standards of forest management. Also as part of its recognized responsibility to assist other nations in the sustainable management of their forests, Canada has instituted a number of model forests. Discussion follows regarding these and other Canadian efforts to contribute to global understanding of the role of forests in sustaining planetary health.

CANADIAN POLICY, PRACTICE, AND PARTNERSHIPS

As the predominant natural resource department of Canada, Natural Resources Canada (NRC) is mandated to promote sustainable development and responsible use of Canada's forests and other resources. The Canadian Forest Service (one of five NRC sectors) provides leading-edge forest science and expertise, and also brought stakeholders together to develop the National Forest Strategy, the Canadian and International Model Forest programs, and criteria and indicators for sustainable forest management. As well, the Canadian Forest Service co-funds research partnerships with other institutes and councils. (For more information, about the Canadian Forest Service, see their home page, their Forest Health Network, and their Forest Biodiversity Network, all listed in the Additional Information Sources section of this chapter.)

As provincial concerns grew about managing forest resources effectively for Canadians, the provinces and territories initiated new approaches to forest management, expanded protected areas, enacted tougher environmental regulations, and invested in forest renewal. Selected examples of these initiatives demonstrate national and provincial commitments to better understand and manage forests for the future (Table 9–6).

The following information about Canada's National Forest Strategy, Model Forest Program, and development of criteria and indicators of sustainable forest management highlights important elements of current forestry policy, practice, and partnerships in Canada.

Canada's National Forest Strategy

After a year of discussion with provincial and territorial governments and organizations representing the interests of naturalists, wildlife, First Nations, foresters, labour, private forest landowners, academics, and forest industries, the Canadian Council of Forest Ministers (1992) released a national forest strategy document. This commitment to sustainable forest management was ratified by the signing of the first Canada Forest Accord on March 4, 1992. Together, these documents represent the broad new directions for forest management in Canada.

agreement, commits Canada to prepare and adhere to a national biodiversity strategy. Part of this commitment is to ensure that a representative sample of Canada's forests is protected, research and education on biodiversity are supported, and Canadian forest management does not affect biodiversity adversely. The Convention on Climate Change, which seeks to stabilize greenhouse gases in the atmosphere to prevent additional threats to climate and to forests, requires Canada to adopt national policies and measures on climate change, limit emissions of greenhouse gases, and report regularly on progress in maintaining emissions levels at early 1990 levels (Forestry Canada, 1993).

While the Earth Summit efforts regarding sustainable forestry have been criticized, international efforts continue to promote sustainable management of forests. In 1995, for example, the United Nations Food and Agriculture Organization's Committee on Forestry confirmed the need for a holistic approach to forests that balances their environmental and developmental functions. In particular, the committee highlighted the need to develop and apply criteria and indicators for sustainable management of all types of forests. Another United Nations agency, the Commission on Sustainable Development, is the body mandated to review and promote implementation of UNCED's decisions in the field of forests. (Additional information on these agencies may be found through a variety of United Nations Web sites, including those for the United Nations Environment Programme and the United Nations System of Organizations listed in the Additional Information Sources section of this chapter.)

Canada has chosen to honour its Earth Summit forestry commitments through involvement in two initiatives aimed at defining criteria and indicators for sustainable forest management. These two initiatives are known

Province/ Territory	Year	Selected Actions toward Sustainable Forest Management
Federal government	1994–95	• The Standing Committee on Natural Resources tabled its report in the House of Commons on clear-cutting (June 1994), concluding that it is an ecologically appropriate practice for most forest types in Canada. The federal government reiterated its commitment to research alternative harvesting practices and to improve scientific knowledge and data on forest ecosystems. • The Canadian Environmental Assessment Act became law (January 1995), possibly requiring mill and forest industry operations to be assessed for potential adverse environmental effects. • The Pulp and Paper Round Table (of 25 national stakeholders) reached consensus on a set of environmental principles for the industry. • All pulp and paper mills indicated commitments to carry out necessary installations to reduce dioxin, furan, and chlorine levels to new standards by the time their extensions expire. • The use of fenitrothion (a chemical insecticide to control spruce budworm) is to be phased out by the end of 1998; research continues on other products.
British Columbia	1994–95	• The Long Beach Model Forest was established on the west coast of Vancouver Island. • Under the Forest Renewal Plan, an estimated $2 billion is to be invested over 5 years in forests and forest workers; a new Crown agency, Forest Renewal BC, was established to oversee this investment. • Since 1992, parks and wilderness areas were doubled by creating 82 new parks and other areas (82 000 km^2 or 8.65% of the province is in protected areas).
	1995–96	• In June 1995, the Forest Practices Code of B.C. and 18 accompanying regulations were brought into force, governing all aspects of sustainable management in B.C.'s public forests. • Large areas of Crown land were placed in reserve under the Forest Land Reserve Act (to help maintain forest land for sustainable resource use in the face of growing urban development and other pressures). • The province committed to have 12% of its land base in parks and protected areas; in 1995, 107 000 hectares of the Stein Valley were protected as Class-A provincial park, to be managed cooperatively by the government and the Lytton First Nation. • Important natural areas in and around the Greater Vancouver region were protected, more than tripling urban green space.
Alberta	1994–95	• The draft conservation strategy for woodland caribou was completed following public consultations. • Companies now pay a sawlog harvest fee based on the market price for the lumber product (formerly a flat rate); stumpage fees doubled and a portion is being reinvested in forests.
	1995–96	• Two popular recreational destinations were nominated for protection; 26 natural areas were designated; the Willmore Wilderness Act was amended to prohibit industrial development inside pristine wildlands; Special Places sites now cover more than 400 000 hectares.
Saskatchewan	1995–96	• Provincial environmental impact assessment legislation required companies wishing to obtain forest management agreements to submit 20-year forest management plans to EIA.

TABLE 9–6
(CONTINUED)

Province/ Territory	Year	Selected Actions toward Sustainable Forest Management
Manitoba	1994–95	• An ecological site classification field guide for forests (to move toward ecosystem management) and a long-term forest management plan was finalized. • With four new protected areas, parklands totalled 5.5% of the province's land base.
	1995–96	• A long-term forest plan was released in 1996 that recognizes multiple uses and values of forests and will guide their management into the next century; partnerships between industry and other stakeholders will be strengthened through development of forest plans that meet ecological and forest management objectives of all.
Ontario*	1994–95	• A new forest policy framework was established that shifted management objectives from managing forests for timber to managing for all values on an ecosystem basis. • Twenty-five thousand hectares of Algonquin Park were set aside as a wilderness zone (no logging). • After more than four years of public hearings, an EIA for timber management on Crown lands was completed; it contains 115 legally binding requirements to change forest management, and includes citizen input, an old-growth forest conservation strategy, and research on the impact of harvesting on forest productivity. • Under a new stumpage system, fees paid to harvest timber on public lands go into trust funds to pay for logging company silvicultural expenses to renew forests (previously fees went into the government's general revenue account). • A $2-million private forests sustainability fund was set up for woodland owners in southern Ontario; community stewardship councils are to be set up to provide owners with woodlot management information. • Thirty new parks and protected areas were established, including 14 old-growth red and white pine forests, created through the 1994 "Keep It Wild" campaign.
	1995–96	• Following a court judgment that lifted a moratorium on development in the old-growth forests in the Temagami region (the centre of a land title dispute), the area is to be opened up gradually for economic development; a commitment was made to preserve areas of old-growth forests and Aboriginal sacred and cultural sites in the region. • Wabakimi Provincial Park was expanded to 891 500 hectares, the largest area of protected boreal forest (woodland caribou habitat) in the province. First Nations, government, the forest industry, tourism outfitters, and environmental and other interest groups cooperated on this initiative.
Quebec	1994–95	• An "inhabited forest" concept—a new approach to managing forests close to populated areas that includes community management responsibilities—was developed. • Quebec released its forest protection strategy—to sustain current levels of forest productivity and socioeconomic activities, protect forest sites, and minimize or eliminate use of pesticides in forests. • Through the Federal Office for Regional Development in Quebec, the federal government provided $6.5 million to private woodlot owners in the Gaspé–Lower St. Lawrence region.
	1995–96	• A forest resource enhancement plan was announced in May 1995, to permit the forest industry to invest $97.5 million directly into the region's economy and strengthen silvicultural efforts to enhance public forest resources. • At the Quebec Summit on Private Forests, representatives from private woodlot owner associations, municipalities, the forest industry, and the provincial government reached consensus on a plan to protect and enhance private forest resources.

* Ontario has in recent years moved toward increased public involvement in forestry planning, new selection systems and ecosystem management approaches, and habitat supply analysis models designed to benefit selected wildlife species (including red-shouldered hawk, moose, and marten). For more on Ontario forestry, see the text updates section of the Web site that accompanies this textbook: environment.nelson.com.

TABLE 9–6
(CONTINUED)

Province/ Territory	Year	Selected Actions toward Sustainable Forest Management
Nova Scotia	1994–95	• A Forest Accord was signed by the minister of Natural Resources and 24 forest sector representatives, committing to continue implementing the National Forest Strategy. • A proposed plan for parks and protected areas and sites was released; a public review committee was to make recommendations.
	1995–96	• A pilot project (which includes extensive public consultation) was initiated to develop an integrated resource management strategy for Crown lands in the north-central region of Nova Scotia, later to be applied to Crown lands throughout the province. • The provincial government is working with the Coalition of Nova Scotia Forest Interests to develop a sustainability strategy for privately owned forests.
New Brunswick	1994–95	• The Federation of Woodlot Owners released a code of practice as part of an initiative to develop stringent land use guidelines and practices. • The federal government contributed $4.9 million to extend the forest agreement. • The province will invest an additional $10.7 million each year to increase the long-term sustainable harvest from Crown lands by 40% (placing greater emphasis on hardwoods).
	1995–96	• In first year of the expanded Crown Land Silviculture Program, $120.7 million enabled forest managers to almost double the area of forests receiving silvicultural treatments. • The federal–provincial forest resource development agreement expired; the province embarked on a $4-million cost-shared program with the New Brunswick Federation of Woodlot Owners to undertake silvicultural improvements on private woodlots. • Five new ecological reserves were created, including areas of eastern hemlock forest, and old balsam fir and old-growth black spruce forest.
Prince Edward Island	1994–95	• A stewardship and sustainability document was released to guide sustainable development and conservation of the Island's natural resources. • The federal government contributed $1.6 million to extend the forest agreement.
	1995–96	• New regulations under the Forest Management Act designated a system of "provincial forests" to ensure public forests are managed to sustain a full range of values, including recreation, wildlife, and wood fibre.
Newfoundland	1994–95	• An ecological classification system was completed for the Western Newfoundland Model Forest. • The Twenty-Year Forestry Development Plan was prepared, setting a new direction for forest management, moving from a timber focus to an ecosystem management focus.
	1995–96	• The public was encouraged to participate in the preparation of forest district ecosystem management plans that are intended to protect wildlife habitat, water quality, nutrient cycling, and other aspects of forest ecosystems.
Yukon	1995–96	• Faced with an unprecedented demand for Yukon timber, the federal Department of Indian Affairs and Northern Development implemented an interim policy to promote sustainability of forest resources; reforestation fees were introduced, a restoration program was established, stumpage fees were increased significantly, and the Yukon Forest Advisory Committee was formed. • A 450 000 m³ ceiling on harvesting was established (for commercial timber permits). • A comprehensive forest policy is to be developed and is to involve public consultation.

SOURCES: Natural Resources Canada, Canadian Forest Service. (1994). *The state of Canada's forests 1993: Forests, a global resource.* Ottawa.

Natural Resources Canada, Canadian Forest Service. (1995). *The state of Canada's forests 1994: A balancing act.* Ottawa.

Natural Resources Canada, Canadian Forest Service. (1996b). *The state of Canada's forests 1995–1996: Sustaining forests at home and abroad.* Ottawa.

Nine strategic priorities were identified in the strategy (Table 9–7); they were meant to ensure that, in addition to protecting ecological integrity and biodiversity, Canada's approach to sustainable forest management included a range of timber and nontimber values. A key goal of the forest strategy was to develop forestry practices that respected a range of values while maintaining the health of forest ecosystems. One of the key commitments Canada made was to implement a national network of model forests where sustainable development principles could be tested and applied (Forestry Canada, 1993).

Canada's Model Forest Program

The model forest program began in 1991 with the selection of 10 working-scale forests between 100 000 and 2 500 000 hectares in size. Each model forest is managed by a partnership of organizations and interested individuals who determine, on a consensus basis, particular objectives for which their forest will be managed.

TABLE 9–7

CANADA'S NATIONAL FOREST STRATEGY: STRATEGIC PRIORITIES

Canada's National Forest Strategy outlines commitments to:

1. Conserve the natural diversity of our forests, maintain and enhance their productive capacity, and provide for their continued renewal

2. Improve our ability to plan and practise sustainable forest management

3. Increase public participation in the allocation and management of forest lands and provide an increased level of public information and awareness

4. Diversify and encourage economic opportunities for the forest sector in domestic and international markets

5. Increase and focus research and technology efforts to benefit our environment and our economy

6. Ensure that we have a highly skilled and adaptable workforce

7. Increase participation by and benefits for Aboriginal people in the management and use of forests

8. Assist private forest owners in continuing to improve their individual and collective abilities to manage and exercise stewardship of their land

9. Reinforce Canada's responsibilities as trustee of 10 percent of the world's forests

SOURCE: Adapted from Canadian Council of Forest Ministers. (1992). *Sustainable forests: A Canadian commitment.* Ottawa, p. 9.

Each model forest has a different number of partners, including provincial governments, forest industries, First Nations, recreational users, community organizations, private landowners, government agencies, environmental and conservation organizations, and academics. The idea behind the partnerships is that full discussion of different viewpoints (as well as any conflicts or tradeoffs) in the earliest stage of forest management planning should lead to an understanding of the important dimensions of the forest and its uses, as well as agreed-on solutions to problems (Forestry Canada, 1993).

The lands involved in model forest projects include national parks, private lands, and First Nations lands, as well as the predominant provincial lands. In each model forest, sustainable development initiatives reflect the issues relevant to each region. For example, wildlife concerns have been addressed in the Western Newfoundland Model Forest, where forest management programs focused on the conservation and protection of the pine marten's mature forest habitat. In the Foothills, Manitoba, and Lake Abitibi Model Forests, the fate of the woodland caribou has been an important concern. Deer monitoring programs (to determine their preferred winter habitat) are under way in the Fundy Model Forest. Similarly, better scientific research about coastal rain forest ecosystems will help stakeholders in British Columbia's Long Beach Model Forest ensure forest conservation.

At the Earth Summit, then prime minister Brian Mulroney announced Canada's intention to expand the concept of model forests to the global level by seeking international partners. With a $10-million commitment from Canada, Mexico became the first international partner (with three sites) in 1993, and Russia became the second in 1994. Malaysia and the United States (with three sites) joined the model forest network in 1995. Canada's contribution to forest management through the Model Forest Program offers promise for building strong international partnerships for sustainable management of the world's forests. (For more details on the Model Forest Program, see Canadian Forest Service [1996] or the Web site for the Model Forest Program listed in the Additional Information Sources section of this chapter.)

Criteria and Indicators of Sustainable Forest Management

Each of Canada's National Forest Strategy, *Agenda 21,* and UNCED Forest Principles recognized the need to formulate scientifically based, internationally accepted criteria and indicators of sustainable forest management. If criteria and indicators were in place, it should be possible to monitor our progress toward the goals established in the National Forest Strategy (as well as in international agreements).

In 1993, officials and scientists from provincial, territorial, and federal governments, academics, and representatives from First Nations, industry, and NGOs

TABLE 9-8

ECOLOGICAL AND SOCIOECONOMIC CRITERIA, INDICATORS, AND CRITICAL ELEMENTS OF SUSTAINABLE FOREST MANAGEMENT IN CANADA

ECOLOGICAL

Conservation of biological diversity

Biological diversity is conserved by maintaining the variability of living organisms and the complexes of which they are part.

- Ecosystem diversity is conserved if the variety and landscape-level patterns of communities and ecosystems that naturally occur on the defined forest area are maintained through time.
- Species diversity is conserved if all native species found on the defined forest area prosper through time.
- Genetic diversity is conserved if the variation of genes within species is maintained.

Maintenance and enhancement of forest ecosystem condition and productivity

Forest ecosystem condition and productivity is conserved if the health, vitality and rates of biological production are maintained.

- Forest health is conserved if biotic (including anthropogenic) and abiotic disturbances and stresses maintain both ecosystem processes and ecosystem conditions within a range of natural variability.
- Ecosystem resilience is conserved if ecosystem processes and the range of ecosystem conditions allow ecosystems to persist, absorb change and recover from disturbances.
- Ecosystem productivity is conserved if ecosystem conditions are capable of supporting all naturally occurring species.

Conservation of soil and water resources

Soil and water resources and physical environments are conserved if the quantity and quality of soil and water within forest ecosystems are maintained.

- Physical environments are conserved if the permanent loss of forest area to other uses of factors is minimized, and if rare physical environments are protected.
- Soil resources are conserved if the ability of soils to sustain forest productivity is maintained within characteristic ranges of variation.
- Water resources are conserved if water quality and quantity are maintained.

Forest ecosystem contributions to global ecological cycles

Forest conditions and management activities contribute to the health of global ecological cycles. This contribution is maintained if:

- The processes that are responsible for recycling water, carbon, nitrogen and other life-sustaining elements are maintained
- Utilization and rejuvenation are balanced and sustained
- Forests are protected from sustained deforestation or conversion to other uses

SOCIOECONOMIC

Multiple benefits to society

Forests provide a sustained flow of benefits for current and future generations if multiple goods and services are provided over the long term. Multiple benefits are maintained if:

- Extraction rates are within the long-term productive capacity of the resource base
- Resource businesses exist within a fair and competitive investment and operating climate
- Forests provide a mix of market and non-market goods and services

Accepting society's responsibility for sustainable development

Fair, equitable, effective, and just resource management choices are in the best interests of present and future generations, including those of particular cultural and/or socioeconomic communities. To achieve these kinds of management choices:

- Aboriginal and treaty rights should be respected in sustainable forest management
- All forest stakeholders and aboriginal communities need to participate and cooperate in achieving sustainable forest management
- All members of society have an obligation and responsibility to understand forest sustainability issues and the positions of others on forest issues

SOURCE: von Mirbach, M. (1997). Demanding good wood. *Alternatives,* 23(3), pp. 10–17.

Radio collars are one of the tools employed in wildlife monitoring programs.

contributed to the Canadian Council of Forest Ministers report on criteria and indicators for sustainable forest management in Canada (Canadian Council of Forest Ministers, 1995). Taken together, the criteria and indicators provide a common understanding of what is meant by sustainable forest management in Canada. At this point in their evolution, the four ecological and two socioeconomic criteria and indicators (outlined in Table 9–8) help us understand the diverse conditions in Canadian forests and forest management. Not only can these criteria and indicators help identify gains made in implementing sustainable forestry (Aplet, Johnson, Olson & Sample, 1993; Maser, 1994), they can also reveal elements of the forest ecosystem that must be sustained or enhanced. In this way, these criteria and indicators lead to improved information for decision makers and the public (Canadian Council of Forest Ministers, 1995).

As these criteria and indicators are implemented in assessing sustainable forest management in Canada, and as experience informs our understanding of which elements of this approach are effective, it is likely that there will be a further evolution in both the criteria and indicators and in the approach toward managing Canada's forests as ecosystems.

Local Partnerships and Responses

Many local responses to forest concerns provide a useful counterpoint and complement to the formal partnerships established to develop national or provincial elements of sustainable forestry management. A few examples are identified here to demonstrate the value of individual actions and partnerships in achieving viable responses to forest-related issues on the local scale.

Wildlife and Forestry Activity Grizzly bear populations in Alberta have declined from an estimated historical population of 6000 to about 800 today, and are at risk

of extinction if their needs are not integrated into land use planning and hunting quotas. The Eastern Slopes Grizzly Bear Research Project began in 1993 as a partnership between researchers at the University of Calgary and about 30 other conservation groups, resource users, and developers such as the cattle and the oil and gas industries, and government agencies. Researchers are attempting to understand grizzly bear habitat as it relates to all human activities. If this understanding can be developed, then it may be possible to design an enduring land use system that would include movement corridors for the endangered bears and enable them to repopulate their former home ranges in Banff National Park and the Kananaskis Country areas.

There are no regulations requiring the Alberta forest industry to demonstrate concern for grizzly bear habitat. However, an Alberta forest products company (Spray Lakes Sawmills Ltd.) became a partner in the Eastern Slopes Grizzly Bear Research Project in 1996, donating $10 000 to support the conservation project (Grizzly study finds forestry friend, 1996). The woodlands manager, aware that logging can be made compatible with other forest values, entered the project with the willingness to develop creative ways to change the company's forest management practices. Committed to learn from researchers about habitat and movement corridors that are important for grizzlies in areas they propose to log, the company expects to gain crucial information for making environmentally responsible decisions.

Clearly, being a partner in this research project helps the company identify how to manage the impact of its forestry operations on sensitive wildlife species such as the grizzly bear. In addition, researchers gain an important opportunity to learn how to integrate grizzly bears' needs into the design of future forest harvesting plans for the eastern slopes of the Rocky Mountains. By protecting grizzly bears and their habitat, this partnership also helps maintain habitat for many other species in healthy ecosystems. The Eastern Slopes Grizzly Bear Research Project is an important demonstration of the win-win situation that can evolve through sharing information about cumulative impacts and being willing to change management practices.

In snowy regions of North America, black bears typically hibernate in dens that are essentially depressions protected by low branches of conifers, in holes excavated under large boulders, in caves, or in hollow trees, stumps, or logs. Seeking secure, warm dens in the wet coastal climate of British Columbia, black bears are particular about the dryness of their winter quarters. A graduate student's research in the Nimpkish Valley on northern Vancouver Island has shown that 55 percent of black bears located their dens in cavities in snags or live trees, primarily cedars. While most dens were in hollows formed at the tree base by heart rot, some dens were as high as 16 metres above the ground and could be reached only by climbing up the outside of the tree trunk.

Most black bear dens were found in trees that were at least 500 years old. Given that much of British Columbia's coastal forest is being converted to second growth that will be harvested on an 80- to 100-year rotation, the future supply of ancient trees for black bear habitat is in serious jeopardy (Backhouse, 1996). Even though the graduate student worked with provincial government biologists and foresters to formulate habitat protection guidelines for coastal black bears, and assisted logging companies to change cut block boundaries when bear dens were located in areas scheduled for clear-cutting, she recognized that protecting trees for bears on a case-by-case basis is an inefficient management approach. Planning at a landscape level is necessary to conserve some old-growth stands that contain existing cavities; so is the management of younger stands to create future tree cavities.

British Columbia's Forest Practices Code gives hope that such a shift in forest management could occur. If it does, part of the credit will belong to dedicated researchers such as the graduate student, whose personal visits to logging companies and government foresters to explain her findings have helped raise awareness of the importance of old-growth trees as bear denning habitat. Cooperative efforts on the part of logging companies also will be required, not only to guarantee an enduring supply of den trees, but also to ensure maintenance of sufficient foraging areas with good production of favourite bear foods, provision of escape trees within clear-cuts to ensure security of females and cubs when they leave the forest to feed, and restriction of human access to bear habitat via logging roads.

White-tailed deer reach the northern limits of their natural habitat in Quebec. Their survival is influenced strongly by availability of winter habitat that provides shelter and food. When establishing their winter habitat, deer seek out mature coniferous stands that provide shelter from the cold and wind. Coniferous stands also facilitate the animals' movements because the trees permit only minor accumulations of snow on the ground. Since twigs constitute the deers' basic winter diet, an abundance of young broad-leaved trees also is necessary. The greater the diversity of food and shelter opportunities within an area, and the shorter the distance deer have to travel during harsh winters, the lower will be their vulnerability to winter weather and predators (Fondation de la faune du Québec, n.d.; Natural Resources Canada, 1995).

To secure this important winter habitat, the forest industry, Quebec government departments, Natural Resources Canada, Wildlife Habitat Canada, and the Fondation de la faune du Québec have developed and funded the Deer Yard Program. The program works in cooperation with the forest industry by increasing woodlot owners' awareness of their land's wildlife potential and by providing landowners with technical and financial assistance to plan timber harvesting and tree-planting regimes that are suitable to the habitat needs of white-tailed deer. The more severe the winter, the more local landowner yards become essential to the survival of the species. The Deer Yard Program initiative is helping to ensure the continued sustainability of Quebec's deer population.

An Ecoadventure in Clayoquot Sound If the Clayoquot Sound area becomes a Biosphere Reserve, it will need to foster a sustainable economy that provides adequate employment for both First Nations and other residents. First Nations women of Ahousaht (pronounced *a-howze-at*) undertook an initiative in ecotourism that provides an important example of the potential to develop sustainable community economies through partnerships (Box 9–6).

FUTURE CHALLENGES

In March 1997, the World Resources Institute reported that only 20 percent of the world's major virgin forests remained, mostly in Canada's far north, in Russia, and in the Amazonia region of Brazil. Only in these areas are the frontier forests large enough to support indigenous species and to survive indefinitely without human intervention—if protection and responsible forest management are put in place now. With only 3 percent of frontier forests remaining, temperate forests are the most threatened. Combining this knowledge with the fact that in North America we use as much wood, by weight, as all metals, plastics, and cement combined (Black & Guthrie, 1994), it is clear that Canada's forests require careful stewardship. Balancing the demands on Canada's forests to attain sustainability requires that the full range of forest values—ecological, economic, and social—should be integrated into decision making. And, in a time when scarcity of forests is an issue, protecting forest ecosystems is paramount.

One way to protect forests and forest ecosystems is to identify an alternative source of fibre, such as hemp (Enviro-Focus 9). New drug-free strains of hemp (marijuana) are revitalizing what once was a major source of fibre for paper, textiles, and other composite materials such as fibreboard. Since hemp is an agricultural crop grown on farms, it has significant implications for providing high-quality fibre with lower costs and fewer environmental impacts, potentially reducing the pressure on Canada's remaining old-growth forests. Other nonwood fibres may be poised for a comeback also (Rosmarin, 1997).

International commitments to protection and monitoring have been implemented also, and new initiatives

BOX 9-6
"WALK THE WILD SIDE": AN ECOADVENTURE PARTNERSHIP

In the spring and summer of 1996, 20 hard-working young Native and non-Native people constructed Ahousaht Wild Side Heritage Trail, a 16-kilometre ocean-side trail on the west side of Flores Island in the heart of Clayoquot Sound. In partnership with the Western Canadian Wilderness Committee, and without government grants, women and men of the Nuu-Chah-Nulth First Nation in Ahousaht have volunteered many hours to develop their "Walk the Wild Side" ecoadventure.

Visitors to the community travel 45 minutes by boat to Flores Island, perhaps seeing grey whales and orcas along the way. From Ahousaht, interpreted forest walks guide visitors through large cedar, fir, and culturally modified trees (those from which the bark has been stripped for basketry, clothing, cordage, and so on). These culturally modified trees can help visitors see forests in a new way and provide concrete examples of traditional Native use of the forest. In the village, the Arts of Paawac gallery offers visitors an opportunity to purchase local, high-quality beadwork, drums, and baskets. Retail products and publications from the Western Canada Wilderness Committee are sold in the gallery, helping Walk the Wild Side to pay the rent.

In partnership with the Western Canada Wilderness Committee, Walk the Wild Side's board of directors was able to upgrade the art galley and set up a World Wide Web home page (the URL is provided in the References section of this chapter). Loans of office and computer equipment, bridge financing, and other support helped the ecoadventure to become a success. In the future, this partnership will repair and extend trails, and build boardwalks in some areas. In addition to the Western Canadian Wilderness Committee's support, the Long Beach Model Forest sponsored Walk the Wild Side's Internet use (since everywhere is long distance from Ahousaht!). This unique partnership demonstrates how, with appropriate skills, equipment, and patience, new nonconsumptive, sustainable forest-based economies may be developed.

continue to be developed. For instance, the Canadian Sustainable Forestry Coalition is promoting the Canadian Standards Association's (CSA) development of an international system of forestry certification using the ISO 14 000 series of Environmental Management Systems standards. The International Organization for Standardization (ISO) focuses on developing systems standards so that quality products of a particular type (such as pharmaceuticals or chemicals) are known to have similar or identical manufacturing histories. With regard to forestry, the ISO emphasizes whether a logging company, for instance, has an adequate forest management planning process in place; the ISO does not focus on their actual on-the-ground performance. (Note, however, that the sustainable forest management system is based on the six Canadian criteria for sustainable forest management outlined in Table 9–8.)

The ISO 14 000 system has been criticized for not requiring a clearly documented and verifiable "chain of custody" back to the forest from which the wood originated. Although participants in this system must define a "designated forest area" where their management system will apply, there is no requirement that the entire output of a specific mill, for instance, must originate from that area. That is, there is no clear link between the products sold by a company and its forest management system (von Mirbach, 1997).

Consumer pressure, especially in Europe, has been driving efforts to establish certification standards or methods to identify forest products that have been produced in ways that do not degrade the environment. As a result, "certified wood" is gaining popularity (Box 9–7).

Hemp: Fibre of the Future?

Humans have used hemp for fibre for thousands of years; in fact, in about 150 B.C., the Chinese made the world's first paper out of hemp. Until about 1850, hemp was used for making textiles, fishing nets, sails, rope, and the caulking between ship planks. More recently, hemp has been held up as an excellent source of biomass for alternative fuels, as a substitute for petrochemicals in the manufacture of some plastics, and in the manufacture of particle board, fibreboard, and other composites used in the construction industry.

Better known as the marijuana plant, hemp used to be grown throughout the western and central provinces of Canada as a textile crop. By 1937, hemp was extremely profitable as the hemp combine and other new machinery had simplified harvesting and made production more cost effective. Manufacturers' interest grew in the byproducts of hemp, including seed oil for paint and lacquer, and "hurds" (the woody inner portion of the stalk) for paper. However, in September 1937, the United States government banned hemp production totally. In spite of the benefits of the plant for industrial uses, and established markets for paper, textiles, and medicine derived from hemp, Canada followed suit, banning production under the Opium and Narcotics Act in 1938. The plant "disappeared" from cultivation for over 55 years.

The U.S. government's reasons for banning such a beneficial plant were purely economic. Timber baron William Randolph Hearst (who controlled large tracts of forested land for pulp and paper), and the multinational DuPont (which owned the patents on new sulphate/sulphite processes for making paper out of wood), stood to lose billions of dollars if low-cost hemp became widely used. Across the United States, Hearst used the newspapers he owned to create a new perception of hemp as "the assassin of youth." Hearst's tactics resulted in the criminalization of hemp.

Although it made a brief comeback during World War II, hemp might never have been heard of again, except that a new strain of the plant was engineered in France. This plant contains very low levels of TCH (the

Textiles made from hemp have multiple uses.

active ingredient responsible for the marijuana "high"). The new "drug-free" hemp was legalized in many parts of Europe and crops were growing again by 1993. In June 1996, the Canadian government amended the Narcotic Control Act to make it legal to cultivate industrial grades of hemp.

There are enormous implications of switching from wood to hemp fibre. Fibreboard industry representatives claim that anything that can be made out of a tree can be made out of hemp, more cost effectively, and with less negative impact on the environment. Since hemp is an annual crop that can be grown on existing farmland, there is no need to build and reclaim expensive logging roads, and no need to clear-cut vast areas of forest using heavy equipment that damages the interconnected elements of the ecosystem and reduces its biodiversity. Hemp fibres are ideal for producing superior quality paper; long and light-coloured, hemp fibres require less bleaching than wood pulp, resulting in the production of lower levels of organochlorines.

If hemp becomes an internationally significant alternative fibre source, it could reduce harvesting pressure on remaining old-growth forests in Canada and elsewhere. The forest industry could then focus on sustainable forest management, value-added production, and community health and sustainability. The viability of the concept of sustainability could become crystal clear to consumers; it makes much more sense to use plant material that grows in 100 days to build a house that lasts 50 years than it does to use plant material that takes between 200 and 500 years to grow to build a house that lasts 50 years. Hemp may be one of the fibres that helps achieve stewardship (conservation) of Canada's forests for the future.

SOURCES: Black, S., & Guthrie, A. (1994). Back to the future: Hemp returns. *Earthkeeper,* 4(3), pp. 18–25.

Herer, J. (1991). *Hemp and the marijuana conspiracy: The emperor wears no clothes.* Van Nuys, CA: Hemp Publishing.

Marck, P. (1997, June 23). Harvesting opportunity. *Calgary Herald,* p. C4.

BOX 9–7
STANDARDS FOR SUSTAINABLE FOREST MANAGEMENT

As public concerns about forests and forest practices have grown, there has been a corresponding growth in industry support for independent assessments of forest operations (to ensure continued or enhanced market access). The objective is to provide purchasers with a form of guarantee that the forest products they buy were managed according to sustainable forest management principles.

The Forest Stewardship Council, an international nongovernmental organization, was established in 1993 with the support of the World Wildlife Fund. Members of the council include representatives of environmental groups, Indigenous peoples, certification organizations, and other nongovernmental groups from 25 countries. The council's goal is to provide consumers with information about forest products and their sources through certification.

There are important similarities between the objectives and approaches of the Canadian Standards Association and the Forest Stewardship Council. For instance, both organizations promote better forest management and require third-party audits. However, there are also important differences in their processes. The Forest Stewardship Council focuses on product labelling and tracking of forest products to their origin (the "chain of custody"). Wood that is guaranteed to have come from environmentally well-managed forests is sometimes called "certified wood" (Polson, 1996). The CSA's registration program does not involve tracing products but assesses a company's ability to manage in an environmentally sound manner and includes performance indicators tailored to specific sites. The Canadian Standards Association process is not an eco-labelling program because the standards do not apply to consumer products at the retail level.

Another difference is that the Forest Stewardship Council's certification is based on a series of principles that they developed independently to apply to all forest types. The CSA's Sustainable Forest Management system is based on both the Canadian criteria and the ISO 14 000 system, which deal with the quality of the management systems, not the quality of the products themselves. CSA's Technical Committee on Sustainable Forest Management has met with Forest Stewardship Council representatives to discuss the potential for aligning the two processes.

SOURCES: Natural Resources Canada, Canadian Forest Service. (1996b). *The state of Canada's forests 1995–1996: Sustaining forests at home and abroad.* Ottawa.

Polson, S. (1996). Cutting with conscience. *E Magazine,* 7(3), pp. 42–43.

von Mirbach, M. (1997). Demanding good wood. *Alternatives,* 23(3), pp. 10–17.

If Canadians wish to have sustainable forests, sustainable forest industries, and sustainable environments, there is a great deal that we have yet to learn, to know, and to predict about forests and forest ecosystems. Knowledge building remains a critical part of developing sustainable forests, sustainable forest communities, and sustainable forest management. This is one reason why Canada's old-growth forests, boreal and temperate, cannot be sacrificed to short-term economic thinking. Old-growth forests must be considered as living laboratories because only they contain the entire genetic code for living, healthy, and adaptable forests, and only they can teach us how we might create sustainable forests for the future (Maser, 1990). As part of this thinking, further study of the strengths and weaknesses of alternative harvesting systems would be a useful addition to sustainable forest management knowledge.

Knowledge-building technology, such as satellite imagery and GIS, can be used effectively to augment our understanding of the impacts of human activities on forest systems. For instance, satellite imagery of the world's forests, evaluated by experts around the world, enabled the World Resources Institute to specify what percentage of natural forests remained on the planet. There is a need, also, to provide and expand these technical forms of assistance to developing nations to enable them to determine what constitutes sustainable forest management.

On a different level, knowledge-building processes such as British Columbia's Committee on Resources and Environment (CORE) help facilitate community understanding of forest uses and values that, ultimately, find expression in community-based land use planning decisions. Knowledge of ways to create sustainable forests and forest-based communities is improved, too, when partnership experiences and successes are shared with others. Overall, there is a critical need to combine science and intuition in our quest for a more sensitive and sustainable relationship between people and forests.

> There are pleasures you cannot buy,
> Treasures you cannot sell,
> And not the smallest of these
> Is the gift and glory of trees.
>
> – Robert Service, "Trees against the sky" (1940)

Chapter Questions

1. In what ways are the falldown effect and the life cycle in old-growth forests interrelated? How might the implications of the falldown effect be alleviated?

2. Outline the range of impacts that human activities have on forests and associated resources. If you live in a community or area in which forestry activities are important, which types of impacts are most visible? Which kinds of impacts are most important? Why? Have there been any efforts to mitigate impacts, either by forest industry companies, local citizen groups, or government agencies? What recommendations might you make to local authorities regarding forest sustainability?

3. Comment on the following statement: clear-cutting is appropriate and necessary for forest management. In what ways would your comments be different for this statement: clear-cutting is appropriate and necessary for forest sustainability?

4. By leasing public lands to large foreign companies that export pulp and logs to their own countries, Canada derives revenue only from raw resources. This is far less than the revenue earned by these same companies when they convert the logs into lumber and pulp into paper. What does this say about Canada's economy and economic future? Does this situation lead to good stewardship on the part of these companies? What would be the costs and benefits to these companies if forest stewardship were a requirement of doing business in Canadian forests?

5. If all the world's remaining tropical forests were to be destroyed, in what ways might your life change? What difference could the loss of all old-growth forests in Canada have on your life and on the lives of your descendants?

6. Discuss the value of the Canadian Council of Forest Ministers criteria and critical elements (outlined in Table 9–8) to achieve sustainability of Canada's forests. Are there additional elements that you would add to the list?

Acharya, A. (1995). Plundering the boreal forests. *World Watch,* (May–June), pp. 21–29.

Amaranthus, M., & Pilz, D. (1996). Productivity and sustainable harvest of wild mushrooms. In D. Pilz & R. Molina (Eds.). *Managing forest ecosystems to conserve fungus diversity and sustain wild mushroom harvests.* (pp. 42–61). Portland, OR: United States Department of Agriculture, Forest Service, Pacific Northwest Research Station: General Technical Report PNW-GTR-371.

Backhouse, F. (1996). Old-growth bears. *Nature Canada,* 25(4), pp. 8–9.

Bakker, E. (1994). Return to Hunstein forest. *National Geographic,* 185(2), pp. 40–63.

Barns, M., & Jacobsen, T. (1997). Ecoforestry: An approach to ecologically responsible forest use. In Schoonmaker et al. (Eds.). *The rainforests of home: Profile of a North American bioregion* (pp. 204–6). Washington, DC: Island Press.

Bequette, F. (1994). Greenwatch: Red alert for the Earth's green belt. *The Unesco Courier,* November, pp. 41–43.

Black, S., & Guthrie, A. (1994). Back to the future: Hemp returns. *Earthkeeper,* 4(3), pp. 18–25.

Canadian Council of Forest Ministers. (1992). *Canada Forest Accord.* Ottawa: Canadian Council of Forest Ministers.

Canadian Council of Forest Ministers. (1992). *Sustainable forests: A Canadian commitment.* Ottawa: Canadian Council of Forest Ministers.

Canadian Council of Forest Ministers. (1995). *Defining sustainable forest management: A Canadian approach to criteria and indicators.* Ottawa: Canadian Council of Forest Ministers.

Canadian Council of Forest Ministers. (1997). *Compendium of Canadian forestry statistics 1996.* Ottawa: Canadian Council of Forest Ministers.

Canadian Forest Service. (1996). *About the CFS: Industry initiatives.* http://www.nrcan.gc.ca/cfs/mandat/facts/ii_e.html

Canadian Forest Service. (1996). *Model forest program.* http://mf.ncr.forestry.ca/

Clayoquot Rainforest Coalition. (1995). Clayoquot Rainforest Coalition overview. http://www.ran.org/ran/ran-campaigns/rain-wood/bc-overview.html

Clayoquot Sound Scientific Panel. (1995). *A vision and its context: Global context for forest practices in Clayoquot Sound.* Report 4 of the Scientific Panel for Sustainable Forest Practices in Clayoquot Sound. Victoria: B.C. Ministry of Forests.

Curtis, M. (1996, August 27). The fight for woods "is over." *Victoria Times Colonist,* pp. A1, A6.

Davidson, B. (1996). Forests: A symbol of national heritage. *World Conservation,* 3 (October), p. 16.

Devall, B. (Ed.). (1993). *Clearcut: The tragedy of industrial forestry.* San Francisco: Sierra Club Books and Earth Island Press.

Diem, A. (1992). Clearcutting British Columbia. *The Ecologist,* 22(6), pp. 261–66.

Drushka, K., Nixon, B., & Travers, R. (1993). *Touch wood: B.C. forests at the crossroads.* Madeira Park, BC: Harbour Publishing.

Eagles, P.F.J. (1995). Environmental management in parks. In P. Dearden & R. Rollins (Eds). *Parks and protected areas in Canada.* (pp. 154–84). Toronto: Oxford University Press.

Earthroots. (1996). Temagami. http://www.sll.fi/TRN/index2.html

Environment Canada. (1995a). *Sustaining Canada's forests: Overview.* Overview SOE Bulletin No. 95-4 (Summer).

Environment Canada. (1995b). *Sustaining Canada's forests: Timber harvesting.* Overview SOE Bulletin No. 95-4 (Summer).

Environment Canada (1996). *Partners in Flight—Canada.* http://www.ec.gc.ca/cws-scf/canbird/pif/p_title.htm

Federation of Ontario Naturalists. (n.d.). *What Is Carolinian Canada?* (Brochure).

Fondation de la faune du Québec. (n.d.). *Deer yard program.* Sainte-Foy, QC: Fondation de la faune du Québec. (Brochure).

Food and Agriculture Organization. (1997). Factfile. Where have all the forests gone? http://www.fao.org/news/FACTFILE/FF9704-E.HTM

Forestry Canada. (1993). *The state of Canada's forests 1992: Third Report to Parliament.* Ottawa.

Franklin, J.F. (1984). Characteristics of old-growth Douglas-fir forests. In *New forests—forests for a changing world.* Proceedings of the 1983 Society of American Foresters Conventions, Bethesda, MD.

Friends of Clayoquot Sound. (1996). Province drops prosecution of Macmillan Bloedel in Clayoquot Sound. News release, October 2, 1996. http://www.island.net/~focs/nr100296.htm.

Gorrie, P. (1994). The enchanted woodland. *Canadian Geographic,* 114(2), pp. 32–42.

Grizzly study finds forestry friend. (1996). *University of Calgary Gazette,* 26(10), p. 6.

Hammond, H. (1991). *Seeing the forest among the trees: The case for wholistic forest use.* Vancouver: Polestar Press.

Hebert, D.M., Sklar, D., Wasel, S., Ghostkeeper, E., & Daniels, T. (1995). Accomplishing partnerships in the boreal mixed wood forests of northeastern Alberta. *Transactions of the 60th North American Wildlife and Natural Resources Conference,* pp. 433–38.

Herer, J. (1991). *Hemp and the marijuana conspiracy: The emperor wears no clothes.* Van Nuys, CA: Hemp Publishing.

Innu Nation. (1995). Adaptive mismanagement proposed for Nitassinan forests. http://www.web.net/~innu/adaptivemm.html

Jardine, K. (1994). Finger on the carbon pulse: Climate change and the boreal forests. *The Ecologist,* 24(6), pp. 220–23.

Kellogg, E. (Ed.). (1992). *Coastal temperate rain forests: Ecological characteristics, status and distribution worldwide.* Occasional Paper No. 1. Portland, OR: Ecotrust/Conservation International.

Kellogg, R.M. (Ed.). (1989). *Second growth Douglas fir: Its management and conversion for value. A report of the Douglas-fir Task Force.* Special Publication No. SP-32. Vancouver: Forintek Canada Corporation.

Kelly, D., & Braasch, G. (1988). *Secrets of the old growth forest.* Layton, UT: Gibbs Smith.

Knudtson, P., & Suzuki, D. (1992). *Wisdom of the elders.* Toronto: Stoddart Publishing.

Leahy, S. (1995). Clayoquot Sound East. *Equinox,* 83 (September/October), p. 14.

Marchak, M.P. (1995). *Logging the globe.* Montreal: McGill–Queen's University Press.

Marck, P. (1997, June 23). Harvesting opportunity. *Calgary Herald,* p. C4.

Maser, C. (1990). *The redesigned forest.* Toronto: Stoddart Publishing.

Maser, C. (1994). *Sustainable forestry: Philosophy, science and economics.* Delray Beach: St. Lucie Press.

McCrory, C. (1995). Canada's forests still "Brazil of the north." *Taiga News,* 14 (June). http://www.sll.fi/TRN/TaigaNews/News14/CanadaUpdate1.html

McGuffin, J. (1997, July 5). Pictographs help tell Temagami story. *Calgary Herald,* p. G8.

McKibben, B. (1996). What good is a forest? *Audubon,* 98(3), pp. 54–63.

McLaren, C. (1993). Heartwood. In T. Leighton. *Canadian regional environmental issues manual.* (pp. 118–25). Orlando, FL: Harcourt Brace.

McPhedran, K. (1997, Spring). Fiddlehead Farm—out of tune? *Beautiful British Columbia Traveller,* p. 7.

M'Gonigle, M., & Parfitt, B. (1994). *Forestopia: A practical guide to the new forest economy.* Madeira Park, BC: Harbour Publishing.

Moffett, M.W. (1997). Climbing an ecological frontier: Tree giants of North America. *National Geographic,* 191(1), pp. 44–61.

Morell, V. (1994). New hope for old growth? *Equinox,* 73 (February), p. 99.

Mungall, C., & McLaren, D.J. (Eds.). (1990). *Planet under stress: The challenge of global change.* Toronto: Oxford University Press.

National Fish and Wildlife Foundation. (n.d.). Neotropical Migratory Bird Conservation. http://www.nfwf.org/nfwfne.htm

National Fish and Wildlife Foundation. (1996). National Fish and Wildlife Fountation. http://www.bev.net/education/SeaWorld/conservation/nfw.html

National Forestry Database Program. http://www.nrcan.gc.ca/cfs/proj/iepb/nfdp

Natural Resources Canada, Canadian Forest Service. (1994). *The state of Canada's forests 1993: Forests, a global resource.* Ottawa.

Natural Resources Canada, Canadian Forest Service. (1995). *The state of Canada's forests 1994: A balancing act.* Ottawa.

Natural Resources Canada, Canadian Forest Service. (1996a). *The boreal forest (poster-map).* Ottawa: Natural Resources Canada.

Natural Resources Canada, Canadian Forest Service. (1996b). *The state of Canada's forests 1995–1996: Sustaining forests at home and abroad.* Ottawa.

Natural Resources Canada, Canadian Forest Service. (1996c). National Forest Week, May 5–11, 1996. http://nrcan.gc.ca/cfs/nfw/nfw_e.html.

Natural Resources Canada. (1997). The sustainable management of forests. http://www.ec.gc.ca/agenda21/97/mono1.htm

Ness, R., & Cooperrider, A.Y. (1994). *Saving nature's legacy: Protecting and restoring biodiversity.* Covelo, CA: Island Press.

Pilz, D., & Molina, R. (Eds.). (1996). Introduction. *Managing forest ecosystems to conserve fungus diversity and sustain wild mushroom harvests.* (pp. 1–4). Portland, OR: United States Department of Agriculture, Forest Service, Pacific Northwest Research Station: General Technical Report PNW-GTR-371.

Pimm, S. (1996). The lonely earth. *World Conservation,* 27(1), pp. 8–9.

Polson, S. (1996). Cutting with conscience. *E Magazine,* 7(3), pp. 42–43.

Quinby, P.A. (1996). A critique of the proposed management of old growth white and red pine forest in Temagami, Ontario resulting from the comprehensive planning process of 1996 with a case study analysis of the Owain Lake old-growth pine stand as a representative ecosystem. http://www.sll.fi/TRN/index2.html

Rainforest Action Network. (1996). Clayoquot Sound landslides add to mountain of evidence against rainforest clearcut. *Rainforest Action News* (February). http://www.ran.org/ran/info_center/press_release/landslide.html

Robinson, B. (1994). Earthly treasure. *Equinox,* 77 (October), pp. 32–45.

Rosmarin, H. (1997). Rethinking paper: Non-wood fibres poised for comeback. *Global Biodiversity,* 7(2), pp. 33–36.

Rowe, J.S. The necessity of protecting landscapes. *Global Biodiversity,* pp. 9–12.

Ryan, J.S. (1990, July/August). Timber's last stand. *World Watch,* pp. 27–34.

PART 3:
RESOURCES FOR CANADA'S FUTURE

Schoonmaker, P.K., von Hagen, B., & Wolf, E.C. (Eds.). (1997). *The rain forests of home: Profile of a North American bioregion.* Washington, DC: Island Press.

Sierra Club of Canada. (1996). Canadian forests fact sheet. http://www.sierraclub.ca/national/forests/forests.html

Swift, J. (1983). *Cut and run: The assault on Canada's forests.* Toronto: Between the Lines.

Taylor, D.M. (1994). *Off course: Restoring balance between Canadian society and the environment.* Ottawa: International Development Research Centre.

Torgersen, T.R., & Torgersen, A.S. (1995). *Save our birds—save our forests.* Portland, OR: United States Department of Agriculture, Forest Service.

United States Geological Survey. (n.d.). Partners in Flight home page. http://www.pwrc.nbs.gov/pif/

Van Patter, M., & Hilts, S. (1990). Natural heritage protection: Voluntary stewardship or planning control? *Plan Canada,* 30(5), pp. 20–28.

von Mirbach, M. (1997). Demanding good wood. *Alternatives,* 23(3), pp. 10–17.

Walk the Wild Side. http://www.web.apc.org/wcwild/wtww.htm

Western Canada Wilderness Committee. (1994). Scientific support increases for preserving Clayoquot's magnificent ancient rainforests. *Western Canada Wilderness Committee Educational Report,* 13(5). http://www.wildernesscommittee.org

Welland, F. (1997). Mushroom madness. *Canadian Geographic,* 117(1), pp. 63–68.

Wigg, M., & Boulton, A. (1989). Quality wood, sustainable forests. *Forest Watch,* 9(7), pp. 7–12.

additional information sources

Aplet, G.H., Johnson, N., Olson, J.T., & Sample, A.V. (Eds.). (1993). *Defining sustainable forestry.* Washington, DC: Island Press.

Barsch, R.L. (1997). Forests, indigenous peoples, and biodiversity. *Global Biodiversity,* 7(2), pp. 20–24.

Canadian Forest Service. Home page. http://www.nrcan.gc.ca/cfs/

Canadian Forest Service. Overview: Forest Health Network. http://www.NRCan.gc.ca/cfs/proj/sci-tech/nets/bpheal_e.html

Canadian Forest Service. Overview: Forest Biodiversity Network. http://www.NRCan.gc.ca/cfs/proj/sci-tech/nets/bpbiod_e.html

Government of the Northwest Territories. (1992). Caribou of the Northwest Territories. http://www.edt.gov.nt.ca/renewable/wildlife/caribou/caribou.htm

Hammond, H. (1997). What is ecoforestry? *Global Biodiversity,* 7(2), pp. 3–7.

Model Forest Program. http://mf.ncv.forestry.ca/

National Heritage League, 10 Adelaide Street East, Toronto, ON M5C 1T3.

National Round Table on the Environment and the Economy (NRTEE). (1997). *State of the debate on the environment and the economy: Private woodlot management in the Maritimes.* Ottawa: NRTEE.

Pruitt, W.O. (1997). Threats to woodland caribou and the taiga. *Global Biodiversity.* 7(2), pp. 25–31.

United Nations Conference on Environment and Development. (1992). The Forest Principles. http://www.tufts.edu/departments/Fletcher/multi/texts/forest.txt

United Nations Environment Programme. http://www.unep.ch/

United Nations Systems of Organizations. http://www.unsystem.org/index8.html

The Woodland caribou: Threatened with extinction in Canada's western provinces. (1996). http://www.afternet.com/~teal/scaribou.html.

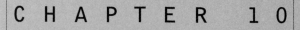

CHAPTER 10

Mining

Chapter Contents

CHAPTER OBJECTIVES   325
INTRODUCTION   325
  Mining in Canada   326
HUMAN ACTIVITIES AND IMPACTS ON
  NATURAL ENVIRONMENTS   326
  Historical Overview   326
  Value and Distribution of Mineral
    Resources in Canada   328
      Canada's First Diamond Mine   329
  Environmental Impacts of Mining   332
    Mineral Exploration   333
    Mine Development and Mineral
      Extraction   336
    Processing of Minerals   338
    Mine Closure and Reclamation   339
RESPONSES TO ENVIRONMENTAL IMPACTS
  AND CHANGE   342
  Market Forces   342
  Partnerships for Environmental
    Sustainability   344
FUTURE CHALLENGES   346
  Stewardship   346
  Protection and Monitoring   347
  Knowledge Building   349
Chapter Questions   350
References   350
Additional Information Sources   351

"Environmentally responsible mining exploration, development, operations and public policies are predicated on maintaining a healthy environment and, on closure, returning mine sites and affected areas to viable and, wherever practicable, self-sustaining ecosystems that are compatible with a healthy environment and with human activities."

Principles and Goals of the Whitehorse Mining Initiative, in <u>Northern Perspectives,</u> 23(3–4)

Chapter Objectives

After studying this chapter you should be able to

- understand the nature and distribution of Canada's mineral resources
- describe the impacts of mining on natural environments
- outline Canadian and international responses to mining issues
- discuss challenges to sustainable mining in Canada

E arth's mineral resources, including sand, gravel, clay, rock, minerals, and fossil fuels, touch almost every aspect of our lives. Mineral products are essential in construction of our homes and workplaces (concrete, bricks, tiles, and structural steel; saw, hammer, and nails), in providing and distributing energy and water to us (coal and uranium; electrical wires and copper pipes), in our transportation (roads, gasoline, trains, and bicycles), in many luxury goods (televisions, stereos, telephones, and computers; gold and diamond jewelry; CDs; aluminum baseball bats, graphite golf clubs), and in medicines, vitamins, and other products to keep us healthy (including zinc, an essential ingredient in sunscreen). Mining is not something we could readily choose not to do!

Even though mineral resources are key components of the global economy, their extraction, transportation, and processing often result in environmental harm and disruption. In Western economies, heightened environmental policies and regulations have prompted the mining industry to improve its practices, to invest in research and development, and to develop new environmental technology. In its activities in developing nations, however, the industry does not always display the same level of concern for sustainability as it does at home.

In many parts of the world, environmental regulations are relaxed (or are minimal) in order to attract foreign investment, generate employment for local people, and expand the industrial base. In fact, many multinational companies exhibiting high environmental standards in the developed world seek out projects in less developed economies with less regard for environmental safety. One example is the 1996 spill of liquefied waste into the Boac and Mogpog rivers on Marinduque Island in the Philippines. A drainage tunnel in the San Antonio copper mine containment pond collapsed, allowing 2.5 million tonnes of waste to spill out, flooding the rivers with silt and mud, smothering fish, and forcing more than 100 residents of the watershed from their homes. Three senior officers of Marcopper Mining Corporation, including the company president, faced criminal charges of reckless imprudence because of property damages and violation of the water code and antipollution law (Philippine mine closed, 1996). The company's environmental clearance certificate was cancelled because Marcopper had failed to stop the flow of mine wastes and had been slow in rehabilitating the damaged rivers.

Despite holding only a 40 percent interest in Marcopper at the time of the accident, Canada's Placer Dome is paying the US$43-million cost of the cleanup (partly in a move to protect the company's reputation). As part of the restoration, Placer Dome plugged the leaking tunnel and built new roads and homes for displaced residents. Activists and area residents are demanding that the mine, which employs 800 people, be shut down permanently to prevent further damage to the island (Spill aftermath, 1997).

Preventive measures, such as upgrading infrastructure and storage facilities, can greatly reduce the likelihood of an environmental disaster. However, preventive actions cost money, and, if not absolutely necessary, mining companies often set aside these kinds of improvements, hoping that there will be no problems. Even if there is an accident, many companies simply write off the environmental liability as a cost of doing business. Environmental destruction caused by corporate disregard for preventive maintenance at the Ok Tedi copper mine in Papua New Guinea is an example.

Operating a mine without **tailings** retention is outlawed in developing countries. Yet, Broken Hill Proprietary (BHP) of Australia (the world's fourth-largest mining company) had been operating the Ok Tedi mine in Papua New Guinea without tailings retention since 1984, when their first tailings dam collapsed due to rugged terrain and high rainfall. Claiming tailings retention was not an option, company mining operations dumped 80 000 tonnes of waste rock per day into the Ok Tedi and Fly rivers. The sediment load, plus a variety of toxic elements in the mine waste, rendered 70 kilometres of the Ok Tedi River almost biologically dead.

In 1996, after many years of struggle, a US$115-million out-of-court settlement was reached between BHP and 15 000 Papua New Guinean downstream landowners on the Ok Tedi and Fly rivers for environmental damages resulting from mine tailings. BHP also agreed to build a full tailings retention system within two years (Papua New Guinea, 1996). It is worth noting, however, that BHP's initial handling of the case earned the company a place on the Multi-National Monitor's List of Worst Corporations for 1995. This distinction was awarded to the company when it was revealed that BHP lawyers had drafted legislation for the Papua New Guinea parliament that would make it illegal to sue BHP!

Accidents such as the San Antonio and Ok Tedi mine spills illustrate some of the dangers mining activities bring to the natural environment. Accidents, however, are only part of the environmental consequences of mining. Even with strong environmental policies and measures in place, all phases of mineral production potentially threaten ecosystem sustainability. During the prospecting phase, drilling and sampling disrupt local ecosystems; in the extraction phase, removing **overburden** (material covering a mineral deposit) and storing mine tailings alter the landscape; and in the processing phase, discharges and emissions pollute water bodies and send toxins into the atmosphere.

MINING IN CANADA

In 1995, mineral exports amounted to more than $40 billion, making Canada the world's leading exporter of minerals. That same year, the mining industry contributed $223 billion to the Canadian economy, or about 4.25 percent of the national gross domestic product. Copper, gold, nickel, and zinc were the four most important metals produced, and potash was the most important nonmetal commodity (Natural Resources Canada, 1996a).

More than 341 000 Canadians are employed directly in the mining and mineral processing industries: 61 000 in mining, 59 000 in smelting and refining, and 221 000 in the manufacture of mineral and metal products. Although Canada does not have accurate data on the nature and extent of land used by the mining industry, in 1982 it was estimated that less than 0.03 percent (279 477 hectares) of Canada's land area was disturbed, used, or alienated by mining activities since metal mining began more than 150 years ago (Government of Canada, 1996a). This intensive use of a relatively small area (less than half the size of Prince Edward Island) produces all the minerals we use every day.

With growing worldwide demand for minerals and mineral products, Canada is faced with the challenge of developing our mineral resources in a way that fosters our economy without compromising the sustainability of our environment. This chapter examines the growth of mineral development in Canada and provides an overview of the environmental hazards and disturbances that result from mining activity. Responses to environmental impacts and change are discussed by outlining some of the strategies that governments, industries, and nongovernmental organizations are using to reduce the environmental impact of mining.

HUMAN ACTIVITIES AND IMPACTS ON NATURAL ENVIRONMENTS

HISTORICAL OVERVIEW

Many communities have strong ties to mineral extraction; in fact, much of Canada's regional and infrastructural development has proceeded in parallel with the development of natural resources. We all have heard tales of the Klondike gold rush where thousands of people from all over the world flocked to the Yukon in the hopes of striking it rich. Despite treacherous conditions, prospectors made their way over icy mountain passes and down the Yukon River to Dawson City. By 1898, three years after the first discovery of gold by George Carmack, more than 40 000 people had set up camp in Dawson.

Then referred to as the Paris of the North, Dawson became a thriving community, creating wealth for both prospectors and the Canadian government. Although few of the men made their fortunes (because the good gold claims had been staked before most prospectors arrived), the tax earnings from gold and alcohol sales prompted the federal government to make the Yukon a separate territory in 1898. Major infrastructure projects, such as the White Pass and Yukon Route Railway (opened in 1900 between Skagway, Alaska, and Whitehorse, Yukon), were constructed to accommodate the growing population.

Unfortunately, not everyone appreciated the economic boom generated by the gold rush. Encroaching populations disrupted traditional ways of life of First Nations people. Miners and other new residents joined in the hunt for game, leaving Aboriginal hunters to travel farther for food. While some First Nations people elected to earn wages packing supplies for miners or cutting fuelwood for steamships, others were forced to leave their lands to escape the growing mining towns.

By 1928, about $200 million worth of gold had been produced in the region, mostly by individual placer mines. For years, gold dredges had operated in the creeks near Dawson City, removing gold until the level of recovery declined sufficiently that it was no longer profitable to run the dredges. Despite the end of the gold rush in the early 1900s, and the depopulation of Dawson City, mining activity remains a valuable component of Yukon economy.

The Yukon gold rush illustrates the boom–bust cycle associated with the mining industry and the history of mining in Canada. Like all sectors of the economy, the mining industry is affected by recession and growth periods within the business cycle. However, mining is especially vulnerable to short-term changes in the supply, demand, and price of an individual commodity. These market conditions have a great deal of influence over the regions and communities where mining takes place.

We know that there is a significant imbalance between the distribution of people (south) and the distribution of natural resources (north) in Canada. This distribution has given rise to a large number of single resource or **one-industry towns,** established to provide a pool of labour to operate and service a mine effectively. When a town's mine is booming, additional workers and support services are required, drawing people into the community. During these good times, one-industry towns are very successful economically with low unemployment and relatively high personal income levels. However, once there is a downturn in the commodity price or reserves are exhausted, mines close, workers leave, and the community is left with little or no economic base. Quite often, entire communities are abandoned, leaving usable facilities and infrastructure behind.

The problems associated with one-industry towns are not as prevalent today as they were in the past. Improvements in air transportation and communication have fostered a regime of **long-distance commuting** (LDC) where miners fly in to a mine to work for a designated period and then are flown back to their homes in larger communities for another period. Workers are provided with food and temporary lodging, but no expensive

In the rush to extract gold, 19th-century mining communities often were erected hastily. This photo of Barkerville, B.C., was taken the day before it was razed by fire in September 1868.

Many of Canada's communities, such as Sudbury, Ont., were founded on the extraction of mineral resources.

infrastructure or support services are constructed at the mine site. Changes in the regulatory environment have also led to fewer one-industry towns being established.

In the past, little attention was paid to community planning; often, the urban environment in single-resource towns was of poor quality. Today, in response to concerns of governments and miners' families, new towns are subject to impact assessment processes, structured planning efforts, and substantial infrastructure investments (Shrimpton & Storey, 1988). These requirements, combined with companies' striving to increase productivity, reduce costs, and rationalize unproductive operations, have led to a movement away from one-industry towns. Even so, mining is the mainstay of employment in over 150 Canadian communities, mostly in rural and remote areas (Natural Resources Canada, 1996b).

From the coal mines of Nova Scotia to the asbestos mines of Quebec, over the years mineral exploration, development, and processing have taken many lives and affected the health of countless mine workers. In the early days of mining, health and safety concerns were of minimal importance to mine operators. Beyond the obvious threats from collapsed mine shafts, equipment failures,

and site explosions, little thought was given to the long-term effects of exposure to hazardous substances, mine dust, and other emissions. Black lung disease, silicosis, asbestosis, and cancer are among the common diseases that miners and other workers have contracted.

Today we recognize these threats; however, we continue to employ workers in conditions that place their health at risk. The mining industry is concerned about worker health and safety, and most mine sites now have programs to monitor exposure to hazardous substances, assess noise impacts, and protect respiratory health. Even so, a key problem confronting the industry is the uncertainty surrounding the long-term, cumulative effects of exposure to mining operations. Governments and industry must continue to strive for continual enhancement of workplace safety through reliable monitoring programs, technical innovation, and enforceable regulatory measures.

VALUE AND DISTRIBUTION OF MINERAL RESOURCES IN CANADA

In 1996, the total value of Canadian mineral production exceeded $49 billion; **mineral fuels** (crude oil and equivalents, natural gas, coal, and natural gas byproducts) accounted for approximately 65 percent of this value. The remaining 35 percent was divided between the other three mineral resource categories—metals, nonmetals, and structural materials (Table 10–1). In 1995, there were about 298 metal, nonmetal, and coal mines; about 3000 stone quarries and sand and gravel pit operations; and about 50 nonferrous smelters, refineries, and steel mills in Canada. Producing mines are found in all provinces and territories except Prince Edward Island (Figure 10–1).

Based on the value of output, the top nonfuel commodities in Canada in 1996 were gold ($2.8 billion), copper ($2.0 billion), nickel ($2.0 billion), zinc ($1.7 billion), iron ore ($1.3 billion), and potash ($1.3 billion). Ontario produces the largest share of nonfuel mineral output, with 32.6 percent of the total value, followed by Quebec (19.5 percent), British Columbia (11.7 percent), and Saskatchewan (10.5 percent) (Natural Resources Canada, 1997). Alberta accounts for the majority of mineral fuels output, producing almost 80 percent of the Canadian total, with Saskatchewan (10.7 percent), and British Columbia (7.0 percent) a distant second and third, respectively.

Precious metals, particularly gold, account for the largest share (40 percent, or $260 million) of total Canadian exploration expenditures. Prompted by the 1991 discovery of diamonds in the Northwest Territories, however, Canada has experienced a significant upward trend in exploration activity. Between 1993 and 1996, the diamond boom accounted for 20 percent of Canada's total

Mining disasters have claimed many lives. The 1992 explosion at the Westray mine in Nova Scotia killed 26 miners.

TABLE 10-1
VALUE OF CANADIAN MINERAL PRODUCTION (1996)

Category/Commodity	Value ($ millions)	Category/Commodity	Value ($ millions)
Metal Mines		**Nonmetal Mines**	
copper	2 037.2	potash	1 263.8
gold	2 803.0	salt	316.2
nickel	1 958.2	asbestos	238.1
zinc	1 652.3	sulphur (elemental)	95.6
iron ore	1 310.5	peat	128.9
uranium	645.8	**total**	**2 042.6**
silver	280.5		
molybdenum	102.9		
cobalt	168.4		
platinum group	146.2		
lead	261.6		
total	**11 366.6**		
Fuels		**Structural Materials**	
crude oil and equivalent	19 008.5	cement	931.5
natural gas	8 718.9	sand and gravel	778.3
coal	1 943.1	stone	552.6
natural gas byproducts	2 456.5	lime	212.3
		clay products	117.1
Total	**32 127.0**	**Total**	**2 591.8**

SOURCE: Adapted from Natural Resources Canada. (1997). *Total value of Canadian mineral production soars in 1996.* http://www.nrcan.gov.ca

exploration expenditures, or $560 million (Natural Resources Canada, 1996a). In 1996, close to 60 companies were active in diamond exploration, attempting to find reserves as lucrative as the BHP mine located northeast of Yellowknife.

Canada's First Diamond Mine

Since the discovery of diamonds, the central region of the Northwest Territories (known as the Slave Geological Province) has attracted intense mineral exploration and development. Encompassing an area approximately one-third the size of Alberta, the Slave Geological Province extends north from Great Slave Lake to Coronation Gulf on the Arctic coast. In three years, roughly 22 million hectares of land were staked by 200 companies—this compares to less than 4 million hectares staked in the previous decade (Department of Indian and Northern Affairs, 1996a).

The Broken Hill Proprietary (BHP) diamonds project, located in the Lac de Gras region 300 kilometres north of Yellowknife, is the largest mineral project in the Northwest Territories and the first diamond mine in North America (Figure 10–2). BHP Diamonds, a subsidiary of the same Australian mining giant referred to earlier in this chapter, owns 51 percent of the Northwest Territories project, Vancouver's Dia Met Minerals owns 29 percent, and Charles Fipke and Stewart Blusson, who discovered the site, each own 10 percent.

On June 21, 1996, a Canadian Environmental Assessment Review Panel (EARP) approved the BHP Diamonds project. Twenty-nine recommendations were made in the EARP report regarding the ecological and social impacts of the mine. Most of these concerns were expected to be satisfied through the terms and conditions of the project's water licence, land lease, and land use permits. However, a number of EARP recommendations fell outside the scope of these regulatory instruments. To satisfy these concerns, the federal government required BHP to enter into an environmental agreement and to negotiate impact–benefit agreements with the Treaty 11 Dogrib, the Yellowknives Dene, the Inuit of Coppermine, and the Mitis Nation who live in various parts of the remote region. The federal government has used similar environmental agreements in the north for several mines in Yukon as well as for the Norman Wells Pipeline.

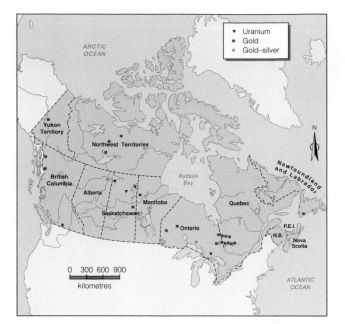

Figure 10–1a

Principal mining regions of Canada: uranium and precious metals mines

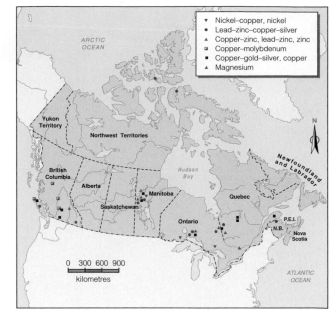

Figure 10–1b

Principal mining regions of Canada: base metal mines

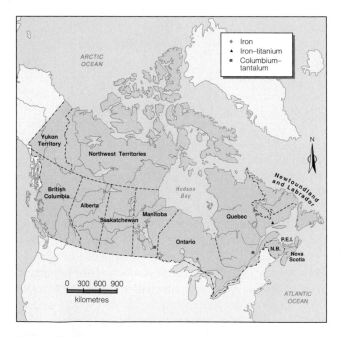

Figure 10–1c

Principal mining regions of Canada: ferrous metal mines

Figure 10–1d

Principal mining regions of Canada: industrial mineral mines

SOURCE: Government of Canada. (1996a). *The state of Canada's environment—1996*. Ottawa. Figure 11.27.

In consultation with the Government of the Northwest Territories and Aboriginal groups, the federal government negotiated the environmental agreement with BHP. The agreement addressed the EARP recommendations and included the following: establishment of an environmental advisory group as well as monitoring and management plans for birds and caribou; submission to the federal gov-

ernment of annual, public monitoring reports on social and environmental preparation of longer term monitoring reports every three to five years; and other water quality issues that were not included in the water licence (Department of Indian and Northern Affairs, 1996b).

These requirements may have been seen as necessary given numerous criticisms of the way in which the

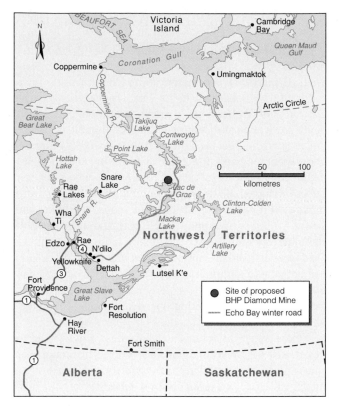

Figure 10–2

Great Slave Lake area and location of proposed BHP diamond mine

SOURCE: Adapted from Wismer, S. The nasty game. *Alternatives,* 22(4), p. 12.

environmental assessment of the diamond project was conducted. Intervenor groups, for instance, noted that BHP's environmental impact statement was deficient in traditional knowledge, monitoring, mitigation, community impacts, and handling of issues related to land claims. Given this and other northern EARP experiences, questions have been raised about the failure of Canada's environmental assessment process to ensure fair, effective, and efficient decision making (Wismer, 1996).

The BHP diamond mining operation is expected to increase the Canadian GDP by $6.2 billion over the 25-year life of the project. More than one-third of this increase (about $2.5 billion) is expected to accrue to the economy of the Northwest Territories, about 60 percent of it in the form of wages and benefits. This is welcome news to many residents as unemployment in the territory is above the national average. BHP expects to create 1000 jobs during the construction of the project, to employ an average of 830 people during the operational phase, and to create another 640 indirect jobs.

According to BHP, two-thirds of the work force will be composed of northern residents and about half of those will be Aboriginal. The company's preference in hiring and

giving on-site training to Aboriginal people is estimated to result in a 10 percent reduction in the unemployment rate in Northwest Territories Aboriginal communities, from 40 percent to 30 percent (Department of Indian and Northern Affairs, 1996c). Currently in the construction phase, the mine operates on a two weeks in/two weeks out, fly-in/fly-out, basis. Although BHP indicates this schedule suits employee needs, it does not provide for a work force that takes time off on a seasonal basis, nor does it account for the costs of social and family disruption and loss of opportunity to participate adequately in community life (Wismer, 1996).

Not everyone is excited about the prospects for mining in Canada's north. While most people appear to favour the BHP diamond project, some environmentalists, Aboriginal leaders, and scientists are concerned about the rapid pace of the approvals process. For example, the World Wildlife Fund (Canada) filed for a judicial review of the EARP's procedures in an effort to obtain commitments for action on protected areas in the region. The international conservation organization was concerned that the diamond mining area is located at the centre of the migration route of the Bathurst caribou herd.

After the governments of Canada and the Northwest Territories committed to produce a Protected Areas Strategy for the entire Northwest Territories by 1998, the World Wildlife Fund withdrew the court action (World Wildlife Fund, 1997). The question of how effective such protected areas might be is illustrated in the case of Tuktut National Park, established in 1996 to protect the tundra hills natural region and the calving grounds of the Bathurst caribou herd: the park also encompasses the BHP diamond mine.

Aboriginal groups also expressed concern over the BHP mining project. The site falls within the traditional hunting and trapping grounds asserted by the Yellowknives Dene and Dogrib Nation. As the mine project was undergoing the approval process, both the Yellowknives Dene and the Dogrib were in the process of

The BHP diamond mine site, Lac de Gras, N.W.T.

negotiating land claims agreements with the federal government. The Yellowknives Dene entered into treaty land entitlement negotiations, while the Dogrib were negotiating a comprehensive land claim and self-government agreement. Both groups were concerned that mining development would compromise the government's ability to conduct negotiations (Department of Indian and Northern Affairs, 1996d).

The Dene were concerned that without a land agreement they risked becoming an "embittered minority" as mining development would attract many new residents to the area (Freeman, 1996). Although BHP has negotiated benefit agreements with Aboriginal groups, there is concern about the enforcement of such agreements because no provision for enforcement has been set out in the EARP recommendations. Attention to equity issues may have been insufficient to ensure that northern people and their communities can remain healthy and sustainable (Wismer, 1996).

Aboriginal leaders also are skeptical of BHP because of the company's environmental performance record, including its problems with the Ok Tedi copper mine in Papua New Guinea. These leaders claim that although BHP may offer monetary compensation for damaging the waters and the land, money does not replace the natural values and opportunities the land provides. In particular, the Yellowknives Dene are concerned about the fuel oil, arsenic, and cyanide that will be hauled on winter roads across their hunting grounds (Wismer, 1996). What troubles many Aboriginal groups and environmentalists is the increased potential for accidents and spills as more and more mining companies show interest in developing the area.

The environmental impact statement prepared by the project's proponents outlined the methods and techniques that were to be used to mitigate environmental damage. Although diamond production avoids the use of toxic chemicals, land and water resources are severely altered by diamond mining. For instance, the mine will have to dig through 6 tonnes of granite for every 1 tonne of kimberlite diamond ore that will be processed. The mine is expected to process about 9000 tonnes of ore per day; that will yield about 2 kilograms of diamonds per day, enough to fill a coffee can (Weber, 1997). In addition, the BHP project will drain 6 lakes and use another for tailings storage. Over the planned 25-year operation of the diamond processing plant, 133 million tonnes of tailings will be impounded at the storage lake (Broken Hill Proprietary, 1996).

Plans exist for up to six new mines in the region where BHP is developing its mine. As delightful as beautiful diamonds may be to look at, they are a luxury; they are not necessary to live a good and happy life. For the northern Aboriginals who see themselves as stewards of their traditional territories, a big question remains: Can mining make a contribution to their longer term health and to the sustainability of their communities? Canadians in general would do well to consider this question.

ENVIRONMENTAL IMPACTS OF MINING

Mineral deposits often are located in areas desirable for other land uses such as forestry, agriculture, and recreation. Using ecosystem-based approaches to make environmental decisions helps us realize that the environmental effects of a mine operation extend far beyond the mine site. Mining has a considerable influence on land surrounding the mine and the range of interaction between mining and other land uses has become increasingly complex. This influence, referred to as the shadow effect, includes all the indirect activities associated with mining such as the construction of roads, rail links, and power facilities (Marshall, 1982). Both the direct uses at the mine site and the accompanying indirect uses in the shadow zone have the potential to conflict with other land use activities (Figure 10–3). As a result, a mining company's responsibility for environmental protection extends beyond its working operations to include neighbouring lands and watersheds.

Increasingly, mineral claims have been staked in areas designated for environmental protection; this action has sparked some intense land use conflicts. For example, a mining development proposed by a subsidiary of the Canadian multinational Noranda Inc., adjacent to Yellowstone National Park, was halted by U.S. president Bill Clinton following a lengthy period of public opposition (Box 10–1). In exchange for all rights to the mining claim, the U.S. government compensated the mine proponents with US$65 million worth of federal lands. Similarly, a proposal to develop a copper mine on British Columbia's Windy Craggy Mountain, in the Tatshenshini watershed, was denied and a land swap compensation package was negotiated in 1993. The region around the Tatshenshini River now is preserved as the Tatshenshini–Alsek Wilderness Park and is permanently closed to mining (Newcott, 1994). In 1994, the area was designated as a World Heritage Site.

Each stage of the mineral production process—from prospecting and exploration to mine development and extraction to refining and processing—introduces potentially disruptive environmental impacts. Figure 10–4 summarizes the waste impacts and potential hazards of mining at each stage of the production process. Table 10–2 highlights a broad range of impact issues.

The extent of environmental impact from a mine depends on a range of factors, from the type of mineral and its chemical properties to the local ecology, geology, and climate characteristics at the mine site. For example, most metal (gold, copper, zinc, and nickel) mines in Canada contain sulphide materials. When exposed to air and water, the sulphide materials oxidize and generate sulphuric acid that results in **acid mine** (or acid rock) **drainage.** (See also the discussion under Mine Closure and Reclamations, below.) Climate variables, such as strong winds and precipitation, may further compound problems of acidic drainage, and increase the risk of freshwater contamination.

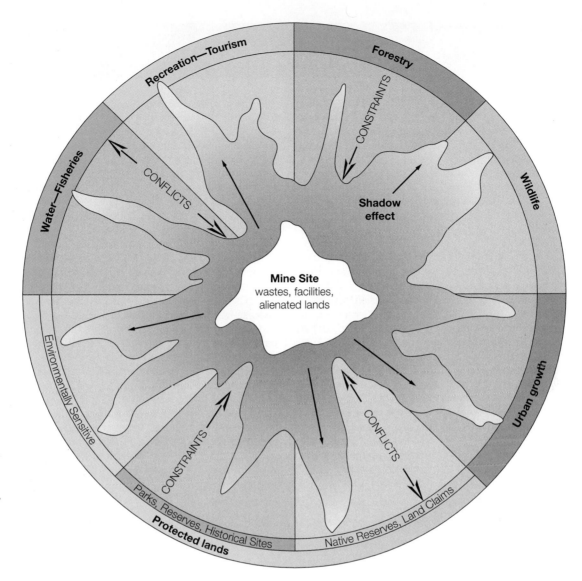

Figure 10–3

Conceptual land use conflicts and constraints for mining

SOURCE: Adapted from Marshall, I.B. (1982). *Mining, land use and the environment: A Canadian overview.* Ottawa: Environment Canada. Land use in Canada series. No. 22–23, p. 194.

Smelting, refining, and fabrication processes use chemicals that may leak or be discharged into the environment. Furthermore, these processing activities require a large amount of energy—the mining industry accounts for about 13 percent of Canadian industrial energy demand (Natural Resources Canada, 1996a). Generally, energy is provided by burning fossil fuels, which releases carbon dioxide and other gases into the atmosphere.

Most mining operations follow a four-stage sequence of development: exploration, development and extraction, processing, and closure and reclamation. The environmental impact at each stage of development varies according to the mineral type, consistency, location, and the form in which the final product is to be delivered.

Mineral Exploration

Mineral **exploration** involves finding geological, geophysical, or geochemical conditions that differ from that of their surroundings (Marshall, 1982). Discovering an anomaly in the landscape may signal the presence of a significant mineral deposit. Even though there are extensive geological mineral records compiled over the past century in Canada, actually detecting an anomaly can be like finding a needle in a haystack. A company's expenditures are high during the exploration stage, and there is no guarantee of turning a discovery into an economically feasible mine.

During exploration, the construction of access roads, trenches, pits, and drill pads disturbs the land surface, and may interfere with wildlife and local drainage. In some instances, where vegetation is stripped to accommodate testing activities, soil erosion and sedimentation (and possible disruption of fish habitat) follow. Constructing roads in areas previously devoid of them opens up access to potentially sensitive areas and permits hunters, wilderness tourists, guides, outfitters, and others to cause potentially significant impacts, ranging from noise to harassment of wildlife. Companies involved in exploration are required to follow guidelines aimed at reducing the disruptive environmental effects of their activities. In addition, most provinces require companies to have reclamation plans and adequate financing to rehabilitate exploration sites.

Having discovered a mineral deposit, a company must first assess the technical and economic requirements of bringing a mine into operation. Costs of extraction, transportation, and processing are considered, as well as costs of environmental controls and reclamation procedures. A company's commitment to operate within an acceptable environmental standard must be demonstrated before a project is approved. As with proposals for many large-scale developments, mining proposals are subject to environmental review. The decision as to whether to proceed with development, modify development, or restrict development is normally reached through the **Environmental Impact Assessment** (EIA) process.

An EIA aims to provide decision makers with scientifically researched and documented evidence to identify the likely consequences of undertaking new developments and changing natural systems (Wiesner, 1995). The magnitude of a review and the requirements to be satis-

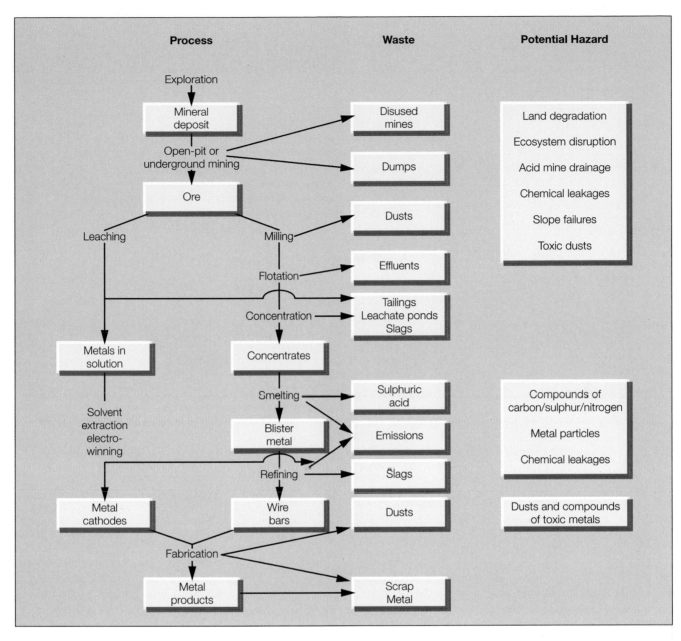

Figure 10–4

The mining process and the environment

SOURCE: Adapted from Warhurst, A. (1994). *Environmental degradation from mining and mineral processing in developing countries: Corporate responses and national policies.* Paris: Organization for Economic Cooperation and Development, p. 14.

fied vary from project to project and from province to province. A key component of the overall EIA process is the preparation of an **Environmental Impact Statement** (EIS). In Canada, it is the responsibility of the project proponent to prepare the EIS and ensure that all provincial and federal policy requirements are satisfied. A balanced EIA should consider the scope of a project from a systems perspective. Table 10–3 outlines the procedural elements involved in the EIA process and highlights basic features of an EIS.

The nature and complexity of the EIA process often leads to frustration for all interested stakeholders. In spite of the possibility of review under the federal Environmental Assessment Act, many people are critical of impact statements because they are commissioned by the developer and prepared by consultants and researchers hired by the developer. For example, the EIS for the BHP diamond mine in the Northwest Territories was described as superficial and totally inadequate in assessing the effects of the mine on the environment (Freeman, 1996).

TABLE 10-2
POTENTIAL ENVIRONMENTAL IMPACTS OF MINING PHASES

Mining phase	Potential impacts
Exploration	• generally low or no impact • when exploration stage requires trenching, drilling, or road access, there is increased habitat disturbance and the potential for discharge of contaminants
Extraction and processing	• acid mine drainage containing contaminants is released to surface water and groundwater; there are particular concerns relating to: – heavy metals that originate in the ore and tailings (their release may be accelerated by naturally occurring acid generation)
• mining and milling	– organic compounds that originate in the chemical reagents used in the milling process – cyanide, particularly from gold milling processes – ammonia • alienation of land as a result of waste rock piles and tailings disposal areas • increased erosion; silting of lakes and streams • dust and noise
• smelting and refining	• discharge to air of contaminants, including heavy metals, organics, and SO_2 • alienation of land as a result of slag • indirect impacts as a result of energy production (most of the energy used in mining processes is used for smelting and refining)
Closure and reclamation[a]	• continuing discharge of contaminants to groundwater and surface water (particularly heavy metals when naturally occurring acid generation exists) • alienation of land and one-time pulse discharge of contaminants and sediment to water as a result of dam failure

NOTE: A particular concern centres on the responsibility for orphaned mine sites; liability falls to society through the government.

[a] Does not apply everywhere.

SOURCE: Adapted from Government of Canada. (1996a). *The state of Canada's environment—1996.* Ottawa: Supply and Services Canada.

Opponents of development projects are not the only ones critical of environmental assessment procedures. In 1996, the Cheslatta Carrier Nation of northern British Columbia obtained documents that revealed "extraordinary corporate pressure to obtain federal approval for the proposed Huckleberry mine near Houston, BC" (Nelson, 1996, p. A5). Japanese investors in the mine opposed "unreasonable delays" in the environmental assessment process and threatened to withdraw from the project and reduce further mining investment in Canada. Such corporate pressure undermines the federal environmental assessment process and may have led to a report entitled "Streamlining Environmental Regulation for Mining" tabled in the House of Commons in November 1996. In the report, the Standing Committee on Natural Resources made 11 recommendations for reforming the federal environmental regulatory regime for mining.

Mine Development and Mineral Extraction

Mining development may have a double impact on the environment, not only as a result of the mine site devel-

opment but also because of the infrastructure put in place to service the mine. As noted above, roads increase access to remote areas and result in additional environmental pressure from nonmining activities such as hunting, fishing, and recreation. Although these activities are beyond the direct control of mining companies, it would be difficult or impossible to undertake them without the mine development.

Effective transportation links are essential for servicing mining operations. Although a large degree of processing occurs at the mine site, large shipments of minerals are transported to smelters, refineries, and other processing locations. Canadian railways earn more than 50 percent of their total freight revenue from transporting mineral products (Natural Resources Canada, 1996a). Environmentalists, and others, are concerned about spills of minerals, mine wastes, and processing chemicals en route to or from mine sites. Roads constructed beside rivers are of special concern as an accident could release toxic substances into the watercourse and threaten aquatic habitat. Mine sites located in areas of seismic activity also are of concern due to the threat of

Gold, coal, potash, and salt are among the minerals extracted in underground mining.

Open-pit mines may have environment impacts beyond land disturbance and aesthetic degradation, including altered surface drainage patterns and the release of harmful trace elements.

an earthquake rupturing tailings ponds and subsequently washing out roads and bridges.

Until the early 1900s, mining activity was concentrated underground. To extract the desired materials, shafts were sunk or tunnels were driven on a slope or horizontally into the ore zone (Figure 10–5). Then the ore could be drilled, blasted, and collected for transport to the surface by ore hoists or wheeled haulage vehicles.

Development of surface mining allowed lower grade ore bodies to be mined over a wider, more dispersed land area. Surface mining involves two basic techniques. In **open pit** mining, ore is extracted from deposits by making a progressively larger and deeper pit from which overburden and waste rock are removed. In **strip mining,** material that lies relatively flat and is not buried too deeply is exposed by shovels or draglines, and the waste materials are thrown back into the previous cut made where the ore or coal was extracted. Placer mining is a form of surface mining, such as panning for gold, that occurs mainly in Yukon and involves mining river- and streambeds for eroded particles of minerals. In 1992, over 70 percent of mineral production in Canada was from surface mining operations.

Open pit mining has allowed mineral companies to exploit economies of scale by using larger mining equipment and large-scale extraction techniques (Warhurst, 1994). However, extensive surface excavations of overburden material may clog streams, create excessive dust, and disturb habitat. In 1989, surface mines produced eight times as much waste per tonne of ore as underground mines (Warhurst, 1994). Land disruption from

TABLE 10–3
THE ENVIRONMENTAL IMPACT ASSESSMENT PROCESS

Procedural Elements in the Environmental Impact Assessment Process	Basic Features of an Environmental Impact Statement
• The developer calls together consultants, regulatory bodies, and other organizations. • An EIS is published and used as a basis for consultation involving regulatory authorities, industry, local residents, and the general public. • The findings of the consultation process are presented to the competent authority reviewing the project. • Any mitigating measures and claims for compensation are considered. • Progressive and postproject monitoring of environmental consequences arising from implementation of the project are set in place.	1. Description of main project characteristics 2. Provision of an analysis of the aspects of the environment likely to be affected by the project 3. Description of the measures envisaged to reduce the harmful effects 4. Listing of alternatives to the proposed project and reasons for their rejection 5. Assessment of the compatibility of the project with environmental regulations and land use plans 6. Systems to be set in place for ongoing and postproject monitoring 7. Nontechnical summary

SOURCE: Adapted from: Wiesner, D. (1995). *The environmental impact assessment process.* Dorset: Prism Press. Used by permission.

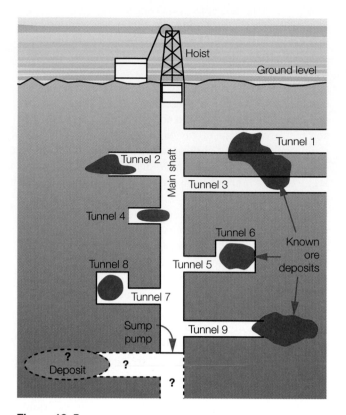

Figure 10–5
Cross-section of a mine shaft

NOTE: Sump pumps keep the mine dry and sophisticated ventilation systems, usually requiring a second shaft, must be installed in most underground mines to remove explosive and radioactive gases and provide fresh air.

SOURCE: Adapted from Castillon, D.C. (1992). *Conservation of natural resources: A resource management approach.* Dubuque, IA: Wm. C. Brown Publishers, p. 325.

surface mining also reduces land available for alternative uses, such as forestry, agriculture, or recreation.

Processing of Minerals

The processing of minerals through milling, smelting, and refining is less land intensive than exploration and extraction; however, the environmental impacts are more significant and long term. The **milling** process involves the crushing and grinding of ores to separate the useful materials from the nonuseful ones. Tailings, the nonuseful materials, are removed from the mill after the recoverable minerals have been extracted. Generally, the amount of concentrate produced per tonne of ore is small in comparison to the amount of rock waste.

Most metal ores require crushing and grinding, plus additional treatment with chemical or biological reagents to extract the desired minerals. Base metal milling commonly uses a flotation process that mixes the ore with chemicals (such as kerosene, organic agents, and sul-

Usually, pure minerals constitute a tiny fraction of the material extracted to obtain them.

phuric acid) and water to produce a fine mineral concentrate (subsequently shipped to a smelter for the next stage of recovery). Following the flotation process, tailings are normally filtered and washed to remove most of the reagents. Once tailing solids have settled, the effluent is discharged to natural water bodies providing it meets regulatory standards.

The milling of gold uses cyanide, which is lethal to fish at concentrations as low as 0.04 milligrams per litre (Government of Canada, 1996b). Once the milling of gold is complete, cyanide must be treated because the retention time in tailing ponds is not normally long enough for cyanide to break down naturally. Various processes are used to treat cyanide in gold mill effluents and tailings pond waters where cyanide concentrations are high. Most

A potash slag heap at Vanscoy, Sask.

The recovery of metallic minerals from the Earth often involves reducing tonnes of rock to mere grams of material, from which products such as copper wire (above) are made.

As the demand for mineral resources continues to increase, the recycling of metals remains an important means to reduce waste. Aluminum products such as these beverage cans are among the most commonly recycled metals.

of the cyanide and metallocyanide complexes can be destroyed or recovered. However, some metallocyanides are more stable and difficult to treat; they may end up in the aquatic environment and harm fish. Provincial regulations specify limits on the amount of cyanide that may be released through effluent discharges.

Usually, mine wastes are treated and stored on site in tailing retention facilities, such as dams and ponds. Effluents containing metals are treated with lime during retention to precipitate the dissolved metals as hydroxides. Such treatment generally removes up to 99 percent of metals and suspended sediments from mine and mill effluent (Government of Canada, 1996a). Serious aquatic damage may result if tailings retention facilities leak or rupture, as was the case with mines in the Philippines and Papua New Guinea. There have been past instances in Canada, too, where leaking or ruptured tailings ponds have affected local water bodies and contaminated community water supplies (such as when the tailings pond at Western Mines discharged into Buttle Lake on Vancouver Island almost 30 years ago).

Production of most base metals (copper, lead, zinc, and nickel), all ferrous metals (iron and steel), and aluminum occurs in smelters and blast furnaces that operate at high temperatures (pyrometallurgy) and emit various pollutants into the atmosphere. Particulate matter, nitrogen oxides, sulphur dioxide, metals, and organic compounds may be deposited locally or transported over long distances. Since the 1970s, stricter emission control standards, new smelting technologies and processes, and voluntary pollution prevention efforts by the mining industry have helped to reduce sulphur dioxide and other emissions (Figure 10–6). However, a substantial portion of the Boreal Shield ecozone continues to receive elevated levels of acidic deposition (Government of Canada, 1996b).

Tailings and waste rock that are naturally high in sulphide materials and are stored at working and abandoned mines can result in acid mine drainage. Acid mine drainage, the most serious control problem facing the Canadian and global mining industry, is discussed in the following section.

Mine Closure and Reclamation

In common with other nonrenewable resources, mineral reserves are finite. Once deposits become depleted or extraction becomes uneconomical, a mine site will close. Efforts to extend the life of a mine include introducing exploration programs to find nearby ore deposits, increasing recovery efficiencies, and providing financial incentives. Regardless of the efforts employed, the eventual closure of a mine is inevitable.

As we have seen with one-industry towns, mine closures can devastate entire communities. In regions dependent on mining, the closure of a mine can lead to the rapid deterioration of social and physical infrastructures. People move to find employment elsewhere and leave behind a small population base with high levels of unemployment and minimal opportunities for diversification. Unless a secondary employer is found early in the life of a mining community, there is little chance of avoiding a rapid decline of the community once a mine closes. In most instances, it is too late to attract a secondary employer once it is known that most of the population is going to disappear soon (Province of Manitoba, n.d.). Governments often provide relocation allowances and retraining programs to help residents of single industry towns.

Some communities have managed to retain a healthy economic base after the closure of a mine. Elliot Lake, Ontario, developed an economic diversification strategy to promote the community for retirement living and outdoor recreation. With the closure of the area's last uranium mine in 1996, Elliot Lake also hoped to position

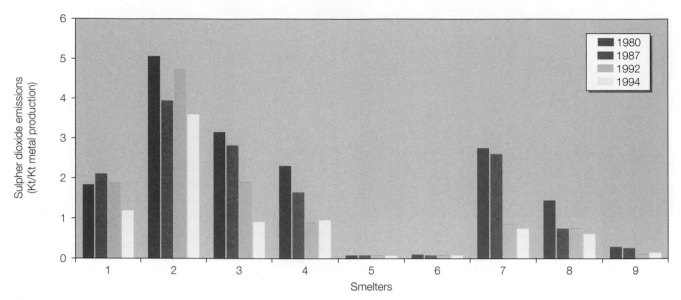

Smelter/location

1. Hudson Bay Mining and Smelting, Flin Flon, Man.[b]
2. Inco Ltd., Thompson, Man.
3. Inco Ltd., Sudbury, Ont.
4. Falconbridge Ltd., Sudbury, Ont.
5. Falconbridge Ltd., Kidd Creek Division, Timmins, Ont.

6. Canadian Electrolytic Zinc (Noranda), Valleyfield, Que.
7. Noranda Minerals Inc., Rouyn-Noranda, Que.
8. Noranda Minerals Inc., Murdochville, Que.
9. Brunswick Mining and Smelting Ltd., Belledune, N.B.

Figure 10–6

Decline in sulphur dioxide emissions per kilotonne of metal production at selected smelters in Eastern Canada for selected years since 1980.[a]

NOTES: a) In this figure, smelting refers to pyrometalurgical processes used in the production of metals from sulphide concentrates, including the roasting of zinc from concentrates,

b) The increase in SO_2 per kilotonne of metal production from 1980 to 1987 is attributable to variability in the sulphur content of concentrates handled at this custom smelter.

SOURCE: Government of Canada. (1996a). *The state of Canada's environment—1996*. Ottawa. Figure 11.32.

itself as an international centre for research on tailings management (Canadian Environmental Assessment Agency, 1996).

Mine closure not only affects the social fabric of a community but can have far-reaching negative impacts on the environment. In the past, in keeping with environmental and mining practices of the day, mine sites were abandoned with minimal or no rehabilitation work. Little, if any, concern was shown for land restoration, environmental stability, or even public safety. Today, most mining projects will be denied approval if the proponents fail to provide a detailed closure plan or do not have the financial security to ensure site rehabilitation. To be effective, these plans must include a long-term monitoring program to safeguard against future environmental damage.

In Canada, jurisdiction over mineral resources is assigned to the provinces. As a result, **reclamation** standards are determined by each province. The federal government has direct responsibility for reclamation in Yukon and the Northwest Territories and in relation to uranium. As well, the federal government influences mine reclamation

issues at the national level through the Fisheries Act, the Canadian Environmental Assessment Act, and through tax policies, and science and technology activities.

Tourism allows communities affected by mine closures, such as Elliot Lake, Ont., to maintain their viability.

Mine reclamation seeks to rehabilitate a mine site to a viable and, wherever practicable, self-sustaining ecosystem that is compatible with a healthy environment and other human activities (Government of Canada, 1996b). Returning land disturbed by mining activity to a condition that is safe, stable, and compatible with adjoining lands requires a well-planned series of activities that incorporate sustainability objectives at all stages of mineral production. In other words, rehabilitation should be a continual activity that occurs over the life of the mine. In addition to initial studies, such as an EIA and closure plan, rehabilitation reports should be prepared annually and the site should be continuously monitored to identify ecological and land use changes.

Mines are no longer abandoned; they are closed following legislated federal or provincial procedures and, when maintained according to these procedures, have few downstream impacts. However, mines were abandoned in the past, and abandoned metal mines potentially introduce the most serious mining-related environmental problems. The tendency of sulphide-bearing rocks to oxidize and generate acidic effluents was noted earlier in the chapter. Every year, the Canadian mining industry generates approximately 650 million tonnes of tailings and waste rock, about half of which are from sulphide ore operations. In the absence of naturally occurring (or applications of) acid-neutralizing materials such as calcite or limestone, toxic metals from surface tailings and mine wastes may leach into nearby watercourses in the form of acid mine drainage. When tailings contain high levels of sulphide material, the potential for acid generation is severe. Untreated acidic wastes also carry toxic concentrations of metals and high levels of dissolved salts. Rainfall and melting snow flush the toxic solutions from waste sites to the surrounding watershed, contaminating watercourses and groundwater.

Although the process of acid mine drainage can be slowed, and the acidic effluent can be treated, it is difficult to prevent completely. Current treatment facilities at mine sites are effective in preventing environmental contamination downstream provided they are well maintained and operated. Unfortunately, acid generation may continue for hundreds of years following mine closure, making treatment plants neither financially nor operationally viable. Furthermore, conventional treatment using lime offers limited long-term benefit as the volume of sludge produced in the treatment process will exceed the volume of tailings in only a few decades.

In 1994, over 12 500 hectares of tailings and 740 million tonnes of waste mine rock were found to be generating acid drainage in Canada. Using these figures, acidic drainage liability in Canada was estimated at between $2 billion and $5 billion. Promoting the growth of vegetation on tailings and waste rock was expected to alleviate acid drainage so that mining companies could abandon sites without future liability. However, it was discovered that the presence of vegetation did little to improve the quality of water drainage. The Canadian mining industry and governments realized that new reclamation technology needed to be developed and in 1986 established a task force to conduct research on acidic drainage.

Recommendations from the task force led to the creation of the Mine Environmental Neutral Drainage (MEND) program in 1989 (Box 10–2). The MEND program has advanced research and led to improved technology for mitigating problems associated with acid mine drainage. The underwater disposal of mine tailings is favoured by many mine operators as part of a decommissioning program. An anaerobic (without oxygen) environment prohibits the production of sulphuric acid in trailings kept underwater. In the long term, natural sedimentation will cover the tailings, preventing their contact with oxygen.

The cost of cleaning up abandoned mine sites across Canada is estimated to be $6 billion (Young, 1996). Unfortunately, a large portion of this total can be attributed to degradation resulting from past practices that are no longer permitted. Abandoned mine sites that represent an unacceptable risk to the environment or human health and safety will have to be rehabilitated. Responsibility for cleaning up many of these abandoned sites rests with the federal government as the previous owner or operator of the property can no longer be identified, is insolvent, or is otherwise unable to pay. Some provincial governments also have begun to survey abandoned or orphaned mine sites to assess the level of degradation and cleanup efforts required.

Mined-out shafts do not necessarily have to be closed and capped as is commonly assumed. For example, a mined-out chamber of a zinc–copper mine in Manitoba has been converted successfully to a thriving garden supporting a wide variety of plant species (Enviro-Focus 10).

In a sustainability context, and as the market for recycled minerals and metals has increased, the recycling of minerals and metals has become an important economic venture. A combination of reuse and recycling practices, as well as the long life span of minerals and metals, can help increase the stock of extracted minerals and metals and reduce the need for primary extraction. Because Canada has developed a large metal smelting and refining capacity, and because scrap and recycled metals follow the same metallurgical pathway through smelters and refineries as do primary metals, Canada has an excellent base for metal recycling.

Already most metal products produced in Canada are made from a mixture of primary and recycled metals. For instance, about 50 percent of the 15 million tonnes of iron and steel produced annually in Canada comes from recycled iron and steel scrap. More than 90 percent of the lead consumed in Canada can be recycled economically; in 1995, about 40 percent of Canada's total refined lead production came from secondary lead sources. On a global

The Mine Environmental Neutral Drainage (MEND) program is a cooperative program financed and administered by the Canadian mining industry, several federal government agencies (including Natural Resources Canada, Environment Canada, and Indian and Northern Affairs), and provincial governments.

The program is a collaborative effort to research and develop technologies that will prevent or substantially reduce environmental problems caused by acid mine drainage and the financial liabilities that accrue to public agencies at abandoned mine sites. However, for the tailings and waste rock piles of many existing and orphaned mines, the best that can be expected is long-term containment and treatment to neutralize acid drainage and remove dissolved metal contaminants.

Since the creation of the program, more than $10 million (42.5 percent contributed by industry) has been spent on research to find ways to reduce the liabilities caused by acidic drainage from reactive tailings and waste rock. Research advances resulting from the MEND program include the following:

- development of precise methods to predict and measure the extent of acidic drainage before it occurs
- subaqueous tailings disposal (such as at the Polaris Mine)
- layered earth covers
- engineered wetlands (such as in Elliot Lake)
- use of solid covers and wet barriers to prevent and control acid runoff
- use of biotechnology to treat small acidic seeps

The MEND program is expected to continue until the end of 1997, at which time more than $18 million will have been spent on acidic drainage research. What has been confirmed in the MEND program is that prevention is the best solution for acidic drainage.

SOURCES: Government of Canada. (1996a). *The state of Canada's environment—1996.* Ottawa: Supply and Services Canada.

Natural Resources Canada. (1996c). Mine environmental neutral drainage program. http://www.emr.ca/mets/mend/

basis, scrap copper accounts for about 40 percent of the raw material input of refined copper production and consumption. The automotive industry is responsible for about 80 percent of the end use of secondary aluminum. In 1971, an average of about 35 kilograms of recycled aluminum was used in the production of each new car; by 1994, that average figure had climbed to 68 kilograms per vehicle (Government of Canada, 1996a).

Metal recycling has significant environmental benefits when compared with primary production of metals. The reduced demand for raw material means more efficient use of minerals and increased energy conservation. Energy savings are gained through the reduced quantity of fossil fuels used to generate electricity or operate smelters. Reduced use of fossil fuels means reduced levels of air emissions such as carbon dioxide, sulphur dioxide, and nitrogen oxides, as well as reductions in effluent discharges. By recycling nonferrous metals, typical energy savings realized are 95 percent for aluminum, 85 percent for copper, 65 percent for lead, and 60 percent for zinc. Producing steel from recycled materials results in energy savings of 74 percent when compared with the energy used in primary production.

Over 1000 companies and about 20 000 people in Canada are involved in the scrap metal recycling industry. They handle over 11 million tonnes and $3 billion worth of metals annually. In 1994, the Canadian trade in recyclable metals exceeded 4 million tonnes and was valued at over $2 billion (cited in Government of Canada, 1996a).

RESPONSES TO ENVIRONMENTAL IMPACTS AND CHANGE

MARKET FORCES

Canada is proud of its position as the global leader in mining and is making great efforts to ensure our number one ranking is secure. Both federally and provincially, policies and guidelines have been adopted to promote the growth of the mining industry. Although sustainable development is recognized as an important component of these strategies, the quest to grow and to achieve international competitiveness often takes precedence. For example, Manitoba's objective for ensuring growth and development in the mining industry is centred on creating a positive business climate. The policy encourages efficient and environmentally sound mineral resource use but places few limitations on exploration and development.

The provincial government feels it must maintain the right to explore and develop mineral properties over as large a prospective land base as possible, must accommodate multiple land use planning principles, and must protect lands with high mineral potential for mineral exploration (Province of Manitoba, n.d.). In addition to

Precious Metals, or Petals?

Exhausted mine shafts and tunnels do not necessarily have to end up abandoned. In a fully operational copper mine in Flin Flon, Manitoba, a rich diversity of plant species flourishes 365 metres below the surface. And with advances in biotechnology, the value of underground gardening is just beginning to take root.

Canada's adventure in underground gardening began in the late 1970s when Inco began growing market vegetables at one of the company's mines in Creighton, Ontario. In 1984, the company switched to growing pine seedlings, replacement trees for those damaged by mine activity. Looking to make use of its kilometres of exhausted mine tunnels, the Hudson Bay Mining and Smelting Co. Ltd. approached Saskatchewan-based Prairie Plant Systems to evaluate the potential of using the spent tunnels for biotechnology research. The mining company also was interested in the possibility of growing plant material for use in mine site reclamation. Despite initial concerns, the underground garden has been extremely successful with some varieties growing almost three times as fast as they would above ground.

The spectacular level of growth may be attributed to the reduced amount of stress plants endure in mine tunnels. Conditions underground—everything from lighting and temperature to moisture and fertilizer—are close to ideal. In the mine, aboveground stresses such as drought, wind, excess sun and water, insects, and disease are avoided. The president of Prairie Plant Systems believes that with conditions such as these, a plant's genetic system is able to direct all its energy toward growth.

The opportunity to expand underground botanical activities may be limited only by the availability of mine sites. Experience in Flin Flon indicates that a mine acts like an artificial growth chamber. Not only do mines speed up the growing process, they also provide an environment that produces good quality plants and trees. Farmers and pharmaceutical companies are attracted by the prospect of perfect plants. For instance, saskatoon berry bushes have become a crop of choice for diversifying western farmers. Although there is a shortage of good quality saskatoon berry bushes, the mine has been able to produce perfect plants that are hardy and produce berries that are uniform in size, flavour, and time of ripening.

Drug companies also are intrigued by the potential of mines to provide high-quality, rapidly growing plants for medicinal purposes. The Pacific yew, for instance, is in high demand because its bark contains taxol, used in the treatment of ovarian cancer (see Enviro-Focus 3). As a result, the Flin Flon mine is cultivating yew trees with the intention of easing pressure on the wild Pacific yew.

SOURCE: Ryan, B. (1995). Roses from rock. *Equinox,* 79 (January–February), pp. 50–55.

this push for mineral development, Manitoba is committed to completing a network of special places where at least 12 percent of the province's land will be protected from commercial logging, mining, hydroelectric development, and other activities that adversely affect habitat.

Unfortunately, environmental policies related to mining are not uniform throughout the world. As a result, countries that have higher environmental standards are often left at a disadvantage when it comes to attracting investment and remaining competitive. In Chile, for example, monitoring and enforcement of environmental laws is rare, obtaining access to information on environment and development impacts is difficult or impossible, and health and safety standards are inadequate (Environmental Mining Council of British Columbia, 1996). Industry leaders, such as Canada's Barrick Gold, praise the attitude of Chile toward mining companies, while others, including the World Bank, are critical of the absence of regulations and administrative obstacles in Chile that make it difficult to assess or enforce environmental standards. The environmental and worker safety conditions that exist at many South American mine sites would not be tolerated in Canada. However, with operating costs averaging about two-thirds that of Canada, South America is gaining a distinct competitive advantage for copper production (Environmental Mining Council of British Columbia, 1996).

PARTNERSHIPS FOR ENVIRONMENTAL SUSTAINABILITY

Major players in Canada's mining industry realize that they have to work hard to overcome a long history of environmental neglect. Abandoned operations, high emissions, and dangerous human health conditions have given the mining industry a reputation that is less socially desirable than that of other forms of economic and land use activities. Government regulations, at both the federal and provincial levels, have prompted mining companies to invest in research and environmental technologies to improve their operations. Environmental nongovernmental organizations (ENGOs), such as the Mining Council of British Columbia, act as environmental watchdogs over industrial practices at home and abroad. In the past decade or so, a variety of cooperative programs and initiatives have been working toward fostering the sustainable development of mining and mineral processing.

The Environmental Mining Council of British Columbia (EMCBC) is a coalition of environmental groups working toward environmentally sound mining laws and practices. A few of the organizations in the EMCBC include the Canadian Nature Federation, the Canadian Parks and Wilderness Society, the West Coast Environmental Law Society, British Columbia Spaces for Nature, and the Yukon Conservation Society. Formed in an effort to advance a coordinated strategy on mining, the EMCBC acts as a clearinghouse for a variety of technical and strategic information on mining. These groups acknowledged that while British Columbia's environmental community had a great deal of depth regarding forestry and wilderness issues, there was a significant gap in their ability to respond effectively to the technically complex and politically distinct world of mineral development. They acknowledged, also, that more work needed to be done to increase awareness of the threats of mining pollution and habitat destruction (British Columbia Spaces for Nature, n.d.)

In response to growing public concern about provincial mining regulations and assessment processes, the EMCBC has initiated an education and advocacy program called BC Mining Watch. The program aims to build the capacity of activists to respond to environmental threats posed by mineral development, from exploration to mine abandonment. The BC Mining Watch project carries out its central objective in three main ways, by (1) supporting effective documentation of environmental mining conflicts, (2) supporting communication and alliance between ENGOs, First Nations, and labour groups on environmental mining issues, and (3) coordinating and communicating a clear agenda for environmentally appropriate mining regulations and practices (British Columbia Spaces for Nature, n.d.). (For more information on the Environmental Mining Council of British Columbia and the BC Mining Watch program, contact any of the participating organizations or reach them at EMCBC's e-mail address listed in the Additional Information Sources section of this chapter.)

One of most successful advances in reducing environmental impacts of mineral processing involves the initiatives that have been taken to lower sulphur dioxide emissions. Ontario's Countdown Acid Rain Program, initiated in 1985, was a key motivator in prompting companies to attain the required reductions in sulphur dioxide emissions. At Inco's nickel smelter in Sudbury, Ontario, the program prompted a 90 percent reduction in emissions. This positive event is tempered by intensification of continuing emissions, however (Box 10–3).

Other efforts to reduce emissions in other parts of Canada are generating positive results also. For instance, at Flin Flon, Manitoba, the Hudson Bay Mining and Smelting zinc smelter uses a new hydrometallurgical pressure process rather than conventional ore roasting. This new process leaches toxic metals and sulphur ore out of wastes in solution. Installation of a new zinc plant resulted in significant emission reductions as up to 98 percent of the sulphur contained in the ore was captured. In addition, use of Gore-Tex™ fabric for filtering purposes greatly reduced particulate emissions. In fact, mine operators are aiming for particulate emissions as low as 16 percent of the allowable limit (Government of Canada, 1996b).

The Accelerated Reduction/Elimination of Toxics (ARET) program is a further initiative that is helping companies reduce emissions of particulate matter and sulphur dioxide from industrial smelters. As part of the ARET program, 13 mining companies representing 83 percent of Canadian base metal production have submitted reduction plans for 12 ARET-listed substances. Between 1988 and 1993, the companies reduced releases by 43 percent, and have committed to total reductions of 71 percent by the year 2000 (Government of Canada,

Over a century of nickel smelting by Inco and Falconbridge near Sudbury, Ontario, devastated the surrounding landscape and waters. The once vast forests essentially disappeared. Much of the worst damage was done in the first 50 years of operation, when ore was smelted over huge, open wood fires. Since the 1970s, new smelting processes and the construction of high smokestacks have reduced the local and overall impacts of emissions.

Between 1965 and 1985, Inco's Sudbury operations reduced emissions of sulphur dioxide by 70 percent, the largest decrease in emission tonnage among North American smelters. In 1985, the Ontario government unveiled its Countdown Acid Rain Program, which required Inco to increase its containment of sulphur dioxide to 90 percent. During the 1980s, Inco invested $530 mil-

lion on related research and developed the necessary new technology. Inco's sulphur dioxide abatement project turned into a wide-ranging facility improvement plan that also generated cost savings of over $50 million per year and reduced carbon dioxide, nitrogen oxides, and particulate emissions, as well as sulphur dioxide emissions.

On January 1, 1994, the company met the government's deadline for reducing sulphur dioxide emissions to a maximum annual level of 265 000 tonnes, setting new standards of environmental stewardship for other companies to follow. This is a considerable achievement, but its effectiveness has been offset somewhat by the fact that sulphur dioxide emissions continue, and their effects have been intensified by other acidifying emissions such as nitrogen oxides.

Facility improvements at the Copper Cliff smelter in Sudbury have reduced atmospheric emissions.

SOURCE: Adapted from Government of Canada. (1996a). *The state of Canada's environment—1996.* Ottawa: Supply and Services Canada.

1996a). (Note that other air-quality initiatives were discussed in Chapter 5.)

Cooperative efforts in the minerals sector extend beyond atmospheric antipollution programs. In 1993, the Aquamin program was initiated to assess the impacts of mining on the aquatic environment. This multistakeholder group included representatives from various federal government departments, eight provincial governments, the Mining Association of Canada, Aboriginal groups, and ENGOs. The final report of Aquamin made a number of key recommendations, including improving federal effluent regulations and updating the Environmental Code of Practice for Mines.

Canada's role in fostering technological development in the mining and metals industry is an important one.

Research activities of federal agencies such as the Canada Centre for Mineral and Energy Technology (CANMET) include the pursuit of sustainable development objectives in advancing mineral science. The federal government also supports stronger links between the scientific community and policy organizations to advance sustainability objectives (Government of Canada, 1996b).

The Ottawa-based International Council on Metals and the Environment (ICME) represents major nonferrous and precious metal producers from five continents. Canadian companies help ICME foster environmentally sustainable economic development by defining environmental management systems for the mining industry, including the ISO 14 000 series of international standards (Box 10–4).

Incorporating an environmental management system (EMS) into an organization's overall business management strategy makes good business sense, especially in light of increased consumer environmental awareness. In addition to attracting environmentally conscientious customers, businesses adopting internal environmental management systems stand to benefit in other areas including the following:

- reduction of liability/risk
- improvement of company image
- pollution prevention and energy savings
- improved insurance coverage
- better resale value of property assets
- attraction of high-quality workforce
- improved internal management methods

In their 1996 Canadian Environmental Management Survey, Canada's largest professional services organization, Klynveld Peat Marwick Goerdeler (KPMG), found that 64 percent of survey respondents reported having an EMS in place. KPMG's study also found that more than half of the respondents without an EMS mitigate environmental issues on an "as required" basis. According to KPMG, organizations that use the latter approach are left at a distinct competitive disadvantage. KPMG recommends that Canadian organizations should move quickly to make management of environmental issues an everyday part of their business by fully integrating environmental risk management into existing management systems.

KPMG's results are particularly important considering the International Organization of Standardization's ISO 14 000 series of environmental management standards. The standards offer a management system that assists companies in identifying deficiencies and improving environmental performance. The standards do not replace Canadian federal and provincial environmental regulations; however, they provide a model that can be used by firms of any size in any industry.

The ISO 14 000 series is expected to affect international trade practices in such a way that many firms, particularly European companies, will refuse to buy or receive bids from suppliers who are not ISO 14 000 accredited. KPMG cautions that Canadian firms looking to conduct business outside Canada should examine immediately the impact of ISO 14 000 standards. KPMG made the recommendation after discovering that, of the natural resource and energy companies surveyed, only 44 percent planned to seek certification.

SOURCES: Standards Council of Canada. (1996). What will be the ISO 14000 series of international standards? http://www.scc.ca.

Klynveld Peat Marwick Goerdeler. (1996). Environmental management survey.
http://www.kpmg.ca/enviro/vL/ensure96e.htm.

The Whitehorse Mining Initiative (WMI) was established in 1992 in order to find solutions to economic and environmental realities in the Canadian and global mining industry. Initiated by the Mining Association of Canada, the WMI accord is perceived as an important key to the future of the Canadian mining industry. The accord advocates change toward a sustainable mining industry within the context of a commitment to social and environmental goals and within the framework of an evolving and sustainable Canadian society (Natural Resources Canada, 1996b).

The vision of the WMI is one of a socially, economically, and environmentally sustainable and prosperous mining industry, underpinned by political and community consensus. In addition to this vision, the accord contains 16 principles, 70 goals, and a statement of commitment to followup action. The principles and goals have been grouped into six main categories: (1) addressing business needs, such as streamlining and harmonizing regulatory and tax regimes, (2) maintaining a healthy environment, by adopting sound environmental practices and establishing an ecologically based system of protected areas, (3) resolving land use issues, beginning by recognizing and respecting Aboriginal treaty rights and guaranteeing stakeholder participation where the public interest is affected, (4) ensuring the welfare of workers and communities by providing workers with healthy and safe environments and a continued high standard of living, (5) meeting Aboriginal concerns by ensuring the participation of Aboriginal peoples in all aspects of mining, and (6) improving decisions through the creation of a climate for innovative and effective responses to change (Natural Resources Canada, 1996b).

The WMI's vision is complex, and its successful implementation requires the full commitment of all stakeholder groups. The WMI is an important initiative for balancing economic and environmental goals and achieving sustainability of Canada's mineral and ecological resources.

FUTURE CHALLENGES

STEWARDSHIP

The cooperation demonstrated by the various parties in preparing the Whitehorse Mining Initiative is an important step toward the stewardship of Canadian mineral resources. Successful implementation of the WMI accord would demonstrate to the world Canada's commitment to environmental sustainability through sound economic, social, and ecological frameworks and policies. Efforts made toward improving the stewardship of minerals in Canada, and other parts of the developed world, should be transferable to the developing world.

The recycling plant in Lachine, Quebec.

Plastic agrichemical containers are recycled into durable fence posts.

Developing nations, often desperate for revenue, fail to legislate (or enforce) sustainable mining policies and regulations. As a result, mining companies, particularly multinationals, must assume a high degree of corporate responsibility when undertaking projects in countries with less stringent environmental regulations. Although it may be economical to cut corners, the risk of accidents, environmental disasters, and injury to mine workers increases if adequate environmental and safety conditions are not followed. In the long term, the initial savings gained by failing to implement proper environmental safeguards may be outweighed by the high costs of accident cleanup and reclamation efforts at a later stage. Corporations that demonstrate effective stewardship of natural resources should be recognized by individuals and governments for their accomplishments.

The stewardship of mineral resources, particularly metals, is demonstrated by efforts to reduce, reuse, and recycle. Recycling extends the efficient use of metals, reduces pressure on landfills and incinerators, and results in energy savings relative to the level of energy inputs

required to produce metals from primary sources. In fact, many minerals and metals can be reused indefinitely because of their value, chemical properties, and durability. Worldwide, approximately 50 percent of lead and steel consumed each year is derived from recycled materials (Peeling, Kendall, Shinya & Keyes, 1992).

PROTECTION AND MONITORING

With increased global competition in the minerals and metals sector, Canada is striving to maintain its role as a leading mineral producer. To attract foreign investment and retain a competitive edge, domestic policy and decision-making processes must be responsive to international factors.

Federal initiatives, such as the streamlining of environmental regulations for mining, are intended to promote a positive investment climate. For the mining industry to remain an important component of the Canadian economy, new mineral deposits must be discovered. Because mineral reserves are finite, exploration will advance into more remote regions of the country and conflicts will arise over key wilderness areas. The Cheviot Mine proposal in Alberta is a case in point (Box 10–5). It is important that the exploration and development of these new deposits is conducted with ecosystem sustainability in mind. Canada must identify and protect areas of significant terrestrial and marine habitat from mineral and other forms of development. Protected areas strategies should be coordinated with the provinces to ensure critical regions are safeguarded. Where mining is permitted, monitoring strategies should be implemented to assess the effect of development on ecosystem health.

BOX 10–5
THE CHEVIOT MINE: STRIP MINING PARADISE?

Jasper National Park is a World Heritage Site, meaning its wilderness and wildlife are of outstanding global significance. However, Cardinal River Coals (CRC) received permission to dig an open pit coal mine less than 2 kilometres from the park boundary. The mine consists of a chain of 26 deep pits extending for 22 kilometres and 1 to 3 kilometres wide. Over a 20-year period, CRC plans to extract about 90 million tonnes of coal, 65 million of which is expected to be marketable, for a total of about US$3.4 billion. About 450 people would be employed directly in the mine.

The huge mine would lie across the headwaters of the McLeod and Cardinal Rivers (the Cardinal Divide), near treeline, at the foot of the front ranges. This location—as environmentally sensitive as it is beautiful—is 10 040 hectares of gently rolling subalpine forest owned by the Crown (public land). The mine's processing plant and some of its pits would be located in the old coal mining area of Mountain Park, which was damaged by mining in the first half of the century and continues to recover. Much of the new mining, however, would occur in undamaged lands.

CRC is a joint venture company consisting equally of Canadian Luscar Ltd. and US Consolidated Coal (the largest coal mining company in the United States). CRC's mine application was reviewed at a joint federal–provincial public hearing in January 1997; two of the three-person panel were members of the Alberta Energy and Utilities Board (not known for turning down projects on environmental grounds), and the third person was appointed by the Canadian Environmental Assessment Agency. CRC justified the Cheviot Mine on the basis that the company's existing Luscar coking-coal mine would exhaust its supply in about four years, and a new mine would be needed to supply the Japanese market.

At the hearing, Parks Canada concluded that the Cheviot Mine proposal has the potential to adversely impact the ecological integrity of Jasper National Park. Concerns relate specifically to the loss or alienation of habitat, to impacts on essential wildlife travel corridors that link Jasper National Park and the high-quality habitat in adjacent provincial lands, and to increases in wildlife mortalities. Over time, the cumulative impacts of this project and other planned or proposed activities such as timber harvesting, access, and oil and gas exploration would result in the extirpation of grizzly bears, wolves, wolverines, and cougars from the region. Expert witnesses from both the company and Parks Canada concluded that the mine would result in the direct loss of quality habitat and wildlife travel routes for at least 100 years.

The Cardinal Divide is a hot spot of biological diversity, an unglaciated area that is home to 76 species of birds, 40 species of mammals, and 1 species of amphibian. There are many rare, disjunct, and threatened species in the proposed mine area; some species have been found nowhere else on Earth. The Upper McLeod River system supports the largest concentration of breeding harlequin ducks known in western Canada. Testimony at the hearing showed harlequin ducks would be affected negatively, as would Alberta's threatened bull trout. Species richness and diversity of song birds is "as high as it gets in North America."

The Cheviot mine area was identified as part of the habitat needed for the recovery of Alberta's grizzlies, but the province has no endangered species legislation to protect them. In addition, the provincial government had identified the proposed mine area as a critical wildlife zone, and scientific assessments recommended the entire Cardinal Divide area should be designated as a Natural Area of Canadian Significance. Western science has pointed to the irreplaceable value of the area, and so has

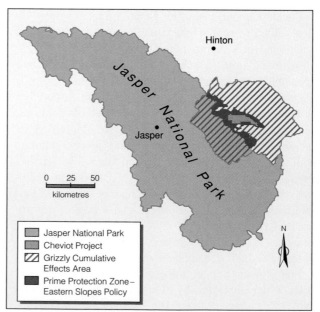

SOURCE: Legault, S. (1997). Coalminer's fodder. *Canadian Geographic,* 117(2), p. 20.

Reprinted by permission of Onjo Graphics.

BOX 10-5
(CONTINUED)

the traditional knowledge of First Nations people who have used medicinal plants from the proposed mine area—plants not found elsewhere.

Reclamation plans call for 14 of the 26 pits to be left partly open to fill with water and function as trout ponds; this mitigation measure does not recreate the diversity of life found in natural streams and along their banks. Neither the bull trout nor the harlequin duck live in lakes. Open pit lakes do not meet the Canadian government policy that requires no net loss of productive fish habitat, nor do they support the international commitments Canada has made to preserve biodiversity.

This mine proposal is not an issue of jobs versus the environment; it is an issue of short-term jobs versus long-term jobs and sustainability. The metallurgical coal in this area is not the only such coal in the region or the province. There are alternatives that would not threaten the World Heritage Site and destroy the Cardinal Divide area. These include accessing the substantial coal reserves remaining deeper in the Luscar mine (by conventional undergound mining and by CRC's inactive hydraulic mine). Alberta's Coal Conservation Act is designed to protect the public from companies that dig up public lands only to take out the coal that is cheapest to reach and then abandon the area and move on to a new site.

In addition, the government's land use planning process identified the need to diversify the region's resource extraction based economy and highlighted tourism as an alternative. The wildlands of the proposed mine area were identified as one of the two key tourism assets in the entire region. The Cheviot Mine will foreclose that option unless international opinion can be mobilized to persuade government officials to reject the $250-million project. Already U.S. environmental groups are involved in lobbying because of Jasper's status as a World Heritage Site and because of the similarities of the Cheviot mine development to the proposed gold mine next to Yellowstone National Park that President Clinton turned down in 1996 (Box 10-1).

SOURCES: Gadd, B. (1997). A hard-nosed look at the proposed Cheviot mine. *Wild Lands Advocate,* 5(2), pp. 4–5.

Legault, S. (1997). Coal miner's fodder. *Canadian Geographic,* 117(2), p. 20.

Pachal, D. (1997). Strip mining paradise. *Encompass,* 1(2), pp. 12–14.

KNOWLEDGE BUILDING

As land-based mines become exhausted and their extraction becomes less cost effective, we may turn to the oceans for many of our mineral requirements. The extraction of mineral fuels from the ocean floor has become a major economic activity; however, deep-sea mining of nonfuels remains in its infancy. As mineral exploration of the seabed increases, we must consider the diverse physical and ecological processes that occur in our oceans and proceed with development on a sustainable basis. Development decisions, both on land and in the ocean, should be based on the precautionary principle.

Research efforts in the mining field focus on all aspects of mineral production, from exploration to processing and site decommissioning. Recently, we have seen important scientific advances in controlling toxic emissions and acid mine drainage. However, much more work needs to be done in the areas of waste management, aquatic effects monitoring, and reduced energy consumption. For instance, there are over 6000 active, abandoned (no longer operating, but owners known), and orphaned (no longer operating, owners unknown) tailings sites in Canada. There is no comprehensive inventory of the risks these sites pose. This is one of the significant gaps in knowledge about the environmental effects of mining that needs to be filled.

The coordination of research efforts through national partnerships may increase technical innovation and allow programs to be delivered with maximum efficiency. International collaboration and the sharing of expertise are essential for meeting the challenge of sustainable development, particularly in the developing world. As a leader in mining, Canada has an important role to play in fostering the global sustainability of mining operations through our research, technology, and policy efforts.

Chapter Questions

1. If mining operations occur on only 0.03 percent of Canada's land surface, why is there so much environmental concern about them?

2. Which of the four phases of mineral development do you think has the greatest environmental impact? Why?

3. What mineral resources are extracted in your local area and in your region? What mining methods are used? What laws and regulations require restoration of the landscape after mining is completed? How stringently are these laws and regulations enforced?

4. Discuss several harmful environmental effects mining and processing minerals have on atmospheric, aquatic, and land environments.

5. Reuse and recycling of mineral and metal resources is one way to extend the availability of these nonrenewable resources. What kinds of mineral and metal recycling occur in your educational institution? In your community? What more could be done in your community or region to encourage reuse and recycling of mineral resources?

6. What are the similarities between the proposed gold mine located near Yellowstone National Park in the United States and the proposed coal mine located near Canada's Jasper National Park? Do you think Canadian public opinion could have a similar effect on the outcome of the political decision to approve the Cheviot Mine as U.S. public opinion did regarding the New World Mine?

references

Adams, J. (1996, August 12). Yellowstone deal elates naturalists. *Calgary Herald*, p. A1.

American Rivers. (1996). President Clinton stops New World Mine. http://www.igc.apc.org

British Columbia Spaces for Nature. (n.d.). http://www.sunshine.net/www/0/sn0004/bc-miningwatch/

BHP Minerals Canada Ltd. and DIA Met Minerals. (1995). *NWT diamonds project: Environmental impact statement/BHP; DIA MET.* Vancouver: BHP Diamonds.

Canadian Environmental Assessment Agency. (1996). *Decommissioning of uranium mine tailings management areas in the Elliot Lake area.* Ottawa.

Castillon, D.C. (1992). *Conservation of natural resources: A resource management approach.* Dubuque, IA: Wm. C. Briwn Publishers, p. 323.

Department of Indian and Northern Affairs. (1996a). Canada's diamond mine project: West Kitikmeot Slave study—a regional study of development impacts. Backgrounder #5. http://www.INAC.ca

Department of Indian and Northern Affairs. (1996b). Canada's diamond mine project: Environmental agreement. Backgrounder #7. http://www.INAC.ca

Department of Indian and Northern Affairs. (1996c). Canada's diamond mine project: Canada's gross domestic product to grow by $6.2 billion. Backgrounder #3. http://www.INAC.ca

Department of Indian and Northern Affairs. (1996d). Canada's diamond mine project: Land claims near the BHP site. Backgrounder #2. http://www.INAC.ca

Environmental Mining Council of British Columbia. (1996). The real story of mining in Chile. http://www.sunshine.net/www/0/sn0004/

Freeman, A. (1996). Government approves largest diamond mine in North America. http://www.igc.apc.org

Gaad, B. (1997). A hard-nosed look at the proposed Cheviot mine. *Wild Lands Advocate*, 5(2), pp. 4–5.

Government of Canada. (1996a). *The state of Canada's environment—1996.* Ottawa: Supply and Services Canada.

Government of Canada. (1996b). *The minerals and metals policy of the Government of Canada.* Ottawa.

Greater Yellowstone Coalition. (1996). President Clinton signs deal to stop New World Mine. http://www.desktop.org/gyc

Klynveld Peat Marwick Goerdeler (KPMG). (1996). Environmental management survey. http://www.kpmg.ca/enviro/vL/ensure96e.htm

Legault, S. (1997). Coal miner's fodder. *Canadian Geographic,* 117(2), p. 20.

Marshall, I.B. (1982). *Mining, land use and the environment: A Canadian overview.* Ottawa: Environment Canada. Land use in Canada series, p. 22.

Natural Resources Canada. (1996a). Canadian mining facts. http://www.nrcan.gc.ca

Natural Resources Canada. (1996b). Whitehorse mining initiative. http://www.emr.ca/ms/sdev/wmi_e.htm

Natural Resources Canada. (1996c). Mine Environmental Neutral Drainage program. http://www.emr.ca/mets/mend/

Natural Resources Canada. (1997). Total value of Canadian mineral production soars in 1996. http://www.nrcan.gov.ca

Nelson, J. (1996, March 14). Environmental review process put under pressure. *Victoria Times Colonist,* p. A5.

Newcott, W.R. (1994). Tatshenshini-Alsek Wilderness Park: Rivers of conflict. *National Geographic,* 185(2), pp. 122–34.

Pachal, D. (1997). Strip mining paradise. *Encompass,* 1(2), pp. 12–14.

Papua New Guinea: BHP agrees to settlement for Ok Tedi spill. (1996). http://www.igc.apc.org

Peeling, G.R., Kendall, G., Shinya, W., & Keyes, R. (1992). Canadian policy perspective on environmental aspects of minerals and metals. In *Minerals, metal and the environment.* (pp. 123–57). London: Elsevier Applied Science.

Philippine mine closed after spill. (1996, June 25). *Calgary Herald,* p. D8.

Principles and goals of the Whitehorse Mining Initiative. Cited in *Northern Perspectives,* 23(3–4), Fall/Winter 1995–96, pp. 9–11.

Province of Manitoba. (n.d.). *Sustainable development: Provincial mineral policies and their application.* Sustainability Manitoba series, MG 3605.

Redbud News. (1996). Two weeks after proposed Headwaters deal, administration offers similar land swap to mining company. http://www.redbud.com/news/paper.html

Ryan, B. (1995). Roses from rock. *Equinox,* 79, pp. 50–55.

Shrimpton, S., and K. Storey. (1988). *The urban miner: Long distance commuting to work in the mining sector and its implications for the Canadian north.* Paper presented to the Canadian Urban and Housing Studies Conference. Institute of Urban Studies, University of Winnipeg.

Spill aftermath: Placer Dome quits Philippine mine after cleanup loss of $43 million. (1997, March 22). *Calgary Herald,* p. B16.

Standards Council of Canada. (1996). What will be the ISO 14 000 series of international standards? http://www.scc.ca

Warhurst, A. (1994). *Environmental degradation from mining and mineral processing in developing countries: Corporate responsibilities and national policies.* Paris: Organisation for Economic Cooperation and Development.

Weber, R. (1997, July 18). Diamond mine rises from tundra. *Calgary Herald,* p. A8.

Wiesner, D. (1995). *The environmental impact assessment process.* Dorset: Prism Press.

Wismer, S. (1996). The nasty game. *Alternatives,* 22(4), pp. 10–17.

World Wildlife Fund. (1997). *WWF Canada withdraws court action on BHP diamond mine.* News release, January 13, 1997.

Young, A. (1996). *Achieving investor security through environmentally sustainable mining.* Speech presented to the Fraser Institute, October 22, 1996.

additional information sources

Environmental Mining Council of British Columbia
emcbc@islandnet.com

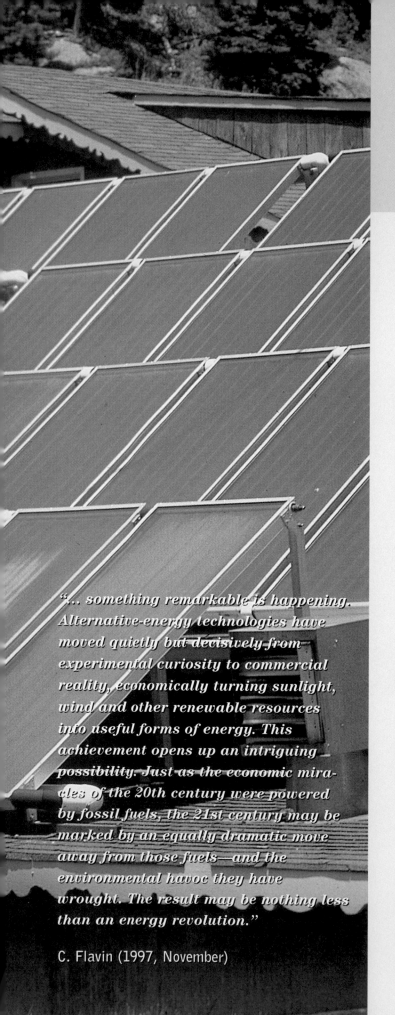

CHAPTER 11

Energy

Chapter Contents

CHAPTER OBJECTIVES   353
INTRODUCTION   353
   A Future without Fossil Fuels?   353
HUMAN ACTIVITIES AND IMPACTS ON
   NATURAL ENVIRONMENTS   354
   Energy Supply and Demand in
     Canada   354
   How Do We Use Energy?   355
     Net Useful Energy   355
   Energy Resources   356
     Fossil Fuels   358
       Oil   358
       Heavy Oil   358
       Coal   361
       Natural Gas   362
       The 1970s Energy Crisis   364
     Biomass   364
     Hydroelectricity   365
     Nuclear   367
RESPONSES TO ENVIRONMENTAL
   IMPACTS AND CHANGE   371
   Emerging Energy Resources   371
     Solar and Wind Energy   371
     Hydrogen   371
   Barriers to the Adoption of Alternative
     Technologies   373
   Improving Energy Efficiency   374
     Transportation Efficiency   374
     Industrial Efficiency   376
     Home Efficiency   376
   Organized Initiatives   378
ENERGY FUTURES   379
Chapter Questions   380
References   380
Additional Information Sources   382

"... something remarkable is happening. Alternative-energy technologies have moved quietly but decisively from experimental curiosity to commercial reality, economically turning sunlight, wind and other renewable resources into useful forms of energy. This achievement opens up an intriguing possibility. Just as the economic miracles of the 20th century were powered by fossil fuels, the 21st century may be marked by an equally dramatic move away from those fuels—and the environmental havoc they have wrought. The result may be nothing less than an energy revolution."

C. Flavin (1997, November)

Chapter Objectives

After studying this chapter you should be able to

- understand the supply and demand of energy resources in Canada
- identify a range of human uses of energy resources
- describe the impacts of human activities related to the production and use of Canada's energy resources
- appreciate the complexity and interrelatedness of energy issues
- outline Canadian and international responses to energy issues
- discuss challenges to sustainable energy production and use in Canada

INTRODUCTION

A FUTURE WITHOUT FOSSIL FUELS?

Imagine the familiar sights and sounds of driving down a crowded highway: engines roaring, horns beeping, and, worst of all, you are hardly moving. Sitting patiently behind the wheel, you stare at the tailpipe of the car in front of you watching drops of water bounce off the asphalt. You think to yourself, if society can build a car that emits nothing but steam and condensed water, why can't we eliminate traffic congestion?

As traffic starts moving, you glance into the blue sky, remembering a story your grandfather told you about smog and air quality warnings. You picture your grandfather's car—although considered fuel efficient at the time, it was powered by gasoline blended with more than 250 hydrocarbons. No wonder air quality warnings were issued back in the 1990s, when transportation was responsible for 30 to 50 percent of all hydrocarbon emissions into the atmosphere. Carbon monoxide, a poisonous gas emitted by incomplete combustion, was a major contributor to the smog your grandfather complained about.

Almost home, you are relieved that the problem of ground level ozone is no longer a major threat in accentuating your asthma problems. As you drive into your parking space and turn off the car's engine, you are relieved by the fact that your trip did not contribute to global warming through the release of carbon dioxide like your grandfather's vehicle used to.

A highway full of vehicles and almost no toxic emissions—could this happen over the course of our lifetime? Perhaps it will, particularly if research into using hydrogen as fuel gains momentum. Even though prototype cars and buses run on our streets today, a number of obstacles must be overcome to make this technology feasible on a widespread basis. This chapter examines some of the obstacles

If electricity for electric vehicles (EVs) is produced by wind and solar technologies, these vehicles are pollution-free. Cars such as the University of Waterloo's Midnight Sun 2 (above) competed recently in a solar-powered-vehicle race from London, Ont., to Montreal, demonstrating the potential of solar technology in transportation.

in adopting new energy sources, such as hydrogen, into our energy use mix. Our reliance on nonrenewable fossil fuels is discussed, as are other energy supplies such as nuclear fission and hydroelectric power. The environmental impact of energy use is investigated along with steps taken to improve energy efficiency. We begin by considering Canada as a producer and consumer of energy.

HUMAN ACTIVITES AND IMPACTS ON NATURAL ENVIRONMENTS

ENERGY SUPPLY AND DEMAND IN CANADA

Canadians consume more energy per capita than any other nation on Earth except Luxembourg. In 1993, despite having only 0.56 percent of the global population, Canadians consumed 2.6 percent of the world's energy (Environment Canada, 1996a). Our high consumption can be attributed to a number of factors including our cold climate, vast distances (which encourage car use), high standard of living, an energy-intensive industrial base, and relatively low energy prices.

Between 1958 and 1992, the total amount of energy consumed in Canada tripled, and in 1994, Canadians consumed 9.72 exajoules of energy, an amount roughly equivalent to 272 billion litres of gasoline (Figure 11–1). Energy resources play a major role in the Canadian economy; for instance, in 1993, more than 7 percent of Canada's gross domestic product (GDP) was attributable to the production of energy. Since the 1950s, growth in Canada's GDP and growth in energy consumption have paralleled each other closely. Recently, however, our energy use per dollar of GDP has been declining. The decline is due to energy

In Canada, long corridors of transmission lines carry power from generating facilities to consumer markets.

conservation practices and improved energy-efficient technologies that have reduced the energy intensity of the economy (Environment Canada, 1994; Statistics Canada & Natural Resources Canada, 1995).

Fossil fuel consumption accounted for approximately 72 percent of total Canadian energy consumption in 1994 (Environment Canada, 1996a). The remaining 28 percent consisted of nuclear energy (10 percent), hydroelectricity (12 percent), and wood (6 percent). In 1992, natural gas surpassed oil as the leading fossil fuel consumed in Canada, climbing from 13 percent of total energy consumed in 1958 to 31 percent in 1992 (Figure 11–2). This increase is due largely to the increased availability of natural gas supplies. Over the same period, Canadian oil consumption showed the largest decline, dropping from 52 percent to 27 percent of total energy consumed. Coal consumption also decreased (by 9 percent) to account for 13 percent of total energy consumed in 1992. Alternative energy technologies, such as solar and wind power, made up less than one ten-thousandth of total energy consumption in Canada.

Thirty cars carry forty people . . .

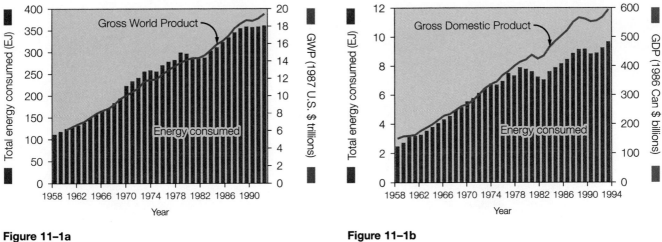

Figure 11–1a

Energy consumption: global

Figure 11–1b

Energy Consumption: Canadian

NOTES:
- Energy consumption includes use of crude oil, natural gas, coal, natural gas liquids, wood, hydro, nuclear, wind, and tidal electricity.
- EJ (exajoules) = 10^{18} joules. One exajoule is roughly equivalent to 28 billion litres of motor gasoline.

SOURCE: Environment Canada. (1996a). Energy Consumption, *SOE Bulletin* No. 96-3 (Spring).

HOW DO WE USE ENERGY?

Of the energy consumed in Canada, it is estimated that transportation uses 27 percent, industry uses 39 percent, and the remaining 34 percent is used in agriculture, homes, and businesses (Natural Resources Canada, 1996a). Five industries—pulp and paper, metal smelting, steel making, mining, and petrochemicals—account for about 70 percent of all energy used by industry.

Net Useful Energy

It takes energy to produce energy and, as described in Chapter 3, converting energy sources into useful energy products leads to waste. This waste is divided almost evenly between degradation of energy to low-quality energy (the second law of energy) and waste brought about by avoidable human practices.

Society unnecessarily wastes a considerable amount of energy. Many Canadians work and live in poorly insulated buildings, drive gas-guzzling motor vehicles, leave the lights on when leaving a room, run the dishwasher when it is only half full, and so on. Reducing the amount of energy we waste is paramount in reducing environmental impacts of our energy consumption. For example, taking the bus, walking to the corner store, or adding an extra blanket instead of turning up the thermostat help to reduce our energy consumption and reduce energy waste.

Improving the efficiency of our energy consumption also reduces the impacts of energy use on the environment. Improving energy efficiency, for example, reduces the amount of low-quality, unusable energy that is lost

. . . but one bus carries forty passengers and takes a lot less space.

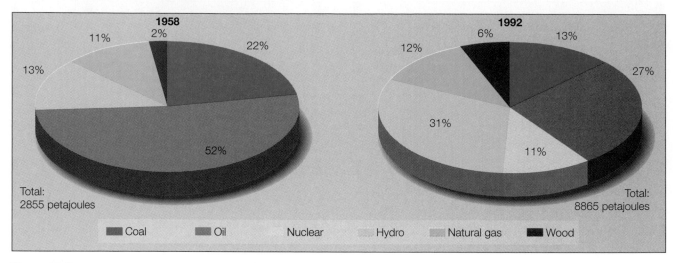

Figure 11–2
Changes in types of energy consumed in Canada: 1958–1992

SOURCE: Environment Canada. (1994, March). Energy consumption. *State of the Environment Bulletin* No. 94-3.

during conversion. Upgrading our appliances to more energy-efficient models, ensuring our homes are properly insulated, and using a hot water heater cover are examples of ways to improve energy efficiency.

Net useful energy is the usable amount of energy available from an energy source over its lifetime. To determine the net useful energy of an energy resource, all losses are subtracted, including those automatically wasted (second energy law) and those wasted in the discovery, processing, and transportation phases. For example, if 10 units of coal energy are required to supply 15 units of electricity, the net useful energy gain is 5 units of energy. If it takes 15 units of coal energy to produce 10 units of electricity, there is a net energy loss of 5 units over the lifetime of the system. Presently, oil has a relatively high net useful energy as it is readily accessible and easily transported; however, as deposits decline and their locations become more remote, net useful energy of oil will decrease. The concept of net useful energy is important in understanding why many alternative technologies, such as hydrogen fuel cells, are not feasible at the present time.

Environmental concern over energy use is reflected throughout the life cycle of the energy source. During exploration and production, there is often disturbance to the land, conflict with other land uses, and the risk of spills or accidents. Delivering energy to the user requires some form of transport (such as that of oil through pipelines or electricity through power lines) that may be intrusive to natural ecosystems. In addition, the risk of accidents or spills increases as the distance or number of transfers increases. At the point of consumption, burning fossil fuels or wood releases emissions that affect air quality, contribute to acid precipitation, and influence global climate. At the end of the life cycle, issues surrounding waste disposal

affect our environment. For example, finding a safe long-term disposal solution for radioactive waste is one of the most controversial issues in energy decision making today.

ENERGY RESOURCES

Canada's economic well-being is tied to the energy sector. The construction of large energy developments, or megaprojects, has been heralded by government and industry as critical in securing Canada's national and international economic success. Government supported ventures, such as the Hibernia oil project off the coast of Newfoundland (Box 11–1), oil sands development in northern Alberta, and the James Bay hydroelectric project in Quebec, offered the promise of jobs and economic security for residents of the respective regions.

Recently, we have backed away from large-scale utility projects; however, the oil and gas industry maintains that bigger is better. The Terra Nova offshore oil project is the second largest oilfield on Canada's east coast, located about 35 kilometres east of Hibernia. A Petro-Canada led venture, the \$2-billion project is expected to begin producing an estimated 400 million barrels of oil by 2001. As oil prices increase and Aboriginal land claims are settled, exploration and development in the Arctic are expected to grow considerably. The North is particularly attractive because large land tracts are available and federal royalty schemes have subsidized companies operating in high-cost environments.

The following section reviews some of the societal benefits and environmental challenges of Canada's primary energy resources: fossil fuels (oil, heavy oil, coal, and natural gas), hydroelectricity, and nuclear power.

On December 11, 1979, Chevron Canada Resources Ltd. announced a major offshore oil discovery at the Hibernia P-15 well. Later, tests on the drilling cores identified three principal oil zones with a producing capability of more than 20 000 barrels per day of light, high-grade crude. Since that day on the Grand Banks, almost 1.6 billion barrels of light oil have been discovered in the Jeanne d'Arc Basin, one of five identified oil-prone basins off Canada's east coast.

To put these finds in perspective, the discovered resources in the Jeanne d'Arc Basin are equal to about 45 percent of established conventional crude oil reserves in western Canada, while the undiscovered potential in the Jeanne d'Arc Basin alone is equal to the remaining light-oil potential in western Canada (the other basins have yet to be evaluated fully). Hibernia is the largest oil field discovered in eastern Canada, the fourth-largest oil discovery ever in Canada, and one of only two fields discovered since 1965 that rank in the top 10. Production from Hibernia's estimated recoverable 615 million barrels is expected to reach peak production of about 135 000 barrels per day in the year 2000.

The major owners and players in the development of the $5.8-billion Hibernia project are Mobil Oil Canada (33 percent), Chevron Canada Resources Ltd. (27 percent), and Petro-Canada (20 percent), while the federal government (9 percent), Murphy Oil Co. Ltd. (of Calgary, at 7 percent), and Norway's Norsk Hydro ASA (5 percent) hold smaller ownership stakes in the project. An illustration of the size of the capital investment required to undertake and develop the Hibernia megaproject, and of the cooperation required among industry and government partners, was the $150-million collaboration of Mobil, Murphy, and Chevron on the design, construction, and financing of one of the two tankers that will move oil from Hibernia to a transshipment point on Newfoundland's Avalon Peninsula. The ships, which will hold up to 850 000 barrels, were designed to operate in the often stormy seas of the Grand Banks.

Geographical conditions on the Grand Banks also meant the partners had to design a production platform that would be iceberg resistant. Research showed that, between February and June each year, a few icebergs weighing up to several million tonnes would enter the Grand Banks in the vicinity of the oil field. Iceberg management involves two approaches: resistance or avoidance. At Hibernia, as elsewhere, avoidance is preferred.

The $5.8-million production platform sits on top of a gravity base structure (GBS) made of concrete and steel. The 1.2-million-tonne GBS, its base surrounded by a 1.4-metre-thick wall featuring 16 force-dispersing teeth, was towed out to the drilling site in June 1997 and ballasted to the ocean floor using iron ore. If tugboats are unable to tow an iceberg off a path that would lead to a collision with the production facility, the GBS was designed to withstand the impact of a 6-million-tonne iceberg travelling at 1 knot. The production system uses a floating platform that looks like a large ship. If necessary, the lines from the drilling rig to the production platform can be disconnected and the platform can sail out of danger if an iceberg collision appears imminent. Drilling started on the first Hibernia well in July 1997, and oil was expected before the end of the year when the drilling would reach about 4000 metres below the ocean floor.

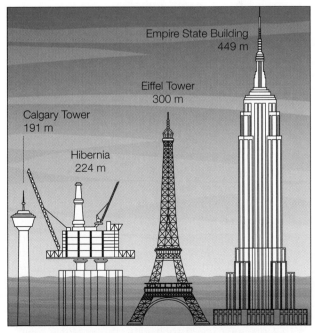

Empire State Building
449 m

Eiffel Tower
300 m

Calgary Tower
191 m

Hibernia
224 m

BOX 11-1
(CONTINUED)

Although the beginning of the project was marred by delays and cost overruns, partners in the project expect about a 10 percent return on their investment (depending on oil prices) over the expected 20-year life of Hibernia. As of 1996, Canadian taxpayers had provided $1.1 billion in grants and $1.8 billion in loan guarantees to the Hibernia project partners. By April 1996, Newfoundland had garnered a 63-percent share of direct employment in the Hibernia project, and the trickle-down effect of expenditures on the project in the province was evident in the significant growth of local businesses. Even though the technology is unique and is unproven in operation in "iceberg alley," hopes are strong that the economic impacts of oil and gas development will equal or exceed those of the fishing industry.

SOURCES: Bergman, B. (1997, March 3). Special report: One of a kind. *Maclean's.* 110 (9), pp. 30–31.

Boras, A. (1996, July 10). It's a win–win project. *Calgary Herald,* p. C2.

MacAfee, M. (1997, July 8). Hibernia ahead of schedule. *Calgary Herald,* p. C8.

Martin, D. (1995, August 30). Last hope. *Calgary Herald,* p. C1.

Martin, D. (1997, July 29). Drilling starts on first Hibernia well. *Calgary Herald,* p. E2.

Fossil Fuels

Oil Oil is a mixture of hydrocarbon compounds, those containing hydrogen, carbon, and other elements. Most oil is found in sedimentary rock located deep below the surface of the land and sea floor; Canada's most important sedimentary basins are illustrated in Figure 11–3. Most **hydrocarbons** are the remains of prehistoric animals, forests, and sea floor life, hence the name **fossil fuels.** Buried in layers of sediment, these plants and animals decomposed very slowly and eventually were converted into crude oil.

Canadians consume roughly 1 665 000 barrels of oil every day. Compared to other energy sources, oil has a high energy value per unit of volume, making it the world's most important traded commodity. In addition, oil is relatively inexpensive (at present) and is transported easily. Mother Nature, however, does not view oil as favourably as our economy does. As we know, the combustion of fossil fuels releases gases that contribute to climate change and acid precipitation. Furthermore, crude oil and other petroleum products often are toxic to wildlife and in some cases can result in drastic changes to wildlife ecosystems. It has been estimated that more than 10 000 cubic metres of oil enters our environment each year through spills and oil well blowouts (Environment Canada, 1996a). An oil spill can occur at any point from production to consumption; spills are most likely, however, during transportation (Box 11–2).

Canadian consumption of energy resources raises concerns about economic and environmental sustainability. We recognize that creating a sustainable economy requires us to use nonrenewable (energy) resources at rates that do not exceed our capacity to create substitutes for them, and to use renewable (energy) resources at rates that do not exceed their capacity to renew themselves. We recognize also that full cost accounting must be in place to ensure that environmental and social costs are accounted for in decisions relating to land, resource use, species depletion, and economics (Taylor, 1994).

These principles suggest that market prices of oil should reflect accurately the actual costs of production, distribution, consumption, and environmental impacts. If market prices were to reflect true costs, it is likely that alternative energy sources such as wind and hydro power would become more viable. Currently these major, renewable sources of energy have virtually no market, while nonrenewable sources such as oil receive government incentives for megaprojects (see Box 11–1). If these incentives were removed, would oil resources continue to dominate our energy industry?

Heavy Oil Oil deposits, in the form of shale and oilsand, are found close to the earth's surface. **Oil shale** is rock that contains a solid mixture of hydrocarbon compounds

Companies extracting bitumen from Alberta's oilsands increasingly employ new technologies, including massive equipment such as this 80-ton shovel, shown here loading a 240-ton truck.

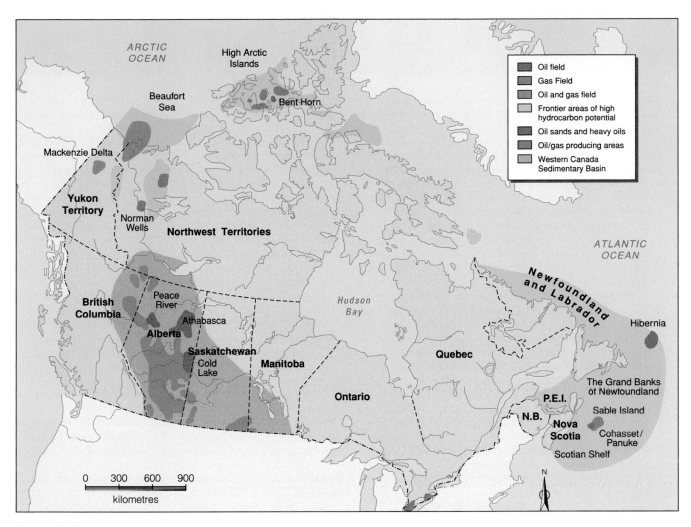

Figure 11–3
Canada's important oil-producing basins

SOURCE: Government of Canada. (1996). *The state of Canada's environment—1996.* Ottawa. Figure 11.43.

called kerogen. Once crushed and heated, kerogen vapour is condensed to form heavy, slow-flowing shale oil. Shale oil is more expensive and difficult to extract and process than conventional oil, and therefore its net useful energy yield is lower. Because oil shale is extracted on land, many of the problems associated with aboveground mining are evident with shale processing. In addition to altering the landscape and interfering with wildlife, salts and toxic compounds from processed shale can leach into watercourses and contaminate groundwater.

Oilsand is a combination of clay, sand, water, and **bitumen,** a black oil rich in sulphur. Removed by surface mining, oilsands are heated and treated with steam to separate the bitumen from other compounds. The bitumen is then treated and chemically upgraded into synthetic crude oil. The net useful energy yield is lower than for conventional oil because more energy is required to extract and process the bitumen. Deriving oil from oil-

sands introduces significant landscape changes, notably the creation of large waste disposal ponds. The process also releases large quantities of sulphur dioxide.

Canada is home to the largest known oilsands deposits in the world. Covering an area about the size of New Brunswick, the Athabasca tar sands lie in the boreal forest zone of northern Alberta. Reserves are estimated at 1.7 trillion barrels of oil, and it is anticipated that 300 billion barrels are recoverable—that's enough to supply Canada with oil for 200 years.

Investment in northern Alberta oilsands projects began in the late 1960s and, since then, industry and government have poured billions of dollars into oilsands research and development. Originally, analysts thought that upgrading the bitumen into usable oil would be profitable only if the price of oil were US$50 per barrel (Boras, 1995). The two major players in Canada's oilsands, Suncor and Syncrude, produce one of every five barrels of oil in

BOX 11-2
OIL SPILLS AND TRANSPORTATION SAFETY

Oil tanker spills—such as the 1989 *Exxon Valdez* spill off the Alaska shoreline or the 1996 *Sea Empress* spill off the Welsh coast—garner a substantial amount of media attention because spills are clearly visible and the potential for environmental damage is clearly evident. However, it has been estimated that tanker accidents account for only 6 percent of the oil released into marine environments (Chivers, 1996) and that 92 percent of all tanker spills occur at the terminal when oil is being transferred (Environment Canada, 1996b). Considering that petroleum is transported by ocean tankers, trains, pipelines, and tanker trucks, the more transfers that occur, the greater is the risk of a spill. In fact, delivering petroleum from the source to the consumer may require up to 15 transfers (Environment Canada, 1996b).

Transportation related accidents and spills account for only a small portion of the total oil that enters the marine environment each year. Oil may enter rivers, lakes, and oceans in many ways, including from oil seeps, offshore oil and gas production, municipal and industrial waste runoff, and atmospheric fallout. Besides human-induced discharges, oil enters the environment naturally. World wide, approximately 200 natural underwater oil seeps have been identified. In Canada, natural seepage has been observed off the north coast of Baffin Island and off the coast of Labrador. All sources considered, municipal and industrial waste runoff are the major sources of oil input into Canada's environment.

Tanker spills are serious because of the large volume of oil that often is spilled and the uncertainty surrounding the nature and extent of environmental damage that may result. Predicting the damage from a spill is difficult because of the number of fac-

tors that must be considered. In addition to the quantity spilled, the location (open sea, close to shore, estuary), weather (temperature, wind speed), tides and currents, grade of oil (crude or refined), and the surrounding environment all play a part in determining the environmental damage. Having the longest coastline in the world, Canada is aware of the risk of oil spills and the responsibility for ensuring safe and effective cleanup. Although it is impossible to eliminate spills completely, Canada supports international initiatives to make transportation safer.

The size of tankers has increased dramatically since the 1950s. For example, ships of 30 000 deadweight tons (dwt) were considered very large in the 1950s. Today, most tankers exceed 250 000 dwt, and some are up to 500 000 dwt. A number of safety measures have been instituted to improve the safety of these larger vessels. For example, individual holding tanks are limited in size to reduce the volume of spill if one tank is ruptured. Technological advances, such as electronic charting and computer imagery, are making it safer for crews to navigate around hazards. In addition, tanker ships built after 1993 are required to have double hulls (bottoms) to reduce the risk of spills if one layer is damaged. At the present time, however, there is minimal global use of double-hulled tankers. For example, more than 90 percent of oil entering American ports is transported in single-hulled vessels. The Natural Resources Defense Council estimates that by the year 2005, only 25 percent of the world's tankers will be double hulled (Chivers, 1996).

Even with improvements in shipping safety regulations, operational requirements, and global conventions and standards, the safety of shipping has not improved since World War II (Frankel, 1995). Major changes in shipping safety standards normally occur following a major disaster. The *Exxon Valdez* spill, for instance, dumped 50 million litres of crude oil into Alaska's marine ecosystem and resulted in the United States introducing the Oil Protection Act in 1990. The act requires the oil industry to pay damage costs resulting from supertanker spills but has been criticized for prompting a transportation shift from tankers to the less regulated tugboat-barge combination. In Canada, the party responsible for the spill is liable for the cleanup costs as well as any economic losses that result from environmental damage. One of the most significant criticisms of the oil transport industry concerns the industry's preoccupation with reducing the amount and impact of accidental discharge and not with preventing accidents in the first place (Frankel, 1995).

Additional information on oil spills in Canada may be obtained from either Environment Canada or the Canadian Coast Guard, an arm of the Department of Fisheries and Oceans. For an overview of oil spills in Canada, including ways in which you can help, check out Environment Canada's Oil, Water and Chocolate Mousse Web site, listed below. The main Web site for the Canadian Coast Guard is identified in the Additional Information Sources section of this chapter; see under Fisheries and Oceans Canada.

SOURCES: Chivers, C. (1996). Troubled waters. *E, The Environment Magazine, 7*(1), pp. 14–15.

Environment Canada. (1996a). Energy consumption. *State of the Environment Bulletin* No. 96-3 (Spring).

Environment Canada. (1996b). Oil, water and chocolate mousse. http://www.doe.ca.

Frankel, E. (1995). *Ocean environmental management: A primer on the role of the oceans and how to maintain their contribution to life on Earth.* Englewood Cliffs, NJ: Prentice-Hall Inc.

Canada. In 1992, it cost the pair of companies $19 per barrel to dig, process, and blend the synthetic oil. In 1995, their costs dropped to below $14 per barrel and by 2000, the target cost is $12 per barrel (Boras, 1995).

With oilsands becoming increasingly price competitive, environmentalists are expressing more concern about Canada's oilsands developments. As of 1995, about $5 billion had been allocated for oilsands expansion in northern Alberta, and an estimated $25 billion is to be invested in new oilsands projects by the year 2020 (Strojek, 1996). Environmentalists are concerned, given projected expenditures and the scope of development, that no federal environmental review has been ordered. The federal government maintained that the oilsands development would not impact areas under their jurisdiction, such as waterways, and referred the matter back to the Alberta government.

In areas where federal reviews are not required, companies prepare environmental assessments and submit them to the province for review before a project licence is issued. According to many environmental groups, company environmental reviews often are narrow and lacking in depth. Consequently, environmental nongovernmental organizations are challenging the federal government to review the impacts of oilsands developments on the boreal forest ecosystem. For instance, the Alberta chapter of the Western Canada Wilderness Committee is concerned that water (drawn from surrounding swamps, lakes, and rivers) used to steam the bitumen will affect the forest's moisture balance, causing some forested areas to dry up and become prone to wildfires (Strojek, 1996).

The Pembina Institute, a watchdog on energy and development issues, is critical of oilsands expansion because of the high concentration of greenhouse gases released during upgrading and processing activities. The institute claims that expansion of production in Alberta's oilsands will make it even harder for Canada to meet its current and future commitments to fight climate change (Chambers, 1996). Attaining international emission targets may be possible in spite of increased production, however. Suncor, for example, has made a commitment to stabilize its carbon dioxide emissions at 1990 levels even though the company is anticipating a 60 percent increase in production (Chambers, 1996).

Acknowledging that world energy markets will be dominated by fossil fuels for some time, the large reserves of oilsands in northern Alberta should provide an important impetus for the Canadian economy. However, further reducing toxic emissions and greenhouse gases, and successfully reclaiming strip-mined lands, are two of the challenges that remain in reducing environmental impacts of this energy megaproject.

Coal Coal is the most abundant fossil fuel in the world with reserves four to five times that of oil and gas combined (Figure 11–4). Coal is burned to generate 20 per-

cent of Canada's electricity, and roughly 45 percent of the world's electricity. Coal has a relatively high net useful energy yield and is highly effective for providing industrial heat. As a result, 75 percent of the world's steel is produced from coal energy. Globally, 4 billion tonnes of coal is consumed per year, 73 million tonnes of which is produced in Canada. Canada's coal industry directly employs about 10 000 people and contributes an estimated $2 billion to $3 billion to the economy.

Of all the fossil fuels, coal burning produces the most carbon dioxide and air pollution per unit of energy. Concern over climate change and acid precipitation has led the coal industry to develop advanced pollution control technologies. Even so, in the United States alone, air pollutants from coal burning kill from 5000 to 200 000 people annually, cause 50 000 cases of respiratory disease, and account for several billion dollars in property damage every year. Extracting coal from underground mines endangers human lives directly through accidents (explosions, shaft collapses) and prolonged exposure to coal dust (black lung disease). Surface coal mining severely alters the landscape, causes soil erosion, and can pollute nearby water supplies. Despite coal's drawbacks, energy analysts forecast it will resume its place as the world's prime energy source within the next 20 years (Coal best long-term energy source, 1995).

For nearly a century, the Sydney steel plant (Cape Breton Island, Nova Scotia) was the lifeblood of the community, providing employment for 1500 workers in its prime. But, virtually every day since 1905, pollution from the plant's coke (coal) ovens poured into the air and untreated effluent from the coking operations was dumped into Muggah Creek. Today, the 34 hectares of tar ponds that once were the tidal flats of the Muggah Creek watershed contain an estimated 500 000 tonnes of toxic coal-tar deposits. Among the contaminants are PAHs, PCBs, and heavy metals (Gjertson, 1997; Hamilton, 1997). With each tide, contaminants are flushed into Sydney harbour; scientists estimate that about 800 kilograms of PAHs are released annually. In 1980, Environment Canada closed the fishery in the harbour's South Arm due to contamination—PAH levels in lobsters were 26 times the norm.

In 1986, federal and provincial government officials signed a $34.3-million cleanup agreement to excavate and incinerate the contaminated tar ponds, and to close the remaining coke ovens in 1988. A number of problems were encountered during the cleanup. The dredging and dumping plan failed, partly because cleanup operators found 10 times more PCBs than had been estimated originally, and partly because the low-temperature fluid-bed incinerator was unsuitable for destruction of PCBs (high-temperature incineration is requied).

After $52 million of taxpayers' money had been spent, federal and provincial government officials abandoned the plan to clean up the tar sands in 1996. Instead

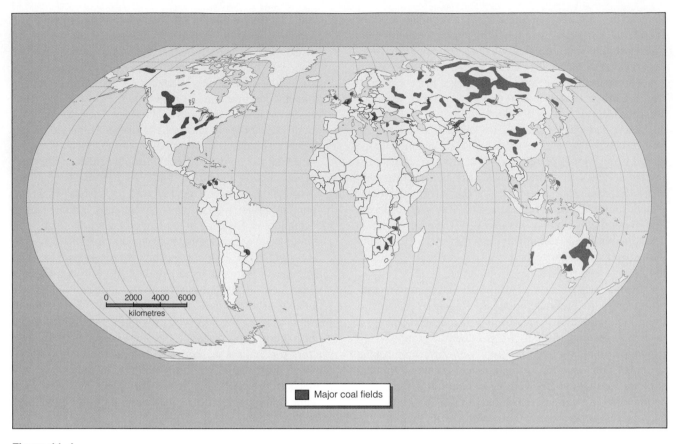

Figure 11–4
World distribution of coal

SOURCE: Hill, R., O'Keefe, P., & Snape, C. (1995). *The future of energy use.* London: Earthscan Publications, p. 87.

of following the original plan, the province announced that it would encase the hazardous waste in slag and pave it over. This plan was shelved due to widespread opposition, and instead a joint action group involving community members was put in place. At the end of January 1997, federal, provincial, and municipal governments announced funding for a variety of studies including further sampling and chemical analysis of the contaminants. Canada's largest toxic dump, the Sydney tar ponds remain a dangerous environmental legacy.

Natural Gas Conventional, or associated, **natural gas** is located underground above most reserves of crude oil and is a gaseous hydrocarbon mixture of methane combined with smaller amounts of propane and butane. When found on its own in dry wells, natural gas is called nonassociated or unconventional natural gas. Approximately 72 percent of world reserves of natural gas are of the nonassociated type and the remaining 28 percent are the associated type. Currently, it is more economical to extract associated reserves; however, advances in extraction technology are improving the cost effectiveness of nonassociated production. Estimated reserves of natural gas are

greater than previously thought and have led to its increased use and popularity. Natural gas is now the leading fossil fuel consumed in Canada.

Many analysts view natural gas as the bridge from "dirty" hydrocarbon-based energy to cleaner renewable

Installation of the Trans-Canada pipeline near North Bay, Ont.

energy. Natural gas burns more efficiently than oil, and produces one-third less carbon dioxide per unit of heat energy and fewer pollutants overall. Simply substituting natural gas for coal in electrical generation facilities could reduce carbon emissions by 50 to 70 percent, depending on efficiency of individual facilities. However, because methane is 30 times more powerful than carbon dioxide as a greenhouse gas, it is critical that turbines and associated machinery in natural gas–burning facilities are sealed against leaks. If only 3 to 4 percent of the methane finds its way to the atmosphere, the lower emission benefit of burning natural gas is nullified (Hill, O'Keefe & Snape, 1995). Natural gas generally is less expensive than oil and transports easily over land through pipelines (Figure 11–5). Pipeline construction, however, can impact sensitive aquatic, grassland, and other environments (see, for example, Wallis, Klimek & Adams, 1996).

The process of flaring also is a source of concern. Flaring is a way of disposing of unwanted, unprocessed natural gas; the industry burns this gas to release hydrogen sulphide (sour gas) and to avoid the buildup of potentially explosive levels of gas at work sites. In Alberta, for instance, only about 1.4 percent of the natural gas processed in the province is flared, but that amount translates into more than two billion cubic metres of gas burned off each year (Francis, 1997). For almost two decades, people living near flares have expressed their concern about the impacts of flaring emissions.

Recent research has revealed that emissions from many flares are greater than was assumed previously, that even though flaring destroys many sulphur compounds others are created, and that the risks to cattle and humans from exposure to many of the emissions from flaring are not well understood. In 1996, the Canadian

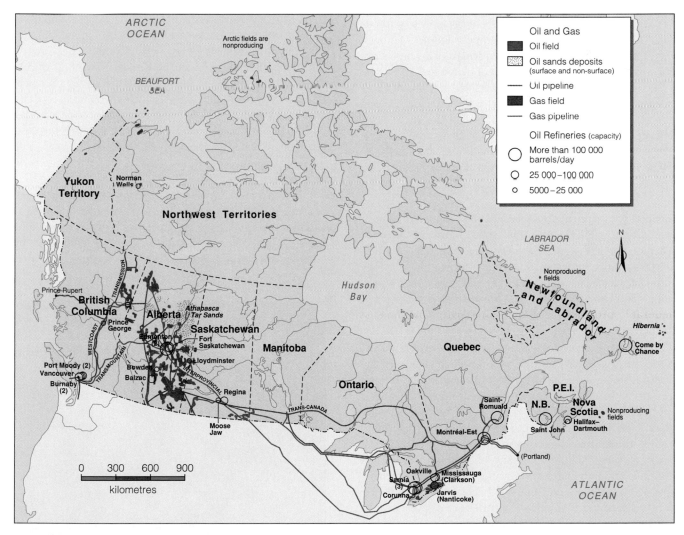

Figure 11–5
Natural gas pipelines in Canada

SOURCE: Adapted from Stanford, Q.H. (Ed.). (1992). *Canadian Oxford world atlas: New edition.* Toronto: Oxford University Press, p. 250.

Cattle Commission noted that flaring eventually should be eliminated, given that flares are Alberta's single largest source of a variety of volatile compounds including PAHs, VOCs (volatile organic compounds), carbon monoxide, carbon dioxide, nitrous oxides, and heavy metals. Following a five-year study, in 1996 the Alberta Research Council identified more than 200 different chemical compounds produced by flaring, including more than 30 varieties of cancer-causing benzene (Francis, 1997). Given the potential seriousness of chronic exposure to these risks, including increased costs of medical care, a precautionary approach is warranted.

The 1970s Energy Crisis In 1973, a then little-known cartel, the Organization of Petroleum Exporting Countries (OPEC), disrupted global supplies of imported oil. The OPEC embargo, combined with the U.S. energy policy, resulted in an energy crisis in the United States that had far-reaching economic, social, and political effects. In addition to high prices and long lines at gas stations, the "oil shock" raised concerns over energy policy, particularly U.S. dependence on imported petroleum.

The energy crisis prompted critical thinking on energy futures in areas such as estimates of global fossil fuel supplies, ways to improve energy efficiency, and use of alternative energy sources. In hindsight, the oil shock helped the North American economy to realize the volatility of energy markets. The energy crisis has been credited with improving our understanding of environmental and societal consequences of energy use (Feldman, 1995).

Biomass

Biomass, organic matter that includes wood, agricultural wastes and manure, and some types of garbage, supplies 15 percent of the world's energy. Canada relies on biomass—principally waste wood chips from pulp mills—to supply about 6 percent of our energy requirements (Environment Canada, 1994). Less developed countries are much more dependent on biomass, relying on it for up to 50 percent of their energy requirements.

Providing trees and plants are replaced at a level equal to or greater than the rate at which they are harvested, biomass is considered a renewable energy resource. In addition, no net increase in atmospheric carbon dioxide occurs if replacement equals harvest. Sound land use management practices must be in place to avoid problems associated with land clearing, such as soil erosion, water pollution, flooding, and habitat loss. Unfortunately, in many parts of the world, harvesting practices are not sustainable and fuelwood shortages occur. Many forested lands in developing countries are disappearing to accommodate agriculture and urbanization, not to provide fuelwood to meet energy needs and demands.

Increasingly, developing countries are turning to agroforestry to meet their energy needs. Agroforestry is a

In Los Angeles in 1979 gasoline rationing resulted in long lineups at local gas stations.

multipurpose land use system that combines indigenous trees (to provide erosion protection and fuelwood) in areas planted with crops and used to graze animals. Land use activities reflect local sociocultural values. Agroforestry initiatives, such as the Kenyan Woodfuel Development Program, have been successful in encouraging farmers to increase the amount of woody biomass on their farms (Hill et al., 1995). The introduction of similar initiatives in other developing countries may improve the sustainability of biomass fuels, enabling people to use wood for fuel while meeting the increasing energy demands of local populations.

Biomass also can be converted into gaseous or liquid **biofuels (ethanol)** and used to power motor vehicles. Ethanol is used directly for fuel but is more commonly used as an octane-enhancing gasoline additive. In Canada, ethanol is available as a blended gasoline with

Making dung fuel cakes in India.

concentrations of between 5 and 10 percent. Ethanol-blended gasoline in concentrations of 10 percent or less can be used in all gasoline-powered automobiles without engine or carburetor modification. Ethanol blends have been found to reduce carbon monoxide emissions by up to 30 percent, especially during the winter months when emissions increase due to colder temperatures. Many U.S. cities mandate use of ethanol-blended gasoline during winter as a measure to reduce carbon monoxide emissions. As a result, use of ethanol-blended gasoline is more widespread in the United States than it is in Canada.

In 1975, Brazil introduced the ProAlcohol program to promote use of ethanol in automobiles. Since then, Brazil has become the world's largest producer of ethanol. More than 90 billion litres are produced each year, reducing Brazil's dependency on imported oil (Hill et al., 1995). Unlike in Europe, the United States, and Canada, in Brazil many automobiles operate on pure ethanol or higher blended concentrations (20 to 22 percent ethanol). In addition to improving Brazil's balance of payment deficit, the ProAlcohol program employs up to 700 000 people directly and many more indirectly. In 1989, five million cars in Brazil operated on pure ethanol and another nine million ran on a 20–80 ethanol–gasoline blend (Hill et al., 1995). Brazil is capitalizing on its success with ethanol development by exporting this technology to developing countries.

Hydroelectricity

Hydroelectric power supplies roughly 5 percent of the world's total commercial energy and about 20 percent of the world's electricity. Canadian consumption of hydropower is above the world average; about 12 percent of our total commercial energy comes from hydroelectric sources (Figure 11–6). Consumption of hydropower increased a marginal 1 percent between 1958 and 1992, indicating low growth potential for further hydroelectric development. Indeed, there are few suitable sites remaining for large-scale hydro projects in Canada, and those that are suitable will introduce massive land use changes and generate strong opposition from resident communities.

Hydroelectric projects are expensive to build but have low operating and maintenance costs. In addition, their lifespans are 2 to 10 times greater than those of coal or nuclear plants. Hydroelectric stations emit no air pollutants or greenhouse gases and help regulate downstream irrigation. Unfortunately, construction of dams to provide hydroelectric power introduces far-reaching landscape changes that displace people and wildlife, destroy cropland and forests, and interfere with aquatic ecosystems. The James Bay Hydroelectric Project in northern Quebec is an example of irreversible environmental damage resulting from a megaproject's construction (see Enviro-Focus 7).

In China, construction site signs announce that on November 15, 1997, the Yangtze River will be dammed, irrevocably changing the landscape of this part of China. In building the world's largest dam across the world's third largest river, China will force at least 1.2 million people to migrate from fertile farmlands along the river and will affect the lives of about one-quarter of the Chinese population (400 million people) who live along its banks. By the time the US$25-billion Three Gorges dam is completed, 140 towns and 326 villages will be submerged under 670 square kilometres of water, along with 657 factories, 953 kilometres of highway, and 139 power stations (Sly, 1997).

Proponents of the dam note that in addition to curbing flooding in the lower reaches of the river, the dam will produce 18.2 million kilowatts of electricity (the equivalent of 18 nuclear power stations) needed for China's economic growth and modernization (Zich, 1997). Critics charge that the dam's ability to control floods may be limited because the river's lower reaches are fed by three other tributaries that also contribute to flooding. A string of smaller dams would have had the same effect on floods and produced as much electricity without as many environmental side effects. The fertile plains that will be flooded downstream of the dam have provided 40 percent of China's grain and 70 percent of its rice crops. People are being moved into previously uninhabited territory, land that is higher, steeper, and less suitable for farming. Many will have to find new ways to earn their living as there is insufficient arable land available for distribution.

Other impacts include the loss of the famous Three Gorges as a landmark; they will be flooded and the ancient (Stone and Bronze Age) archeological sites they contain will be submerged. Also, the river supports numerous endangered species, including the Yangtze dolphin, Chinese sturgeon, finless porpoise, giant panda, and the Siberian white crane. How many of these species will survive in the dramatically changed environment is not known.

The energy conservation movement and advancements in energy-efficient technologies have reduced the demand for large power-producing utility projects in the Western world. Supporters of utility megaprojects maintain they provide economies of scale necessary to meet the energy requirements of future populations.

In reality, however, many hydroelectric megaprojects across North America have fallen far short of expectations. Demand estimates have generally been on the high side, resulting in surplus electricity (Freeman, 1996). The northeastern United States, which buys a portion of its electricity requirements from Quebec, has sharply reduced its imports of Canadian power during the last decade. Ontario, Quebec, New England, and New York state presently operate with surplus electricity. Many analysts believe that construction of utility megaprojects would be a thing of the past if it were not for political motivation that aims to create jobs through dam building.

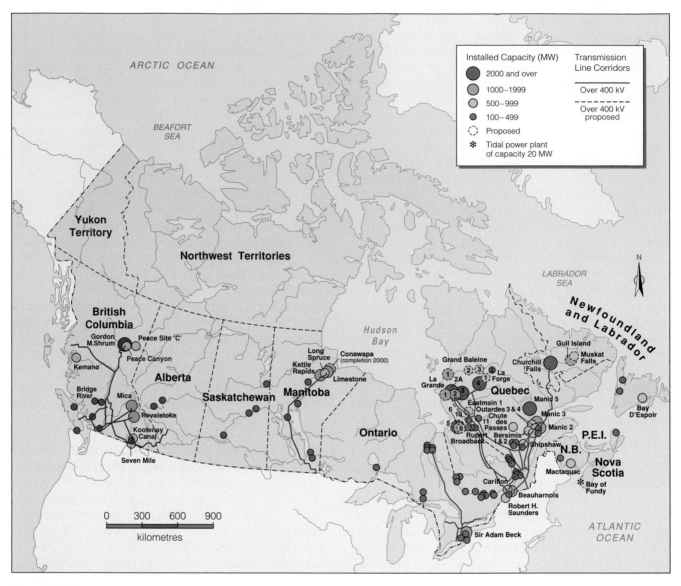

Figure 11–6
Major hydroelectric dams in Canada

SOURCE: Adaped from Stanford, Q.H. (Ed.). (1992). *Canadian Oxford world atlas: New edition.* Toronto: Oxford University Press, p. 23.

One Canadian ENGO whose objectives include stopping unnecessary hydroelectricity plants is the Energy Probe Research Foundation (EPRF). Incorporated in 1980 (but originating in 1970 as the Energy Team of Pollution Probe), EPRF is financially independent of governments and corporations, and receives the majority of its funding from the general public. The goals and objectives of EPRF include educating Canadians about the benefits of sound resource use (Energy Probe Research Foundation, 1995). Often viewed as a maverick because of its stand against "ill-advised projects," EPRF promotes democratic processes by encouraging individual responsibility and accountability, and provides business, governments, and the public with information on energy, environmental, and related issues.

Energy Probe is the division of EPRF dedicated to research and advocacy in Canada's energy sector. In 1980, Energy Probe established a model for the electricity industry that separated the transmission component of the business from the generation component. This allowed electrical generation to become a competitive industry with electrical transmission maintained as a separate, regulated monopoly. The Energy Probe model is becoming the dominant organizational structure throughout the world.

Following an extensive study of hydroelectric water pricing, both in Canada and internationally, Energy Probe concluded that our provincial governments undervalue Canada's rivers. This has led to overexploitation of hydroelectric power through such megaprojects as the James Bay project in Quebec and the Peace River project in British Columbia. Energy Probe also is working to promote competition in the Canadian electricity sector in an effort to stop unnecessary electricity plants. The organization suggests that an increasingly competitive system would eliminate new coal and nuclear generation facilities and hydro dams and favour conservation, renewable resources, and high-efficiency gas technologies while improving the economy at the same time. (For more information on their activities, contact Energy Probe or the Energy Probe Research Foundation at the address provided in the Additional Information Sources section of this chapter.)

Nuclear

Nuclear energy generates approximately 90 million megawatt-hours of electricity in Canada each year and accounts for 11 percent of the total energy consumed in Canada. This is equivalent to about 60 percent of all electricity consumed in Ontario and is worth roughly $6 billion (Stothart, 1996). The nuclear industry is an important aspect of Canada's economy, generating more than $250 million in export income annually, and providing employment for over 26 000 people. Canada has developed a strong competitive advantage in the nuclear technology sector, primarily through development and export of the CANDU reactor. Atomic Energy of Canada Limited (AECL), a Crown corporation, generates about 60 percent of its revenue through export of nuclear expertise, technology, and services to foreign governments and utilities (Stothart, 1996).

Despite these statistics, development of Canada's nuclear industry has been very expensive. Between 1947 and 1994, government support of AECL totalled $9.4 billion with no compensating return to the federal government (Lermer, 1996). The government subsidy tab is expected to escalate even further because of the high costs associated with site decommissioning and long-term storage of spent reactor fuels. Construction of Canada's nuclear power plants also has been very costly. For example, construction costs of Ontario's Darlington plant were between 186 and 340 percent higher than initial budget forecasts. Cost overruns add to consumer cost of power and, when combined with massive government subsidies, suggest that nuclear generated electricity is more expensive than major alternatives such as hydro and coal.

The capacity of nuclear fission to provide the world with energy has not lived up to expectations. In the 1950s, researchers predicted that 1800 nuclear power plants would supply 21 percent of the world's commercial energy by the end of the century. Today there are about 420 commercial reactors world wide producing less than 5 percent of global energy. Government subsidies, cost overruns, accidents, and public concerns about safety have impacted growth of the nuclear industry.

Given safe operation, generating electricity through nuclear reactors produces no greenhouse gas emissions and adds minimal disturbance to land. The entire fuel cycle, from mining uranium ore to storing wastes, adds about one-sixth as much carbon dioxide per unit of electricity as does use of coal. Finding suitable facilities to store **radioactive wastes** is problematic, however. Depending on their half-life (see Chapter 3), some wastes emit radiation for tens of thousands of years; no wonder few communities volunteer to act as landfill sites for radioactive waste storage.

After more than 15 years of study and more than a year of public hearings, the federal government is expected to decide during the fall of 1997 whether to go ahead with a plan to permanently bury Canadian nuclear waste in a vault excavated 500 to 1000 metres below the surface in the granite of the Canadian Shield. Critics of this plan note, among other things, that the geographic area under consideration is largely traditional land of First Nations people (with whom minimal consultation has occurred), and that the integrity of the disposal site is suspect, given there is a constant flow of water through the fractured rock of the Canadian Shield (Plummer, 1996).

Regardless of the decision, energy experts concur that rising stocks of nuclear waste from civilian energy programs are a great challenge for the future. Not only is there concern about passing on to future generations the need to look after radioactive waste, but also the potential that nuclear waste could become a resource as technology continues to identify alternatives to terminal disposal solutions.

Nuclear reactors are constructed with multiple safety systems to keep highly radioactive materials inside the reactor core. However, accidents such as occurred at Three Mile Island in Pennsylvania and at Chernobyl in the former Soviet Union, illustrate the harmful effects of even a partial release of radioactive material.

In 1979, a series of human errors and mechanical failures resulted in loss of coolant water to one of the two reactor cores at the Three Mile Island plant. The reactor core was partially uncovered and was not cooled adequately for a period of 16 hours. Absence of cooling water resulted in overheating and eventual rupture of the uranium fuel rods, turning a significant portion of the reactor core to rubble. Unknown quantities of radioactive materials escaped through an open valve to the containment building inside the reactor and then to the atmosphere through leaky pipes in the building's exhaust system. Two

A concrete sarcophagus encloses the damaged reactor at Chernobyl.

days after the accident, 200 000 people within a 40-kilometre radius were evacuated from the area. Officially, no deaths were linked to the Three Mile Island accident (although some contradictory claims exist). This incident sparked the antinuclear movement and severely reduced public trust in nuclear power.

The world's worst commercial nuclear accident occurred April 26, 1986, at the Chernobyl nuclear power plant in the former Soviet Union (now the Ukraine). In spite of the fact that the reactor type was known to be very unstable at low power settings (a design flaw), the Chernobyl reactor crew prepared to test how long the turbines would spin and supply power following loss of their main electrical supply. The crew disabled the reactor's automatic shutdown mechanism, the key safety feature, prior to the test.

When the reactor experienced a dramatic power surge during the test, the fuel elements ruptured, and the steam explosion that followed lifted the cover plate off the reactor, releasing fission products to the atmosphere. A second explosion ejected fragments of burning fuel and graphite from the core and allowed air to rush in, causing a graphite fire that burned for nine days. The main release of radioactivity into the environment came from the burning graphite; about 5 percent of the reactor core was

released into the atmosphere. Winds carried radiation particles thousands of kilometres from the site.

Soviet officials were slow to respond to the accident and did not evacuate the area until three days following the explosion. The world did not hear of the disaster for two days when Moscow acknowledged Swedish reports that 10 000 times the normal amount of Caesium 137 (a low-dose, long-lasting radioactive element) had been recorded in that country's airspace. The Chernobyl accident released an estimated 30 to 40 times the radioactivity of the bombs dropped on Hiroshima and Nagasaki during World War II.

Had the safety system been in operation, the reactor would have shut down, preventing the explosion and release of radioactivity. Investigators concluded the Chernobyl accident was the result of a very flawed reactor design that was operated with inadequately trained personnel and without proper regard for safety (Uranium Information Centre, 1996). World analysts consider the Soviet-designed RDMK type reactor to be unsafe. Although similar reactors continue to operate at the Chernobyl site and in Russia and Lithuania, it is fortunate that this type of reactor was never exported outside the former Soviet Union. In addition to its instability at low power settings, the RDMK reactor at Chernobyl was built without containment shells (walls that prevent escape of radioactive material in the event of an accident).

Two of the three remaining reactors at Chernobyl continue to produce nuclear energy (the third was closed following a 1991 fire). The ill-fated reactor number four sits in a concrete sarcophagus, described as "neither strong nor durable" (Uranium Information Centre, 1996). Approximately US$400 million has been spent to increase the safety of the remaining reactors. In April 1995, the Ukraine announced that Chernobyl would be permanently closed by the year 2000 when two new reactors are scheduled to be operational.

Ten years after the Chernobyl accident, the total amount of radioactive material present in the environment had decayed to approximately 1 percent of the total amount released (Dreicer & Alexakhin, 1996). Even so, the effects of Chernobyl on natural environments remain difficult to gauge (Box 11–3 provides information on an international conference designed to clarify what is known about the accident). In the 30-kilometre exclusion zone, some plants and animals suffered lethal doses of radiation while others showed little signs of contamination. Reproductive functions were damaged in many species after the accident but most appear to have recovered fully. However, the long-term health effects on specific populations remain difficult to estimate. Interestingly, the relocation of people out of the 30-kilometre zone has even helped some animals flourish because of the absence of human interference. On the other hand, cleanup procedures, including soil and water

PART 3:
RESOURCES FOR CANADA'S FUTURE

In April 1996, 10 years after the Chernobyl nuclear accident, an international conference, "One Decade after Chernobyl: Summing up the Consequences of the Accident," was held in Vienna, Austria. Attended by more than 800 experts from 71 countries and 20 organizations, the purpose of the conference was to reach an international consensus on the accident's consequences, to agree on proven scientific facts, and to clarify information and prognoses in order to dispel confusion (Gonzalez, 1996). The major findings of the conference are summarized here.

Radioactive Fallout

- Radioactive fallout from the accident was estimated at 10^{19} becquerels (units of activity).

- Caesium 137 was the most significant of the radioactive elements. It is a long-lived nuclide whose activity falls by half every 30 years; it was transported long distances through the atmosphere and deposited variably throughout the entire northern hemisphere; and it was the main cause of whole-body, long-term radiation exposure.

- Iodine 131 is a short-lived radioactive isotope whose activity falls by half every eight days. Radioiodines were responsible mainly for irradiating the thyroid glands of people living in nearby regions shortly after the accident.

Radiation Doses

Of the 237 "liquidators" (plant workers, firefighters, and others who helped with the aftermath), 134 were diagnosed with acute radiation syndrome (they received doses in the thousands of millisieverts).[1]

- Twenty-eight liquidators died, their deaths attributed directly to radiation injuries; some years after the accident, 14 more of these people died (but their deaths were not attributable, necessarily, to radiation exposure).

- Over 100 000 people who were evacuated or who still live in contaminated areas will receive low, whole-body doses of radiation (but these doses are thought to be comparable with lifetime doses from natural sources of radiation). Up to the end of 1995, there were more than 800 cases of thyroid cancer reported in children, mostly in Belarus. Doses in local ecosystems also were high.

Environmental Damage

- Lethal doses of radiation were reached in some radiosensitive local ecosystems within a few kilometres of the accident. Coniferous trees and voles suffered the greatest effects. No sustained severe impacts on the environment have been observed and the ecosystems appear to have recovered.

- Foodstuffs produced in contaminated areas remained above the maximum level of contamination permitted by international standards for some time after the accident, but have returned to acceptable levels. Wild food products, including berries, mushrooms, game, and fish remain above the international acceptable limit for contamination.

Economic and Social Impacts

- Economic losses related to the Chernobyl incident are in the hundreds of billions of dollars. Losses of capital assets and production, population resettlement, forest protection, water conservation, soil decontamination, and compensation payments to the affected population account for the majority of expenditures.

- Economic losses to Belarus alone were estimated at US$235 billion (the equivalent of 32 annual budgets of the republic).

- Significant psychological symptoms, such as anxiety, depression, and other forms of mental distress, are high in the region; however, it is difficult to ascertain if these symptoms are solely a result of the accident at Chernobyl.

Future Outlook

- Radiation levels that can still be detected in most affected areas are sufficiently low to permit the resumption of normal economic and social activities.

- Health effects have not been as catastrophic as feared, but a number of radiation effects did occur and more are expected to occur.

- The main source of future doses will be due to the gathering of food and to recreational activities in natural and seminatural ecosystems.

NOTE: 1. Radiation damage is a result of the dosage incurred by people and biota. Dosage is measured in sieverts, or more commonly millisieverts (one-thousandth of a sievert). Natural background radiation accounts for an average annual dose of 2.4 millisieverts of radiation per person.

SOURCES: Dreicer, M., & Alexakhin, R. (1996). *Post-Chernobyl scientific perspectives: Social, health and environmental effects. IAEA Bulletin.* http://www.iaea.or.at/worldatom.inforesource/bulletin/bull383/dreicer.html

Gonzalez, A. (1996). *Chernobyl—ten years after: Global experts clarify the facts about the 1986 accident and its effects.* http://www.iaea.or.at/worldatom/inforesource/bulletin/bull383/gonzalez.html

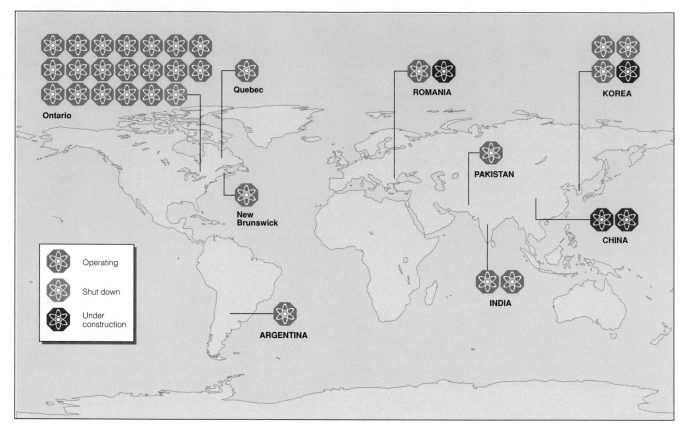

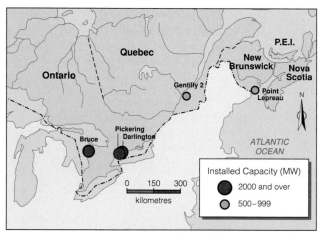

Figure 11–7

a) Canadian nuclear plant locations around the world

NOTE: Plant locations are current as of August 1, 1997.

SOURCE: Adapted from Wells, J. (1997). Meltdown. *Maclean's,* 110 (34), p. 15.

b) CANDU reactors in Canada

SOURCE: Adapted from Stanford, Q.H. (Ed.). (1992). *Canadian Oxford world atlas: New edition.* Toronto: Oxford University Press, p. 23.

The nuclear power station at Pickering, Ont.

remediation, have had negative effects on many species because these activities drastically alter habitat. (For more information, see Savchenko in the Additional Information Sources section of this chapter.)

In Canada, nuclear plants (Figure 11–7) have not been problem-free either. The troubled Pickering nuclear plant that supplies about 20 percent of Ontario's electricity, for instance, has had at least one fire, failure of safety systems, and botched repairs. Reports from the Atomic Energy Control Board, the agency that regulates nuclear power in Canada, pinpointed years of poor practices at Pickering—workers even ate in radioactive hazard areas (Shape up or else, 1996).

Responses to Environmental Impacts and Change

EMERGING ENERGY RESOURCES

If Canada continues to rely on hydrocarbon-based energy, we may damage our long-term competitiveness in the world energy market. In other parts of the globe, **alternative energy** is price competitive with fossil fuels. For example, California wind turbines produce electricity for the same cost as nearby coal-fired plants, and India is on target to be the world's fastest growing installer of wind turbines. More than 40 countries are estimated to employ geothermal power, including Nicaragua and the Philippines where presently 25 percent of their power is generated from geothermal sources.

Regardless of these advances, nonrenewable energy sources are likely to dominate for some time. However, world oil reserves are estimated to be economically feasible as an energy source for only another 40 to 80 years. Currently, nuclear power does not seem to be a feasible alternative as issues such as radioactive waste storage and reactor accidents have made society wary of nuclear energy.

Although they are renewable resources, wood and other forms of biomass often are exploited to produce energy without concern for the pollutants released through burning, the low net useful energy yield, or the long-term sustainability of the resources. Except for microhydro opportunities, expanded use of hydroelectricity in North America is unlikely as there are few ideal sites remaining, construction costs are high, and alteration of landscapes introduces significant ecological and social concerns. Work of researchers and scientists continues to improve the feasibility of alternative energy technologies. The following section discusses some of the research advances in developing alternative technologies as well as barriers to their adoption.

Solar and Wind Energy

> Few ventures have produced more noble failures than the quest to power civilization with renewable energy from geophysical forces—the winds, the tides and, most of all, the sun's rays. (Linden, 1994, p. 50)

The sun provides Earth with close to 99 percent of its heat energy requirements. Just imagine the benefits possible if we could harness the sun's energy to provide our (commercial) energy needs. If we were able to combine **solar energy** with other renewable energy sources, such as wind, flowing water, and biomass, our energy production would cause much less environmental damage and pollution per unit of energy than any fossil fuel.

Solar power gained most of its strength at the height of the energy crisis in the late 1970s. At that time, it was anticipated that solar energy would provide the United States with 2 to 5 percent of its energy requirements (but by 1994, roughly 0.5 percent came from solar sources). In Canada, solar and wind power combined provide only one ten-thousandth of our energy consumption (Environment Canada, 1994). Part of the reason is that the return to stable oil prices following the energy crisis greatly reduced corporate and government funding of solar power research and development.

Once again, the quest to improve the viability of renewable energy, particularly solar and wind power, is gaining momentum. Shell International Petroleum in London predicted that renewable energy will dominate world energy production by 2050 (Linden, 1994). Canada appears to be in support of developing renewable energy resources despite our economic ties to fossil fuels. In 1996, Canada's Energy minister unveiled a renewable energy strategy that included tax breaks and incentives aimed at encouraging research and development of renewable energy technology. A key aspect of the renewable energy strategy is to increase market demand for "green power" (Canadian Renewable Fuels Association, n.d.). To that end, the federal government plans to use more renewable energy at its own facilities and encourage other levels of government to do the same.

Corporations also are investing more money in research and development of energy alternatives. For example, Honda Canada acquired a minority interest in Ovonic Battery to help facilitate its production of electric cars; a University of Calgary professor teamed up with a manufacturer in Regina, Saskatchewan, to export Canadian wind turbine technology to Africa; and builders of Canada's R-2000 homes are incorporating solar energy devices in their house designs.

Hydrogen

Hydrogen is a colourless, odourless gas that makes up 75 percent of the mass of the universe. Industry uses hydrogen to manufacture ammonia and to refine petroleum. Hydrogen is an important component of the NASA space program; space shuttles are fuelled with hydrogen and fuel cells convert hydrogen to electricity to provide astronauts with heat, light, and drinking water. The commercial use of hydrogen as a power source would provide us with a virtually inexhaustible source of energy while reducing our dependency on nonrenewable fossil fuels. So why is this nonpolluting and abundant element not being used to fuel our vehicles, power our airplanes, and provide electricity to our homes and offices?

A number of complexities, both technical and socioeconomic, are working against the mass commercialization of hydrogen as an energy source. Despite its abundance, hydrogen is found only in combination with other elements, primarily oxygen, carbon, and nitrogen. Hydrogen must be separated from these elements to be a useful energy source. A substantial amount of energy is required to isolate hydrogen; if this energy comes from fossil fuels or nuclear power, the environmental benefit of using hydrogen is negated. However, the production efficiency of hydrogen improves when renewable energy sources (solar and wind power) are used, and fewer stresses are placed on the environment. Currently, producing hydrogen from these sources is expensive and the production efficiency, while improving rapidly, is not yet commercially viable.

Other technical obstacles in moving toward a hydrogen-based economy involve concern over the safe storage of hydrogen and the lack of infrastructure to support its widespread use. Hydrogen usually is stored as a compressed gas or cryogenic liquid. The volatility of hydrogen gas is prompting researchers to develop storage systems that not only improve safety but also increase capacity per unit volume. For example, researchers at the National Renewable Energy Laboratory (a division of the United States Department of Energy) are developing a solid-state storage system that binds hydrogen to microscopic carbon tubes. The hydrogen attaches to the surface of the carbon and is released by changing temperature and pressure levels. In another experiment, engineers at Lawrence Livermore National Laboratory in California have found that under pressurized conditions, small glass bubbles absorb hydrogen then release it when crushed or heated (Frenay, 1996).

To achieve a commercial market for hydrogen, effective infrastructure and distribution networks are required. Establishing these networks will take time and may involve lengthy transition periods. Government and business leaders need to consider carefully the alternative methods of supplying hydrogen to meet growing consumer demands. For example, the extensive natural gas pipeline network throughout North America could be converted to carry hydrogen. At the other end of the scale is localized production, where automobile owners produce their own hydrogen using home reformers or on-board hydrogen converters (Frenay, 1996). Developing safe and economical production, infrastructure, and storage systems will help bring hydrogen one step closer to commercial use. However, once these technical challenges have been mitigated, the most restrictive barriers remain, those of economic and political will.

The economic success of many nations depends on the production and delivery of fossil fuels. As the world's most traded commodity, oil has given the petroleum industry considerable economic and political influence world wide. Convincing oil companies to invest in hydrogen research is difficult because most consider hydrogen as a serious threat to their short-term economic well-being. Furthermore, many oil companies are opposed to large-scale government funded hydrogen research. As a result, government supported hydrogen research is lower in nations whose economies are strongly tied to the petroleum sector. For example, compared with Japan and Germany, the United States allocates about one-seventh of the funding those countries do to hydrogen research. Additional reasons working to slow investment in hydrogen research include uncertainty surrounding the short-term prospects for its widespread use and the estimated lengthy transition period to convert the population to **hydrogen power.**

Despite uncertainty and objections from major petroleum companies, hydrogen research is drawing the attention of governments and the private sector. In 1996, although there were across-the-board funding cuts to budgets for solar and other renewable energy research, American federal funding for hydrogen research increased (Congress ups hydrogen funding 1996). A "hydrogen corridor" is taking shape in the desert basin east of Los Angeles where Xerox operates a $2.5-million hydrogen production complex (Frenay, 1996). The facility in El Segundo, California, is North America's largest solar converter of water into hydrogen. The use of hydrogen-powered golf carts on local California streets has been legalized, and the community of Palm Desert is looking into building two fuelling stations that will use hydrogen produced from a local wind farm.

In the near term, the transportation sector is likely to benefit most from hydrogen power. Current technology enables combustion engines to be fuelled directly with pure hydrogen or hydrogen blended with natural gas. Vehicles powered with hydrogen fuel cells are three times

The 275-hp Ballard Fuel Cell engine fits into the same space as the diesel engine; these buses meet performance requirements of transit authorities without emitting any pollution.

more efficient than gasoline powered engines (National Renewable Energy Laboratory, 1996). A Canadian company, Ballard Power Systems, is front and centre in developing hydrogen as a fuel source for commercial transportation.

In 1995, Ballard supplied the city of Chicago with three transit buses powered by their hydrogen fuel cell. During a public ceremony, Mayor Daley enjoyed a "glass of exhaust" collected from the tailpipe of an idling Ballard bus. The taste test was performed to illustrate the environmental cleanliness of the exhaust—nothing but steam and condensed water. Providing the $5.8-million test program is successful, the conversion of all of Chicago's buses to fuel cell models will be considered as buses become due for replacement.

Ballard Power Systems also made an $8.6-million deal with the Province of British Columbia and British Columbia Transit in 1996. As in the Chicago demonstration, Ballard supplies three fuel cell buses, spare buses, fuel, and program support. Once testing opportunities have proven successful, the company expects to begin full-scale commercial production of the fuel cell transit bus engine.

Ballard uses a type of fuel cell known as a proton exchange membrane (PEM). The PEM fuel cell is one of five fuel cell types currently available that produces energy from a hydrogen reaction. With a PEM cell, hydrogen is directed through one side of a central core that is divided by a proton-permeable membrane. Oxygen is directed into the other side of the core and attracts the hydrogen protons to move through the membrane. The hydrogen protons then bond with the oxygen to form water. With the absence of protons on the hydrogen side, the hydrogen electrons are drawn to a metal electrode creating a charge that provides energy. The PEM cell operates at temperatures below boiling and is presently the most suitable choice to power a motor vehicle with hydrogen.

Through Natural Resources Canada, the federal government supports projects aimed at making fuel cell technology a practical energy option. In addition to funding a project to improve the cost effectiveness of the Ballard fuel cell, Natural Resources Canada facilitated a utility demonstration program between Western Economic Development (a federal funding agency), the Government of British Columbia, and Ballard to develop a fuel cell electricity generating plant (Natural Resources Canada, 1996b).

BARRIERS TO THE ADOPTION OF ALTERNATIVE TECHNOLOGIES

Advances in solar, wind, hydrogen, and other renewable energy sources are occurring rapidly. In some locations, homes can be heated fully using solar power, entire communities are powered from wind farms, and freeway signs are being illuminated by hydrogen fuel cells (Box 11–4).

Despite these advances, renewable technologies often are considered small-scale alternatives that are incapable of providing large populations with affordable energy. Localized renewable energy provision also is contrary to contemporary corporate megathinking and the quest to achieve economies of scale (through pipelines, hydroelectric plants, nuclear power stations, and so on). Utility companies generally prefer large-scale projects because of the perceived benefits of lower costs and more customers. In addition, megaprojects often have fewer players, and therefore the utilities and other large companies have more control over a region and its energy. However, as society is beginning to learn, bigger is not always better, and cooperation among energy producers can provide benefits.

Advances are being made in wind turbines to make them operate effectively in Canada's climate. North America's largest operating wind turbine, a 600-kilowatt

BOX 11-4
LIGHTING UP THE ROAD: IMPROVING TRAFFIC SAFETY WITH HYDROGEN

The use of a variable message sign (VMS) is an important component of highway safety. A VMS alerts motorists to potential hazards, construction areas, and lane closures. Commonly powered by a diesel generator, VMS signs consume up to 19 litres of fuel per day.

Improved alternative energy technology has led to an increasing number of VMS signs being powered by solar energy. Fitted with solar panels, the sun's energy is captured to charge a battery that operates the highway sign. Although environmentally efficient, the sign shuts down when sunlight cannot keep the battery charged. In 1996, H Power Corporation introduced a retrofitted VMS that operates on solar and fuel cell power. The U.S. fuel cell manufacturer teamed up with the New Jersey Department of Transportation to demonstrate the improved highway sign.

The combination of solar and fuel cell power allows the VMS to be placed in any location under all weather conditions. When low battery conditions exist, a built-in controller switches the sign to fuel cell power. The fuel cell operates using electrochemical reactions, which convert hydrogen and air into electricity. The process produces no emissions and is noise free. The fuel cell can operate the sign and recharge the batteries for up to three weeks without any solar power. H Power Corporation estimates a 50 percent cost saving when operating a VMS with hydrogen fuel rather than diesel fuel.

Fuel cell technology offers promise for improving the energy efficiency of all highway signage, including commercial billboards. Combination solar–hydrogen signs offer an added benefit in remote regions where the alternatives are to use diesel or extend power lines.

machine in Kincardine, Ontario (installed in 1995 near Ontario Hydro's Bruce nuclear plant), is reliably feeding enough electricity into Ontario Hydro's grid to meet the electrical needs of 150 to 200 homes (Bright & Salaff, 1996). Residents of Cambridge Bay, N.W.T., where a wind farm was built in 1987, have found that their 80-kilowatt wind turbine reduces their costly reliance on diesel power. And plans have been set for large-scale installation of cold-weather turbines on Quebec's Gaspé Peninsula.

Fifty-two windmills near Pincher Creek in south-western Alberta constitute the Cowley Ridge Windplant. Erected in 1993–94, the 19-megawatt wind farm supplies power to the provincial grid. The wind plant comprises two joint venture projects, one (with 25 windmills) between a Pincher Creek and a California wind-power company, the other (with 27 windmills) between a Calgary-based wind energy developer and the Peigan Nation of Brocket, Alberta. As a result of political lobbying, renewable energy producers were given the right, in 1994, to generate 125 megawatts of the 7200-megawatt Alberta Interconnected System (Tulley, 1994). In 1994, however, TransAlta Utilities spent 3 cents per kilowatt-hour to generate coal-fired power, and paid 5.2 cents for wind-generated power. Wind-power advocates maintain that when the costs of environmental degradation and health problems are factored into energy pricing, wind power is actually cheaper than coal-fired electricity.

Since the wind plant was installed, the Pincher Creek community has worked diligently to attract wind energy development (including wind turbine manufacturing) and to integrate it into its economic, education, and tourism base. Wind producers charge that governments and utilities in Alberta perpetuate false market mechanisms to avoid real total cost competition of wind power with fossil fuel-generated power (Johnson, 1997). Perceptions of protectionism and the lack of a level playing field for new electrical generation projects may be seen as barriers to the encouragement of energy sustainability. For renewable energy resources to be accepted by the public, prices must be comparable and quality of service must parallel current sources.

The implementation of alternative energy sources likely will reduce the dominant market position of many large utilities. For this reason it is difficult to convince these companies to invest in alternative energy sources. Instead, utilities have worked to keep their costs down and promote energy efficiency to keep their product more affordable than a renewable alternative. Even so, renewable energy resources will be developed to serve an increasing number of people as they become cost effective.

The potential to capitalize on alternative energy offers developing nations a double opportunity. Besides reducing dependency on oil imports, developing nations can manufacture many of the components of wind and solar energy systems, thus creating jobs and expanding their industrial base. In both developed and developing nations, the world's major oil, utility, and automotive companies bring strong political and economic influences to bear on decision-making processes; these influences may jeopardize widespread research and implementation of alternative energy technologies. The execution of Nigerian author Ken Saro-Wiwa may be a case in point (Box 11–5).

IMPROVING ENERGY EFFICIENCY

Although roadblocks stand in the way of adopting renewable energy sources for widespread use, Canadians increasingly are conscious of the environmental and cost-saving benefits of using energy wisely. The implementation of energy-efficient technology is helping to reduce the environmental burden of energy use in our transportation, industrial, and residential requirements.

Transportation Efficiency

The best way to improve energy efficiency in transportation is to increase the fuel efficiency of motor vehicles. For the period 1973 to 1985, the average fuel efficiency of all new domestic cars doubled, and the efficiency of imports improved by 54 percent. Since that time, however, only slight gains in fuel efficiency have been observed.

Advances in electric vehicles and hydrogen fuel cell technology promise further improvements in transportation efficiency. For example, the Sunrise—a preproduction, prototype electric vehicle built by Solectria of Massachusetts—achieved a fuel efficiency record of 70.7 miles per equivalent gallon of gasoline at the 1995 American Tour de Sol electric vehicle race (Northeast Sustainable Energy Association, 1995).

Another way to improve energy efficiency in transportation is to examine the types of vehicles we use to ship goods and products. For instance, transporting durable goods by planes and transport trucks wastes a

A patented power unit provides a unique method for the Ecorail to carry truck trailers.

PART 3:
RESOURCES FOR CANADA'S FUTURE

BOX 11-5
THE POLITICS OF OIL: THE EXECUTION OF KEN SARO-WIWA

On November 10, 1995, Nigerian author and environmentalist Ken Saro-Wiwa was executed by the military-led Nigerian government. Along with eight others, Saro-Wiwa was charged with murdering leaders of his own ethnic community—the Ogani.

Saro-Wiwa was a leader of the Movement for the Survival of the Ogani People (MOSOP), a group committed to halting the environmental devastation of Rivers state, a part of Nigeria near the delta of the Niger River. The Ogani lands are important for a number of reasons, including their fertility and vast crude oil reserves. Oil production began in the region in 1958; since that time more than 900 million barrels of crude oil have been extracted (Earthline Africa, 1996). More than 80 percent of Nigeria's revenue comes from oil production.

Saro-Wiwa's death sparked an international backlash; Nigeria was suspended from the Commonwealth, and protests were held by organizations such as Amnesty International and Greenpeace. Criticisms from these groups were aimed largely at oil companies, especially the Anglo–Dutch petroleum giant Shell Oil. Shell produces about half of all the oil in Nigeria and, through taxes and royalties, contributes 45 percent of the country's foreign earnings (Shell Nigeria, 1996).

Almost half of all recorded spills from Shell's worldwide operations (in over 100 countries) occurred in Nigeria. An independent study claimed that from 1982 to 1992, Shell Oil spilled more than 6.4 million litres of oil in 27 separate incidents (cited in Greenpeace, 1996). In addition to oil spills, another major criticism directed at Shell Nigeria was that for more than 30 years the company had flared natural gas instead of reinjecting it into underground reservoirs as is required in most countries (Greenpeace, 1996).

Shell Nigeria admits to a poor environmental record, particularly throughout the Niger Delta. Shell Petroleum Development Company (SPDC) confirmed that oil spills are common and blames many of them on aging infrastructure (Shell Nigeria, 1996). Shell Nigeria reports spending $150 million a year on infrastructure improvements and environmental projects. In 1996, the company began a liquefied natural gas project to reduce the one billion cubic feet per day of gas that is flared during oil production (Shell Nigeria, 1996).

Human rights activists strongly urged all Commonwealth nations and the United States to boycott oil imported from Nigeria. Although economic sanctions were not adopted because of the unemployment, poverty, and other social problems that would result from such an action, they were favoured by Nigerian opposition groups (Cable News Network, 1995). The United States, which purchases half of Nigeria's oil exports, banned military sales and imposed travel restrictions on Nigerian government officials, but stopped short of considering an oil embargo (Cable News Network, 1995).

Saro-Wiwa was an outspoken critic of Nigeria's military regime and leader General Sani Abacha. His efforts to protect the Ogani people and their lands earned him a Nobel Peace Prize nomination, Sweden's Right Livelihood Award, and a Goldman Environmental Foundation Prize.

For more information on oil production in Nigeria, the Ogani peoples, and the activities of Ken Saro-Wiwa, consult the Web sites for Earthline Africa, Greenpeace Canada, the Sierra Club, and Shell Nigeria listed in the Sources section below.

SOURCES: Cable News Network. (1995). Nigeria given two-year democracy deadline. http://www.cnn.com/WORLD/9511/nigeria/11-12/index.html.

Earthline Africa. (1996). Execution of Ken Saro-Wiwa. http://www.gem.co.za/ELA/ken.html

Greenpeace Canada. (1996). Shell in Nigeria. http://www.web.apc.org/~embargo/shell.htm

Shell Nigeria. (1996). About Shell in Nigeria—people, oil and politics. http://www.shellnigeria.com/abshell/oil.html

Sierra Club. http://www.sierraclub.org

considerable amount of energy. Increasing the use of trains and ships, as well as improving the fuel efficiency of transport trucks, promises rapid gains in energy savings to the transport sector.

One example of innovative thinking is Ecorail, a trailer train that cuts transportation costs by moving truck trailers on rails. Ecorail combined a mini locomotive and steel wheel sets called *bogies* to pull a string of truck trailers on the tracks. Ecorail carried truck trailers down the Quebec–Ontario corridor for more than a year until a legal dispute between the three owners shut it down in the fall of 1996, putting about $10 million in international orders for the units on hold (Feud may kill Ecorail, 1997).

The inventor of Ecorail (who spent eight years and $15 million developing the technology) holds one-third ownership with equal partners Canadian National Railway (CN) and SGF, a Quebec funding agency. Despite the legal impasse, CN continued to operate Ecorail using regular locomotives. The inventor believes CN will let Ecorail go out of business but keep the technology. It is unfortunate that ideas such as Ecorail that promote energy efficiency and long-term sustainability potentially could founder on legal and economic grounds.

Industrial Efficiency

Industrial uses account for almost one-third of all energy consumed in Canada. Unfortunately, industry wastes a large percentage of the energy it uses through inefficient motors and boilers, improper use of lighting, and machine operation at higher settings than required. There are a number of ways industries can reduce their consumption and waste of energy at the plant level. In addition to installing energy-efficient lighting and equipment, industries can use computer-controlled energy management systems to turn off equipment and lighting when not required.

District heating through co-generation is another option industries and governments can explore to maximize energy efficiency. Under normal operating conditions, fossil-fuel-powered electrical generating stations produce more waste energy than electricity. For example, the Tufts Cove Generating Station in Dartmouth, Nova Scotia, uses only about 35 percent of the energy that is available from fossil fuels to produce usable electrical energy. The remainder is lost to the environment as waste heat in the form of hot flue gases, and as warm water, which is released into Halifax Harbour.

In an effort to recapture some of the waste heat and convert it to usable energy, Nova Scotia Power Inc. has begun a feasibility study of applying district heating to Metropolitan Halifax. In a district heating process, the steam cycle is modified so that the steam is extracted and used to produce hot water. The water then would be pumped through pipes to surrounding buildings (such as offices, schools, and shopping malls) to supply heat.

Producing two useful forms of energy from the same source is known as **co-generation** or combined heat and power (CHP). To initiate a district heating project, a variety of infrastructure improvements must be made. A closed-loop delivery system of pre-insulated pipe must be constructed between the plant and selected buildings. This allows hot water to flow from the plant to customers and then to return for reheating. Receiving buildings also require a heat exchanger to transfer energy to their heating systems. Customers with steam heating also may have to retrofit their systems to use hot water. Because of the substantial costs associated with such improvements, district heating systems normally are phased in over time.

District heating can produce a number of economic and environmental benefits. Proponents of the Halifax study cite that the more efficient use of fuel will decrease dependence on burning fossil fuels, thereby reducing greenhouse gas emissions. Furthermore, oil-fired boilers in the buildings targeted for district heating would no longer be needed, reducing the risk of fires and soil contamination. Employing the energy-saving benefits of co-generation would give North Americans a chance to catch up to Western Europe where co-generation has been used extensively since the 1970s.

Home Efficiency

When we think of the ways human activities influence the release of greenhouse gases into the atmosphere, we commonly blame our cars and factories, not our homes and offices. However, the average Canadian home produces four tonnes of carbon dioxide per year. Much of this can be avoided by improving the energy efficiency of our homes through insulation, better quality windows and doors, and heating rooms and water more effectively.

Canada's foray into improving home energy efficiency began during the energy crisis. At that time, the federal government began the Super Energy-Efficient

The solar panels and SunPipe® are two of the features of Ash House in Calgary.

Home program to promote improvements in residential heating, insulation, and ventilation. In 1984, the Department of Energy, Mines and Resources (now Natural Resources Canada) introduced the R-2000 housing system in partnership with the Canadian Home Builders Association (CHBA). The R-2000 "environmentally friendly" home can generate up to 50 percent savings in energy consumption over a traditional house of the same size. Advantages of R-2000 homes are identified in Box 11–6.

The central feature of an R-2000 home is the heat recovery ventilator (HRV) or the air-to-air heat exchanger. Located near the furnace, an HRV unit draws fresh air into the house while expelling existing air. As the air streams pass each other, incoming air is either heated or cooled by outflowing air, resulting in improved heating and cooling efficiency. R-2000 standards require an HRV unit to exchange all the air in a house at least once per hour. Although the placement of windows, doors, and roof overhangs is taken into consideration in energy efficient homes, virtually any house design can accommodate the R-2000 approach.

By 1992, about 6000 R-2000 homes had been built in Canada, a small number compared to the 150 000 to 200 000 new homes built here each year. Although R-2000 construction costs are about 2 to 5 percent higher than those encountered in building conventional housing, the R-2000 system has not lived up to expectations. Higher construction costs, as well as the administrative process imposed by R-2000 construction, may be responsible for the limited number of registered homes.

Such homes must be constructed by qualified R-2000 homebuilders (there are about 4000 in Canada), and the dwelling must be tested during construction and inspected upon completion to be certified. It is possible that three or four times as many R-2000 "clones" exist as there are certified houses; contractors may apply R-2000 techniques but avoid strict construction standards by not applying for official certification (Lougheed, 1992).

Energy-efficient homes have captured the attention of homeowners in the Maritimes, where high-cost electric heating dominates. Heating costs in East Coast R-2000 homes have been reduced by up to 50 percent, while resale values are estimated to be 5 percent higher than conventional houses (Lougheed, 1992).

Natural Resources Canada (1996c) estimated that the average Canadian homeowner could reduce heating costs by up to 25 percent per year by performing a variety of reasonably priced home renovations to increase energy efficiency. Prompted by the $19 billion Canadians spent on home renovations in 1995, the federal government entered into a sponsorship agreement with Home Hardware stores to encourage energy-efficiency renovation projects. Launched in 1996 under the brand name Reno$ense, how-to videos and publications on topics such as insulating your home and buying energy-efficient windows, doors, appliances, and lighting were displayed in Home Hardware stores nationwide. Natural Resources Canada plans to enter into a variety of other joint ventures with the retail industry to promote energy efficiency.

Efforts also are being made globally to improve heating efficiency in homes and businesses. The World Wide Fund for Nature (WWF) estimated that Britain's infamous drafty houses and apartments contributed one-third of the country's carbon dioxide emissions, while homes in the Netherlands were responsible for 10 percent of that nation's carbon dioxide emissions. On average, one-fifth of Europe's carbon dioxide emissions come from households.

In Britain, building regulations now require that the efficiency of water and space heating devices in new homes be specified (on a scale of 1 to 100). This initiative places pressure on builders to meet purchasers' demands for lower heating costs and thereby encourages competition to make homes more energy efficient (Russell, 1996).

In 1995, WWF-Netherlands signed an agreement with the country's five largest property developers to build 200 energy-efficient houses in a period of two years (Russell, 1996). Similar to construction standards for an R-2000 home, Dutch developers must conform to a rigid set of building specifications, including the use of solar-powered boilers, solar cells, blown fibre wall cavity insulation, water tank jackets, double-glazed windows, and energy-efficient light bulbs. In return, WWF will actively promote the advantages of the homes to municipal authorities and prospective buyers and tenants.

Ground-source heating and a new aquifer thermal energy storage project in Canada are considered briefly in Enviro-Focus 11.

BOX 11–6

ADVANTAGES OF AN R-2000 HOME

- Careful sealing against air leakage
- High levels of insulation
- Advanced heating systems
- Solar energy gains
- Energy efficient windows and doors
- Heat recovery ventilation (HRV) system
- Advanced sound proofing
- Less dust and pollen than conventional houses

So why the name R-2000?

The "R" is a value normally assigned to the insulation capacity of a building surface, such as R-35 walls, and the 2000 represents the futuristic building standard the federal government wanted to see in place by the year 2000.

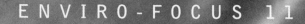
Ground-Source Heating and Cooling

Both earth and water maintain a relatively constant temperature below the surface, making them an ideal heating source in the winter months or cooling source in the summer months. Tapping back yards, ponds, or lakes for geothermal energy is an environmentally friendly and efficient way to heat and cool many types of buildings.

Tapping geothermal energy is basically a way of moving (rather than generating) heat. A sealed or closed-loop system, in which a water-based solution is pumped through a polyethylene pipe extending vertically or horizontally below the Earth's surface, can operate effectively with ground temperatures ranging from –5°C to 38°C.

In the winter, for example, the solution absorbs heat and carries it to a geothermal unit, which compresses the heat to a high temperature (similar to the process used in conventional refrigerators) and delivers it to the home or building. A small electric pump operates the system, but the energy generated is often four or five times greater than the energy used. (In comparison, if a conventional natural gas furnace achieves a one-to-one ratio, it is considered to be highly efficient.)

The idea of geothermal energy use in Canada is not a new one. Open-loop heat pumps, which use the water and discard it, have been used in Canada since 1912, and closed-loop technology has been available since the 1940s. A 300-room hotel in Winnipeg has used geothermal power since the 1930s, and it is used extensively in British Columbia.

Although startup costs of geothermal systems are about 40 percent higher than for conventional systems, savings in operating costs usually make up for the difference in three to five years. Because there is no combustion of fossil fuel (and no greenhouse gases), geothermal systems are safe. They produce less dust and provide better indoor air quality. Ground-source heating maintains a relatively constant heating in winter, greater control over humidity in summer, and is suitable for use in private residences and commercial and public buildings such as schools.

In Sussex, New Brunswick, an aquifer thermal energy storage (ATES) system at the Sussex Hospital complex began in 1992 and has been fully operational since the spring of 1996. The hospital uses the ATES system to reduce the cost of preheating air and save approximately $86 000 in energy consumption annually.

The system works by using two well fields, one cool (7.5°C) and the other warm (10°C), located on either side of the hospital complex. During the cooling season, the groundwater is transferred from the cool well field through the exchange systems within the buildings to the warm well field; the process is reversed during the heating season. In the cooling season, heat is transferred from the air through, for example, a water-to-air coil to the groundwater, thus reducing the temperature of the air in the supply system.

Using a hospital to demonstrate the ATES concept is significant because hospitals depend on secure energy supplies for heating and cooling. Monitoring of this project is ongoing, but officials expect to be able to apply the ATES process to other community buildings and to demonstrate the potential for other community-based underground thermal energy sources.

SOURCES: Burke, D. (1997, March 18). Ground-source heating: The wave of the future? *Canmore Leader*, p. A14.

Cruickshanks, F. (1997). Underground thermal energy in Sussex, New Brunswick. *Water News*, 16(2), pp. 3–6.

Cruickshanks, F., & Sponagle, J.L. (1997). Underground thermal energy rises to future challenges. *Technical Bureau Supplement, Water News*, June, pp. i–viii.

ORGANIZED INITIATIVES

Canadians expect that heat and light for our homes, fuel for our vehicles, and power to operate our businesses and factories will be available on demand. In Western society, much of this energy comes from nonrenewable fossil fuels. Use of oil, coal, and natural gas is a major cause of air and water pollution, land disruption, and long-term changes in global climate. Similarly, use of other common energy sources, such as hydroelectricity, nuclear power, and biomass energy, also impact the natural environment and can have devastating effects on ecosystem sustainability.

In response to the detrimental environmental effects of energy use, Canada has developed a number of initiatives, and has become a partner in international agreements aimed at conserving energy, reducing the output of greenhouse gases (discussed in Chapter 5), and developing renewable energy sources.

Many nations that ratified the United Nations Convention on Climate Change will not meet the carbon dioxide stabilization target by the year 2000. In fact, at the end of 1995, Canada's carbon emissions were 9 percent above 1990 levels (Gherson, 1996). Despite missing the target, several nations are beginning to take the matter seriously and initiate specific objectives and rules. Germany, for example, aims to reduce one-third of its carbon dioxide emissions by 2005, while Denmark, the Netherlands, and Britain have imposed fuel taxes to encourage energy conservation (Alexander, 1994).

Canada and the United States also are making efforts to reduce their contributions to climate change. In 1997, the two nations agreed to work together to encourage and adopt cleaner, more efficient transportation, and to promote the use of innovative market strategies to reduce greenhouse gas emissions (Environment Canada, 1997). One such strategy involves the use of tradable **emissions permits** where companies buy and sell from each other the right to release greenhouse gases. Tradable emissions permits also may be used between nations that export and import clean-burning fuels. For example, when the United States imports natural gas from Canada, the burning of oil and coal is reduced, subsequently lowering U.S. carbon emissions. Canada would receive a credit from the United States, which would offset the environmental cost of extracting and transporting the natural gas.

Canada has instituted a variety of national programs that work toward reducing emissions of greenhouse gases. Emissions targets developed under the Motor Vehicle Safety Act, for example, are among the most stringent in the world. In 1996, the federal government also passed legislation (Bill C-29) to ban the fuel additive MMT (methylcyclopentadienyl manganese tricarbonyl). The controversial fuel additive is supposed to boost the octane rating of gasoline to reduce engine knock and nitrous oxide emissions. Introduced in Canada in 1976, MMT was considered a replacement for leaded gasoline, which was phased out in 1990 to improve urban air quality. Almost all Canadian refiners used MMT and were opposed to the ban because of added operational costs. Car manufacturers, however, lobbied for the ban because MMT clogs pollution monitoring components. With built-in diagnostic systems and emission control equipment becoming more sophisticated, and pollution standards more stringent, the MMT ban was necessary to ensure automobiles perform up to government and industry expectations.

The federal government also has made strides in promoting energy efficiency and developing alternative energy sources. The Efficiency and Alternative Energy program comprises 33 initiatives that are directed toward improved energy efficiency and the use of alternative energy in all end-use sectors (equipment, buildings, industry, and transportation). Included in the program is the 1993 Energy Efficiency Act, which sets minimum efficiency standards for energy-using equipment. In 1996, the federal government introduced a renewable energy strategy that includes tax breaks, funding for private sector research, and initiatives to increase market demand for green power.

ENERGY FUTURES

What are the best options for meeting our energy requirements, and how do we meet these requirements without jeopardizing environmental sustainability? In the short term, we likely will continue to depend on fossil fuels. Oil is the lifeblood of our economy and despite its environmental hazards, remains inexpensive (compared to its alternatives), has a relatively high net useful energy, and is easy to transport. However, the Earth's fossil fuels are diminishing. During the last century, we have consumed massive reserves of coal, oil, and natural gas, reserves that took eons to accumulate.

Combined with global deforestation, our burning of fossil fuels has upset the natural balance of the carbon cycle. We have been warned about the potential effects of human-induced climate change. Even so, most (if not all) of the world's richest economies will be unable to meet the target of reduced greenhouse gas emissions by the year 2000. Our inability to meet this internationally negotiated objective emphasizes how attached we have become to fossil fuels, and how difficult it is to move away from their use.

Fortunately, we are trying to kick the fossil fuel habit. We have little choice. At current usage rates, fossil fuels are expected to become uneconomical for use at some point in the next century. Improvements in energy efficiency, increased use of coal, and co-generation efforts will help to extend the life of fossil fuels a little longer; however, their use is finite. As the availability of fossil fuels decreases (and costs escalate), the use of alternatives will increase.

Alternatives may include sources we are using already, such as nuclear, biomass, and hydropower. As we have discovered, however, there are limits on these sources as well. The construction of hydroelectric dams results in widespread landscape and ecological changes, and few sites remain that would be accepted on both environmental and economic grounds. Nuclear power is an option that has suffered in popularity, especially in Western nations. The events at Chernobyl, potential for further accidents, and storage of radioactive wastes are issues detracting from the suitability of nuclear power to satisfy global energy requirements. Nuclear power also is not sustainable over the long term as uranium is a nonrenewable resource. Although renewable, the widespread use of biomass for energy would not be feasible unless harvest were equal to replacement. In addition, effective land use controls are required to maintain soil nutrients and prevent excessive soil erosion. Biomass also has a low net useful energy and is expensive to collect and transport.

In the longer term, it is likely that our communities will draw on a much wider variety of energy resources, depend much less on imported energy, and instead make optimal use of locally available renewable resources. Advances in technology and energy-efficiency measures are providing the bridge to transport us from nonrenewable fossil fuels to alternative, renewable energy sources.

Despite our appetite for oil and gas, we have begun making the transition to renewable energy. Although it is in its infancy, there are positive signs that this transition is taking place. International efforts to reduce the release of greenhouse gases are prompting countries to increase research budgets for renewable energy, levy fuel taxes, and offer incentives for energy conservation. Increased government funding for hydrogen research in the United States and the success of the Ballard hydrogen fuel cell battery are examples of the steps being taken toward wider use of alternative energy sources.

Chapter Questions

1. Identify the range of negative impacts associated with fossil fuels; which do you think is the most serious? Why?

2. An advantage of various forms of renewable energy (wind and solar energy, for instance) is that they cause no net increase in carbon dioxide. Is this true for biomass? Why or why not?

3. Excluding fossil fuels, what other forms of energy have the greatest potential where you live? What might be some of the barriers to developing these energy sources?

4. Discuss the reasons why or how energy conservation and improved energy efficiency might be considered major "sources" of energy.

5. Why is the permanent storage of (high-level) radioactive wastes such a problem in Canada (and elsewhere)?

6. What kinds of energy conservation measures could you adopt for each of the following aspects of your life: washing dishes, doing laundry, lighting, bathing, cooking, buying a car, driving a car?

references

Alexander, C. (1994). Two years after the Earth Summit it's time to take the pulse of the planet. *Time,* November 7, pp. 43–47.

Bergman, B. (1997, March 3). Special report: One of a kind. *Maclean's,* 110(9), pp. 30–31.

Boras, A. (1995, November 18). Golden sands—amazing oilsands revival taking place. *Calgary Herald,* pp. C1, 2.

Boras, A. (1996, July 10). It's a win–win project. *Calgary Herald,* p. C2.

Bright, D., & Salaff, S. (1996). Wintry power play. *Equinox,* 85 (February), p. 13.

Burke, D. (1997, March 18). Ground-source heating: The wave of the future? *Canmore Leader,* p. A14.

Cable News Network. (1995). Nigeria given two-year democracy deadline. http://www.cnn.com/WORLD/9511/nigeria/11-12/index.html

Canadian Renewable Fuels Association. Green fuels home page. http://www.greenfuels.org

Chambers, A. (1996, June 5). Watchdog calls for strict control of emissions. *Calgary Herald,* p. C2.

Chivers, C. (1996). Troubled waters. *E, The Environment Magazine,* 7(1), pp. 14–15.

Coal best long-term energy source. (1995, September 12). *Calgary Herald,* p. C4.

Congress ups hydrogen funding, sends Walker Bill to White House for Clinton signature. (1996). *Hydrogen and Fuel Cell Letter,* 11(10). http://www.ttcorp.com/nha/thl/jan_97.htm

Cruickshanks, F. (1997). Underground thermal energy in Sussex, New Brunswick. *Water News,* 16(2), pp. 3–6.

Cruickshanks, F., & Sponagle, J.L. (1997). Underground thermal energy rises to future challenges. Technical Bureau Supplement, *Water News,* June, pp. i–viii.

Dreicer, M., & Alexakhin, R. (1996). Post-Chernobyl scientific perspectives: Social, health and environmental effects. *IAEA Bulletin.* http://www.iaea.or.at/worldatom.infosource/bulletin/bull383/dreicer.html

Earthline Africa. (1996). Execution of Ken Saro-Wiwa. http://www.gem.co.za/ELA/ken.html

Energy Probe Research Foundation. (1995). *1995 Annual Report.* Toronto: Energy Probe.

Environment Canada. (1994, March). Energy consumption. *State of the Environment Bulletin* No. 94-3.

Environment Canada. (1996a). Energy consumption. *State of the Environment Bulletin* No. 96-3 (Spring).

Environment Canada. (1996b). Oil, water and chocolate mousse. http://www.doc.ca

Environment Canada. (1997). Minister Marchi announces Canada–U.S. actions to protect the environment. http://www.doe.ca

Feldman, D.L. (1995). Revisiting the energy crisis: How far have we come? *Environment,* 37(4), pp. 16–20, 42–44.

Feud may kill Ecorail. (1997, July 1). *Calgary Herald,* p. C1.

Flavin, C. (1997, November). Clean as a breeze. *Time,* 150(17A), pp. 46–49.

Francis, W. (1997). Burning questions about gas flares. *Environment Views and Network News,* 1(1), pp. 18–19.

Frankel, E. (1995). *Ocean environmental management: A primer on the role of the oceans and how to maintain their contribution to life on Earth.* Englewood Cliffs, NJ: Prentice-Hall.

Freeman, S.D. (1996). *Put energy conservation front and centre. Policy Options,* 17(3), pp. 11–13.

Frenay, R. (1996). Water power. *Audubon,* 98(3), pp. 24–26.

Gherson, G. (1996, November. 10). Move environment to Ottawa's front burner. *Calgary Herald,* p. A7.

Gjertson, H. (1997). Still the worst. *Alternatives,* 23(3), p. 5.

Gonzalez, A. (1996). Chernobyl—ten years after: Global experts clarify the facts about the 1986 accident and its effects. http://www.iaea.or.at/worldatom/inforesource/bulletin/bull383/gonzalez.html

Government of Canada. (1996). *The state of Canada's environment—1996.* Ottawa: Supply and Services Canada.

Greenpeace Canada. (1996). Shell in Nigeria. http://www.web.apc.org/~embargo/shell.htm

Hamilton, G. (1997, February 16). Emblem of death. *Calgary Herald,* p. A13.

Hill, R., O'Keefe, P., & Snape, C. (1995). *The future of energy use.* London: Earthscan Publications.

Johnson, D. (1997). The answer is blowing in the wind. *Encompass,* 1(2), pp. 21–22.

Lermer, G. (1996). The dismal economics of Candu. *Policy Options,* 17(3), (April), pp. 16–20.

Linden, E. (1994). Bright alternatives. *Time,* November 7, pp. 50–51.

Lougheed, T. (1992). R-2000. *Canadian Consumer,* (May/June), pp. 24–28.

MacAfee, M. (1997, July 8). Hibernia ahead of schedule. *Calgary Herald,* p. C8.

Martin, D. (1995, August 30). Last hope. *Calgary Herald,* p. C1.

Martin, D. (1997, July 29). Drilling starts on first Hibernia well. *Calgary Herald,* p. E2.

National Renewable Energy Labratory. (1996). Hydrogen research at NREL. http://www.nrel.gov.lab/pao/hydrogen.html

Natural Resources Canada. (1996a). *Energy efficiency trends in Canada.* Ottawa.

Natural Resources Canada. (1996b). Anderson announces funding for Ballard fuel cell technology. http://www.nrcan.gc.ca/css/imb/hqlib/0610.htm

Natural Resources Canada. (1996c). New initiative will encourage energy-efficient home renovations. http://www.emr.ca/hqlib/9611.htm

Northeast Sustainable Energy Association. (1995). Electric cars proven twice as efficient as gasoline models. http://nesea.nrel.gov

Plummer, D. (1996). Nuclear waste: Coming soon to a hole near you? *Canadian Dimension,* 30(5), pp. 52–54.

Russell, S. (1996). Making eco-friendly houses. *WWF Newsletter,* (March). http://www.panda.org

Shape up or else, plant told. (1996, June 21). *Calgary Herald,* p. A15.

Shell Nigeria. (1996). About Shell in Nigeria—people, oil and politics. http://www.shellnigeria.com/abshell/oil.html

Sierra Club. http://www.sierraclub.org

Sly, L. (1997, January 18). Upheaval on the Yangtze. *Calgary Herald,* p. C3.

Standford, Q.H. (Ed.). (1992). *Canadian Oxford world atlas: New edition.* Toronto: Oxford University Press.

Statistics Canada & Natural Resources Canada. (1995). *Energy statistics handbook* (Catalogue 57-601). Ottawa.

Stothart, P. (1996). Nuclear electricity: The best option given the alternatives. *Policy Options,* 17(3), pp. 14–16.

Strojek, S. (1996, December 5). Oilsands alarm. *Calgary Herald,* p. D2.

Taylor, D.M. (1994). *Off course: Restoring balance between Canadian society and the environment.* Ottawa: International Development Research Centre.

Tulley, A. (1994). The age of wind power dawns in Alberta. *Canadian Geographic,* 114(2), p. 12.

Uranium Information Centre. (1996). Chernobyl and Soviet reactors. http://www.uic.com.au/nip22.htm

Zich, A. (1997). China's Three Gorges: Before the flood. *National Geographic,* 192(3), pp. 2–33.

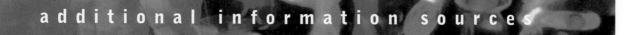

additional information sources

Energy Probe Research Foundation
225 Brunswick Avenue
Toronto, ON M5S 2M6

Fisheries and Oceans Canada. (1997). Canadian Coast Guard. http://www.ccg-gcc.gc.ca/main.htm

Savchenko, V.K. (1995). *The ecology of the Chernobyl catastrophe.* Man and the Biosphere Series, 16. New York: Parthenon.

Wallis, C., Klimek, J., & Adams, W. (1996). Nationally significant Sage Creek Grassland threatened by Express pipeline. *Action Alert,* 7(4), 4 pp.

CHAPTER 12

Wild Species and Natural Spaces

Chapter Contents

CHAPTER OBJECTIVES   384
INTRODUCTION   384
   The Importance of Biodiversity   388
HUMAN ACTIVITIES AND IMPACTS ON
CANADIAN SPECIES AND NATURAL
ENVIRONMENTS   389
   Human Activity and Biodiversity   389
      Habitat Alteration Due to Physical
         Changes   389
         Forestry, Agriculture, and Other
            Human Activities   389
         Fragmentation   390
         Chemical Changes   390
         Climate Change   390
      Habitat Alteration Due to Competition
         from Non-Native Biota   393
      Habitat Alteration Due to
         Harvesting   393
      Habitat Alteration Due to Toxic
         Contaminants   393
      Habitat Alteration Due to Cumulative
         Agents of Change   393
   Species at Risk   394
   Spaces at Risk   397
RESPONSES TO ENVIRONMENTAL IMPACTS
AND CHANGE   402
   International Calls to Action   402
      International Treaties   402
      In Situ Conservation   404
         Protected Areas   404
         Restoration and
            Rehabilitation   408
      Ex Situ Conservation   409
         Plants   409
         Animals   410
      Sustainable Use of Biological
         Resources   410

"The endangered spaces that must be loved and protected are the irreplaceable landscapes and waterscapes whose mosaics contribute to the health, beauty, permanency, and productivity of the globe. To perceive native landscapes and waterscapes, parks and wildernesses, as beyond price, as sacrosanct, is the saving goal that humanity must pursue."

J.S. Rowe (1989), in Hummel (Ed.)

Improving Understanding of
Biodiversity   411
Canadian Law, Policy, and Practice   411
Protecting Canadian Species   412
Protecting Canadian Spaces   412
Partnerships for the Future   413
FUTURE CHALLENGES   415
Chapter Questions   416
References   417
Additional Information Sources   418

Chapter Objectives

After studying this chapter you should be able to

- understand the biodiversity concerns relating to Canada's species and spaces

- identify a range of human uses of wild species and natural spaces

- describe the impacts of human activities on wild species and their habitats and environments, including protected areas

- appreciate the complexity and interrelatedness of wild species, habitat, protected areas, and biodiversity issues

- outline Canadian and international responses to the need for protection of wild species and spaces

- discuss challenges to a sustainable future for wild species and protected areas in Canada

INTRODUCTION

Once the most widespread frog species in North America, the northern leopard frog experienced a population crash in the mid-1970s all across the continent. "Piles of dead and dying frogs were reported from many Lake Manitoba shorelines, [and] heaps nearly a metre high were recorded from the major frog holes" (Zolkewich, 1995, p. 3). By 1989, the realization that a variety of frog species had disappeared almost simultaneously from large, well-protected national parks and nature reserves around the world raised particular concern. Golden toads, for instance, disappeared from the Monteverde Cloud Forest Reserve in Costa Rica, and gastric breeding frogs vanished from a remote national park in Australia; both may now be extinct (Dunn, 1996). Recent research has shown that red-legged frogs have disappeared from pristine habitat near Yosemite National Park, California (Drost & Fellers, 1996).

Most previously observed amphibian (frog, toad, salamander, and newt) population declines and extirpations were attributed directly to habitat destruction by logging, urbanization, and drainage of wetlands, and indirectly to pollutants. Local amphibian populations also could have been affected greatly by factors such as weather (particularly drought), predation, and extensive commercial harvest such as occurred with bullfrogs in Algonquin Provincial Park, Ontario (Brooks & MacDonald, 1996; Orchard, n.d.).

The loss of frogs from geographically dispersed and apparently pristine protected areas, however, suggested one or more global agents might be adversely affecting amphibians (Declining Amphibian Populations Task Force, n.d.; Dunn, 1996). Possible candidates for the causes of these global declines include an increase in UV-B radiation resulting from ozone layer depletion; chemical contamination including the effects of acid precipitation, pesticides, herbicides, and fertilizers; introduction of exotic competitors and predators; and disease (Declining Amphibian Populations Task Force, n.d.; Dunn, 1996).

Frogs and other amphibians are highly sensitive to a variety of environmental stressors and are good indicators of ecological problems. Their permeable skins, through which they breathe, make them extremely vulnerable to both airborne and waterborne pollutants. In addition, their low mobility and complex life cycles (involving both aquatic and terrestrial habitats) make them vulnerable to subtle habitat changes. Of all the vertebrate classes, they may be the best indicators of ecological health, able to pinpoint degradation of terrestrial and aquatic habitats better than even the more commonly monitored bird populations (Bishop et al., 1994).

Amphibians, such as frogs, toads, newts, and salamanders, are highly sensitive to a variety of environmental stressors.

Why does the loss of amphibians matter? Vanishing amphibians are not only a loss of biodiversity (a cause of concern in itself) but also may indicate "profound environmental change affecting all life on earth" (Dunn, 1996, p. 4). There is a sense that if frogs are in trouble, humans are not far behind (Zolkewich, 1995). In addition to their significance as a measure of the health of the environment, amphibians are an important part of the ecological balance of many habitats. As predators, frogs and salamanders consume many times their weight in invertebrates, including many pest species, and as prey, they control the abundance, distribution, and health of numerous aquatic and terrestrial predators (Bishop et al., 1994). Amphibians also have biomedicinal value: for example, we are just beginning to appreciate the potential and value that the skins of amphibians have in yielding drugs useful to medicine.

In spite of their ecological significance, scientists have only a rudimentary understanding of amphibian population dynamics, and baseline data on the populations of the 140 salamanders and 90 frogs and toads occurring in Canada and the United States are almost nonexistent (Bishop et al., 1994). Since the populations of most amphibian species exhibit large natural fluctuations, extensive research and long-term monitoring are necessary to determine whether the extirpations and large population declines are following natural patterns or are accelerating.

In response to the international declines in frog populations, the IUCN (World Conservation Union) Species Survival Commission struck the Declining Amphibian Populations Task Force (DAPTF) in 1991. Over 3000 scientists and conservationists now belong to the network of 90 working groups around the world (including one in Canada) attempting to determine the nature, extent, and causes of global declines of amphibians, and to promote means by which the declines can be halted or reversed and species diversity maintained (Orchard, 1997; Wilkinson, n.d.).

The documented disappearance of amphibian species emphasizes the urgency of establishing reliable inventories and long-term monitoring programs in general, and of establishing them in national parks and other protected areas in particular. Inventorying in Mount Revelstoke and Glacier national parks in British Columbia, for example, has revealed the presence of two amphibian species (western toads and spotted frogs) that have undergone severe population declines elsewhere. Monitoring these species within the parks should contribute data to a national database and help analysts identify and understand both the internal and external threats to biodiversity and ecological integrity (Dunn, 1996). (For further information about amphibian monitoring programs in Canada, see Box 12–1.)

BOX 12-1
AMPHIBIAN MONITORING IN CANADA

In 1992, volunteer observers began monitoring the mating calls of male amphibians in Canada. By 1995, over 400 observers were involved in large-scale monitoring programs in Nova Scotia, Quebec, Ontario, Manitoba, and Saskatchewan. Each night for three minutes during the April to July mating season, observers report on the species calling and the intensity of the calling. Observers choose their own monitoring sites, which can be a favourite pond or marsh, a rural road, or even their own back yard. This program has become very popular with the general public, partly because volunteers are sent tapes of the frog calls, and people enjoy the opportunity to learn the calls of animals other than birds.

In Ontario, the Long Point Bird Observatory and Environment Canada's Marsh Monitoring Program combine sight and sound surveys of marsh birds and amphibians in Great Lakes wetlands to assess the need for rehabilitation of a marsh or to determine whether a rehabilitation project has been successful. In 1995 and 1996, 5502 amphibian choruses were recorded on 256 routes.

In Nova Scotia, the monitoring program focuses on the spring peeper; volunteers call the provincial museum on the first date of spring that they hear the spring peepers. These data collected by volunteers not only provide information on the presence or absence of the spring peeper, but also promote awareness because the locations of the first dates of calling are reported on television weather maps.

There is an extensive cooperative amphibian monitoring program between Canada and the United States, also. The North American Amphibian Monitoring Program (NAAMP), established in 1994, is a collaborative effort of the amphibian research and conservation community in North America.

The broad goal of NAAMP is to develop a statistically defensible program to monitor the distribution and abundance of amphibians. So far, provinces and states have focused on implementing calling surveys and establishing herpetological (reptile and amphibian) atlases. Collaboration among researchers and volunteers is important to the success of projects such as Saskatchewan's Amphibian Monitoring Program (initiated in 1993) and Herpetology Atlas Project (initiated 1996). For instance, NAAMP provides data reports to the atlas project, and the atlas project assists the monitoring program through analysis of data, development of additional survey routes, and a "frog watch" program.

Participants in NAAMP's monitoring programs come from federal governments, provincial and state natural resource groups, national parks, wildlife refuges, academia, NGOs, and the public. Both the Canadian and North American amphibian monitoring programs rely to a considerable extent on partnerships between professional biologists and volunteer observers. These partnerships serve also as educational and training opportunities, as volunteers learn how to identify the calls of adult amphibians and develop other skills in order to help collect high-quality data.

For additional information, the following sources should prove useful.

Organization	Publication/Web site	Contact
Canadian Amphibian and Reptile Conservation Network	*The Boreal Dip Net,* semiannual newsletter	Canadian Wildlife Amphibian Service Environment Canada Box 5050 Burlington, ON L7R 4A6
Declining Amphibian Populations Task Force (Canada)	*FROGLOG,* quarterly newsletter	1745 Bank Street Victoria, BC V8R 4V7
North American Amphibian Monitoring Program	third annual meeting was held on Internet: http://www.im.nbs.gov/naamp3/naamp3.html	Biological Resources Division U.S. Geological Survey 12100 Beech Forest Road Laurel, MD 20708-4038 e-mail: frog@nbs.gov
Nova Scotia FrogWatch	http://www.cciw.ca/ecowatch/FROG/FRGW1B2.HTM or http://www.ednet.ns.ca/educ/museum/mnh/educ/frogwtch/index.htm	
Saskatchewan Amphibian Monitoring and Herpetology Atlas Projects		Coordinator Saskatchewan Amphibian Monitoring Program P.O. Box 1574, Saskatoon, SK S7K 3R3

ACKNOWLEDGMENT: Stan A. Orchard, Canadian National Co-ordinator of the Species Survival Commission of IUCN (World Conservationi Union)/Task Force on Declining Amphibian Populations in Canada, kindly provided extensive background information.

Saving remaining populations and their habitat also is critical to the survival of some amphibian species, and Ducks Unlimited is one organization that has been active in this area. Their Prince's Spring project, a northern leopard frog breeding colony located about 190 kilometres southeast of Hanna, Alberta, is a protected site where this species has a good chance for survival. The frog population has remained stable since the early 1980s, when Ducks Unlimited constructed two dykes to create a spring-fed freshwater marsh, and built five nesting islands within the marsh (Zolkewich, 1995).

In addition to amphibians, there are many other wild animal and plant species in Canada whose continued healthy existence is threatened by loss and degradation of habitat through human economic development activities. Unrestricted clear cut logging, agricultural expansion, wetland drainage, urban growth, pollution, global climate change, unsustainable use of some wildlife populations, and poaching and illegal trade are among the key threats to species biodiversity.

In April 1997, the Committee on the Status of Endangered Wildlife in Canada (whose primary mandate is to develop a national listing of Canadian species at risk) identified a total of 291 mammal, bird, reptile, fish, mollusc, lepidoptera (butterfly and moth), and plant species that were at risk across Canada (Environment Canada, 1997b; Maxwell, 1996). Species on the list are found in every part of Canada, but most are found in the Okanagan Valley of south-central British Columbia; on the Prairies of Alberta, Saskatchewan, and Manitoba; in southwestern Ontario; in southern Quebec; and on Nova Scotia's Atlantic coastal plain (World Wildlife Fund Canada, 1996a). Figure 12–1 illustrates areas of risk to biodiversity in Canada.

Just as important as the threatened wild species themselves are the wild spaces (landscapes) they inhabit. From the coasts of Newfoundland to the rain forests of British Columbia, and from the prairie grasslands to the Arctic tundra, Canada is losing wilderness at the rate of more than one acre every 15 seconds (World Wildlife Fund Canada, 1996b). Since all species rely on a healthy natural world that includes intact wild places, the consequences of this loss for wild species and humans potentially are far reaching.

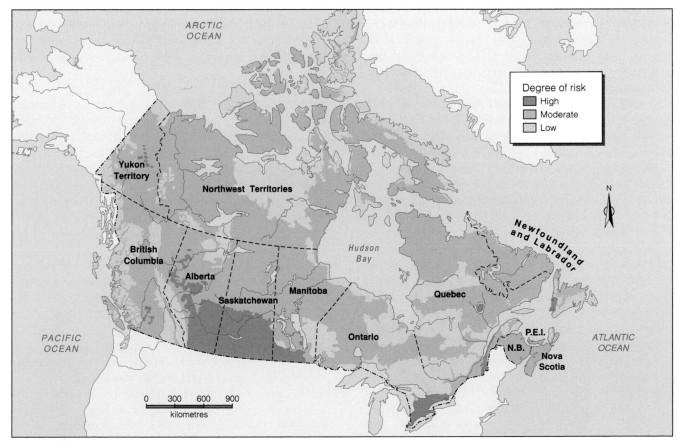

Figure 12–1
Risk to biodiversity for Canada

SOURCE: Adapted from Western Canada Wilderness Committee. (1995, Spring). *Protect Canada's Biodiversity,* 14(4), pp. 4–5. Based on Minister of Supply and Services. (1995). *Biodiversity in Canada: A science assessment for Environment Canada.* Ottawa, p. 2.

THE IMPORTANCE OF BIODIVERSITY

The diversity of life in Canada and on this planet supports vital ecological processes including oxygen production, water purification, conversion of solar energy into carbohydrates and protein, and climate moderation. Even though society has not completely understood that human health depends on these ecological processes, and has not fully valued them, conserving biodiversity has become an essential part of Canada's efforts to achieve sustainability. Beyond its ecological processes, biodiversity is important for at least three additional reasons: employment, spiritual inspiration and identity, and insurance for the future.

The diversity of Earth's life forms enables people to satisfy many of their needs, including that for gainful employment. Millions of people who work in the fishing, forestry, agriculture, tourism and outdoor recreation, pharmaceutical, and biotechnological industries depend directly on high-quality biological resources to earn their living. Particularly in the north of Canada, many Indigenous communities derive a large portion of their food and income from sustainable harvesting of biological resources.

As we have seen in the cases of east coast fishers and Indigenous and First Nations peoples, loss of wildlife species or their habitats affects traditional lifestyles and reduces the quality or availability of country foods, as well as opportunities to undertake other hunting, gathering, and guiding activities. The attendant economic repercussions are important also.

In part, the Canadian cultural identity has been shaped by the wild, elemental beauty of our natural landscapes. Indigenous cultures developed intimate relationships with nature, and many non-Indigenous Canadians also have found that the country's diversity of species and spaces provides spiritual, emotional, and artistic inspiration. Painters, writers, and musicians have captured landscape and wildlife elements in their work and have helped define Canada domestically as well as internationally.

Many Canadians believe that each wild species that inhabits our landscape has **intrinsic value**—a value based on the inherent qualities of that species, independent of its value to humans. This suggests that human society should be built on respect for the life that surrounds us, and that biodiversity should be conserved for its own sake, regardless of its economic or other values. Loss of biodiversity in wild species and spaces means that certain intangible values also are lost, ranging from relationships with the natural world to aesthetics.

A distinct advantage of maintaining Canada's (and the Earth's) biodiversity, and using biological resources sustainably, is that we will maximize our options in the event that we need to respond to unforeseen and changing environmental conditions. "Maintaining our potential as a country to be creative, productive, and competitive will also provide us with opportunities for discov-

First Nations people on Canada's west coast derive distinctive art forms from their close relationship with wildlife species.

ering and developing new foods, drugs, and industrial products" (Government of Canada, 1996). One example of this is the potential to use the genetic material contained in many of our native plants (that enables them to endure both cold winters and hot summers) to develop agricultural crops that can withstand even greater temperature ranges.

If Canadians fail to conserve biodiversity, we foreclose future options, flexibility, and economic opportunities, and pass on the enormous costs of this failure to future generations. Given the current rate of environmental change, and the likelihood that species of unknown (but valuable) ecological, medical and economic potential are vanishing before their existence has even been confirmed, striving to conserve biodiversity is an investment in the future and makes good business sense. Conserving biodiversity also is one way to help provide for intergenerational equity.

Conversely, loss of habitat or loss of access to habitat reduces potential employment, income, or trade opportunities. In the recreational field, increased use of wildlands for both consumptive (hunting, fishing, resort development) and nonconsumptive uses (wildlife viewing, photography, hiking) may have negative local impacts. When coupled with infrastructural requirements to support outdoor recreational activities, such impacts could compound the potential for destruction of the resources on which these activities depend.

Given the desirability of preventing a reduction in the benefits of biodiversity, Canada has an important stewardship role for major portions of the world's tundra, temperate forest, and aquatic ecosystems, as well as in the protection of smaller areas of grassland and cold-winter desert ecosystems. The fact that relatively fewer species

Wildlife viewing and nature photography may cause local environmental stress.

inhabit Canadian landscapes (compared to other nations) does not diminish the importance of the species that are present, particularly if they are **endemic** species found only in particular geographic regions of Canada and nowhere else in the world.

Unfortunately, a major global threat to species diversity is that many of the areas richest in endemics—such as Vancouver Island and the Queen Charlotte Islands in British Columbia—also are prime targets for intensive economic development including forestry. In other areas, such as the large sand dunes on the south shore of Lake Athabasca, Saskatchewan, the 10 endemic plant species that occur there could be put at risk by large-scale removal of sand, or unrestricted use of all-terrain vehicles.

Having briefly reviewed some reasons to protect the biodiversity and sustainability of Canada's species and spaces, the following sections note the nature of Canada's wildlife species and protected areas, and highlight relevant concerns regarding biodiversity and sustainability. As we shall see later in the chapter, national and international efforts are being made to address the loss of species diversity and wild spaces.

HUMAN ACTIVITIES AND IMPACTS ON CANADIAN SPECIES AND NATURAL ENVIRONMENTS

HUMAN ACTIVITY AND BIODIVERSITY

Globally, the numbers of species in most **taxonomic** groups tend to decrease from equatorial to polar latitudes; thus, in spite of its large size, and because it consists mainly of polar and temperate ecosystems, Canada has less species richness than many other nations. Brazil, for instance, has close to 55 000 known species of flowering plants, while Canada has only about 4039 known species of higher plants, including about 2980 species of native flowering plants and about 930 introduced flowering plants.

With regard to the total wildlife population in Canada (that is, the total of all plants, animals, and micro-organisms, of both terrestrial and aquatic ecosystems), estimates are that there are more that 138 000 species in Canada (Government of Canada, 1996). This total includes the 4039 plants noted above, plus nearly 1800 vertebrate animals and more than 44 000 invertebrates (Table 12–1).

Beginning with European settlement, Canada's ecosystems have been altered significantly through settlement, cultivation, industrial and domestic pollution, and harvesting of commercially valuable life forms such as fish and trees. Habitats have been altered through physical changes, competition from non-native biota, and other cumulative agents of change. Figure 12–2 provides an overview of the level of human activity occurring on Canada's ecosystems; note the overlap with areas of risk to biodiversity shown in Figure 12–1 (refer also to Figure 3–6). Table 12–2 indicates in summary form some of the key areas, characteristics, and environmental stresses relating to biodiversity within Canada.

The state of wild species and natural spaces in Canada reflects natural changes, such as periodic fluctuations in populations due to disease, weather events, naturally occurring fires, competition among species, and predation, as well as human activities that alter habitats or introduce non-native species. Major types of habitat alteration, as well as their causes and effects, are outlined briefly in the following sections.

Habitat Alteration Due to Physical Changes

Forestry, Agriculture, and Other Human Activities
Physical changes to habitats have resulted from activities in forestry, agriculture, and other human pursuits. In forestry, logging and clear-cutting result in loss or fragmentation of habitat for certain species but may enhance habitat for other species. In addition, replanting and reseeding are based on commercial preferences of the forest industry and are not likely to reproduce the original species mix and balance. This results in simplified, evenly aged forests of the tree-farm variety. Fire suppression activities deter the return to early or pioneer stages of natural succession; this has implications for species reliant on young-growth forest. Fire suppression also may change the species composition of the climax forest in the area affected.

Agriculture has distorted the original habitat balance of forests, grasslands, and wetlands as they were converted to agricultural lands. Over time, however, previously farmed lands that proved to be marginal for agriculture have been allowed to return to their wild state, while other marginal agricultural lands have been

TABLE 12-2

(CONTINUED)

Area	Key Characteristics and Environmental Stresses
	• Forest ecosystems filter and purify the atmosphere; provide a living substrate for complex communities of organisms (such as insects, birds); protect watersheds against soil erosion; and moderate impacts of extremes of temperature, wind, and precipitation. Living trees contribute oxygen to the atmosphere, and breakdown of their leaves and other organic debris sustains microorganisms and invertebrates that contribute to soil formation.
	• In Canada, forest biodiversity is threatened by reductions in the extent of forest types (such as southern Ontario's Carolinian species, northern boreal forests, and British Columbia's old-growth forests that provide habitat for specialized species such as the spotted owl).
	• Logging and clear-cutting result in fragmentation of forested habitat areas so that forests can no longer support species that rely on large contiguous forest habitat.
Grassland diversity	• Grassland biomes represent about 20 percent of Earth's land area; most have been altered dramatically by human activities.
	• At the time of European settlement, prairie grassland ecosystems covered about one-half million square kilometres of western Canada, sustaining a rich, highly specialized floral and faunal community.
	• Since then, more than 80 percent of Canada's grasslands have been converted to agricultural use; their original diversity has been altered profoundly—only about 1 percent of Canada today remains in grassland ecosystems.
	• An important part of the conservation challenge is to protect and enhance native prairie biodiversity within modern agricultural landscapes.
Wetland diversity	• Canada has about 24 percent of the world's wetlands as well as a much greater proportion of its boreal fens and bogs.
	• Wetlands are among the world's most varied and biologically productive ecosystems, supporting a great diversity of plants and providing ideal breeding and feeding sites for many kinds of invertebrates, fish, amphibians, and waterfowl.
	• Wetlands also perform important ecological functions, including water retention and purification, and flood and erosion control.
	• Removal of wetlands for agricultural or urban development eliminates habitat for wetland-dependent wildlife species and can seriously disrupt the seasonal supply of fresh water over large areas.
Freshwater diversity	• Canadian runoff to the sea is about 9 percent of the world's freshwater runoff; freshwater ecosystems cover more than 7 percent of Canada's surface area, having significant climatic effects (cooling the summer heat, moderating the winter cold).
	• Canada's freshwater ecosystems sustain about 180 fish species, a rich variety of aquatic plants, and many invertebrates, including some groups of arthropods that appear to achieve greatest diversity in temperate latitudes.
	• Pollution by industrial activities and urban wastes is a significant threat to the quality of freshwater habitats; point-source release of industrial effluents, discharges from urban settlements, and airborne pollutants that fall as wet (acid rain) or dry deposition are of concern.
Marine diversity	• Globally, the range and diversity of marine ecosystems is only beginning to be understood and measured.
	• Canada has five major marine ecozones spread over five million square kilometres of ocean; these ecozones contain some of the most productive marine ecosystems in the northern hemisphere; the total marine food web contains thousands of different kinds of organisms.
	• Threats to Canada's marine ecosystems include overfishing, by-catch (nontargeted species in the catch), destruction of habitat, pollution, and global environmental changes such as climate, temperature, and ocean current changes. Thinning of the ozone layer globally places phytoplankton (the biological foundation of the marine ecosystem) at risk.

SOURCE: Government of Canada. (1996). *The state of Canada's environment—1996*. Ottawa: Supply and Services Canada. Chapters 10, 14.

wildlife habitats. For instance, coastal wetlands could be displaced or created as sea levels rise; aquatic and semi-aquatic habitats could recede as wetlands dry up; and boreal forest plants and animals could shift northward.

Habitat Alteration Due to Competition from Non-Native Biota

Non-native (alien, exotic, nonindigenous, or introduced) species can become established in Canada intentionally or accidentally; in either case, native species must compete with non-native species for space, water, food, and other essentials of life. Virtually every region of the country has an introduced species that is actively displacing a native, rare, or endangered species. Released in Central Park, New York, the European starling has spread throughout North America, displacing native species that require tree holes or other cavities for nests.

Similarly, raccoons released on the Queen Charlotte Islands (to provide local trappers with a new species to harvest) have put sea bird colonies at risk, killing about 10 percent of the breeding colonies of burrow-nesting alcids (auklets, guillemots, and ancient murrelets—the latter is listed as a vulnerable species) in only five years. Plants, such as Scotch broom, purple loosestrife, and crested wheatgrass, also have competed aggressively with and replaced native species. Currently, about 23 percent of wild flora (mostly weeds) and about 1 percent of fish in Canada are exotic species.

Habitat Alteration Due to Harvesting

Harvesting has the potential to cause short- and long-term changes in populations and species composition, regardless of the type of wildlife harvested or the methods employed. Logging, for example, causes tempo-rary (sometimes permanent) reduction in tree populations, which affects trees' delivery of ecological functions such as habitat provision, carbon fixation, and oxygen production. Logging also affects the structure of the forest community as older growth stands are replaced with younger trees. Harvesting of fish not only targets large, older specimens, but also extracts enor-mous numbers from the population pools of aquatic species (in 1993, for example, commercial landings of fish were more than 1.1 million tonnes). Harvesting of species for collection purposes cannot be overlooked; some butterfly species and at least nine nationally endangered plants already at risk face some threat from collectors.

Habitat Alteration Due to Toxic Contaminants

Toxic substances may occur naturally (mercury, lead) or anthropogenically (industrial discharges, municipal waste, agricultural and forestry activities, etc.); these contaminants may spread over great distances through air and water currents. Mercury and lead do not appear to have any nutritional or biochemical function; at higher concentrations, however, they can adversely affect plant and animal growth and health.

Lead poisoning of waterfowl and other birds occurs when ducks and other bottom-feeding species ingest the lead pellets from lead shot used in hunting ammunition. Lead enters the gizzard and becomes available for absorp-tion into the body. Ten to 15 percent of the mortality of golden and bald eagles has been attributed to secondary lead poisoning (from feeding on waterfowl carrying lead pellets embedded in their bodies). Beginning in 1997 there is to be a national ban on the use of lead shot for all migratory game bird hunting.

Use of lead sinkers in recreational fishing also causes secondary lead poisoning; when fish escape from anglers with the "hook, line, and sinker" attached, loons or other fish-eating birds can swallow the fish whole, including the lead sinkers, and subsequently die of lead toxicosis. Starting in the fall of 1996, it was illegal to use lead fishing sinkers or jigs (weighted lead hooks) in Canada's national parks and national wildlife areas.

Persistent organochlorines and metals are two notable groups of toxic substances. Organochlorines include pesticides, industrial chemicals, and byproducts of certain industrial processes that take decades or cen-turies to break down naturally (thus their persistence). This persistence and their high solubility in fat leads to bioaccumulation in animal tissues, which are then passed on through food webs, reaching very high concentrations in the tissues of predators at the top of the food web (bio-magnification).

Flooding for hydroelectric developments resulted in mercury contamination as naturally occurring inorganic mercury in submerged organic material was converted into methylmercury by anaerobic bacteria. Methylmer-cury easily bioaccumulates in many organisms and also biomagnifies through food webs. Advisories regarding human consumption of fish above certain sizes from both reservoirs and natural lakes have been given.

Habitat Alteration Due to Cumulative Agents of Change

Wildlife and habitat change frequently is the result of a combination of factors that act directly or indirectly to cause change. Insect populations, for example, can be reduced through habitat loss, pesticide applications, and other factors. Loss of insects also can have a domino effect on the total functioning of the ecosystem and can have ecological and economic repercussions. For example, use of the insecticide fenitrothion (used to con-trol spruce budworm) appears to have caused native wild bee populations to plummet, affecting the success of pol-lination and cross-pollination.

SPECIES AT RISK

It is clear that without adequate and healthy habitat, wildlife (terrestrial and aquatic plants, animals, and microorganisms) cannot survive. This section uses several illustrations of human-related changes in the Arctic and elsewhere to highlight how species may be put at risk by habitat change.

Resource extraction, such as mineral and diamond mining in the Northwest Territories and oil and gas exploration in the Arctic, raises a variety of concerns related to wildlife. The Arctic National Wildlife Refuge (ANWR) in Alaska, often called the Serengeti of North America, sustains vast wildlife populations and also is a potential source of crude oil. Concerned about the fate of the Porcupine caribou herd that overwinters in Canada and migrates each spring to the coastal plain of the ANWR, Canadian conservationists have debated with American government officials about whether oil exploration should be permitted. Caribou show reduced calf production and lower calf survival rates around oil development areas; oil exploration could cause a 20 to 40 percent decline in the size of the herd, and cause economic hardship to the 7000 Aboriginal people who depend on the caribou for their survival (Oil exploration, 1997).

According to the Canadian Wildlife Federation, if the United States did open up the wildlife refuge to oil exploration and drilling, it would be violating four international accords: the Migratory Birds Convention (1916), the Agreement on the Conservation of Polar Bears (1976), the North American Waterfowl Management Plan (1986), and the Porcupine Caribou Agreement (1987) (Oil exploration, 1997). Until 1995, President Clinton had respected his campaign pledge to protect the refuge from drilling. However, because the petroleum industry indicates that advances in drilling mean less land is disturbed during the process now (Bloomberg, 1997), the Canadian Wildlife Federation remains committed to press President Clinton to honour his country's international obligations (Oil exploration, 1997).

Canada's first diamond mine, the Broken Hill Proprietary diamonds project at Lac de Gras, N.W.T., received regulatory approval from the federal government in January 1997. Observers predict that within 15 years there will be 6 to 10 new diamond, base, and precious metal mines in the region, transforming a large portion of the Canadian Arctic (Fenge, 1996).

The Canadian Arctic Resources Committee and the Canadian Wildlife Federation, among other organizations, are concerned about the cumulative effects that these future developments will have on wildlife and other resources as well as on Aboriginal people. The minister of Indian Affairs and Northern Development wrote to the Canadian Wildlife Federation, indicating that his and other federal departments would cooperate to develop a protected areas strategy by 1998, and provide $750 000 per year over five years for collection of baseline data that could help determine the cumulative effects of other potential mineral developments in the area (Canadian Wildlife Federation, 1997a).

The Arctic already has experienced the environmental impacts of actions taken by other people thousands of kilometres away. These impacts include those of pollutants, borne by wind and water currents, that enter the food chain, biomagnify, and end up in Inuit and other Aboriginal people who eat what they hunt. As well, the predicted severe climatic consequences of global warming for the Arctic could result in a shift in location of many wildlife habitats.

Economically, the Arctic is connected to global events also. For many years the Inuit, Dene, and Métis people have relied on the sale of pelts and skins to world markets as a source of cash to purchase market goods and hunting equipment. In turn, the hunting equipment was used to provide food for their families. In 1976, seal skins contributed $1.5 million to the economies of Inuit communities in the Northwest Territories, Quebec, and Labrador. During the 1980s, as Western European and United States governments banned or restricted imports of fur and skins, the economic effect on small communities in the Canadian north was devastating. In 1980, for instance, one seal skin could bring in $23; in 1985, the value dropped to $7. As a result, all types of social pathologies increased—suicides, spousal assault, and alcoholism (Fenge, 1996).

As industrial development proceeds in the north, protecting habitat important for wildlife is likely to be an issue of increasing importance. A comprehensive network of parks, reserves, and protected areas will be needed to ensure environmental protection and wildlife sustainability, as well as cultural and social sustainability. Protecting habitat does not mean excessive hunting by Aboriginal people will occur. In fact, cooperative management of aquatic, marine, and terrestrial animals by government and Aboriginal peoples, agreed on pursuant to land claim and self-government agreements, is attracting interest from many nations because it helps ensure that harvesting remains within sustainable limits. Co-management also encourages people to integrate traditional and scientific knowledge in a quest for better management of the environment, including protection of wild species and spaces.

Northern Aboriginal people consider sustainability as a means to safeguard their cultures and economies as well as the natural environment on which they depend so heavily. Even though involvement of the federal government provides some assurance that sustainability may be implemented domestically, there is a concern that action within Canada alone will not be sufficient to achieve the desired ends. In this case, the eight Arctic Inuit nations in

Inuit hunters during an annual whale hunt.

Canada, Greenland, Alaska, and Chukotka are implementing an environmental protection strategy that they agreed on during their 1991 Circumpolar Conference. In effect, they are undertaking a global effort to ensure sustainability Arctic-wide, including the future of the Canadian Arctic and its wildlife (Fenge, 1996).

The Arctic is not the only area where wild species are at risk because of human activities. A variety of threats face wildlife in ecosystems across Canada; while some species have been impacted negatively by agricultural and industrial activities, acid precipitation, or contaminants, other species have been affected by hunting pressure and recreational and residential impacts. Some species, such as the peregrine falcon, have been brought back from the brink of extinction while others, such as the whooping crane, remain at risk in their Canadian ranges.

Brief stories of four selected species at risk illustrate the threats from human actions facing wild species in ecosystems across Canada (the stories are based on information from Canadian Geographic Enterprises, 1997). The threatened marbled murrelet is a small sea bird, a member of the auk family, whose nesting behaviour had been a mystery to researchers for nearly 100 years. It was not until 1993 that the first occupied murrelet nest in Canada was located in the dense coastal rain forest of British Columbia. Marbled murrelets forage for small schooling fish in nearshore areas (where they are at risk from gill nets and oil spills), and nest only on broad, moss-covered branches of mature conifers within 30 kilometres of the ocean (many similar species of sea birds nest in colonies on coastal cliffs). Only one egg is laid each year; to elude predators, the nest is relocated every year. As logging in the old-growth forests in valley bottoms continues, murrelet numbers have dropped as their prime nesting habitat has disappeared. As forest cover shrinks, opportunistic ravens and Stellar's jays find the murrelet eggs and chicks easy prey; in Clayoquot Sound, the mur-

relet population has declined by about 20 percent since 1982. Legislation is proposed to oblige logging companies to survey their cutting areas and to set aside a minimum of 10 to 12 percent for nesting marbled murrelets.

First identified in Canada in 1920, the endangered pink coreopsis is a pink and yellow perennial herb that is scattered along the shorelines of Nova Scotia's southwestern lakes. In Canada, this coastal plain plant occurred exclusively in the Tusket River valley at six separate locations, all but one on private land. Three of those sites have been lost to residential development. The remaining sites are at risk because the hardy and stress-tolerant coreopsis thrives in gritty, sandy, and seasonally flooded soil on the shorelines of lakes. This locational preference makes the plant vulnerable to activities of cottagers and off-road drivers. Efforts are under way to educate landowners about this plant and to protect the pink coreopsis and other biologically associated plant species in remote areas where it is still found.

Living on the Queen Elizabeth Islands in the Northwest Territories, endangered Peary caribou are the only members of the deer family adapted to life in the Canadian High Arctic. During the summer, the Peary caribou graze river valleys and plains for grasses, sedges, herbs, and willows. During winter they move to higher areas where winds sweep snow away from vegetation; some travel across the frozen sea to search for food. Caribou numbers have dropped from 25 000 in 1961 to fewer than 3000 in 1997 because heavier snowfall and freezing rain during the past decades have increased the caribou's vulnerability to starvation. On some islands, hunting and wolf predation have accelerated the herd's decline. Local Inuit communities that have relied on the caribou for generations voluntarily have reduced their hunting. A national park on Bathurst Island has been created to protect calving areas, and a captive breeding program at the Calgary Zoo also was initiated (but has not been implemented because inclement weather prevented capture of the caribou).

The aurora trout is a colourful brook trout known to live only in two remote lakes (Whirligig and Whitepine) in the Temagami region north of Sudbury. By 1961, the aurora trout had been extirpated from both lakes, because their high elevation and their sensitive geological setting made them prone to acidification that killed trout fry within weeks of hatching. Fortunately, the aurora trout escaped becoming the first casualty of acid precipitation because, a few years prior to 1961, researchers had collected over 3600 eggs to form the basis of a brood stock. This stock has been maintained for about 40 years. Attempts to introduce the species into lakes other than the species' native ones failed; rehabilitation of the trout's native lakes began prior to 1990 when water in the 11-hectare Whirligig was neutralized with 21 tonnes of powdered lime. In 1990, 950 fish were reintroduced to Whirligig, and today both lakes are successfully stocked with hatchery-raised aurora trout. As

Among Canada's threatened and endangered species are the marbled murrelet, pink coreopsis, aurora trout, and Peary caribou.

we know, emissions causing acid precipitation have been reduced substantially, but nevertheless the water quality of the fish habitat is monitored constantly. Twice since 1990 the recovery team has had to intervene and add more lime to Whirligig. (For further information on the threats faced by a variety of wild species, see the following sources listed in the Additional Information Sources section of this chapter: Bildstein, Brett, Goodrich & Viverette; Fair; Gayton; Henry; Schneider; and Wood.)

Toxic contaminants in the environment may occur naturally (mercury and lead in bedrock and soils) or through human activities; wild species may be affected by both sources of toxins. Concerns raised in the early 1960s about the bioaccumulation and biomagnification of persistent organochlorines resulted in a ban or severe restrictions on their release into North American ecosystems. Interestingly, certain wildlife species are used as environmental indicators to monitor levels of organochlorines and toxic contaminants in ecosystems. Researchers use the eggs of one of these species, the double-crested cormorant, to monitor concentrations of selected compounds in ecosystems (see Box 12–2 for

further information on use of wildlife indicators to track toxic contaminants).

Perhaps one of the best illustrations of the cumulative impacts of many human activity pressures is found in the case of grizzly bears in the Banff–Bow Valley area of Alberta. This saga, outlined briefly in Enviro-Focus 12 and Box 12–3, emphasizes the competition bears face with humans for critical montane habitat, and the habitat fragmentation and barriers that human development, land use, and transportation systems have on bear populations located within protected areas (in this case, a national park).

Initiated in 1977, the Committee on the Status of Endangered Wildlife in Canada (COSEWIC) is the agency responsible for identifying the status of all wild species in Canada. COSEWIC employs a seven-category set of status definitions (outlined in Table 12–3); these designations help to monitor the condition of wild species known to be at risk of eventual extinction from one or more agents of change. Table 12–4 provides a summary of the numbers of species at risk in Canada in 1997, as well as those known to be extinct.

PART 3:
RESOURCES FOR CANADA'S FUTURE

Indicators are selected key statistics that represent or summarize some aspect of the state of ecosystems. By focusing on trends in environmental change, they convey how ecosystems are responding to both stresses and management responses.

The insecticide DDT was widely used in Canada between 1947 and 1969 to control agricultural and forest insects. The main breakdown product of DDT is dichlorodiphenyldichloroethylene (DDE), a compound that interferes with enzymes necessary for the production of calcium carbonate in female double-crested cormorants and other birds. Eggshells with less calcium carbonate are thinner and more likely to crack or break during incubation. Because of these and other toxic properties, most uses of DDT were banned in Canada by the mid-1970s. Concentrations of DDE have declined substantially since the 1970s. In recent years, declines have levelled off, possibly as a result of the slow release of contaminant residues from bottom sediments or long-range atmospheric transport from countries still using DDT.

Certain toxic organochlorines, including DDE, PCBs, and some dioxins and furans, have been monitored in species of wildlife since the early 1970s. Tracking concentrations in wildlife simplifies the detection of some chemicals that are present in extremely low concentrations in air and water and are therefore difficult to measure directly. Levels of some organochlorine contaminants in the eggs of fish-eating birds, for example, may be as much as 25 million times the concentrations in the waters in which the fish live, because of the processes of bioaccumulation and biomagnification.

The double-crested cormorant has been selected as a national indicator species for organochlorine levels in wildlife because of its broad distribution across southern Canada, especially in areas of concentrated human activity, and because it is a top predator that eats lives fish. A disadvantage of using the double-crested cormorant as an indicator, however, is that, like many Canadian birds, it migrates south in the winter. It is therefore not known what proportion of the contaminants measured in its eggs comes from non-Canadian sources.

The double-crested cormorant (*Phalacrocorax auritus*) is an excellent swimmer and diver. In pursuit of its fish prey it may remain underwater for 30 seconds or longer, sometimes using its wings for propulsion in addition to its webbed feet. It nests in colonies and builds its nest on the ground or in a tree.

SOURCE: Government of Canada. (1996). *The state of Canada's environment—1996*. Ottawa: Supply and Services Canada.

SPACES AT RISK

The health, biodiversity, and sustainability of wild species is closely connected to the availability and quality of the natural spaces they occupy. Principally because of the extent and natural character of its grasslands, as well as the concentration of rare, threatened, and endangered species it supports, Sage Creek, Alberta, is a nationally significant environmental area.

Hundreds of species of prairie plants and animals occur in this contiguous, 5000-square-kilometre area in the southeastern part of Alberta, including such familiar threatened wildlife species as the burrowing owl, swift fox, and sage grouse, as well as rare plant species such as Pursh's milk vetch and the plains boisduvalia. Sage Creek also is recognized as one of the most diverse areas in North America for breeding grassland birds, and is home to the threatened mountain plover, fewer than 10 breeding pairs of which exist in Alberta (Wallis, Klimek & Adams, 1996).

In March 1996, the Alberta Energy and Utilities Board (AEUB) recognized that Sage Creek's native prairie grassland ecosystems were important, vulnerable, and disappearing rapidly. In spite of awareness that the cumulative long-term impacts of all development in such grasslands, including that of oil and natural gas, can be

Grizzly Bears and Humans in Banff National Park and Area

In spite of the fact that national parks were created in part to protect wildlife, "Banff National Park is a dangerous place to live, if you are a grizzly bear. Researchers have learned that of the 73 grizzlies known to have died in the park from 1971 to 1995, 52 were either destroyed or removed in the interests of public safety. Ninety percent of the grizzlies died close to developed areas, and 56 percent of those were females, since females with curious cubs are the most likely to run into trouble with people" (Marty, 1997, p. 37).

These few statistics highlight some important dimensions of the competition between wild species and humans for habitat. Grizzly bears, whose numbers are estimated to be between 60 and 80 in Banff National Park, are 80 percent vegetarian and range widely in search of food sources such as berries, roots, grasses, and other plants, as well as carrion. Male bears require up to 2000 square kilometres to survive and females need between 200 and 500 square kilometres.

The Banff–Bow Valley area contains montane habitat (valley bottom and open forest of trembling aspen and Douglas fir) that is critical for wildlife survival, including that of grizzlies. Only 3 percent of Banff National Park's 6641 square kilometres is montane habitat, and half of that portion lies in the Bow Valley where wildlife compete for the most productive habitat with humans and their developments. For instance, in the Bow Valley, people have built towns such as Banff, Lake Louise, and Canmore, and associated ski resorts, golf courses, shopping malls, industrial parks, campgrounds, and an airstrip, leaving only a remnant of their former range for bears to roam.

In placing their infrastructure within the valleys, humans have obstructed the traditional north–south and east–west links or corridors that wild species have used for centuries to move north and south within their range between the Yukon and Yellowstone ecosystems. Genetic pathways for regional gene flow, these movement corridors also are fractured by the Trans-Canada Highway, which carries about 20 000 vehicles per day (one every six seconds), and the Canadian Pacific Railway. Bears do

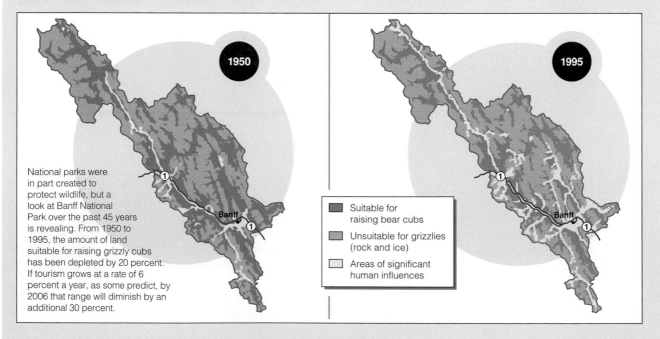

National parks were in part created to protect wildlife, but a look at Banff National Park over the past 45 years is revealing. From 1950 to 1995, the amount of land suitable for raising grizzly cubs has been depleted by 20 percent. If tourism grows at a rate of 6 percent a year, as some predict, by 2006 that range will diminish by an additional 30 percent.

Legend:
- Suitable for raising bear cubs
- Unsuitable for grizzlies (rock and ice)
- Areas of significant human influences

Impacts of human development on grizzly bear habitat in Banff National Park and area.

SOURCE: Marty, S. (1997). Homeless on the range: Grizzlies struggle for elbow room and survival in Banff National Park. *Canadian Geographic*, 117(1), pp. 35, 36.

ENVIRO-FOCUS 12
(CONTINUED)

not like crossing highways or using the underpasses that Parks Canada provided for big game animals (see Box 12–3 for further information on highway and railway impacts on wildlife).

Biologists working on the Eastern Slopes Grizzly Bear project are concerned about habitat fragmentation in Banff National Park and the Bow Valley area and have sensed a general decline in bear numbers. Sensitive to human incursions, grizzly bears are an indicator species (when they are in trouble, the entire ecosystem usually is out of balance). Essentially, the Banff–Bow Valley area now provides only a fraction of its former potential for large mammals. While bears, wolves, and cougars still travel through the Banff–Bow Valley movement corridors, biologists warn that more development will cause wary animals to avoid this area, potentially placing the continued survival of these populations at risk (Canadian Parks and Wilderness Society, 1997).

Human development and land use practices relating to "world class tourism" and the millions of visitors it draws annually to Banff National Park have had significant impacts on wild species, their behaviour and survival, and their habitat in the Banff–Bow Valley area. For instance, until improved garbage management systems were available in 1981, habituated bears (human-food addicts) frequently were relocated or destroyed. Although tourists feed bears less frequently than they did 20 years ago, finding finances and workers to deal effectively with habituated wildlife remains a problem.

Another example of human development impacts on wildlife is that until recently, the policy of fire suppression to protect visitors and property in the park reduced the amount of feeding habitat for grizzly bears. The species remains slow to recover because mortality rates for female bears remain high (females do not breed until they are between 4 and 8 years old, and average 0.5 cubs per year after that). Also, there is concern that the grizzly bear population on the east slopes of the Rocky Mountains could become genetically inbred and isolated from other subpopulations farther south as mate selection and other biological necessities are constrained by human barriers to bear movement.

In addition to the relatively recent developmental pressures being put on bears in the Banff–Bow Valley area, grizzlies were extirpated from the Prairies near the turn of the century. Current population estimates for Alberta suggest there are between 500 and 800 grizzlies in the province; the provincial goal is to reach 1000. Even though grizzly bears are identified as a vulnerable species in the province, and are considered to be at risk of becoming endangered, the Alberta Fish and Wildlife Department allows 150 individuals to obtain hunting licences for the annual Alberta grizzly bear hunt (Lunman, 1997). In 1996, 18 grizzlies were harvested in this sport or trophy hunt (it is illegal to sell bear parts, such as gall bladders or paws). Even though some parties support this hunt, public concern has raised questions about the wisdom of continuing it.

Harmonizing human developments with wild species' habitat needs requires people to realize that some of their attitudes and actions are directly detrimental to the long-term survival of grizzly bears and other wild species. If we can't make room for the grizzly bear in our national parks and surrounding lands, then where can the wilderness that sustains the grizzly find protection? If wild places cannot find protection, then biodiversity—and humans, too—clearly are threatened.

SOURCES: Banff–Bow Valley Study. (1996). *Banff–Bow Valley: At the crossroads. Technical Report of the Banff–Bow Valley Task Force* (R. Page, S. Bayley, J. D. Cook, J. Green & J.R.B. Ritchie). Ottawa.

Canadian Parks and Wilderness Society (CPAWS). (1997). *The Bow Valley: A very special place.* Calgary: CPAWS.

Lunman, L. (1997, March 28). Province defends grizzly bear hunt. *Calgary Herald*, p. B3.

Marty, S. (1997). Homeless on the range: Grizzlies struggle for elbow room and survival in Banff National Park. *Canadian Geographic*, 117(1), pp. 28–39.

CHAPTER 12:
WILD SPECIES AND NATURAL SPACES

399

As a place where one can view wild animals close up, Banff National Park has become a favourite vacation destination for Canadian and international visitors alike. However, the pressure on the transportation network that brings about five million visitors to Banff annually is increasing, as are collisions and congestion on the highway. To cope with the expected increase in visitors and the anticipated 3 to 4 percent annual increase in traffic on the Trans-Canada Highway through 2015, a decision was made to extend the twinned (expanded from two to four lanes) portion of the highway.

The Trans-Canada Highway has serious effects on wildlife populations in the park: not only does the highway fragment habitat and act as a barrier to natural movements in the Bow Valley, it also is a significant factor in wildlife mortality. About half of the reported wildlife deaths in the park can be attributed to highways—statistical records confirm that known wildlife losses are in the thousands for several species. This is ironic, given the park's role as a core refuge for wildlife protection.

Upgrading and twinning of the Trans-Canada Highway in Banff National Park began in 1980. To date, 45 kilometres have been twinned; the next 18-kilometre section was scheduled for completion in late 1997. Wildlife exclusion fencing was erected to keep animals off the highway right of way, as records showed that fencing the Trans-Canada Highway reduced ungulate (principally elk) mortality by 96 percent. Bears, however, infrequently crossed the divided highway to reach other portions of their fragmented habitat, and the effectiveness of the highway crossing structures for bears and other species was questionable.

The latest section of the highway to be twinned incorporates two experimental overpasses to enable wildlife to cross the highway. Costing over $2 million each, these 50-metre-wide overpasses are based on successful European overpasses.

A wildlife overpass under construction (before landscaping).

Within terrain limitations, they are constructed along known wildlife corridors and will be blended into the landscape using ground cover, shrubs, and other vegetation selected for wildlife security. Whether bears will use these overpasses to cross the highway remains to be seen, but if the overpasses are successful, two more will be considered.

Another transportation corridor passing through Banff National Park is the Canadian Pacific Railway line and right of way. The railway, too, is a source of considerable wildlife mortality, although little research has been done on railway impacts on wildlife populations. At a 1997 "Roads, Rails and Environment Workshop" in Revelstoke, British Columbia, a locomotive engineer presented some observations about train-killed wildlife on the main line between Field and Revelstoke, British Columbia. The collected statistics indicated that trains killed two species of birds (bald eagle and great horned owl) and 12 species of mammals, including black bear, cougar, beaver, bighorn sheep, elk, wolf, and wolverine. Numerous other small mammals and birds were killed also.

It appears that birds are attracted to the railway track to feed on the mice that are eating the various grains that spill from passing grain trains. Other wildlife come to the tracks to feed on the carcasses of large animals killed by trains (carcasses are not removed as they are along the Trans-Canada Highway and in national parks). For example, the engineer observed that all bald eagles and almost all coyotes and wolves were killed near carcasses. Other factors such as snow depth, wildlife using the railway right of way as a travel corridor because it is plowed in winter, and the type of seed with which cleared slopes and right of ways are planted (such as clover and other grasses—nutrient-rich food sources that attract bears) contribute to wildlife kills by trains. Changing some of the current management strategies, such as removing train-killed animals from the railway right of way, would help reduce the number of wildlife killed.

An example of a wildlife underpass.

SOURCES: Clevenger, A. (1997). Highway effects on wildlife in Banff National Park. *Research Links,* 5(1), pp. 1, 6.

Wells, P. (1997). *Wildlife mortality on the Canadian Pacific Railway between Field and Revelstoke, British Columbia.* Paper presented at the Roads, Rails and Environment Workshop, April 9–10, Revelstoke, B.C.

TABLE 12-3

THE COMMITTEE ON THE STATUS OF ENDANGERED SPECIES IN CANADA (COSEWIC): STATUS DEFINITIONS (REVISED 1994)

Status Category		Definition
V	vulnerable	• a species of special concern because of characteristics that make it particularly sensitive to human activities or natural events
T	threatened	• a species likely to become endangered if limiting factors are not reversed
E	endangered	• a species facing imminent extirpation or extinction
XT	extirpated	• a species no longer existing in the wild in Canada, but occurring elsewhere
X	extinct	• a species that no longer exists
NAR	not at risk	• a species that has been evaluated and found to be not at risk
I	indeterminate	• a species for which there is insufficient scientific information to support status designation

SOURCE: Committee on the Status of Endangered Species in Canada (COSEWIC). http://blizzard.cc.mcgill.ca/Redpath/cosewic.htm

TABLE 12-4

THE COMMITTEE ON THE STATUS OF ENDANGERED SPECIES IN CANADA (COSEWIC): SUMMARY OF SPECIES AT RISK IN CANADA, 1997

Group	Number of Species				
	Vulnerable	Threatened	Endangered	Extirpated	Extinct
terrestrial mammals	18	5	6	3	1
birds	21	7	16	2	3
fish and marine mammals	47	16	10	4	5
molluscs	–	1	–	–	1
vascular plants, mosses and lichens	35	38	30	2	–
reptiles and amphibians	9	3	4	1	–
lepidoptera	1	-	1	1	–

SOURCE: Environment Canada. Canadian Wildlife Service. (1997a). *List of species at risk in Canada as designated by the Committee on the Status of Endangered Wildlife in Canada (COSEWIC), 1997.* http://www.ec.gc.ca/envcan/docs/endanger/table.html

very significant, the AEUB recommended to the National Energy Board (NEB) that Express Pipeline be granted approval to construct and operate a crude oil pipeline in the Sage Creek area. The NEB granted that approval. When the pipeline construction began in August 1996, one of the most extensive grasslands left in North America began to be fragmented.

Having opposed the approval of this pipeline proposal, the Alberta Wilderness Association (AWA) remains "very concerned about further fragmentation and loss of threatened grassland ecosystems and is very disappointed in the apparent rubber stamping that seems to occur in regulatory hearing processes" (Wallis et al., 1996, p. 4). As one of the "crown jewels of prairie biodiversity," the AWA believes that the failure of the National Energy Board and the Canadian Environmental Assessment Agency's hearing process to deny Express Pipeline's application and reroute the pipeline through less sensitive terrain "demonstrates clearly the need to have a legislated system of areas that are protected from industrial activity" (Wallis et al., 1996, p. 4).

Most biologists agree that the best way to protect species is to protect native habitats, that saving species starts with saving spaces for them. If, as Canadians, we value protected areas, ecosystem integrity, biodiversity, and sustainability, then habitat conservation must be a priority nationally, as well as locally. We need full understanding of the interrelationships between species and spaces. In the following section of this chapter, some of the responses to the need to conserve biodiversity for the future, globally and in Canada, are noted.

RESPONSES TO ENVIRONMENTAL IMPACTS AND CHANGE

There is broad international recognition that wild species, ecosystems, and natural spaces are under increasing pressure from a growing human population and a wide range of human activities. If, as predicted, as much as one-quarter of the world's species could be extinct within 40 years, our future options for food, fibre, and medicines could be compromised severely. This prospect lends additional credence to the need for protection and preservation of biological diversity, and of the quality and quantity of suitable habitat, as vital international goals. Accordingly, numerous international agencies, national governments, and other parties have instituted treaties, policies, strategies, legislation, and programs in response to the need to protect biodiversity.

INTERNATIONAL CALLS TO ACTION

Since 1980, a series of important documents have influenced international thinking about and responses to the issues of conservation of biodiversity and sustainable use of biological and other resources. Five of these documents are the following: *World Conservation Strategy* (1980); *Our Common Future* (1987); *Caring for the Earth* (1991); *Global Biodiversity Strategy* (1992); and *Agenda 21* (1992). The Canadian government has been influenced by these documents, too, and our national efforts to conserve biodiversity involve international treaties, *in situ* conservation, *ex situ* conservation, sustainable use policies, and improvement in understanding of biodiversity. Each of these approaches is considered briefly in the sections that follow.

International Treaties

The World Conservation Monitoring Centre (WCMC), located in Cambridge, England, is an international centre of excellence in the location and management of information on conservation and sustainable use of the world's living resources (World Conservation Monitoring Centre,

1997). Of the more than 80 multilateral treaties the WCMC lists relating to conservation and management of biodiversity, Canada is involved in about 20 treaties, including 9 out of 10 global conventions. These 9 international treaties are specified and their objectives noted briefly in Table 12–5. (The URL for the WCMC Web site is listed in the Additional Information Sources section of this chapter.)

The 1992 United Nations Convention on Biological Diversity is the basis for much of the current international action on biodiversity. The objectives of the convention are to conserve biological diversity; to attain sustainable use of ecosystems, species, and genetic material; and to ensure the fair and equitable sharing of benefits arising from genetic resources.

As a leading proponent of the Convention on Biological Diversity, Canada (like all the other signatories) was responsible for developing a national strategy for the conservation and sustainable use of biological resources. The outcome—the Canadian Biodiversity Strategy—was derived by a working group comprising federal, provincial, territorial, and nongovernmental representatives.

The working group identified five strategic goals for the Canadian Biodiversity Strategy: to conserve biodiversity and use biological resources in a sustainable manner; to improve Canada's understanding of ecosystems and increase our resource management capacity; to promote public understanding of the need to conserve biodiversity and use biological resources in a sustainable manner; to maintain or develop incentives and legislation that support these goals; and to work with other countries to achieve the objectives of the convention (Government of Canada, 1996). The Canadian Biodiversity Information Network (CBIN) (see the CBIN Web site listed in the Additional Information Sources section of this chapter), provides support for the Convention on Biological Diversity and *Agenda 21*.

Another important international treaty that deals with protection of wild species is the Convention on Interna-

Bears killed illegally to satisfy specific market are confiscated by authorities.

TABLE 12-5
CANADA'S PARTICIPATION IN SELECTED GLOBAL TREATIES THAT HELP PROTECT BIODIVERISITY

Global Treaty	Treaty Objectives
International Plant Protection Convention (Rome), 1951	• to maintain and increase international cooperation in controlling pests and diseases of plants and plant products; to prevent introduction and spread of these pests and diseases across national boundaries
Convention on Fishing and Conservation of the Living Resources of the High Seas (Geneva), 1958	• to improve conservation of the living resources of the high seas and prevent overexploitation
Convention on the High Seas (Geneva), 1958	• to codify the rules of international law relating to the high seas
Convention on Wetlands of International Importance Especially as Waterfowl Habitat (Ramsar), 1971	• to stem the progressive encroachment on and loss of wetlands; to recognize ecological functions of wetlands and their economic, cultural, scientific, and recreational value
Convention Concerning the Protection of the World Cultural and Natural Heritage (Paris), 1972	• to establish an effective system of collective protection of cultural and natural heritage of outstanding universal value, organized on a permanent basis and in accordance with modern scientific methods
Convention on International Trade in Endangered Species of Wild Fauna and Flora (Washington), 1973	• to protect, via import/export controls, certain endangered species from overexploitation
United Nations Convention on the Law of the Sea (Montego Bay), 1983	• to set up a comprehensive new legal regime for the sea and oceans as far as environmental provisions are concerned; to establish material rules concerning environmental standards as well as enforcement provisions dealing with pollution of the marine environment
International Tropical Timber Agreement (Geneva), 1983	• to provide an effective framework for cooperation and consultation between countries producing and consuming tropical timber; to promote the expansion and diversification of international trade in tropical timber; to improve structural conditions in the tropical timber market; to promote research and development; to promote sustainable utilization and conservation of tropical forests and their genetic resources; to maintain the ecological balance in regions concerned
United Nations Convention on Biological Diversity (Rio de Janeiro), 1992	• to conserve biological diversity, the sustainable use of its components, and the fair and equitable sharing of the benefits arising out of the utilization of genetic resources, including, by appropriate access to genetic resources and by appropriate transfer of relevant technologies, taking into account all rights over those resources and technologies, and by appropriate funding

SOURCE: Government of Canada. (1996). *The state of Canada's enviroment—1996*. Ottawa: Supply and Services Canada. Table 14.7.

tional Trade in Endangered Species of Wild Fauna and Flora (CITES). As signatories to CITES, Canadian and international law enforcement agents are able to target poaching, smuggling, and illegal trade in wildlife species, their parts, and derivatives. For instance, the Canadian Wildlife Service is responsible for implementing CITES in Canada against poachers who illegally kill bears to obtain gall bladders and paws for sale to international markets.

Enforcement of CITES internationally is necessary to eliminate trade in illegally obtained animals and plants. CITES enforcement is essential to reduce the pressure of poaching and smuggling of rhino horn that has reduced the world's rhinoceros population by close to 85 percent since 1970. The black rhino has been hardest hit; its numbers dropped from at least 65 000 to fewer than 4000 in only 20 years.

A new Canadian federal law proclaimed in 1996, the Wild Animal and Plant Protection and Regulation of International and Interprovincial Trade Act (WAPPRIITA) protects Canadian and foreign species from illegal trade. It also protects Canadian ecosystems against the introduction of designated harmful species (Environment Canada, 1996).

In Situ *Conservation*

In situ conservation is the conservation of ecosystems and the maintenance and recovery of viable populations of species in their typical surroundings. Three main methods are associated with in situ conservation: protection of spaces that are large enough to support ecosystem processes and species diversity; re-creation of those spaces through species recovery programs; and sustainable use of biological resources outside of protected areas.

Protected Areas Protected areas are known by a number of names including ecological areas, wildlife management areas, parks, and conservation areas. Each type of protected area has a different set of management objectives ranging from almost complete protection of biotic and abiotic components from human disturbance, to protection that is offered only to selected ecosystem components (such as wildlife or soils). Conserving biodiversity through the use of protected areas involves careful management of human activities and prohibition of activities that could harm ecological processes or ecosystem integrity.

The World Conservation Union (IUCN, in keeping with the organization's *original* mane) is the only global organization that unites nations, government agencies, and NGOs in conserving the integrity and diversity of nature. The IUCN has categorized protected areas into six types (I to VI). Table 12–6 identifies these categories, their defining characteristics, and the management goals or practices associated with each type. Comparison of various types of protected areas found in Canada with those found in other countries shows slightly more protected areas in Canada are in IUCN classes IV to VI than in categories I to III which, involve the highest level of protection. This means the Canadian system affords a slightly lower level of biodiversity protection than the systems of other nations.

Most of Canada's protected areas traditionally have been held in public ownership. Provincial parks and our national park system (Figure 12–3) constitute the largest portion of protected land in Canada. NGOs, however, have made important contributions to conserving biodiversity.

The success of the North American Waterfowl Management Plan in protecting thousands of hectares of productive wetland ecosystems has been generated partly through incentives to private landowners to conserve wetlands for wildlife, and partly by the stewardship actions of partner NGOs such as Ducks Unlimited. By 1993 NGOs owned or managed over one million hectares of conservation lands in relation to Canadian biodiversity efforts.

Growth in protected areas is one measure of the commitment to protect ecosystems. Since about the mid-1970s, protected lands have more than doubled in area until, in 1994, about 8 percent of Canada, or almost 800 000 square kilometres, was protected area. Only about half that land will not be subject to major resource extraction activities, however, as only about half the area is protected under designations that correspond roughly to IUCN categories I to III (Government of Canada, 1996). Proportions of different types of federally and provincially protected areas, and other conservation areas, are shown in Figure 12–4.

In November 1992, federal, provincial, and territorial ministers responsible for environment, parks, and wildlife issued a joint commitment that they would attempt to complete Canada's network of protected areas for land-based natural regions by the year 2000. By 1995, 146 of Canada's 217 terrestrial ecoregions were protected to some degree by some form of legislation. More than 12 percent of 33 of these regions was protected at a high level (by IUCN categories I to III); however, 71 ecoregions had received no protection (Table 12–7).

Part of the impetus for this push to protect areas representing all of Canada's natural regions came from the 1989 Canadian Wilderness Charter (Box 12–4). Part of the Endangered Spaces Campaign of World Wildlife Fund Canada, the Canadian Wilderness Charter has a broad base of support—by the winter of 1995, more than 550 000 individuals had signed the charter. Following the recommendation in *Our Common Future,* the charter specified that at least 12 percent of Canadian lands and waters should be protected (thus the importance of the 12 percent figure in Table 12–7). (The Endangered Spaces Campaign is considered in more detail in a later section of this chapter.)

Canada's best-represented areas are ecoregions of the montane, boreal, and Arctic cordillera ecozones, while major gaps in ecosystem representation occur in the southern prairies, most of the ecoregions of the southern Arctic and the three taiga ecozones, as well as the most densely populated regions of Ontario and Quebec. It is difficult to protect underrepresented ecosystems in southern Canada because they frequently have been modified highly through human settlement and economic activities, and because they usually are owned privately (Government of Canada, 1996). The role of private stewardship is emphasized in such settings.

IUCN Category	Defining Characteristics	Management Goals or Practices	Canadian Example
I. Natural reserve or wilderness area			
a. Nature reserve	• areas possessing some outstanding or representative ecosystems, geological or physiographic features, or species	• scientific research or ecological monitoring primarily	Oak Mountain Ecological Reserve (New Brunswick)
b. Wilderness area	• large areas, unmodified or slightly modified, retaining their natural character and influence, without permanent or significant habitation	• preservation of natural conditions	Bay du Nord Wilderness Area (Newfoundland)
II. National park (or equivalent)	• areas designated to sustain the integrity of one or more ecosystems, exclude exploitation or intensive occupation, and provide a foundation for scientific, educational, recreational, and visitor opportunities, all of which must be ecologically and culturally compatible	• ecosystem protection and recreation	Banff National Park (Alberta)
III. Natural monument	• areas containing one or more specific natural or cultural features of outstanding or unique value because of inherent rarity, representation of aesthetic qualities, or cultural significance	• protection of specific outstanding natural features, provision of opportunities for research and education, and prevention of exploitation or occupation	Parrsboro Fossil Cliffs (Nova Scotia)
IV. Habitat/species management areas	• areas important for ensuring the maintenance of habitats or for meeting the requirements of certain species	• securement and maintenance of habitat conditions necessary to protect species and ecosystem features where these require human manipulation for optimum management	Watshishou Migratory Bird Sanctuary (Quebec)
V. Protected landscape or seascape	• areas where interactions of people and nature have produced a distinct character with significant cultural or ecological value and often with high biodiversity	• conservation, education, recreation, and provision of natural products aimed at safeguarding the integrity of harmonious interactions of nature and culture	Algonquin Provincial Park (Ontario)
VI. Managed resource and protected areas	• predominantly natural ares that are large enough to absorb sustainable resource uses without harming long-term maintenance of biodiversity	• long-term protection and maintenance of biodiversity and other natural values and the promotion of sound management practices for sustainable production purposes	Battle Creek Community Pasture (Saskatchewan)

SOURCE: Government of Canada. (1996). *The state of Canada's environment—1996.* Ottawa: Supply and Services Canada. Box 14.4.

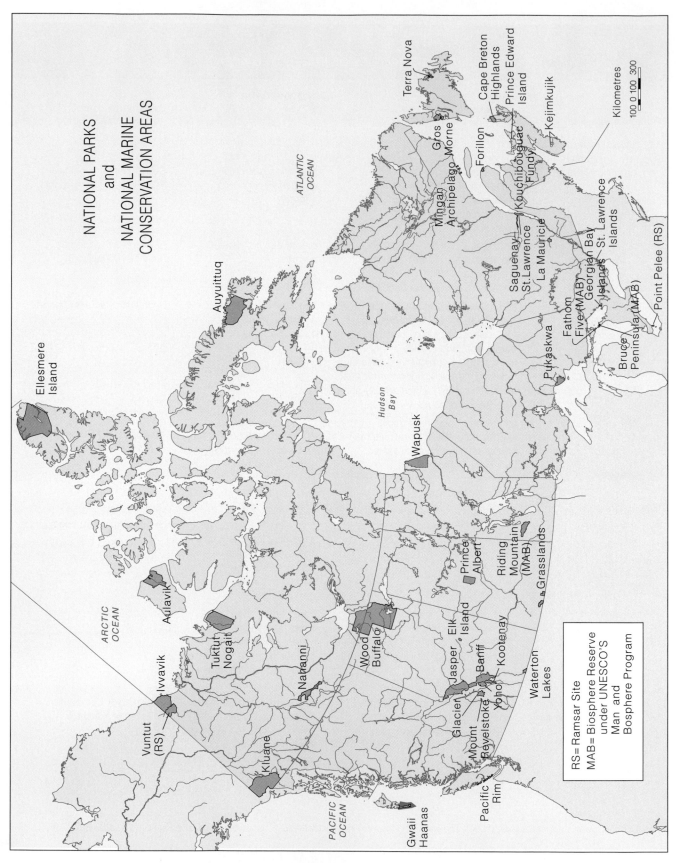

Figure 12–3
Canada's national park system

SOURCE: Reprinted courtesy of Department of Canadian Heritage, Parks Canada.

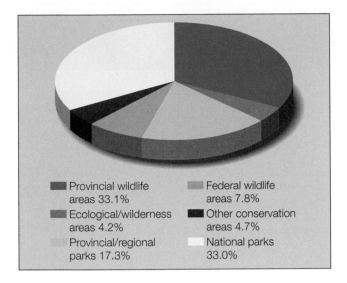

Figure 12–4
Proportion of federal, provincial, and other protected areas in Canada

- Provincial wildlife areas 33.1%
- Federal wildlife areas 7.8%
- Ecological/wilderness areas 4.2%
- Other conservation areas 4.7%
- Provincial/regional parks 17.3%
- National parks 33.0%

SOURCE: Government of Canada. (1996). *The state of Canada's environment—1996.* Ottawa. Figure 14.8.

Although protection of marine ecosystems is as important as protection of terrestrial ecosystems, Canada has lagged behind some other developed nations in achieving the desired protection. Recent efforts have been directed toward establishment of marine conservation areas: currently there are three National Marine Conservation Areas (NMCA). One is the Gwaii Haanas NMCA off the Queen Charlotte Islands in British Columbia, and a second is Fathom Five National Marine Park located in Georgian Bay, Ontario. At the confluence of the Saguenay and St. Lawrence rivers, another marine park has been established to protect whales, marine mammals, and endemic plant species. In

order that commercial fishing may continue, conservation areas are designed to include sustainable use zones.

The Canada Oceans Act also provides for establishment of marine protected areas (see Chapter 8). In addition to the federal marine protection efforts, British Columbia has established ecological reserves in marine areas to protect unique and representative nearshore resources from degradation and exploitation. The province also will assist restoration of marine ecosystems.

Some of Canada's protected areas are designated under the terms of international treaties or agreements. The Ramsar Convention (see Box 7–6) protects wetlands of international importance within Canada, and World Heritage Sites (including areas of particular scientific or aesthetic value as well as the habitats of endangered species) are designated under the Convention Concerning the Protection of World Cultural and Natural Heritage. Ramsar and World Heritage sites may be designated without being protected formally (this helps identify candidate sites for formal protection in the future). In 1997, there were 12 World Heritage Sites in Canada, 34 Ramsar sites, and 6 Canadian Biosphere Reserves (Figure 12–5).

Biosphere Reserves are established under the United Nations Educational, Scientific and Cultural Organization's (UNESCO) Man and the Biosphere (MAB) Programme. These reserves have a wide range of objectives in addition to conservation, including scientific research, training, monitoring, and demonstration. Typically, Biosphere Reserves consist of a strictly protected core area surrounded by a buffer for control of intrusive activities. Surrounding the core and buffer is a large "zone of cooperation" where a wide range of human activities occurs and where ecological restoration and sustainable resource use can be demonstrated. Biosphere Reserves increasingly are seen as one type of model area for conservation and sustainability (Government of Canada, 1996).

TABLE 12–7
STATUS OF CANADIAN ECOREGION PROTECTION BASED ON AMOUNT OF PROTECTED AREA, 1995

% of Ecoregion Protected by IUCN Categories I to III	Number of Ecoregions	% of Canada	% of Ecoregion Protected by IUCN Categories IV to VI	Number of Ecoregions	% of Canada
0	87	40	0	71	33
>0–3	49	22	>0–3	51	23
>3–6	23	11	>3–6	28	13
>6–9	16	7	>6–9	19	9
>9–12	9	5	>9–12	10	5
>12	33	15	>12	38	17
Total	217	100	Total	217	100

SOURCE: Government of Canada. (1996). *The state of Canada's environment—1996.* Ottawa. Figure 14.8.

BOX 12-4
CANADIAN WILDERNESS CHARTER

1. Whereas humankind is but one of millions of species sharing planet Earth and whereas the future of the Earth is severely threatened by the activities of this single species,
2. Whereas our planet has already lost much of its former wilderness character, thereby endangering many species and ecosystems,
3. Whereas Canadians still have the opportunity to complete a network of protected areas representing the biological diversity of our country,
4. Whereas Canada's remaining wild places, be they land or water, merit protection for their inherent value,
5. Whereas the protection of wilderness also meets an intrinsic human need for spiritual rekindling and artistic inspiration,
6. Whereas Canada's once vast wilderness has deeply shaped the national identity and continues to profoundly influence how we view ourselves as Canadians,
7. Whereas Canada's aboriginal peoples hold deep and direct ties to wilderness areas throughout Canada and seek to maintain options for traditional wilderness use,
8. Whereas protected areas can serve a variety of purposes including:
   a) preserving a genetic reservoir of wild plants and animals for future use and appreciation by citizens of Canada and the world,
   b) producing economic benefits from environmentally sensitive tourism,
   c) offering opportunities for research and environmental education,
9. Whereas the opportunity to complete a national network of protected areas must be grasped and acted upon during the next ten years, or be lost,

We the undersigned agree and urge:

1. That governments, industries, environmental groups and individual Canadians commit themselves to a national effort to establish at least one representative protected area in each of the natural regions of Canada by the year 2000,
2. That the total area thereby protected comprise at least 12 percent of the lands and waters of Canada as recommended in the World Commission on Environment and Development's report *Our Common Future,*
3. That public and private agencies at international, national, provincial, territorial and local levels rigorously monitor progress toward meeting these goals in Canada and ensure that they are fully achieved, and
4. That federal, provincial and territorial government conservation agencies on behalf of all Canadians develop action plans by 1990 for achieving these goals by the year 2000.

SOURCE: Hummel, M. (1989). *Endangered spaces: The future for Canada's wilderness.* Toronto: Key Porter Books, p. 275. Reprinted with permission.

Restoration and Rehabilitation There is not much point in expending time, energy, and finances on species recovery or restoration if the ecosystem that is meant to support them is not rehabilitated also. This is why Canada reviews the status of certain classes of native flora and fauna under COSEWIC. A complementary program, Recovery of Nationally Endangered Wildlife (RENEW), develops recovery plans for more than 30 terrestrial vertebrate species that have been designated by COSEWIC as extirpated, endangered, or threatened. RENEW and similar programs recognize the need to, but do not have the knowledge base to respond effectively to, threats to plants, invertebrates, fungi, and algae, even if many of these species perform more vital ecological functions than the vertebrates.

Encouraging results have been attained from several species protection or reintroduction programs. Sea otters have been reintroduced to Vancouver Island's west coast kelp forests; peregrine falcons have been restored to territories from which they had been extirpated; the ferruginous hawk has been downlisted from threatened to vulnerable, and the wood bison has been downlisted from

endangered to threatened. The American white pelican and the prairie long-tailed weasel, two prairie species that had been listed as threatened, are among those that have been removed from the COSEWIC list.

Some efforts to reintroduce Canada's Pacific sea otters have been successful.

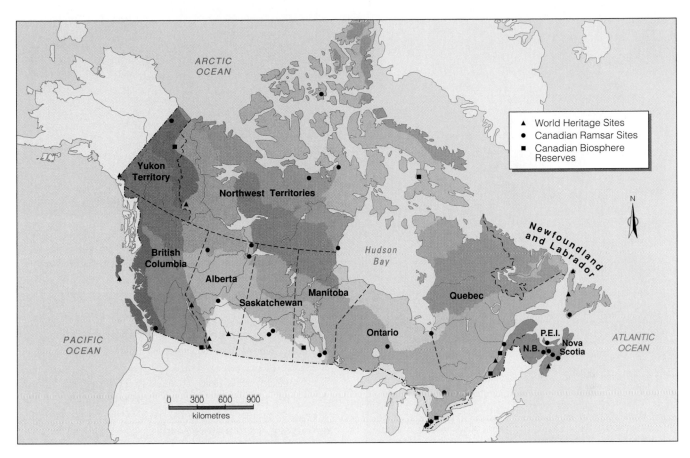

Figure 12–5

Distribution of internationally designated protected areas within Canada

SOURCE: Adapted from Government of Canada. (1996). *The state of Canada's environment—1996.* Ottawa. Figure 14.10.

Ex Situ *Conservation*

Ex situ conservation of biodiversity is the conservation of species or genetic materials under artificial conditions, away from the ecosystems to which they belong. As the supply of natural habitats has declined, maintaining captive populations (or cultivated populations in the case of plants) has been accepted as one of the few ways that survival of increasing numbers of species can be ensured until the long-term goal of restoring them to the wild (in at least some of their original ranges) is attained.

Among the advantages of *ex situ* facilities such as zoos, aquariums, aviaries, and botanical gardens are opportunities for scientific study as well as public education opportunities about species on display. In turn, this can help build broader public support (and provide fundraising opportunities) for species conservation *in situ.* The majority of conservation biology opinion, however, indicates that captive breeding programs are not the answer to conservation needs.

There are many reasons why not, including the fact that *ex situ* protection is expensive, and, as natural habitats continue to disappear, too many species require

housing. Within *ex situ* facilities, animals often become domesticated and lose their wild behaviours. Lack of natural selection of mates is an issue that also may contribute to inbreeding problems such as depression. Another loss associated with *ex situ* facilities is the inability to pass on to captive-born young their hunting strategies or migration routes.

Plants As of 1995, Canada had about 50 zoos, 15 aquariums, and 15 aviaries; these facilities hold hundreds of species of mammals, birds, reptiles, fish, and invertebrates. About 800 of the world's 1500 botanical gardens are committed to conserving rare, endemic, or other threatened plant species. Canada's 60 botanical gardens contain close to 40 000 plant species native to Canada and from around the world, including at least 11 endangered, rare, or vulnerable native plant species. In 1995, no plants were being propagated specifically for reintroduction.

Seed banks can be important *ex situ* facilities for conservation of plant species and genetic diversity. Many of the world's 528 seed bank facilities are coordinated through the International Board for Plant Genetic

Captive breeding programs in zoos help conserve genetic diversity but are not a substitute for natural, functioning ecosystems. The black-footed ferret (above) is being re-introduced to North American grasslands.

Rare species, such as the Seychelles coco-de-mer palm tree, may be protected in ecological reserves.

Resources. Both Agriculture and Agri-Food Canada, and the Canadian Forest Service, maintain seed stocks for use in plant breeding or in sustainable use programs. The Heritage Seed Program is a nongovernmental initiative that maintains a large variety of vegetable species, and "Seedy Saturday" (a concept that began in Vancouver and since has spread throughout British Columbia, Alberta, and recently Ontario) promotes springtime sharing of seeds and seed stories among backyard gardeners, farmers, and others. This is an informal but effective way to preserve old varieties of garden vegetables and family farm livestock (Penstone, 1997).

Animals More than 870 zoos and aquariums worldwide, housing over one million vertebrate specimens, are involved in global efforts to preserve both wild and native animal diversity *ex situ.* The focus in many of these institutions is no longer on entertainment but on provision of living conditions that simulate various species' natural habitats accurately enough to promote breeding. This is seen to be particularly important for species whose numbers in the wild are so low that survival depends on cap-

tive breeding programs to build up population numbers to the point where species can be returned to their native ecosystems.

Canadian zoos hold at least 12 endangered, threatened, or vulnerable animal species, including the whooping crane, ferruginous hawk, eastern massasauga rattlesnake, spotted turtle, grizzly bear, and polar bear. Canadian captive breeding programs have provided swift foxes and peregrine falcons for reintroduction programs (Government of Canada, 1996; Henry, 1994). Some Canadian zoos participate in international breeding programs of non-Canadian species for reintroduction to native ecosystems in other countries. Not all species can be propagated successfully in captivity, however.

At the University of Alberta, a poultry conservation program to conserve the genetic diversity of six breeds of chickens that contributed to our past or present meat and egg stocks has been ongoing since 1992. This program is a bit like an insurance policy; it is a conscious effort to sustain the genetic variability of the old-fashioned birds against the danger that today's commercially bred chickens are becoming more genetically uniform and may develop traits that will limit their viability (Robinson, 1997).

In spite of some benefits obtained through *ex situ* protection, it is not sufficient merely to save seeds, extract and freeze sperm, and protect some species in "stationary arks." Rather, we need to save wild species and natural ecosystems in intact, natural spaces if we hope to protect biodiversity and sustainability on this planet.

Sustainable Use of Biological Resources

Growing human populations and increases in resource consumption continue to intensify the pressures on biodiversity, *in situ* and *ex situ* conservation efforts notwithstanding. Given the consensus that current and projected consumption levels are unsustainable (World Commission on Environment and Development, 1987), the best way to satisfy basic human economic needs without compromising biodiversity is the rigorous adoption of sustainability policies in all resource sectors.

In Canada, this means that agriculture, forestry, and fisheries are of particular significance in developing sustainable use practices that will conserve genetic resources. In forestry, for instance, conserving the natural diversity of trees (and associated wildlife) not only requires better knowledge of forest ecosystems and species, but also requires less aggressive and more selective harvesting as well as protection of old-growth forests.

Improving Understanding of Biodiversity

If we are to be successful in conserving biodiversity and using biological resources sustainably, adopting ecological management principles is necessary. Ecological management directs human activities so that the biotic and abiotic components of ecosystems, and the processes that sustain them, continue. To manage effectively, it is necessary to have adequate understanding of ecosystems, species, and human impacts on them; unfortunately, the current state of this knowledge is inadequate. This means there needs to be a strong commitment to research.

Research needs include reliable baseline data, indicators for conserving biodiversity, standardized protocols for conducting surveys and inventories, and indicators of biodiversity change (for trend prediction). Gap analysis is a research tool used to evaluate and complete representative protected areas networks (see Rowe, Kavanagh & Iacobelli, 1995). Using ground surveys, inventories, satellite imagery, and Geographic Information System (GIS) technology, gap analysis identifies missing dimensions in the representation of biodiversity. Hot spot analysis is a related tool that locates areas of species or endemic richness that should have priority for protection, sustainable use, or new biotechnologies. Biodiversity prospecting, the search for wild species that may yield new medicines or add vigour to food crops, provides economic reasons for conservation (rather than consumption) becoming the more effective way of dealing with nature and natural areas (Government of Canada, 1996).

Efforts to monitor the status of biodiversity also are ongoing. The federal Ecological Monitoring and Assessment Network (EMAN) program, for example, monitors a wide variety of ecosystem and species parameters to assess the interactions and sustainability of regional ecosystems. In addition to the research needs noted above, it is necessary to develop "an energetic program of public education" that promotes awareness of biodiversity and develops strategies to reduce resource consumption levels.

CANADIAN LAW, POLICY, AND PRACTICE

With the growth of international concern and action relating to biodiversity issues (species and spaces), and Canada's active participation in global efforts to preserve biodiversity, the national response has involved strengthening and augmenting existing laws, policies, and practices as well as instituting new partnerships. Table 12–8 highlights selected examples of Canada's approach to protecting biodiversity. To illustrate Canadian efforts to protect Canadian species and spaces, the following sections comment briefly on the proposed Endangered Species Protection Act and the Endangered Spaces Campaign of World Wildlife Fund Canada.

TABLE 12-8 PROTECTING BIODIVERSITY IN CANADA: EXAMPLES OF POLICIES, STRATEGIES, AND LEGISLATION	
National/ Regional	Canadian Biodiversity Strategy (proposed) Canada Endangered Species Protection Act
	Federal Policy on Wetland Conservation
	Canadian Environmental Protection Act
	National Accord for the Protection of Species at Risk
	Committee on the Status of Endangered Wildlife in Canada
	North American Waterfowl Management Plan
Wildlife	RENEW (Committee on the Recovery of Nationally Endangered Wildlife)
	Wildlife Policy for Canada
	Canada Wildlife Act
	CITES (Convention on International Trade in Endangered Species of Wild Fauna and Flora)
	WAPPRIITA (Wild Animal and Plant Protection and Regulation of International and Interprovincial Trade Act)
	Endangered Species Recovery Fund
Birds	Migratory Birds Convention Act
Plants	Canada Forest Accord
	National Forest Strategy
	Agricultural Weed Biocontrol Program

Protecting Canadian Species

Wildlife management in Canada is "a complex, almost precarious system of shared responsibilities between the federal government and the provinces and territories" (Protecting Canadian Species, 1996). The legislative basis of shared responsibility places migratory birds, fish, and marine mammals within federal jurisdiction; the majority of wildlife protection responsibilities lie with the provincial and territorial governments. In spite of this, interjurisdictional cooperation—such as is seen in COSEWIC—and informal agreements have been a hallmark of wild species protection in Canada.

As useful as COSEWIC's designations of species at risk are in raising both public awareness and the political will to protect wildlife, the designations are less effective than they might be simply because they have no legal status. The proposed Canada Endangered Species Protection Act, tabled in Parliament on October 31, 1996, would have been the first federal legislation to protect endangered species. The purposes of the act were to "prevent wildlife species from being extirpated or becoming extinct, and to provide for the recovery of wildlife species that are extirpated, endangered, or threatened as a result of human activity" (Environment Canada, 1997c).

Unfortunately, however, before royal assent could be obtained in the spring of 1997, an election was called, Parliament was dissolved, and the legislation was not enacted. Nevertheless, a few comments about provisions of this act are in order.

The proposed Endangered Species Protection Act recognized COSEWIC as a source of independent advice on the status of nationally imperilled species, and supported the listing of species at risk according to COSEWIC's current categories. Besides designating species at risk, COSEWIC was assigned additional functions that legitimized its role in species protection. However, the Canadian Wildlife Federation had criticized the proposed act for two main reasons: the act did not address adequately the greatest threat to wildlife—habitat loss; and the act reflected traditional thinking in its species-by-species approach, rather than adopting an ecosystem approach to protection (Canadian Wildlife Federation, 1997c). Habitat conservation plans would help in the recovery of species at risk and prevent other species from becoming endangered in the first place. Whether these issues will be addressed in the subsequent sitting of Parliament remains to be seen.

Protecting Canadian Spaces

Protecting our "natural capital" is essential if future generations of Canadians are to experience a healthy and prosperous environment. This is why the World Wildlife Fund Canada's Endangered Spaces Campaign, based on the Canadian Wilderness Charter (see Box 12–4), is pushing governments to complete the promised nation-wide system of protected areas (see Hummel, 1989). In this 10-year campaign, begun in 1989, conserving representative areas of the country's diverse lands and waters is a critical first step toward a sustainable future (Hackman, 1996).

Setting aside ecologically representative terrestrial and marine areas, whether they are in Ontario's hardwood forests or on Newfoundland's Grand Banks, means that these areas are to be free from activities likely to cause large-scale or long-term habitat disruption. Mining, logging, oil and gas drilling, hydroelectric developments, and bottom trawling and dragging would not be permitted. Instead, the benefits of wilderness would prevail.

Wilderness benefits which in general are inadequately considered during land use decisions, convincingly support the case for protection of representative spaces (sites). Wilderness-related activities, such as hiking, fishing, camping, and canoeing, put millions of dollars into regional economies. In British Columbia, for example, the parks system contributes about $400 million per year to the provincial gross domestic product, sustaining more than 9000 direct and indirect jobs over widely distributed communities and regions (Hackman, 1996). In Ontario, tourists spend $8 million annually in the region of the Bruce Peninsula National Park and Fathom Five Marine Park (Bayly & Ives, 1997).

Establishing parks and protected areas creates a growing number of jobs that can last indefinitely and help to diversify regional economies. In Alberta, for instance, a study for Alberta Environmental Protection found that parks and recreation created more than three times more jobs than the forestry sector (Engman, 1997). This is an important benefit given that jobs in forestry, mining, and other resource industries are being lost to mechanization and other factors (Hackman, 1996). Canada's wilderness areas, like tropical rain forests, contain genetic materials that may provide new opportunities for the pharmaceutical industry.

In the bigger picture, as global markets shift from traditional resource extraction to knowledge-based industries, ecosystems offer new opportunities for research, tourism, and sustainable economies. Canada's large share of the world's diminishing wilderness potentially gives us a competitive advantage in developing these business opportunities. Most Canadians understand this connection, too: a 1996 national survey by the Environics Research Group revealed that 86 percent of the respondents believed that a network of protected natural areas would make a major or moderate contribution to Canada's long-term economic health (cited in Hackman, 1996).

The Endangered Spaces Campaign of World Wildlife Fund Canada has a strong science base, rooted in concepts such as ecological integrity and ecosystem management. The healthy state, or integrity, of an ecosystem is one in which the ecosystem is complete and functions properly. To have integrity, an ecosystem must have all its native species, complete food webs, and naturally functioning ecological processes, and it must be able to persist over time. Ecosystem management is a holistic approach, recognizing that the well-being of parks and human communities alike depends on the ecological state of larger landscapes.

Leading conservation biologists, major corporations, and organizations such as the Canadian Council on Ecological Areas assisted in development of the scientific approach of the Endangered Spaces Campaign. "A core network of protected lands and waters will help maintain or restore native species in their natural patterns of distribution and abundance, and sustain natural processes. If complemented by sustainable use of the rest of our lands and waters, this network of protected areas will ensure that the full range of Canada's biodiversity is preserved" (Hackman, 1996, p. 14).

BOX 12-5
THE 1996/1997 ENDANGERED SPACES REPORT CARD

The Endangered Spaces Campaign has a specific measurable goal; to help conserve Canada's biological diversity by protecting a representative sample of each of the country's terrestrial and one-third of its marine natural regions by the year 2000, and to complete the marine protected areas system by 2010. Following are the "grades" received by federal, provincial, and territorial governments for 1996/97 (and 1995/96, for comparison purposes).

	Federal Grades	
	1996/97	1995/96
Terrestrial	A–	C
Marine-Pacific	C–	C
Marine-Arctic	D–	D–
Marine-Atlantic	D–	D+
Marine-Great Lakes	D	D

	Provincial and Territorial Grades	
	1996/97	1995/96
Alberta	D+	B
British Columbia	C	A
Manitoba	B+	D–
New Brunswick	F	F
Newfoundland	C–	D
Nova Scotia	C–	A
Northwest Territories	C–	D
Ontario	C–	F
Prince Edward Island	B	C+
Quebec	D–	C–
Saskatchewan	F	C
Yukon	C–	D

SOURCE: World Wildlife Fund Canada. (1997). Measuring progress in the Endangered Spaces Campaign. http://www.wwfcanada.org/spaces/x-004.html

---

Each year, to measure progress in the Endangered Spaces Campaign, World Wildlife Fund Canada grades the provincial, territorial, and federal governments on their progress toward completing the goal. The 1996/1997 Report Card shows the final grades assigned to each jurisdiction for their progress in establishing the protected areas system (Box 12–5). Not only does this simple measure capture year-to-year differences in provincial, territorial, and federal progress in setting aside protected areas, it also is a means for Canadians to compare performance across political jurisdictions over time. (In 1995, the Sierra Club of Canada used a similar report card approach to rate the federal, provincial, and territorial governments on their progress in keeping the commitments they made at the 1992 Earth Summit regarding climate change and protection of biodiversity.)

PARTNERSHIPS FOR THE FUTURE

Growing concern over wildlife and wild spaces issues has caused a broad range of groups—government agencies, private sector interests, NGOs, and individuals—to work together to preserve and protect wildlife and to sustain Canada's ecosystems. The involvement of this range of groups helps ensure that resources are used wisely and that efforts are directed to the best possible use.

The policies, strategies, and legislation identified in Table 12–8, as well as numerous provincial and territorial conservation and sustainability strategies, wetland and wildlife policies, forest management plans, and protected areas strategies, are evidence that cooperation and collaboration can provide positive outcomes for wildlife and wild spaces. The Canadian Biodiversity Strategy, Canada's first effort to implement the United Nations Convention on Biological Diversity, sets the stage for all jurisdictions in Canada to identify the actions required, individually as well as in partnership with others. The Canadian Biodiversity Strategy also establishes a comprehensive planning framework within which Canadians can participate in the effort to conserve biodiversity (Government of Canada, 1996).

While every province and territory in Canada has management policies, programs, and laws in place to protect wildlife, 291 species remained on COSEWIC's 1997 list of species at risk. In order to prevent any species from becoming extinct as a consequence of human activities, and to institute a harmonized national approach to conservation of species at risk, federal, provincial, and territorial governments have signed a National Accord for the Protection of Species at Risk in Canada.

An underlying precept of this approach is that all Canadians must share responsibility for the conservation of wildlife at risk. A second precept is that if it is to be effective and complete, a national endangered species framework must be able to address all nondomesticated living organisms native to Canada. RENEW (see Table 12–8) coordinates recovery programs for COSEWIC. Under RENEW's umbrella, between 1988 and 1995, 199 federal, provincial, and territorial government agencies and NGOs spent nearly $13 million on recovery programs for 34 terrestrial vertebrates. Whooping cranes, swift foxes, and piping plovers are among the species to have benefited from activities of RENEW partners (Environment Canada, 1996).

Canada and the United States have signed several agreements to improve the management of birds that migrate between the two countries, and to deal with questions of fairness in regulating waterfowl harvests among Alaskan and Canadian Aboriginal peoples. Recently, a Framework for Cooperation that will protect shared endangered species was signed by Canadian Environment Minister Marchi and U.S. Interior Secretary Babbitt. Probably the most well-recognized cooperative effort, the billion-dollar North American Waterfowl Management Plan (NAWMP) is the combined initiative of Canada, the United States, and Mexico. NAWMP is implemented through regionally based joint ventures that, in turn, involve federal, provincial, territorial, and state government agencies, NGOs such as Ducks Unlimited and Wildlife Habitat Canada, the private sector, and landowners all cooperating together. Regional habitat management in Canada is undertaken through the Prairie Habitat, the Eastern Habitat, and the Pacific Coast joint ventures. Initially conceived as a waterfowl plan, the NAWMP has expanded to include multispecies and biodiversity objectives.

The Canadian Coalition for Biodiversity, the Natural Heritage League, the Canadian Parks Partnership, Wildlife Habitat Canada, and the Canadian Parks and Wilderness Society (CPAWS) are among many citizen-based ENGO groups across Canada whose collaborative and cooperative efforts to preserve and protect wild species and spaces have made a difference at the national level. The current Yellowstone to Yukon Biodiversity Strategy project involving CPAWS, and the reintroduction of the swift fox to the southern Alberta and Saskatchewan prairie and the timber wolf to Montana, are examples of projects that exemplify the range of actions possible through various forms of cooperation and collaboration.

On the provincial scale, organizations such as the Federation of Ontario Naturalists and the Nature Trust of British Columbia demonstrate how coordination of focused energies of multiple groups can magnify the effectiveness of local biodiversity conservation efforts. For example, acting as a partner with The Nature Trust of British Columbia, the Pacific Estuary Conservation Program was able to purchase Englishman River Flats on the east coast of Vancouver Island in 1992. This partnership, and the cooperation of the provincial government, enabled protection of a key feeding and resting area along

The whooping crane is one species that has benefited from wildlife protection policies and strategies. It nests in Wood Buffalo National Park, in the Northwest Territories, and winters on the gulf coast of Texas.

British Columbia's coast for up to 30 000 brant (geese) that fly from Baja to Alaska and Russia. The Englishman River Estuary also is a wintering area for the trumpeter swan and other waterfowl; more than 110 bird species have been recorded in the estuary, which also provides essential rearing habitat for steelhead trout and salmon (Nature Trust of British Columbia, 1993).

Another illustration of the success that cooperation brings is the focus on alternative silviculture techniques to better integrate grizzly bear habitat requirements with timber harvesting in British Columbia. After a coastal valley bottom is logged, many of the plants that grizzlies feed on are among those that compete for growing space and sunlight with regenerating tree seedlings. Not only does this competition make it difficult to reestablish a new crop of commercial trees, it also can affect seriously the short- and long-term availability of grizzly forage (when grizzly food sources are treated with herbicides to reduce competition).

Grizzly bears depend on diversity; coastal valleys generally consist of clusters of mature conifers with numerous groupings of deciduous trees, open brushy areas, and skunk cabbage swamps. Knowing this, wildlife biologists proposed ways to produce forested stands that

The sustainability of timber wolves (top) and swift foxes depends partly on the cooperative and collaborative actions of groups and individuals.

Early results of these efforts, and the guidelines that have been produced to help silviculturalists integrate grizzly bear habitat and silviculture needs, have been promising. Cooperation between the Forest Service, British Columbia Environment, and participating forest companies has been good (I'Anson, 1995). In conjunction with British Columbia's Forest Practices Code and the 1995 provincial Grizzly Bear Conservation Strategy, the silviculture guidelines are a very important development in helping to maintain the grizzly's coastal habitats and ensure the survival of the species.

British Columbia's CORE process (Committee on Resources and Environment) and Alberta's Special Places 2000 programs also brought together government, industry, academic, environmental, and other resource interests to identify priority areas for wilderness protection. Although the outcomes of both processes have not always satisfied participants' objectives, the principle of cooperative participation was paramount in identification of Canadian spaces that needed protection.

FUTURE CHALLENGES

How important are wildlife and wilderness to the future of Canada and Canadians? As the rich heritage and diversity of Canada's wild species and natural landscapes continue to be placed at risk through human demands for expansion of urban, industrial, agricultural, recreational, and other activities, the importance of wildlife and wild spaces to the future sustainability of Canadian society cannot be underestimated. Continued stewardship and actions on the part of individual Canadians, NGOs, the private sector, and governments are vital if Canadians are to achieve completion of the national parks system and establishment of the network of protected areas across the country (Noss, 1995). At least the same levels of energy, dedication, enthusiasm, and partnerships displayed across the country to complete the Trans Canada Trail (see the References list for the URL for the Trans Canada Trail Web site) are required to ensure sustainability of Canada's wild species and wildlands.

In part, the achievement of these goals is dependent on continued development, application, and enforcement of legislation and regulation. International and national legislation, including Canada's proposed Endangered Species Protection Act, RENEW, CITES, WAPPRIITA, and the Migratory Birds Convention Act, provide important directions for protecting the future of biodiversity. These directions require continued monitoring, not only of the effectiveness of the legislation, but also of the species and spaces that are the subject of this legislation. As well, continued development of creative conservation programs

more closely resembled the natural ground cover found in the wet valleys prior to logging, while continuing to produce high-value timber. Since these new methods had not been tried before, a series of field projects was established beginning in 1992 to test the different techniques of planting. Because of the uncertainty about the most economical and effective techniques, and the need for site-specific flexibility, an adaptive management approach was used.

and conservation research efforts (such as endangered species and spaces campaigns, and gap analysis) that include, but are not limited to species currently protected under legislation, will be necessary.

If Canadians are to achieve balanced sustainable use and protection of wild species and spaces, in national parks or elsewhere, there is a need to shift from individual species management to a more holistic landscape management approach. The knowledge-building requirements to meet that challenge are ongoing, from use of traditional ecological knowledge to data collection by individual volunteers and scientists, to analysis and interpretation of data by academics in universities and research institutes, to the new information that GIS and other remote sensing technologies generate. The contributions that both phys-

ical and social sciences have to make to wild spaces and species in Canada must be supported and incorporated in actions at all scales if the global mission of conservation of biodiversity is to be attained.

However, remember that actions do not have to be big and expensive to be significant. As scores of Canadians have already found out, making a big difference to Canada's species and spaces can start in our own back yards. Learning more about spaces and species and translating that knowledge into action is a good start. Sometimes, starting small and working at the local level is the most appropriate action to take. What we believe, and what we do, influences others around us; each of us can be stewards of Canada's wild species and natural spaces.

Chapter Questions

1. Review the ways in which habitat alteration can occur. In your local area, identify examples of current habitat alteration. Which types or sources of habitat alteration do you think are most important in your region? Justify your choice.

2. Discuss the reasons why it is necessary to save (endangered) species by saving their habitat and ecosystem.

3. Using Environment Canada's lists of Canadian species at risk (check the URLs in the References section), and other sources that are available to you, try to identify examples of species that are at risk in the region where you live. Are there any activities under way to try to protect, preserve, or rehabilitate these species and their habitats? If so, who is undertaking these efforts, what specific

actions are being taken, and what is the rationale for these actions? If not, describe what you think needs to be done to achieve protection for these species.

4. If you are "pro-nature" does that mean you are "antidevelopment"? Discuss your reasoning.

5. Discuss the pros and cons of *in situ* and *ex situ* conservation approaches.

6. One of the ways each of us can help the world preserve its biological diversity is by talking about the problem with our friends. In what ways could talking about the problem help reverse the decline in global biodiversity? In what ways would modifying our consumption habits help protect wild species and natural spaces?

Banff–Bow Valley Study. (1996). *Banff–Bow Valley: At the crossroads. Technical Report of the Banff Valley Task Force* (R. Page, S. Bayley, J.D. Cook, J. Green & J.R.B. Ritchie). Ottawa.

Bayly, S., & Ives, S. (1997). Seeing the forest for the jobs. *Encompass,* 1(3), pp. 6–7.

Biodiversity Assessment Team. (1994). *Biodiversity in Canada: A science assessment for Environment Canada.* Ottawa: Environment Canada.

Bishop, C., et al. (1994). A proposed North American amphibian monitoring program. http://www.im.nbs.gov/amphib/naampneeds.html

Bloomberg. (1997, May 3). Chevron shareholders approve Arctic drilling in wildlife refuge. *Calgary Herald,* p. E2.

Brooks, R.J., & MacDonald, C.J. (1996). Ranid population monitoring in Algonquin Provincial Park. *Froglog,* 16 (February). http://acs-info.open.ac.uk/info/newsletters/FROGLOG-16-5.html

Canadian Biodiversity Information Network
http://www.ec.gc.ca/ecs/biodiv/biodiv.html

Canadian Geographic Enterprises. (1997). *Wildlife at risk.* Vanier, ON: Canadian Geographic Enterprises.

Canadian Parks and Wilderness Society. (1997). *The Bow Valley: A very special place.* Calgary: CPAWS.

Canadian Wildlife Federation. (1997a). Diamond mining in the Northwest Territories. http://www.cwf-fcf.org/current/curmain.htm

Canadian Wildlife Federation. (1997b). What are CWF's key recommendations relating to the Canada Endangered Species Act? http://www.cwf-fcf.org/current/curmain.htm

Clevenger, A, (1997). Highway effects on wildlife in Banff National Park. *Research Links,* 5(1), pp. 1, 6.

Committee on the Status of Endangered Species in Canada (COSEWIC). http://blizard.cc.mcgill.ca/Redpath/cosewic.htm

Declining Amphibian Populations Task Force. (n.d.). What are amphibian declines and their causes? http://www.open.ac.uk/OU/Academic/Biology/J_Baker/DAPTF. What_are_ADs.html

Drost, C.A., & Fellers, G.M. (1996). Collapse of a regional frog fauna in the Yosemite area of the California Sierra Nevada, USA. *Conservation Biology,* 10, pp. 414–25.

Dunn, P. (1996). The need for amphibian monitoring in protected areas. *Research Links,* 4(3), pp. 4, 10.

Engman, K. (1997, April 21). Fewer jobs in forestry than in parks—study. *Calgary Herald,* p. A4.

Environment Canada. Canadian Wildlife Service. (1996). Endangered species in Canada. http://www.doe.ca:80/envcan/docs/endanger/endanger.html

Environment Canada. Canadian Wildlife Service. (1997a). List of species at risk in Canada as designated by the Committee on the Status of Endangered Wildlife in Canada (COSEWIC), 1997. http://www.ec.gc.ca/envcan/docs/endanger/table.html

Environment Canada. Canadian Wildlife Service. (1997b). Canada's list of species at risk updated. http://www.ec.gc.ca/cws-scf/es/97nr_e.htm

Environment Canada. Canadian Wildlife Service. (1997c). Endangered species in Canada. http://www.ec.gc.ca/cws-sct/es/default.htm

Fenge, T. (1996). The Arctic comes in from the cold. *World Conservation,* 3, pp. 11–12.

FROGLOG: Newsletter of the Declining Amphibian Populations Task Force of the World Conservation Union (IUCN) Species Survival Commission. Issue 16 (February 1996) focuses on Canadian amphibian population research. http://acs-info.open.ac.uk/info/newsletters/FROGLOG.html

Geist, V., & McTaggart-Cowan, I. (1995). *Wildlife conservation policy: A reader.* Calgary: Detselig Enterprises.

Government of Canada. (1996). *The state of Canada's environment—1996.* Ottawa: Supply and Services Canada.

Hackman, A. (1996). Protecting wild places. *World Conservation,* (3), pp. 13–14.

Hummel, M. (Ed.). (1989). *Endangered spaces: The future for Canada's wilderness.* Toronto: Key Porter Books.

I'Anson, B. (1995). *Saving berries for the bears.* Victoria: British Columbia Environment.

International Union for the Conservation of Nature and Natural Resources, United Nations Environment Programme, & World Wildlife Fund. (1980). *World conservation strategy: Living resource conservation for sustainable development.* Gland, Switzerland.

Lunman, L. (1997, March 28). Province defends grizzly bear hunt. *Calgary Herald,* p. B3.

Marty, S. (1997). Homeless on the range: Grizzlies struggle for elbow room and survival in Banff National Park. *Canadian Geographic,* 117(1), pp. 28–39.

Maxwell, C. (1996). A voice in the wilderness. *Canadian Wildlife Federation Bulletin,* p. 1.

Nature Trust of British Columbia. (1993). PCEP purchase of Englishman River Flats "jewel" triggers creation of rare wildlife management area. *Natural Legacy,* 6 (Summer), pp. 1–3.

Noss, R. (1995). *Maintaining ecological integrity in representative reserve networks.* Toronto: World Wildlife Fund Canada/World Wildlife Fund United States.

Oil exploration in the Arctic. (1997). *Canadian Wildlife Federation Bulletin,* pp. 6, 7.

Orchard, S. (n.d.). Why are most amphibians declining? http://www.cuug.ab.ca:8001/~animal/AD.html

Orchard, S. (1997). *E-mail communication.* 29 April.

Penstone, S. (1997). Seedy Saturday. *Environment Views/Environment Network News,* 1(1), p. 14.

Protecting Canadian Species. (1996). *World Conservation,* (3), p. 9.

Robinson, F.E. (1997). Where have all the chickens gone? *Environment Views/Environment Network News,* 1(1), p. 15.

Rowe, S., Kavanagh, K., & Iacobelli, T. (1995). *A protected areas gap analysis methodology: Planning for the conservation of biodiversity.* Toronto: World Wildlife Fund Canada.

Trans Canada Trail. http://www.tctrail.ca.home_page.htm

Wallis, C., Klimek, J., & Adams, W. (1996). Nationally significant Sage Creek grassland threatened by Express Pipeline. *Action Alert,* 7(4). 4 pp.

Wells, P. (1997). *Wildlife mortality on the Canadian Pacific Railway Between Field and Revelstoke, British Columbia.* Paper presented at the Roads, Rails and Environment Workshop, April 9–10, Revelstoke, BC.

Western Canada Wilderness Committee. (1995, Spring). *Protect Canada's biodiversity,* 14(4), pp. 4–5.

Wilkinson, J.W. (n.d.). The Declining Amphibian Populations Task Force (DAPTF) Home Pages. http://www.open.ac.uk/OU/Academic/Biology/J_Baker/JBtxt.htm

World Commission on Environment and Development. (1987). *Our Common Future.* Toronto: Oxford University Press.

World Wildlife Fund Canada. (1996a). Endangered species program. http://www.wwfcanada.org/home-two.html

World Wildlife Fund Canada. (1996b). Endangered Spaces campaign. http://www.wwfcanada.org/spaces/x-001.html

World Wildlife Fund Canada. (1997). Measuring progress in the Endangered Spaces campaign. http://www.wwfcanada.org/spaces/x-004.html

Zolkewich, S. (1995). Leopard frogs abound at DU project. *Ducks Unlimited Canada Conservator,* 16(1), p. 3.

additional information sources

Bildstein, K.L., Brett, J., Goodrich, L., & Viverette, C. (1993). Shooting galleries. *American Birds,* 47(1), pp. 38–43.

Canadian Amphibian and Reptile Conservation Network. Canadian Wildlife Amphibian Service, Environment Canada, Box 5050, Burlington, ON L7R 4A6.

Fair, J. (1994). Last call? *Equinox,* 77 (October), pp. 52–59.

Gayton, D. (1997). Terms of endangerment. *Canadian Geographic,* 117(3), pp. 30–41.

Henry, J.D. (1994). Home again on the range. *Equinox,* 76 (August), pp. 46–53.

North American Amphibian Monitoring Program, Biological Resources Division, U.S. Geological Survey, 12100 Beech Forest Road, Lanvel, MD 20708-4038. E-mail frog@nbs.gov

Nova Scotia FrogWatch. http://www.cciw.ca/ecowatch/FROG/FRGW1B2.HTM or http://www.ednet.ns.ca/educ/museum/mnh/educ/frogwtch/index.htm

Saskatchewan Amphibian Monitoring and Herpetology Atlas Projects, Coordinator, Saskatchewan Monitoring Program, P.O. Box 1574, Saskatoon, SK S7K 3R3

Schneider, D. (1994). Return of the ospreys. *Canadian Geographic,* 114(4), pp. 20–26.

Wood, D. (1996). Cougars on the rebound. *Beautiful British Columbia,* 38(4), pp. 20–31.

World Conservation Monitoring Centre. (1997). World Conservation Monitoring Centre. http://www.wcmc.org.uk:80/

Getting to Tomorrow

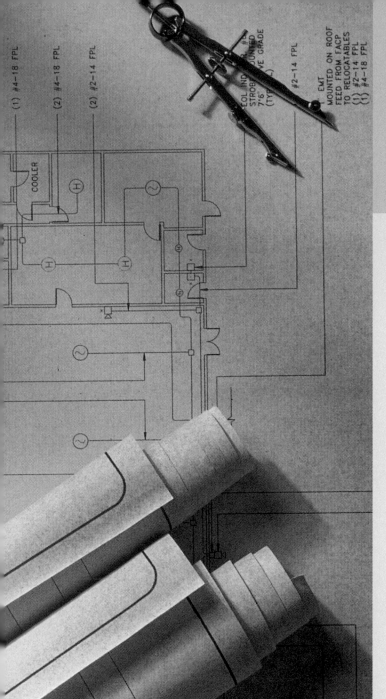

"... if our acceptance of the entire industrial experiment has been a mistake, whether viewed from the social or ecological perspective, how do we escape from the mess? It is not complicated. The first step is to gain consciousness, and stop the process which is killing us and killing the planet. The we need to recover viable practices to reverse it."

J. Mander (1997), in Drengson & Taylor (Eds.)

Lifestyle Choices and Sustainable Communities

Chapter Contents

CHAPTER OBJECTIVES   421
INTRODUCTION   421
URBAN ENVIRONMENTAL CONDITIONS
   AND TRENDS   421
   Atmosphere and Climate   422
      Microclimate   422
      Air Quality   423
   Noise   424
   Water   425
      Cities and the Hydrologic Cycle   425
      Water Supply and Water Quality   425
      Water Use and Wastewater
         Treatment   426
      Water and Recreation   428
   Energy   429
      Sustainable Housing   429
      Depending Less on Our Cars   430
   Materials Use   432
      Solid Waste   432
      Land Contamination   434
   Urbanization of Land   435
      Green Space in the City   435
      Loss of Agricultural Land   437
TOWARD SUSTAINABLE
   COMMUNITIES   439
   Cities and Sustainability   439
   Making Canadian Cities More
      Sustainable   439
      Urban Form   440
      Conservation   441
         Water Conservation   441
         Energy Conservation   441
         Conservation of Materials   441
      Conservation of Ecosystems and
         Natural Features   442

Reduction of Environmental Impacts   442
    Air Quality   442
    Water Quality   444
    Waste Management and Cleaning
        Up   444
    Transportation   444
    Planning   445
PROGRESS TOWARD URBAN
    SUSTAINABILITY?   445
Chapter Questions   446
References   447
Additional Information Sources   448

Chapter Objectives

After studying this chapter you should be able to

- understand the main issues and concerns relating to urbanization and ecosystems in Canada

- identify the impacts of urbanization on the environment around us

- appreciate the complexity and interrelatedness of issues relating to urbanization and the environment

- appreciate the impacts our lifestyle choices have on our environment

- understand the types of efforts Canadians have made toward more sustainable communities

INTRODUCTION

The development of sustainable cities is the key to ensuring the future," said Sergio Marchi, Minister of the Environment, at a meeting of the Federation of Canadian Municipalities, in Ottawa, on June 8, 1997. And indeed the 21st century will bring the dawn of the urban millennium when, for the first time, more than half the human population will be living in urban areas. Although Canada's cities occupy only about 0.2 percent of the country's total land area, already more than 75 percent of Canadians live in communities of over 1000 persons. We often seem to forget that our cities are part of the ecosystem and that urbanization has had a high impact on productive land, aquatic systems, forested lands, and other valued components of regional and local ecosystems. As we draw closer to and prepare to enter the 21st century, we continue to face challenges in balancing the demands of our urban lifestyles while also maintaining and improving ecosystem health (Hancock, 1996).

In this chapter we identify some of the major kinds of impacts our urban ways of life have on the environment, consider what efforts have been made to take the sustainability of the environment into account in urban planning, and comment on future directions for more sustainable communities.

URBAN ENVIRONMENTAL CONDITIONS AND TRENDS

In 1997, for the fourth consecutive year, Canada was ranked number one among all countries in the world on the United Nation's Human Development Index. This index measures people's well-being according to three indicators: life expectancy, knowledge (derived from adult literacy and mean years of schooling), and standard of living (the per-capita gross national product adjusted for the local cost of living) (Government of Canada, 1996). Canada, with a score of 0.96 out of 1.0, was followed by France (0.946), Norway (0.943), and the United States (0.942) (Beltrame, 1997). As useful as they are, neither the Human Development Index nor other similar measures take into account the environmental stresses that are involved in maintaining this high quality of life.

When we realize that Canadians use water and energy and generate household garbage at rates similar to those of residents in other developed countries (Figure 13–1), and when we realize that lifestyle choices are influential elements in achieving environmental sustainability, the importance of new technologies as well as

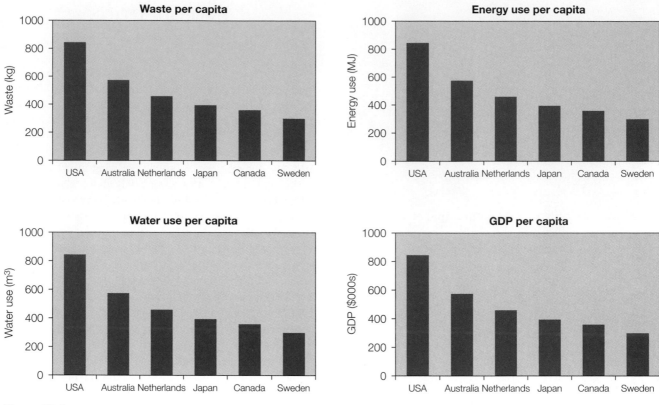

Figure 13–1

Per capita urban solid waste production, energy use, water use, and gross domestic product in Canada, 1991

NOTE: Waste figures for Canada refer to residential waste. Comparisons are difficult, as waste is defined and measured differently between countries. GDP values are from 1990.

SOURCE: Government of Canada. (1996). *The state of Canada's environment—1996.* Ottawa: Supply and Services Canada.

new attitudes becomes clear. A high quality of life with reduced waste, energy use, and pollution is both a goal and a challenge that can be assisted by new technologies that improve the resource and energy efficiencies of our activities. At the same time, attitudes that espouse less wasteful choices and less stress on the environment are necessary. This is apparent when we acknowledge that environmental factors as well as economic (material) and health factors contribute to our high quality of life.

If we consider environmental, material, and health factors, we realize that Canadian urban areas create environmental stresses that have interrelated and cumulative impacts on atmosphere, water, energy, materials, and land, on both regional and global scales. These and other stresses are discussed briefly below, as are illustrations of efforts being made to enhance sustainability of our communities.

ATMOSPHERE AND CLIMATE

Since our ancestors learned how to use fire, humans have been adding pollutants to the atmosphere and affecting its quality. Today, as the threat of global warming has demon-strated, not even climate is immune from human influence. Cities, because of their structure and form and because of the results of various activities taking place within them, modify the local climate and create their own microclimates.

Microclimate

Five main factors shape a city's microclimate. These are the storage and reradiation of heat by buildings and streets, reduction of wind speed (which reduces the wind's cooling effect in summers), human-made sources of heat, rapid runoff of precipitation (which reduces the cooling effect of evaporation), and the effects of atmospheric pollutants. The net result of the influence of these factors is the urban **heat island** effect, where temperatures are one to two degrees Celsius higher in the city than in the surrounding rural area. Two implications of the heat island effect are that cities need less energy for heating but more for cooling, and that in using cooling devices that contain chlorofluorocarbons (CFCs) or CFC substitutes, we generate emissions with known (and unknown) impacts on the ozone layer.

Air Quality

Although many sources of air pollution are located outside cities (refineries, pulp mills, forest fires), there is a concentration of many different sources in cities. In 1990, for example, air emissions in the Greater Vancouver area included 385 000 tonnes of carbon monoxide (CO), 85 000 tonnes of volatile organic compounds (VOCs, including various solvent and fuel vapours), 53 000 tonnes of nitrogen oxides (NO_x), almost 8000 tonnes of sulphur oxides (SO_x), 19 000 tonnes of particulate matter (soot, fly ash, and dust), and many other hazardous air pollutants such as benzene and lead. Most of this air pollution was produced by motor vehicles.

When the wind cannot disperse the more than 600 000 tonnes of pollutants produced in the Greater Vancouver area, the result is photochemical smog that can stretch more than 50 kilometres out to Abbotsford and beyond. This smog can have serious health effects on humans, wildlife, and livestock, and damage natural vegetation and buildings. Asthmatic attacks can worsen, risk of contracting respiratory diseases such as bronchitis can increase, and the danger of developing certain types of cancer can increase as well (Government of Canada, 1996; Greater Vancouver Regional District, 1994). As much as we receive immediate and individual benefits from hopping in the car and driving wherever we want to go (rather than face the inconvenience of waiting for the bus), we are beginning to appreciate that the results of our personal choices have diffuse and sometimes hidden environmental costs (such as in diseases related to air pollution).

Canada's National Air Pollution Surveillance (NAPS) network measures atmospheric levels of five common pollutants in cities. These pollutants are sulphur dioxide (SO_2), suspended particles, ground-level ozone, carbon monoxide (CO), and nitrogen dioxide (NO_2). Atmospheric pollutant data from NAPS are compared with the National Ambient Air Quality Objectives (NAAQOs) set out in the Canadian Environmental Protection Act.

Motorcyclists wear masks in Pontianuk, on the Indonesian Island of Kalimantan, in September 1997, to filter the polluted air caused by huge forest fires on neighbouring islands.

The NAAQOs define the maximum desirable, maximum acceptable, and maximum tolerable levels for each pollutant. Maximum desirable levels specify the long-term goal; maximum acceptable levels specify those at which there is adequate protection of human comfort and well-being, as well as adequate protection of soils, water, and vegetation; and maximum tolerable levels are those beyond which action is required to protect human health. The NAAQOs do not include standards for greenhouse gases such as carbon dioxide that contribute to global warming (Government of Canada, 1996).

Environment Canada indicated that, from 1979 to 1993, average levels of most of the pollutants measured by the NAPS network (calculated as a percentage of the respective maximum acceptable levels) declined: CO by 56 percent, SO_2 by 46 percent, NO_2 by 28 percent (in spite of a 13 percent increase in distance travelled by passenger vehicles), and airborne particles by 38 percent (cited in Government of Canada, 1996). During that same time period, however, ground-level ozone concentrations increased by 29 percent.

The number of hours when pollution exceeded maximum acceptable levels declined for each of SO_2, CO, airborne particles, and, to a lesser extent, NO_2. Much of this reduction was achieved through the use of catalytic converters in cars, cleaner burning engines, cleaner gasoline, more and better scrubbers on industrial smokestacks, and greater overall energy efficiency. Generally, air quality is good in Canadian cities for most of the year, and from 1979 to 1993, air quality in the larger Canadian cities (where vehicles are a significant source of air pollution) improved noticeably.

While very small airborne particles may be cause for concern about human health (because they are thought to contain unburned pieces of carbon originating from fossil fuel combustion in vehicles and heating of buildings), ground-level ozone is Canada's most serious urban air pollution problem. The seriousness of the problem varies regionally across the country, depending on each city's land use, industrial base, commuting patterns, topography, weather conditions, prevailing winds, and location relative to other sources of ozone. Given these factors, settled rural areas downwind from large cities generally experience higher average annual ozone levels than do urban areas themselves.

As we know from previous chapters, not all air pollution in every Canadian city is derived entirely from activities taking place within the city. Air quality in some Canadian cities is affected by the long-range transport of pollutants from other areas, principally the United States. The Lower Fraser Valley (affected by Vancouver area ozone), the Windsor–Quebec corridor (affected by local and U.S. Great Lakes and Midwest sources), and the Fundy region of southern New Brunswick and western Nova Scotia (affected by sources in the northeastern

United States), are the three ozone problem areas in Canada (Canadian Council of Ministers of the Environment, 1990). Neither Victoria nor Prairie cities have the density of vehicles or the prevailing winds from industrial areas needed for ozone problems to develop. Figure 13–2 illustrates, for selected Canadian cities, the number of hours air quality objectives for ground-level ozone were exceeded from 1985 to 1994.

As a precautionary measure, other toxic chemicals in the air such as benzene (a VOC) are being monitored in large urban areas. Benzene, a known carcinogen that initiates tumours and has been linked to a specific form of leukemia, has been monitored since 1989. Transportation sources account for more than 85 percent of the benzene released into the atmosphere in urban areas. However, since 1989, average airborne benzene concentrations have fallen by one-third, due largely to better emission controls on vehicles and more efficient engines. Although Canada does not have a health standard for airborne benzene, and very little is known about human health effects of prolonged exposure to trace amounts of benzene in city air, breathing city air is the most common form of exposure. (This excludes cigarette smoking, which is by far the principal source of adult exposure to benzene.) Also, as of July 1995, Environment Canada announced that it would limit benzene in gasoline to a maximum of 1 percent by volume (Government of Canada, 1996).

With the exception of ground-level ozone, air quality in Canada's urban areas is generally good. Since 1979, average levels of the main air pollutants have declined, and very small airborne particles and toxic chemicals such as benzene are being monitored. But, as long as car ownership and use continue to rise, and traffic congestion continues to grow (at a pace that outstrips per vehicle reductions in energy use and airborne emissions), it is not likely that overall levels of air pollution will continue to decline.

NOISE

Modern society is getting louder. From the high-powered stereo systems in "boom cars" (the ones so loud they make your car vibrate when they pull alongside), to leaf blowers, vacuums, dishwashers, highway traffic, personal watercraft, helicopters, snowmobiles, "surroundsound" big-screen TVs, and portable stereos and earphones, the Canadian population is exposed to more noise than we ever have been. Hearing loss is increasing; tests by the British Columbia Workers Compensation Board, for example, show that close to one-third of the young people entering the work force already are showing signs that their hearing has been affected to some extent by noise (Patterson, 1995).

One of the factors leading to increased hearing loss is the ability to make much more powerful sound equip-

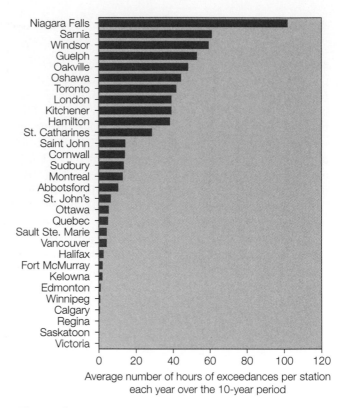

Figure 13–2

Ground-level ozone in selected Canadian cities, 1985–1994: Average number of hours in excess of the maximum acceptable level

NOTE: Refers to the average number of hours in excess of the maximum acceptable level at stations within each urban area. Values in centres with more than one station have been averaged for each year first. Stations in rural areas or small towns, and with insufficient records over the 10-year period have not been included. Measurements are generally taken hourly, April through September. Measurements have been normalized to 100% of readings per station to compensate for missing readings, for each month during this period each year. Maximum acceptable level is 82 ppb (1h).

SOURCE: Government of Canada. (1996). *The state of Canada's environment—1996.* Ottawa: Supply and Services Canada. Figure 12.10.

ment; rock concerts today are more powerful than they were 20 or 30 years ago. Rock concerts frequently are measured at 110 to 128 decibels—about the same level as a pneumatic drill or military jet, respectively. The higher the decibel level, the less time it takes before sound receptor cells start dying and permanent hearing damage occurs. At 130 decibels, after 75 seconds, you're at risk for permanent damage to your hearing; at 135 decibels, exposure time for permanent damage drops to 37.5 seconds (cited in Shideler, 1997). Sound levels in boom cars have been measured at up to 138 decibels. In addition to loudness, both the length of exposure and the proximity to the source increase the damaging effects.

Most noise-induced hearing loss is preventable with proper use of protective ear devices. However, because hearing damage may not show up until years later, promoting safe hearing is a "tough sell," particularly among high school students, and especially when advertisers encourage young adults to play music and video games at loud levels. Even though the idea of ear plugs at rock concerts has little appeal, Hearing Education and Awareness for Rockers (H.E.A.R.) worked with radio stations around the United States and Canada to give out over 60 000 earplugs during the 1996 Lollapalooza Tour, the first major music tour ever to give out earplugs. Some rock bands, such as Motley Crue, are beginning to sell ear protectors at their concerts. (For more information about H.E.A.R. and its interactive Web site, HEARNET, see Box 13–1.)

Noise, or unwanted sound, "is the 'silent' environmental issue of the 1990s" (City of Vancouver, 1997). Second-hand noise (experienced by people who did not produce it), just like second-hand smoke, can have negative impacts on people without their consent. Although people do not bleed, limp, or get sick as a result of noise exposure, there is evidence that noise causes increased stress and blood pressure levels, disrupted sleep patterns, altered heart function, and difficulties in concentrating (Fried, 1996; Patterson, 1995). Hearing loss caused by noise and the natural aging process is cumulative over a lifetime, so people over 50 years of age are impacted particularly severely.

Although noise pollution often is not thought of as an air quality problem, particularly in comparison to the ozone hole or the greenhouse effect, it is an increasingly serious problem for urban populations. Other noise issues in rural areas, such as the concern of the Innu in Labrador and Quebec regarding noise impacts on wildlife and human health from low-level military training flights over their traditional lands, or the concerns of backcountry hikers about noise from helicopters ferrying tourists into prime wilderness areas, are increasing also (Canadian Environmental Assessment Agency, 1995).

WATER

Cities and the Hydrologic Cycle

The relationship of cities to the hydrologic cycle is a good illustration of the way cities are linked to the larger ecosystem. Generally, a city withdraws water (which may be contaminated) from a lake or river and treats the water to make it potable. As it is used, the water receives pollutants, including human wastes, that require the water be treated again prior to its return to the hydrologic system (where natural processes further clean the water). Downstream, other communities that depend on the river or lake for their water supply put the water they withdraw through a similar succession of treatment processes. Some, per-

haps, discharge untreated wastewater. Eventually the river carries the water and any remaining pollutants into the ocean. There, the natural processes of evaporation, transportation (as clouds), and precipitation continue the hydrological cycle.

Water Supply and Water Quality

Surface water supplies most Canadian cities, although nearly 10 percent of the population is served by municipal systems that rely on groundwater (cited in Government of Canada, 1996). As we saw in Chapter 7, supplies of both surface water and groundwater are susceptible to problems of availability and quality. Residents of cities that rely on surface water, such as Victoria, sometimes face seasonal and temporary shortages of or restrictions on water use, whereas residents of cities that rely on groundwater, such as in Prince Edward Island and southern Ontario, may face the possibility of a long-term decline in supply. In Kitchener–Waterloo, Ontario, for example, the search for alternative water supply sources has led to consideration of a 120-kilometre water pipeline from Georgian Bay, part of Lake Huron. Cities such as Regina, where supply sources of surface water are of questionable or declining quality, also may have to find a new supply source or raise the treatment levels of the water they use.

Many sources of contamination may affect both surface water and groundwater supplies: drainage or seepage from industrial, commercial, residential, and recreational land uses, including waste disposal sites; runoff or seepage of farm manure, chemical fertilizers, and other agricultural chemicals; spills and discharges from shipping; and deposition of atmospheric pollutants. To be safe for human consumption, water affected by such contamination must be filtered and treated chemically prior to entering a city's distribution system.

Although water quality generally is good in Canadian cities, quality does differ across the country. The city of Toronto's Department of Public Health (1990), for example, determined that tap water in the city contained very low levels of many of the chemicals detected in the water, sediments, and biota of the Great Lakes ecosystem. Although levels of these chemicals were not a health concern, a recommendation was made to reduce exposure to certain of the chemicals detected, including lead, aluminum, and trihalomethanes (a byproduct of the chlorination of organic matter in raw water).

While urban water quality may be good generally, there are numerous instances where water treatment plants serving residents of smaller Canadian communities either do not meet provincial guidelines on treated water quality or on treating bacteria, or have not performed sufficient testing for bacteria and toxic chemicals to determine if the guidelines have been met. Even in some of the largest communities—Vancouver, for instance—tap water is safe to drink but no longer meets the new, more stringent Canadian Drinking Water Quality guidelines set by Health Canada. In thinking about the sustainability of drinking water for their children and for future generations, officials of the Vancouver Regional District recognized the need to act on supply and quality issues before they became problems. A proposed $500-million improvement plan would deal with four specific areas of concern to health: inadequate disinfection of water sources; seasonal coliform bacteria; seasonal turbidity; and natural acidity or corrosiveness (Greater Vancouver Regional District, 1993).

Water Use and Wastewater Treatment

Over 10 percent of the water withdrawn from natural sources in Canada supplies municipal systems used by residents, businesses, and some industries. More than half the water in municipal systems supplies residential consumption; between 1983 and 1994, residential consumption increased by almost 23 percent (even though the population grew by less than 16 percent). As noted in Chapter 7, most water within the home is used in the bathroom, but on peak days in the summer, lawn and garden watering and car washing can drive water use up by 50 percent.

This is just one way in which Canadians have become the second highest per-capita users of water in the world (see Figure 13–1). Our low water prices and flat-rate pricing contribute to our profligate use. Since water consumption declines as its cost increases, it may be possible to reduce consumption by having water charges reflect the amount of water used. In the past, for example, when most Calgary residents paid a flat rate for their water, they consumed up to 60 percent more water per capita than did residents of Edmonton, a similar sized city that used water meters to charge for water according to the volume people used. Since 1989, however, Calgary waterworks

Leaking water supply systems and overwatered lawns and gardens are emblematic of Canadians' wasteful way with water.

officials have been encouraging reduced wastage through a water meter incentive program. Now, 64 percent of residential water use is on a metered billing system (Engman, 1997), and per capita consumption has declined.

The construction of cities affects the water cycle that, in turn, affects soils, plants, and animals. Cities may receive 5 to 10 percent more rainfall than the surrounding areas because the particulates and dust above cities provide nuclei for condensation of raindrops. But, the concrete, stone, and asphalt streets, and other impervious building materials, prevent water infiltration and induce rapid runoff directly into storm water systems. Local flooding events may increase, and the frequency of downstream flooding may increase also. In addition, hard surfaces prevent water in the soil from evaporating; in natural ecosystems evaporation is an important process that cools the surface.

Most of the water used in urban areas is employed to remove domestic, industrial, and commercial wastes, including human sewage. Treatment to remove impurities is needed to safeguard human health, but the large and increasing volumes of treated wastewater may stress aquatic ecosystems. Some cities such as Vancouver do not separate their storm and sanitary (sewage) waters. Even if separate storm and sewer systems exist, heavy storm drainage flows may overload a treatment plant's capacity and cause either or both storm and sewage discharges to leave the plant untreated or insufficiently treated.

The number of Canadians served by municipal wastewater treatment plants has been increasing steadily (Table 13–1), but the level of treatment varies widely. For instance, many coastal cities as well as those on the lower St. Lawrence River discharge their wastewater directly into oceans or rivers. Most Ontario cities must discharge into smaller rivers or the Great Lakes, while Prairie cities discharge solely into rivers. By 1994, no sewage was left totally untreated in Ontario or Prairie communities with treatment systems. The situation in Atlantic Canada was very different, however, as more than 50 percent of the

The effects of localized urban flooding may range from the inconvenience of being unable to use a pathway to paying for costly repairs to residences and public property.

population with sewage systems were not served by any form of wastewater treatment. In Quebec by 1994, following construction of new treatment systems in Montreal and other cities, 84 percent of the population with sewage systems were also served by treatment plants (compared with 56 percent in 1991) (Government of Canada, 1996).

Although more Canadians than ever before are served by increasingly higher levels of sewage systems (Figure 13–3a), regional variations in levels of treatment are evident. By 1994, almost 80 percent of Ontario residents and about 30 percent of Prairie residents were served by tertiary treatment systems (Figure 13–3b). The high level of tertiary treatment in Ontario is due to provincial regulations that require phosphate removal systems. In contrast, a minimal percentage of the municipal population in the Atlantic region was served by tertiary treatment. Large volumes of wastewater, including sewage from cities such as St. John's, Newfoundland, and Halifax, Nova Scotia (as well as from Victoria, British Columbia) are discharged into the ocean untreated or after only primary treatment. As noted previously in Chapter 7 and Chapter 8, such practices have adverse effects on local shellfish grounds, coastal wetlands, and shorelines.

			TABLE 13–1		
INCREASING POPULATION SERVED BY WASTEWATER TREATMENT FACILITIES IN CANADA					
Date	Population Served by Sewage Systems	Population Served by Sewage Treatment	Population Served by Tertiary Treatment	Untreated Wastewater
1983	18.2 million	13.0 million	5.0 million	5.2 million
1994	21.2 million	19.6 million	8.2 million	1.6 million

SOURCE: Government of Canada. (1996). *The state of Canada's environment—1996.* Ottawa: Supply and Services Canada. Chapter 12 and Figure 12.13.

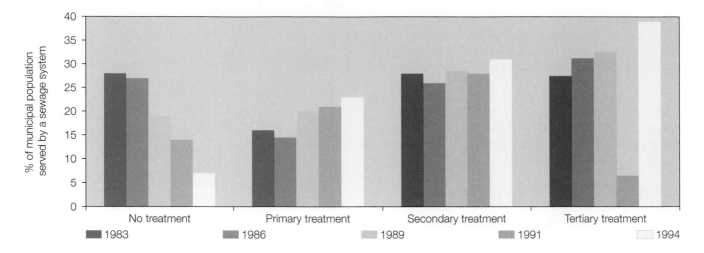

Figure 13–3a

Municipal population served by type of sewage system in Canada

SOURCE: Government of Canada. (1996). *The state of Canada's environment—1996.* Ottawa. Figure 12.13.

Water and Recreation

Recreational pursuits—even those that seem environmentally friendly—can have impacts on the environment. These impacts range from use of resources such as land for golf courses and ski areas, to chemicals used to purify water in swimming pools, to energy consumed and emissions produced by use of vehicles to get to the cottage or recreational event. Clearly, recreational pursuits are important in Canadians' health and quality of life. It is equally important, however, that more of us learn how we can minimize impacts on the environment of our recreational activities.

One way to consider the sustainability of our recreational activities is to examine how much energy, use of materials, emissions, and waste are involved. In general, activities that are fuel dependent (snowmobiling, motorcycling, and power boating) are more harmful to the environment than are human-powered activities (hiking, skiing). If hikers stay on designated trails and follow other environmentally friendly practices, they can enjoy the outdoors without causing much damage to it. However, the cumulative effects of human-powered activities on the environment potentially are significant given that about 20 percent of Canadians participate in each of skating, downhill skiing, running or jogging, and golf (Gauthier & Haman, 1992).

In some recreational pursuits, fuel-dependent activities predominate. Pleasure boating in Canada, for example, involves more than five times as many motor boats and yachts (693 500) as sailboats (124 000). Power boats are estimated to consume 1 373.90 litres of fuel per vessel; a typical 5.2-metre (17-foot) runabout consumes about 25 to 30 litres of fuel per hour and averages about 1

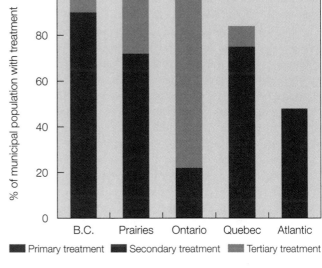

Figure 13–3b

Total population served by a sewage system in Canada

NOTE: Insufficient data to include the Northwest Territories and Yukon.

SOURCE: Government of Canada. (1996). *The state of Canada's environment—1996.* Ottawa. Figure 12.14.

to 2 kilometres of travel per litre of fuel (automobiles attain an average of over 8 kilometres per litre) (Government of Canada, 1996). In addition, power boats cause noise, air, and water pollution; as much as 8 percent of total hydrocarbon emissions in the Quebec–Windsor corridor are estimated to be released from power boats. When aging or improperly maintained engines are included, air pollution from power boat engines may be 25 to 30 percent higher.

Water pollution may be exacerbated by power boat use in some areas, and the wakes (waves) from these vessels can disturb aquatic wildlife and erode vulnerable shorelines. The practice of releasing raw sewage from boat heads (toilets), particularly into sheltered bays and coves where boats tend to anchor and people swim and fish, also is problematic. In the past, and prior to improved regulations, houseboats on Shuswap and Okanagan lakes were among the pleasure craft that contributed to serious sewage contamination problems.

Canadians can choose less environmentally damaging recreational activities, and can choose to carry out leisure time activities in less damaging ways. Doing so increases the likelihood that we can maintain the benefits of leisure activities at the same time as we reduce the long-term environmental impacts of our recreational activities.

ENERGY

Canadians use a lot of energy to cope with our cold climate, to travel the long distances between population centres, and to satisfy our lifestyle choices (such as our preference for detached, single-family houses). Nearly 30 percent of total energy consumption in 1992 was used in the transportation sector, while residential use accounted for nearly 20 percent. As noted in Chapter 11, the production and consumption of fuels and electricity in cities lead to local and global environmental stresses. Automobile use, home heating, and commercial enterprises cause local air pollution from emissions of NO_x, VOCs, SO_2, and particulate matter; as well, they contribute to global warming through release of CO_2. Ecosystems also experience stress from production, transport, and use of energy.

While it is difficult to compile a picture of municipal energy use in Canada (because the data are not collected by municipalities), it is known that per capita use of energy in the inner city is lower than in suburban areas, and lower still than in small towns and rural areas. This seems to suggest that, given its higher population density, the inner city is a more energy-efficient form of settlement. The extensive, enclosed environments in large cities mean that people can travel from their homes and jobs to go shopping, dining, or to attend to business without ever going outdoors. While these environments

provide convenience and comfort, they require heavy energy consumption for heating, cooling, and ventilating the system. Typically, industrial energy users do not locate in large cities, but in Toronto and Ottawa, commercial and institutional sectors account for one-third of all energy use. This is double the national average and suggests that these businesses are good targets for energy management efforts.

Sustainable Housing

The Alberta Sustainable Home/Office in Calgary is a three-bedroom, 170-square-metre (1820-square-foot) house designed and built to demonstrate sustainability in cold climate housing. "An inventory of ideas," the house reflects concern for environmental stewardship, occupant health, resource conservation, the use of appropriate technologies and alternative energy sources, and self-sufficiency (Checora, 1996). The project was undertaken on the initiative of a small group of individuals who are partners in the business ASH—Autonomous and Sustainable Housing, Inc. To demonstrate its marketability and financial feasibility, the project was funded by a conventional mortgage without government assistance.

The first of its kind in Canada, the project has three distinct phases: the sustainable stage, the autonomous stage (when the house no longer needs any city water or sewage treatment), and the energy-credit stage (when surplus electricity produced by the photovoltaic panels on the roof will be sold to the power company). The house was built to achieve these goals in Calgary's cold climate without a conventional forced-air furnace or boiler—the house is not even connected to natural gas. Instead, the passive solar design of the home allows its occupants to take advantage of Alberta's year-round sunny climate.

Even in Calgary's cold winters, about 60 percent of the home's space heating requirements are met simply by allowing the sun to shine through the expanse of south-facing windows onto the dark ceramic and recycled-glass floor tiles. Placed on top of a five-inch-thick concrete slab, these materials constitute a substantial thermal mass that helps store the heat from the sun. To keep the heat stored in the thermal mass in the house, the walls are insulated with cellulose to R-50 and the roof cavity to R-74 (well beyond the current building code). Any backup heat required comes from the highly efficient, wood-burning masonry heater that can be used for baking as well as future electrical generation. As the two-year sustainable phase neared completion in 1996, the total purchased energy requirements of this house averaged about 6 percent of those required by an ordinary house (Checora, 1996).

High performance windows throughout the house, including one with an R-16.6 value (developed in Winnipeg), complete the building's envelope. Some of the other technology in the project, much of which was donated by more than 220 leading-edge companies from

Regulations prohibit houseboat users from discharging raw sewage wastes directly into Shuswap Lake, B.C.

around the world, includes nonadditive concrete, "Eco-stud" wall trusses, nontoxic drywall mud, waterless (composting) and ultralow flush toilets, a solar hot water collector, two types of greywater heat exchangers, an air-to-air heat exchanger, and radiation-shielded, full-spectrum, and electroluminescent lighting.

As the autonomous stage of the project begins, research continues on hydrogen fuel cells, co-generators, high-performance ground-coupled heat pumps, in-house sewage treatment, and other technologies for a conserver lifestyle and energy independence. There is no oven in the house; most of the cooking is done in a solar oven (made in Saskatoon) that sits on the front porch facing the sun. When the connection to the city's water supply is shut off, all water for the house will be rainwater collected from the roof and stored in a 14 500-litre cistern buried in the back yard. Experiments on a number of filtration and purification processes (to produce potable water) are ongoing, as are strategies to treat and reuse the greywater produced in the household. When the waterless composting toilet is operational, it is expected to save about 200 000 litres of purified drinking water from being polluted every year.

Education is a large part of ASH Inc.'s mandate, and the house is open to the public every Saturday afternoon. Prior to the end of 1996, more than 16 000 people from Africa, Asia, Europe, and North America had toured the house. This house is an important reminder that today's possibilities can become tomorrow's trends.

A similar demonstration project—the Toronto Healthy House—is a three-bedroom infill home that harvests its own energy, collects rainfall and purifies it for drinking, and biologically treats its own waste. Part of the Canada Mortgage and Housing Corporation's (CMHC) Healthy Housing initiative, the house has low operating costs and is affordable. In Red Deer, Alberta, in 1994, Healthy Housing principles were applied to the renovation of a 1905 home, demonstrating environmental responsibility through such elements as material selection, energy efficiency, airtightness, and equipment selection.

Among other trends in sustainable housing are the use of straw bales, recycled tires, packed dirt, and mud. Straw bale construction is an old technology, used in Europe 300 years ago and pioneered in North America in the sandy, treeless Nebraska prairie in the 1890s. Then, building homes from bales of straw was a necessity; now, as the world is concerned about running short of wood, straw bale construction of residences, workshops, and garages creates a new use for straw (normally an almost useless byproduct of such grains as wheat, oats, flax, and barley).

Straw bale construction has many advantages over conventional wood frame construction, including the fact that straw is a low-cost, renewable, easy-to-use material with high insulation value (Table 13–2). For example, buying and transporting the bales for a 2200-square-foot home built in 1996 near Millarville, Alberta, cost $1000

(King, 1996). Stacked like huge bricks, straw bales are easy to build with and walls go up quickly. The frame of the Millarville area house used corner posts and beams, and the walls were built by stacking straw bales horizontally and pushing them into floor-to-ceiling threaded metal rods, clamped at the top. The insulation value of the straw bale walls approaches R-50. A two-storey straw bale workshop in Nova Scotia made construction history when it became the first "code-approved" load-bearing straw building in Canada (Wood, 1997).

"Earthships," built from recycled tires, packed dirt, and mud, are another type of sustainable housing finding a new use for "waste" material (tires, cans, and bottles). More common in the United States than in Canada (although a 4000-square-foot, $500 000 earthship exists outside Edmonton), these homes use passive solar heat to reduce utility bills by about 75 percent compared with conventional construction methods (Hope, 1995). Typically, water is supplied from catchment systems in the earth roof (stored in cisterns for future use), and other environmental technology such as solar toilets that turn sewage into dust are common also. Some earthships also include domestic food production.

Sustainable housing leaves a much smaller footprint on the ecosystem than do conventional single-family homes. Depending on their design and construction, sustainable houses may increase efficiency in land use and energy and water consumption, and provide healthy indoor environments. By overcoming most of the environmental problems of single-family homes (such as high energy use and high costs of infrastructure services), as well as by being affordable, sustainable housing may become more common in the future.

Depending Less on Our Cars

Still other opportunities exist to reduce the environmental impact of housing, including planning for better use of land and of transit and infrastructure systems. The spread-out nature of Canadian suburban development helps keep us dependent on the automobile. This means that use of energy for transportation in suburban and fringe areas is particularly high, which in turn highlights the need to ensure that vehicles are maintained (to reduce smog), that public transit systems are promoted and are convenient alternatives to driving, and that bicycle paths are provided for commuting and recreational use.

Although the single most important contribution that individuals can make to reducing environmental impacts of cars is to use them less, all over Canada people have taken various actions to reduce energy use in urban transportation. Environment Canada's Action 21 "Down-to-Earth Choices" program identified a range of actions taken by community groups, environmental groups, individuals, municipalities, and employers. From special events to promote alternative transportation and "clean-

CMHC'S HEALTHY HOUSE IN TORONTO

A WINNING DESIGN:

Martin Liefhebber Architect Incorporated
Creative Communities Research Inc.

CMHC ❄ **SCHL**
Helping to house Canadians
Question habitation, comptez sur nous

1. Rooftop solar panels generate electric energy, which can be stored for later use.

2. Airtight wall construction reduces heat loss, eliminates drafts, and minimizes the entry of moisture and pollutants.

3. Thermally efficient windows are situated to provide natural light and passive solar heat, reducing lighting and heating costs.

4. The building envelope features high levels of insulation to improve energy efficiency.

5. Low-volume toilets and low-flow shower heads and aerator faucets help to conserve water

6. Materials used to furnish and decorate the house (countertops, cabinets, paints, etc.) emit few chemicals.

7. Rainwater is collected, filtered, purified, and stored for drinking and washing. It is then recycled for use in the tub, washing machine, shower, or toilet.

8. Wastewater from the dishwasher, washing machine, and toilet is filtered and biologically treated before being discharged. This prevents contamination of waterways.

9. The first-floor design is ideal for a home office. Working at home reduces the need for transportation and so reduces pollution.

10. The house design is appropriate for construction on infill lots. This promotes the efficient use of land and reduces urban sprawl.

Figure 13–4

Toronto Healthy House

SOURCE: Canada Mortgage and Housing Corporation brochure, provided courtesy of CMHC and Martin Liefhebber Architects. Reproduced by permission. Actual house design may vary from design shown.

Each of Canada's 15 million cars and light truck emits over 4 tonnes of pollutants into the atmosphere every year.

Bicycle paths for commuters and recreational cyclists promote pollution-free travel and physical fitness.

Although highly dependent on their vehicles, many Canadians are choosing to reduce their energy consumption by driving less and increasing their use of bicycles and public transit.

air commuting," to a group of volunteers who devised a "walking school bus" (children are walked to school holding a loop on a rope instead of using a seat on the bus), many Canadians have shown they are willing to reduce their car use. Some have even worked together to halt roads (see, for instance, Verrall, 1995). Examples of this range of actions may be found at several of Environment Canada's Green Lane Web sites, including Action 21 and Halifax's Metro Transit Park & Ride Public Transit Program, which are listed in the Additional Information Sources section of this chapter.

Every year, each of the 15 million cars and light trucks on Canada's roads emits over 4 tonnes of pollutants into the atmosphere. In 1997, for the twelfth consecutive year, Environment Canada will hold its voluntary emissions inspection clinics. The program is aimed at raising awareness about the importance of proper vehicle maintenance in reducing air pollution and protecting the environment and the health of Canadians. (For more information on the program, check Environment Canada's Green Lane Web sites "Check-Up for Clean Air" and "Emissions Inspection Clinics," listed in the Additional Information Sources section of this chapter.)

MATERIALS USE

Solid Waste

Throughout Canada, generating and managing solid wastes is an expensive environmental and social issue. From an ecosystem perspective, waste materials that enter landfills or are incinerated represent energy and resources that have not been used fully and that could have been recycled, reused, or reduced at their source, thereby reducing the need to extract and process new resources. From an economic perspective, solid wastes cost municipalities more than $3 billion annually for their collection, transportation, and disposal. In community and environmental terms, continuing generation of waste leads to the need to find new landfill sites when the old ones fill up. Finding and approving new sites is becoming harder, in part because of the "nimby" (not in my backyard) syndrome.

Landfilling and incinerating wastes almost always are controversial land use decisions because neither is free of environmental impacts. Even though technology has improved, landfills emit methane and other gases (some toxic) and there is as yet no method that is 100 percent efficient in capturing and containing these gases. Inadequate engineering, too, can result in leachates (leaking liquid) contaminating surface water or groundwater. Incineration produces both air emissions that contain toxic contaminants and particulates, and solid residues that are hazardous and require further disposal in specialized facilities. With a combination of high-temperature incineration

PART 4:
GETTING TO TOMORROW

TABLE 13-2
ADVANTAGES OF STRAW BALE CONSTRUCTION

- Straw bales are cheap to buy. Considered an agricultural waste product, straw is available annually. Rather than plow it under or burn it in the fields and thus create air pollution, straw can be baled and turned into an energy-efficient resource.

- Straw bales have a high insulation value (R-2.7 per inch; an 18-inch-wide bale has an R value of 48).

- Straw bale buildings have lower heating and cooling requirements, resulting in reduced fossil fuel use and reduced CO_2 emissions.

- Straw bale construction is low-tech, easy, and requires few power tools.

- Lumber use is reduced.

- Straw bales are nontoxic and, when finished with natural plaster, allow a gradual transfer of air through the walls, promoting good indoor air quality.

- Straw bale buildings are soundproof: one Nebraska pioneer family, found playing cards in the kitchen, was unaware that a tornado had just roared through the town.

- Straw bales resist combustion: because of the thickness and lack of oxygen available, it takes two hours to burn through a plaster, straw, and stucco wall (double the resistance of most wood-frame homes).

- With the proper foundation, roof, and finish plaster, straw bale buildings can last indefinitely (some Nebraska historic homes are still standing).

- Anecdotal evidence indicates that there are no problems with bugs in straw bale buildings.

SOURCES: Black Range Films. (n.d.). *Straw bale construction*. Kingston, NM.

King, F. (1996, May 11). Hay, there's a new way to build a house! *Calgary Herald,* p. I10.

Oosterom, N. (1995, October 25). Piggy's idea recycled: straw replaces scarce wood. *Calgary Herald,* p. A2.

Council of Ministers of the Environment set a national target for annual reduction of solid waste at a 50 percent reduction from 1988 levels (on a per capita basis) by the year 2000. By 1992, total solid waste generation per person in Canada had declined by just over 16 percent (in part due, perhaps, to the economic recession of 1990–92), while municipal solid waste alone declined by nearly 11 percent (due to an almost 174 percent increase in recycling and composting by municipalities, households, and businesses).

The challenge remains to reduce the waste stream even further; in 1992, only about 17 percent of municipal waste was recycled or composted while the remaining 83 percent was landfilled and incinerated (78 percent and 5 percent, respectively) (Government of Canada, 1996). By weight, the main materials in municipal solid waste were paper and paperboard (25 percent), food wastes (19 percent), yard wastes (13 percent), and plastics (12 percent). Asphalt, concrete, rubble, and wood dominate the construction and demolition waste stream and suggest the importance of transportation infrastructure in cities. Figure 13–4 displays the composition of both municipal and construction waste streams in 1992.

From 1988 to 1992, the highest levels of recovery of solid waste materials were for metals, paper and paperboard, and glass, but in no case did the recovery exceed 40 percent. Recycling of plastics and wood from the municipal solid waste stream—which had been nonexistent in 1998—remained at low levels through 1992. Likewise, rates of municipal and individual composting of yard waste (10.5 percent) and food waste (2.2 percent) illustrate how much opportunity Canadians have to improve their performance in solid waste management. (See Box 13–2 for examples of waste management efforts in the workplace.) Availability and accessibility of community recycling facilities, effectiveness of recycling technologies,

A straw bale house under construction near Millerville, Alberta.

methods and emission controls, problems of air emissions could be solved (Environment Canada, 1991). However, because high volumes of waste are required to make incineration economical, municipalities could have less incentive to "reduce, reuse, and recycle" their waste materials.

Although comparisons with other countries are difficult, Canadians are cited frequently as being among the world leaders in per-capita waste production—in 1992, Canadians generated 18.1 million tonnes of municipal solid waste. This is 637 kilograms per person per year, or 1.7 kilograms daily; about one-half of that is from residential sources. If we add construction and demolition waste, the estimates of solid waste in Canada rise to 29.3 million tonnes or 1030 kilograms per person (Government of Canada, 1966). Given these statistics, the Canadian

Of the material we send to landfills, how much could we reuse, recycle, or compost?

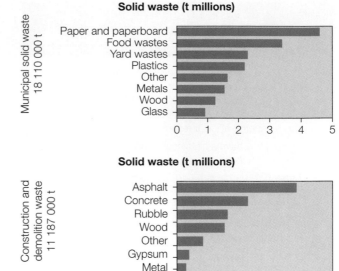

Figure 13–5

Materials in the solid waste stream, 1992

NOTES: 1. Municipal solid waste consists of residential, industrial, commercial, and institutional waste.
2. Other municipal waste consists of rubber and leather, textiles, miscellaneous inorganic wastes, and other.
3. Other construction and demolition waste consists of paper, building material, and other.

SOURCES: Franklin Associates Ltd.; Government of Canada. (1996). *The state of Canada's environment—1996*. Ottawa. Figure 12.17. Reproduced by permission of Senes Consultants Ltd., Thornhill, Ont.

markets for manufactured postconsumer waste products, and levels of awareness and willingness to recycle on the part of consumers, businesses, and institutions are the main reasons for variations in recycling or in composting of waste materials.

The amount of household or residential solid waste collected for disposal varies by region and size of municipality across Canada. Smaller municipalities with populations between 5000 and 29 999 averaged 415 kilograms per person annually whereas municipalities with populations over 30 000 collected an average of just over 300 kilograms per person annually. Lowest per-capita rates were recorded in British Columbia, and the highest in Quebec and Atlantic Canada. In spite of improvements, management of solid wastes remains a serious challenge within Canada's urban areas.

Land Contamination

An important urban waste management problem has arisen on old industrial and other sites where toxic materials were deliberately dumped or accidentally spilled or leaked from underground storage tanks. On these sites, contamination levels of certain persistent compounds and metals, such as lead, cadmium, chromium, and nickel, prevent redevelopment for residential, recreational, or even commercial use without a costly cleanup. Numerous examples exist across the country, including the Expo 86 site in False Creek in Vancouver, and the Ataratiri housing project in Toronto (dropped in the late 1980s when cleanup costs were estimated to be over $30 million).

This problem is not confined to large cities; soils in the town of Trail, British Columbia, may be contaminated by deposition of dust containing lead from the town's smelters. In northern Canada, contaminated sites are associated with abandoned U.S. military facilities such as the 21 Distant Early Warning (DEW) Line radar sites. High levels of PCBs, heavy metals, and POLs (petroleum,

oil, and lubricants) constitute a toxic legacy, and are known to be entering the Arctic food chain. Cost estimates to clean up only four U.S. military installations range from $350 million to more than $1 billion,

Easily accessible community facilities are one way Canadians may be encouraged to increase their recycling of solid wastes.

Provided that a company workplace is supportive of employee efforts to implement environmental initiatives, employees can have important effects on company practices. Whether as individuals, members of committees, or managers, many people have helped their companies to become greener in such areas as purchasing, environmental codes of practice, nonsmoking buildings, and conservation strategies for water, energy, and waste.

Support for bicycle commuting (including provision of shower facilities in the workplace) and contributions to events such as community tree planting and river cleanups have become meaningful company activities. Many of these activities have resulted from people sharing information about the importance of individual attitudes, actions, and impacts on our environment.

Within the workplace, individuals and environmental committees can influence other employees to participate in initiatives such as recycling programs. With the advent of computers in the workplace, the paperless office was predicted as the way of the future. However, as a result of people using more paper by printing more drafts of their work, paper use actually increased in 50 percent of Canadian companies surveyed in 1994. Fortunately, many companies and employees now participate in efforts to reduce paper use and to recycle used paper. In the same survey, it was noted that 83 percent of respondents participated in efforts to recycle paper, 60 percent used 2-sided photocopying, 56 percent used the backs of paper sheets, and 55 percent used the computer for revisions to their documents rather than printing a new hard copy (Government of Canada, 1996; Pitney Bowes, 1994).

Telework or telecommuting is a trend that may be positive for the environment. As some corporations offer their employees the opportunity to work at home and connect to the office via computer and telecommunication technologies, reductions of air emissions and other environmental stresses due to commuting are expected. In addition, as employees spend less time in the office, telework can allow more people to share office space. This reduces the need for land for buildings as well as the heating and cooling costs associated with such real estate.

Environmental stewardship also is reflected in Canadian Pacific Hotels and Resorts (CPH&R) Green Program. Started in 1991, this program includes waste recycling programs in the kitchens, reuse of damaged tablecloths as aprons for kitchen and housekeeping staff, donation of leftover pastries and hot foods to food kitchens, and giving leftover shampoos and conditioners to hostels. The Royal York Hotel in Toronto, for example, installed an $800 000 Hobart Press waste disposal system in their kitchen to turn food scraps from their dining rooms into a mash for use by a local pig farmer. Each morning, the farmer collects six to ten 64-gallon bins to feed his 600 to 700 pigs. Without the Hobart Press, this material would have gone to the landfill (and incurred disposal charges for CPH&R).

Anne Checkley, director of communications and environmental affairs for CPH&R, indicated that there was "absolutely no down side to having an environmental program" (Beale, 1996, 24). Even though hotel occupancy has increased during the past decade, waste management costs have decreased. In fact, CPH&R publishes "The Green Partnership Guide," a collection of tips from its environmental committees that is sold around the world. This is another indication that greening of business can be profitable.

SOURCES: Beale, J. (1996). Canadian Pacific Hotel's enviro-initiatives. *Ecolutions,* Winter, pp. 24–25.

Government of Canada. (1996). *The state of Canada's environment—1996.* Ottawa.

Pitney Bowes. (1994). *Pitney Bowes fourth annual green office survey.* Toronto: Pitney Bowes.

---

depending on the standards used for cleanup (Canadian Arctic Resources Committee, 1997). (For additional information on the agreement Canada and the United States negotiated regarding cleanup of these sites, see the Canadian Arctic Resources Committee's Web site listed in the Additional Information Sources section of this chapter.)

As we saw in the case of creosote contamination of the Bow River (Chapter 7), toxic substances also may migrate from old industrial sites to contaminate other areas through groundwater movement. Chemical fertilizers and pesticides, often applied to lawns and gardens in quantities greater than are applied in agricultural operations, enter the ecosystem through leaching into the ground or entering the wastewater disposal system. In response to public concerns about use of pesticides and herbicides, many municipal governments have developed integrated pest management plans and reduced or eliminated use of chemicals on public lands such as parks.

URBANIZATION OF LAND

Green Space in the City

Until relatively recently, green space in the city was not accorded much value other than for utilitarian purposes such as space for buildings and roads. As a result of this lack of value accorded to green space, many natural areas and stream valleys were used as convenient locations for dumping garbage and for highway routes, many watercourses were used as storm sewers, and many waterfronts were cut off from public access for use by industries, railways, and roads (Turner, 1996).

Even the creation of parks in the city caused destruction of the natural environment as, for example, when productive wetlands were transformed into sports fields, playgrounds, manicured lawns, flower displays, and other planted areas using exotic species. Golf courses and other formal parks often are fertilized, treated with pesticides, and irrigated. Such treatments often eliminate remaining natural characteristics and add polluted runoff to lakes, streams, and rivers.

Apart from its important social benefits, most urban outdoor recreational space has very little conservation, ecological, or environmental value. Only when large wild areas are preserved (such as Stanley Park in Vancouver or Nose Hill Park in Calgary) is there a potential for protection of environmental values. Even then, heavy use of Stanley Park has resulted in severe erosion of some of the area's original natural characteristics. Certain of the wildlife found in Nose Hill Park may not survive over the long term as their corridors into the park now are virtually surrounded by urban development.

Other species of wildlife, wildflowers, and trees, however, are able to survive and even thrive in urban environments. Ravines, woods, and other vegetated areas within cities are important in providing habitat for a variety of wildlife and plants and in reducing or preventing soil erosion. In addition, natural areas help moderate urban microclimates, decrease air pollution (trap particles and absorb carbon), and reduce storm flows (thus reducing the overload on sewers and treatment plants). Urban forests also are important recreational resources. Seventy-seven percent of Canadians live in cities and, perhaps unknowingly, derive considerable environmental, economic, and social benefits from the trees that grow in their parks, on their street boulevards, and in their own back yards. Some of the benefits trees bring to human health and well-being are identified in Box 13–3.

As the ecosystem approach to green space within cities has developed, many communities have established systems of interconnected natural areas that permit reproduction and migration of many species of plants and wildlife and continuation of some or most ecosystem functions. While natural green spaces provide residents and visitors with aesthetically pleasing surroundings for recreation, relaxation, or contact with nature, the longer term view is that such natural heritage systems would become the focus around which cities develop, rather than providing just a backdrop for development.

In spite of growing awareness of the multiple values of urban green space, city land use controls do not always afford green areas or natural spaces the protection they require to remain functional in an ecological or ecosystem

While socially important, manicured green spaces in cities have fewer environmental benefits than natural areas.

sense. Many private developers and public agencies continue to view green space as unused or underused land and as prime sites for buildings and other facilities. Additional pressure on urban green space comes from efforts to increase the intensity of occupancy of urban land in order to reduce infrastructure costs and increase energy efficiency. From 1966 to 1986 (the last year for which Canada-wide data are available), the rate of conversion of rural and prime agricultural land to urban uses varied according to the population size of urban centres—the 9 largest centres (over 500 000 population) accounted for 42.9 percent of the conversion (Warren, Kerr & Turner, 1989).

Growth in urban populations during the coming decades is inevitable, as is continued urban expansion. The impacts of continued expansion could be enormous; for example, a conservative estimate indicates that by the year 2021, even if the most compact growth is pursued, the Greater Toronto area is expected to grow an additional 23 percent or 350 square kilometres (from a 1988 area of 1520 square kilometres). If current, dispersed trends were to continue, the increase would be 900 square kilometres or 59 percent (IBI Group, 1990).

One of the major contributing factors to this rate of land occupation is the popularity of the detached, single-family house surrounded by its own lot. Curvilinear street patterns (rather than the more compact grid layout) also have reinforced the spread-out form of urban development. Single-family detached housing remains popular; in Canadian urban areas of more than 100 000 people, the proportion of housing starts for single-family detached homes rose from 31.4 percent in 1971, to 44.5 percent in 1981, and to 52.8 percent in 1994 (with a peak of 57.0 percent in 1986). Prairie cities tend to have the highest proportion of single-family detached housing starts, with West Coast and most Quebec centres slightly lower. However, there has been an increase in the average density of

BOX 13-3
URBAN FORESTS

Trees greatly influence the health of the urban environment; they are a source of beauty and help to purify the air, abate noise, modify heat, stabilize soil, reduce flood risks, and provide wildlife habitat as well as recreational settings for residents. The urban forest includes not only large stands of native trees, such as are found in Stanley Park in Vancouver, British Columbia, and in C.A. Pippy Park in St. John's, Newfoundland, but also the millions of native and exotic trees lining our streets, in our yards, parks, and plant nurseries, and on the edges of some of our newest neighbourhoods.

One reality of life for urban trees is that many get a great deal less water than trees in rural settings do (streets, gutters, and sewer systems channel water away quickly). Urban trees also experience higher average temperatures, air and soil pollution, and the constant threat of root or stem damage from human traffic or heavy equipment. As a result, their lifespans are less than trees in rural areas. A tree planted in the black-top jungle of downtown Vancouver will survive an average of 13 years, while those planted in large treed gardens may survive up to 60 years (Forest Alliance of British Columbia, n.d., p. 2). While an average life expectancy of 32 years for trees in the Vancouver area is significantly less than the average lifespan of trees in rural areas, trees in urban areas naturalize built landscapes and provide important psychological benefits also.

The benefits of trees (rural and urban) to human psychology are difficult to quantify, but they contribute noticeably to human health and well-being. Research has shown, for instance, that patients recover more quickly if their hospital room has a view of trees and natural landscapes (Ulrich, 1979). Urban trees shade and cool streets and buildings in summer, moderating the higher temperatures experienced in cities. If coniferous trees are placed strategically to buffer winter winds, they can help reduce heat loss from buildings in winter and contribute to fuel savings of 20 percent or more (Forest Alliance of British Columbia, n.d.).

Each tree in the urban forest removes pollutants and other particulates from city air. Carbon, chlorine, fluorine, ozone, sulphur dioxide, peroxyacetylnitrate (a component of photochemical smog), and other gases are absorbed by these trees. Every year, each city tree removes about 6 kilograms of carbon dioxide from the atmosphere. Simply because of their high emission locations, urban trees are 5 to 15 times more beneficial than wilderness trees with regard to the purification of the air we breathe. Similarly, trees filter airborne particulates, resulting in 27 to 42 percent less ground-level dust in treed areas than in open areas, an important health benefit for people sensitive to dust or allergic to pollen (Forest Alliance of British Columbia, n.d.). Ultimately, however, air pollution will damage forest health; the decline in the health of German forests noted previously, and the loss of ponderosa pine forests near Los Angeles due to smog, attest to this fact.

For all of the above reasons, as well as the fact that they increase property values by 5 to 20 percent or more, "trees are not mere niceties, they're necessities" (Krakauer, 1990). We need to remember this as our cities grow—in Canada every day, forests are cleared to make way for new subdivisions, shopping centres, roadways, agriculture, and grazing lands. Population growth within cities means city trees also are lost to development changes designed to accommodate new residents. While not a total substitute for natural forests, urban tree planting, such as that encouraged by the Green Streets Canada Program (an initiative of Tree Plan Canada), is an important greening activity. By 1994, more than 40 million trees had been planted in rural and urban areas (Natural Resources Canada, 1995).

SOURCES: Forest Alliance of British Columbia. (n.d.). The urban forest. *Choices*, 4(1), p. 2.

Krakauer, J. (1990). Trees aren't mere niceties—they're necessities. *Smithsonian*, 21 (April), pp. 160–71.

Natural Resources Canada, Canadian Forest Service. (1995). *The state of Canada's forests 1994: A balancing act.* Ottawa.

Ulrich, R.S. (1979). Visual landscapes and psychological well-being. *Landscape Research*, 4, pp. 17–23.

new residential developments, in part because frontage of single-family detached lots has decreased from the 15 to 18 metres (50 to 60 feet) common up until the 1970s to about 9 to 12 metres (30 to 40 feet) common in the 1990s.

Loss of Agricultural Land

Both historically and today in Canada, much of the expansion of settlement occurs on fertile agricultural land. About 25 percent of Canada's high-capability (class 1 to 3) agricultural land is located within 80 kilometres of the 23 largest cities; this includes more than 50 percent of our prime, class 1 agricultural land. While it may seem that the amount of agricultural land lost to urbanization is quite small, there are two important factors that we need to remember. One factor in this complex issue is that in some parts of Canada urbanization affects specialty crop areas. The Okanagan Valley in British Columbia, the Niagara Peninsula in Ontario, and the horticultural lands adjacent to Vancouver and Montreal are areas that account for only a tiny proportion of the total amount of productive land in Canada. In these areas, however, urbanization has far more significant impacts than in other parts of Canada.

The second factor is that urban growth affects agriculture in many indirect ways. Agricultural regions experience significant economic and social impacts when extensive industrial sites, gravel pits, golf courses, recreational facilities, and residential estates are developed. Sometimes called urban shadow effects, these impacts extend over large areas and cause declines in agriculture in urban regions (Gertler, Crowley, & Bond, 1977). The problem seems to be that once agricultural production is discouraged, even land that is not needed for urban growth comes to be occupied by nonagricultural uses or is abandoned. In efforts to combat this problem, Quebec and British Columbia have had protective agricultural zoning in place for years, and other provinces have adopted policies that regulate urban expansion in agricultural areas.

In addition to agricultural land loss, removal of woodlands, disruption of wildlife corridors, destruction of habitat, and accelerated soil erosion, urban expansion has resulted in the loss of wetlands. By 1981, for instance, 98 percent of the original wetlands in the vicinity of Windsor, Winnipeg, and Regina had been converted to other uses. In the Toronto and Montreal areas, 88 percent of wetlands had been filled or drained by 1981, and a similar fate had claimed 78 percent of wetlands in the vicinity of St. Catharines–Niagara Falls, Calgary, and Vancouver (Environment Canada, 1988).

Other environmentally sensitive areas may be threatened (and sometimes are destroyed) by urban expansion, including aquatic habitats if groundwater and surface water bodies are polluted by storm runoff or septic tank and landfill seepage. Air quality, too, may be affected by the operation of gravel pits and landfills, including the con-

Increasingly heavy use of even large protected areas, such as Stanley Park, presents sustainability challenges.

tinuous truck traffic they generate. These and previously noted effects of human activities associated with the city remind us that our ecological footprint (see Chapter 1) is impressed on the productive output of a land area many times larger than the geographic size of our cities. If we are to continue to support people's demands for food, water, forest products, and energy, and to assimilate the wastes resulting from our urban activities, then actions to ensure sustainability of our communities and to protect the environment that maintains them are vital. (See Box 13–4 for information on urban agriculture.)

BOX 13–4
URBAN AGRICULTURE

For most Canadians, food is plentiful and we are among the best-fed people in the world measured by caloric intake. However, Canadians living in urban areas rarely think about where their food comes from or about the environmental issues associated with the abundance of food seen in the supermarket. For instance, food prices tend not to incorporate fully the long-term environmental costs of production and transportation—it has been estimated that it takes three times as much energy to truck a head of lettuce from California to Toronto as it does to grow it locally in season (cited in Government of Canada, 1996). (For an in-depth look at the environmental implications of one of our most common food choices, the hamburger, see Environment Canada's State of the Environment Fact Sheet No. 95-1.)

Concerns about the sustainability of Canada's resource-intensive food production system, as well as health concerns

surrounding the use of additives and preservatives, have sparked increased interest in organic farming, and in gardening in the city (urban agriculture). Since 1978, City Farmer, a non-profit society, has promoted urban food production and environmental conservation from their small office in downtown Vancouver and from their demonstration food garden in a residential Kitsilano neighbourhood.

Montreal's Community Gardening project is recognized as the largest and best organized city gardening program in the country. The program's work in the 1990s has involved composting research, donating food to community kitchens, providing access for disabled gardeners, and horticultural therapy projects. (For more information on the Kitsilano and the Montreal projects, see the City Farmer Web sites listed in the References section of this chapter.)

SOURCE: City Farmer. (1997). *Montreal's community gardening program.* http://www.cityfarmer.org./Montreal13.html#ontreal

City Farmer. (1997). *Urban Agriculture Notes.* http://www.cityfarmer.org/urbagnotes1.html#notes

Environment Canada. (1995). *Connections: Canadian lifestyle choices and the environment.* State of the Environment Fact Sheet No. 95-1. Ottawa.

Government of Canada. (1996). *The state of Canada's environment—1996.* Ottawa: Supply and Services Canada.

TOWARD SUSTAINABLE COMMUNITIES

If cities did not grow, many of the ecological impacts noted above might not occur. However, we have come to appreciate that many consequences of urban growth could be avoided, or their impacts reduced, if we paid more careful attention to and incorporated stricter controls in land use planning. Similarly, if our attitudes toward our consumption patterns and lifestyles consciously reflected an awareness of our dependence on the natural environment for our own (and the planet's) well-being, our decisions, behaviours, and choices might be different and more environmentally friendly than they are now.

Before we consider examples of actual actions undertaken to move toward more sustainable communities, it is worthwhile outlining what is meant by sustainability in an urban context.

CITIES AND SUSTAINABILITY

The density, form, and structure of Canadian cities, as well as the activities of people within cities, are the principal sources of stress to the ecosystem in urban areas. Achieving more sustainable communities implies that these sources of stress are reduced. This does not mean that cities should strive to be self-sufficient within their own boundaries, but rather that cities should meet the needs of society while simultaneously using resources and generating wastes at levels that are compatible with ecological sustainability within their region. In addition, cities should strive for no overall loss of environmental capital within both the nation and the planet (Mitlin & Satterthwaite, 1994).

This means that cities need not only to perform the economic functions that are the basis of their existence but also to evolve to meet changing social and economic needs. In practice, citizens need to place a high priority on the condition of the environment and to ensure that city administrators not only recognize the need for continuing economic and physical development and revitalization in the city, but also provide water and sewage treatment plants, clean up contaminated land, and preserve open spaces. In short, environmental protection and resource conservation must be recognized as integral components of urban form and function.

Potentially, cities may be better for environmental protection and resource conservation than dispersed settlement patterns because cities may achieve economies and efficiencies in water, sewage, and waste disposal (including recycling and reuse), in energy use (through district heating), in use of land (through compact development), and in transportation (substituting walking, bicycling, and

transit for car use) (Government of Canada, 1996). However, if urban sustainability is to be an objective of Canadian cities, we need to recognize that some obstacles exist.

Among the major obstacles is the fact that we still lack certain kinds of information on which to base long-term decisions about the future of our urban areas. For instance, we do not know the long-term consequences of climate change, or the implications of certain air and water pollutants for human and ecosystem health, nor the best physical form or appropriate density for residential occupation. Lack of full knowledge, however, is never an excuse for inaction on any of these issues.

We do know that Canadians continue to prefer single-family detached housing over higher density housing, and that they prefer to use their cars rather than public transit. Changing ingrained social values, and personal lifestyle and economic attributes such as these, always is difficult. And, as numbers of the oldest and relatively prosperous segment of the Canadian population grow, resistance to change may increase (Government of Canada, 1996). Such social and demographic factors suggest that, to date, the concept of environmental sustainability has not been a significant influence for change in the complex field of urban development.

Another reason we have been slow to move to a sustainable communities approach to urbanization is because of the great expense and long life of the buildings, expressways, sewage treatment plants, public transit systems, and other facilities that make up our urban fabric. It would be very costly, both socially and financially, if we decided to quickly and radically alter this urban fabric. Particularly given current fiscal constraints, slow evolution toward more sustainable communities is the most likely scenario for change.

Another obstacle is that political control and administration of cities in Canada is not well suited to achieving sustainable communities. Different federal, provincial, and municipal policies and programs, the lack of coordination between them, and the lack of cooperation among the three levels of government affect communities differentially. Sometimes, for instance, governmental policies make it difficult to balance social, economic, and environmental aspects of urban development, or to weigh the specific interests of a small part of the population against more diffuse interests of everyone. Fortunately, government departments and agencies are working to improve their cooperation and coordination so that progress toward sustainable communities may advance.

MAKING CANADIAN CITIES MORE SUSTAINABLE

In spite of the difficulties in striving for urban sustainability, there are signs of progress in urban form, conservation, reduction of environmental impacts, transportation, and planning. In the sections that follow, we consider some examples of actions that have been taken to help make Canadian cities more sustainable.

Urban Form

Current thinking is that urban sustainability will be advanced through a more compact urban form. A more compact urban form is expected to lead to more economical use of land, water, energy, and materials, and to reduce our dependence on cars in the city. Several municipalities across Canada, including the city of Halifax, the regional municipality of Hamilton–Wentworth, Metropolitan Toronto, and the city of Regina have revised their planning policies deliberately to support the shift to more compact urban forms. The kinds of changes that are envisioned for sustainable cities in Canada in the future are identified in Table 13–3.

Carma Developers' McKenzie Towne in Calgary uses neighbourhood squares containing a civic monument, a location for community gatherings, and a public transit stop—all within a five-minute walk.

TABLE 13–3
CHARACTERISTICS OF CANADIAN "SUSTAINABLE CITIES" IN THE FUTURE

Changes to the form of the city (the pattern and density of its physical fabric) are expected to advance urban sustainability. In the future, sustainable cities in Canada would be expected to have the following characteristics:

- A substantially higher average density than today's city
  - Land is used more fully; abandoned or underused sites are redeveloped.
  - Obsolete industrial and commercial buildings are converted to residential use.
  - Single-family detached housing (low density) largely is replaced by more dense, compact forms.
  - Compact, affordable, and adaptable housing, such as the narrow, two-storey rowhouse (Grow Home) designed at McGill University's School of Architecture, provides ground-level access and some private outdoor space.

- A network of viable, linked subcentres
  - These subcentres and the downtown area are linked by mixed-use corridors and high-capacity, rapid transit.
  - Each centre provides a range of services plus employment opportunities and moderate- to high-density housing.

- A mixed land use pattern
  - Residential and other uses are mixed (more than we see now) with compatible, nonpolluting industries located in or adjacent to subcentres.
  - This mixed-use development, including a mix of different housing types and sizes, reduces the need for travel.

- A citywide transit system and a network of bicycle routes
  - Convenient, efficient, and reliable city public transit system results in restrictions on the use of private cars, particularly in the downtown area and core of the subcentres.
  - Safe bicycle routes also are constructed.

- A range of housing choices in every residential district
  - All houses are built to high standards of energy and water efficiency.
  - Residents walk safely and conveniently to transit and cycle routes and to local schools, shops, and parks.

- Corridors of open space
  - Open space corridors are left in their natural condition and run through the entire city.
  - These provide recreational opportunities and ecological links to parks and the open countryside.

- A well-defined edge of the city
  - Carefully planned urban expansion is compact and has no scattered urban infiltration into the surrounding rural area.
  - Expansion is mainly in the form of physically separate satellite communities developed around their own subcentres and served by the city's rapid transit system.

Planners feel that such reshaping of the city is attainable and would go a long way toward conserving land, natural ecosystems, energy, and water, and would reduce air pollution. As well, it would provide an extremely liveable urban environment.

SOURCE: Government of Canada. (1996). *The state of Canada's environment—1996*. Ottawa: Supply and Services Canada. Chapter 12.

Some of these changes are being put in place now; for example, in Greater Toronto and Greater Vancouver, suburban town centres on high-capacity transit networks are being developed to house commercial and institutional activities that once were concentrated downtown. Kitchener and Winnipeg have adopted urban growth boundaries. In communities such as Bamberton (near Victoria), McKenzie Towne in Calgary, and Cornell (near Toronto), new community developments have been planned explicitly to achieve conservation and environmental protection goals in addition to social goals. Each of these developments features relatively high densities and encourages movement by foot, bicycle, and transit rather than by car. Also, the Historic Properties in Halifax, Montreal's Vieux Port, Toronto's St. Lawrence neighbourhood, The Forks in Winnipeg, and False Creek in Vancouver are examples of the cleanup and transformation of obsolete industrial, rail yard, and warehouse areas for different purposes including housing, office buildings, and parkland.

In addition, intensification (developing or redeveloping land at higher densities) is an issue that is being worked out through building conversions, neighbourhood rehabilitation, and infill construction. In cities as diverse as Toronto, St. John's, Sudbury, Montreal, and Vancouver, places of employment and residence are being integrated in mixed-use neighbourhoods. Higher intensity land use is being achieved also through the use of infill housing, smaller lots in new suburban areas, and by Main Street initiatives that encourage residential development above retail establishments. (For further information on density and mixed use, see Newman, 1996, in the Additional Information Sources section of this chapter.)

Conservation

Water Conservation Water and energy conservation programs have been put in place in many Canadian municipalities. Water conservation programs typically involve city programs such as leak detection and repair, metering, public education, and use restrictions. Major centres such as Toronto, Ottawa–Carleton, Laval, and Edmonton have broad water management plans in place, as do many smaller urban centres such as Cochrane, Ontario, and Rosemère, Quebec. Communities also contemplate alternatives: in considering how their area could move toward sustainability, the Greater Vancouver Regional District has proposed that rainwater be collected for flushing toilets and for use in gardens (Balcom, 1997). Both municipal and community actions are important in water conservation.

Energy Conservation Like water conservation programs, energy conservation efforts focus both on reduction of city costs for fuel and electricity, and on community-wide initiatives that contribute to economic, social, and environmental objectives such as local economic development, improved air quality, and reduced CO_2 emissions. Common energy conservation initiatives include changing streetlighting, adopting energy standards for buildings, retrofitting municipal buildings, and converting municipal vehicles to alternative fuels (Federation of Canadian Municipalities, 1995).

Energy audits and energy controls in municipal buildings, and energy reviews of newly designed municipal facilities, are among the ways both large and small communities can identify energy-saving possibilities. Quebec, for example, has had a provincial law on energy efficiency in new buildings since 1983. In other parts of the country, community partnerships with utility companies such as Ontario Hydro have enabled smaller communities to identify opportunities for managing energy demand and to implement energy and cost-saving measures.

Increasingly, municipalities have become involved in urban energy management, and have linked with broader community environmental efforts. Ontario's Green Communities program is one example where the focus was on smaller centres such as Guelph, Sarnia, and Peterborough. Domestic energy conservation measures also are being adopted both through retrofitting of older buildings and in new construction (including R-2000 standards; see Chapter 11).

Conservation of Materials Many Canadian municipalities now offer recycling programs, compost collection, and other waste reduction services. Typically, emphasis is on the "3Rs"—reduction of the volume of waste at its source, reuse of materials, and recycling and composting. Some cities, including Sherbrooke, Montreal, Toronto, and Vancouver, have firm waste reduction targets; some, such

Readily available and affordable, recycled-plastic compost bins are an increasingly common sight.

Collecting rainwater in barrels or other containers is an effective way for individuals and communities to augment municipal water supply systems.

as Toronto and Vancouver, are trying to establish controls on packaging; and still others have placed limits on the amount of garbage the city will collect from each dwelling.

Access to recycling programs of various types has increased throughout Canada; in 1994, 69.6 percent of Canadian households had access to a paper recycling program either through curbside collection or recycling depots. While paper recycling is the most widely available program, access to recycling programs for glass bottles (67.4 percent), metal cans (67.2 percent), and plastics (62.8 percent) also increased. Also, 40.2 percent of communities offer special hazardous waste disposal opportunities for paints, chemicals, and batteries. Since the early 1990s, when large cities generally had programs in place, access to recycling facilities has increased most in larger urban areas in Quebec and Atlantic Canada as well as in smaller centres in Ontario and western Canada. At least through 1994, more than 81 percent of households with access to recycling programs continued to use them. In spite of its strong potential to reduce the amount of organic material entering the municipal waste stream, composting has not been accepted as readily as other recycling programs; in 1994, only 23 percent of households used a compost heap (Statistics Canada, 1995).

Conservation of Ecosystems and Natural Features

Cities are moving away from the traditional view of urban parks as green areas for recreation and toward conservation of natural areas, environmentally sensitive areas, and natural habitats. Although the biodiversity values of wetlands, shore zones, forests, and wildlife corridors have begun to be recognized, their protection is just beginning at the local level.

To encourage wildlife population growth and restoration of natural ecosystems, cities including Ottawa,

Edmonton, Toronto, and Montreal have begun to create or restore green corridors by linking small natural areas, cemeteries, waterfronts, transmission line right of ways, and other open spaces. Nationally, the Trans Canada Trail Foundation is overseeing the creation of a cross-country trail that conserves and preserves our natural heritage (see Enviro-Focus 13). The city of Calgary employs its Natural Area Management Plan to help protect existing natural environments and to identify potential areas for future conservation prior to their development. Many cities now practice urban forestry, encourage naturalization of vegetation, and substitute integrated pest management for chemical pesticides. From Gander, Newfoundland, to Fort Saskatchewan, Alberta, experiments have been undertaken with sheep and other herbivores to replace gasoline-powered lawnmowers (Federation of Canadian Municipalities, 1995).

Some recent municipal legislation has focused on achieving ecosystem based planning. The ecosystem approach—land use planning that is based on natural boundaries and respect for ecosystem integrity (Table 13–4)—is more promise than practice at the moment. However, outstanding examples of the application of the ecosystem approach are the Fraser River Estuary Management Program, Saskatoon's Meewasin Valley Authority (see the Web site listed in the Additional Information Sources section), and the Hamilton Harbour Remedial Action Plan (Tomalty, Alexander, Fisher & Gibson, 1994).

Reduction of Environmental Impacts

Ideally, cities should be free of activities that harm the health of other people or natural ecosystems. In reality, however, financial, jurisdictional, and behavioural barriers arise that affect progress toward air and water quality, waste management, and cleanups of harmful sites or substances.

Air Quality The main way to lower concentrations of ground-level ozone (the leading urban air quality problem in Canada) is to reduce the emissions of its precursors (nitrogen oxides and VOCs) by motor vehicles. Federal and provincial governments largely control air pollution action—such as banning leaded gasoline and regulating vehicle emissions—through the federal Motor Vehicle Safety Act and other provincial regulations. Federal and provincial governments continuously review quality standards and regulations (the NAAQOs), and some cities are taking action to improve air quality.

As of June 1997, 30 municipalities across Canada had joined the Twenty Percent Club, each with its own plan to reduce emissions that contribute to global climate change and stratospheric ozone depletion. In reducing the amount of fossil fuel burned in city facilities, and in encouraging individual homeowners to conserve energy, municipal programs are working to reduce greenhouse gas emissions by 20 percent from their 1988

The Trans Canada Trail: A Legacy for Future Generations

When the main trunk of the 15 000-kilometre Trans Canada Trail is completed, on June 21, 2000, it will be the longest trail in the world. A shared-use recreational trail that will link all provinces and territories, the Trans Canada Trail is a community-based project that will preserve and protect the environment; promote physical fitness and well-being; provide a safe and secure place for recreational activity; act as a stimulus for local economies (such as bed-and-breakfast operations); educate people by bringing them closer to nature and their historical roots; and foster eco-tourism opportunities.

Since 1994, when the Trans Canada Trail Foundation was launched publicly as an independent registered charity, about $2.5 million (of the estimated $42 million required) has been raised toward the building of the trail. Over 70 000 Canadians have donated an average of just under $60 each to the building of the trail. By 1996, individuals had raised about 65 percent of the donations, corporations had raised 30 percent, and governments, 5 percent. Through local trail and community groups, about 1.5 million people across Canada are volunteers with the trail councils in their region and their organizations have united to fulfill a shared vision of making the Trans Canada Trail a reality.

Built on provincial and federal park and Crown lands, on abandoned railway lines, alongside railway lines, and on private land, the trail will accommodate five core activities: walking, cycling, horseback riding, cross-country skiing, and (where possible or desired) snowmobiling. In 1996 about 800 kilometres of the trail were dedicated to the Trans Canada Trail, including the Galloping Goose Trail in Victoria, B.C. (a 60-kilometre former rail line, considered the first "rails to trails" conversion in Canada); the Caledon Trailway, Jackson Creek Kiwanis Trail, Elora Cataract Trailway, and Grand River Trails in Ontario; several sections of trail in the National Capital Commission area (Ottawa–Hull); Le Petit Temis (between Cabano, Quebec, and Edmundston, N.B.), Guysborough Trail in Nova Scotia; and Confederation Trail in Prince Edward Island. The foundation expects to have opened over 1200 kilometres of trail by the end of 1997.

Metre by metre, Canadians are making the Trans Canada Trail happen. If you would like to be a part of this important undertaking, you can find more information by e-mail (info@tctrail.ca) or by phone (1-800-465-3636), as well as at the Web site noted below.

SOURCE: Trans Canada Trail Foundation. *The Trans Canada Trail*. http://www.tctrail.ca/home_page.htm

levels by the year 2005. In May 1997, Toronto became the first city in North America to report that it had stabilized its greenhouse gas emissions at 1990 levels (Marchi, 1997).

Several cities have policies and programs relating to the use of alternative fuels as well as the reduction of emissions of sulphur dioxide, carbon dioxide, and nitrogen dioxide. Vancouver directs attention toward reduction of greenhouse gas and ozone-depleting emissions, Montreal's strategy focuses on reducing emissions and use of CFCs and halons, and Toronto has specific targets for reducing SO_2 emissions by 2006.

Since, in an ecosystem, everything is connected to everything else, an ecosystem approach should

- encompass natural, physical, social, cultural, and economic considerations, and the relationships among them

- focus on understanding interactions among air, land, water, and living organisms, including humans

- emphasize the dynamic nature of ecosystems

- recognize the importance of living species other than humans, and of future generations

- work to restore and maintain the integrity, quality, and health of the ecosystem

SOURCE: Government of Canada. (1996). *The state of Canada's environment—1996.* Ottawa: Supply and Services Canada. Adapted from Box 12.4.

Water Quality Ideally, when treated water is released to the receiving body of water, the treated water should be at least as clean as when it entered the supply system or fell as natural precipitation. This idea that there should be no increase in the net level of impurities in the hydrologic cycle has been interpreted to mean that cities should (1) provide secondary or tertiary treatment of all wastewater, including storm drainage, (2) prevent overloading of treatment plants in heavy storms, and (3) make necessary improvements to their collection system to prevent leakages resulting from age and deterioration.

Although variable, the level of wastewater treatment has increased across Canada. Montreal recently has completed a major sewage treatment scheme, while smaller centres such as Banff, Portage la Prairie, and others use innovative methods of sewage treatment including biological processes and ultraviolet disinfection. However, on the argument that health risks and harm to the environment are negligible if the discharge pipe is located at sufficient depth and distance from shore, and if currents are suitable, some coastal cities discharge sewage into the sea after only low levels of treatment. Victoria's practice of discharging untreated sewage waste into the Strait of Juan de Fuca has, for years, generated continuing complaints from Washington state.

Waste Management and Cleaning Up Good urban waste management programs help protect the environment and conserve materials by reducing the total quantity of waste that must be assimilated into the environment. Because everything is connected to everything else, any disposal method will have some adverse

environmental effects. While we cannot eliminate them, we can work to minimize these effects. On this basis, in addition to promoting the 3Rs, many cities locate their landfills in such a way that truck traffic is minimized; locate, design, and construct landfills so that leaching and gas emissions are prevented and so that, ultimately, landfills may be restored as usable land; employ the best incineration technology (if used); and involve the public in planning of disposal programs.

Cleaning up past environmental legacies of activities within a city sometimes entails dealing with contaminated land (by removing, treating, or disposing harmlessly of the soil), or finding ways to use the site that will not endanger human health. Outside the city, it might be necessary to deal with old garbage dumps and tire disposal sites that may affect groundwater and pose health risks or fire hazards. Vancouver, Calgary, Toronto, Ottawa, and Montreal have developed comprehensive inventories of contaminated sites and have review processes in place to control development on or near these sites (Federation of Canadian Municipalities, 1995).

Transportation

Apart from walking and human-powered vehicles such as bicycles, all forms of transport entail significant consumption of resources and impacts on the environment, particularly on air quality. Because transportation decisions affect urban environments in so many ways, transportation is a key area for action. Some of the many ways cities can and have achieved greater sustainability in their transportation systems are outlined in Table 13–5. In 1993 it was determined that if we could apply the kinds of measures identified in Table 13–5, even without changes in urban structure or improved emission control and fuel efficiency, the average energy use could be reduced by 29 to 36 percent by the year 2000 (IBI Group, 1993). In addition, we have the lessons from northern European ecological community design to assist us in reducing dependency on our vehicles (Saunders, 1996).

Throughout the country, in both large and smaller urban centres, a variety of initiatives to improve transportation have been undertaken and are under way. These initiatives may be categorized as urban structure and urban design policies, transportation infrastructure, demand management, traffic and transit management, and cleaner vehicle technology (Irwin, 1994). Specific municipal policies and programs to improve transit services have been implemented in St. John's, Dartmouth, Montreal, and Toronto; reserved bus lanes have been established in Vancouver, Toronto, Ottawa, and Montreal; parking-related measures have been proposed in Montreal, Toronto, and Vancouver; and bicycle and pedestrian networks exist in Calgary, Vancouver, and other cities.

TABLE 13 – 5
ACTIONS TO ACHIEVE MORE SUSTAINABLE URBAN TRANSPORTATION

- Shift budget and program priorities from road systems to transit systems.

- Provide diverse transit options such as rapid transit, commuter rail, and surface transit networks, special facilities for high-occupancy vehicles such as car and van pools and cycle and pedestrian pathways.

- Improve efficiency, speed, reliability, and general attractiveness of transit through dedicated lanes for buses, transit priority at intersections, schedule reliability, provisions of up-to-the-minute travel information, and integration of fares and schedules between routes and systems.

- Encourage more efficient use of infrastructure and vehicles such as travelling at off-peak time, combining trips, substituting transit for car use, sharing vehicles, and using less congested routes.

- Discourage unnecessary automobile use in local residential areas by such means as traffic calming street design.

- Provide public outreach, awareness, and education programs.

- Improve vehicle technology by designing lighter, more aerodynamic vehicles and smaller, more fuel-efficient engines, and by developing alternative fuels.

- Reduce the need for vehicular movement by implementing urban designs in which land use and transportation are integrated to create pedestrian-friendly streets and compact centres of intensive mixed activity linked by mixed-use corridors.

SOURCE: Government of Canada. (1996). *The state of Canada's environment—1996.* Ottawa: Supply and Services Canada. Chapter 12.

Planning

Deliberate movement toward urban sustainability implies "a more holistic, ecosystem-based approach to urban policy and governance than has been usual in Canada" (Government of Canada, 1996). This kind of approach means that attention would be paid at the local level to developing and implementing urban sustainability goals, standards, and criteria, and that progress toward sustainability would be monitored and reported on in regular, municipal state-of-the-environment reports. In addition, sustainability goals would be supported by appropriate provincial (and sometimes federal) fiscal policies and economic development policies that are consistent with sustainability goals and principles. This approach also implies integrated, effective planning for the entire urban region.

Examples of municipal cooperation in planning for sustainability are found in the official plan of the Regional Municipality of Ottawa–Carleton, the regional Municipality of Sudbury's land reclamation program, and the Greater Vancouver Regional District's Livable Region Strategy. Other municipalities are moving toward more comprehensive sustainable development or environmental policies. The city of Halifax, and the Regional Municipality of Hamilton–Wentworth, among others, are implementing their broad visions of sustainability for the future (Pearce, 1995). Many cities now have environmental offices and interdepartmental environmental committees composed of municipal staff. Others, such as Calgary, have developed environmental advisory committees that value public representation and input. Severe budgetary cutbacks in some municipalities, however, likely portend reductions in environmental programs.

Several municipalities have produced (or are in the process of preparing) state-of-the-environment reports, while other cities have completed reports on the quality of life, state of the city, or environmental issues. Following the lead of the city of Ottawa, many municipalities might attempt to produce comprehensive municipal environmental evaluation procedures for review of development applications.

Regarding citizen action, it has been the persistent and frequently well-informed and skillful lobbying of environmental advocacy organizations that often has helped bring about new or improved policies and programs within cities. In addition, some municipalities try to involve residents in environmental actions ranging from community cleanups, to tree-planting and park naturalization efforts, to bird counts. Similarly, the healthy communities movement in Quebec, Ontario, and British Columbia has the common (and provincially supported) goal of socially, economically, and environmentally healthy communities. In short, hundreds of communities across Canada have developed a variety of achievable and practical sustainability strategies through involvement of local citizens and municipal representatives.

PROGRESS TOWARD URBAN SUSTAINABILITY?

Although it is not possible to provide a definitive answer to the question of whether Canadian cities are being planned and managed in ways that are moving them toward greater sustainability, there are signs that some resource demands and some stresses on both local ecosystems and the global ecosphere are being reduced. If we accept various reservations and exceptions, progress is evident in air and water quality and waste management areas. Although more can be done with regard to the conservation of water, energy, and materials, progress also has been made. Municipalities also are continuing to make substantial efforts to conserve and protect environmentally sensitive areas, green space, and natural systems.

As intensification has become a major policy goal, there has been increasing restraint on low-density expansion in the urban fringe. Cities are trying numerous approaches to have citizens use transit, bicycles, and their feet instead of cars. And new techniques and approaches such as environmental assessment, sustainable development policies, and state-of-the-environment reporting are appearing more frequently in municipal operations (Government of Canada, 1996).

In spite of these successes, however, there is concern that continuing improvement in energy conservation and in air quality depends on attaining a more compact urban form and a substantial shift in modes of transportation. Municipal and provincial action being taken may not be sufficient to achieve the required changes. For instance, in light of the cuts to transit expenditures being experienced by many cities (budget cutbacks), how likely is it that costly, substantial improvements to transit systems will be authorized? Given current and foreseeable future market forces and consumer preferences, how likely is it that large numbers of people will choose more compact types of housing, or switch from cars to buses or subway trains? Demographic trends do not suggest encouraging changes, and yet our cities, and the number of cars within them, continue to grow.

If global warming impacts occur, the implications for Canadian cities include flooding, depletion or degradation of water supply, increased energy demands and deteriorating air quality, and even the potential for serious impacts on the economic base in some areas. And because cities in Canada (and elsewhere) are dependent on the depleting and increasingly less diverse resources from the "global hinterland," they are made even more vulnerable to these long-term threats. In short, while there are signs of progress, there also are signs of concern that the recent municipal movement toward an ecosystem-based approach to land use planning may not come to full fruition. The words of Roberta Bondar (1994), Canada's first female astronaut, are worth remembering: "Good intentions and expressions of concern are not enough. Protecting the environment is the most serious challenge we face today. Every Canadian can and must get involved, not just today, but every day." Long-term change comes about when we all care about the future world we will inhabit and act on our environmental convictions.

Chapter Questions

1. How do cities change their own environment and affect the environment of surrounding areas? How can we plan cities to minimize some of these effects?

2. In what ways is a high-quality life, with reduced waste, reduced energy use, and reduced pollution, both a goal and a challenge?

3. Discuss the ways in which sustainable housing can leave a smaller footprint on the ecosystem than conventional single-family homes. Are there ways in which existing housing in your community can be made more sustainable?

4. Comment: Natural area habitats in city parks and preserves will become more important as wilderness decreases.

5. All over Canada, people are taking action to encourage and promote healthy neighbourhoods. Consider your neighbourhood. What are some of the actions that have been taken—or could be taken—to reduce the impact of "the car culture"? What could you do to take the lead in your neighbourhood to reduce the impact cars have on the environment and on our health?

6. One of the challenges facing Canadians in urban areas is to reduce the waste stream. How would you design a program for your community that would achieve a 50-percent reduction of the waste stream? What would be the most important factors to take into account?

Balcom, S. (1997, April 12). West coast experiments with sustainable housing. *Calgary Herald,* p. 113.

Beale, J. (1996). Canadian Pacific Hotel's enviro-intiatives. *Ecolutions,* Winter, pp. 24–25.

Beltrame, J. (1997, June 12). Canada is still the best place to live. *Calgary Herald,* p. A5.

Black Range Films. (n.d.). *Straw bale construction.* Kingston, NM.

Bondar, R. (1994, April 18). Earthweek only first step in campaign to save environment, Dr. Roberta Bondar says. *Canada News Wire.*

Canadian Arctic Resources Committee. (1997, Spring). Letter from Chair.

Canadian Arctic Resources Committee. http://www.carc.org

Canadian Council of Ministers of the Environment. (1990). *Management plan for nitrogen oxides (NO$_x$) and volatile organic compounds (VOCs).* Phase 1. Winnipeg: CCME.

Canadian Environmental Assessment Agency. (1995). *Military flying activities in Labrador and Quebec. Report of the Environmental Assessment Panel.* Ottawa.

Checora, G. (1996). Calgary house goes beyond sustainability. *Alternatives,* 22(4), pp. 5–6.

City Farmer. Urban agriculture notes. *Montreal's Community Gardening Project.* http://www.cityfarmer.org/urbagnotes1.html#notes

City Farmer. Urban agriculture notes. *The Demonstration Garden* (Kitsiano). http://www.cityfarmer.org/Montreal13html#ontreal

City of Vancouver. (1997). *City noise: Report of the Urban Noise Task Force.* Vancouver, BC: City of Vancouver.

Engman, K. (1997, June 15). Water meter levels rising. *Calgary Herald,* p. A3.

Environment Canada. (1988). *Wetlands of Canada.* Ecological Land Classification Series No. 24. Ottawa: Environment Canada, National Wetlands Working Group, Canada Committee on Ecological Land Classification.

Environment Canada. (1991). *The national incinerator testing and evaluation program.* Ottawa.

Environment Canada. The Green Lane. Vehicle Emissions Inspection Clinic Program. http://www.ec.gc.ca/special/emissions_e.htm

Federation of Canadian Municipalities. (1995). *Canadian municipal environmental directory: municipal government actions for a sustainable environment: A compendium of environmental initiatives.* Ottawa.

Forest Alliance of British Columbia. (n.d.). The urban forest. *Choices,* 4(1), p. 2.

Fried, J.J. (1996, January 6). Noise. *Calgary Herald,* p. B4.

Gauthier, P., & Haman, A. (1992). Amateur sport in Canada. *Canadian Social Trends,* Summer, pp. 21–22.

Gertler, L.O., Crowley, R.W., & Bond, W.K. (1977). *Changing Canadian cities: The next 25 years.* Toronto: McClelland and Stewart.

Greater Vancouver Regional District. (1993). *Drinking water quality improvement plan: Discussion paper.* Vancouver.

Greater Vancouver Regional District. (1994). *Let's clear the air: Draft air quality management plan—summary document.* Vancouver.

Hancock, T. (1996). Healthy, sustainable communities: Concept, fledgling practice and implications for governance. *Alternatives,* 22(2), pp. 18–23.

HEARNET. (1997). May 1997 HEARNET. http://www.hearnet.com/

Hope, M. (1995, June 3). Earthship Alberta: Construction method uses recycled tires, compacted soil. *Calgary Herald,* p. H3.

IBI Group. (1990). *Greater Toronto area urban structure concepts study—summary report.* Toronto: Greater Toronto Coordinating Committee.

IBI Group. (1993). *Initiatives to limit transportation energy consumption and emissions in Canadian cities.* Ottawa: Natural Resources Canada.

Irwin, N. (1994). *A new vision for urban transportation: Current Canadian initiatives.* In Transportation Association of Canada, Federation of Canadian Municipalities, and Canadian Institute of Planners, Ottawa. *Proceedings: New visions in urban transportation. (Part 3).* Ottawa: Transportation Association of Canada.

King, F. (1996, May 11). Hay, there's a new way to build a house! *Calgary Herald,* p. I10.

Krakauer, J. (1990). Trees aren't mere niceties—they're necessities. *Smithsonian,* 21 (April), pp. 160–71.

Mander, J. (1997). Foreword. In A.R. Drengson & D.M. Taylor (Eds.). *Ecoforestry: The art and science of sustainable forest use.* Gabriola Island, BC: New Society Publishers, p. 12.

Marchi, S. (1997). Making our cities sustainable. http://www.ec.gc.ca/minister/speeches/fcm_s_e.htm

Mitlin, D., & Satterthwaite, D. (1994). *Cities and sustainable development: Background paper prepared for Global Forum '94.* London: International Institute for Environment and Development, Human Settlements Program.

Natural Resources Canada, Canadian Forest Service. (1995). *The state of Canada's forests 1994: A balancing act.* Ottawa.

Oosterom, N. (1995, October 25). Piggy's idea recycled: Straw replaces scarce wood. *Calgary Herald,* p. A2.

Patterson, B. (1995, November 14). Sound off. *Victoria Times Colonist,* p. C1.

Pearce, B. (1995). Hamilton–Wentworth region's sustainable community initiatives. *Plan Canada,* 35(5), pp. 26–27.

Peck, K. (1997). Letter from executive director. May 1997 HEARNET. http://www.hearnet.com/text/mainframe.html

Pitney Bowes. (1994). *Pitney Bowes fourth annual green office survey.* Toronto: Pitney Bowes.

Saunders, T. (1996). Ecology and community design. *Alternatives,* 22(2), pp. 24–29.

Shideler, K. (1997, March 15). Common noise and "boom cars" cause hearing loss. *Calgary Herald,* p. C9.

Statistics Canada. (1995). *Households and the environment 1994.* Statistics Canada Catalogue No. 11-526. Ottawa: Statistics Canada, Household Surveys Division.

Tomalty, R., Alexander, D.H.M., Fisher, J., & Gibson, R.B. (1994). *Planning with an ecosystem approach in Canadian cities.* Toronto: Intergovernmental Committee on Urban and Regional Research Press.

Trans Canada Trail Foundation. (n.d.). The Trans Canada Trail. http://www.tctrail.ca/home_page.htm

Turner, J. (1996, August 28). Tide is turning against industrial waterfront. *The Globe and Mail* (Toronto), p. A2.

Ulrich, R.S. (1979). Visual landscapes and psychological well-being. *Landscape Research,* 4, pp. 17–23.

Verrall, C. (1995). A tale of community activism: Residents work together to halt the Brantford Southern Access Road. *Alternatives,* 21(4), pp. 47–49.

Warren, C.L., Kerr, A., & Turner, A.M. (1989). *Urbanization of rural land in Canada 1981–1986.* SOE Fact Sheet No. 89-1. Ottawa: Environment Canada, State of the Environment Directorate.

Wood, G. (1997). The first little pig was right. *Alternatives,* 23(3), pp. 7–8.

additional information sources

Canadian Arctic Resources Committee. http://www.carc.org

Environment Canada. The Green Lane. Action 21. http://www.ns.doe.ca/action21.menu.html

Environment Canada. The Green Lane. Park & Ride Public Transit Program (Halifax). http://www.ns.doe.ca/sucess/046.html

Environment Canada. (1997). Check-up for clean air. http://www.ec.gc.ca/special/check-up_e.htm

Environment Canada. (1997). Environment Canada to sponsor Emissions Inspection Clinics for the 12th year. http://www.ec.gc.ca/press/emissions_n_e.htm

Government of Canada. (1996). *The state of Canada's environment—1996.* Ottawa: Supply and Services Canada.

Meewasin Valley Authority. http://www.saskriverbasin.ca.

Metro Transit, Halifax. (n.d.). "Park & Ride" public transit program. http://www.ns.doe.ca/success/046.html

Newman, P. (1996). Greening the city. *Alternatives,* 22(2), pp. 10–16.

"To continue to survive, Canadians—along with the other members of the human global family—have no alternative but to adapt their behaviour and institutions to the imperatives of environmental stewardship and sustainability."

D.M. Taylor (1994)

CHAPTER 14

Meeting Environmental Challenges

Chapter Contents

CHAPTER OBJECTIVES   450
INTRODUCTION   450
PROGRESS IN SAFEGUARDING CANADA'S
   ENVIRONMENT   451
   Air Quality Issues   451
   Water Quality Issues   451
   Biological Diversity   452
   Climate Change   452
   Sector Industries   453
      Agriculture   453
      Forests   453
      Minerals and Metals   454
      Energy   454
      Fisheries   454
REGULATORY EFFORTS TO SAFEGUARD
   OUR ENVIRONMENT   455
   Atlantic Canada   455
   Central Canada   455
   Western Canada and the North   457
ENGO ACTIONS TO SAFEGUARD OUR
   ENVIRONMENT   460
CHALLENGES FOR THE FUTURE   463
   Resources Management   463
   Conservation 464
   Waste Reduction   465
   Urban Centres and Transportation
     Systems   465
   Pollution Control   466
   Cleanup of Past Environmental
     Problems 467
   Changes in Decision-Making
     Processes 467
THE IMPORTANCE OF INDIVIDUALS 470
Chapter Questions   473
References   473
Additional Information Sources   474

INTRODUCTION

Every day, each Canadian makes lifestyle choices that have substantial environmental impacts, choices that relate to the kind of housing we live in, the foods we eat, the appliances we use, the household products we select, and the means of transportation we favour. Every one of these choices may seem insignificant, but cumulatively (especially if many people make choices with negative impacts) these choices may result in serious damage to, and may influence the sustainability of, our future environment. The same is true of the kinds of decisions that governments, corporations, and public institutions make in their daily operations.

Protecting and sustaining the quality of our environment is a serious challenge for all Canadians. Balancing economic and social well-being and the integrity of the ecological systems that support our economy and society requires all of us to come to grips with the fundamental issues involved in achieving sustainability. Not only do we need to think globally and act locally, cognizant of the impacts our actions may have on others and on our environment, but also we need to work together in a cooperative and collaborative fashion. Achieving sustainability goals requires new, greener ways of thinking and making decisions. Will we meet the challenge?

In the sections that follow, we briefly review the trends in key environmental issues and sectors and indicate the kinds of actions taken and progress made in safeguarding Canada's environment. The chapter ends with a review of the challenges that remain, and some suggestions about what we as individuals can do to live in a more Earth-sustaining manner.

Have we done everything we can to "reduce, reuse, and recycle"? From individual effort comes advances in our collective well-being.

Chapter Objectives

After studying this chapter you should be able to

- appreciate the general trends in environmental issues and sectors

- outline the broad range of Canadian efforts to safeguard our environment

- identify those challenges that remain in our quest for sustainability

- appreciate some of the Earth-sustaining actions we can take

PROGRESS IN SAFEGUARDING CANADA'S ENVIRONMENT

Since the 1970s, environmental awareness, conservation, and protection have become increasingly important elements in economic and social decision making. As scientific understanding of ecosystem dynamics and complexity has grown, the need to take an ecosystem approach to environmental issues has been impressed on many decision makers. As a result, in addition to legislative and technical solutions, Canadians began to promote cooperation among governments, industry, ENGOs and communities. Public education and action also were fostered, various economic instruments developed, and voluntary codes of conduct established. These changes enabled progress on certain environmental issues, but in other areas we have fallen short of our goals.

AIR QUALITY ISSUES

Regulatory changes by the federal and provincial governments, supported by technological advances in the private sector as well as by partnership actions involving industries, NGOs, and communities, are among the efforts that have brought about reductions in the production and emission of many air contaminants. On an international level, for instance, Canada has exceeded its commitments to reduce ozone-depleting substances, and is meeting or exceeding both domestic and international targets for emissions that contribute to acidic precipitation.

Canada participates in other international efforts that are expected to improve air quality, including control of the long-range transport of pollutants (including heavy metals, pesticides such as DDT, and persistent organic contaminants such as PCBs). Domestically there have been some important improvements in air quality such as the virtual disappearance of lead from Canadian air following the 1990 phase out of lead as a gasoline additive for road vehicles.

Nevertheless, smog levels and particulate matter remain important air quality issues. The Bay of Fundy, Lower Fraser Valley, and Windsor–Quebec corridor are subjected to elevated smog levels partly because of their geographic locations and partly because of pollutants generated in industrial, transportation, and energy production activities. The expectation that use of the more than 12 million cars in Canada will increase means that ground-level ozone problems could worsen. Another important issue is the particulate matter in our air that constitutes a known public health issue. In order to have Canadian objectives for particulate levels in our air reflect current understanding of health effects, a federal–provincial working group was expected to recommend new objectives during 1997.

WATER QUALITY ISSUES

Both freshwater bodies and oceans have benefited from efforts to clean up and prevent pollution from cities, industries, and agriculture. As a result of stronger laws, increasing demands for greener products, and behavioural changes, there have been important reductions in the levels of many emissions. The forest industry's reduction in discharges of dioxins and furans is illustrative of the improvements made. Some impacts of the minerals and metals industry on watersheds have been reduced also. Public participation in watershed management and rehabilitation efforts has been an important factor in reduction of pollutants entering fresh and ocean waters.

However, significant stresses on our aquatic ecosystems continue to challenge us. Our per capita levels of water use remain among the highest in the world, even though commercial and industrial users have improved their efficiency and reduced consumption. We still have untreated municipal and industrial wastewater entering water bodies, and both surface water and groundwater supplies continue to be subject to contamination. Fish

Education is central to the making of appropriate and sustainable decisions.

and wildlife are known to be experiencing reproductive problems as a result of endocrine disruptors entering water bodies; this could endanger the survival of some species (Colborn, vom Saal & Soto, 1993).

BIOLOGICAL DIVERSITY

The decline in biodiversity in Canada is a continuing concern: the 291 species determined to be at risk by the Committee on the Status of Endangered Wildlife in Canada include 10 that are extinct and 13 that are no longer found in the wild in Canada. When it is enacted, the proposed Canada Endangered Species Protection Act (CESPA), in conjunction with the National Accord for the Protection of Species at Risk, is expected to provide much of the requisite protection. CESPA emphasizes cooperation among all parties, from the territorial and provincial governments to Aboriginal peoples, farmers, scientists, environmental groups, and industry.

When passed, CESPA also will fulfil part of Canada's obligations under the United Nations Convention on Biological Diversity. (Note that the Permanent Secretariat of the United Nations Convention on Biological Diversity is located in Montreal.) Building on a range of existing initiatives, the Canadian Biodiversity Strategy involves and draws on the commitment of a broad range of interests (Environment Canada, 1995). Quebec and British Columbia were the first provinces to report formally on how they were implementing the strategy and the convention.

Another of the trends in Canadian efforts to protect biodiversity has been the increase in protected space. In 1970, 23 parks made up the Canadian national parks system; by 1997, there were 38 parks in the system. Growth in the establishment of protected areas in Canada is illustrated in Figure 14–1. Individual provinces have added to their protected spaces also; between 1990 and 1995, for instance, British Columbia added about 8.6 million hectares as part of its effort to preserve species at risk and conserve

Each action has an environmental impact.

Healthy communities and healthy environments are interdependent.

representative ecosystems. Although federal tax law changes now encourage donations of ecologically sensitive land, there are many ecosystems (particularly in the more heavily populated parts of the country) that continue unprotected. We continue to lose lands due to urban expansion, and the protection of wetland habitats remains uncertain.

CLIMATE CHANGE

The Intergovernmental Panel on Climate Change has demonstrated the international consensus that human activities clearly are influencing global climate. If projections are correct, and Canada does experience greater temperature changes than most regions of the world, the implications could be numerous. More heat waves; increased storms, floods, and droughts; major shifts in fisheries, forestry, and agricultural resource bases; and damage to northern ecosystems are among the potentially severe consequences.

The challenges we face in reducing anthropogenic sources of greenhouse gases are significant. With approximately 89 percent of total greenhouse gas emissions in Canada attributed to transportation and fossil fuel production and consumption, and with our large land mass, cold climate, and increasing population, reducing use of fossil fuels is difficult.

While progress has been made in fuel efficiency, and in reducing carbon dioxide emissions, Canada's greenhouse gas emissions have risen steadily since the 1980s (Figure 14–2). Unless additional steps are taken, forecasts are that Canada's greenhouse emissions will exceed 1990 levels by about 8 percent in the year 2000. This means Canada will not meet its commitment under the United Nations Convention on Climate Change.

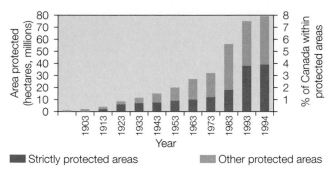

Figure 14–1

Growth in establishment of protected areas in Canada

NOTES: 1) Strictly protected areas include nature reserves, wilderness areas, national parks many provincial parks, and natural monuments.

2) Other protected areas include habitat/species management areas, protected landscapes and seascapes, and managed resource areas.

SOURCE: Government of Canada. Department of Foreign Affairs and International Trade. (1997). *Building momentum: Sustainable development in Canada.* Ottawa, p. 5.

In an effort to improve this performance, new initiatives were announced in 1996 including research and education, an enhanced Climate Change Voluntary Challenge and Registry Program, as well as new regulatory measures. Federal–provincial–territorial cooperation will be important in strengthening and expanding the National Action Program on Climate Change.

SECTOR INDUSTRIES

All of Canada's primary sector industries depend on the existence and continuation of natural capital stocks. All of these industries have been subject to efforts to improve

As stewards of our environment, we need to connect with the natural world.

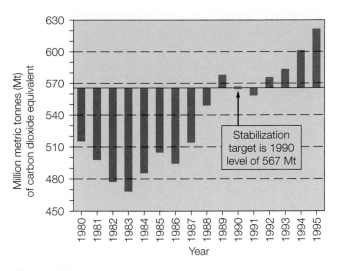

Figure 14–2

Greenhouse gas emissions 1980–1995: comparison to stabilization target

SOURCE: Government of Canada. Department of Foreign Affairs and International Trade. (1997). *Building momentum: Sustainable development in Canada.* Ottawa, p. 5.

sustainability and reduce negative environmental impacts. Here, too, there have been varying levels of success in attaining sustainability goals.

Agriculture

Healthy ecosystems, and the quality of soil, water, and air, are fundamental to agriculture. While Canada's total farmland area has remained relatively constant over the past 25 years, there have been losses of prime agricultural land due to urban expansion and other activities. Through increasingly intensive use, however, the productivity of farmland has increased during the past two decades. Improvements in fertilizers and Integrated Pest Management approaches have helped to offset some of the impacts of this intensive use.

As awareness of the linkages between farm operations and the larger ecosystem have been recognized, concern for human health and off-farm environmental effects have begun to alter the approach to agriculture in Canada. In particular, water quality has become an important concern. Efforts to maintain and improve water quality have entailed improvements in management of soils, nutrients, manure, and pesticides. In addition, more sustainable land management practices are being adopted, such as conservation tillage methods that reduce soil erosion.

Forests

A highly significant component of Canada's environment, economy, and culture, forests also have benefited from

Do we know where our water comes from and where our wastes go?

efforts to improve sustainability. Although disagreements remain about harvesting practices such as clear-cutting, efforts have been made to reduce logging impacts on watersheds and to protect some sensitive areas. While pollution from pulp and paper mills has decreased in general, concern continues regarding specific emissions such as organochlorines.

The 1992 National Forest Strategy, protection legislation and policies, the Canadian Council of Forest Ministers' criteria and indicators of sustainable forest management, and various industry codes of practice and standards are among the actions taken to improve forest management and move toward sustainability. The model forests are important testing grounds for sustainable practices. However, more research is needed regarding forest ecosystems and ecosystem management, as well as assessment of clear-cutting and alternative harvesting practices. For the future, implementation of an international forest convention promoting sustainable forest management also is seen as important.

Minerals and Metals

Canada is the world's leading mineral exporter, and the minerals and metals industry is an important contributor to the Canadian economy. Canada's mining, smelting, and refining processes, however, frequently cause environmental impacts such as surface disruption, toxic and non-toxic air emissions, and discharge of liquid effluents. The multistakeholder Aquamin process recommended that a national environmental protection framework be established and that effluent quality regulations be revised.

The minerals and metals industry has made technological advances, changed their regulatory regime, and developed voluntary measures in efforts to improve their mining practices. The environmental policy that commits members of the Mining Association of Canada to sustainable development is one example. In addition, the Whitehorse Mining Initiative illustrates the industry's effort to involve stakeholders in defining what is meant by a socially, economically, and environmentally sustainable mining industry. Nevertheless, continuing concerns regarding environmental and social impacts of mining (such as those affecting Aboriginal people) remain to be resolved.

Energy

Canada's energy sector contributes significantly to the national economy and economic well-being through jobs. The energy sector also is the largest contributor to carbon dioxide emissions in Canada. For this reason, strategies to manage the energy sector in a sustainable manner have been developed, including environmental management systems, federal tax law changes to promote investment in energy efficiency, and green procurement practices.

If sustainability is to be achieved, however, additional efforts and research are required in such areas as development of alternative energy sources and technologies. As well, ways to achieve reductions in consumption levels need to be determined, and consumer support for energy efficiency (as in R-2000 homes) needs to be encouraged (National Energy Board, 1994).

Fisheries

Coastal and northern communities in particular receive important economic and social benefits from access to fisheries resources. However, as the closure of the groundfish fishery, including that of the northern cod, has demonstrated, it is critical to practise sustainability in use of these resources. Unsustainable harvesting practices and changing oceanic conditions are among the reasons for declines in the fish resource that subsequently led to the closure of the fishery, and resulted in severe socio-economic impacts on coastal communities.

Consulting residents with knowledge of local ecosystems is a critical component of the decision-making process.

PART 4:
GETTING TO TOMORROW

To avoid similar situations, governments, the fishing industry, and communities have undertaken a variety of initiatives to promote more sustainable fisheries. Canada's Oceans Act and the Code of Conduct for Responsible Fishing are among the efforts undertaken to help ensure ocean resources are used sustainably. Notably, the Oceans Act is built on the precautionary principle.

REGULATORY EFFORTS TO SAFEGUARD OUR ENVIRONMENT

To illustrate governmental action and concern for our environment, the author asked each provincial and territorial minister of Environment (or equivalent) as well as the federal minister of the Environment to specify the policy, legislative, and other initiatives that were being taken to resolve the major environmental issues they were facing. Not unexpectedly, given Canada's vast space and political diversity, the environmental issues identified as "major" differed from province to province. Even so, a number of common environmental problems affected most regions of Canada.

Recurring issues identified included water quality, solid waste disposal, and greenhouse gas emissions. In addition, many jurisdictions had made efforts to improve the integration of environmental, economic, and social considerations into decision-making practices. For instance, the federal government established a Commissioner of the Environment and Sustainable Development in 1996. Interestingly, the commissioner's first report noted that in many areas the federal government's performance fell short of its stated environmental and sustainable development objectives. Common to many governments, there is an "implementation gap," a failure to translate policy direction into effective action. (The Web site for the Commissioner of the Environment and Sustainable Development is listed in the Additional Information Sources section of this chapter.)

ATLANTIC CANADA

In Atlantic Canada, waste management was identified as a central environmental concern. In Nova Scotia, only 10 percent of the province's 623 000 tonnes of solid waste is recycled each year. As a result, a solid waste strategy has been developed to help Nova Scotia meet the Canadian target of a 50 percent reduction in solid wastes by the year 2000. New Brunswick identified completing a regional network for solid waste management as the province's highest priority in protecting the quality of land-based resources. The waste management network includes the construction

of sanitary landfills as well as initiatives aimed at promoting waste reduction, reuse, recycling, and composting. Prince Edward Island also identified waste management as a concern and addressed the problem in a 1994 document, "Stewardship and Sustainability, a Renewed Conservation Strategy for Prince Edward Island."

Other environmental concerns identified by the Atlantic provinces included groundwater contamination (P.E.I., N.S.), air pollution (N.B.), wastewater management (Nfld.), environmental impacts of agriculture (P.E.I.), and water resources management (N.S., N.B.). Examples of the kinds of regulatory activities relating to environmental issues that affect the four Atlantic provinces are identified in slightly more detail in Table 14–1. Regulatory activities are highlighted because they provide an important impetus for change.

CENTRAL CANADA

In the province of Quebec, pollution, exploitation of resources, and unrestricted energy use were identified as the three principal sources of stress on the environment. Quebec was concentrating its environmental efforts on reduction of solid wastes as well as on developing a sustainable development plan. These efforts, as well as a fuller range of Quebec's regulatory efforts, are noted in Table 14–2.

At the time the Environment ministers were contacted, Premier Harris of Ontario recently had taken office. Although no specific environmental problems were identified, the response outlined the approach the newly elected government would take with respect to environmental laws, policies, and programs. A key aspect of the new government's approach was to have the government set environmental standards while allowing the private sector and municipalities to determine the best and most cost-effective ways of meeting those standards.

How well are we monitoring the impact we have on our environment?

TABLE 14-1
EXAMPLES OF PROVINCIAL REGULATORY ACTIVITY IN ATLANTIC CANADA

Province/Year	Regulatory Activity
Newfoundland	
1995	• Initiatives were under way to deal with wastewater management.
1996	• A multimaterials packaging stewardship program was established, starting with a deposit/refund system for beverage containers effective January 15, 1997.
	• All provincial environmental legislation was being overhauled.
1997	• A draft 20-year forestry plan was released, which outlined a shift from a timber management to an ecosystem management approach.
	• Work was under way on draft regulations for waste oil, hazardous wastes, and ozone-depleting substances.
Prince Edward Island	
1995	• A wildlife policy was approved by the executive council.
	• A new agricultural irrigation policy set a minimum amount of water that must be maintained in streams and ponds.
1996	• The Department of Agriculture increased enforcement of the Pesticides Control Act.
	• Public participation began on a new Wildlife Act.
	• The Interim Report of the Round Table on Resource Land Use and Stewardship called on the provincial government to better monitor water resources.
1997	• Developed by the Forest Partnership Council, a new voluntary code of practice for the forest industry took effect April 1.
Nova Scotia	
1996	• A new provincial strategy for solid waste management was approved and regulations adopted.
	• Guidelines for the management of contaminated sites were approved.
1997	• A tire recycling program began on January 2.
	• The province's first state-of-the-environment report was expected in 1997.
	• An Endangered Species Act was introduced.
	• New sewage regulations for subdivisions took effect April 1.
	• A pollution prevention strategy was in the works.
New Brunswick	
1996	• A new Clean Air Act was introduced in the legislature.
	• A tire collection and recycling program began October 1, administered by the New Brunswick Tire Stewardship Board.
	• A waste oil stewardship program was being developed.
1997	• The Clean Air Act received royal assent in March 1997.
	• Under the draft waste oil stewardship program, effective April 1, collectors of oil must be approved by the province.
	• An interdepartmental panel was revising a proposed flood plain policy after reviewing public comments; a river classification program was being developed.

SOURCE: Menyasz, P., Pole, K., & Ray, R. (Eds.). (1996–97). *Environment Policy and Law,* 6(9)–8(2). Reprinted by permission of IOS Press, Amsterdam.

TABLE 14-2
EXAMPLES OF PROVINCIAL REGULATORY ACTIVITY IN QUEBEC

Province/Year	Regulatory Activity
Quebec 1996, 1997	• A new regulation subjected major industrial projects to environmental assessment.
	• Two government policy papers were released: Strategic Vision 1996–2001—The Issues, and Strategic Vision 1996–1998—The Choices (perhaps representing a "cultural revolution" in the way governments view regulation to promote environmental protection).
	• Public review was under way on a new forest management regulation covering the size of clear-cuts and the construction of roads and stream crossings.
	• Work was under way on contaminated sites guidelines.
	• A draft policy to guard against contamination of underground water was being developed.
	• A draft regulation regarding the handling of incineration and garbage dumps was being circulated.
	• Hazardous materials regulations and a contaminated lands policy were before the environment minister for consideration.
1997	• An action plan, scheduled for implementation late in 1998, was being prepared for management of household and industrial waste.
	• After more than a year of public hearings, the Bureau d'audiences publiques released a 477-page report on the management of "residual matters" (waste).

SOURCE: Menyasz, P., Polc, K., & Ray, R. (Eds.). (1996–97). *Environment Policy and Law,* 6(9)–8(2). Reprinted by permission of IOS Press, Amsterdam.

One of the first initiatives undertaken by Ontario's Conservative government was to call for a review of all environmental regulations in an effort to reduce the barriers that government actions posed to doing business in Ontario. With less than one year in office, the Harris government acted to dismantle the Interim Waste Authority and return power to the municipalities; end the previous government's policy prohibiting incineration by municipalities; release a new policy establishing limits on government access to self-initiated environmental evaluations; and release a new regulation, which was designed to stimulate growth in the mining sector, protecting prospectors from cleaning up historic environmental contamination. As noted in Table 14–3, Ontario's Environment Commissioner criticized the government for eliminating environmental safeguards too quickly and noted that cost cutting compromised the ministry's ability to protect the environment.

WESTERN CANADA AND THE NORTH

In the west, Manitoba was in the process of drafting a Sustainable Development Act to integrate sustainable development considerations into existing legislation. The province also had released two state-of-the-environment reports, one in 1993 and another in 1995. The 1995 report provided a comprehensive summary of the natural and socioeconomic environments of Manitoba with a special focus on agriculture.

The government of Saskatchewan linked most of its environmental problems to the resource- and agriculture-based economy of the province. With only 24 percent of

Is our technology environmentally friendly?

TABLE 14–3
EXAMPLES OF PROVINCIAL REGULATORY ACTIVITY IN ONTARIO

Province/Year	Regulatory Activity
Ontario 1996	• The Ontario government suspended parts of the province's Environmental Bill of Rights.
	• A major review of the provincial environmental regulatory system was under way.
	• New guidelines for an incineration policy were being developed.
	• Under the "Common Sense Revolution," Ontario's Ministry of Environment and Energy lost one-third of its budget and 389 staff members but promised "no compromise in environmental quality" in its 1996–97 business plan. This plan proposed development of broader measures to address urban smog.
	• Ontario was loosening rules on pollution.
	• Ontario's Environment Commissioner criticized the government for eliminating environmental safeguards too quickly.
	• Bill 76, the Environmental Assessment and Consultation Improvement Act, received royal assent.
1997	• Work continued on reforms to Ontario's energy and environment regulations.
	• Municipalities took control of water and sewage treatment.
	• A report on climate change initiatives was released.
	• Ontario's Environmental Commissioner criticized government ministries for "an alarming lack of environmental vision" in 1996. The commissioner indicated that government cost cutting compromised ministries' ability to protect the environment, including testing of the quality of drinking water, Ontario's acid rain program, and the inspection of pits and quarries.
	• A report on environmental spills in the Great Lakes was released.
	• Work continued on reforms to Ontario's energy and environment regulations.

SOURCE: Menyasz, P., Pole, K., & Ray, R. (Eds.). (1996–97). *Environment Policy and Law,* 6(9)–8(2). Reprinted by permission of IOS Press, Amsterdam.

its natural grasslands remaining, a key challenge for Saskatchewan was to preserve examples of the provincial landscape. Wetland drainage and conversion complicated efforts aimed at protecting biodiversity. Saskatchewan was concentrating on initiatives that encouraged cooperation and public involvement to address environmental issues. A sustainable communities program was developed along with a co-management strategy for consulting with the public on resource use decisions. Other regulatory activities, including those in Manitoba, are identified in Table 14–4.

The government of Alberta identified water allocation, forest management, protection of representative ecosystems, air pollution, First Nations involvement in resources management, and solid waste as the major environmental issues affecting the province. Alberta introduced a new Water Act and was developing a forest conservation strategy. Efforts aimed at protecting key wilderness areas in Alberta, such as the Special Places Program, were progressing slowly with development often taking precedence over conservation (Table 14–5).

Have we introduced our children to the wonders of nature?

Not surprisingly, British Columbia identified sustaining the province's forestry sector as a top priority. Protecting natural areas and biodiversity, controlling urban air pollution in the Vancouver area, and reducing global

PART 4:
GETTING TO TOMORROW

TABLE 14 – 4
EXAMPLES OF PROVINCIAL REGULATORY ACTIVITY IN MANITOBA AND SASKATCHEWAN

Province/Year	Regulatory Activity
Manitoba	
1996	• Work was under way on a used oil regulation.
	• Bill 34, legislation to clean up contaminated sites, was tabled in the legislature and approved, and was expected to be in force in early 1997.
	• A review of 48 environmental regulations was completed; implementation was expected to take about two years.
	• A draft white paper on the Sustainable Development Act was released for discussion.
	• A new Provincial Parks Act was proclaimed.
	• Public input was sought on draft ambient air quality guidelines for formaldehyde.
	• Bill 19, which amends dangerous goods handling and transportation regulations, was in force.
1997	• The used-oil regulation was approved by the government.
	• Bill 34 was approved and was expected to take force in the spring of 1997.
	• The government was scaling back its proposed Sustainable Development Act after harsh criticism (about ending municipal control over land use, for example) and was developing a new strategy to incorporate the principles of sustainable development into all government processes.
Saskatchewan	
1996, 1997	• The provincial government and Saskatchewan Scrap Tire Corp. signed a partnership agreement formalizing a cooperative approach to management of scrap tires in the province.
	• A Forest Resources Management Act was passed (improving use, management, and protection of forests).
	• Regulations for a used oil management program were approved.
	• The petroleum industry adopted new waste management guidelines.
	• Work was ongoing regarding liability regulations for contaminated sites.

SOURCE: Menyasz, P., Pole, K., & Ray, R. (Eds.). (1996–97). *Environment Policy and Law,* 6(9)–8(2). Reprinted by permission of IOS Press, Amsterdam.

TABLE 14 – 5
EXAMPLES OF PROVINCIAL REGULATORY ACTIVITY IN ALBERTA AND BRITISH COLUMBIA

Province/Year	Regulatory Activity
Alberta	
1996	• Alberta's Environmental Protection department unveiled its Regulatory Reform Action Plan, a simpler, more efficient regulatory regime.
	• A new Water Act was approved and accompanying regulations received public input.
	• A task force was drafting a policy for logging on private lands.
	• A new timber permit system was put in place.
	• Spending cuts of $50.2 million were identified in the 1996–99 business plan; 526 jobs were eliminated.
	• A state-of-the-environment report was released focusing on the successes of the province's waste management initiatives.
	• Codes of practice to replace approvals for activities with low environmental impact were to take effect September 15.
1997	• The Alberta Energy and Utilities Board released requirements for management of oilfield waste.

TABLE 14-5
(CONTINUED)

Province/Year	Regulatory Activity
British Columbia 1996	• New regulations forced auto makers to build cleaner cars.
	• New regulations to phase out beehive burners were introduced.
	• A new pollution prevention program was launched in conjunction with five major industrial companies and the Canadian Chemical Producers Association.
	• Paint recycling regulations were tightened after the paint industry failed to meet the objectives of the Post-Consumer Stewardship Program.
	• The B.C. Water Quality Status Report indicated the importance of non–point sources of pollution; water quality protection was identified as a major priority.
	• Pharmaceuticals became part of B.C.'s household hazardous waste collection program.
	• The province requested the addition of 50 bodies of water to the federal Pleasure Craft Sewage Pollution Prevention regulation.
	• A review of water licences at all B.C. Hydro facilities aimed to ensure that environmental values were considered.
British Columbia 1997	• The State of Environment Indicator on groundwater quality was released.
	• A public awareness campaign was launched on water quality protection ("Clean Water: It's Up to You"); Environmental Youth Team interns will help at public seminars and workshops.
	• Work was under way on a fish protection act to deal with habitat protection and water use plans.
	• Contaminated site legislation took effect April 1.
	• Environment enforcement officers were given power to ticket for a wider range of environment related offences.
	• A discussion paper on clean air and water law was expected.

SOURCE: Menyasz, P., Pole, K., & Ray, R. (Eds.). (1996–97). *Environment Policy and Law,* 6(9)–8(2). Reprinted by permission of IOS Press, Amsterdam.

atmospheric problems also were identified as key environmental concerns by the government of British Columbia (see Table 14–5).

The Yukon and Northwest Territories are in a unique position as the federal government takes responsibility for a number of program areas that directly affect environmental quality. The importance of sustaining traditional Aboriginal ways of life in light of growing developmental pressure was identified as the overriding concern. The long-range transport of airborne pollutants into the north from other areas also continues to be a major concern of the territorial governments. The devolution of responsibility for forest, land, and water resources was identified by the Yukon as important in helping them catch up to the rest of the country with respect to environmental initiatives. Additional regulatory activities undertaken by the Yukon and Northwest Territories are identified in Table 14–6.

ENGO ACTIONS TO SAFEGUARD OUR ENVIRONMENT

At the same time that ministers of the Environment were asked for information, 74 selected environmental non-governmental organizations (ENGOs) were asked about their group's objectives and activities, about how well they felt provincial and federal government initiatives promoted environmental sustainability, and about the ways that they and other ENGOs could show leadership in contributing to environmental sustainability in Canada. Small and large organizations, working on a variety of environmental issues, were selected from all regions of Canada; almost 40 percent responded to the request for information.

TABLE 14–6
EXAMPLES OF REGULATORY ACTIVITY IN YUKON AND NORTHWEST TERRITORIES

Province/Year	Regulatory Activity
Northwest Territories	
1996, 1997	• The Guideline for Industrial Waste Discharges and the Guideline for the General Management of Hazardous Waste were adopted.
	• An ozone-depleting substances guideline was adopted.
	• Regulations to control air emissions from gold roasting operations were developed and circulated for public consultation.
	• A study on the use of economic instruments to influence environmental practices was completed.
	• Guidelines on specific hazardous wastes such as asbestos and lead-based paint were developed to complement the general guideline on Management of Hazardous Wastes; public input was received and the guidelines were revised.
	• Pesticides regulations under the Pesticides Act were updated to be consistent with other jurisdictions; public consultation was to follow.
	• Three departments were amalgamated into a new superministry (the Department of Resources, Wildlife, and Economic Development) to blend economic growth with preservation of the environment. Administrative costs were to be reduced through the loss of 100 jobs.
	• The Pollution Prevention Recognition Program will reward firms that meet pollution reduction targets.
Yukon	
1996	• Ozone-depleting substances regulations were approved by Cabinet.
	• New beverage container regulations were approved.
	• Regulations for underground storage tanks, air emissions, and hazardous materials spills were circulated for public comment.
	• Bill C-6, An Act to Amend the Yukon Quartz Mining Act and the Yukon Placer Mining Act, was prepared to replace 70-year-old legislation that contained no environmental protection measures.
1997	• Administrative regulations, which were needed to operate fully the environmental protection programs under the Environment Act, took effect on Feb. 17.

SOURCE: Menyasz, P., Pole, K., & Ray, R. (Eds.). (1996–97). *Environment Policy and Law,* 6(9)–8(2). Reprinted by permission of IOS Press, Amsterdam.

Although governments play important roles in environmental protection, governmental actions (or lack thereof) often are criticized by environmental groups that play important roles as watchdogs of environmental protection and related activities. In response to the question of how well ENGOs felt government initiatives promoted environmental sustainability for the future, most comments received from those national and regional ENGOs surveyed were negative ones (see Table 14–7). While the ENGO responses included in the table do not constitute a representative sample of ENGO opinion, the marked consistency of their comments points to the potential for governments to further enhance their sustainability actions. However, as noted in previous chapters, fewer fiscal resources have resulted in reduced environmental spending and services.

Some groups identified in Table 14–7 are very outspoken and confrontational in their dealings; others are more collaborative in their approach and work toward influencing government policies through cooperative means, including increasing public awareness, youth education, stewardship, and partnership initiatives. Other ways ENGOs indicated they could demonstrate environmental leadership included contributions of scientific research, development of creative potential solutions to sustainability issues, and incorporation of public values in political decision making (perhaps through additional round tables dealing with environmental, social, and economic issues).

Some groups felt they could be involved in monitoring environmental policies or projects; others felt they could generate funding (nongovernmental) to help support unbiased work on sustainability issues; and yet others

TABLE 14-7

HOW WELL DO GOVERNMENT INITIATIVES PROMOTE ENVIRONMENTAL SUSTAINABILITY FOR THE FUTURE? A SUMMARY OF SELECTED ENGO RESPONSES

National Organizations	Response
Canadian Environmental Defence Fund	• Government initiatives appear to be in retreat.
Canadian Institute for Environmental Law and Policy	• On the whole, provincial and federal initiatives are not promoting sustainable futures.
	• Government actions are eroding the present foundation of legislation.
Canadian Parks and Wilderness Association	• Governments can play a strong role; the pace of action must be accelerated.
	• Governments promote unsustainable forestry and mining.
Ducks Unlimited Canada	• In recent years, governments have made significant strides in developing land and resource use policies, but much more could be done on land owned or controlled by governments.
	• Governments often provide funds for activities that are not ecologically friendly or sustainable.
Environment Probe	• Governments have given thousands of reasons not to trust them (forests, fishing, pollution, etc.).
Environmental Youth Alliance	• Governments promote sustainability in partnership with local groups.
Greenpeace Canada	• On what standard should success be measured? Sometimes governments make good decisions, sometimes poor ones.
Harmony Foundation	• While some successes should be noted, government initiatives are often impediments; they waste money, trivialize issues, and block creativity.
Ocean Voice International	• Government capacity to promote sustainable futures has been reduced because of job cuts and reduced funding.
	• Corporate agendas have been eroding the established degree of environmental protection.
	• Steps forward are possible as actions in several provinces regarding biodiversity and parks have shown.
Sea Shepherd Conservation Society	• Governments do not envision problems or solutions further than the next election.
	• Governments serve industry first, the elite second, the people third, the environment fourth, and nonhuman species last.
Wildlife Habitat Canada	• International competitiveness negatively affects the ability of government to practise stewardship.
	• Governments are less effective due to reduced budgets.

Regional Organizations	Response
Alberta Wilderness Association	• Governments have done very poorly.
	• Decentralization of federal responsibilities to the provinces will leave the federal government with few powers over natural resources.
Forest Alliance of British Columbia	• Some programs are excellent, others are not.
Recycling Council of British Columbia	• Some initiatives are significant, others appear to be at cross-purposes to sustainability.
Saskatchewan Environmental Society	• Several initiatives are headed in the right direction.
	• Governments espouse sustainability yet hand out huge subsidies to unsustainable industries.

Regional Organizations	Response
Society Promoting Environmental Conservation	• Action is slow despite meetings, reports, and newsletters.
	• Corporations get around environmental legislation.
The Clean Nova Scotia Foundation	• There is always room for improvement in promoting sustainable futures.
Western Canada Wilderness Association	• Provincial and federal initiatives are woefully inadequate.
	• Initiatives are not strong enough to be effective, particularly regarding biodiversity and ecosystem health.

noted they could encourage successful governmental and industry initiatives, particularly those that employ ecosystem-based planning. In fact, shared responsibility has become an important perspective as agencies (governmental in particular) realize that innovative arrangements are needed to respond to the cutbacks in programs due to scarce financial resources.

Many of the ENGOs in Canada have been in existence for decades and are likely to remain active in a variety of ways to raise public awareness of environmental issues, to challenge governments and industries to deal with the root causes of ecosystem problems, and to mount partnerships and promote stewardship activities that will lead to sustainable practices. These grassroots activities are important given that Canadians continue to leave a large ecological footprint on the planet (Wackernagel & Rees, 1996). In fact, if all humans on Earth used the same levels of energy and other resources as Canadians do, it would take three planet Earths to supply the resources for them (Figure 14–3).

The following sections review briefly the challenges that remain in Canada's progress toward sustainability.

Figure 14–3
Wanted: three planet Earths

SOURCE: Adapted from Wackernagel, M., & Rees, W. (1996). *Our ecological footprint: Reducing human impact on the earth.* Gabriola Island, BC: New Society Publishers, p. 15.

CHALLENGES FOR THE FUTURE

Seven major types of challenges face Canadians as we try to respond effectively to current and future environmental sustainability issues. These challenges are found in our approach to resources management; the need for conservation of resources, species, and ecosystems; waste reduction requirements; the need to design urban areas and transportation systems for greater sustainability; pollution control requirements; the cleanup of past environ-

mental problems; and changes in decision-making processes (Government of Canada, 1996a). Each of these challenges is considered briefly below.

RESOURCES MANAGEMENT

We know that resources management must involve affected stakeholders in the planning and implementation of resource development projects. Not only does this

Do we strive for consistency in our daily actions?

involved. Some developers have complained about these delays; one of the challenges we face is to develop a process that minimizes delays and yet ensures adequate time to make appropriate and effective decisions. Other challenges include the need for further research into the effects of resource management practices, and the need to create partnerships that can address key issues.

CONSERVATION

Collapse of the northern cod stocks provided concrete evidence of how important it is to "live within our means"—to have resource management strategies and regulations that act to conserve resources. This is a challenge that, to some degree, has been reflected in the Atlantic Groundfish Strategy and the Oceans Management Strategy, as both have given important emphasis to conservation. Living within our means—finding economically and environmentally sound ways to use resources—results in challenges for the future such as generating adequate and scientifically sound knowledge on which to base decisions about sustainable use, undertaking appropriate monitoring, and strictly enforcing regulations regarding specific resources. If solutions to these sustainability challenges can be met, then it should not be necessary to take such drastic measures as closure of the fishery.

Although awareness is growing, another challenge is to ensure that the need for effective conservation is understood by more people across the spectrum of natural resources. To some extent this has begun: we can see the effectiveness of such changes as urban water pricing based on volume consumed, the Permanent Cover program returning marginal cropland to pasture, and the stewardship of landowners supporting wildlife habitat conservation (through such organizations as Ducks Unlimited, Wildlife Habitat Canada, and the Nature Conservancy of Canada, as well as through programs such as the North American Waterfowl Management Plan). Part of this challenge to improve public understanding of the importance of conservation involves extending awareness of the need for conservation to nonrenewable resource sectors also.

In the past, a variety of governmental and other programs resulted in unintended consequences because the quest for increased production was encouraged without full consideration or understanding of environmental side effects. Examples include subsidizing the removal of natural areas, encouraging cultivation on slopes, and promoting wetland drainage. The challenge of restoring the biological diversity of areas affected by these kinds of decisions and removing inappropriate subsidies to prevent these impacts from occurring is beginning to be met.

reduce the risk of community opposition, public involvement also reduces the likelihood of raising legal challenges to projects. Though not perfect, environmental review procedures in many provinces and territories now provide considerable public involvement opportunities. Public involvement permits compromise and development of a consensus on appropriate solutions to environmental issues (and may be particularly important in contentious issues such as Clayoquot Sound forestry practices). Public participation also may enhance explicit consideration of the needs of future generations (Nickerson, 1990).

Public involvement also can lead to initiatives that promote sustainable resource management. Examples include the decision to use co-management approaches and practices in northern communities, the Model Forest Program, and the Aquamin and MEND programs in mining. These and other resource management initiatives not only reflect public input but also provide insight into the effects of resource management processes (helpful in improvement of future decisions).

While public participation promotes integration of environmental, social, and economic values, decisions often take a long time to be reached when the public is

PART 4:
GETTING TO TOMORROW

WASTE REDUCTION

Although Canadians are among the world's leading producers of domestic waste, since the early 1990s there have been gains in recycling through blue box and other community programs, and small improvements in the amount of home composting. One challenge is to ensure there are markets for recycled materials so that the rates of recycling of paper, glass, metals, and plastics can increase. Another challenge is to ensure recycling opportunities are convenient and readily available to all residents.

At the national level, a variety of targets have been established to stimulate waste reduction by households, industries, and government. For instance, the Canadian Council of Ministers of the Environment has developed the National Packaging Protocol and the National Solid Waste Management Program. The latter program has as its objective the reduction in Canadian per-capita output of solid waste to 50 percent of the 1988 level by the year 2000. By 1992, disposal of municipal, construction, and demolition waste had decreased by 23.2 percent per capita from the 1988 baseline year.

One of the challenges in the waste reduction field is to have more firms reduce risks and potential liabilities by adopting environmentally sound waste management practices (which may be economically advantageous as well). In responding to this challenge, the private sector has developed some highly innovative waste management programs. The 3M Corporation, for example, saved itself $1 million by reducing waste disposal volumes (from 2800 to 115 tonnes per year) at an Ontario manufacturing plant. A U.S. company, Malden Mills, developed a Recycled Series of fleece fabrics in which at least 89 percent of the material comes from postconsumer recycled pop bottles. Not only does it take less energy to make the fibres that go into this fabric, it creates 17 times fewer air pollutants. An average-sized jacket keeps 25 two-litre pop bottles out of landfills; every year a pile of pop bottles "the size of a few dozen Boeing 747s gets recycled instead of going to waste" (Malden Mills Industries, Inc., 1994).

Ecosystem health is threatened directly by hazardous wastes; in 1990, 4 of the top 10 Canadian hazardous waste generators were manufacturing industries. There are some indications that these industries are taking their responsibilities regarding hazardous waste more seriously. For instance, a voluntary initiative is the Canadian Manufacturers Association's Improving Manufacturing Environmental Performance Program. This program assists small- and medium-sized manufacturing operations to improve their environmental performance.

Hazardous wastes require special treatment and disposal to make them less dangerous. The Alberta Special Waste Treatment Centre in Swan Hills is Canada's first and only fully integrated hazardous waste treatment facility. For additional information on this facility, see Box 14–1.

BOX 14-1
THE SWAN HILLS SPECIAL WASTE TREATMENT CENTRE

Opened in 1987, the Swan Hills Special Waste Treatment Centre treats all forms of waste except biomedical, radioactive, and explosive materials. Typically, wastes are burned or chemically treated to make them relatively innocuous, and the remaining residues are buried in secure landfills or injected deep underground. Since 1995, the government of Alberta has permitted hazardous wastes to be imported from other provinces for treatment at the privately operated site.

In mid-July 1997, Health Canada announced it was doing a study to see how the Swan Hills plant affects First Nations people who eat wildlife living near the plant. This announcement followed a late-1996 warning from Alberta Health that meat taken within a 30-kilometre radius of the plant should not be eaten. The warning had been issued as a result of a plant accident (in October 1996) that leaked toxic gases into the atmosphere, as well as concern on the part of First Nations people in the area that toxic chemicals released by the plant could be to blame for a greater incidence of meat infested with parasites.

About 1 week after Health Canada's announcement of its study, an explosion at the Swan Hills plant released PCBs measured at 1.38 parts per billion, or more than 9 times the normal rate (but still within the established safety margin) into the air. This major accident, the second in 9 months, raised concern about the safety of the plant and led the opposition party to call for a full study into the environmental impact of pollution from the plant, including its effects on ground water.

One of the implications of these events is the need to encourage reduced use of consumer and industrial goods that contain toxic materials. Also, the safe disposal or recycling of hazardous materials must be ensured.

SOURCES: Chase, S. (1997, May 16). Animal toxin levels elevated. *Calgary Herald,* p. A3.

Chase, S. (1997, July 23). Explosion forces closure of Swan Hills plant. *Calgary Herald,* p. A4.

Chase, S. (1997, July 26). Swan Hills PCBs nine times normal. *Calgary Herald,* p. A4.

Lund welcomes federal study of Swan Hills plant. (1997, July 14). *Calgary Herald,* p. B4.

URBAN CENTRES AND TRANSPORTATION SYSTEMS

Urban centres supply their residents with food, clothing, housing, recreation, and other amenities; in providing these goods and services, Canadian cities often are the source of many environmental stresses. The water, food, fibre, energy, and minerals that flow into our cities come from surrounding ecosystems; flowing back out into those

Do we know which elements of our lifestyles are harmful or beneficial to the Earth?

ecosystems are waste water, garbage, air contaminants, and urban residents seeking recreation and natural areas.

Cities also can be catalysts in deriving solutions to environmental stresses. For instance, providing clean water, effective sewage treatment systems, and recycling programs is easier, more efficient, and less costly when people are concentrated in smaller areas rather than dispersed. Recycling programs, for example, can run more efficiently in densely populated centres because large amounts of waste glass, paper, plastic, and aluminum cans can be collected from a small area. Large urban population bases also provide a larger group of people who can provide environmental leadership; this is one reason why municipalities often have led the way in developing and implementing new initiatives and programs to promote environmental sustainability.

As we saw in previous chapters, there has been mixed success in efforts to improve the sustainability of urban environments. Some of the encouraging results include trends toward smaller, more energy-efficient homes, more home-based businesses (reduced transportation demands), tighter land use controls and green community planning processes, and growing support of mixed land uses and intensification policies (such as infill and redevelopment of land to support higher population densities). Also, the increasing importance attached to protecting ecologically sensitive areas in urban landscapes has grown even though government resources have declined.

Some of the less encouraging trends include the continued Canadian preference for single-family, detached housing located in low-density neighbourhoods; the establishment of many new businesses in low-density business parks; and the resultant reliance on our vehicles and a transportation infrastructure focused less on public transit and more on the automobile. In fact, numerous efforts have been made by municipalities to increase use of public transportation services. Many of these actions, including higher parking fees and use of preferential lanes for buses and car pools, have not been very effective in changing people's behaviour. As essential as transportation is to Canada's socioeconomic well-being, Canadians' transportation practices seem particularly environmentally unsustainable with regard to pollution and fuel supply.

The importance of environmentally sustainable transportation has been reflected in international agreements (such as the Nitrogen Oxide Protocol, the Volatile Organic Compounds Protocol, and the Canada–United States Air Quality Agreement), national efforts (such as the Canadian Environmental Protection Act [CEPA] regulations regarding benzene content of gasoline), as well as regional and local level initiatives (such as the Twenty Percent Club and the Air Care Program in British Columbia's Lower Mainland). However, these actions may be insufficient to reverse long-standing trends toward increased transportation activity. In the short term, it appears that even technological changes (such as lighter materials in vehicles, improved fuel efficiency, use of alternative fuels, hydrogen cells, and electric vehicles) will have only limited effects on fuel use and emissions. Fortunately, research is continuing in these areas.

POLLUTION CONTROL

The Canadian public continues to place high priority on a clean and healthy environment, and expects that public and private institutions will take the necessary actions to achieve environmental quality. Since the early 1990s, higher fines for pollution offences, concerns over personal and corporate environmental liability, and considerations of corporate image, as well as demands from insurance and lending institutions, have been important elements in pollution reduction. Perhaps additional education is required to encourage corporate officials to act less out of fear of reprisal and more out of understanding of the need for and importance of pollution control measures in attaining environmental sustainability.

Canada's participation in the United Nations Convention on Climate Change, our National Action Program on Climate Change, and federal initiatives such as the Efficiency and Alternative Energy Program have helped to reduce energy-related greenhouse gas emissions, but have proved insufficient to reach established goals. Clearly, further action is necessary.

In relation to acidic deposition, Canada has surpassed its emission reduction target for sulphur dioxide. Additionally, a National Strategy on Acidifying Emissions for beyond the year 2000 will help protect air clarity and human health as well as acid-sensitive areas. This strategy will replace the Canadian Acid Rain Control Program when it expires in 2000. Local air pollution control efforts, too, are being assessed with an eye to required changes for the future.

The Ocean Dumping Control Action Plan was initiated in 1991 to strengthen regulations, improve surveillance, and set up a national program to reduce persistent plastics in the marine environment. This plan enhances national efforts to regulate disposal at sea (by permit under CEPA and the Ocean Disposal Regulations) and to comply with the 1972 London Convention. Continued diligence in application and enforcement of this and other regulatory initiatives is an important challenge in achieving a sustainable future.

The toxic pollutants list in the National Pollutant Release Inventory (NPRI) is part of the large task of identifying, monitoring, and controlling toxic pollutants in Canada. One of the benefits of collecting data on pollutants being released into Canada's environment is that, over time, these data will provide a solid basis for comparison and enable trends to be identified and analyzed. For instance, the 1994 data (released in 1996) indicated that there was a 16 percent decrease in the amount of pollutants discharged to Canada's water and air compared to 1993. In 1994, Ontario had the highest on-site releases (57 191 tonnes) but recorded a 9 percent decrease from 1993. Alberta ranked second in releases (44 927 tonnes) but this represented a 40 percent increase over 1993. Quebec, with 39 838 tonnes in 1994, managed a 56 percent decrease from 1993. (The Web site for the NPRI is listed in the Additional Information Sources section of this chapter.)

Because of the difficulty in determining the safety of the large number of chemical products already in existence—more than 110 000—and because of the 1000 or so new substances added each year, regulations (under the New Substances Notification Regulation of CEPA) now require manufacturers and importers to provide toxicological information on new commercial substances introduced into Canada. Knowledge of these substances is important as it forms the basis for action and regulation directed at their control. More industrial responses such as the Responsible Care® program of the Canadian Chemical Producers' Association (which manages chemicals from "cradle to grave") will be necessary to help reduce total pollution from toxic substances (Canadian Chemical Producers' Association, 1994).

New approaches to managing toxic substances are being developed; the life-cycle concept (Box 14–2), and "industrial ecology" (which manages industrial impacts from a more holistic perspective) are among these new developments. Site assessments and environmental auditing also are becoming more common. In fact, the federal government has adopted an overall pollution prevention strategy that incorporates these ideas (Government of Canada, 1995a).

Policies such as the Toxic Substances Management Policy (a precautionary, proactive, and science-based management framework to be applied to all areas of fed-

eral responsibility) and the National Pollutant Release Inventory are making it easier to track pollutant releases, to identify pollution sources, and to more effectively promote management of polluting processes and their conversion to more sustainable processes (Government of Canada, 1995b).

CLEANUP OF PAST ENVIRONMENTAL PROBLEMS

In 1991, Environment Canada reported that (in 1989) there were an estimated 10 000 sites in Canada that potentially were contaminated with environmentally harmful substances (Government of Canada, 1991). Harbour bottoms, fuel storage areas, former gasoline stations, closed metal mines, former industrial facilities, railyards, former military bases, Distant Early Warning Line sites, and waste disposal areas are among these sites. Many are orphan sites; no responsible party could be found that was capable of paying for remediation. The remaining sites require rehabilitation by governments and responsible local landowners.

As the soil under many of these sites must be cleaned or removed if the site is to be sold or used for other purposes, rehabilitation can be very costly. Costs of cleaning up leaking underground storage tanks, for example, have averaged about $150 000; some sites cost millions of dollars, particularly where aquifers are contaminated by hydrocarbons or other chemicals.

Owners of properties with past and current environmental liabilities, who are facing stronger laws regarding contamination and rising civil settlements for damages, are turning to environmental auditing to identify these liabilities. Environmental auditing allows remedial or preventive actions to be taken before civil damages or noncompliance with regulations result in high costs. Governments, too, are using remedial action plans to clean up areas where the risk is greatest (such as the remaining 16 Areas of Concern on the Canadian side of the Great Lakes).

Experience with cleaning up past environmental problems has led to the development of new and more affordable remediation technologies. One of the most promising areas of research involves the use of bacteria and other microbes normally present on contaminated sites (some of which have adapted to the presence of the contaminants and are able to use them as a carbon source) to clean up the pollutants (Enviro-Focus 14).

CHANGES IN DECISION-MAKING PROCESSES

Decision-making processes that integrate environmental, economic, and social considerations in the management of natural resources and ecosystems are the basis of achieving sustainability in Canada. Examples of the kinds

BOX 14-2
THE LIFE-CYCLE CONCEPT

The life-cycle concept is a "cradle to grave" approach to thinking about products, processes, and services. The concept recognizes that all life-cycle stages (from extracting and processing raw materials to manufacturing, transportation and distribution, use and reuse, and recycling and waste management) have environmental and economic impacts.

Public policymakers as well as industrial and private organizations can use the life-cycle concept to help them make decisions about environmental design and to make improvements in resource efficiency and pollution prevention. In addition, the life-cycle approach can be used as a scientific tool for gathering quantitative data to inventory, weigh, and rank the environmental burdens of products, processes, and services.

In contrast to the specific approaches to environmental management that occur at the "end of the pipe" or "within the plant gate," decision makers can apply the life-cycle approach to all of the upstream and downstream implications of site-specific actions. For instance, decision makers could examine the changes in emission levels that would result from changing a raw material in the production process.

There are a variety of specific life-cycle tools that have been developed to help decision makers make a difference, including life-cycle assessment (LCA), design for environment, life-cycle cost accounting, total energy cycle assessment, and total fuel cycle assessment. Industries increasingly are using LCA to improve their environmental performance. A life-cycle assessment quantifies energy and resource inputs and outputs at all stages of a life cycle, then determines and weighs the associated impacts to set the stage for improvements.

The accompanying figure shows the breakdown of a product life-cycle inventory (LCI) into inputs and outputs for material and energy, as well as environmental releases. An environmental engineer might use LCIs to baseline the operation's performance against generic data and help guide pollution prevention and

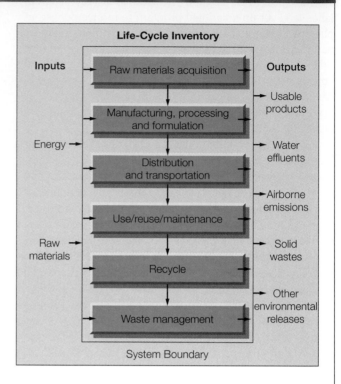

process improvements. Similarly, a manufacturer might provide consumers with environmental profiles of finished products based on input/output accounts of its own activities, its materials and energy use, and external data. This could influence product users and also help a manufacturer to meet changing customer requirements.

SOURCES: Environment Canada. (1996). What is life-cycle management? http://www.ec.gc.ca/ecocycle/whatis/index.html

Young, S.B. (1996). LCM across the life cycle—considering your role in the total life cycle of products and services. *Ecocycle,* Issue 4. http://www.ec.gc.ca/ecocycle/issues/issue4/index.html

of environmentally sensitive decision making required range from the Crombie Commission in Toronto, to Vision 2020 statements from diverse communities such as Hamilton, Ontario, and Canmore, Alberta, to the University of British Columbia's Task Force on Healthy and Sustainable Communities. These planning efforts, as well as concepts championed in such documents as the World Conservation Strategy, *Our Common Future*, and Agenda 21, have resulted in improved understanding of the need to make changes in consumption patterns, wealth distribution, and resource planning. Some of this understanding is reflected in Canada's annual Report(s) to the United Nations Commission on Sustainable Development (see, for example, Government of Canada, 1996b).

National and provincial round tables (Box 14–3), community initiated programs, and voluntary initiatives by private industry are important signs that at least some environmental ethics have been internalized among Canadians and in the business world (National Round Table on the Environment and the Economy, 1995). In addition, there is more of an effort now for environmental problems to be anticipated and prevented (rather than simply reacted to). Part of this new way of acting is the result of much more consistent public consultation on the design and implementation of decision-making strategies. Also, with better ways of disseminating information (such as Environment Canada's Green Lane Web site listed in the References section of this chapter), both the public and

Toxin-Munching Bacteria and Microbes

Underground aquifers often contain naturally occurring bacteria capable of breaking down petroleum derivatives such as toluene and benzene. In environmental microbiologist Barbara Butler's lab at the University of Waterloo, a new technique is being developed to boost the natural bacterial action on petroleum products.

Ultimately hoping to be able to eliminate contaminants that result from leaking underground gasoline storage tanks, or from industrial spills that have percolated down into groundwater, Butler monitors decomposition speed and identifies the nutrient shortages that limit the process. She is able to supply the deficient elements and can increase the rate at which the bacteria break down the contaminants into carbon dioxide and water. Even when partially broken-down products flow

into naturally oxygenated groundwater, they may be quite degradable.

This promising process is being field tested to determine if nutrient delivery systems developed by the university's earth sciences department will allow Butler's techniques to deal successfully with drinking water sources contaminated by gasoline, dry cleaning fluid, or tannery wastes.

Two U.S. researchers have found that *Desulfovibrio sulfuricans* effectively and efficiently removes dissolved uranium from wastewater. Enzymes in the microorganism convert (metabolize) dissolved uranium to uraninite, an insoluble form of the mineral that can be removed easily from wastewater. *D. sulfuricans* has been used successfully to decontaminate groundwater from a nuclear waste site. The microbe can be used to treat wastewater from uranium mining and milling operations, uranium-contaminated surface water and groundwater, and solvents used in the nuclear fuel processing cycle.

SOURCES: Long, V. (1996). Better bacteria munch toxics. *Alternatives*, 22(2), p. 3.

Microbe eats nuclear waste. (1993). *Alternatives*, 19(4), p. 3.

BOX 14-3
THE NATIONAL ROUND TABLE ON THE ENVIRONMENT AND THE ECONOMY

Created in 1988 as one of Canada's main institutional responses to the challenges of sustainable development, the National Round Table on the Environment and the Economy (NRTEE) consists of a chairperson and 24 distinguished Canadians appointed by the prime minister. The NRTEE was established to generate awareness of environment–economy issues by identifying, explaining, and promoting the principles of sustainability to government, business, and the broader community.

Proclamation of the Round Table Act in 1994 established the NRTEE as a key forum for discussion of sustainability issues. Other functions of the NRTEE were to help government address public policy questions relating to sustainable development, to provide a neutral meeting ground where stakeholders together could tackle natural resource and environmental issues, and to produce a broad range of information and publications to encourage grassroots initiatives.

local decision makers are better informed and able to contribute significantly to decisions.

Education also is a major influence on how Canadians understand and react to environmental issues and is a key to ensuring sustainability will become a reality. State-of-the-environment reports (from provinces, municipalities, corporations, and other bodies), environmental modules in school curricula, and other educational materials help ensure that future decision makers will be better informed about potential consequences of actions than were their predecessors.

Environmental indicators (or indicators of sustainability) are another tool for improving decision making. They provide concise, understandable, scientifically credible information that profiles the state of the environment and helps measure progress toward the goal of sustainable development. Economic instruments such as pollutant emission charges ("green taxes") have been implemented much more slowly, and have been used mostly to pay for the environmentally safe disposal of a product (Macdonald, 1996).

Government cutbacks and reductions or terminations to programs have resulted in reduced availability of environmental data, reduced monitoring capability, and the loss of national baseline data and ecosystem-specific information required for decision making. This makes it difficult to know whether Canada is on an environmentally, economically, and socially sustainable path. Clearly, challenges remain: problems resulting from our increasing population, continuing dependence on natural resource use to promote economic growth, generally unchanged consumption patterns, and expectations require continuing effort, commitment, dialogue, and innovation to be resolved. Some comments about how individual Canadians can address sustainability concerns are provided in the following section.

THE IMPORTANCE OF INDIVIDUALS

From the outset of this book, we identified the ecological realities of our individual actions and the challenges we face in shifting our thinking and actions toward sustaining our environment. We noted that individual and combined actions do make a difference to the environmental, social, and economic sustainability of our environment. Even though many people look to governments to show leadership and commitment in these areas, the responsibility for sustainability is shared among all members of Canadian society.

Given these realities, each one of us faces a number of fundamental choices as we look toward the future of the Canadian environment: What kind of future do we want? How can we live a life that helps to sustain the Earth? How can we get where we want to be in the future? What kind of legacy will we leave for our children, grandchildren, and succeeding generations? Knowing that each small action we take is important—because, fundamentally, healthy human communities and healthy environments are interdependent—we need to understand what our own attitudes and values are. If need be, we must change our view of the world and adopt new ways of thinking and acting.

It is important that we accept, both intellectually and emotionally, that humanity is dependent on nature, and that there are limits to the Earth's carrying capacity. While much of the world seems committed to the expansionist path, ecological footprint analysis (among other analyses) has challenged the assumptions driving that model of development and has noted the need for a shift in social consciousness. Just as the Canadian government indicates that sustainable development is an essential goal of public policy and has demonstrated (through such actions as "green government") the political will to work toward at least certain dimensions of sustainability (see Government of Canada, 1995c), so too individual Canadians need to demonstrate actively that we believe we are the stewards of our environment.

As stewards, we must ensure not only that we are (re-)connected with the natural world, but also that we learn to understand, respect, and work with one another toward sustainability objectives. As part of our stewardship, we must recognize that the material and energy consumed by each Canadian is part of the depletion of natural capital (ecological deficit) occurring globally and reduce our resource consumption accordingly. Devising a truly different way for people to exist in the world is a most important challenge to human creativity. Out of the exercise of our individual and composite intelligence, insight, and innovation, we should be able to develop many successful approaches to sustaining our Earth.

Because there is no one right approach to achieving sustainability of our environment—indeed, in diversity we find the greatest potential to adapt to Earth's ever-changing conditions—our choices will be predicated on each individual *learning* about the place where they live, *caring* about the air, water, soil, wild plants, wild animals, wild places, and people of the place where they live (as well as beyond the immediate area), and *acting* on that caring. Since acting on one's own is not always conducive to long-term change, many people find it important to get involved with ENGOs or other grassroots organizations that are dedicated to helping and empowering local people bring about change in their own lives and communities.

Taken together, Figure 14–4 and Table 14–8 provide a summary overview of major components of Earth-sustaining actions. The elements of Figure 14–4 are expanded

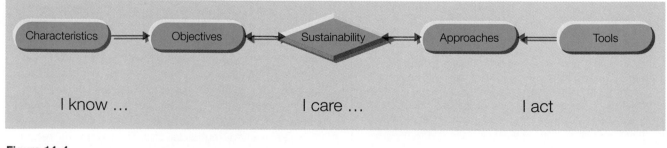

Figure 14–4
Toward environmental sustainability

PART 4:
GETTING TO TOMORROW

TABLE 14 – 8

MAJOR COMPONENTS OF EARTH SUSTAINING ACTIONS

Sustainability Characteristics	Sustainability Objectives	Sustainability Approaches	Sustainability Tools

• an ethical principle
• commitment to equality
• quality of life and well-being
• integrated approach to planning and decision making
• legacy left to future generations
• an international concept
	• sustain our natural resources
	  – sustainable renewable resources development
	  – efficient use of non-renewable resources
	• protect the health of Canadians and ecosystems
	  – eliminate toxic substances
	  – adopt a pollution prevention approach
	  – protect representative areas
	• meet our international obligations
	  – protect the ozone layer
	  – reduce greenhouse gas emissions
	  – conserve biodiversity
	  – reduce acidic precipitation and long-range transport of hazardous materials
	  – improve management of high seas fisheries and forestry
	• promote equity
	  – ensure fair distribution of costs and benefits between generations
	  – ensure fair distribution of current costs and benefits of sustainability
	• improve quality of life and well-being
	  – improve productivity through environmental efficiency (waste minimization, energy, and water efficiency)
	  – support innovation toward sustainability (long-term time horizon, flexibility)
	  – include nonmonetary dimensions of progress
		• integrated approach
		  – full cost accounting (social, economic, and environmental)
		  – environmental assessment (social, economic, and environmental)
		  – ecosystem management
		• sound science and analysis (regarding key issues, goals, etc.) including traditional ecological knowledge
		• collaboration and cooperation among
		  – individuals
		  – private sector
		  – governments and Aboriginal people
			• policy tools
			  – voluntary actions of groups, individuals, industry, or communities
			  – economic instruments
			  – government expenditure
			  – legal tools
			  – environmental auditing
			• information and awareness tools
			  – labelling programs
			  – technology sharing
			  – sustainability indicators
			  – quality standards

SOURCE: Adapted from Government of Canada. (1995). A guide to green government, pp. 4–17.

What legacy do we want to leave for succeeding generations?

on in Table 14–8; while not comprehensive, the table is meant to demonstrate the ways in which sustainability tools support sustainability approaches and, in turn, how sustainability approaches help achieve sustainability objectives (that reflect at least some of the characteristics of sustainability that stewards attempt to practise and achieve).

Individuals and their cooperative actions matter when it comes to environmental sustainability. Whether we lead by example (for instance, in picking up litter from our streets, showing a neighbour how our backyard compost works, or volunteering for an executive position in an ENGO), or whether we lead by working within existing economic and political systems, the power of one-on-one communication to influence environmental change within political elites, among other elected officials, and in our circle of friends, family, and neighbourhood members should not be underestimated.

To ensure that we live as sustainably as we can (leave the lightest possible footprints on the planet) and make good decisions with respect to environmental sustainability, a number of practical and philosophical considerations may guide our thinking and actions. These considerations include the following:

- Critical assessment to determine in what ways development proposals are sustainable: Do they deplete Earth's capital? Do they preserve biodiversity? Do they enhance cultural diversity? Do they promote self-reliance on the part of individuals and communities? Is the precautionary principle useful to help ensure we use resources efficiently and live off Earth's income?

- Use of appropriate technology: To what degree are design-with-nature concepts employed? Are they simple, resource-efficient, and culturally adaptable technologies? Do they rely mostly on local sources of resources (recycled) and labour?

- Information and education: Are we teaching people (and learning, ourselves) how to think holistically, in a systematic, integrated, multidisciplinary fashion about planet Earth? Are we listening to the variety of sources of knowledge about Earth? Do we know where our water comes from, where our wastes go, what kinds of soils support our food production, and how long our growing season is?

- Simplicity: Have we reduced, reused, recycled, and refused (unnecessary products) wherever possible? Have we eliminated unnecessary consumption and waste of energy and other resources? Do we know what elements of our lifestyles are harmful or beneficial to the Earth?

Each small action we take in support of environmental sustainability is important in helping to sustain Earth's life-support systems for ourselves and all life. Perhaps, in working with others in our neighbourhoods and communities, our actions will help promote stewardship and acceptance of responsibility for sustainability. It is not too late to learn how to work with Earth's ecosystems; if we really care, together our thoughts and actions will help achieve a sustainable society.

Chapter Questions

1. Looking at the area where you live, identify examples of issues where progress has been achieved in reaching environmental goals, as well as examples where less progress has been achieved. What might some of the reasons be for the differential success?

2. Identify (name) any ENGOs that are active in your region. What are their objectives and what are some of the environmental issues they are concerned about? What kinds of actions do they take? Have they been successful in achieving their goals?

3. In October 1996, at the World Conservation Union's first World Conservation Congress in Montreal, Deputy Prime Minister Sheila Copps said: "We believe in good, tough environmental regulations. We need good laws to protect the gains we have made." Do you agree with these statements? Why or why not?

4. Comment on this statement: "A strong correlation is emerging between environmental and economic success." If you were to develop a complete response to this question, what additional information would you need to confirm that this statement was correct (or not)?

5. Using the information contained in Tables 14–1 through 14–6, inclusive, identify which issues and which sectors received the greatest attention from regulators. Which issues or sectors received the least attention? Are there issues or sectors of concern that you feel have not been recognized by the regulators? What actions could you take to bring these issues to their attention?

6. Draw up a two-column list of the economic goods you use; in one column identify those economic goods that meet your basic needs and in the other column, those that satisfy your wants. Are there any of these economic wants you would be willing to give up? Are there any that you believe you should give up but are unwilling to? Are there any of these wants that you hope to satisfy in the future? Will any of these improve the quality of your life (if not, what will)? Relate the results of your analysis to your personal impact on the environment. How do your results compare with others in your class?

references

Canadian Chemical Producers' Association. 1994. *Reducing emissions: A Responsible Care® initiative. 1993 emissions inventory and five year projections.* Ottawa.

Colborn, T., vom Saal, F.S., & Soto, A.M. (1993). Developmental effects of endocrine-disrupting chemicals in wildlife and humans. *Environmental Health Perspectives,* 101(5), pp. 378–84.

Commissioner of the Environment and Sustainable Development. http://www.oag-bvg.gc.ca

Environment Canada. (1996). What is life-cycle management? http://www.ec.ca/ecocycle/whatis/index.html

Environment Canada. (1995). *Canadian Biodiversity Strategy.* Ottawa.

Environment Canada. The Green Lane. http://www.doe.ca

Government of Canada. (1991). *The state of Canada's environment—1991.* Ottawa: Supply and Services Canada.

Government of Canada. (1995a). *Pollution prevention: A federal strategy for action.* Ottawa.

Government of Canada. (1995b). *Toxic substances management policy.* Ottawa.

Government of Canada. (1995c). *A guide to green government.* Ottawa.

Government of Canada. (1996b). *Report of Canada to the United Nations Commission on Sustainable Development.* Ottawa.

Government of Canada. Department of Foreign Affairs and International Trade. (1997). *Building momentum: Sustainable development in Canada.* Ottawa, p. 5.

Long, V. (1996). Better bacteria munch toxics. *Alternatives,* 22(2), p. 3.

Macdonald, D. (1996). Beer cans, gas guzzlers and green taxes. *Alternatives,* 22(3), pp. 12–19.

Malden Mills Industries, Inc. (1994). *Cool stuff to know about Polartec® fabrics.* Lawrence, MA: Malden Mills Industries.

Menyasz, P., Pole, K., & Ray, R. (Eds.) (1996–1997). *Environment Policy and Law,* 6(9)–8(2).

Microbe eats nuclear waste. (1993). *Alternatives,* 19(4), p. 3.

National Energy Board. (1994). *Canadian energy supply and demand 1993–2010, trends and issues.* Calgary.

National Pollutant Release Inventory.
http://www.ec.gc.ca/pdb/npri.html

National Round Table on the Environment and the Economy. (1995). In Hodge, T., Holtyz, S., Smith, C., & Hawke, K. (Eds.). *Pathways to sustainability: Assessing our progress.* National Round Table Series on Sustainable Development: Ottawa.

Nickerson, M. (1990). *Planning for seven generations—guideposts for a sustainable future.* Merrickville, ON: Bakavi School of Permaculture.

Taylor, D.M. (1994). *Off course: Restoring balance between Canadian society and the environment.* Ottawa: International Development Research Centre.

Wackernagel, M., & Rees, W. (1996). *Our ecological footprint: Reducing human impact on the earth.* Gabriola Island, BC: New Society Publishers.

Young, S.B. (1996). LCM across the life cycle—considering your role in the total life cycle of products and services. *Ecocycle,* Issue 4. http://www.ec.gc.ca/ecocycle/issues/issue4/index.html.

additonal information sources

Commissioner of the Environment and Sustainable Development. http://www.oag-bvg.gc.ca

Government of Canada. (1996a). *The state of Canada's environment—1996.* Ottawa: Supply and Services Canada.

National Pollutant Release Inventory.
http://www.ec.gc.ca/pdb/npri.html

GLOSSARY

abiotic. The nonliving components of an ecosystem such as water, air, solar energy, and nutrients necessary to support life in a given area. Compare *biotic*.

acclimation. The adjustment of a species to slowly changing conditions in an ecosystem, such as temperature. See also *threshold effect*.

acid mine drainage. Acidic water that drains from mine sites and sometimes enters streams and lakes.

adaptation. Any genetically controlled characteristic—structural, physiological, or behavioural—that enhances the chance for members of a population to survive and reproduce in its environment. See also *mutation*.

aerobic respiration. A complex chemical process that drives the life processes of living things, by using oxygen to convert nutrients such as glucose back into carbon dioxide and water. The opposite of photosynthesis.

aesthetic arguments. A rationale for the conservation of nature based on its beauty and aesthetic qualities. Compare *utilitarian justification, ecological justification, moral justification*.

age-specific rate. The number of live births per 1000 women of a specific age group per year.

agroforestry. The raising of trees or shrubs together with crops and/or animals on the same parcel of land.

alternative energy. Renewable energy sources, such as wind, flowing water, solar energy and biomass, which create less environmental damage and pollution than fossil fuels, and offer an alternative to nonrenewable resources.

alternative livestock. The raising together of non-native animal species and domesticated native species.

aquaculture. The breeding and raising of fish under controlled conditions, with the goal of high level production for food or recreational purposes.

atmosphere. A thin layer of gases consisting mostly of nitrogen and oxygen which completely surrounds the solid and liquid earth. See also *troposphere, stratosphere*.

atomic number. The number of protons in an atom's nucleus, which distinguishes it from the atoms of other elements.

atoms. The smallest particles that exhibit the unique characteristics of that particular element.

autotrophs. See *producers*.

background extinction. The continuous, low-level extinction of species that has occurred throughout much of history. Compare *mass extinction*.

barrier islands. Long, low, offshore islands of sediment that run parallel to much of North America's Atlantic and Gulf coasts and help protect coastal wetlands and habitats from storm damage.

bellwether species. See *indicator species*.

benthic environment. The ocean floor, one of the two main divisions of the open sea environment. See also *pelagic environment*.

biodiversity. The diversity of life on earth, consisting of genetic diversity, species diversity and ecosystem diversity.

biofuels. See *ethanol*.

biogeochemical cycles. See *nutrient cycles*.

biological evolution. The change in inherited characteristics of a population from generation to successive generation.

biological oxygen demand (BOD). The amount of oxygen needed during the time it takes for waste material to be oxidized. Water quality is directly affected by this; some organisms thrive on a higher BOD and some suffocate for lack of oxygen.

biomagnification. The accumulation and concentration of certain substances in organisms, such as chlorinated organic compounds (DDT and PCBs) in the fatty tissues of predators in the Arctic marine system.

biomass. The amount of living or organic matter contained in living organisms.

biome. A broad, regional type of ecosystem characterized by distinctive climate and soil conditions and a distinctive biological community adapted to those conditions.

biosphere. That part of the earth inhabited by plants and animals, and their interactions with the atmosphere, hydrosphere, and lithosphere.

biotechnology. The use of a living organism (or a part thereof) to create some different product, whether cheese to eat, a vaccine to combat disease, or a plant or animal with novel attributes. Genetic engineering is a more recent aspect of biotechnology.

biotic potential. The maximum rate a population can increase under ideal conditions.

biotic. The living components of an ecosystem including plants, animals, and their products (secretions, wastes, and remains) and effects in a given area. Compare *abiotic*.

bitumen. A black oil rich in sulphur that is found in oilsand. It can be treated and chemically upgraded into synthetic crude oil, though the net useful energy yield is lower than for conventional oil because more energy is required to extract and process it. See also *oilsand*.

carnivores. Organisms that feed indirectly on plants by eating the meat of herbivores. Most carnivores are animals, but a few examples are in the plant kingdom, such as the Venus flytrap. See also *herbivores, omnivores*.

carrying capacity. The number of organisms that an ecosystem can support indefinitely, while maintaining its productivity, adaptability, and capability for renewal.

cash crop. A crop grown to be traded in a marketplace.

chemical change. A change in which a chemical reaction is produced and a new substance created, as when gasoline is burned to produce carbon dioxide. Compare *physical change*.

chemical contamination. The presence of a chemical that makes something unfit for its intended use. Pesticide contamination, for example, makes soil unfit for food production.

chemosynthesis. The process in which some organisms (usually certain types of bacteria) convert, without sunlight, inorganic chemical compounds into organic nutrient compounds—food energy for their own use. Contrasts with photosynthesis.

chemotrophs. Producers, including algae and bacteria, which convert the energy found in inorganic chemical compounds into more complex energy, without the use of sunlight. See also *producers, consumers*.

clear-cutting. A system of tree harvesting that removes all the trees in a given area, as opposed to selective cutting that leaves some trees standing . Replanting after clear-cutting can be difficult.

climax community. The mature stage of succession in a particular area, in which all organisms and nonliving factors are in balance.

coal. The most abundant fossil fuel in the world, with reserves four to five times that of oil and gas combined. It has a relatively high net useful energy yield and is highly effective for providing industrial heat.

coastal wetlands. Coastal area that provides breeding grounds and habitats for many marine organisms as well as for waterfowl, shorebirds, and other wildlife.

coastal zone. The area where the ocean meets the land, which constitutes 10 percent of the ocean's area but contains 90 percent of all marine species.

co-generation. The production of two useful forms of energy from the same source, such as heat and power. See also *district heating*.

commensalism. An interaction between species in which one benefits and the other is neither helped nor harmed. See also *mutualism, symbiosis*.

community. An area where different species interact, such as an alpine community or a prairie community. See also *habitat*.

community shared agriculture (CSA). A shared-risk venture in which local people buy a share of a farm's produce prior to the growing season.

competitive exclusion principle. When two species are competing for the same resources, one must migrate to another area if possible, shift its feeding habits or behaviour, suffer a sharp decline in population numbers, or become extinct.

compounds. One of the basic forms of chemical composition, which involves two or more different elements held together in fixed proportions by the attraction in the chemical bonds between their constituent atoms. See also *mixtures, elements*.

consumers. Those organisms that eat the cells, tissues, or waste products of other organisms. Animals are common consumers. See also *producers, chemotrophs*.

controlled experiment. An experiment designed to test the effects of independent variables on a dependent variable by changing one independent variable at a time.

coral reefs. Found in warm tropical and subtropical oceans, these formations are rich in life and may contain more than 3000 species of corals, fish, and shellfish.

country food. Food grown by people in small communities living in harmony with their local environment.

crude birth rate. The annual number of live births per 1000 population, without regard to age or sex composition.

crude death rate. The annual number of deaths per 1000 population.

crude growth rate. The net change, or difference, between the crude birth rate and the crude death rate.

decomposer. See *microconsumers*.

deductive reasoning. Drawing conclusions from observations of the natural world by means of logical reasoning. Compare *inductive reasoning*.

deforestation. To clear an area of forests or trees, usually for commercial use of the lumber or agricultural use of the land.

demographic transition. A four-stage model of population change that links industrial development with zero population growth, and suggests a post-industrial phase that would focus more on sustainable forms of economic development.

demographic trap. A state in which a nation or population is stuck in the second stage of demographic transition, with a low death rate, a high birth rate, and increasing demand on available resources.

demography. The study of the characteristics and changes in the size and structure of human populations.

dependency ratio. A measure of the number of dependents, young and old, that each 100 people in their economically productive years must support. It is used to forecast the condition of the future human population.

detritus feeders. See *detritivores*.

detritivores. Consumers that ingest fragments of dead organic material. Examples are earthworms and maggots.

differential reproduction. The ability to produce more offspring with the same favourable adaptations as the parents, which will allow them to survive under changed environmental conditions.

dissolved oxygen content. The amount of oxygen dissolved in a given volume of water at a particular temperature and pressure. This can be a limiting factor on the growth of aquatic populations.

district heating. An effort to maximize energy efficiency in power generating stations, which involves a steam cycle that is modified so that the steam is extracted and used to produce hot water. The water is then pumped through pipes to surrounding buildings to supply heat. See also *co-generation*.

doubling time. The length of time required for a population to double in size.

drainage basin. The area of land that contributes water and sediment to a river.

ecological diversity. The variety of biological communities, such as forests, deserts, grasslands, and streams, that interact with one another and with their physical and chemical (nonliving) environments. See also *species diversity*.

ecological footprint. A link between human lifestyles and ecosystems, which allows people to visualize the impact of their consumption patterns and activities on ecosystems.

ecological justification. A rationale for the conservation of nature based on the idea that the environment provides specific functions necessary to the persistence of our life. Compare *utilitarian justification, aesthetic arguments, moral justification*.

ecological niche. The role an organism plays within the structure and functions of an ecosystem, and the way it interacts with other living things and with its physical environment.

ecology. The study of the interactions of living organisms with one another and with their nonliving environment of matter and energy.

ecosphere. See *biosphere*.

ecosystem. A community and its members interacting with each other and their nonliving environment.

electrons. Negatively charged ions that continually orbit the nucleus of an atom and are held in orbit by attraction to the positive charge of the nucleus. See also *protons, neutrons*.

elements. One of the basic forms of chemical composition. All matter is built from the 109 known chemical elements; these are the simplest building blocks of all matter. See also *compounds, mixtures*.

emissions permits. A strategy developed to reduce greenhouse gas emissions, where companies buy and sell from each other the right to release greenhouse gases.

endemic species. A species that is native to a particular geographic region.

energy quality. The measure of an energy source's ability to perform useful work, such as running electrical devices or motors. See also *high-quality energy, low-quality energy*.

energy. The ability or capacity to do work. Energy enables us to move matter and change it from one form to another.

environment. The surroundings in which plants and animals live, affected by various physical factors such as temperature, water, light, and food resources.

environmental ethics. A new discipline that analyzes the issues regarding our moral obligations to future generations with respect to the environment.

environmental impact assessment (EIA). A process that aims to provide decision makers with scientifically researched and documented evidence to identify the likely consequences of undertaking new developments and changing natural systems. See also *environmental impact statement*.

environmental impact statement (EIS). A key component of an environmental impact assessment, an EIS provides a nontechnical summary of the study, including the main project characteristics, aspects of the environment likely to be affected, possible alternatives, and suggested measures and systems to monitor or reduce any harmful effects. See also *environmental impact assessment.*

environmental resistance. The limits set by the environment that prevent organisms from reproducing indefinitely at an exponential rate.

estuaries. A body of coastal water partly surrounded by water, with access to the open sea and a large supply of fresh water from rivers. These conditions provide excellent conditions for many important shellfish and fin fish species.

ethanol. A fuel converted from biomass materials and used to power motor vehicles, either directly as fuel or as an octane-enhancing gasoline additive. Ethanol can reduce carbon monoxide emissions from regular gasoline blends.

eukaryotic. Cells with a high degree of internal organization, including a nucleus (genetic material surrounded by a membrane) and several other internal parts surrounded by membranes. See also *prokaryotic.*

eutrophic. A lake enriched with nutrients in excess of what is required by producers. See also *oligotrophic, mesotrophic.*

eutrophication. An increase in the concentration of plant nutrients in water. Natural eutrophication is a slow process, but human-induced eutrophication (as from fertilizers used in agricultural) may accelerate the process and make water unfit for human consumption.

exclusive economic zone. An area of exclusive fishing rights granted to Canada in the 1982 United Nations Convention on the Law of the Sea. It came into force in 1994.

exotic. A species that enters an ecosystem from a different part of the world through introduction (deliberately or accidentally) by humans.

exponential growth. Growth in a species that takes place at a constant rate per time period.

extinction. The process whereby a species is eliminated from existence when it cannot adapt genetically and reproduce successfully under new environmental conditions. See also *mass extinction, background extinction.*

fact. An observation that all (or almost all) scientists agree is correct.

first law of energy. See *first law of thermodynamics.*

first law of thermodynamics. During a physical or chemical change, energy is neither created nor destroyed. See also *second law of thermodynamics.*

food chains. The sequence of who feeds on or decomposes whom in an ecosystem.

food web. A complex network of feeding relationships in which the flow of energy and materials through an ecosystem takes place. That flow occurs on the basis of a range of food choices on the part of each organism involved.

fossil fuels. The remains of prehistoric animals, forests, and sea floor life that have become buried in layers of sediment and decomposed very slowly, eventually being converted into crude oil. See also *hydrocarbons.*

fundamental niches. The full range of physical, chemical, and biological factors each species could use if there were no competition from other species. See also *interspecific competition.*

gene pool. The sum of all genes possessed by the individuals of a population.

general fertility rate. The number of live births per 1000 women of childbearing age per year.

generalist species. The ability to live in many different places while tolerating a wide range of environmental conditions. Humans are considered a generalist species. See also *specialist species.*

genes. Segments of various deoxyribonucleic acid (DNA) molecules found in chromosomes. Genes impart certain inheritable traits to organisms.

genetic diversity. The diversity within a given population that shares common structural, functional, and behavioural traits but varies slightly in genetic makeup and so exhibits slightly different behaviours and appearances.

global warming potential. A concept developed to take into account the differing times that gases remain in the atmosphere, in order to evaluate the potential climate effects of equal emissions of each of the greenhouse gases.

gross primary productivity. The rate at which producers in an ecosystem capture and store chemical energy as biomass. Compare *net primary productivity.*

groundwater. Water that has accumulated beneath the Earth's surface in cracks, the pores of rocks, and other spaces. It can reach down from above or rise up from below. Compare *surface water.*

habitat. The place where an organism or population lives, such as an ocean, a forest or a stream. See also *community.*

heat island. A microclimate in which the air temperature is slightly higher than in the surrounding area. In an urban heat island, for example, the temperature in the city is 1–2°C higher than in the rural area around it.

herbivores. Organisms that eat green plants directly as a source of nutrients. Deer are common herbivores. See also *carnivores, omnivores*.

heterotrophs. See *consumers*.

high-quality energy. Concentrated energy sources such as electricity, gasoline, and food, which enable people and machines to perform useful tasks. See also *low-quality energy, energy quality*.

high-quality matter. Material such as coal or salt deposits commonly found near the Earth's surface in an organized or concentrated form, so that its potential for use as a resource is great. See *low quality matter*.

highgrading. An unsound practice associated with selective cutting techniques that involves logging the highest-quality and most accessible timber first.

human cultural diversity. The variety of human cultures that represent our adaptability and survival options in the face of changing conditions.

hydrocarbons. Any of a class of compounds containing only hydrogen and carbon, which include fossil fuels. See also *fossil fuels*.

hydroelectric power. Electrical power generated from the energy of falling water or any other hydraulic source.

hydrogen power. A source of energy that converts hydrogen to electricity to provide heat, light, and power. Though hydrogen is readily available, the production of hydrogen power is expensive and not yet commercially viable.

hydrological cycle. The movement of water between the atmosphere and the oceans, through evaporation, runoff from streams and rivers, and precipitation.

hydrosphere. The Earth's supply of moisture in all its forms: liquid, frozen, and gaseous. This includes surface water, underground water, frozen water, water vapour in the atmosphere, and moisture in the tissues and organs of living things.

hypothesis. An explanation that is based on testable observations and experiments, and that can be accepted until it is disproved.

igneous rock. Rock formed from molten materials crystallizing at the Earth's surface (such as lava from volcanoes), or beneath the surface (such as granite). See also *sedimentary rock, metamorphic rock*.

immigrant species. Those species that migrate into or are introduced into an ecosystem, deliberately or accidentally, by humans.

independent variable. A condition that is deliberately manipulated by scientists to test the response in an experiment. See also *responding variable, operational definitions*.

indicator species. Those species that provide early warnings of environmental damage to communities or ecosystems.

inductive reasoning. Drawing a general conclusion based on a limited set of observations. Compare *deductive reasoning*.

infant mortality rate. The ratio of deaths of infants under 12 months per 1000 live births.

inferences. Conclusions derived either by logical reasoning from premises and/or evidence, or by insight or analogy based on evidence.

instream uses. Water used in its natural setting for hydroelectric power, transportation, fisheries, and other applications. See also *withdrawal uses*.

interspecific competition. Competition from other species for one or more of the same limited resources of food, sunlight, water, soil, nutrients, or space. See also *fundamental niches*.

intrinsic value. A value placed on the inherent qualities of a species, independent of its value to humans.

invertebrates. Animals without backbones, such as jellyfish, worms, insects, and spiders. Compare *vertebrates*.

ions. Subatomic, electrically charged particles in an atom. See also *protons, neutrons*.

keystone species. Those species that play a crucial role in helping to maintain the ecosystems of which they are a part, by pollination, regulation of populations, or other activities.

kinetic energy. Energy associated with the movement of matter and mass. A moving air mass such as wind has kinetic energy, as do flowing streams, moving cars, heat, and electricity. See also *potential energy*.

law of conservation of matter. Matter is neither created nor destroyed, but is combined and re-arranged in different ways.

law of tolerance. The presence, number, and distribution of a species in an ecosystem are determined by whether the levels of one or more physical or chemical factors fall within the range tolerated by the species. See also *limiting factor principle*.

limiting factor principle. Too much or too little of any abiotic factor can limit or prevent growth of a population even if all other factors are at or near the optimum range of tolerance. See also *law of tolerance*.

limnetic zone. The open water area away from the shore of a lake or pond, with less light penetration and fewer producers. See also *littoral zone, profundal zone*.

lithosphere. The upper zone of the Earth's mantle and the inorganic mixture of rocks and mineral matter in the Earth's crust.

littoral zone. The shallow water and vegetated area along the shore of a lake or pond, and the most productive zone of the lake. See also *limnetic zone, profundal zone*.

logistic growth curve. The idea that the population increases exponentially at the outset and then levels out as the carrying capacity of the environment is reached.

long-distance commuting. The practice of flying miners into a mine to work for a designated period and then flying them back to their homes in larger communities for another period.

low-quality energy. Dispersed energy, such as the heat stored in the oceans, with little capacity to perform useful tasks. See also *high-quality energy, energy quality*.

low-quality matter. Hard-to-reach matter, such as that dispersed or diluted in the atmosphere or oceans. See also *high-quality matter*.

macroconsumers. Organisms that feed by ingesting or engulfing particles, parts or entire bodies of other organisms, living or dead, including herbivores, carnivores, omnivores, scavengers, and detrivores.

macronutrients. The main constituents of the complex organic compounds required by all living organisms. The six major macronutrients are carbon, oxygen, hydrogen, nitrogen, phosphorus, and sulphur. See also *micronutrients*.

mangrove swamp. A collection of tropical evergreen trees with stiltlike aerial roots that cause thick undergrowth and provide habitat for marine organisms, waterfowl, and other coastal species.

manipulated variable. See *independent variable*.

mass extinction. The disappearance of numerous species over a relatively short period of geological time. See also *background extinction*.

matter. Anything that has mass and takes up space, including everything that is solid, liquid, or gaseous.

mesotrophic. A lake that falls in the mid-range between the two extremes of nutrient enrichment required by producers. See also *oligotrophic, eutrophic*.

metamorphic rock. Formed when existing rocks lying deep below the Earth's surface are subjected to high temperatures, high pressures, chemically active fluids, or a combination of these agents, causing the rocks' crystal structure to change. See also *igneous rock, sedimentary rock*.

microconsumers. Organisms that live on or within their food source, completing the breakdown of complex molecules into simpler compounds (which we call rot or decay).

micronutrients. The trace elements of complex organic compounds required by all living organisms. These include boron, copper, zinc, and others. See also *macronutrients*.

milling. In the processing of minerals, the crushing and grinding of ores to separate the useful materials from the nonuseful ones. See also *tailings*.

mineral exploration. Finding geological, geophysical, or geochemical conditions that differ from those of their surroundings.

mineral fuels. Crude oil and equivalents, including natural gas, coal, and natural gas byproducts. In 1996, they accounted for approximately 65 percent of the total value of Canadian mineral production.

mixtures. One of the basic forms of chemical composition. A combination of elements, compounds or both.

molecules. Particle formed when two or more atoms of the same or different elements combine.

moral justification. A rationale for the conservation of nature based on the idea that elements of the environment have a right to exist, independent of human desires. Compare *utilitarian justification, moral justification, aesthetic arguments*.

mutation. The random and unpredictable changes in DNA molecules that can be transmitted to offspring and produce variability. See also *adaptation*.

mutualism. A symbiotic relationship in which both interacting species benefit, as when honeybees pollinate flowers as they feed on the flower's nectar. See *also symbiosis, commensalism*.

native species. See *endemic species*.

natural gas. A gaseous hydrocarbon mixture of methane combined with smaller amounts of propane and butane. The conventional or "associated" type is located underground above most reserves of crude oil, while the nonassociated type is found on its own in dry wells.

natural selection. The tendency for only the best adapted organisms to survive and reproduce in a given environment.

net primary productivity. The rate at which organic matter is incorporated into plant bodies so as to produce growth. See also *gross primary productivity.*

net useful energy. The usable amount of energy available from an energy source over its lifetime.

neutrons. Uncharged or electrically neutral ions, which cluster with protons in the centre of an atom and comprise its nucleus. See also *electrons, protons, ions.*

nitrogen fixation. A part of the nitrogen cycle in which atmospheric nitrogen is converted into other chemical forms available to plants.

nonrenewable resources. Resources such as coal, oil, and other fossil fuels that are finite in supply and replaced so slowly that they are soon depleted. Compare *renewable resources.*

nuclear energy. The energy released by reactions within atomic nuclei, such as nuclear fission or nuclear fusion. See also *radioactive wastes.*

nutrient cycles. The means by which the nutrient elements and their compounds cycle continually through Earth's atmosphere, hydrosphere, lithosphere and biosphere.

nutrients. The materials that an organism must take in to enable it to live, grow, and reproduce.

observations. Information gathered through any of our five senses or instruments that extend these senses.

oil shale. Rock that contains a solid mixture of hydrocarbon compounds called kerogen. Once crushed and heated, kerogen vapour is condensed to form heavy, slow-flowing shale oil.

oilsand. A combination of clay, sand, water, and bitumen. Canada is home to the largest know oilsand deposits in the world. See also *bitumen.*

oligotrophic. A lake with minimal levels of nutrients required for producers. See *eutrophic, mesotrophic.*

omnivores. Consumers that eat both plants and animals, such as black bears, pigs, and humans. See also *carnivores, herbivores.*

one-industry town. A community whose existence depends on the exploitation of a single resource.

open-pit mining. A type of mining in which minerals are extracted from the Earth by digging that leaves a large pit in the surface. Compare *strip mining.*

operational definitions. Set of criteria that tell scientists what to look for or what to do in order to carry out the measurement, construction, or manipulation of variables. See also *independent variable, responding variable.*

organic farming. Farming that uses natural soil-forming processes and crop rotation rather than synthetic inputs.

organism. A complex organization of cells, tissues, organs, and body systems that work together to create a multicellular individual such as a bear, whale, human, or orchid.

overburden. The layers of rock and soil that overlay mineral deposits. These layers are removed during surface mining.

ozone. A gas (O_3) that is an air pollutant in the lower atmosphere but beneficial in the upper atmosphere. See *ozone layer.*

ozone layer. The layer of ozone in the stratosphere that filters out harmful ultraviolet radiation from the sun.

parasitism. A symbiotic relationship in which the parasite benefits by obtaining nourishment from the host and the host is weakened or killed by the parasite.

pelagic environment. The ocean water, one of the two main divisions of the open sea environment. See also *benthic environment.*

permafrost. A permanently frozen layer of subsoil, characteristic of the tundra biome.

physical change. A change from one state to another, as when water changes from ice to its liquid state. See also *chemical change.*

polar stratospheric clouds. Formed in extremely cold temperatures within the polar vortex as it matures, cools, and descends, these clouds have been linked to depletion of the ozone layer.

polar vortex. An atmospheric condition that occurs during the polar winter night when the Antarctic air mass is partially isolated from the rest of the atmosphere and circulates around the pole.

polynyas. An area of unfrozen sea water, created by local water currents in northern oceans. They act as biological hotspots and serve as vital winter refuges for marine mammals.

population age structure. The distribution of the population by age, used in analysis of demographic trends.

population lag effect. See *population momentum.*

population momentum. When a population achieves replacement fertility, that population continues to grow for several generations before stabilizing.

population. A group of individuals of the same species living and interacting in the same geographic area at the same time.

potential energy. Energy stored and potentially available for use, such as the chemical energy stored in gasoline or food molecules. See also *kinetic energy*.

precious metals. Metals, such as gold and silver, that are valuable to humans because of their rarity or appearance.

predation. When members of a predator species feed on parts or all of an organism of a prey species.

predator–prey relationships. The most obvious form of species interaction, which occurs when one organism (the predator) feeds on another (the prey).

predator. An organism, usually an animal, that feeds on other organisms, as when a turtle eats a fish in a freshwater pond ecosystem.

prey. The organism consumed by a predator.

primary consumer. See *herbivores*.

primary succession. The development of biotic communities in a previously uninhabited and barren habitat with little or no soil. Compare *secondary succession*.

primary treatment. The lowest level of treatment in the management of municipal wastes, which involves the mechanical removal of large solids, sediment, and some organic matter. See also *secondary treatment, tertiary treatment*.

principle of connectedness. Everything in the natural world is connected to and intermingled with everything else, and a change in environmental conditions will have multiple effects.

producers. Those self-nourishing organisms that perform photosynthesis by converting relatively simple inorganic substances such as water, carbon dioxide, and nutrients into complex chemicals such as carbohydrates, lipids, and proteins. Green plants and phytoplankton are common producers. See also *chemotrophs, consumers*.

profundal zone. The deepest zone of a lake, where lack of light means that no producers can survive. See also *littoral zone, limnetic zone*.

prokaryotic. Cells that lack a nuclear envelope and other internal cell membranes, including bacteria. Compare *eukaryotic*.

protons. Positively charged ions, which cluster with neutrons in the centre of an atom and comprise its nucleus. See also *electrons, neutrons, ions*.

qualitative data. Non-numerical records of independent and dependent variables kept during experiments.

quantitative data. Numerical records of independent and dependent variables kept during experiments.

radioactive wastes. Radioactive by-products from the operation of a nuclear reactor or from the re-processing of depleted nuclear waste. See also *nuclear energy*.

realized niche. That portion of a fundamental niche actually occupied by a species, which results from the sharing of resources in a given ecosystem.

reclamation. The rehabilitation of a site (a disused mine, for example) in order to make it a viable and, if possible, self-sustaining ecosystem that is compatible with a healthy environment.

regional sustainability. An alternative to the globalization of the food-production system in which developing countries would be encouraged to grow food first for themselves and then for export.

renewable resources. Resources such as forests, solar energy, and fisheries that can be replaced by environmental processes in a time frame meaningful to humans. Compare *nonrenewable resources*.

replacement fertility. The fertility rate needed to ensure that the population remains constant as each set of parents is replaced by their offspring.

resource partitioning. The division of scarce resources in order that species with similar requirements can use the resources in different ways, in different places, and at different times.

responding variable. A condition that responds to changes in the independent variable in an experiment. Also referred to as a dependent variable. See also *independent variable, operational definitions*.

salinity. The amounts of various salts dissolved in a given volume of water. This can be a limiting factor on the growth of aquatic populations.

salinization. The accumulation of salts in soil—a process that may result in soil too salty to support plant growth.

scavengers. Consumers that eat dead organic material (consuming the entire dead organism), such as vultures and hyenas.

scientific method. Systematic methods used in scientific investigations of the natural world, which include designing controlled experiments, gathering data, developing and testing hypotheses.

second law of energy. See *second law of thermodynamics*.

second law of thermodynamics. With each change in form, some energy is degraded to a less useful form and given off into the surroundings, usually as low quality heat. See also *first law of thermodynamics*.

secondary consumers. See *carnivores*.

secondary succession. The development of biotic communities in an area where the natural vegetation has been removed or destroyed but where soil is present. See also *primary succession*.

secondary treatment. The second level of treatment in the management of municipal wastes, which employs biological processes by which bacteria degrade most of the dissolved organics, about 30 percent of the phosphates and about 50 percent of the nitrates. See also *primary treatment, tertiary treatment*.

sedimentary rock. Rock formed when small bits and pieces of matter and sediments are carried by wind or rain and then deposited, compacted, and cemented to form rock. See also *igneous rock, metamorphic rock*.

soil compaction. A form of structural degradation in soil in which soil is packed so tightly that its air spaces are closed, reducing aeration and infiltration and thus reducing the ability of the soil to support plant growth. Caused mainly by the repeated passing of heavy machinery over wet soil.

solar energy. Energy derived from the sun in the form of solar radiation.

specialist species. The ability to live in only one type of habitat, eat only a few types of food, or tolerate a narrow range of climatic or environmental conditions. See also *generalist species*.

speciation. The formation of two or more species from one as the result of divergent natural selection and response to changes in environmental conditions.

species diversity. The number of different species and the relative abundance of each in different habitats on Earth. See also *ecological diversity*.

species. A group of organisms that resemble one another in appearance, behaviour, chemical makeup and processes, and genetic structure, and that produce fertile offspring under natural conditions.

stewardship. The concept that mankind has an ethical responsibility to care for plants, animals, and the environment as a whole, due to our superior intellect and power to change the natural world.

stratosphere. The layer above the troposphere that contains the ozone layer and protects life on Earth's surface by absorbing most incoming solar ultraviolet radiation. See also *troposphere, atmosphere*.

strip mining. Surface mining in which heavy machinery strips away the overlying layer of rock and soil to create a trench that exposes the mineral resource below. Compare *open-pit mining*.

surface runoff. Precipitation that flows on the land (instead of soaking into it) and into bodies of surface water. May carry contaminants.

surface water. All bodies of water, such as lakes, rivers, streams and oceans, that lie on the surface of the Earth. Compare *groundwater*.

sustainability. The ability of an ecosystem to maintain ecological processes, functions, biodiversity, and productivity over time. See also *sustainable development*.

sustainable development. Maintaining environmental resources so that they continue to provide benefits to living things and the larger environment of which they are a part. See also *sustainability*.

sustainable yield. The greatest productivity that can be yielded from a renewable resource without depleting the supply in a given area.

symbiosis. Any intimate relationship between two or more different species. The fur of the three-toed sloth is often occupied by algae and insects that feed on the algae. See also *mutualism, commensalism*.

tailings. The nonuseful materials removed from the mill after the recoverable minerals have been extracted in the processing of minerals. See also *milling*.

taxonomic. The classification of organisms according to evolutionary relationships.

tertiary consumers. Carnivores that eat other carnivorous (or secondary) consumers.

tertiary treatment. The third level of treatment in the management of municipal wastes, which involves a chemical process that removes phosphates, nitrates, and other contaminants not removed during secondary treatment. See also *primary treatment, secondary treatment*.

theories. Models based on currently accepted hypotheses that offer broadly conceived, logically coherent, and very well supported concepts.

threshold effect. The harmful or even fatal reaction to exceeding the tolerance limit of a species in a given ecosystem. See also *law of tolerance, acclimation*.

Total Allowable Catch (TAC). A limit set by the Northwest Atlantic Fisheries Organization (NAFO), an agency of the United Nations Food and Agricultural Organization, to ensure that groundfish stocks were not depleted.

total fertility rate (TFR). The average number of children expected to be born to a woman during her lifetime.

trophic level. Each organism is assigned a feeding or trophic level depending on whether it is a producer or a consumer and on what it eats or decomposes.

troposphere. The lowest layer of the atmosphere and the zone in which most weather events occur. See also *atmosphere, stratosphere.*

utilitarian justification. A rationale for the conservation of nature based on the idea that the environment provides individuals with direct economic benefits. Compare *ecological justification, moral justification, aesthetic arguments.*

vertebrates. Animals with backbones, including fish, amphibians, reptiles, birds, and mammals. Compare *invertebrates.*

volatile organic compound (VOC). Most VOCs are hydrocarbons, such as methane, propane, chlorofluorocarbons, and benzene. They are found also in the vapours of substances such as gasoline, solvents, and oil-based paints. VOCs result primarily from the combustion of fossil fuels in motor vehicles.

water resources. The network of rivers, lakes, and other surface waters that supply water for food production and other essential human systems.

watershed. A region of high ground that lies between and determines the flow of two unconnected drainage systems, such as the Continental Divide, which is formed by the Rocky Mountains.

wetlands. Transitional areas between aquatic and terrestrial ecosystems, usually covered with fresh water for part of the year, with characteristic soils and vegetation.

withdrawal uses. Water that is removed from its natural setting for municipal use, irrigation, manufacturing, and other applications. See also *instream uses.*

worldview. A set of commonly held values, ideas, and images concerning the nature of reality and the role of humanity within it.

COPYRIGHT ACKNOWLEDGMENTS

PHOTO CREDITS

Chapter 7: **Page 184** Evan Turner; **Page 186** Natural Resources Canada; **Page 188** Dianne Draper; **page 189** Tourism Saskatchewan; **page 194** Canapress; **Page 197** Canapress; **Page 200** top: Central Experimental Farm/Agriculture and Agri-Food Canada, Ottawa, centre and bottom: PhotoDisc; **Page 201** Dianne Draper; **Page 204** Flip Nicklin/Minden Pictures/First Light; **Page 208** Frank M. Hanna/ Visuals Unlimited; **Page 209** top: Courtesy of Department of Fisheries and Oceans, lower: Bob Semple; **page 213** Vicki Gould; **Page 217** S.H. Draper

Chapter 8: **Page 222** Gustav Verderker/Visuals Unlimited; **Page 224** Canapress; **Page 227** S. McCutcheon/Visuals Unlimited; **Page 230** Bob Semple; **Page 232** Canapress; **Page 233** Al Harvey/The Slide Farm; **Page 237** Canapress; **Page 238** Canapress; **Page 240** Bob Semple; **Page 243** Dianne Draper; **Page 245** Dianne Draper; **Page 254** Peter Ziminski/Visuals Unlimited; **Page 256** Victoria Times Colonist; **Page 258** Canapress; **Page 262** Al Harvey/The Slide Farm

Chapter 9: **Page 272** John D. Cunningham/Visuals Unlimited; **Page 275** Natural Resources Canada; **Page 276** both: Courtesy of Western Canada Wilderness Committee; **Page 277** 1: Steve McCutcheon/Visuals Unlimited, 2: Kirtley-Perkins/Visuals Unlimited, 3: Brooking Tatum/Visuals Unlimited, 4: Steve McCutcheon/Visuals Unlimited, 5: Berndt Wittich/Visuals Unlimited; **Page 284** top: John Oohlden/Visuals Unlimited, lower: Mark E. Gibson/Visuals Unlimited; **Page 293** Courtesy of the Museum of Anthropology, University of British Columbia, Vancouver, Canada; **Page 300** Photo sequence compiled by Richard G. Thomas, Alberta Environmental Protection—Air Photo Services, Edmonton Phone: (403) 427-3520; **Page 301** Laurie Wierzbicki; **Page 302** top left: Carlyn Galati/Visuals Unlimited, bottom right: IDRC; **Page 303** Arthur R. Hill/Visuals Unlimited; **Page 305** Dianne Draper; **Page 306** top: Allen H. Benton/Visuals Unlimited, bottom: Mary Cummins/Visuals Unlimited; **Page 309** The Vancouver Sun; **Page 315** Paul Jones; **Page 317** Dianne Draper; **Page 318** The Calgary Herald

Chapter 10: **Page 324** Science VU/API/Visuals Unlimited; **Page 327** left: B.C. Provincial Archives, right: Victor Last/Geographical Visual Aids; **Page 328** Canapress; **Page 331** Natural Resources Canada; **Page 337** top: Al Harvey/The Slide Farm, lower: Victor Last/Geographical Visual Aids; **Page 338** both: Natural Resources Canada; **Page 339** top: Science VU/Visuals Unlimited, lower: Alcan Aluminium; **Page 340** City of Elliot Lake; **Page 343** Patrice Halley; **Page 345** both: INCO LIMITED, Ontario Division Copper Cliff, Ontario; **Page 347** left: Alcan Aluminium, right: Crop Protection Institute

Chapter 11: **Page 352** Visuals Unlimited; **Page 353** Canapress; **Page 354** top: Al Harvey/The Slide Farm, bottom (both): Toronto Transit Commission; **Page 355** both: Toronto Transit Commission; **Page 357** Canapress; **Page 358** The Calgary Herald; **Page 360** Reuters/Eriko Sugita/Archive Photos; **Page 362** Comstock; **Page 364** top: Corbis-Bettman, bottom: Sylvan H. Wittwer/Visuals Unlimited; **Page 368** Canapress; **Page 370** Ontario Hydro Corporate Archives; **Page 372** Ballard Power Systems Inc.; **Page 374** Canapress; **Page 375** Canapress; **Page 376** Dianne Draper

Chapter 12: **Page 383** Elizabeth DeLaney/Visuals Unlimited; **Page 385** top left: Thomas Gula/Visuals Unlimited, top right: John Gerlach/Visuals Unlimited, lower left: R. Lindholm/Visuals Unlimited, lower right: Joe McDonald/Visuals Unlimited; **Page 388** Victor Last/Geographical Visual Aids; **Page 389** John Gerlach/Visuals Unlimited; **Page 395** Steve McCutcheon/Visuals Unlimited; **Page 396** top left: Mark Hobson/Viewpoints West Photofile Ltd., top right: William J. Weber/Visuals Unlimited, lower left: Bernd Wittich/Visuals Unlimited, lower right: Nada Pecnik/Visuals Unlimited; **Page 397** Arthur Morrison/Visuals Unlimited; **Page 399** PhotoDisc; **Page 400** both: Dianne Draper; **Page 402** Canapress; **Page 408** Al Harvey/The Slide Farm; **Page 410** left: Dianne Draper, right: Metro Toronto Zoo; **Page 414** Arthur Morris/Visuals Unlimited; **Page 415** top: Joe McDonald/Visuals Unlimited, lower: Stephen J. Lang/Visuals Unlimited

Page 419 Michael G. Gabrigde/Visuals Unlimited; Chapter 13: **Page 420** G.K. and Vikki Hart/The Image Bank; **Page 423** Canapress; **Page 426** left: Dianne Draper, right: Al Harvey/The Slide Farm; **Page 427** Dianne Draper; **Page 429** Al Harvey/The Slide Farm; **Page 432** top: Canapress, centre: Dianne Draper, bottom left: Al Harvey/The Slide Farm, bottom right: The Calgary Herald; **Page 434** top: Dianne Draper, bottom: Dianne Draper; **Page 436** Al Harvey/The Slide Farm; **Page 438** Al Harvey/The Slide Farm; **Page 440** Courtesy of Carma Developers Ltd.; **Page 441** Dick Hemingway; **Page 442** John Cunningham/Visuals Unlimited; **Page 443** Dianne Draper

Chapter 14: **Page 449** Ducks Unlimited Canada; **Page 450** Dianne Draper; **Page 451** Dianne Draper; **Page 452** both: Dianne Draper; **Page 453** Dianne Draper; **Page 454** top: Dianne Draper, bottom: Steve McCutcheon/Visuals Unlimited; **Page 455** Scott Berner/Visuals Unlimited; **Page 457** Daphne Kinzler/Visuals Unlimited; **Page 458** The Orleans Preschool; **Page 464** Dianne Draper; **Page 466** NASA; **Page 472** Dianne Draper

INDEX

Abiotic, 61
Aboriginal land claims, 159, 160
    Gwich'in Comprehensive Land
        Claim Agreement, 160
    See also First Nations view of
        natural world
Abortion, 109, 110
Abyssal zones, 78
Accelerated Reduction/Elimination
    of Toxics (ARET) program, 344
Accidents, shipping, 233
Acclimation, 65
Acid mine drainage, 332
Acid rain, 137–42
Acid Rain National Early Warning
    System (ARNEWS), 138
Acidic deposition, 137–42, 204
Acinic keratoses, 120
Activated sludge process, 195
Adaptation, 83
Adaptive radiation, 84
Aeration tank digestion, 195
Aerobic respiration, 64
Aerosols, 134
    sulphate, 134
Aesthetic arguments, 45
Agenda 21, 14
    forests, 308
    fresh water, 208
    oceans/fisheries, 262
    overview, 15
Age-specific fertility rate, 105
Aggressive generalists, 291
Agricultural activities,
    nontraditional, 176–78
Agricultural biotechnology, 177, 178
Agricultural uses of land resources,
    154–83
    aboriginal land claims, 159, 160
    agricultural biotechnology, 177,
        178
    biodiversity, 164, 166
    Canadian initiatives, 172–80
    changes in agricultural use,
        157–59
    community shared agriculture
        farms, 176
    economic/environmental/social
        issues, 181
    energy use, 168
    future challenges, 180, 181

game farming, 176, 177
greenhouse gases, 166–68
integrated pest management,
    167
international initiatives, 169–71
jurisdiction/tenure, 159
Manitoba, sustainable
    agriculture in, 172–74
nontraditional agricultural
    activities, 176–78
organic farming, 176
resources and, 156
responses to environmental
    impacts, 168–80
soil quality, 161–63
water quality, 163–65, 200–2
Agroecosystems, 157
Agroforestry, 176
Ahousaht Wild Side Heritage Trail,
    317
AIDS, 99
Air quality, 141, 423, 424, 442, 443
Airborne contaminants, 142
Alachlor, 200
Alberta Sustainable Home/Office,
    429
Algoma Highlands, 305
Alkylated lead, 199
Allowable annual cut (AAC), 286
Alternative energy, 371
Alternative live stock production,
    176
Amphibians, 56, 384–86
    North American Amphibian
        Monitoring Program
        (NAAMP), 386
    See also Frogs
Anderson, David, 247
Angel Glacier, 132
Animalia, 61, 62
Antarctic ozone depletion, 124
AOC, 210
Aquatic biomes, 77–81
Aquifer thermal energy storage
    (ATES) system, 378
Arctic diversity, 391
Arctic National Wildlife Refuge
    (ANWR), 394
Areas of concern (AOC), 210
ARET program, 344
Argon, 56

Arntzen, Charles, 31
Artificial diving reef, 256
Ash House, 376, 429
ATES system, 378
Athabasca tar sands, 359
Atlantic Coastal Action Program
    (ACAP), 265
Atmosphere, 54, 55
Atmospheric changes, 116–53
    acidic deposition, 137–42
    airborne contaminants, 142
    Canadian law/practice, 145–49
    climate change, 126–37
    community responses, 149
    future challenges, 149, 150
    international responses, 143–45
    stratospheric ozone depletion,
        121–26
Atomic Energy of Canada Limited,
    367
Atomic number, 52
Atoms, 51, 52
Automobile use, 430, 432
Autotrophs, 62, 63

Backus Woods, 306, 307
Bacteria, 61
    toxin-consuming, 469
Ballard Power Systems, 373
Banff National Park, 398–400
Barrier islands, 78
Bathyl zones, 78
BC Mining Watch project, 344
Bears, grizzly, 398, 399
    Eastern Slopes Grizzly Bear
        Research Project, 315
Beautiful British Columbia, 146
Beetle, Colorado, 178
Behavioural adaptation, 83
Belugas, 204
Benthic environment, 78
Benzene, 424
Benzo(a)pyrene, 199
Beyond the Limits, 96
BHP diamond mine, 329–32
Bighead Conservation Tillage Club,
    175
Biocentric equality, principle of, 41
Biodiversity, 60, 84, 388
Biogeochemical cycles, 71–76
Biological evolution, 83

Biomagnification, 227, 228
Biomass, 364, 365
Biome, 59, 76
     aquatic, 77–81
Biosphere, 55, 59
Biosphere II, 82
Biosphere reserves, 407
Biotechnology, 177
     agricultural, 177, 178
Biotic, 61
Biotic potential, 81
Birds. *See* Cormorant; Eagles; Hawk;
     Murrelet; Songbirds, migratory;
     Warbler, Cape May; Waterfowl
Birth control, 109, 110
Birth rate, 94
Blue Box recycling campaign, 43
Boating, 428
Bondar, Roberta, 446
Boreal forest, 76
Botanical gardens, 409
Boundary Waters Treaty, 209
Bourassa, Robert, 206
Bovine spongiform encephalopathy
     (BSE), 99
Boyce Thompson Institute for Plant
     Research, 31
Braer, 255
Breast-feeding, 109
Brechtel, Steve, 67
Brewer ozone spectrophotometer,
     121
British Columbia's CORE process,
     180, 320, 415
Broken Hill Proprietary (BHP), 326,
     329
Bruntland Report, 14, 16
Butler, Barbara, 469

Canada Centre for Inland Waters
     (CCIW), 212
Canada Centre for Mineral and
     Energy Technology (CANMET),
     345
Canada Endangered Species
     Protection Act (CESPA), 412, 452
Canada Forest Accord, 309
Canada–Manitoba Agreement for
     Agricultural Sustainability
     (CMAAS), 173
Canada Oceans Act, 263
Canada–Spain turbot dispute,
     236–38
Canada Water Act, 210
Canadian Aboriginal Economic
     Development Strategy, 160

Canadian Acid Rain Control
     Program, 142
Canadian Biodiversity Information
     Network (CBIN), 402
Canadian Biodiversity Strategy, 413
Canadian Council of Ministers of the
     Environment (CCME), 147
Canadian Drinking Water Quality,
     guidelines for, 194, 213
Canadian Environment Week, 41
Canadian Environmental Protection
     Act (CEPA), 145
Canadian Food Inspection Agency
     (CFIA), 177
Canadian Heritage Rivers System
     (CHRS), 192
Canadian Organic Growers (COG),
     176
Canadian Pacific Hotels and Resorts
     (CPH&R) Green Program, 435
Canadian Ramsar Network, 209
Canadian regulatory efforts. See
     Regulatory efforts
Canadian Wilderness Charter, 408
Canada's Green Plan, 178, 179
Canada's national forest strategy,
     309, 313
Cancer, skin, 118–20
CANDU reactors, 367, 370
Captive breeding programs, 410
Carbon cycle, 71, 73
Carbon dioxide, 56, 127
Carbon monoxide, 56
Carbon tetrachloride, 122
Cardinal Divide, 348
Cardinal River Coals (CRC), 348
Caribou, Peary, 395, 396
Caring for the Earth, 16
Carmack, George, 327
Carnivores, 63
Carolinian forest, 306, 307
Carrying capacity, 20, 21, 81, 100
Carson, Rachel, 36, 39
Census, 92
Certified wood, 319
CFCs, 122, 128, 143
Challenges for the future. *See*
     Future challenges
Change, 81
Changes in population sizes, 81–83
Chaudière, 256
Checkley, Anne, 435
Chemical change, 54
Chemical contamination, 163
Chemical notations, 52, 53
Chemosynthesis, 62

Chemototrophs, 62
Chernobyl nuclear accident, 368,
     369
Cheviot mine development, 348, 349
China, 134, 135
     one-child policy of, 110
Chlorofluorocarbons (CFCs), 122,
     128, 143
Chloroquinine, 102
Cholera, 103
Citemene, 171
CITES, 403
Cities. *See* Urban living
City Farmer, 438
Classification, five-kingdom system
     of, 60–62
Clayoquot Sound, 275, 276
Clean Rural Environment (ACRE),
     175
Clear-cutting, 282
Climate, 76
Climate change
     El Niño, 134, 135
     enhanced greenhouse effect,
          130–32
     future trends, 135–37
     general circulation models, 129
     global warming potential, 135,
          136
     greenhouse gases, 126–28
     indicators/effects, 130–34
     predicting, 128–30
     sulphates/sulphur emissions,
          134
Climax community, 84
Clinton, Bill, 332, 334
Co-generation, 376
Coal, 361, 362
Coastal zone, 78
Coastal zone management, 264
Cod, northern, moratorium, 238–42
Coffee plantations, 167
Collingwood Harbour, 213
Combined heat and power (CHP),
     376
Commensalism, 67, 68
Commission on Resources and
     Environment (CORE), 180, 320,
     415
Commission on Sustainable
     Development, 309
Committee on the Status of
     Endangered Wildlife in Canada
     (COSEWIC), 298, 396
Community, 57
Community gardening, 438

Community shared agriculture (CSA) farms, 176
Commuting, long-distance, 327
Competitive exclusion principle, 66
Compost bins, 441
Compounds, 51, 52
Comprehensive claims agreements, 160
Condom use, 109
Confederation Bridge, 258, 259
Connectedness, principle of, 85
Conservation Authorities Act, 214
Conservation Cover Program, 173
Conservation movement, 36–39
Conservation tillage, 174, 175
Conservation tillage clubs, 175
Consumers, 62
Contraceptives, 109
Convention Concerning the Protection of the World Cultural and Natural Heritage, 403
Convention on Biological Diversity, 308
Convention on Climate Change, 309
Convention on Fishing and Conservation of the Living Resources of the High Seas, 403
Convention on the High Seas, 403
Convention on Wetlands of International Importance Especially as Waterfowl Habitat, 403
Convention to Combat Desertification, 171
Coon-Come, Daniel, 206
Coon-Come, Matthew, 34
CORE, 180, 320, 415
Coreopsis, pink, 395, 396
Cormorant, double-crested, 397
Corner Brook Pulp and Paper Limited, 247, 252
COSEWIC. See Committee on the Status of Endangered Wildlife in Canada
Countdown Acid Rain Program, 344, 345
Counter-Enlightenment period, 36
Cow. See Mad cow disease, 99
Cowley Ridge Windplant, 374
Creosote, 203
Critical thinking, 33
Cropland, 158
Crown land, 159
Crown Land Silviculture Program, 312
Crust, 55

CSA farms, 176

Dams, 204–6
DDT, 397
Death rate, 94
Declining Amphibian Populations Task Force (DAPTF), 385
Decomposers, 63
Deductive reasoning, 28
Deep ecology, 41
Deer Yard Program, 316
Deforestation, 284
Demographic transition, 97–99
Demographic trap, 98
Demography, 91
Denis, Paul-Yves, 6
Dense nonaqueous phase liquids (DNAPLs), 203
Dependency ratio, 105
Dependent variable, 30
Desertification, 169–71
Deserts, 76
Desulfovibrio sulfuricans, 469
Detritus feeders, 63
Detrivores, 63
Developed countries, 90
Developing countries, 90
Diamond, Billy, 206
Diamond mine, BHP, 329–32
Dichlorodiphenyldichloroethylene (DDE), 397
Dieldrin, 199
Differential reproduction, 83
Dinoflagellates, 102
Disease epidemics, 99
Dissolved oxygen content, 65
District heating, 376
Diversions, 204–6
DNA, 83
DNAPLs, 203
Dobson units (DU), 121
Dolly, 32
Domtar Specialty Fine Papers, 252
Doubling time, 95
Drinking water, 194–96
contamination of, 195
Ducks Unlimited, 174, 216, 387

Eagles, bald, 72
Earth, 55
Earth Charter, 16
Earth Summit, 14
Earth Summit +5, 145
Earth-sustaining actions, 470, 471
Earth's freshwater resources, 186
Earth's life-support systems, 50–87

aquatic biomes, 77–81
biodiversity, 60
Earth's major components, 54–57
ecology, 57–60
ecosystems. See Ecosystems
energy, 53
matter, 51–53
organisms, 60, 61
physical/chemical changes in matter, 54
responses to environmental stress, 81–84
terrestrial biomes, 76, 77
working with nature, 85
Earthships, 430
Eastern Slopes Grizzly Bear Research Project, 315
Ecofeminism, 41
Ecological diversity, 60
Ecological footprints, 17–19
Ecological justification, 44
Ecological maturity, 285
Ecological Monitoring and Assessment Network (EMAN), 212, 411
Ecological niche, 66
Ecological Science Cooperative (ESC), 212
Ecological succession, 84
Ecological sustainability, 16–21
Ecological worldview, 36, 38
Ecology, 57
deep ecology, 41
industrial, 467
social, 41
Economic maturity, 285
Economic sustainability, 21, 22
Ecorail, 376
Ecosphere, 55, 59
Ecosystem approach, 18
Ecosystems, 4, 57
components/structure, 61–65
energy flow, 69–71
human impacts, 84, 85
limiting factors, 65
matter cycling, 71–76
species, 65–69
Ecozones, 59, 60
Efficiency and Alternative Energy Program, 148, 379
Ehrlich, Paul, 90
EIA process, 334, 335, 337
Elño and the Southern Oscillation, 134, 135,
Electrons, 51, 52
Elements, 51

Elk farming, 176, 177
    North American Elk Breeders
        Association (NAEBA), 176,
        177
EMAN, 212, 411
Emissions permits, 379
Endangered Spaces Campaign, 412,
    413
Endangered species. *See* Wild
    species/natural spaces
Endangered Species Protection Act,
    412, 452
Endemic species, 65
Energy, 53, 352–82
    alternative, 371–73
    barriers to adopting alternative,
        373–75
    biomass, 364, 365
    Canadian initiatives, 378, 379
    Chernobyl, 368, 369
    coal, 361, 362
    crisis (1970s), 364
    first law of, 54
    future trends, 379, 380
    geothermal, 378
    ground-source heating, 378
    heavy oil, 358–61
    Hibernia oil project, 357, 358
    high-quality, 53
    home efficiency, 376, 377
    hydroelectric power, 365–67
    hydrogen, 371–73
    improving efficiency, 374
    industrial efficiency, 376
    low-quality, 53
    natural gas, 362–64
    net useful energy, 355, 356
    nuclear energy, 367–70
    oil, 358
    oilsands, 359, 361
    second law of, 54
    solar/wind power, 371
    supply/demand, 354
    Three Mile Island, 367
    transportation efficiency, 374,
        376
    types, 53
    urban life, 429–32
Energy balance, 57
Energy flow, 56
Energy Probe, 366, 367
Energy Probe Research Foundation
    (EPRF), 366
Energy quality, 53
ENGOs, 460–63

Enhanced greenhouse effect, 127,
    130–32
Enlightenment, 35
Environment Week, 41
Environmental decision making, 34,
    35
Environmental ethics, 45, 46
Environmental impact assessment
    (EIA), 334, 335, 337
Environmental impact statement
    (EIS), 335, 337
Environmental management system
    (EMS), 346
Environmental Mining Council of
    British Columbia (EMCBC), 344
Environmental nongovernmental
    organizations (ENGOs), 460–63
Environmental problems, causes of,
    7–13
    abuse of resources/natural
        systems, 11, 12
    human population growth, 10,
        11
    pollution, 12
Environmental resistance, 81
Environmental stewardship, 22
Environmental stress, responses to,
    81–84
Environmental values, 44, 45
Environmentalism, 39–44
    first wave of, 39, 40
    second wave of, 40, 43
Enviropark, 213
Epidemics, 99
Erosion, 161, 162
Estai, 236–38
Estuaries, 78
Ethanol, 364, 365
Ethanol-blended gasoline, 365
Ethics, 18
    See also Environmental ethics
Eukaryotic cells, 61
Euphotic zones, 78
Eutrophic lake, 79, 80
Eutrophication, 164
Evolution, 83
Ex situ conservation, 409, 410
Exclusive economic zones (EEZs),
    261
Exotic species, 65
Expansionist worldview, 35, 38
Experiment, controlled, 30
Exponential growth, 94
Extinction, 84
Exxon Valdez spill, 360

Fact, 29
Fagi, Achmad, 170
Falldown effect, 286–88
False conclusions, 28
Family planning services, 109, 110
FAO fishing area boundaries, 261
Farming for Tomorrow, 173
Farming, rice-fish, 170
Farmland, 158
Fathom Five National Marine park,
    407
Federal/Provincial Committee on
    Land Use, 179
Fernow, Bernhard, 294
Fertility rates, 105–8
Fertilizer use, 167
Fiddlehead Farm, 305
Final Agreements on the Tunngavik
    Federation of Nunavut, 160
Final Agreements with the Council
    for Yukon Indians and Four First
    Nations, 160
First Nations view of natural world,
    192
    See also Aboriginal land claims
Fish
    northern cod moratorium,
        238–42
    Pacific herring, 243–45
    rice-fish farming, 170
    salmon stocks, 245–47
    turbot war, 236–38
    wasted, 239
    world's most-fished species, 234
    See also Oceans and fisheries.
Fisheries. *See* Oceans and fisheries.
Fisheries Resources Conservation
    Council (FRCC), 242
Fishing zone, 200-mile exclusive,
    240
Flaring, 363, 364
Flight Plan, 299
Flin Flon mine, 343
Flood damage reduction program,
    214
Floods, 193–94
Food chain, 69
Food web, 69, 70
Forest diversity, 391
Forest Practices Code, 316
Forest Renewal Plan, 310
Forest Stewardship Council, 319
Forests, 272–23
    Agenda 21, 308
    agroforestry, 176

allowable annual cut, 286
birds, neotropical migratory, 299
Canada's national forest strategy, 309, 313
Canadian Council of Forest Ministers criteria/critical elements, 314
Canadian forests, 278–82
Canadian policy/practice, 309–16
Carolinian forest, 306, 307
Clayoquot Sound, 275, 276
ecosystem-based values, 274
endangered wildlife, 296–99
falldown effect, 286–88
forest zones, world's principal, 278
forests, tropical, 300–3
future challenges, 316–20
global distribution, 277
harvesting systems, 282–84
history of forest industry, 293–95
indigenous peoples, 304
international initiatives, 307–9
local initiatives, 315, 316
model forest program, 313
pollution, 303, 304
provincial initiatives, 310–12
rain forests, temperate, 76
sociocultural dimensions, 304
standards, 317, 319
temperate deciduous, 76
timber bias, 284–86
tourism and recreation, 304, 305
tree plantations, 284
trees, Canada's tallest, 277
trees, old-growth, 286, 289–92
tropical forests, 300–3
UNCED forest principles, 307, 308
Fossil fuels, 358
Framework Convention on Climate Change (FCCC), 143
Fraser River Action Plan (FRAP), 215, 265
Fraser River Estuary Management Program (FREMP), 264
Fresh water, 184–21
    acidic deposition, 204
    Agenda 21, 208
    agricultural uses, 200–2
    beluga whales, 204
    Canadian law/policy, 210
    Canadian resources, 186–88
    common link, water as, 192
    domestic/urban uses, 194–99

drinking water, 194–96
Earth's freshwater resources, 186
Ecological Monitoring and Assessment Network, 212
environmental quality guidelines, 194, 212, 213
flood damage reduction program, 214
floods, 193, 194
Fraser river action plan, 215
future challenges, 218
Great Lakes, 197–99
Great Lakes Cleanup Fund, 213
Great Lakes 2000 program, 213
groundwater contamination, 202, 203
hydroelectric generation, 204–7
industrial uses, 202–4
Inquiry on Federal Water Policy, 211
international initiatives, 208–10
nature sanctuaries, 216
North American waterfowl management plan, 216
Northern River Basins Study, 213, 214
pressures on water quality, 190, 191
Ramsar Convention, 208, 209
recreational uses, 207, 208
remedial action plans, 210
source of conflict, water as, 192, 193
U.S.–Canadian agreements, 209, 210
uses of water, 188–90
watershed planning, 214, 215
zebra mussels, 191
Freshwater diversity, 392
Freshwater ecosystems, 79
Freshwater rivers/streams, 80
Frogs, 384–86
Fuel cell engine, Ballard, 372, 373
Fulton, Frederick, 294
Fundamental niches, 66
Fungi, 61, 62
Future challenges
    cleanup of past problems, 467
    conservation, 464
    decision-making processes, 467–70
    individual participation, 470–72
    pollution control, 466, 467
    resources management, 463, 464

urban living, 465, 466
waste reduction, 465

Gaia hypothesis, 43
Game farming, 176, 177
Gardening, community, 438
Garrison Diversion project, 206
Gases, 56
Gene pool, 83
General circulation models (GCMs), 129
General fertility rate, 105
General systems theory, 41
Generalist species, 66
Genes, 83
Genetic diversity, 57
Genetic engineering, 31
Genus, 61
Geographic information systems (GISs), 29, 180
Geographic isolation, 83
Geographic variations, 76
Geothermal energy use, 378
Global Forum, 14
Global warming, 130–37
Global warming potential (GWP), 135, 136
Gold rush, Klondike, 326, 327
Golf courses, 207, 208
Gophers, 67
Goshawk, Queen Charlotte, 296, 297
Government-sponsored family planning, 110
Grassland diversity, 392
Grasslands, 76
Gravity, 56, 57
Great Lakes Action Plan, 213
Great Lakes Cleanup Fund, 213
Great Lakes–St. Lawrence Basin Project, 149
Great Lakes–St. Lawrence River basin, 197–99
Great Lakes 2000 program, 213
Great Lakes water quality agreements, 209, 210
Great Whale project, 207
Green alternatives, 41
Green Lane web sites, 432
Green Plan, Canada's, 178, 179
Green space, 435–37
Green Streets Canada Program, 437
Greenhouse effect, 126–37
    See also Climate change
Greenhouse gas emissions, 379
Greenhouse gases, 126–28

Gross primary productivity, 70
Ground-level ozone, 424
Ground-source heating, 378
Groundwater, 186, 187
    contamination, 202, 203
Growing ecological footprints, 20
Growth rate, crude, 93, 94
    exponential, 94
Guidelines for Canadian Drinking
    Water Quality, 194, 213
Gulls, herring, 72
Gwaii Haanas NMCA, 407
Gwich'in Comprehensive Land Claim
    Agreement, 160

Habitat, 57
Habitat fragmentation, 390
Habitat joint ventures, 216
Habitat/species management areas,
    405
Halons, 122
Harvesting systems, 282–84
Hawk
    Queen Charlotte goshawk, 296,
    297
    Swainson's, 6
Hearing Education and Awareness
    for Rockers (H.E.A.R.), 425
Hearing loss, 424, 425
HEARNET, 425
Hearst, William Randolph, 318
Heat island effect, 422
Heavy oil, 358–61
Helium, 56
Helsinki Process, 309
Hemp, 318, 319
Herbivores, 63
Heritage Seed Program, 410
Herring, Pacific, 243–45
Herzberg, Gerhard, 7
Heterotrophs, 62, 63
Hexachlorobenzene (HCB), 199
Hexachlorocyclohexane (HCH), 142
Hibernia oil project, 357, 358
Highgrading, 282, 283
Highly developed countries (HDC),
    90
Hobart Press waste disposal system,
    435
Home energy efficiency, 376, 377
    See also Sustainable housing
Houseboats, 429
Human cultural diversity, 60
Human demography, 91
Human development index, 421

Human–environment connections,
    10
Human population, 88–113
    age structure, 100–5
    carrying capacity, 100
    cultural factors, 107, 108
    demographic transition, 97–99
    demography, 91
    dependency ratio, 105
    diseases, 99
    environmental sustainability,
    and, 111
    exponential growth, 94
    fertility rates/lag-time effects,
    105–8
    future trends, 106
    historical overview, 92
    limiting factors, 100
    population dynamics, 93, 94
    projecting future growth, 95, 96
    solutions to population problem,
    108–11
    technological issues, 89–91
    world population growth, 93
    zero population growth, 99, 100
Human population growth, 10, 11
Humans, 7
Hunters and gatherers, 92
Hydro-Québec, 206, 207
Hydroelectric generation, 204–7
Hydroelectric power, 365–67
Hydrofluorocarbons (HCFCs), 122
Hydrogen, 56, 371–73
Hydrogen corridor, 372
Hydrologic cycle, 74, 75
Hydrosphere, 54, 55
Hypotheses, 27, 29

Immigrant species, 65
Improved cropland, 158
Improved pasture, 158
In situ conservation, 404
Incineration, 433
Independent variable, 30
Indicator species, 65
Individual participation, 470–72
Inductive reasoning, 28
Industrial ecology, 467
Industrial efficiency, 376
Industrial Revolution, 92
Infant mortality rate, 94
Inferences, 29
Inhabited forest concept, 311
Inland wetlands, 80, 81
Inquiry on Federal Water Policy, 211

Instream uses, 188
Integrated pest management (IPM),
    167
Interbasin diversions, 205
Intergovernmental Panel on Climate
    Change (IPCC), 130, 145
International Centre for Agricultural
    Science and Technology (ICAST),
    178
International Conference on
    Population and Development
    (ICPD), 110
International Co-operative for
    Environmental Leadership, 149
International Council on Metals and
    the Environment (ICME), 345
International Day for the
    Preservation of the Ozone Layer,
    143
International Development Research
    Centre (IDRC), 169, 308
International Geographical Union's
    Commission on Climatology
    (IGU), 145
International Geosphere Biosphere
    Program (IGBP), 145
International Human Dimensions
    Program (IHDP), 145
International Joint Commission
    (IJC), 209
International Planned Parenthood
    Federation, 110
International Plant Protection
    Convention, 403
International Tropical Timber
    Agreement (ITTA), 307, 403
Intrinsic value, 388
Invertebrates, 61
Ions, 51
Irving Whale recovery project,
    223–25
Islands Trust, 266
ISO 14 000 system, 317, 319, 346
IUCN, 404

J curve of population growth, 81
James Bay project, 206, 207

Kenyan Woodfuel Development
    Program, 364
Kerogen, 359
KEY Foundation, 148
Keystone species, 65, 66
Kinetic energy, 53
Klondike gold rush, 326, 327

Knowledge of the Environment for Youth (KEY) Foundation, 148
Krypton, 56

Lag-time effects, 105, 106
Lake Erie, 191
    See also Great Lakes–St. Lawrence River basin
Lakes, 79, 80
Land accounts, 179
Land Claim Agreement of the Sahtu Dene and Métis, 160
Land claims. *See* Aboriginal land claims.
Land contamination, 434, 435
Land Drainage Act, 172
Land ethic, 45
Land resources, 156
    See also Agricultural uses of land resources
Landfills, 432
Law of conservation of matter, 54
Law of tolerance, 64
Leopold, Aldo, 36, 39, 45
Less developed countries (LDCs), 90
Levels of biological organization, 57
Life-cycle assessment, 468
Life-cycle concept, 468
Life-cycle inventory, 468
Life expectancy, 108
Light bulb, incandescent, 54
Limiting factor principle, 65
Limits to adaptation, 83
Limits to Growth, The, 96
Limnetic zone, 79
Lithosphere, 54, 55
Littoral zone, 79
Living systems, 85
Logistic growth curve, 97
Long Beach Model Forest, 310
Long-range transport of pollutants (LRTP), 227, 229, 249
LOS conferences, 261
Lovelock, James, 43
LRTP contaminants, 227, 229, 249

MAB programme, 407
Machine age, 92
Mackenzie, 256
McLaren, Digby, 7
Macroconsumers, 62, 63
Macronutrients, 71
Mad cow disease, 99
Malaria, 102

Malden Mills, 465
Malthus, Thomas Robert, 100, 101
Man and the biosphere (MAB) programme, 407
Managed resource and protected areas, 405
Manipulated variable, 30
Manitoba, sustainable agriculture in, 172–74
Marchi, Sergio, 421
Marcopper Mining Corporation, 325
Marine diversity, 392
Marsh, George Perkins, 36
Mass extinction, 84
Mass numbers, 52
Matter, 51–53
    cycling, 56, 71–76
    quality, 53
Meewasin Valley Authority, 215
Mcfloquine, 103
Melanoma, 118
Melanoma skin cancer, 120
MEND program, 341, 342
Mercury, 199, 229
Mesotrophic lakes, 80
Metals, precious, 328
Methane, 56, 127, 128
    cattle as source of, 155
Methyl bromide, 122
Methyl chloroform, 122
Methylmercury, 393
Michener, Gail, 67
Microconsumers, 63
Micronutrients, 71
Migration, 111
Milling process, 338
Milner, Brenda, 7
Mine Environmental Neutral Drainage (MEND) program, 341, 342
Mineral fuels, 328
Mining, 324–51
    accidents, 325, 326, 328
    acid mine drainage, 332
    BHP diamond mine, 329–32
    Canadian environmental initiatives, 344–46
    Cheviot mine proposal, 348, 349
    closure and reclamation, 339–42
    development and extraction, 336–38
    distribution of resources, 328, 329
    economic market forces, 342–44
    ENGOs, 344

    environmental impact, 332, 333, 336
    exploration, 333–36
    future challenges, 346–49
    Klondike gold rush, 326, 327
    knowledge building, 349
    MEND program, 341, 342
    New World Mine, 334
    one-industry towns, 327, 328
    processing, 338, 339
    protection/monitoring, 347
    recycling, 347
    stewardship, 346, 347
    surface, 337
Miramichi River Environmental Assessment Committee (MREAC), 266
Mirex, 199
Mixtures, 51
MMT, 379
Moats, Lee, 175
Model forest program, 313
Moderately developed countries (MDCs), 90
Modern era, 92
Mole, atypical, 120
Molecules, 52
Molina, M., 122
Monesin, 155
Monoculturing, 284
Montreal Process, 309
Montreal Protocol, 143, 144
Moral justification, 45
Mortality rate, 94
Motley Crue, 425
Movement for the Survival of the Ogani People (MOSOP), 375
Muir, John, 36, 38
Mulroney, Brian, 313
Municipal wastewater treatment, 195
Muntemba, Shimwaayi, 171
Murrelet, marbled, 395, 396
Mushroom, pine, 301
Mussels, zebra, 65, 191
Mutations, 83
Mutualism, 67
Mycota, 301
Mysak, Lawrence, 7

NAAMP, 386
NAAQOs, 423
Narwhals, 227
National Action Plan for the Recovery, Recycling and Reclamation of CFCs, 146, 148

National Action Program on Climate Change (NAPCC), 147
National Agriculture Environment Committee, 179
National Air Pollution Surveillance (NAPS), 423
National Ambient Air Quality Objectives (NAAQOs), 423
National birth rate reduction programs, 110, 111
National Contaminated Sites Remediation Program, 203
National marine conservation areas (NMCA), 407
National parks, 404–6
    Banff National Park, 398–400
National Pollutant Release Inventory (NPRI), 467
National Round Table on the Environment and the Economy (NRTEE), 469
National Soil Conservation Program, 179
National Water Research Institute (NWRI), 212
Natural gas, 362–64
Natural monument, 405
Natural selection, 83
Natural spaces. See Wild species/natural spaces
Nature reserve, 405
Nature sanctuaries, 216, 217
NAWMP, 216, 414
Neon, 56
Nestucca, 233
Net primary productivity, 70, 71
Net useful energy, 355, 356
Neutrons, 51
New World Mine, 334
1992 Rio de Janeiro Earth Summit, 14
Nitrogen, 56
Nitrogen cycle, 71–73
Nitrogen dioxide, 56
Nitrogen fixation, 71
Nitrous oxide, 128
No tillage, 174
Noise, 424, 425
Non-point sources, 247
Nonrenewable resources, 11
North American Amphibian Monitoring Program (NAAMP), 386
North American Elk Breeders Association (NAEBA), 176, 177

North American Waterfowl Management Plan (NAWMP), 216, 414
North Fraser Harbour Environmental Management Plan, 266
Northern cod moratorium, 238–42
Northern River Basins Study (NRBS), 213, 214
Northern Telecom, 149
Northumberland Strait, 258
NPRI, 467
NRTEE, 469
Nuclear energy, 367–70
Nucleus, 52
Nutrient cycles, 71–76
Nutrients, 71

Observations, 29
Ocean dumping, 255
Ocean Dumping Control Action Plan, 466
Ocean Voice International, 267
Oceans, 77, 78
Oceans and fisheries
    abandoned mines, 253
    Agenda 21, 262
    Arctic Ocean environment, 225–29
    artificial reefs, 256
    Atlantic Ocean environment, 230–32
    atmospheric change, 260
    Canadian law/practice, 262–67
    coastal development, 256–59
    concerns facing ocean regions, 233
    Confederation Bridge, 258
    El Niño, 244, 247
    future challenges, 266, 267
    hydrocarbon exploration/production, 259, 260
    industrial effluent, 247–54
    international initiatives, 261, 262
    Irving Whale recovery project, 223–25
    killer spike, 239, 240
    local initiatives, 265–67
    marine shipping, 255
    municipal sewage, 254, 255
    northern cod moratorium, 238–42
    ocean dumping, 255
    Pacific herring, 243–45

    Pacific Ocean environment, 229, 230
    plastics, 255, 256
    pollution, 247–55
    salmon stocks, 245–47
    shipping accidents, 233
    turbot war, 234–36
    urban runoff, 256–58
    wasted fish, 239
    world's most-fished species, 234
Oil, 358
Oil shale, 358, 359
Oil spills, 358, 360
Oilsands, 359, 361
Ok Tedi copper mine, 326
Old-growth trees, 286, 289–92
Oldman River flood, 201
Oligotrophic lake, 79, 80
Omnivores, 63
One-industry towns, 327, 328
Ontario Land CARE, 175
Open pit mining, 337
Operational definitions, 30
Organic farming, 176
Organisms, 57
Organization of Petroleum Exporting Countries (OPEC), 364
Organochlorines, 393, 397
Our Common Future, 14, 16
Overharvesting, 22
Overuse of antibiotics, 99
Owain Lake stand, 292
Oxygen, 56
Ozone, 56, 121, 126
Ozone-depleting substances, 122, 123
Ozone-Depleting Substances Products Regulations, 146
Ozone depletion. *See* Stratospheric ozone depletion
Ozone hole, 122, 124
Ozone layer, 55, 118, 121
Ozone Layer Protection Program, 145

Pacific yew, 68
Palm tree, Seychelles coco-de-mer, 410
Paralysis by analysis, 34
Parasitism, 67
Parizeau, Jacques, 207
Park
    Banff National, 398–400
    Tatshenshini-Alsek Wilderness, 332

496   INDEX

Wabakimi Provincial, 311
Partners FOR the Saskatchewan
    River Basin, 215
Partners in Flight program, 299
Patch cutting, 282, 283
Peace–Athabasca delta, 205
Pearse, Peter, 295
Pelagic environment, 78
PEM fuel cell, 373
People, 7
Perfluorocarbons (PFCs), 128
Permanent Cover Program, 179
Personal exposure monitoring, 141
Phosphorus cycle, 73, 74
Photosynthesis, 57
Physical change, 54
Physiological adaptations, 83
Phytoplankton, 124, 126
Pinchot, Gifford, 36, 38
Plantae, 61, 62
Polar stratospheric clouds, 124
Polar vortex, 124
Pollution, 12
    point source of, 247
Pollution Prevention Awards
    program, 147
Polyani, John, 7
Polychlorinated biphenyls (PCBs),
    199
Polynyas, 225
Population, 57
    age structure, 100–5
    bomb, 10, 11
    change, 81–83
    growth, world, 93
    lag effect, 106
    momentum, 106
    See also Human population
Population times technology
    equation, 90
Potatoes, "hairy," 178
Potential energy, 53
Prairie Care Project, 179
Prairie Farm Rehabilitation Act
    (PFRA), 179
Prairie Plant Systems, 343
Precautionary principle, 22
Precious metals, 328
Predation, 66–67
Preindustrial agriculture, 92
Preservationists, 36, 38
Primary consumers, 63
Primary succession, 84
Primary treatment, 195
ProAlcohol program, 365

Probability, 28
Producers, 62, 63
Profundal zone, 79
Progress on environmental issues
    agriculture, 453
    air quality, 451
    biological diversity, 452
    climate change, 452, 453
    energy, 454
    fisheries, 454, 455
    forests, 453, 454
    minerals/metals, 454
    water quality, 451
Prokaryotae, 61, 62
Protected areas, 404, 405
Protected landscape seascape, 405
Protista, 61, 62
Proton exchange membrane (PEM),
    373
Protons, 51
Provincial regulatory efforts. See
    Regulatory efforts
Pseudoscience, 31

Qualitative data, 30
Quantitative data, 30

R-2000 housing system, 377
Radioactive wastes, 367
Rain forests, 76
Ramsar Convention, 209
Random errors, 29
RDMK type reactor, 368
Reagan, Ronald, 110
Realized niche, 66
Recovery of Nationally Endangered
    Wildlife (RENEW), 408
Recreational pursuits, 428, 429
Recycling programs, 442
Reef, artificial diving, 256
    coral reefs, 78
Rees, William, 19, 20
Regional sustainability, 169
Regulatory efforts
    Alberta, 458, 459
    British Columbia, 458, 460
    Manitoba, 457, 459
    New Brunswick, 455, 456
    Newfoundland, 455, 456
    Northwest Territories, 460, 461
    Nova Scotia, 455, 456
    Ontario, 455, 457, 458
    Prince Edward Island, 455, 456
    Quebec, 455, 457
    Saskatchewan, 457–59

Yukon, 460, 461
Remedial Action Plans (RAPs), 210
RENEW, 408
Renewable energy resources, 371
Renewable resources, 11
Replacement fertility, 106
Reproduction strategies, 82
Resource partitioning, 66, 69
Resources, 11
Responding variable, 30
Rice-fish farming, 170
Righteous management
    conservationists, 36, 38
Rio Declaration, 16
River basin planning, 215
River flow, 186
Rivers, 77
Rock concerts, 424, 425
Rocks, 75
Romanticism, 36
Roots, Betty, 7
Rotation period, 286
Roundwood, 296
Rowland, F.S., 122

S curve of population growth, 81
Sage Creek, 397
Salinity, 65
Salinization, 163
Salmon stocks, Chinook, 245–47
San Antonio copper mine, 325
Sand County Almanac, A, 45
Saro-Wiwa, Ken, 375
Savannas, 76
Scavengers, 63
Schindler, David, 137
Science, 26
    basic assumptions, 28
    complexity/values/worldviews,
        33, 34
    deductive reasoning, 28
    defined, 27
    environmental decision making,
        34, 35
    inductive reasoning, 28
    language, and, 31
    methods of, 29, 30
    misunderstandings, 31–34
    scientific measurements, 28, 29
    scientific method, 32, 33
    value-free, 31
Scientific Committee on Problems of
    the Environment (SCOPE), 145
Scientific measurement, 28, 29
Scientific method, 32, 33

Scientific revolutions, 30
Scorecard. *See* Progress on
    environmental issues
Scrap It program, 149
Secondary consumers, 63
Secondary succession, 84
Secondary treatment, 195
Seed banks, 409
Seed tree cutting, 283
Seedy Saturday, 410
Selection cutting, 282, 283
Self-realization, principle of, 41
Serengeti of North America, 394
Sewage treatment, 195
Shadow effect, 332
Shelterwood cutting, 282, 283
Shrinking earthshares, 20
Shrublands, 76
Sick buildings, 141
Sifton, Clifford Victor, 36–38
Single-family detached housing, 436,
    437
Single-resource towns, 327, 328
Ski resorts, 207, 208
Skin cancer, 118–20
Sloan, Gordon, 295
Social ecology, 41
Social sustainability, 21
Soil
    compaction, 162, 163
    quality, 161–63
    salinization, 163
    structure, 162, 163
Solar energy, 371
Solid waste, 432–34
Songbirds, migratory, 167, 299
Southeast Anatolian Project, 193
Special Places 2000 programs, 415
Specialist species, 66
Speciation, 83, 84
Species, 57
Species biodiversity, 84
Species diversity, 60
Spot check, 120
St. Lawrence Action Plan, 247
St. Lawrence Vision 2000 program,
    247
State of the Ozone Layer over
    Canada, 125, 153
Stewardship, 22
Stratosphere, 55
Stratospheric ozone depletion
    antarctic ozone depletion, 124
    impact on atmosphere, 124, 125
    mid-latitude ozone depletion,
        124

ozone-depleting substances,
    122, 123
ozone layer, 121
tropical ozone depletion, 124
ultraviolet radiation, 125, 126
volcanoes, 123
Straw bale construction, 430, 432
"Streamlining Environmental
    Regulation for Mining," 336
Streams, headwater, 80
Strip cutting, 283
Strip mining, 337
Structural adaptations, 83
Succession, 84
Sulphates, 134
Sulphur dioxide, 56
Sulphur emissions, 134
Summerfallow, 158
Sun sensitivity test, 120
Surface runoff, 163
Sustainability, 13, 14
    social, 21
Sustainability challenges
    ecological sustainability, 16–21
    economic sustainability, 21, 22
    environmental stewardship, 22
    milestones, 16
    monitoring for sustainability, 22,
        23
    precautionary principle, 22
    social sustainability, 21
    sustainability/sustainable
        development, contrasted, 13,
        14
Sustainable development, 13, 14, 41
Sustainable housing, 429, 430
    See also Home energy
        efficiency
Sustained yield, 285
Swamps, mangrove, 78
Swan Hills Special Waste Treatment
    Centre, 465
Swan Lake Christmas Hill Nature
    Sanctuary, 216, 217
Symbiosis, 67

Taiga, 76
Tatshenshini-Alsek Wilderness Park,
    332
Taxol, 68
TCDD, 199
TCDF, 199
Telecommuting, 435
Temagami, 292
Terra Nova offshore oil project, 356
Terrestrial biomes, 76, 77

Tertiary consumers, 63
Tertiary treatment, 195
Theories, 30, 31
Theory of evolution, 83
Thermodynamics, 54
Three Gorges dam, 365
3M Corporation, 465
Three Mile Island, 367
Threshold effect, 65
Tillage erosion, 161
Timber bias, 284–86
Timber volume production, 285
Tobin, Brian, 231, 236–38, 246, 264
Tolerance ranges, 64, 65
Toronto Healthy House, 430, 431
Total fertility rate (TFR), 105–7
Toxaphene, 199
Toxic substances management
    policy, 467
Toxins, 72
Tradable emissions permits, 379
Trans Canada Trail, 442, 443
Transportation efficiency, 374, 376
Treaties protecting biodiversity, 403
Tree farm licences (TFLs), 295
Tree harvesting, 282, 283
Tree plantations, 284
Trent–Severn Waterway, 198
Troposphere, 54, 55
Trout, aurora, 395, 396
Tundra, 76
Turbot war, 236–38
Twenty Percent Club, 148, 442
2,3,7,8-tetrachlorodibenzop-dioxin
    (TCDD), 199
2,3,7,8-tetrachlorodibenzofuran
    (TCDF), 199

UNCED forest principles, 307, 308
UNCLOS, 261, 262
Underground gardening, 343
United Nations Convention on
    Biological Diversity, 403
United Nations Convention on the
    Law of the Sea (UNCLOS), 261,
    262
Urban agriculture, 438
Urban forest, 437
Urban living, 420–49
    agricultural land loss, 437, 438
    air quality, 423, 424, 442, 443
    automobile use, 430, 432
    compact urban form, 440
    conservation, 441, 442
    energy, 429–32, 441
    future considerations, 445, 446

green space, 435–37
land contamination, 434, 435
microclimate, 422
natural areas, 442
noise pollution, 424, 425
planning, 445
recycling/composting, 441, 442
sick buildings, 141
single-family detached lots, 436, 437
solid waste, 432–34
sustainable communities, 439–46
sustainable housing, 429, 430
transportation, 444, 445
trees, 437
waste management, 432–34, 444
water, 424–29, 441, 444
Urban runoff, 256–58
Utilitarian justification, 44
UV-A rays, 125
UV-B radiation, 118, 125, 126
UV-C rays, 125
UV Index, 118, 119
UV radiation, 118, 125, 126

Vaccines, banana, 31
Variable message sign (VMS), 373
Variables, 30
Velvet, 176, 177
Vertebrates, 61
VMS signs, 373
Volatile organic compounds, 142
Volcanoes, 123
Voluntary Challenge and Registry
    Program, 147

Wabakimi Provincial Park, 311
Wackernagel, Mathis, 19, 20
Waldsterben, 303
Walk the Wild Side ecoadventure, 317
Walking school bus, 432
Wallis, Cliff, 67

WAPPRIITA, 404
Warbler, Cape May, 298
Waste management, 432–34, 444
Waste, radioactive. 367
Water
    agriculture/farming, and, 163–65,
        200–2
    urban living, 424–29, 441, 444
Water cycle, 74, 75
Water erosion, 161, 162
Water terror, 193
Water vapour, 56, 126
Waterfowl. *See* North American
    Waterfowl Management Plan
    (NAWMP)
Watershed planning, 214, 215
WEDNET, 171
Westray mine disaster, 328
Wetland diversity, 392
Wetlands, coastal, 78
Whales, beluga, 204
Whitehorse Mining Initiative (WMI),
    346
Whole tree harvesting, 283
Wild Animal and Plant Protection and
    Regulation of International and
    Interprovincial Trade Act
    (WAPPRIITA), 404
Wild species/natural spaces, 383–18
    Canadian law/policy, 411–15
    Canadian wild species, 389, 390
    ex situ conservation, 409, 410
    future challenges, 415, 416
    habitat alteration, 389–93
    highways, 400
    in situ conservation, 404–8
    international documents, 402
    international treaties, 402–4
    protected areas, 404, 405
    research needs, 411
    spaces at risk, 397–402
    species at risk, 394–97

Wilderness area, 405
Wildlife management areas, 404, 405
Wildlife underpass/overpass, 400
Wind erosion, 161, 162
Wind power, 371
Winnipeg floods, 193, 194
Wise management conservationists,
    36, 38
Withdrawal uses, 188
Wood products development, 288
Wordsworth, William, 36
World Conservation Monitoring
    Centre (WCMC), 402
World Conservation Strategy, 13,
    16
World Conservation Union (IUCN),
    404
World Scientists' Warning to
    Humanity, 6, 8, 9
World Water Council, 42
World Water Day, 42
Worldviews and values
    conservationist movement,
        36–39
    ecological worldview, 36, 38
    environmentalism, 39–44
    expansionist worldview, 35, 38
    worldviews, defined, 35

Yellowstone-to-Yukon (Y2Y)
    Conservation Initiative, 334
Yew, Pacific, 68
Yucca plant, 67
Yukon gold rush, 326, 327

Zer-O-Zone project, 149
Zero population growth, 99, 100
Zero tillage, 174, 175
Zooplankton, 126
Zoos, 409, 410

To the owner of this book

We hope that you have enjoyed *Our Environment,* and we would like to know as much about your experiences with this text as you would care to offer. Only through your comments and those of others can we learn how to make this a better text for future readers.

School _____ Your instructor's name _____

Course _____ Was the text required? _____ Recommended? _____

1. What did you like the most about *Our Environment?*

_____
_____
_____

2. How useful was this text for your course?

_____
_____
_____

3. Do you have any recommendations for ways to improve the next edition of this text?

_____
_____
_____

4. In the space below or in a separate letter, please write any other comments you have about the book. (For example, please feel free to comment on reading level, writing style, terminology, design features, and learning aids.)

_____
_____
_____
_____

Optional

Your name _____ Date _____

May ITP Nelson quote you, either in promotion for *Our Environment* or in future publishing ventures?

Yes _____ No _____

Thanks!

You can also send your comments to us via e-mail at
college_arts_hum@nelson.com

PLEASE TAPE SHUT. DO NOT STAPLE.

TAPE SHUT

TAPE SHUT

FOLD HERE

MAIL POSTE
Canada Post Corporation
Société canadienne des postes
Postage paid   Port payé
if mailed in Canada si posté au Canada
Business Reply   **Réponse d'affaires**

0066102399   01

Nelson

0066102399-M1K5G4-BR01

ITP NELSON
MARKET AND PRODUCT DEVELOPMENT
PO BOX 60225 STN BRM B
TORONTO ON M7Y 2H1

TAPE SHUT

TAPE SHUT